DYNASTIES

The Tudor and Early Stuart Monarchs

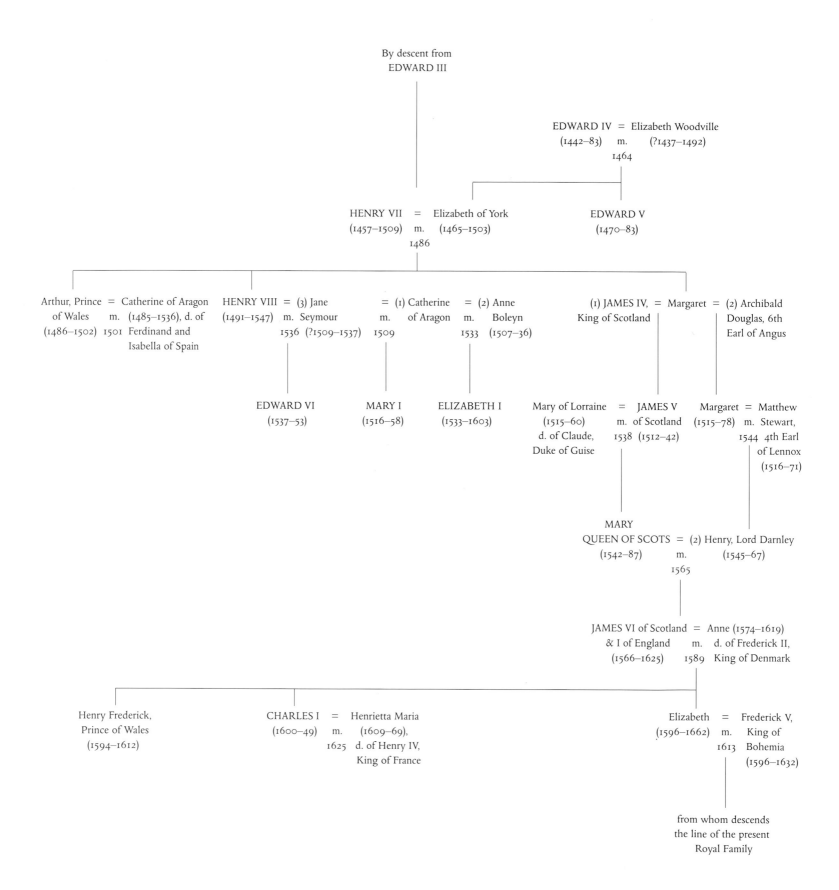

By descent from
EDWARD III

EDWARD IV = Elizabeth Woodville
(1442–83) m. (?1437–1492)
1464

HENRY VII = Elizabeth of York   EDWARD V
(1457–1509) m. (1465–1503)   (1470–83)
1486

Arthur, Prince = Catherine of Aragon   HENRY VIII = (3) Jane   = (1) Catherine   = (2) Anne   (1) JAMES IV, = Margaret = (2) Archibald
of Wales   m. (1485–1536), d. of (1491–1547) m. Seymour   m.   of Aragon   m.   Boleyn   King of Scotland   Douglas, 6th
(1486–1502) 1501 Ferdinand and   1536 (?1509–1537) 1509   1533 (1507–36)   Earl of Angus
               Isabella of Spain

                              EDWARD VI   MARY I   ELIZABETH I   Mary of Lorraine = JAMES V   Margaret = Matthew
                              (1537–53)   (1516–58)   (1533–1603)   (1515–60)   m. of Scotland (1515–78) m. Stewart,
                                                                                   d. of Claude,   1538 (1512–42)   1544 4th Earl
                                                                                   Duke of Guise   of Lennox
                                                                                                                                   (1516–71)

                                                                            MARY
                                                                 QUEEN OF SCOTS = (2) Henry, Lord Darnley
                                                                 (1542–87)   m.   (1545–67)
                                                                                1565

                                                        JAMES VI of Scotland = Anne (1574–1619)
                                                        & I of England   m.   d. of Frederick II,
                                                        (1566–1625)   1589 King of Denmark

Henry Frederick,   CHARLES I = Henrietta Maria   Elizabeth = Frederick V,
Prince of Wales   (1600–49) m. (1609–69),   (1596–1662) m. King of
(1594–1612)   1625 d. of Henry IV,   1613 Bohemia
                                        King of France   (1596–1632)

                                                                                        from whom descends
                                                                                        the line of the present
                                                                                        Royal Family

DYNASTIES

Painting in Tudor and Jacobean England 1530–1630

EDITED BY KAREN HEARN

TATE PUBLISHING

Exhibition sponsored by Pearson plc

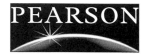

ISBN 1 85437 169 X (cloth)
ISBN 1 85437 157 6 (paper)

A catalogue record for this publication is available
from the British Library

Published by order of the Trustees 1995
for the exhibition at the Tate Gallery
12 October 1995 – 7 January 1996
© Tate Gallery 1995 All rights reserved
Designed and typeset in Columbus by Caroline Johnston
Printed in Great Britain on Parilux silk by Balding + Mansell,
Peterborough, Cambridgeshire

Contents

Foreword

Dynasties is the first exhibition to study the full range of painting from Tudor and Jacobean times since Sir Roy Strong's ground-breaking exhibition *The Elizabethan Image*, shown at the Tate to much acclaim in 1970. This was a period both of great political change and major cultural achievements but the paintings remain comparatively unknown.

The term dynasties is generally associated with monarchs and the great families that rose to power during the course of the century, but the term is equally applicable to the artists themselves whose standing rose significantly in the period. Unusually, the exhibition sets the British art of this time in a European context, a theme that we are keen to emphasise. British art has special qualities but it cannot be isolated from international developments.

The understanding, generosity and enthusiasm of lenders, both private and public collections, has been overwhelming. Without their support the exhibition could not have been realised. Paintings of this period are often fragile, many of them being painted on panel. A study of the behaviour of panels and their care in changing environments has been the subject of considerable research in our Conservation Department and this has helped to reassure owners. We are particularly grateful to Her Majesty The Queen and to the National Portrait Gallery for agreeing to lend so many works from their collections. These have provided a backbone for the exhibition.

The exhibition has been selected by Karen Hearn, Assistant Keeper in the British Collection, who has also acted as general editor of the catalogue. Her research has brought to light not only works not seen in this country for many years but new information both about the artists and the sitters. She has been ably assisted by her colleague in the British Collection, Tabitha Barber. A number of other scholars contributed catalogue entries on works that fell into their particular area of research, and we are grateful to them. We should also like to thank Neil Cuddy, Christopher Brown, Susan Foister and Rica Jones for their essays, which expand our knowledge of a number of aspects of the period, art historical, social and technical.

An exhibition of this scale and ambition would have been impossible without the generous assistance of Pearson. Their enthusiasm and commitment both to the exhibition and the conservation research have been significant factors in the realisation of the project. Pearson have been sponsors of exhibitions at the Tate Gallery in 1982 and 1984 and we are extremely grateful for their continuing support for the activities of the Gallery.

Nicholas Serota
Director

Sponsor's Foreword

This is the fourth exhibition that Pearson has sponsored at the Tate Gallery since 1982, when we helped to put on the *Sir Edwin Landseer* exhibition. That was the Tate's first commercially sponsored exhibition as well as our own, and paved the way for our sponsorship of an exhibition at one or other of the great national galleries every year since. We are delighted to be involved with *Dynasties*, which illuminates an exciting political and cultural period in British history. The exhibition and this accompanying catalogue include many well-known works that will both delight the eye and encourage a better understanding of the age. I very much hope that you will enjoy the exhibition as much as we have enjoyed being involved in its preparation.

Michael Blakenham
Chairman, Pearson plc

Acknowledgments

My principal thanks go to Pearson plc, without whose generosity this exhibition could not have taken place. In my task of selecting and curating *Dynasties*, I had considerable assistance from the Tate Gallery Conservation department, and above all from Rica Jones, whose collaboration on numerous visits much enriched the project. I am most grateful to all those who allowed us to examine their paintings, sometimes hung in almost inaccessible positions, and who with great good humour provided ladders, coffee, and power points for our equipment. We are still trying to find out which potential lender first tagged us 'the Ladies with the Lamp'.

The generosity of Sir Oliver Millar to other scholars in the field is legendary, and I am very glad to acknowledge his valuable suggestions, particularly at the outset of the project. Thanks are due to all the contributors to the catalogue; I have benefited especially from my discussions with Susan Foister and Lorne Campbell. In the later stages, research assistance was provided by Susan Bracken, whose reliability and professionalism were matched only by her unfailing good humour.

For help and advice, I should like also to thank Simon Adams, Janet Arnold, Alexander Bell, Warren Boutcher, Xanthe Brooke, Christine Byers, Charlotte Crawley, Sarah Cove, Ellen Chirelstein, Katherine Coombs, Catherine Cullis, Keith Cunliffe, Jane Cunningham, Peter Day, Diana Dethloff, Elizabeth Drey, Mary Edmond, Claire Gapper, Philippa Glanville, Anthony Griffiths, John R.S. Guinness, Yvonne Hackenbroch, Kate Harris, the Hon. Lady Hastings, Wendy Hefford, Steffen Heiberg, Paula Henderson, Elizabeth Honig, Maurice Howard, Alex Kidson, Wouter Th. Kloek, Caroline Knight, Olaf Koester, Alastair Laing, Susan Lambert, Christopher Lloyd, Stephen Lloyd, Rosalind K. Marshall, Olivier Meslay, Hessel Miedema, Andrew Moore, Cathal Moore, Theresa-Mary Morton, Jane Munro, A.V.B. Norman, Sheila O'Connell, Jacqueline Penniall-Boer, Aileen Ribeiro, the Hon. Mrs Hugh Roberts, Sara Rodger, Malcolm Rogers, Francis Russell, Sidney Sabin, Cécile Scaillierez, Diana Scarisbrick, David Scrase, Jacob Simon, Helen Smailes, Kiffy Stainer-Hutchins, Christopher Taylor, Paul Taylor, Duncan Thomson, Mark Weiss, Lavinia Wellicome, Aidan Weston-Lewis, Timothy Wilks, Richard Williams and Jeremy Wood.

I should like also to express particular gratitude to my former supervisor, John Newman, and to his colleagues at the Courtauld Institute, Katie Scott and David Solkin.

At a key stage in my research, I benefited greatly from a four-week Fellowship at the Yale Center for British Art, New Haven. I wish to thank the staff there for their help, and also those of the Institute of Historical Research, Courtauld Institute and Tate Gallery libraries. A particular debt is owed to Jonathan Franklin and the team at the National Portrait Gallery Library and Archive. Assistance was also received from the Roberts Library at the University of Ontario; the Royal Ontario Museum Library; the Centre for Reformation and Renaissance Studies, Victoria University in the University of Toronto; and the Pontifical Institute of Medieval Studies, Toronto.

Within the Tate Gallery, I have been grateful for the support and encouragement of my colleagues in the British Collection, particularly of Tabitha Barber, Elizabeth Einberg, and the Keeper, Andrew Wilton. The tremendous drive of the Exhibitions department – Ruth Rattenbury, Emma Jones, and primarily Sarah Tinsley – brought the exhibition to fruition, while Judith Severne, Tim Holton and Susan Lawrie of Tate Publishing, together with the designer, Caroline Johnston, have turned this catalogue into a reality.

Finally, I wish to thank my family – Audrey, Andrew, Jonathan and Suzanne Hearn, and my late father, Clive Hearn – for their patience and forbearance. Paul Petzold has been a constant enthusiast and support.

Karen Hearn

Introduction

KAREN HEARN

The images in this catalogue span just over a hundred years – broadly the century between the arrival of the German artist Hans Holbein the Younger, in search of employment at the court of Henry VIII, and that of the Flemish Anthony Van Dyck, invited to England by Charles I.

This period saw immense political and religious changes throughout Europe. In 1603, the crowns of Scotland and England were united. Throughout the century, c.1530–1630, British drama, literature and music flourished. Yet, apart from certain portraits of the well-known figures – particularly the monarchs – the visual arts of the period are curiously unfamiliar. Some of the reasons for this are purely practical. Images have been lost simply through the passage of time. Painted on such materials as wooden panels or linen cloth and liable to damage from damp, heat or excessive light, they have decayed or been thrown away. Or, they may have been deliberately destroyed in the iconoclasm of the sixteenth and mid seventeenth centuries. Or, again, in the course of time they may have seemed hopelessly out of fashion, and perhaps suffered so much overpainting during the following three to four hundred years that it is now difficult to be certain how much of the original image remains. Nevertheless, many of the best paintings of this period have a power and a directness that is still irresistible today. They also suggest a slippery secret world of private allusions with which our late twentieth-century postmodernist sensibility is particularly in tune.

One question that this catalogue attempts to address is – how English was painting in England at this time? There are extremely distinguished indigenous artists – Bettes, Hilliard, Gower, Peake – but they are heavily outnumbered by those from overseas, particularly from the Low Countries.

The 'dynasties' of the title are not only those of the Tudors and Stuarts, and of the great families that rose to power (and, in some cases, fell again) in the course of the century. They are also the dynasties among the artistic networks that served them. Many of the artists represented here were from families in which members of successive generations were painters, and they made family alliances that reinforced professional connections within their own, or other allied crafts. Apprenticeships, too, were almost like family bonds. Thus, the close network of the foreign-born Gheeraerts, de Critz and Oliver families (see e.g. nos.41, 45, 118, 79, 89) encompassed painting, limning and sculpture. Similar networks are being discovered among the families of English-born painters, such as that of the Elizabethan Serjeant Painter William Herne with the Cutler family, and the extent of the Wright, Hethe, Isaackson and Potkin painter dynasties.

This close and familial structure was, in fact, a reflection of professional patterns on the Continent, and it was one that could accommodate the skills of women family members, too (no.68). Such networking encouraged the establishment of studios and workshops where painters may have collaborated, and between which they may have moved. The little documentary material that exists suggests that this may have been the practice.

Rather in the way that the English have not prized their native cooking tradition, but have placed a greater value on, say, that of France, there seems during the centuries in question to have been a real cachet in employing a 'foreign' artist. This may explain why in the few cases where artists in England sign their works, they add their nationality: Gerlach Flicke as 'Gerlacus flicus Germanus', in 1545–6 (no.12), or Quentin Metsys's 'ANT', for Antwerp, in 1583 (no.40). What do we make of the signature of Marcus Gheeraerts the Younger, brought to settle in England as a child, but who, forty years later, added to his signature the Latin word 'Brugiensis' (i.e. 'from Bruges')?

The nature of the training available to artists in England is not clear, but if this was problematical it may help to account for the preponderance of non-native artists and the enthusiasm of clients for their services. It is, for instance, known that John de Critz the Elder was apprenticed in London to a fellow-Netherlander, Lucas de Heere.

While this catalogue principally examines easel paintings, miniatures and, to a certain extent, works on paper (excluding prints – a complex area which deserves to be examined in its own right), clients of the period commissioned a wide range of painted work. Painted cloths or hangings, in some cases imitating the much more expensive woven form, tapestry, were common. These, however, were so ephemeral that a mere handful of fragments survive. Wall-paintings were also popular. Generally decorative in nature, sometimes consisting of texts or narrative images, they were often based on engraved sources.

Contrary to the general impression, not every painting made or owned in England during the sixteenth century was a portrait. Narrative – including religious – images continued to be owned and, certainly in some cases, displayed, well after the full impact of the Reformation had been felt. Existing inventories and surviving accounts of interiors emphasise that people also displayed maps, painted genealogies and coats of arms.

The early part of the century under review saw, with the advent of the Reformation, the gradual end of the native industry of painted alabaster carving of religious subjects. There is, however, evidence of subsequent interest in painted terracotta sculpture, practised by Italian and later by Netherlandish or Germanic visitors.

Nevertheless, the vast majority of extant works are painted portraits – a galaxy of faces of the famous, the obscure, the infamous and the unknown. Portraits served practical purposes as demonstrations of political or familial affiliation, or as memorials. They reinforced the bonds of duty and affection.

The period as a whole witnesses an ebb and flow in the desire for naturalistic representation. It is powerfully realised in the work of Holbein, increasingly in retreat during the course of Hans Eworth's career, returning only gradually with the work of Marcus Gheeraerts the Younger.

Portraits, however, were more than mere records of features – even though contemporary comments on images may praise them in terms of their 'likeness' to the living subject. They were intended partly as documents to proclaim the sitter's station. Backgrounds or settings sometimes convey an appropriate context for the individual depicted. Often, however, by the inclusion of text written across the picture plane, the portrait is removed from reality – from depicted space. The information thus supplied is generally the sitter's age, the date and perhaps a motto, either in English or Latin, or occasionally Greek, Italian or French. Such inscriptions usually relate to the sitter – a signature (or even a monogram) by the artist is exceptionally rare in the sixteenth century. The post-Romantic preoccupation with artistic originality would have been an unfamiliar notion to contemporary patrons. With a rise in connoisseurship, however, came a greater emphasis on individual artistic style. Where, previously, repeat versions of the same image might be ordered, sometimes over several years (see no.119), or an earlier portrait might be borrowed by a friend or relative of its owner for a copy to be made, towards the end of the period copies might be made for more complex reasons. An interesting measure of the growth of antiquarian taste and a new concept of artistic value lies in Lucy Harington's desire to purchase in about 1618 the Bacon family's ancestral portraits which she thought were by Holbein: 'If any copies of them be desired, I will retorne such as he must extraordinarily well know paintinge, that shall distinguish them from the originals.' (*Cornwallis Correspondence*, 1842, pp.50–1).

The display of heraldic arms and their quarterings – presumably instantly identifiable to well-informed contemporaries – fixed the sitter's exact identity, as well as his or her dynastic position – but if added later and erroneously can cause great confusion (see no.28) to the modern observer.

The costume selected for depiction was another vehicle for meaning. Its opulence, cost and fashionableness convey messages about status, of course, but there would be additional resonances: the Earl of Surrey, Italianate poet, was portrayed in Italian attire (no.14); the French queen, Catherine de'Medici took it as a compliment when she received from England a portrait of Elizabeth I dressed in the French style.

The veracity of surviving portraits is hard to ascertain. It has already been noted that this was not necessarily required: for instance in an age when smallpox, often disfiguring, was rife, portraits never convey the havoc it wrought. Sir Philip Sidney's acned compexion was a matter of record yet survivng portraits of him show no sign of it. Specific blemishes do sometimes appear, however, such as that in Ketel's portrait of Joan Fanshawe (no.60). Mytens's portrait of the Earl of Arundel (no.140) emphasises his warts, while they are characteristically almost smoothed away by Van Dyck (no.146). Military disfigurements are seldom in evidence: the battle scar displayed by Captain Thomas Lee in 1594 (no.120) carries a very specific message.

The images that have come down to us reveal not only changes in intention and function, but also a viewpoint that, however remotely, we can begin to identify with our own. The relatively small market for top-level patronage was distributed among artists many of whom had taken the grave step of journeying to a foreign country. Within that small circle there flourished an internationalism that countered Britain's island status – as effectively as the Channel Tunnel may do today.

Dynasty and Display:
Politics and Painting in England, 1530–1630

Neil Cuddy

Royal marriages fill today's front pages because most people are fascinated by the private deeds and misdeeds of the rich and famous – and it matters little whether the royalty in question is a Presley or a Windsor. But in the century covered by this exhibition, the marriage policy of royalty really was an important issue. On it depended England's internal political stability, the nature of its church, the identities and fortunes of its chief ministers, peace, war, and its alliances and interests abroad: indeed in 1603, it turned Tudor England into Stuart Britain. More important still, royalty stood at the head of a landed elite which thought, and behaved, in a similarly dynastic way. 'Dynasty', which originally meant 'power', came to mean a family which *holds* power (and wealth), over successive generations. From kings to mere gentlemen, the collection of family firms that was 'England' all played the game of dynastic ambition and aggrandisement. Dynastic preoccupations shaped that elite's culture. Part of that culture, new and increasingly significant, was the commissioning, collecting, and display, of paintings. And to understand those paintings, it will help to understand the world in which they were produced.[1]

The rules of the dynastic game were well established in the England of 1530. Out of a population of about two and a half million, there were perhaps three thousand gentry families. They were defined by a combination of lineage – their right to bear a coat of arms; and lifestyle – their ability to live wholly at leisure on their landed rents, and keep up the state of a gentleman, with a substantial 'seat' (or country house), decently lavish hospitality, and adequate attendance. By European standards, the gentry were 'noble'. But in England, 'nobility' proper was restricted to a tiny elite at the apex of this group: the peerage. During the sixteenth century there were usually about fifty peers, since only the head of each house held the title (in ascending rank, of lord, viscount, earl, marquis, duke). And though some lesser peers were not as rich as some greater gentry, the division in status between the two groups did reflect a real difference in wealth. Uniquely in Europe, the English

gentry and peerage had no fiscal exemptions, and even peers enjoyed only minor, personal legal privileges. But this was compensated by their right to rule the localities in the crown's name. The major gentry shared out amongst themselves both the local government of the shires as justices of the peace (JPs), and the vast majority of seats in the House of Commons. Peers' dominance of their counties was formalised after the 1550s by their appointments as Lords Lieutenant; and of course their titles carried the duty to sit in the House of Lords. Moreover, the peerage periodically recalled its claim, advanced repeatedly in its medieval struggles with the crown, to be *consiliarii nati* – councillors with a hereditary right to be consulted about the realm's affairs.[2]

Managing this landed elite, and their formidable local power and prestige, was always a chief task of monarchy; and it was always management from within. The crown, as an inherited office, descending by the same rules as the older peerages, was part of the nobility: indeed, at times in the fifteenth century, the crown could appear to be little more than an additional title, to be claimed, and won, by peers and their retinues. But by 1530, the Yorkist and early Tudor refoundation of the crown had elevated it above the nobility. Reviving the crown's formal legal and financial power was one aspect of this: and the law courts and administrative departments that saw to that revival are what we think of as 'government'. But this formal machine largely provided the raw material of power. Power was asserted – and cash spent – in ways less familiar to us. The English court long ago vanished as a political power-centre: but in this period, it was *the* continuing centre of power. One cause of the Wars of the Roses had been the court's eclipse, in size and wealth, by other noble households. But the Yorkists and Tudors created a household that outstripped all others, 'the house of houses principal of England': and until 1642, the crown invested most of its peacetime expenditure in it. There were two main activities – magnificent feasting, and the 'retaining' of the politically important – and two departments to organise them. The Household 'below stairs' provided fine dining on a daily basis, at scores of court tables, supplied by about five hundred (mostly menial) servants, working in twenty service departments (Kitchen, Buttery, Pantry, etc.). The Chamber, under the Lord Chamberlain, ensured this magnificence was acted out with due ceremony, in the 'above stairs' court chambers; served the king as he ate, dressed, and slept; and kept him company. Chamber servants were mostly gentlemen and better, and there were many more than was strictly necessary – perhaps four hundred including supernumeraries. To us, all this looks like extravagance: but to them, it was hard-headed investment. Feasting certainly displayed royal wealth: but it also had a precise political function, for the hierarchical arrangement of the court tables demonstrated and cemented the power relationships, and bonds of loyalty, between the king, those who presided over the tables, and those who ate at them. The Chamber was heavily overmanned because it provided the focus of the crown's 'retinue', its direct power base of loyal 'retainers'– gentlemen who served three months at court as Gentlemen of the Chamber, Esquires of the Body, Carvers, Cupbearers and so on, and spent the rest of the year in their country seats. Recruited from all over England, they took home to their counties the prestige of their court service, and royal patronage for themselves, their kin, and in turn their own 'retainers': they brought back their own local influence, and knowledge of county matters. Indeed, the royal court possessed political resonance because it resembled in form and function the households of the nobility and gentry, who themselves kept up both hospitality, and 'retines' drawn from the ranks below them. And attaching peers to the court, who could add their followings to the crown's, was vital for the royal dynasty's stability. Some peers served at court (as Lord Chamberlain, Lord Steward, Master of the Horse), or as heads of administrative departments (Lord Treasurer, Lord Admiral, Lord Privy Seal). Others might attend on state occasions – receptions of ambassadors or visiting princes, openings of parliament – or on anniversaries, such as the accession day jousts. And after 1540, a Privy Council dominated by the peerage attended at court.[3]

So the royal dynasty – in the fullest sense of its power, its lineage, its connections with the families that served it – was physically embodied in the royal court, just as a noble or gentry household embodied a peer's or gentleman's 'house'. That embodiment was physical because visual display was everywhere; in feasting; in ceremonial attendance; and not least, in the setting within which all this took place. Coats of arms and badges covered the insides of palaces, halls and chambers, and the outsides of servants and retainers. Indeed, dynasty and display shaped both parts of the interchange on which this household politics was based – an interchange of service by those below, in return for reward from those above. Families were linked in service and lordship over generations, and their allegiances permanently expressed. Gentlemen's houses often contained oriel windows in their great (or dining) chambers, displaying the coats of arms of their lineage: they might also display the badges of a lord and patron, or of the royal house if they were directly retained by the crown – the mullet of the Earls of Oxford, the sun of York, the Tudor rose (see no.16), and so on. Retainers also wore their lords' badges – the Collar of SS worn by Sir Thomas More in Holbein's portrait (and Lockey's later miniature copy, no.76), was a badge of service to the royal house of Lancaster. Or a retainer might signal allegiance by turning out in his team's colours, or livery. In 1566 the followings of the Duke of Norfolk and the Earl of Leicester massed at court in a competitive show of strength, one side in yellow stripes, the other in blue.[4] Ambition for reward was conceived dynastically too. Peers and gentry aspired to increase the wealth and status, not of themselves in the here and now, but of their 'houses' as institutions stretching forward through future generations. Prudent estate management was essential to this, but alone – even in a century of rising agricultural prices – it was unlikely to move a family up in the world: 'it is impossible for a mere country gentlemen to … raise his house … by only following the plough' thought one contemporary. Here the favour of a patron – a pension, an office in his gift, a grant or beneficial lease of land – made a difference. And in a world where 90 per cent of wealth was in the land, and where it was mostly inherited, marriage was the landed elite's most effective point of leverage for 'raising their houses'. A prosperous yeoman – one of the social group below the gentry, often as wealthy, but who did not affect a gentry lifestyle, and farmed land directly – might enter the gentry by marrying a local gentleman's daughter: more likely their son would be accepted as a gentleman. Daughters endowed with marriage portions were essentially negotiable commodities in a marriage market among the gentry and nobility, at once sources of mobile wealth, and pledges of alliance between families. And the most spectacular coups came when a powerful patron could rig the marriage market in his own, or his client's, favour. On average, succession from father to son failed after three generations: property then went either to junior male branches of the family, or to one or more heiresses. The latter were the prizes in the marriage market. Royal (or noble) influence could be decisive in arranging a marriage with an heiress of full age. But if a man died leaving an under-age heir or heiress, their landlord took charge of the child's marriage, and (temporarily) its lands – its 'wardship'. The crown exploited the wardships of its tenants in chief in several ways: a ward's marriage could be granted as a favour to a follower; it could be sold for cash on the market; or it could be sold back to the family, at a rate depending on how well-disposed the crown (or the Master of the Wards) was towards them. The results of playing this market with consistent prudence, favour, and luck, over a few generations, were spectacular accumulations of lands and titles. The Howards became Dukes of Norfolk by marrying the female heiress of the Mowbray Dukes: over this century they went on to collect (through heiresses) the Arundel, Audley, and Talbot inheritances. The rise of the Habsburg dynasty, from obscure roots in the 1100s to world empire, and a collection of crowns, in the 1500s, is only the most dramatically successful outcome of a strategy common to the landed elites of Europe.[5]

Growing wealth called for a rise in status: and though control of this was theoretically a royal monopoly, in practice peers and greater gentry could act as intermediaries at court for the promotion of their followers. At the lowest level of the gentry, crown heraldic visitations examined claims to gentility itself, and issued coats of arms. Knighthoods conferred precedence on individual gentlemen over their rivals: though military commanders could also bestow knighthoods on the field of battle (and the Earl of Essex did so in abundance in the 1590s). The crown also created peers: but, like all their predecessors, the Tudors did so very sparingly, and usually in accordance with rules of lineage (if sometimes leavened with royal favour). Wholly new creations were rare, and almost always in recognition of military service. A handful of peerages rewarded purely administrative servants, such as Henry VIII's Thomas Cromwell, and Elizabeth's Lord Burghley. In France such men formed the *noblesse de robe*: but they were never numerous enough in England to be considered a separate social group. If they survived the resentment of the blood nobility – Cromwell was degraded and executed at their hands, and Burghley and his son Robert Cecil had to outface and survive aristocratic combinations in the 1560s and 1590s – they were assimilated into it by marriage within two generations. And if other so-called Tudor 'new men' began as mere gentlemen, and amassed wealth in crown service, they also had blood claims to their peerages – Henry VIII's Pembroke from the wrong side of the blanket; Edward VI's Northumberland, Elizabeth I's Leicester and Essex, by transmission through female heiresses. Promotion was one aim: but in the meantime, precedence over one's equals also mattered. Within any rank, this normally went by age of lineage, or of creation: but it could be adjusted. For the nobility, the Council reforms of 1539 established the great offices as prizes. To be Lord Treasurer, for example, was not only lucrative (the Sackville Earl of Dorset who held the place was nicknamed 'lord fill-sack'); it gave its holder precedence over his fellow earls. The four inheritable great offices

similarly enabled their holders to leap-frog over their colleagues, and in special circumstances (according to medieval theory), also carried quasi-regal powers: houses nursed claims to them over generations – successive Earls of Essex to be Constable, Earls of Pembroke to be Lord High Steward, Dukes of Norfolk to be Earl Marshal, and Earls of Oxford to be Lord Great Chamberlain – the first two houses with mixed results, the latter two with more consistent success.[6]

After Henry VII gained the throne in battle in 1485, it was according to these rules that he established, then strengthened the Tudor dynasty. His claim to the throne (and, in 1483–5, much of the wealth that had made him a contender for it) came through his mother, the great Lancastrian heiress Lady Margaret Beaufort. But for any who doubted that claim, Henry's marriage to Elizabeth, daughter of Edward IV and now heiress to the Yorkist claim (and following), in any case made him king in right of his wife, as her consort: and their offspring inherited both claims. This union of the two houses was the foundation of the Tudor dynasty, as successive Tudors, and indeed Stuarts, repeatedly stressed. From there, Henry VII proceeded to establish his dynasty further. In 1501 a feast to celebrate the marriage of Arthur, Prince of Wales (see no.1) with Catherine of Aragon took place in the Great Hall of the splendid new palace of Richmond – beneath a chronological series of portraits of English monarchs, culminating in Henry himself. The Tudors were placing their new dynasty in context: the successor to the old English royal houses; the equal of the oldest European ones.[7]

The establishment of the dynasty was continued by Henry VIII. He quickly began war with France (and resumed it in the 1520s and 1540s), setting himself forth as legitimate successor, not only to the English crown, but also to its claim (by female transmission) to the French throne. But for most of the reign Henry engaged in more settled dynastic competition, with the revived France of François I, and the Habsburg Charles V (King of Spain, Duke of Burgundy, and Holy Roman Emperor). Since François had four times, and Charles V more than five times, Henry's annual revenue, Henry could only compete on external marks of splendour. At first, this was sub-contracted to Cardinal Wolsey, whose proxy 'court', of practically royal dimensions, supplemented the King's, and whose direction of highly visible diplomatic epics, like the Field of the Cloth of Gold, did enable England to 'punch above its weight' in Europe. But on Wolsey's fall in 1529, Henry took over the director's chair (together with Wolsey's palaces) himself: and his subsequent orgy of palace building resumed his father's assertion of dynasty, in an architectural setting continuing to respond to European fashion. There were two developments, already underway: first, a retreat into greater privacy, with the introduction of a separate staff of private royal body servants, in a Privy Chamber, and still more private and extensive 'Privy Lodgings'; second, the building of 'galleries' – broad windowed corridors, at first connecting buildings but by now purpose-built for indoor recreation, which became a chief setting, in palaces and country houses, for the display of pictures. Whitehall, the main London palace built after 1530, combined the two: its hub was a long Privy Gallery, running from the Privy Chamber, through the main range of Privy Lodgings.[8] The most costly furnishings here (and in the more public apartments which led up to them) were silk hangings, tapestries (laced with gold and silver thread), and gilded panelling and ceilings. Paintings, which usually contained no precious metals, were by comparison cheap (in the 1620s a set of tapestries cost as much as fifty Van Dycks, for example). But with Charles V patronising Titian, and François I patronising Leonardo, fashion dictated that Henry attract a first-rate exponent of the new art: this was Holbein, from Basel. The staff of royal 'painters' – including Holbein – were still mainly occupied in painting heraldic devices, for palaces and court pageants: but as we have seen, Henry VII was already using portraits. In the 1530s, with Holbein pre-eminent, portraiture blossomed at court, and spread from there throughout the landed elite: henceforth, portrait collections in galleries supplemented heraldic decoration, displaying, and now individualising, the dynastic links between houses. Kings now exchanged portraits as part of diplomacy: marriages were as ever central to this, and in 1539–40 Henry VIII married Anne of Cleves sight unseen, on the evidence of Holbein's portrait of her (no.66). (That Henry had the marriage annulled after seeing her in the flesh only attests to Holbein's power as an image-maker.) Domestically, the royal portrait became essential to the collections of nobility and gentry, who presented, and requested, pictures of each other.[9] At Whitehall, Holbein's great mural hammered home the message of Tudor legitimacy and continuity. Painted in 1537 (see no.5), either in the Privy Chamber or another room in the Privy Lodgings, it showed a life-sized Henry and his third wife Jane Seymour (who that year died after giving birth to his male heir, Edward), with Henry VII and Elizabeth of York behind them, the founders of the dynasty overseeing its continuation. The mural's survival until Whitehall burnt down in 1698, symbolises Henry's achievement in creating the infrastructure of Tudor and Stuart monarchy.[10] At his death he possessed fifty-five houses: the few additions to that total, and the many losses, before 1642, meant that subsequent English monarchs would largely perform on Henry VIII's stages, and – with his legacy of tapestry, plate and hangings – to a great extent with his props.[11]

But Henry's stature as founding father also depends on the comparative meagreness of his children's achievements – which, ironically, was partly due to Henry's other, less material, legacies. First there was religious division, the consequence of his break with Rome and divorce. This made it difficult for his successors to maintain universal dynastic appeal; it led to half a century of rebellions and plots to change ministers and policies, or depose the monarch, on religious grounds; and it factionalised the most powerful of the nobility and higher gentry, as they inclined towards different religions, Catholic and Reformed. Second, there was the peculiar late-Tudor succession: despite Henry's Herculcan efforts as a husband, he provided only a boy and two women to follow him. Royal minorities were a familiar, if infrequent problem in England: but in a patriarchal society, two Queens regnant (the second of whom did not marry), faced unprecedented difficulties in managing a divided realm. The reigns of the precociously Protestant boy-king Edward VI (1547–53) (see no.13), and of Mary (1553–8) (see no.24), a bitterly committed Catholic, simply shifted power from one religious 'side' to the other; Elizabeth spent a long reign (1558–1603) trying to avoid, ultimately with little success, becoming a figurehead for a regime run by a small group of Protestant magnates. Third, the crown's power was fundamentally undermined by a shift of landed wealth, away from the crown (and the church), towards the nobility and higher gentry. It began with Henry's dissolution of the monasteries (1536–9), a patronage bonanza shared between 'old' and 'new' religious camps among the existing elite (with some additions); it continued during Edward VI's minority, when those in control – a newly forming Protestant 'establishment', of Seymours, Dudleys, Russells, Sidneys, Herberts, and their followers – awarded themselves high titles and broad acres (see no.31). Inflation exaggerated the effect during Elizabeth's long, conservative reign: as prices doubled, crown land revenue increased by only a third, and customs revenues stayed flat; while war with Spain in the 1580s led to land sales, permanently diminishing capital. Elizabeth relied on parliament for a quarter of her ordinary expenditure by the 1570s, and war increased her dependence: yet during her reign the value of the subsidy fell by 70 per cent in real terms, partly due to inflation, but also because the Protestant establishment which voted and paid the tax progressively under-assessed itself.[12]

For the Elizabethan nobility and gentry, by contrast, this was indeed a prosperous age, most visibly in building. Throughout the Protestant elite, new seats arose, 'so magnificent and stately as the basest house of a baron doth often match in our days with some honours of princes in old time', thought an observer in the 1570s. The courtier nobility built 'prodigy houses', big enough to house the Queen and her court – who indeed spent the summers on progress around them, sponging off her greatest subjects. The crown by contrast built nothing: and so had nothing to compare with Holdenby or Theobalds (see p.16), scarcely smaller than Hampton Court, but built in the most modern style – for, unlike the ageing royal palaces, these new houses took account of the changing habits of the landed elite. Privacy had taken hold: halls were omitted, or placed on the ground floor with the servants' departments, for them to eat in; houses became more compact, often arranged vertically, introducing the classic 'upstairs-downstairs' division between servants and family. The latter ate in the Great Chamber on the first floor, and had accommodation beyond it, and on the floor above, in private lodgings. And here the Long Gallery became both the architectural centrepiece, and the setting for display – especially of pictures.[13] All this reflected the changing structure and function of noble and gentry households. Public feasting and hospitality declined, along with the number of servants below-stairs. Upstairs, numbers also shrank, as chamber service ceased to express a political bond between a great man and his followers, and became simply a job for an emerging 'gentlemanly profession of serving men'. By 1605 most of the nobility were said to prefer being served in their bedchambers, and at table, by 'pages and groomes', rather than by 'that estate which belongeth to their degree' – that is, important knights. Great noblemen still had powerful followers among the gentry, and under Elizabeth many of them still wore livery. But the bond of personal household service was disappearing, followed soon by the wearing of livery itself – which by the 1610s was seen as a demeaning sign of dependence, fast becoming the mark of the professional servant.[14]

The causes of these changes in social and political behaviour are complex. Historians once tried to relate them to a fundamental shift of power and wealth, from a 'feudal' 'aristocracy' in 'crisis', to a rising class of 'capitalist' gentry. It does seem that by 1600, against a doubling of population (to perhaps five million), the number of families claiming gentility had disproportionately quintupled (to about fifteen thousand). But such class-based explanations have failed to convince: these changes affected the common lifestyle of the noble-gentry elite as a whole.[15] More persuasive are qualitative explanations, relating particularly to the impact of religious division on politics. As politics became a matter of personal conscience and principles; as the elite gained literacy and education, at the universities and inns of court; as print and newsletters created a more nationally centred politics; so noble and gentry factions became 'national' and ideological, where they had once been more directly local and personal. A religious stance broadened a great nobleman's power, and gave a Leicester (no.49) or an Essex (no.121) a national following –

and indeed a European profile. Leicester gave livery to men all over the country, and disciplined them if they wore the colours of their actual landlord. Essex's following was similarly widespread. But if the bonds of magnificent hospitality and direct personal service were weakening, these new political and religious groupings were still based on dynastic loyalty, and on patronage in exchange for service. From the 1550s to the 1640s, leadership of the Protestant cause was passed on from Edward VI's minister Northumberland, to his son Leicester, to his stepson Essex, and from him to his son: and the key noble and gentry families which followed them were equally continuous, and cross-linked by intermarriage.[16] On the Catholic side, dynastic continuity was similar – to grim effect. Between 1547 and 1589, four successive senior representatives of the Howard (Norfolk) line were attainted for treason, and two executed (nos.14, 27): nevertheless, the next in line, Arundel (no.146), continued to lead Catholic sympathisers into the 1640s.[17] The infusion of dynastic allegiances with personal principles can indeed be paralleled culturally, in the growing use of 'emblems' and 'devices', adaptations and extensions of heraldry to display not just the lineage of a man's house, but his personal qualities, policies, and religious stance. They became the currency of Elizabethan politics – in court literature, in masques and jousts, in architecture (a gentleman could have a house built in the shape of his initials), and of course in miniatures and paintings (see nos.23, 120).[18]

Underlying all these developments was the growth of London, as a national politics developed in step with a metropolitan elite culture. Between 1550 and 1600 London's population grew from about eighty thousand to about two hundred thousand, making it ten times bigger than its nearest rivals, Bristol and Norwich.[19] And as its mass increased, so did its gravitational attraction for the prospering county gentry and nobility. Partly they came, as they always had, for litigation, or the court, or for parliaments: but now the development of coaches enabled whole families to travel up, and they stayed for months on end to enjoy the London 'season' – for the theatre, to visit each other, to buy luxuries obtainable only in the great centre of craftsmen's skills and imported goods. Great nobles took over former bishops' palaces along the Strand, between the City and Whitehall, or built anew on their sites: their townhouses contained 'all the amenities of a country house packed on to a town site', with halls, great chambers, galleries and lodgings. Substantial gentlemen rented houses, or apartments, as residential development in the West End met the demand. By making large retinues unnecessary and impractical, the metropolitanisation of the elite accompanied and confirmed the decline in the size of households.[20] It also created a large urban market for culture: for plays, of course (the Globe theatre held about three thousand), but also for paintings. Townhouses, such as Arundel's between 1607 and 1642 (see nos.140, 141), became arenas for the display of collections of pictures and antiquities, more accessible than country seats for those they were designed to impress. London's size attracted immigrant artists, especially refugees from Catholic persecution in the Dutch religious wars (Hoefnagel, de Heere, Ketel) – and in its trading patterns, London was still essentially an outlier to the Netherlands' concentration of great cities. With the gentry accessibly gathered in London, artists now produced for this market, both through commissions – witness the number of (to us) 'unknown ladies' painted in this period – and in mass-produced portraits of the great, which were sold from stalls.[21]

Elizabeth's court was a big exception to the trend towards smaller and more functional households. Most ordinary crown expenditure still went on the court tables' costly magnificence, which was losing resonance for those it had been designed (in 1471 and 1526) to impress. But despite continuing her father's household, and inhabiting his palaces, she remained a dynastic anomaly, as an unmarried Queen regnant. This could only be assumed to be temporary, however, and in the 1560s the possibility of her marriage, and consequent ambiguity about the succession, enabled Elizabeth to balance religious conservatives and Protestants at court. Yet compared to her European contemporaries – France under Catherine de'Medici and Henri III, the Habsburg Emperors Maximilian II and Rudolph – whose dynastic court culture was designed deliberately to surmount religious division, Elizabeth's regime lacked direction: in Sir Roy Strong's words, 'the portraiture of the first ten years of her reign is as tentative as her government'.[22] But then came the reign's watershed. In 1567, Alva's huge Spanish army took up station across the Channel, to put down Protestant revolt in the Netherlands. Mary, deposed Catholic Queen of Scots but still Elizabeth's obvious heir, arrived as an exile in England in 1568. Catholic plots, centred on Mary and Alva's army, began – the Northern Rising in 1569, the 4th Duke of Norfolk's (see no.27) plot to marry Mary in 1571. Their failure, and Norfolk's execution in 1572, combined to remove 'conservative' voices from court and Council. Yet Elizabeth clung to the idea that dynasty must come before religion, and almost until the Armada hove into view, she continued saying no to the 'confessional' policies of her now dominant Protestant Councillors: no to executing Mary, for plotting her deposition (1572–87); no to persecuting her own Catholic subjects (1571–82); no to aiding Dutch Protestants against their lawful Catholic sovereign (1578–85). Elizabethan court culture takes on identifiable themes after 1570, but less under direct royal initiative than as part of her Protestant Councillors' political pressure campaign.

The first essays in allegorical royal image-making are by Dutch refugees, patronised by major courtiers, urging Elizabeth to stand firm for the Protestant cause, and linking it dynastically back to Edward VI and Henry VIII (nos.29, 35). This lobbying reached a crescendo in the late 1570s and early 1580s, as relations with Spain reached a crisis: and only now was Elizabeth appropriated as an icon of the cult of a Protestant Virgin Queen – but again, largely under the direction of her Protestant courtiers, who after decades of pressing her to marry, in 1579–80 stopped the Alençon match, Elizabeth's last realistic chance to marry, which she wanted to take (see no.40). The fashion for wearing the royal portrait (in miniature and/or cameo) began only in 1585, at a time of maximum threat from Spain. But for all her Councillors' efforts, it was only the inescapable fact of Spanish aggression which persuaded Elizabeth at last to act: in 1585 to send Leicester with troops to aid the Dutch (no.42), in 1587 to allow Mary's execution. With the Armada defeated in 1588, the cult of *Eliza Triumphans* took off in the 1590s (nos.43, 45). It is not surprising that the Protestant establishment believed God was an Englishman: if their future was safe at last, that was largely due to the providences of Elizabeth's remarkable longevity, and the 'Protestant wind' that scattered the Armada.[23]

So Elizabeth ended a figurehead, formidable at times, but dependent upon a shrinking board of directors, and their patronage networks, at court and on her Council – a 'monarchical republic' in Professor Collinson's phrase. For forty years she largely sub-contracted the job of managing them to William Cecil (fig.1), first as her Secretary (as he had once been to Edward VI), later as Lord Treasurer, and throughout, as Master of her Wards – which at once gave him his chief source of personal wealth, and a point of leverage over the elite. By his death in 1598, he was being called *pater patriae* (father of his country), a tag usually reserved for kings.[24] The myriad galleries of Theobalds, one of two great houses he built, displayed this unique status to the world. A lower gallery depicted Cecil forebears and their (necessarily) invented 'notable acts under different reigns'; in a gallery above came portraits of the Caesars, English kings (Henry V to Henry VII), leaders of the Dutch revolt, and others 'chief in Europe'. Another gallery contained more 'common' portraits; a mural in another depicted Elizabeth's coronation. Then came three galleries of mural maps of the English counties, depicting their natural resources and towns, with trees alongside each displaying the arms (and inter-marriages) of the key noble and gentry families: here was the control centre for Cecil's management of the Elizabethan establishment.[25] He was purely Elizabeth's creation: and since both believed in a tightly restricted nobility of blood, both hesitated before he became Lord Burghley, in 1571 – for

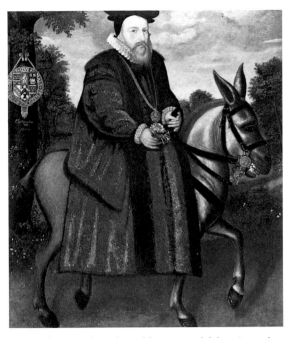

fig.1 'William Cecil, Lord Burghley on a Mule', late sixteenth century, oil on canvas. *The Bodleian Library, University of Oxford*

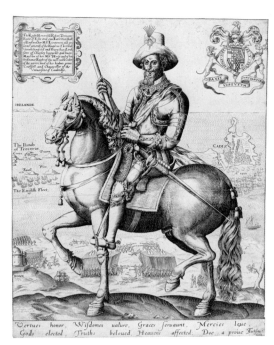

fig.2 Thomas Cockson, 'The 2nd Earl of Essex on Horseback', engraving *Trustees of the British Museum*

despite his family's later claim to descend from ancient Roman aristocrats, its recent origins were in fact scarcely gentle. Leicester and Norfolk alike resented him as an upstart in the 1560s: yet time, and the Queen's unwavering support, obliged the blood nobility to accept and work with him. But in the 1590s, when Burghley's exceptional status became hereditary in his second son, Robert Cecil (no.119), there was a more serious reaction. Essex, Leicester's heir as military leader, opposed Cecil's hold on counsel and patronage, and stood for active crusade against Spain. Essex claimed to be Constable – that is, hereditary leader of the armed forces, a claim partially recognised when Elizabeth gave him the lesser post of Earl Marshal (forfeited by the Howards), and the command of what expeditions she did allow. Essex also attracted other excluded 'ancient nobles' as allies and followers. By 1600, all this combined in a stance that appeared semi-royal – explicitly so in Cockson's engraved portrait (which was suppressed by the Council) (fig.2). But Robert Cecil manoeuvred Essex out of court, into a botched coup attempt, and so in 1601 to his execution. Crowds might lament Essex, and deride the Cecils as 'pen-gents': but of course it was Cecil who had survived, to mastermind James VI of Scotland's accession, as James I of England, in 1603 (no.125).[26]

It was as Cecil's guest, at Theobalds, that James first met his English Council, and began organising his new regime. But rather than be king solely by the grace of Robert Cecil, James first broadened, then tried to unite (through marriage alliances) what he later described as a 'state in faction'. Immediately, the Howards returned, faithful supporters of, and sufferers for, the Stuart dynastic claim – as expected: in 1603, mass-produced portraits of Mary Queen of Scots were selling strongly in London. The 4th Duke of Norfolk's brother, and younger son, gained Earldoms (of Northampton, and Suffolk, respectively) and high office; Arundel, heir to the main Norfolk line (no.146), regained lands and titles (except the Dukedom), and later the family's Earl Marshalship. The surviving Essex faction – Essex's friend, Southampton, Essex's young son, the 3rd Earl – were also restored.[27] And with the regime as inclusive as it had been in the 1560s, in 1605–6 the newly broadened establishment was tied together in a flurry of royal-sponsored marriages. Essex married one of Suffolk's daughters; Cecil's heir married another (no.90); and Suffolk's heir married the heiress of a new key figure, the Earl of Dunbar, James's chief Scottish minister, and most intimate confidant, as Gentleman of the Bedchamber (a new, and almost wholly Scottish, department, monopolising the king's body service within the Privy Lodgings).[28] Turning his dynastic union of England and Scotland into a practical one was James's other preoccupation, and to that end he encouraged other Anglo-Scottish couples to the altar at Whitehall, amid celebratory court masques pointing the weddings' wider meaning. He also tried to obtain Union legislation, especially to recognise that his accession had automatically naturalised Scotsmen in England, as British subjects. But here James found that the English establishment, which he had broadened and united, was broadly united against him in parliament, to deny his dynastic union any practical effect on the England they knew, and were used to dominating. James pressed ahead by proclamation (assuming the style 'King of

Great Britain'), and with a test case affirming his accession's effect in naturalising the Scots. But suspicion of James's high claims for his prerogative, aroused by this Union campaign and fanned by resentment of the patronage bestowed on Scots like Dunbar, spread to issues of finance. The result was the chaotic dissolution of his first parliament in 1610.[29]

And after 1610, James's reaction was to loosen the stranglehold of the Elizabethan establishment, through an unprecedented assault by the new dynasty on the exclusiveness and autonomy of the existing English peerage. Ignoring the Tudor conventions that had tightly restricted new creations, James exercised his prerogative to fix the status of his subjects as he set the values of his coin. Robert Carr, younger son of minor Scottish gentry, was promoted to the position of Bedchamber favourite (vacated by Dunbar's death in 1611), matched into the house of Suffolk, and promoted to an English royal earldom (of Somerset). English peerages followed for other Scots. And after Somerset's fall, in 1615, James took this discipline still further. By 1617, a new Bedchamber favourite, George Villiers (a younger son of minor English gentry), had been promoted to the royal earldom of Buckingham. In 1618 he became a Marquess, in 1623 a Duke, outranking the entire English peerage, however ancient (no.115). And now, rather than match his favourite with the existing establishment, James created a new network centred around Buckingham, who became by proxy the dynastic lynchpin for the Stuarts among the English elite. For James (and indeed later Charles I, even after Buckingham's assassination) insisted that marriage into Buckingham's own extensive (and until recently, totally obscure) kin, be the condition of royal promotion – whether for a newly risen financier like Lionel Cranfield to became Lord Treasurer, or for the mighty 3rd Earl of Pembroke (no.138) to secure the long-sought Lord Stewardship. Still more radically, peerages were put on sale, with Buckingham as chief broker: the criterion for an earldom was no longer a reasonable blood claim, or exceptional military service, but rather £10,000 in cash. So, where there had been fifty-five peers in 1603, there were 126 by 1628. Together with James's reliance on other kinds of prerogative finance (impositions, wardship, purveyance, monopolies), and his habit either of doing without parliaments, or declaring their meetings void (as in 1614 and 1621), the policies of 1610–25 set the scene for the following fifteen years.[30] First came the parliamentary storms of the later 1620s, as the survivors and heirs of the Elizabethan elite assaulted Buckingham, the sale of peerages, and extra-parliamentary prerogative finance, using the classic Elizabethan charge of 'popish plotting' to bolster popular support – not (as in 1571–1605) against the royal regime's Catholic enemies, but now rather against the 'evil counsellors' of Charles I's regime itself, as alleged sub-

verters of the Elizabethan church and constitution. After the deceptive calm of the 1630s – Charles's comprehensive attempt to escape the clutches of the Elizabethan establishment, by doing without parliaments, and ruling through his prerogatives – these earlier issues re-erupted in 1637–42, as a British crisis which began in Scotland, split the Stuart and Elizabethan establishments in England. Arundel led Charles I's forces against Protestant Scotland in the First Bishops' War; Essex and Pembroke led the assault, first on Charles I's ministers, then on Charles himself, in 1640–2.[31]

So in its management of British dynastic politics, James I's court was highly innovative – and highly disruptive. But culturally, it was less original. Robert Cecil tried to use the opportunity of a new reign to abolish the court tables (and divert the money to adjust salaries for inflation, for the first time in seventy years): but in 1610 James rejected that, along with Cecil's wider attempt to create a monarchy based on parliament (a solution that had to wait until the Restoration, in 1660–3). So magnificent hospitality (whose utility was now compared by one courtier to putting money down the privy) remained the biggest item of peacetime expenditure: indeed, after 1614 James began a proclamation campaign (which Charles I continued in the 1630s), that told the nobility and gentry to keep traditional hospitality in their country seats, and removed them from London. When James himself fled his capital, however, as he did for long periods, it was to hunt and read theology, surrounded by his Scots Bedchamber in intimate hunting lodges. If all this chimed with James's personal tastes, it also formed another, defensive aspect of his struggle with the Elizabethan status quo, as the Stuart court, in Scotland a remote satellite of Paris and London, now at Whitehall risked being swallowed by London's large and well-established metropolitan culture.[32] But if James was a hunting king, his wife, Anne of Denmark (nos.130, 139) was a dancing queen: she was responsible for the court's chief cultural innovation, masques, whose ubiquitous theme was dynastic Anglo-Scottish union, and in which (according to Franco-Scottish fashion) the royal family – apart from James – performed. Indeed it was James's wife and sons who made contact most actively with the English cultural mainstream, which itself was now changing through the reception of Italian renaissance ideals of art, architecture and 'virtuoso' collecting. Inigo Jones's designs for masque settings were among the earliest signs of this, soon to be translated into real buildings (see no.108).[33] Jones was employed as Master of the Works by James's elder son Prince Henry (who died in 1612) (see nos.84, 127). Henry formed a large picture collection which, while still dominated by portraits, showed a new appreciation of who had painted them, and how well. Arundel shared these interests, and after his Italian visit with Jones in

1613–14, became the chief conduit both for connoisseurship, and the works of European masters (both old, and in Rubens and Van Dyck, new).³⁴ Fuelled by competition and emulation, the new attitude spread through the elite: Bedchamber favourites (Somerset and Buckingham) and ancient nobility (Pembroke as well as Arundel) alike assembled such collections. Above all, Prince Charles (no.128) took up where his dead brother had left off, spurred in 1623 by direct experience of rival collections in Paris and Madrid, and culminating after his accession as King in 1625 with his purchase of the great Mantuan collection in 1627.³⁵ This new connoisseurship stood in contrast to the greatest Elizabethan picture collections, whose purpose, in Strong's words, had been 'not aesthetic but dynastic; … for most … Elizabethans, the idea of painting as a work of art perhaps never existed; … it was primarily an expression of rank and class.' Lord Lumley's collection, for example, inventoried only subjects' names, seldom artists' (no.105).³⁶ Yet we should not exaggerate the shift in perception. The arrangement of Charles I's collections at Whitehall married new taste with traditional function. Paintings in the fully private Privy Lodgings were arranged by artist, with little attention to subject matter (Titian's naked 'Venus with an Organ Player' hung almost next to his 'Entombment of Christ'). But the galleries, slightly more public, were arranged by sitter – albeit efforts were made to ensure the portraits were by the best masters, often by means of ambitious attributions. A traditional series of the Caesars hung at St James's: the difference now was that they were by Titian.³⁷ Similarly, commissions from the new masters continued the traditional demands of dynastic display – in Rubens's 'Banqueting House Ceiling' (stressing James I's Anglo-Scottish Union) (no.151), or his 'Buckingham on Horseback' (which hung in the Duke's Great Chamber at York House), in Van Dyck's 'Charles I, Henrietta Maria and their Children' (fig.3) (placed at the end of the Whitehall Privy Gallery), and 'Charles I Riding through a Triumphal Arch' (at the end of the Gallery at St James's). But if, after the long interim following Holbein and Henry VIII, the 1630s saw the royal dynasty 'heroicised' again, Van Dyck was available to do the same for the great dynasties beneath the throne, in his family groups of both Pembroke and that proposed for Arundel (figs.4, 5). Whereas Henry VIII had faced rivalry only from his fellow monarchs in the splendour of his court culture, Charles I's court (like Henry VI's) ended in competition with his greatest subjects.³⁸

The pictures at this exhibition, then – predominantly portraits, of sitters surrounded by trappings of wealth, symbols of power, and badges of descent – are not art for art's sake; still less art for God's sake; they are rather art for the sake of power, wealth, and lineage – for the sake of dynasty.

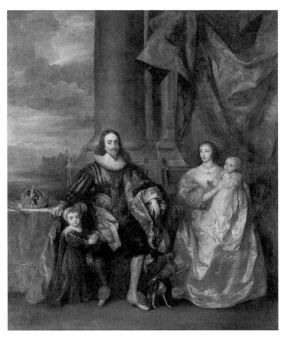

fig.3 Anthony Van Dyck, 'Charles I, Henrietta Maria and Children' 1632, oil on canvas. *The Royal Collection, Her Majesty The Queen*

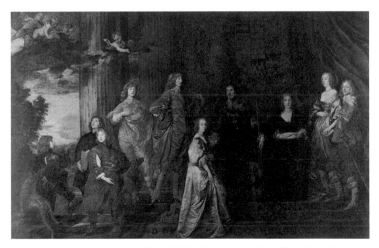

fig.4 Anthony Van Dyck, 'Family of Philip Herbert, 4th Earl of Pembroke' 1635–6. *Collection of the Earl of Pembroke, Wilton House*

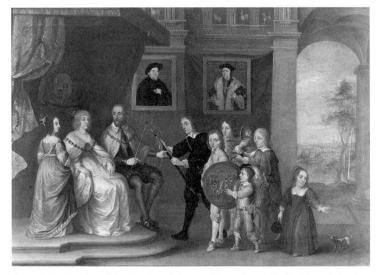

fig.5 Philip Fruytiers, 'The Family of Thomas Howard, 14th Earl of Arundel', oil on copper. *Reproduced by permission of His Grace The Duke of Norfolk*

Notes

1 R. Bonney, *The European Dynastic States, 1494–1660*, Oxford 1991, especially chap.10, and D. Starkey (ed.), *Rivals in Power: Lives and Letters of the Great Tudor Dynasties*, 1990, are useful treatments of the dynastic theme.

2 D. Starkey, 'The Age of the Household, 1350–1550', in S. Medcalf (ed.), *The Later Middle Ages*, 1981; M. Bush, *The English Aristocracy: A Comparative Synthesis*, Manchester 1984; L. Stone, *The Crisis of the Aristocracy, 1558–1641*, Oxford 1965; D. Starkey, 'Court, Council and Nobility in Tudor England', in R.G. Asch and A.M. Birke (eds.), *Princes, Patronage, and the Nobility: The Court at the Beginning of the Modern Age, c.1450–1650*, Oxford 1991.

3 Starkey in Medcalf (ed.) 1981; in D. Starkey *et al.*, *The English Court, from the Wars of the Roses to the Civil War*, 1987; S. Thurley, *The Royal Palaces of Tudor England*, New Haven 1993, chaps.2, 3; K. Mertes, *The English Noble Household, 1250–1600*, Oxford 1988; F. Heal, *Hospitality in Early Modern England*, Oxford 1990; J. Guy, *Tudor England*, Oxford 1988, pp.164–73.

4 Starkey in Medcalf (ed.) 1981; Thurley 1993, chap.6, pp.98–102; J.E. Neale, *Queen Elizabeth I*, 1934, p.147.

5 L. Stone, *An Open Elite? England 1540–1880*, Oxford, abridged ed. 1986, especially pts.ii and iv; J. Hurstfield, *The Queen's Wards*, 1958.

6 H. Miller, *Henry VIII and the English Nobility*, Oxford 1986, chap.1; Stone 1965, chap.3; W.H. Dunham, 'William Camden's Commonplace Book', *Yale University Library Gazette*, vol.43, 1969, pp.148 et seq.; Starkey in Asch and Birke (eds.) 1991; J. Adamson, 'The Baronial Context of the English Civil War', *Transactions of the Royal Historical Society*, vol.40, 1990. On claims to individual peerages and hereditary offices, cf. G.E. C[ockayne], *The Complete Peerage*, ed. V. Gibbs et al., 1910–59, s.nn; 11, App.D; X, app.F.

7 Thurley 1993, pp.28–9.

8 D. Starkey, *The Reign of Henry VIII: Personalities and Politics*, 1985; D. Starkey (ed.), *Henry VIII: A European Court in England*, 1991; Thurley 1993, p.31, chaps 4, 8.

9 Thurley 1993, chap.13; S. Foister, 'Holbein as Court Painter', in Starkey (ed.) 1991; S. Foister, 'Foreigners at Court: Holbein, Van Dyck and the Painter-Stainers Company', in D. Howarth (ed.), *Art and Patronage in the Caroline Courts*, Cambridge 1993; R. Strong, *The English Icon: Elizabethan and Jacobean Portraiture*, 1969, pp.43 et seq.

10 Thurley 1993, pp.208–9; R. Strong, *Holbein and Henry VIII*, 1967, *passim*, and his revised views in *Lost Treasures of Britain*, 1990, chap.11.

11 Starkey (ed.) 1991; Thurley 1993.

12 The up-to-date and comprehensive general account is Guy 1988, figures from pp.38, 380.

13 M. Girouard, *Robert Smythson & the Elizabethan Country House*, 1983, especially introduction and p.4; J. Summerson, *Architecture in Britain, 1530–1830*, Harmondsworth 1991, chap.4.

14 M. Girouard, *Life in the English Country House*, 1978, p.85; Starkey in Medcalf (ed.) 1981 and 'Introduction: Court History in Perspective', in Starkey et al. 1987, pp.22–4; Stone 1965, chaps.5, 10; Mertes 1988, especially. pp.183–93.

15 L. Stone (ed.), *Social Change and Revolution in England, 1540–1640*, 1965, is a useful collection of edited highlights from the 'gentry controversy' of the 1950s and 1960s.

16 F. Levy, 'How Information Spread among the Gentry, 1550–1640', *Journal of British Studies*, vol.21, 1982; R. Cust, 'News and Politics in Early Seventeenth Century England', *Past & Present*, vol.112, 1986; A. Hughes, *The Causes of the English Civil War*, 1991, chaps.2, 3; Stone 1965, pp.211, 257–63; S. Adams, 'The Dudley Clientèle, 1553–63', in G. Bernard (ed.), *The Tudor Nobility*, Manchester 1992; S. Adams, 'The Protestant Cause … 1585–1630', unpublished Oxford D.Phil thesis, 1973; R. McCoy, *The Rites of Knighthood*, Berkeley, Calif., 1989; Adamson 1990.

17 Six chapters on the Howards by D. MacCulloch and S. Gunn, in Starkey (ed.), 1990; N. Williams, *A Tudor Tragedy: Thomas Howard, Fourth Duke of Norfolk*, 1964; D. Howarth, *Lord Arundel and his Circle*, 1985; C. Hibbard, *Charles I and the Popish Plot*, Chapel Hill, NC, 1983, on Arundel's Catholic connections, alleged and real.

18 Girouard 1983, pp.24 et seq.; Strong 1969, pp.29 et seq., and R. Strong, *Artists of the Tudor Court: The Portrait Miniature Rediscovered*, 1983, especially p.10; Summerson 1991, p.73.

19 A.L. Beier and R. Finlay (eds.), *London 1500–1700: The Making of the Metropolis*, 1986, introduction and chap.1; B. Coward, *The Stuart Age*, 1994, p.29.

20 Summerson 1991, pp.92–3; Stone 1965, chap.8 and pp.385–98, 566; L. Stone, *Family and Fortune: Studies in Aristocratic Finance*, Oxford 1973, chap.3; L. Stone, 'The Residential Development of the West End of London in the Seventeenth Century', in B. Malament (ed.), *After the Reformation*, Manchester 1980.

21 T. Cogswell, 'Thomas Middleton and the Court: *A Game at Chesse* in Context', *Huntington Library Quarterly*, vol.47, 1984; Howarth 1985, pp.57–9, 102–6;

Strong 1969, s. nn; S. Foister, 'Foreigners at Court', in Howarth (ed.) 1993. Gower and Hilliard had established clienteles before entering royal service.

22 F. Yates, *Astraea: The Imperial Theme in the Sixteenth Century*, 1975, pt.iii; H. Trevor-Roper, *Princes and Artists: Patronage and Ideology at Four Hapsburg Courts, 1517–1633*, 1991 ed., chap.3; R. Strong, *Gloriana: The Portraits of Queen Elizabeth I*, 1987, p.61.

23 C. Haigh, *Elizabeth I*, Harlow 1988; Strong 1987; P. Collinson, *The Birthpangs of Protestant England*, New York 1988, chap.1.

24 P. Collinson, 'The Monarchical Republic of Queen Elizabeth I', *Bulletin of the John Rylands Library*, vol.69, 1987; Hurstfield, *Queen's Wards*, 1958, chaps.11–13.

25 G. Groos (ed. and trans.), *The Diary of Baron Waldstein*, 1981, pp.83–7; H. Scott (ed.), *The Journal of Sir Roger Wilbraham, 1593–1616*, Camden Society, 3rd Series, 4, Miscellany x, 1902, pp.22–3; Summerson 1991, pp.67–70.

26 A. Hawkyard, 'The Cecils', and 'Robert Devereux, Earl of Essex' in Starkey (ed.0) 1990; M. James, 'At the Crossroads of the Political Culture: The Essex Revolt, 1601', in his *Society, Politics and Culture*, Cambridge 1986; McCoy 1989; Adamson 1990 on Essex's son as Constable.

27 N. Cuddy, 'The Revival of the Entourage: The Bedchamber of James I, 1603–25', in Starkey et al. 1987; *Commons Journal*, i. 309, 15 May 1606; J. Peacock, 'The Politics of Portraiture', in K. Sharpe and P. Lake (eds.), *Culture and Politics in Early Stuart England*, 1994, p.199; L. Peck, *Northampton*, 1982; Stone 1973, chap.9; N. Cuddy, 'The Divided Loyalties of a 'vulger counselor': The 3rd Earl of Southampton, 1597–1624', in J. Morrill, P. Slack and D. Woolf (eds.), *Public Duty and Private Conscience: Essays Presented to Gerald Aylmer*, Oxford 1993.

28 N. McClure (ed.), *The Letters of John Chamberlain*, Philadelphia, Pa. 1939, 1, 211–12; *Calendar of State Papers Venetian* x (1603–07), 308; Stone 1965, pp.652, 657. Cuddy in Starkey et al. 1987, pp.185–95, and Cuddy in Morrill, Slack and Woolf (eds.) 1993, pp.126 et seq.

29 N. Cuddy, 'Anglo-Scottish Union and the Court of James I, 1603–25', *Transactions of the Royal Historical Society*, vol.39, 1989; Cuddy in Morrill, Slack and Woolf (eds.) 1993, pp.125–39; M. Butler, 'Britain and Britishness in the Early Stuart Masques', forthcoming in proceedings of the conference *Europe and Whitehall, 1603–85* held at Amherst, Mass., Oct. 1993, eds. R.M. Smuts and N. Maguire.

30 Cuddy 1989, cf. p.122, Cuddy in Starkey et al. 1987; Cuddy in Morrill, Slack and Woolf (eds.) 1993; R. Lockyer, *Buckingham*, 1981; Stone 1965, chap.3; GEC, *Complete Peerage*, s.vv. Buckingham, Somerset.

31 C. Russell, *Parliaments and English Politics, 1621–29*, Oxford 1979; C. Russell, *The Causes of the English Civil War*, Oxford 1990; C. Russell, *The Fall of the British Monarchies, 1637–42*, Oxford 1991; Hibbard 1983; Adamson 1990.

32 N. Cuddy, 'The Structure and Political Function of the Stuart Court, 1603–88', forthcoming in the proceedings of a *Colloquium on the Stuart Courts in the Reigns of James I–James II*, Sept. 1994, ed. E. Cruickshanks for the Voltaire Society; R.M. Smuts, 'Cultural Diversity and Cultural Change at the Court of James I', in L. Peck (ed.), *The Mental World of the Jacobean Court*, Cambridge 1991, has to expand 'court culture' to include that of London, and of the English elite as a whole, in order to find a subject.

33 See works cited by Smuts in Peck (ed.) 1991, p.298, n.1; L. Barroll, 'The Court of the First Stuart Queen', also in Peck (ed.) 1991; Peacock in Sharpe adn Lake (eds.) 1994, especially. pp.212–13.

34 R. Strong, *Henry Prince of Wales and England's Lost Renaissance*, 1986, pp.86 et seq., 184 et seq.; Howarth 1985, especially chap.2.

35 R.M. Smuts, *Court Culture and the Origins of a Royalist Tradition in Early Stuart England*, Philadelphia, Pa., 1987, chaps.5–7; R. Lightbown, 'Charles I and the Tradition of Princely Collecting', in A. MacGregor (ed.), *The Late King's Goods*, Oxford 1989; A. Braunmuller, 'Robert Carr, Earl of Somerset, as collector and patron', in Peck (ed.) 1991.

36 Strong 1969, pp.43–50, p.44.

37 F. Haskell, 'Charles I's Collection of Pictures' in MacGregor (ed.) 1989, especially pp.203–6; Peacock in Sharpe and Lake (eds.) 1994, pp.215–20.

38 P. Palme, *The Triumph of Peace*, Stockholm 1956; O. Millar, *The Age of Charles I*, exh. cat., Tate Gallery 1972, p.19; O. Millar, *Van Dyck in England*, exh. cat., National Portrait Gallery 1983, pp.27–8, 32, 46, 50; Howarth 1985, pp.164–7 (the Van Dyck of Arundel's family, commissioned to commemorate his command of the army against Scotland in the First Bishops' War, was never finished). Smuts 1987, convincingly demolishes earlier attempts to read the early seventeenth century in terms of a cultural split between 'court' and 'country', and to appropriate Van Dyck, Jones, etc. to the 'court' side of that equation.

The Production and Reproduction of Holbein's Portraits

Susan Foister

In 1524 Erasmus sent two versions of a portrait of himself by Holbein to England, one of which was probably destined for his friend and patron, the Archbishop of Canterbury, William Warham. When Holbein first came to England in 1526–8 Warham may have reciprocated, sending back a version of his own portrait by Holbein.[1] On his second visit in 1532–43 Holbein was extremely busy producing portraits for his English clients, many of whom may also have wanted repeat versions of their portraits to give to relatives and friends. Holbein was well-equipped to make such replicas, for he could re-use his own preparatory drawings, over eighty of which survive (see nos.93–7).

Although copies of many of Holbein's English portraits do exist, the extraordinarily high quality of Holbein's own work is hard to match. Little attention has generally been paid to such copies once it has been established they are not the work of Holbein himself, although a number can claim – on grounds of provenance or technique – to be sixteenth-century paintings and some are of good quality. Could any be paintings produced under Holbein's own supervision, in a workshop headed by him? Or were they produced in the decades after his death? It is usually argued that Holbein's style of portraiture had little following in sixteenth-century England, being succeeded by a taste for the work of Netherlandish-trained artists and then the more stylised productions of English-born painters. Very little is known about painters' workshops of the time. Is it possible that replicas of Holbein's portraits were produced in one or more of them, perhaps at a period when the prevailing taste was for quite a different type of portrait?

The workshop system was undoubtedly as common in England as in Europe. Most painters who had worked in European towns in the sixteenth century and arrived in London would immediately have recognised the ways in which their craft was organised and regulated, whether Holbein arriving from Basel in the early sixteenth century, or one of the immigrants from the Low Countries or France late in the century. Like other occupations, painting was governed by guild regulations lay-ing down the number of years that apprentices should serve under a master before becoming fully qualified, and the numbers of both apprentices and journeymen that could be employed.

Painters coming from abroad would also have recognised the barrage of legislation intended to make life for such immigrants as difficult as possible, and to boost the position of native workers who feared their competition. It was normal in the Low Countries for instance for painters who were not born in a town to have to become citizens and pay higher fees to enter the guild than those born there; the most favourable fees were normally reserved for the sons of painters who would carry on the family workshop.[2] Indeed, Holbein's particular circumstances, as a foreign national with an address in the City of London in the parish of St Andrew Undershaft, would have barred him from legally running a workshop. Aliens were only entitled to set up new workshops in any craft after 1529 if they took on English nationality or denizenship, and they were then limited to English apprentices. In London alien immigration was a highly sensitive issue. There had been riots on 'Evil May Day' in 1517 and one of the complaints of the rioters concerned the importation of foreign goods and the presence of foreign workmen. Restrictive legislation was constantly framed to help maintain the position of English workers. Those who worked in the visual arts found themselves particularly badly affected. The London Company of Painter-Stainers carried on a constant struggle on all fronts throughout the sixteenth century, against foreigners as well as against competitors such as heraldic painters.[3]

Holbein's contemporary and fellow employee at the court of Henry VIII, the Netherlandish artist Lucas Horenbout, who was probably responsible for the portrait miniatures of the King, became a denizen or English citizen in 1534 and is recorded as employing four foreign assistants.[4] Holbein never became a denizen and there is no record of him obtaining privileges. Nevertheless it is possible that his position as a valued employee of the King may have helped protect him from normal legal requirements, just as elsewhere in Europe artists escaped the restrictions of guild regulations by working for the courts. The actual existence of a Holbein workshop thus remains an open question, but much remains to be discovered by analysis and comparison of surviving paintings by and after Holbein.[5]

What were the methods of production in use in painters' workshops in Holbein's time? Paintings made to commission were only part of the livelihood of most painters: the sale of ready-made paintings was increasing in the sixteenth century. The repetition of images was necessarily a part of such production, and was common northern European workshop practice in the sixteenth century. Some workshops made replicas of small compositions on an almost industrial scale and sold them at the large fairs in the Netherlands.[6]

Replicas were easily made using patterns kept in the workshop. The outlines were transferred by tracing or by pricking small holes and pouncing, shaking charcoal dust through them. These outlines could then be filled in with further reference to the main pattern and perhaps to other patterns, as well as to studio props such as lengths of fabric for drapery patterns, and books of heraldry. In particular circumstances such as portraits those commissioning the work might have lent clothing or even jewellery in order for it to be incorporated into the final painted image.

Why should portraits have been repeated? We have seen that Holbein's own sitters may have ordered more than one portrait of themselves. The likenesses of some sitters such as kings and queens or famous Protestants were collected because of their fame and out of loyalty to the causes they represented. In the second half of the sixteenth century, after Holbein's death, many of Holbein's sitters had become notable men or women, whose portraits were now collected, and Holbein's image of them was in many cases the only likeness. In addition, descendants were often eager for portraits of their ancestors: the descendants of Sir Thomas More commissioned several portraits of More and his family in which Holbein's images were combined with portraits of the Mores of Elizabeth's reign.[7]

Holbein certainly used his own portrait drawings to produced his painted portraits, a practice throughout his career as the survival of drawings and corresponding paintings from as early as 1516 demonstrates.[8] Many of these head and shoulders portrait drawings include Holbein's notes on colours and fabrics which are reflected in surviving painted portraits. But the relationship between drawings and paintings was closer than this. Comparative measurements of a number of drawings and paintings have shown correspondences between the two so close that a method of transferring the outlines of the drawing

to the panel must have been used, probably using a sixteenth-century equivalent to modern carbon paper.[9] As we shall see, such close correspondences also occur in the case of replicas as well as Holbein's originals.

It should not be surprising that Holbein kept the portrait drawings made in preparation for his painted portrait for future reference. But would they have been available for use by a workshop after his death in 1543? It is unfortunately not clear what the fate of the drawings was on Holbein's death. It seems possible however that they were immediately taken into the King's collection, and bound as a book. According to the inventory of the Lumley collection (no.105), into which they had passed by 1590, they were in royal hands by the reign of Edward VI.[10]

If these drawings were not available to painters after Holbein's death, how then were paintings made which reflect so precisely the size of the portraits painted by Holbein himself? The answer perhaps lies both in patterns made after the drawings themselves, such as the pattern produced after Holbein's drawing of Bishop Fisher (no.98) and in patterns made from the paintings. Further patterns could have been made from replicas. Some examples may help to illustrate how such processes of reproduction were carried out.

Two versions of Holbein's portrait of Henry VIII with the Barber-Surgeons Company survive, the damaged and over-painted original owned by the Barbers' Company, and the completely over-painted cartoon for it in the Royal College of Surgeons.[11] Apart from the dominating figure of Henry VIII, the group includes two portraits of figures closely associated with Holbein, the royal physicians Dr Butts (fig.6) and Dr Chambers. Dr Chambers was painted by Holbein in a portrait now at Vienna which is very similar to the group portrait, but no drawing for it survives. Infrared reflectograms however show underdrawing which suggests the likeness was traced from a drawing in Holbein's usual fashion.[12] Dr Butts, with the addition of a hat, and his wife, Margaret Lady Butts, were portrayed by Holbein in paintings now in Boston. A drawing for the portrait of Lady Butts survives in the Royal Collection which closely matches the Boston picture in size. Presumably a corresponding drawing for Dr Butts has been lost.

At least two other versions of the portrait of Dr Butts survive, one of which has a pendant of Lady Butts, and which appear close to the Barber's Company portrait of Dr Butts.[13] One of these independent portraits of Dr Butts is in the National Portrait Gallery, London, and has been described as a 'good near contemporary version' of the Boston picture 'probably produced for a junior branch of the family'. The other portrait comes from a private collection.[14] Both paintings are on panel, and seem to be of sixteenth-century manufacture.

Both are competently painted, but neither is of outstanding quality.

Infrared photographs and reflectograms show that the portrait in a private collection was produced from a pattern using pouncing. The dotted chalk marks are clearly visible along all the main outlines of the picture, including the folds of skin at the neck (fig.7) There are no such marks in the National Portrait Gallery picture, or indeed any evidence of drawing or incised lines at all. This would suggest that if a pattern was used the method of transference was similar to the carbon paper method probably used by Holbein, but no trace of such schematic outlines could be found.[15] Both portraits, though evidently produced by different methods, are virtually identical in outlines, as was shown when a tracing of the NPG portrait was placed over the other; there was only a slight variation in the area of the chin, which protruded slightly more in the NPG picture.

When the tracing was placed over a same-size photograph of the Barbers' Company head made from Holbein's cartoon, again the correspondence was extremely close, with just a slight variation in the line of the profile. It is therefore apparent that a portrait pattern of Holbein's image of Dr Butts was in use in sixteenth-century England. The recurrence of the hat – worn in the Boston portrait but not in the cartoon – suggests this image derived from the individual portrait rather than the cartoon head, though Holbein probably used one drawing for both.

The portrait of Lord Cobham (no.9) was probably produced in a similar fashion from a portrait pattern. The portrait matches almost exactly a facsimile of the preparatory drawing by Holbein at Windsor Castle. It differs only in the line of the hat and in the costume, which is more complete in the painting. The contours of the face match exactly. As it seems likely that Lord Cobham would have wanted to be shown fully dressed in his portrait rather than in an open shirt as he is drawn by Holbein (fig.8), this portrait may have been made after a pattern taken from the finished portrait, the dimensions of which would then have followed the drawing precisely. A certain amount of preparatory underdrawing was visible with the aid of infrared reflectography (fig.9) There was no indication of the method of transfer of the pattern, such as the pouncing found in the versions of Dr Butts. The details were drawn freehand, and hatching indicates shading on the left-hand side of the face and eyes. None of this is comparable to Holbein's own underdrawing, where lines tend to be much bolder, nor to his original drawing, where the shadows are much stronger.

Also in the National Portrait Gallery and in Lambeth Palace are versions of the portrait of the Archbishop of Canterbury William Warham by Holbein which hangs in the Louvre. The

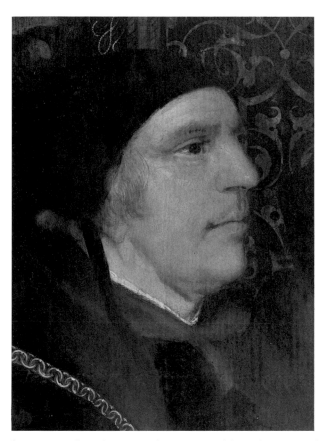

fig.6 Hans Holbein the Younger, 'Henry VIII and the Barber-Surgeons' (detail of head of Dr William Butts), oil on panel. *Barbers' Company.* Photo: Hamilton-Kerr Institute

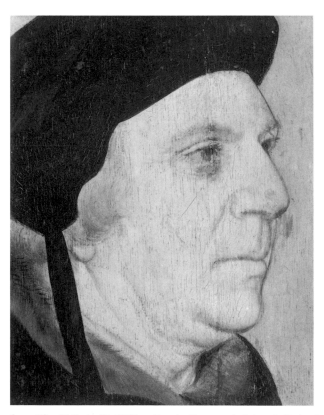

fig.7 After Holbein, 'Dr William Butts', oil on panel. *Private Collection.* Infrared photograph of detail of face

[23]

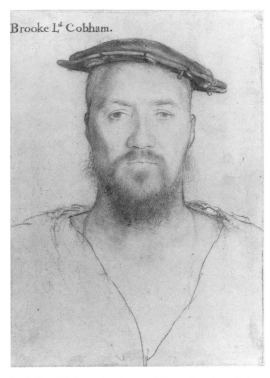

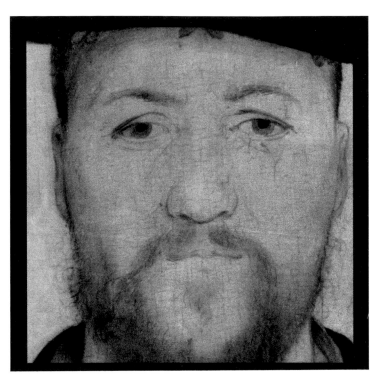

fig.8 Hans Holbein the Younger, 'George Brooke, 9th Baron Cobham', black and coloured chalks, pen and black ink and some metalpoint on pink prepared paper. *The Royal Collection, Her Majesty The Queen*

fig.9 After Holbein, 'George Brooke, 9th Baron Cobham'. Infrared reflectogram detail of face by Rachel Billinge

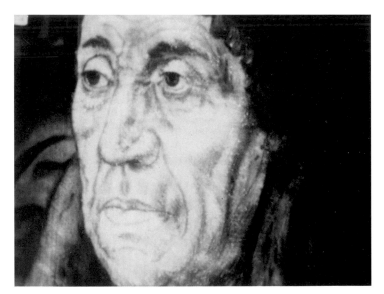

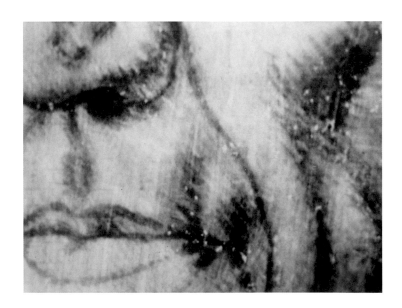

figs.10 and 11 After Holbein, 'William Warham, Archbishop of Canterbury', oil on panel, *Lambeth Palace*. Infrared reflectogram details of face, reproduced by kind permission of His Grace the Archbishop of Canterbury

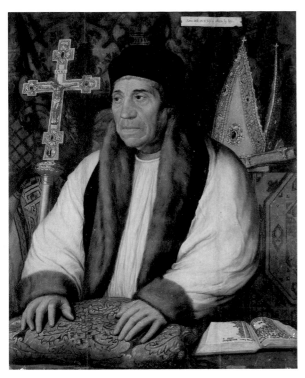

fig.12 After Holbein, 'William Warham, Archbishop of Canterbury', oil on panel. *National Portrait Gallery, London*

Lambeth Palace version has been supposed to be that commissioned to replace the original in the late sixteenth century, though the circumstances are far from clear.[16] The NPG version has no provenance taking it beyond the seventeenth century, though it is very probably of sixteenth-century manufacture. The heads of all three paintings are very close indeed in size,[17] suggesting that the NPG and Lambeth Palace pictures were produced from a pattern.

The Lambeth Palace version has a very detailed and mechanical kind of underdrawing (figs.10, 11) apparently in a fluid medium, using extensive hatching and going over every single wrinkle of the face, in a manner very different from the way in which Holbein himself approached the wrinkles of the faces of Lady Butts or Dr Chambers.[18] A pattern was clearly used, but the elaboration of detail is very unlike a Holbein underdrawing.

The NPG painting (fig.12) also has a very detailed underdrawing (figs.13, 14). It is executed in a dry medium, probably black chalk, and the underdrawing extends to the hands as well as to the face. The style of drawing, with its insistent emphasis on Warham's wrinkles, and its use of hatching, and a curious zigzagging convention, especially on the upper lip, does not follow the style of Holbein's own drawing of

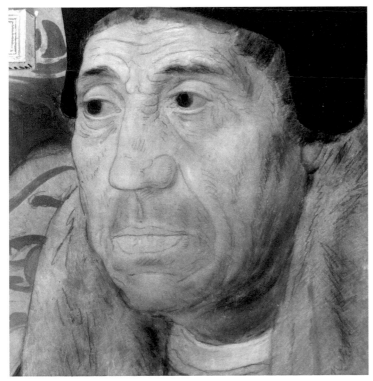

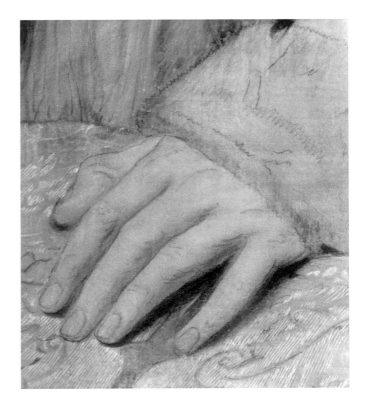

figs.13 and 14 After Holbein, 'William Warham, Archbishop of Canterbury', oil on panel. *National Portrait Gallery.* Infrared reflectogram detail of face and hands by Rachel Billinge

Warham. Nor does it copy exactly the lines of that drawing: it includes more wrinkles than are there, describes some of them quite differently, and is linear in a way appropriate to recording the essential elements of an established portrait rather than a human head in three dimensions, which had been Holbein's task.

The outlines of the NPG painting follow almost exactly those of the drawing by Holbein, as can be established by placing a tracing of the outlines of the painting over a facsimile of the drawing. However, since the underdrawn details of the face of the NPG portrait seem to follow the painted original rather than the drawing, it is probable that the painter of the NPG portrait followed a pattern made from the painted portrait, from which he would also have been able to take details of the hands, rarely included in Holbein's own drawings. But the painter also needed to copy background details, since both versions of the Louvre painting follow these details very closely indeed. It is possible that Holbein's original painting was made available to the first of the copyists, for while it was a simple matter for a painter of a replica portrait to supplement a head and shoulders pattern by reproducing a plain painted background of the type Holbein used later, it is improbable that the painting of Warham could have been replicated simply by the use of such a pattern.[19] The fact that the painter of the NPG portrait at first misplaced Warham's fur collar is perhaps a further indication that he did not have a pattern of the entire portrait which he could transfer.

All the examples above show that patterns taken directly or indirectly from Holbein's portraits were used to create new portraits. Such patterns would have been used by painters who employed their own techniques of transference in the preparatory work for portraits, not necessarily the tracing associable with Holbein's use of his drawings, and whose style of painting was often merely workmanlike, rather than a close imitation of Holbein's own. The study of such replicas however suggests that Holbein's portraits had an after-life of their own in sixteenth-century England, even after his death, and that painters were active in fulfiling demand by reproducing them.

Notes

Some of the material in this essay appeared in a different form in S. Foister, 'Workshop or Followers? Underdrawing in some Portraits Associated with Hans Holbein the Younger', in *Le Dessin sous-jacent dans la peinture: Colloque IX 1991*, Louvain-la-Neuve 1993. I am grateful to my colleagues Rachel Billinge and David Bomford at the National Gallery, London, for making the reflectograms and helping me to examine the pictures discussed, and to the owners of the pictures for allowing us to do so.

1   J. Rowlands, *The Paintings of Hans Holbein the Younger*, Oxford 1984, pp.128, 133–4, nos.13, 27; the portrait of Erasmus is currently on loan to National Gallery, London.

2   See L. Campbell, 'The Art Market in the Southern Netherlands in the Fifteenth Century', *Burlington Magazine*, vol.118, 1976, p.191.

3   See S. Foister, 'Foreigners at Court: Holbein, Van Dyck and the London Painter-Stainers Company', in D. Howarth (ed.), *Art and Patronage at the Caroline Courts*, Cambridge 1993, pp.32–50, and D. Ransome, 'The Struggle of the Glaziers' Company with the Foreign Glaziers 1500–1550', *Guildhall Miscellany*, II, 1960, pp.12–20.

4   See L. Campbell and S. Foister, 'Gerard, Lucas and Susanna Horenbout', *Burlington Magazine*, vol.128, 1986, p.722.

5   For further comment see S. Foister, 'Workshop or Followers? Underdrawing in Some Portraits Associated with Hans Holbein the Younger', in *Le Dessin sous-jacent dans la peinture: Colloque IX 1991*, Louvain-la-Neuve 1993.

6   See L. Campbell, 'The Early Netherlandish Painters and their Workshops', in *Le Dessin sous-jacent dans la peinture: Colloque III 1979*, Louvain-la-Neuve 1981; J. Wilson, 'Workshop Patterns and the Practice of Painting in Sixteenth Century Bruges', *Burlington Magazine*, vol.132, 1990, pp.523–7; H. Mund, 'Le Peintre et son métier: La Copie', in R. van Schoute and B. de Patoul (eds.), *Les Primitifs flamands et leur temps*, Louvian-la-Neuve 1994, pp.125–41 with bibliography pp.631–2.

7   For versions of the More family portraits see J.B. Trapp and H. Schulte Herbrüggen, *'The King's Good Servant': Sir Thomas More*, exh. cat., National Portrait Gallery 1977, pp.18, 86–7.

8   See S. Foister, *Drawings by Holbein from the Royal Library, Windsor Castle*, London and New York 1983, pp.13–25.

9   See S. Foister, 'Holbein and his English Patrons', unpublished PhD thesis, University of London 1981, pp.511–12 for tabulated comparisons of measurements, Foister 1983, pp.21–5 for further discussion of transference, and M. Ainsworth, '"Paternes for Phiosioneamyes" Holbein's Portraiture Reconsidered', *Burlington Magazine*, vol.132, 1990, pp.173–86, especially pp.176–8 for traced comparisons. Holbein's individual portrait drawings (as opposed to the cartoons for large commissions) are not, with one exception – that of a drawing of Sir Thomas More – pricked for transfer by pouncing. On portraits with evidence of pouncing: see Ainsworth 1990, pp.176–8, and for Anne of Cleves see E. Foucart-Walter, *Les Peintures de Hans Holbein le jeune au Louvre*, exh. cat., Louvre, Paris 1985, pp.57–8.

10   For the history of the drawings after Holbein's death see Foister 1981, pp.3–12.

11   R. Strong, 'Holbein's Cartoon for the Barber-Surgeons Group Rediscovered – A Preliminary Report', *Burlington Magazine*, vol.105, 1963, pp.4–14.

12   See Ainsworth 1990, pp.184–5.

13   I am grateful to the Barbers' Company for inviting me to be present at a detailed examination of the picture and to Herbert Lank for his comments and for making a photograph available to me.

14   R. Strong, *Tudor and Jacobean Portraits*, National Portrait Gallery 1969, I, p.33–4.

15   Compare Ainsworth 1990, fig.24, Lady Rich.

16   For differing interpretations of the evidence see Rowlands 1984, pp.133–4, R. Strong, 'Holbein in England – III to v', *Burlington Magazine*, vol.109, 1967, pp.698–701 and Foucart-Walter 1985, pp.73–4.

17   See Foister, 1981, p.512.

18   See Foister 1983 and Ainsworth 1990.

19   It is worth noting the existence of what appears to be an early traced copy of Holbein's original drawing of Warham, sold Christie's, 4 July 1984, lot 139, from the collection of Lord Astor of Hever, also a copy noted by Foucart-Walter 1985, p.74.

British Painting and the Low Countries 1530–1630

CHRISTOPHER BROWN

One of the most striking features of the period 1530–1630 is the large number of foreign artists who came to work in Britain and the dominance they exerted over the development of art here. Indeed, the period can be defined by the arrival of foreign artists: it begins with the arrival of Hans Holbein in London (for the second time) in 1532 and closes with the arrival of Anthony Van Dyck (also for the second time) in 1632. During the intervening century dozens of artists from France, Germany, Italy, but above all from the Low Countries, came to work in Britain.

Simply to make a list of some of the most outstanding of the foreign artists who settled in Britain is to tell a large part of the story of British art in these years: Bartolommeo Penni, Girolamo da Treviso, Antonio Toto del Nunziata, the Horenbout family, Levina Teerlinc and Holbein at the court of Henry VIII; Guillim Scrots, Hans Eworth and Gerlach Flicke during the reign of Edward VI; Steven van der Meulen, Arnold Bronckorst, Hieronimo Custodis, Cornelis Ketel, the de Critz and Gheeraerts families under Elizabeth; Paul van Somer, Abraham van Blijenberch, Daniel Mytens and Cornelius Johnson working for James I; and Francis Cleyn, Orazio and Artemisia Gentileschi, Hendrick van Steenwijk and Van Dyck in the service of Charles I. This is not to mention the many distinguished artists who came for short, though often very influential, stays: Lucas de Heere, Federico Zuccaro, Joris Hoefnagel, Cornelis van Poelenburgh, Gerrit van Honthorst and Peter Paul Rubens.

This foreign domination of British art was a constant cause of complaint. In his *The Boke Named The Governor* of 1531 Sir Thomas Elyot lamented that the English 'be constrayned, if we wyll have any thinge well paynted, kerved, or embrawdred, to abandon our own countraymen and resort unto straungers'.[1] His sentiment is echoed a century later by Henry Peacham in his *Treatise on Drawing and Limning* of 1634: 'I am sorry that our courtiers and great personages must seek far and near for some Dutchmen or Italian to draw their pictures, our Englishmen being held for Vauniens.'[2]

Unsurprisingly, the resentment against the presence of so many foreign artists was felt most intensely by the Painter-Stainers' Company, which constantly complained that foreigners received commissions which should by rights go to its own members and that this had led to the decay of art in Britain.[3] Bans on the opening of new shops by anyone other than natives and denizens – foreigners who had submitted themselves to the lengthy process of obtaining citizenship – and restrictions on the employment of foreign-born apprentices in order to protect the livelihoods of native painters were enacted early in the sixteenth century. In 1575 the Painter-Stainers presented a petition to the Queen calling for increased powers to counter the influx of foreign artists and these were granted in their royal charter of 1581. They petitioned on this subject again and again, notably to Charles I in 1627 when they named foreigners such as Mytens, Gentileschi, van Doort and Steenwijk, who were threatening the ability of their members to earn a living. Since all these artists were in the royal service, the petition had little chance of success.

The truth, however, was that few native artists of real distinction emerged during this period. The great exceptions are, of course, the miniaturists Nicholas Hilliard and Isaac Oliver, but George Gower, Sir William Segar, Robert Peake and William Larkin represent the best of the home-grown talent. A key reason for the failure of a vigorous native school to develop was, as Peacham suggested, a desire by the monarch and the aristocracy to employ more fashionable foreign artists. There was a strong sense throughout the century that the significant artistic developments were taking place in France, especially at Fontainebleau; in Italy, especially in Florence, Rome and Venice; and in the Low Countries, especially in Antwerp, and towards the end of this period, in Amsterdam. There was a general feeling that it was easier to share in these developments by importing the artists (and the paintings) into Britain than by encouraging young British artists to travel abroad in order to study them. The idea of an aristocratic patron sponsoring a young artist to travel on the Continent did not take hold to a

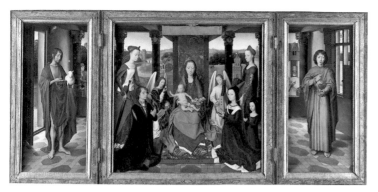

fig.15 Hans Memlinc, 'The Virgin and Child with Saints and Donors' (The Donne Triptych) c.1475, oil on panel. *The National Gallery, London*

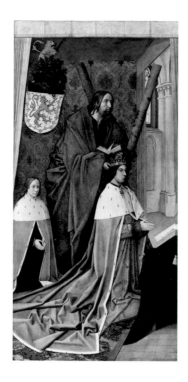
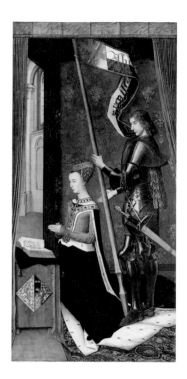
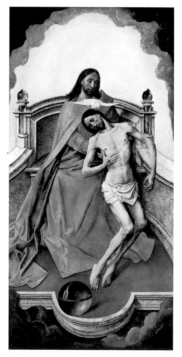
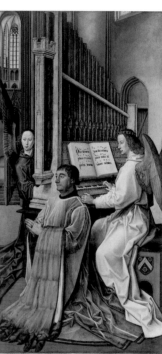

fig.16 Hugo van der Goes, the Trinity Altarpiece, c.1480, oil on panel. *The Royal Collection, Her Majesty The Queen*

significant extent during this period: Hilliard's one visit to France was for the very specific purpose of painting the portrait of the duc d'Alençon, a potential bridegroom for the Queen. Only at the end of this period did Inigo Jones travel to Italy with the Earl of Arundel in order to absorb the lessons to be learnt there and put them into practice on his return. Nor were British artists sent to be apprenticed on the Continent. We know of one case: on 29 April 1613 a certain Michiel Austine, living in London, apprenticed his son Nataniel, who was then sixteen years old, for five years with the Amsterdam painter Jan Teunissen, 'omme te leren het schilderen met alle den aencleven van dyen, voor sooveele de voorn. Jongman sal cunnen aennemen en begrijpen' (in order to learn painting with all that pertains to it in so far as the above-mentioned youth is able to take it in and understand it).[4]

Although German, French and Italian artists came to Britain, the most important and consistent artistic axis during the sixteenth century was with the Low Countries and especially with Antwerp. After 1585, Antwerp's pre-eminent place in this respect was to some extent usurped by Amsterdam, just as her position as the leading economic centre in the Netherlands was also usurped by the Dutch city. The principal reason for this British–Flemish artistic relationship was economic. Antwerp was the nearest large town on the Continent – its population had risen from thirty thousand in 1500 to almost a hundred thousand in 1565 – and the English cloth trade was based there. London took its lead from Antwerp in many respects. Sir Thomas Gresham's Exchange was modelled on the Antwerp Bourse and, significantly, its inauguration was marked by the publication of a series of prints by a Flemish artist, Frans Hogenberg. Gresham served as the financial agent of the English crown in Antwerp from 1552 until 1567. His favoured portraitist was Antonis Mor, who painted him there (no.18).

Flanders had been Britain's single most important trading partner since the late Middle Ages. Much of the prosperity of the so-called 'Three Pillars of Flanders', the towns of Bruges, Ghent and Ypres, had been founded on the importation and weaving of English wool, acknowledged to be the best in Europe. British merchants and diplomats in Flanders in the fifteenth century had their portraits painted by local artists and bought religious paintings. The triptych commissioned from Hans Memlinc in Bruges by Sir John Donne of Kidwelly (fig.15), a diplomat in the service of Edward IV who was regularly in Flanders between 1468 and 1483, is an outstanding example of British patronage of Flemish artists. Another is the Trinity Altarpiece ordered from Hugo van der Goes in about 1480 by Sir Edward Bonkil for the Collegiate Church of the Holy Trinity in Edinburgh (fig.16). Portraits include that of Edward Grimston by Petrus Christus (fig.17), painted in Bruges in 1446, and the portraits of Lord Berners attributed to Ambrosius Benson (fig.18 and no.3). There was also a considerable number of small altarpieces bought in Flanders, often in Antwerp, in the early sixteenth century and carried back to Britain. Others came to this country with refugees like the Flemish merchant Sir Thomas Coteel, who presumably brought the small altarpieces now at Cotehele in Cornwall.[5] The appearance of such works in Britain together with, in far greater numbers, illuminated books from Flanders, created an immense respect for the techniques of the Flemish artists and, consequently, a great enthusiasm for their work. In this sense art followed trade routes, as it often does, and works of art were imported by merchants for the British market.

Further impetus was given to this close artistic relationship as the religious and political destinies of Britain and the Low Countries became even more intimately entwined during the course of the sixteenth century. In 1534 Henry VIII was recognised as the Supreme Head of the Church in England and the Protestantisation of the country was under way. When the eleven provinces of the Netherlands revolted against their Spanish Habsburg rulers – a conflict which arose out of a desire for freedom of Protestant worship as much as political independence – their natural ally was the Protestant kingdom across the North Sea which had for so long been such an important trading partner. Elizabeth considered the Netherlanders to be rebels against their lawful king and was very reluctant to be drawn into war with Spain. However, although she declined the proferred crown, she was unable to avoid some involvement, making generous loans to the Netherlanders and sending the Earl of Leicester and a British force to their assistance in 1586. Although Leicester's expedition was unsuccessful, the death of Sir Philip Sidney at Zutphen gave it an aura of Elizabethan chivalry and forged even closer bonds

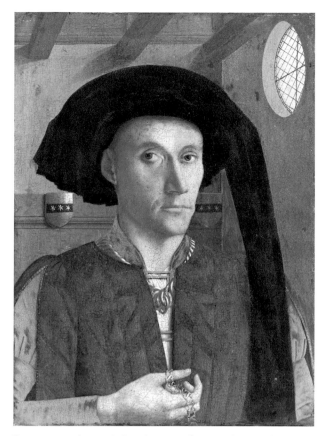

fig.17 Petrus Christus, 'Edward Grimston' 1446, oil on panel. *On loan to the National Gallery, London, from the Earl of Verulam*

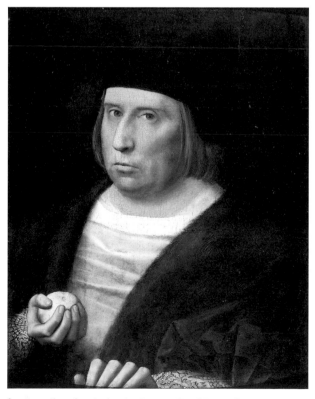

fig.18 attributed to Ambrosius Benson, 'Lord Berners' c.1520–6, oil on panel. *National Portrait Gallery, London*

of affection between the two countries. In artistic terms, these political events which brought Britain and the Low Countries closer together tended at the same time to distance Britain from France and Italy, both of whom were (for the most part) in the Spanish camp, and so opportunities both for travel to and trade with those countries were circumscribed. When Lord Howard of Effingham wanted to commemorate the defeat of the Armada, he turned not to a Frenchman or an Italian but to a Dutch artist, the famous marine painter Hendrick Vroom of Haarlem.[6]

For Flemish and Dutch artists, coming from countries with lively artistic traditions and often cut-throat competition for available commissions, the incentive was usually quite straightforward. It was, as Erasmus wrote in the famous letter recommending Holbein to Sir Thomas More, 'ut corrodat aliquot Angelatos' (to scrape together some angels, i.e. money).[7] According to Karel van Mander in his *Lives of the Netherlandish and German Painters* (in his *Schilderboek* of 1604), Lucas Cornelis de Kock 'dewijl het hem te Leyden onghelegen was overmits dat uyt t'schilderen den cost qualijck wilde vallen verstaende dat ten tijde van den Coningh van Engelandt Henricus de 8e de Const daer in't landt in weerden en wel begheert was vertrock hy derwaerts met Wijf en kinderen die hy wel tot 7. oft 8. in getal hadde' ('As things did not go well for him in Leiden, because he could hardly make a living from painting, and as he understood that art at that time was valued and much sought after in the England of King Henry the Eighth, he travelled there with his wife and children, of whom he had at least seven or eight').[8] This must have been in the 1530s.

The outbreak of the Revolt of the Netherlands thirty years later and the consequent bitter war with Spain had a devastating effect on the demand for works of art in the Low Countries. Cornelis Ketel wished to remain in his native Gouda, 'Doch also door den krigh daer van schilderen niet te doen viel vertrock A[nn]o 1573 nae Enghelandt en quam te London' ('But since, owing to the war, there was no painting work there, he left in 1573 for England and arrived in London').[9] For some, the move was a success. Ketel flourished, receiving major portrait commissions from merchants and courtiers, including one to portray the Queen herself, but no more is known of the fate of Lucas de Kock and his large family. Much later, in 1750, Johan de Gool was to warn Dutch artists that they should not expect too much of Britain 'want dat het in Engelant zo breet met de schilders niet gestelt is, als men melkanderen wel zoekt wys te maken, en dat de weifelende kunstfortuin daer alzo wel haere vieze nukken heeft als hier' ('because artists are not as well off in England as people tend to say, and fickle fortune has her whims there as much as here').[10]

Religion was a second factor in the movement of artists to

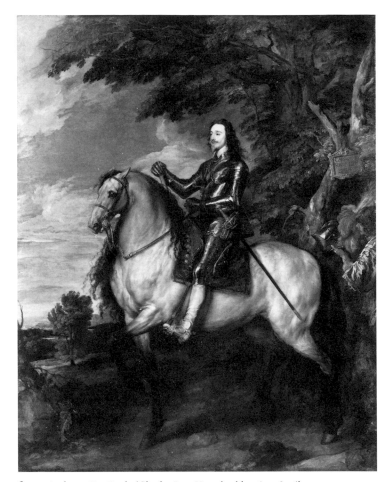

fig.19 Anthony Van Dyck, 'Charles I on Horseback' *c*.1637–8, oil on canvas. *The National Gallery, London*

England. A number of Protestant artists fled here to practise their faith. Lucas de Heere, who was born in Ghent in 1534, came to England in the late 1560s, following the Duke of Alva's crushing of the rebellion against the Spanish crown in 1567. He was to serve as an elder in the Dutch Church in London in 1571, but returned home soon after the Pacification of Ghent in 1576. The reconquest of Antwerp by the Spanish in 1585 led to the emigration of many Protestants, artists among them, to the north Netherlands, Germany and also to England. Finally, there were professional reasons. Van Dyck was undoubtedly flattered by the invitation to work for a patron and collector as discerning as Charles I and tempted by the honours and wealth which were promised, but there was also a strong desire to escape from the overpowering presence of Rubens in his native Antwerp and establish his own independent artistic personality.

In viewing the phenomenon of the emigration of Netherlandish artists to Britain in the sixteenth and seventeenth centuries from a Netherlandish rather than a British perspective, it is important to remember that this was not an isolated phenomenon. It is true that the native school was relatively weak and that the court favoured foreign artists, but this emigration was just one aspect of the emigration of Netherlandish artists throughout Europe during this period.[11] Netherlandish artists can be found working in all the major courts of Germany – not just in the nearby Rhineland, but in Berlin and Munich. They were also in demand at the Danish court in Copenhagen as well as in Prague and Vienna. There were Netherlandish artists' communities in Paris and Lyon as well as in Rome, Naples and Sicily. This remarkable diaspora was at its height in the early seventeenth century but many Netherlandish artists of earlier generations travelled abroad to find work and Britain was only one of their destinations.

These Netherlandish artists, whether in London, Düsseldorf, Prague or Copenhagen, worked principally for the court. They travelled at the invitation of the monarch or a courtier, or, lured by the possibilities of court patronage, they came to offer their services in the hope of lavish rewards. They were working for a relatively restricted, if prominent, clientele. In Britain, it was not until after the Restoration in 1660 that a substantial number of Dutch painters came to work for a growing non-aristocratic market. Artists like Gillis Tilborch and Gerard Edema, for example, found employment with merchants and country gentry rather than at court. In the period we are concerned with, however, there was effectively a two-tier system of artistic patronage in operation, with the court favouring foreign, especially Netherlandish, artists and less socially elevated patrons having their portraits painted by native artists.

James I was even less keen than Elizabeth to become involved in the Continental war. Even the pleas of his son-in-law, the Elector Palatine Frederick V, the Protestant hero who had been forced to flee Prague and go into exile in The Hague, fell on deaf ears. However, James continued to look to the Netherlands for his court artists: Daniel Mytens and Paul van Somer were among those who came to London to work for him. It was his son Charles I, with his far more sophisticated taste, who broke the Flemish mould. His visit to Madrid with Buckingham in 1623 had opened his eyes to Venetian painting and his collecting taste – like that of the Earl of Arundel, which to some extent shaped the King's – was directed towards Italy rather than the Netherlands. Ironically, Charles's enthusiasm for Van Dyck, whom he invited to London in 1632 on terms unprecedented in the history of royal patronage in England, was based on Van Dyck's profound understanding of Titian, the King's favourite painter. Van Dyck came to England, not in the first place as a Flemish painter, but a disciple of an Italian painter, as *Titianus Redivivus*.

Notes

For encouragement and generous assistance with this foray into often unfamiliar territory I am most grateful to Karen Hearn and my colleague Susan Foister.

1 H.H.S. Croft (ed.), *Sir Thomas Elyot: The Boke Named The Governor*, 1888, I, pp.139, 140.
2 Quoted by H. Gerson, *Ausbreitung und Nachwirkung der Holländischen Malerei des 17. Jahrhunderts*, 1942, 2nd ed., Amsterdam 1983, p.369.
3 S. Foister, 'Foreigners at Court: Holbein, Van Dyck and the Painter-Stainers Company', in D. Howarth (ed.), *Art and Patronage in the Caroline Courts: Essays in Honour of Sir Oliver Millar*, Cambridge 1993, pp.32–50.
4 A. Bredius, 'Archiefsprokkelingen', *Oud Holland*, vol.52, 1935, p.288.
5 *Cothele, Cornwall* (National Trust Guidebook), 1991, pp.74–5.
6 M. Russell, *Visions of the Sea: Hendrick Vroom and the Origins of Dutch Marine Painting*, Leiden 1983, pp.116–40.
7 P.S. Allen (ed.), *Opus Epistolarum Des. Erasmi Rotterodami*, Oxford 1906–58, VI, no.1740, p.392.
8 H. Miedema (ed.), *Karel van Mander: The Lives of the Illustrious Netherlandish and German Artists*, Doornspijk 1994, I, pp.128–9 (fol.217v)
9 Ibid., p.358 (fol.275r)
10 Quoted by P. Hecht, 'Dutch Painters in England: Readings in Houbraken, Weyerman and Van Gool', in S. Groenveld and M. Wintle (eds.), *Britain and the Netherlands XI: Religion, Scholarship and Art in Anglo-Dutch Relations in the 17th Century*, Zutphen 1994, p.162 n.21.
11 The best general account of this fascinating phenomenon is still Gerson's *Ausbreitung* (see above, n.2), published in 1942.

Catalogue

Explanations

Authorship of the entries is indicated in the following way:

AT   Anne Thackray
AW-C   Anthony Wells-Cole
CM   Catharine MacLeod
CW   Christopher White
GM   Gregory Martin
JW   Joanna Woodall
KB   Kathryn Barron
KH   Karen Hearn
MG   Mireille Galinou
SB   Susan Bracken
SF   Susan Foister
TB   Tabitha Barber
TC   Tom Campbell
TS   To Schulting

Details of medium, support, size, inscriptions and provenance are given as fully and accurately as possible, combining our own information and research with collection and museum records.

Measurements. Height is given before width, centimetre size before inches (the latter in parentheses); for irregularly shaped surfaces, the maximum extent is cited.

Medium. Artists often used a variety of media to produce miniatures and works in paper. Where there is any uncertainty the medium has been omitted.

Provenance ('PROV'). At the beginning of the provenance line, three full points are used to indicate ignorance of the work's history before the first owner named; the same device is used for gaps in our knowledge of its later history.

Exhibition history ('EXH'). Only the most important exhibitions are cited.

Literature ('LIT'). The literature cited is selective. Exhibition catalogues are not listed under 'LIT' if the exhibitions in question have already been cited under 'EXH'. Occasionally details of a publication have been omitted in order to maintain a private collector's anonymity. Place of publication is London unless otherwise stated.

Illustrations. The illustrations for nos.12, 98 and 102 show the works before conservation. Nos.53 and 54 are shown before the removal of varnish and overpainting.

Abbreviations: General

bt   bought
b.l.   bottom left
b.r.   bottom right
exh.   exhibited
exh. cat. exhibition catalogue
repr.   reproduced
t.l.   top left
t.r.   top right
CSP   Calendar of State Papers
NPG   National Portrait Gallery, London
PRO   Public Record Office
RA   Royal Academy, London
V&A   Victoria and Albert Museum, London

Abbreviations: Exhibitions

Arts Council 1973
The King's Arcadia: Inigo Jones and the Stuart Court, Arts Council, London 1973

Leicester and London 1965–6
Hans Eworth: A Tudor Artist and his Circle, City of Leicester Museums and National Portrait Gallery, London 1965–6

London and Belfast 1988–9
Armada, National Maritime Museum, Greenwich, and Ulster Museum, Belfast 1988–9

Manchester 1857
Art Treasures Exhibition, Manchester 1857

V&A 1980
Princely Magnificence, Victoria and Albert Museum, London 1980

RA 1950–1
Holbein and other Masters of the Sixteenth and Seventeenth Centuries, Royal Academy 1950–1

South Kensington Museum 1866
Catalogue of the First Special Exhibition of National Portraits Ending with the Reign of James II, South Kensington Museum 1866

Tate Gallery 1969–70
The Elizabethan Image, Tate Gallery 1969–70

Tate Gallery 1972
The Age of Charles I: Painting in England 1620–1649, Tate Gallery 1972

Washington 1985–6
The Treasure Houses of Britain, National Gallery of Art, Washington 1985–6

V&A 1947
Nicholas Hilliard and Isaac Oliver: An Exhibition to Commemorate the 400th Anniversary of the Birth of Nicholas Hilliard, Victoria and Albert Museum 1947 (catalogue reprinted 1971)

V&A 1983
Artists of the Tudor Court: The Portrait Miniature Rediscovered 1520–1620, Victoria and Albert Museum 1983

Abbreviations: Literature

Arnold 1988
Arnold, J., *Queen Elizabeth's Wardrobe Unlock'd*, Leeds 1988

Auerbach 1954
E. Auerbach, *Tudor Artists*, 1954

Auerbach 1961
E. Auerbach, *Nicholas Hilliard*, 1961

Auerbach and Adams 1971
E. Auerbach and C. Kingsley Adams, *Paintings and Sculpture at Hatfield House*, 1971

Bayne Powell 1985
R. Bayne-Powell, *Catalogue of the Portrait Miniatures in the Fitzwilliam Museum, Cambridge*, Cambridge 1985

Campbell 1990
L. Campbell, *Renaissance Portraits: European Portrait-Painting in the 14th, 15th and 16th Centuries*, New Haven and London 1990

Clark 1981
J. Clark, 'The Buildings and Art Collections of Robert Dudley, Earl of Leicester', unpublished MA report, Courtauld Institute 1981

Cornwallis Correspondence
Lord Braybrooke (ed.), *The Private Correspondence of Jane Lady Cornwallis*, Audley End 1842

Cust 1913–14
L. Cust, 'Marcus Gheeraerts', *Walpole Society*, vol.3 1913–14, pp.9–45

Cust 1917–18
L. Cust, 'The Lumley Inventories', *Walpole Society*, vol.6, 1917–18, pp.15–35

Edmond 1978–80
M. Edmond, 'Limners and Picturemakers – New Light on the Lives of Miniaturists and Large-scale Portrait-painters Working in London in the 16th and 17th Centuries', *Walpole Society*, vol.47, 1978–1980

Edmond 1983
M. Edmond, *Hilliard and Oliver*, 1983

Finsten 1981
J. Finsten, *Isaac Oliver: Art at the Courts of Elizabeth I and James I*, New York and London 1981

Foister 1981
S. Foister, 'Paintings and Other Works of Art in Sixteenth-Century English Inventories', *Burlington Magazine*, vol.123, 1981, pp.273–82

Gent and Llewellyn 1990
L. Gent and N. Llewellyn (eds.), *Renaissance Bodies: The Human Figure in English Culture c.1540–1660*, 1990

Hearn 1990
K. Hearn, 'The Patronage of Lucy Harington, Countess of Bedford', unpublished MA report, Courtauld Institute 1990

Hervey 1921
M. Hervey, *The Life, Correspondence and Collections of Thomas Howard, Earl of Arundel*, Cambridge 1921

Hilliard
N. Hilliard, *The Arte of Limning*, ed. R.K.R. Thornton and T.G.S.Cain, Manchester 1992

Howarth 1985
D. Howarth, *Lord Arundel and his Circle*, London and New Haven 1985

Howarth 1993
D. Howarth (ed.), *Art and Patronage in the Caroline Court: Essays in Honour of Sir Oliver Millar*, Cambridge 1993

MacGregor 1989
A. MacGregor (ed.), *The Late King's Goods*, 1989

Miedema 1994
K. van Mander, *The Lives of the Illustrious Netherlandish and German Painters: from the first edition of the Schilder-boeck (1603–4)*, ed. Hessel Miedema, Doornspijk 1994

Millar 1958–60
O. Millar (ed.), 'Abraham van der Doort's Catalogue of the Collections of Charles I', *Walpole Society*, vol.37, 1958–60

Millar 1963
O. Millar, *The Tudor, Stuart and Early Georgian Pictures in the Collection of Her Majesty The Queen*, 1963

Millar 1970–2
O. Millar, 'The Inventories and Valuations of the King's Goods 1649–1651', *Walpole Society*, vol.43, 1970–2

Murdoch, Murrell, Noon and Strong 1981
J. Murdoch, J. Murrell, D.J. Noon, and R. Strong, *The English Miniature*, New Haven and London 1981

Orgel and Strong 1973
S. Orgel and R. Strong, *Inigo Jones: The Theatre of the Stuart Court*, London, Berkeley and Los Angeles 1973

NPG 1969
R. Strong, *Tudor and Jacobean Portraits*, 2 vols., National Portrait Gallery 1969

Parker 1945
K.T. Parker, *The Drawings of Hans Holbein at Windsor Castle*, 1945, reprinted 1983

Piper 1992
D. Piper, *The English Face*, rev. ed. 1992

Poole 1913–14
Mrs R.L. Poole, 'Marcus Gheeraerts, Father and Son, Painters', *Walpole Society*, vol.3, 1913–14, pp.1–8

Reynolds 1988
G. Reynolds, *English Portrait Miniatures*, rev. ed. Cambridge 1988

Rowlands 1985
J. Rowlands, *Holbein*, Oxford 1985

Rye 1865
W.B. Rye, *England as Seen by Foreigners*, 1865

Sharpe and Lake 1994
K. Sharpe and P. Lake, *Culture and Politics in Early Stuart England*, Basingstoke 1994

Stainton and White 1987
L. Stainton and C. White, *Drawing in England from Hilliard to Hogarth*, exh. cat., British Museum 1987

Strong 1963
R. Strong, *Portraits of Queen Elizabeth I*, Oxford 1963

Strong 1969
R. Strong, *The English Icon: Elizabethan and Jacobean Portraiture*, London and New York 1969

Strong 1983
R. Strong, *The English Renaissance Miniature*, 1983

Strong 1986
R. Strong, *Henry Prince of Wales and England's Lost Renaissance*, 1986

Strong 1987
R. Strong, *Gloriana: The Portraits of Queen Elizabeth I*, 1987

Varkonda-Bishop 1979
L.K. Varkonda-Bishop, 'Haunce the Drawer', unpublished Ph.D dissertation, Florida State University 1979

Vertue
G. Vertue, *Note Books*, vols.I–VI, *Walpole Society*, vols.18, 20, 22, 24, 26, 30

Waterhouse 1978
E.K.W. Waterhouse, *Painting in Britain 1530–1790*, Harmondsworth 1978

Whinney and Millar 1957
M. Whinney and O. Millar, *English Art 1625–1714*, Oxford 1957

Wilks 1987
T.V. Wilks, 'The Court Culture of Prince Henry and his Circle 1603–1613', unpublished D.Phil thesis, Oxford University 1987

1 Holbein and his Predecessors

Few independent paintings made in England have survived from before the arrival of Hans Holbein the Younger in 1526. Apart from manuscript illuminations and some wall-paintings, there remains only a handful of panels painted with the figures of saints and other religious images.

The early paintings that have come down are mainly portraits (see no.1), and mostly of royal sitters. Even these are not always as old as was once thought. The fine portrait of Edward IV (no.3) is now known to have been painted in about 1520. The sixteenth-century fashion for owning sets of portraits meant that earlier prototypes were copied.

The identities of the painters of these early works are largely lost and it is impossible to link surviving pictures with such names as are known from documents. One possible exception may be Joannes Corvus (Jan de Rave) from Bruges, whose name was once on the now-lost frame of a portrait of Bishop Richard Foxe (Waterhouse 1978, pp.14–15). The early portraits that do survive are in the Flemish tradition.

Henry VIII was born at Greenwich on 28 June 1491, the second son of Henry VII, the first Tudor king. The death of his elder brother Arthur (no.1) in 1502 made him heir apparent, and he succeeded his father in 1509.

Following the accession of François I, Henry embarked on a programme of political and cultural rivalry with the French king. Artists from overseas were welcomed at Henry's court. The Italian sculptor Pietro Torrigiano and his team were employed from 1512–18 to create the Renaissance tomb of Henry's parents in Westminster Abbey. Other Italian court artists included the painter and sculptor Giovanni da Maiano, Vincent Volpe, Nicholas Bellini da Modena, and two Florentines, Bartholomew Penni and Antonio di Nunziato d'Antonio, known in England as 'Toto' and who presented narrative paintings to the King.

Holbein came to England in the autumn of 1526 as a speculative venture. By the following year he was working for Henry VIII on large paintings on cloth for the entertainment of the French envoys in the Greenwich banqueting house. One of these depicted the Battle of Thérouanne (The Battle of the Spurs) in which the English had defeated the French in 1513. Holbein's picture does not survive but another depicting the same encounter, does (fig.20). Images recording significant military and political events evidently enjoyed a vogue during Henry VIII's reign and private individuals as well as the monarch owned pictures of the Battle of Pavia (in which François I had been defeated and captured in 1525).

Holbein returned to Basel in 1528 but by 1532 he was again back in England. His earlier clients had either died or fallen from power and on this return visit his clients included the merchants of the German Steelyard, the London office of the Hanseatic League. The finest surviving Steelyard portrait is that of 'Georg Gisze' of 1533 (fig.21). Flemish artists were also busy at Henry's court. Gerard Horenbout of Ghent, illuminator of manuscripts, visited c.1528–31 and his kinsman Lucas Horenbout (see no.65) made his career there from c.1526. Levina Teerlinc, from Bruges (see no.68) entered Henry VIII's service as a painter in 1546.

Painters were principally required at court to carry out decorative work. Artists' names – particularly those that seem to be of English origin – most frequently appear in the surviving royal records and accounts in connection with such decorative tasks – painting interiors, furniture, banners, a royal boat. The English painters were frequently members of the London Painter-Stainers Company or guild. At this period the king's official painter – the Serjeant Painter – was basically responsible for managing such decorative projects. At first, he was generally a member of the Company, but as the century wore on, this was no longer always the case; the Painter-Stainers increasingly complained about the tide of foreign painters entering London and threatening their livelihood.

The most striking decoration of Henry VIII's interiors would not have been paintings, but tapestries. He owned a great number – more than two thousand – and an idea of their richness can be gained from the 'Abraham and Isaac' set which can be seen in the Great Hall at Hampton Court Palace (fig.22). Tapestries were favoured throughout the period by the nobility, with painted hangings the less costly alternative.

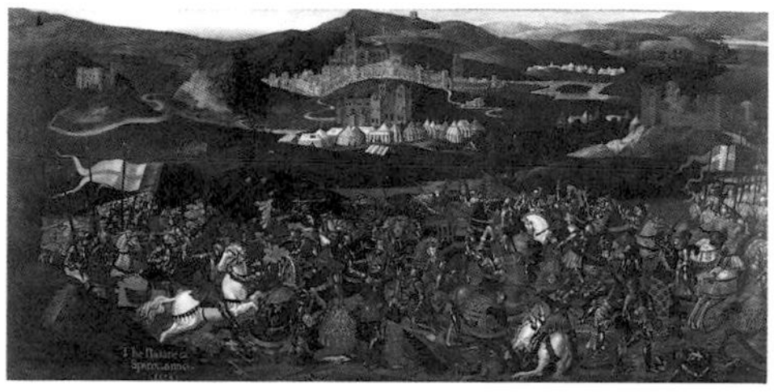

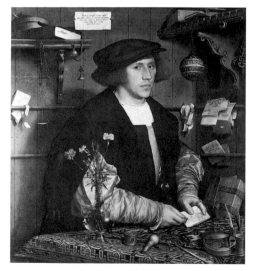

fig.20 'The Battle of the Spurs', 16th century, oil on canvas. *The Royal Collection, Her Majesty The Queen*

fig.21 Hans Holbein the Younger, 'Georg Gisze' 1532, oil on panel. *Staatliche Museen zu Berlin-Preußischer Kulturbesitz Gemäldegalerie*

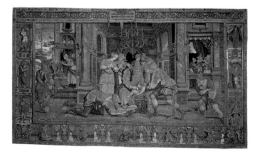

fig.22 After ?Bernard van Orley, 'Circumcision of Isaac' c.1547, tapestry. *The Royal Collection, Her Majesty The Queen*

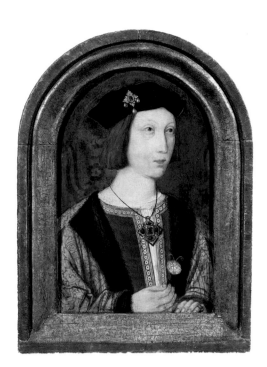

ANGLO-FLEMISH SCHOOL

1 Arthur, Prince of Wales *c.*1500

Oil on panel 27.9 × 17.8 (11 × 7)
PROV: ...; Earls of Granard collection,
Castle Forbes, Ireland by whom sold 1993;
Historical Portraits Ltd
Private Collection

Prince Arthur (1486–1502) was Henry VII's
eldest son and would have succeeded to the
throne of England, but for his early death at
the age of fifteen. In 1501, after protracted
negotiations, he was married to Catherine of
Aragon, the daughter of Ferdinand and
Isabella of Spain. Following Arthur's death,
his younger brother Henry became heir to the
throne and in 1509, after his accession as
Henry VIII, also married Catherine.

Marriage negotiations often called for the
creation and exchange of portraits. In the present work Arthur holds a white gilliflower, a
relative of the carnation, flowers symbolic
respectively of purity and betrothal.

The present portrait fits the description of
Prince Arthur recorded in Charles I's collec-
tion: 'Princ Arthure in his minoritye | In a
black capp and goulden habbitt houlding | in
his right hand a white gillifloore in a reed
pintit | goulden frame' which measured 11 ×
7 inches, approximately the same dimensions
as this one (see Millar 1958–60). Records of a
portrait of Arthur in the royal collection continue until 1714, after which they cease. It is
not currently known when the present portrait entered the Granard collection.

This appears to be the only surviving contemporary portrait of Arthur, and later versions such as one in the late-sixteenth-century
corridor set of royal portraits at Syon House,
and one formerly at Weston Park and now
known through an engraving, appear to have
been based on it. The portrait formula – a
head-and-shoulders image, against a stencilled
decorative background, with hands resting on
a ledge – is ultimately of Flemish origin. It is
similar to other surviving royal portraits of
about the same date, such as 'Henry VII'
*c.*1490–1500 (private collection) and 'Elizabeth of York' *c.*1502 (The Royal Collection).
Stylistically, it resembles a portrait of Elizabeth Woodville, also in the Royal Collection,
which is possibly a copy of an image of
*c.*1470–5.

A portrait, tentatively identified as of
Arthur, Prince of Wales, and with the sitter
wearing a collar of York and Lancastrian
roses, survives in the Royal Collection. In
attire, pose and position of the hands it is
very close to the present work, but the sitter
appears older and it is perhaps a slightly later
portrait of Arthur's brother Henry. Its identity
may have become confused as early as 1542
when it was recorded as of Arthur in an
inventory of Henry VIII's collection (see
Shaw 1937), where a second portrait of Arthur
is also listed. Its sitter's appearance, however,
agrees fairly well with the portrait of *c.*1520
of 'Henry VIII' by an unknown artist (National Portrait Gallery, London).

LIT: W.A. Shaw, *Three Inventories of the years 1542, 1547
and 1549–50 of Pictures in the Collections of Henry VIII
& Edward VI*, 1937, p.41; Millar 1958–60, p.30; Millar
1963, p.53; Christopher Lloyd and Simon Thurley,
Henry VIII: Images of a Tudor King, 1990, pp.14–16;
Piers Davies, 'The Granard Portrait: Portrait of Arthur,
Prince of Wales', unpublished paper, 1993

KH and TB

ANGLO-FLEMISH SCHOOL

2 Edward IV *c.*1520

Oil on panel 67.9 × 47.9 (26¾ × 18⅞)
Inscribed across the top, in a later hand:
'K.Edward ye 4th'
PROV: Possibly the 'table with the picture
of King Edward the IIIjth' first recorded in
the collection of Henry VIII in 1542;
recorded by Van der Doort among the
'Nyne old heades' in the collection of
Charles I, 'a Lardger picture … without a
beard putting a ring uppon his left hand
… Saide to be king Edward ye 4th in a
reed & guilded frame'; in the collection of
Charles II, recorded as 'Henry 5th holding
up his hands with a ring' (see Millar 1963,
p.50)
Her Majesty The Queen

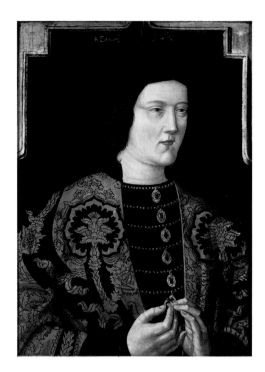

This is not a contemporary portrait but is a
good example of a posthumous one, intended
as part of an historical set of English kings
and queens. Such series, most of them commissioned *en bloc*, were popular until at least
the beginning of the seventeenth century, and
are illustrative of the antiquarian interest in
history, genealogy and lineage that was prevalent at the time. Among the earliest surviving
panel portraits are those dated *c.*1500 in the
Society of Antiquaries, and some of the panels
in the Royal Collection. The latter do not
form a uniform series, being produced at
different times and by different hands, but by
1639 they were definitely seen as a unity,
'Nyne old heades' being recorded by Van der
Doort hanging together in the Privy Gallery
at Whitehall (Millar 1958–60, p.27). Edward
IV is notably larger than the other panels
which would indicate a slightly later dating.
Dendrochronological analysis put it at
*c.*1534–40, although this is not always a
reliable dating method and it could well be
earlier.

Edward IV (1442–1483) was the son of the
Duke of York and the Lancastrian, Cecily
Neville, and was crowned king in 1461. In
1470–1 he had to seek refuge in the Nether-
lands from the armies of his cousin Richard
Neville, Earl of Warwick, and Margaret of
Anjou, who supported Henry VI's brief
restoration to the throne. He was succeeded
by his son Edward V, one of the ill-fated
Princes in the Tower, and afterwards by his

brother Richard III. His daughter Elizabeth of
York became the wife of Henry VII.

The portrait is Burgundian in character,
and it has been suggested that it is a copy
after a contemporary portrait *c.*1470–5, commissioned when the king was in exile in
Bruges. Evidence for this is an engraving of
Edward IV (Bayerische Staatbibliothek,
Munich – formerly called the Emperor Ferdinand III until reidentified by Anzelewsky)
which is remarkably similar to this portrait
and which is believed to have been taken
from the same source, but with a crown, orb
and sceptre added. It has been dated to the
early 1470s. It is possible that the original
portrait had as a pair one of Edward's queen,
Elizabeth Woodville, of which the one in the
Royal Collection *c.*1500–20 is an early copy.
The costumes in both seem to date from
*c.*1470–5, for instance Edward's black cap,
which was originally smaller and has been
enlarged, and his brocaded cloth-of-gold with
stylised plant forms (an Italian cloth that was
used all over northern Europe), which ties in
with Philippe de Commynes's eye-witness
description of the King at the signing of the
Treaty of Picquigny in 1475.

Extensive political, mercantile and cultural
links existed between England and Burgundy
during Edward IV's reign, strengthened by
the marriage of his sister Margaret of York to
Charles the Bold, Duke of Burgundy, in 1468.
In 1470–1, during his exile, Edward would
have seen for himself the sophistication of the
Burgundian court, and in 1478–80 seems to
have embarked on a concerted programme to
emulate its magnificence. He acquired expensive Burgundian tapestries in bulk, and, guid-
ed by the famous bibliophile Louis de
Gruuthuse with whom he had stayed in
Bruges, commissioned Flemish illuminated
manuscripts. However, it has been argued that
instead of a wholesale importation of Burgundian culture, a far more selective process was
in operation, the texts of the manuscripts
being carefully chosen and altered in accordance with English taste. It is possible that
the portrait of Edward IV was Burgundian-
inspired, but executed in England. Pamela
Tudor-Craig notes how the pinched mouth
and elongated eyes are firmly within the traditions of English draughtsmanship, although
the pose is Flemish.

Other portraits of Edward seem to derive
from the same source as this one, although
some, for example that at the National Portrait Gallery, show him in reverse, as in the
engraving.

EXH: Pamela Tudor-Craig, *Richard III*, NPG 1973,
p.82, cat.P8
LIT: Millar 1963, p.50; Fedja Anzelewsky, 'An Unidentified Portrait of King Edward IV', *Burlington Magazine,* vol.109, 1967, pp.702–5; NPG 1969, pp.86–7;
John Fletcher, 'Tree Ring Dates for Some Panel Paint-
ings in England', *Burlington Magazine*, vol.107, 1974,
pp.250–8; Lorne Campbell, *The Early Flemish Pictures in
the Collection of Her Majesty the Queen*, 1985, pp.xiv–xv;
Frederick Hepburn, *Portraits of the later Plantagenets*,
1986, pp.54–70; Scot McKendrick, 'Edward IV: An
English Royal Collector of Netherlandish Tapestry',
Burlington Magazine, vol.129, 1987, pp.521–4; Scot
McKendrick, 'The Romuléon and the Manuscripts of
Edward IV', in Nicholas Rogers (ed.), *Harlaxton
Medieval Studies IV: England in the Fifteenth Century*, 1994

TB

ATTRIBUTED TO AMBROSIUS BENSON *c.*1495–1550

3 John Bourchier, 2nd Baron Berners *c.*1521–6

Oil on panel 53.5 × 26.5 (21 × 10⅜)
PROV: …; by 1952 Sir Geoffrey Frederick
Neill Palmer, 11th Bart decd. (when attrib-
uted to Gerlach Flicke); sold Christie's 11
Dec. 1959 (136, as by Holbein), bt Agnew;
sold Sotheby's 11 March 1964 (111, as by
Isenbrandt); …; private collection
Private Collection, Paris

Berners (1467–1533) came of an eminent family and was descended from King Edward III.
A soldier, courtier and diplomat, he is principally remembered as the translator of chivalric
romances and histories from French and
Spanish originals, particularly Jean de Frois-
sart's fourteenth-century *Chronicles*.

Berners served at the siege of Boulogne in
1492, distinguished himself at the siege of
Thérouanne in 1513, became Chancellor of
the Exchequer in 1516 and in 1518 was sent
on a special mission to Spain to negotiate an
alliance between Henry VIII and Charles V. In

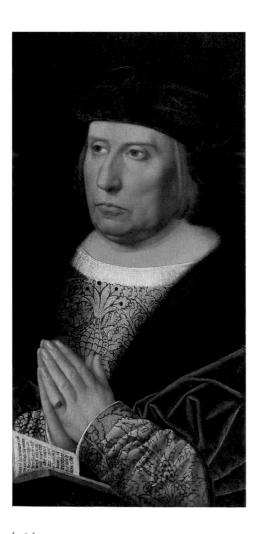

1519 he and his wife attended Henry at the
Field of the Cloth of Gold. In December 1520
he was appointed Deputy, or governor, of
Calais, at that time English territory. He
returned to England on his retirement on 1
October 1526, but in March 1531 was reap-
pointed Deputy of Calais, where he died and
was buried in March 1533. As he died in debt,
his effects were seized by the King's officers
who made an inventory that still survives
(PRO S.P.1/82, ff.294–304). The inventory
shows that he lived in great style, possessing
over eighty books (a large number for an
individual at this date) and, among his furniture 'iiij pictours', about which no precise
information is given. All Berners's literary
work seems to have been carried out after his
appointment to Calais, and the two volumes
of his immensely popular translation of Frois-
sart were first published in 1523 and 1525.
Berners married Catherine (died *c.*1536),
daughter of John Howard, Duke of Norfolk.
Of their two daughters only Joan (or Jane),
who married Edmund Knyvet Esq, survived
her father and had children of her own. Berners also mentions in his will his four illegitimate children by Elizabeth Bakyn.

This portrait, stylistically by an artist working in Bruges, may have been painted while
Berners was in Calais. The short distance
between the two cities and their close trading
links make this not unlikely. It appears that
the same sitting resulted in a second half-
length portrait of Berners (fig.18 on p.29), in
which Berners grasps a lemon and gazes
directly out at the viewer, which implies that
it was conceived as an independent portrait. It
has been suggested that the lemon, which
appears in other portraits attributed to Benson, was thought to safeguard against disease
and might have been included to express the
sitter's gratitude for escape after a time of
plague. Berners certainly appears to have
suffered much ill-health.

In the present portrait, Berners gazes to the
left, his hands joined in devotion above what
appears to be a prayer-book. It may well have
originally formed part of a diptych, an adjoining panel to the left showing, perhaps, Christ,
the Virgin Mary or a saint of especial significance for Berners. Such diptychs were frequently made in Bruges but the panel has
been trimmed at the sides, so no evidence of a
hinge on the left edge now remains.

This painting has been attributed to various artists, but Ambrosius Benson is the like-
liest. He is first recorded joining the artists'
Guild in Bruges in 1519: 'Hambrosus Benson,

ende was hut Lombardie [who was from Lom-
bardy]' (Marlier 1957, p.14, who notes that in
other documents the name is given in explicitly Italian forms, such as 'Benzone', 'Bensoni'
and 'de Bensoni'). Benson, who had a successful career in Bruges as a painter of religious and genre subjects and portraits, lived
as a young man in the house of the painter
Gerard David, for whom he worked as a jour-
neyman. Benson became engaged in a dispute
with David about two trunks that he had left
there, containing painters' materials and patterns, a small model-book with heads and
nude figures and three paintings, two finished
and one unfinished. Benson testified that
some of the patterns were borrowed from
Adriaen Ysenbrandt and others from Ael-
brecht Cornelis (Jean C. Wilson, 'Workshop
Patterns and the Production of Paintings in
Sixteenth-Century Bruges', *Burlington Magazine*, vol.132, 1990, pp.523–7). The case provides an insight into the way in which a
young artist built up a stock of patterns and
the value that was attached to these. There is
good reason to think that this was equally the
case with artists working in England (see
nos.98, 102). It has been suggested that Benson was the 'Ambros' who was sent to England in 1532 as 'painter to the Queen of
Navarre' (Auerbach 1954, p.150), but there is
no evidence that he ever worked for her. Benson's oeuvre is not easily established but he is
thought to be the author of two paintings
monogrammed 'AB': a triptych of 'St Anthony
of Padua' (Musées Royaux, Brussels) and a
'Holy Family' (formerly Germanisches Museum, Nuremberg), and these works have been
used as the basis for other attributions.

Another portrait with an English provenance and also attributed to Benson, now in
the Musée des Beaux-Arts, Brussels, is traditionally called 'George Hastings, Ist Earl of
Huntingdon' and Marlier records the remains
of an inscription '… ASTIN …'. No other
portraits of Hastings survive to enable the features to be compared. Hastings and Berners
had been companions on a French campaign,
and a preface to the third edition of Berners's
Boke of Huon of Bordeaux explicitly names
Hastings as 'a continuall spurre' to Berners in
his translation work.

Benson had two sons whom he trained as
artists. One of them, Hans (or 'John') certainly
came to England, where he became a denizen
(that is, became naturalised) in 1567. He
was described as 'a paynter upon tables' but
no works by him in England are known to
survive (Cust 1903, p.27). He is thought to

have died in Bruges before January 1581 (information from Elizabeth Drey).

The early history of the present portrait is unknown but a label on the back for the colourmen and framers Charles Roberson & Co. suggests that it may have been cleaned or reframed there between 1840 and 1853 (information on dates, Sally Woodcock, Hamilton Kerr Institute). A second label, in a nineteenth-century hand, identifies the sitter.

A cruder head-and-shoulders version of this portrait was sold anonymously at Christie's 30 Oct. 1959 (112) and again on 12 July 1963 (172). An extended version of it by a later hand, and which is thought to have come from the collection of the 1st Lord Clarendon where it was erroneously called 'Sir Thomas More' was sold at Christie's 16 July 1954 (32). The whereabouts of both are currently unknown. A larger and apparently later copy of the NPG portrait with lemon (photograph in NPG archive) may have been in the possession of Lord Berners's descendant The Hon. H. Tyrwhitt Wilson, Keythorpe Hall, in 1882. A further probable image of this sitter was sold at Sotheby's 6 July 1983(5).

EXH: Apparently Leicester Art Gallery 1937, but not listed in catalogue; *Paintings in the Low Countries*, Demedts Museum, St Baafs-Vijve 1986
LIT: On Benson: G. Marlier, *Ambrosius Benson et la peinture à Bruges au temps de Charles Quint*, Damme 1957; M. Friedländer, *Early Netherlandish Painting*, XI, Leyden and Brussels 1974

KH

Hans Holbein the Younger
1497/8–1543

4 A Lady with a Squirrel and a Starling

Oil on panel 56 × 38.8 (22 × 15¼)
PROV: ...; bt Jan Six, Amsterdam sale 6 April 1702; Pieter Six; by descent; sale of Willem Six, Burgomaster of Amsterdam, 12 May 1734 (11), acquired Pieter Six; ...; at one time in 'Monsieur Slingeland's Collection' according to Prestage and Hobbs, Sir William Hamilton sale 20 Feb. 1761 (75), acquired by the 3rd Earl of Cholmondeley; by descent to the Marquess of Cholmondeley; purchased by the National Gallery, London 1992
Trustees of the National Gallery, London

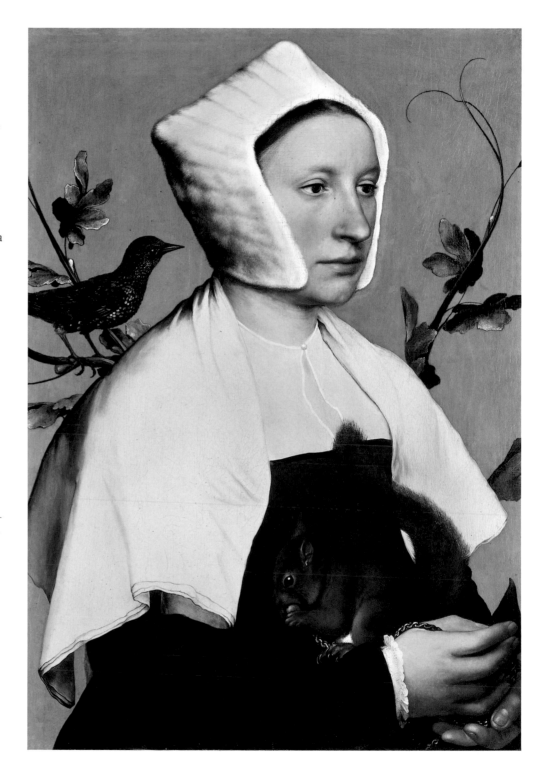

This is an outstanding example of the skills as a painter of portraits which won Holbein an extensive and prestigious clientele in England. From the exquisite control of the brush shown in the undulating black lines indicating the edges of the sitter's shawl, to the carefully arranged composition anchored in the lower right-hand corner by her tightly arranged hands, Holbein shows unfaltering confidence and authority. The restraint and economy of the pose lend a quiet dignity to the sitter which is reinforced both by her averted gaze and by the lack of idealisation which Holbein characteristically applies to his female portraits.

Holbein painted several portraits in which the sitters are varied in their poses but shown against a background of a similar intense blue with vine branches scrolling behind them. All represent sitters known to have been painted in England, and it is therefore highly probable that the sitter in no.4 is English. In style it is most closely comparable to the portraits Holbein painted during his first visit to England in 1526–8. The portraits of Sir Henry Guildford of 1527 (The Royal Collection) and of his wife Lady Guildford (St Louis Art Museum) provide the closest parallel.

The sitter has frequently been confused with the subject of a drawing by Holbein in the Royal Collection of Sir Thomas More's foster daughter, Margaret Giggs. Both women wear the same type of fur cap, apparently an English fashion, but their features, especially their noses, as well as their costumes and poses, are quite distinct. There is no need to assume that the sitter in this portrait was related to the Mores, as even in 1526–8 Holbein found favour with a range of patrons at court.

The most unusual feature of this portrait is the presence of two animals: a starling perched on a branch and the bright-eyed squirrel nibbling a nut. Among portraits of male sitters by Holbein are two who hold birds of prey (see no.7), as well as a drawing of a boy holding a marmoset (Kupferstichkabinett der Offentlicher Kunstsammlung, Basel). Like the latter, the squirrel here is clearly a pet and wears a chain around its neck; squirrels were kept as pets in England from as early as the fourteenth century. Recent technical examination has found that the squirrel was a late addition to the composition. X-radiographs show that the position of the sitter's arm had to be adjusted in order to accommodate the crouching animal, which had presumably been the subject of a separate sketch. The inclusion of the starling is less easily explained, and may conceivably have featured in the sitter's coat of arms or otherwise symbolically allude to her name. A possible Arundel collection provenance for this painting will be discussed by the author in a forthcoming article.

EXH: RA 1950–1 (32); *The Houghton Pictures*, Agnew's, 6 May–June 1959 (12)
LIT: P. Ganz, 'An Unknown Portrait by Hans Holbein the Younger', *Burlington Magazine*, vol.47, 1925, pp.113–15; F. Grossmann, 'Holbein Studies – II', *Burlington Magazine*, vol.93, 1951, pp.111–14; Rowlands 1985, no.28; S. Foister, A. Roy and M. Wyld, 'Hans Holbein's "Lady with a Squirrel and a Starling"', *National Gallery Technical Bulletin*, vol.15, 1994, pp.6–19; S.A.C. Dudok van Heel, 'Een Holbein uit de collectie Six', *Amstelodamum*, 1992, pp.51–5

SF

REMIGIUS VAN LEEMPUT 1607–1675 AFTER HANS HOLBEIN THE YOUNGER

5 Henry VII, Elizabeth of York, Henry VIII and Jane Seymour (The Whitehall Mural) 1667

Oil on canvas 88.9 × 99.2 (35 × 39)
Inscribed: See Rowlands 1985
PROV: Painted for Charles II and continuously recorded in the Royal Collection
Her Majesty The Queen

This small painting provides the only complete record of Holbein's great wall-painting at Whitehall Palace, which was destroyed when the palace was burned down in 1698. It was made for Charles II by the Flemish painter van Leemput who worked for him principally as a copyist.

Henry VIII and his third wife Jane Seymour, the mother of his only son Edward, Prince of Wales (no.6) are shown standing in front of Henry's parents, Henry VII and Elizabeth of York. In the centre of the composition is a tablet with the date 1537 and Latin verses celebrating the Tudor dynasty. It has been argued that this tablet was invented by Leemput and was not part of Holbein's original

painting, but the recent discovery of a visitor's description of the painting in 1600 which includes a complete transcription of the verses establishes that they were always an integral part of the design.

The Whitehall wall-painting was one of four large-scale commissions which Holbein received when he was in England, the others being the portrait of the family of Sir Thomas More, the 'Triumphs of Riches and Poverty' for the Hanseatic merchants (both on cloth and now lost) and the portrait of Henry VIII and the Barber-Surgeons Company (Barber-Surgeons Hall, much damaged); this is the only mural. Works with illusionistic architectural settings were part of Holbein's stock-in-trade as a Basel artist, but he seems to have had little opportunity for this kind of work in England. Like the More family portrait this composition sets the figures in a highly convincing interior space, so that if the painting occupied one wall, the figures would appear to be part of the room space. How far the interior that Holbein shows is to be taken as a realistic representation of an interior in the Palace of Whitehall, however, is doubtful: the

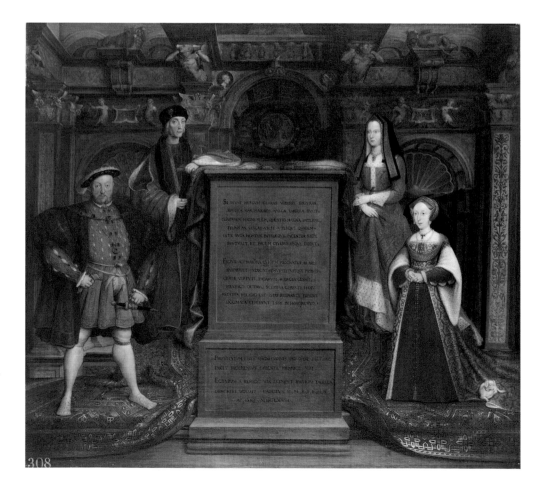

308

large head at the top is taken from an engraving by Bramante much used by German artists, although the frieze may bear some relation to what is known of Tudor palace decoration. Holbein's painting is sometimes known as the Privy Chamber painting, but references to it in this room go back only as far as the late seventeenth century when the Palace of Whitehall had been much altered, and the use of rooms had changed. If the painting was not made for Henry VIII's Privy Chamber, a relatively private room where Henry dined, it is certainly likely to have been made for one of the adjacent rooms in the King's Lodgings, perhaps a more public one.

The full-length figures in the portrait are arranged around the central tablet, a composition which recalls Holbein's 'Ambassadors' of 1533 (National Gallery, London). A cartoon survives for the left-hand part of the composition (National Portrait Gallery) and shows that the figure of Henry VIII has undergone some modification in the way his face is shown. In the cartoon he is in three-quarter face, as he is shown in the Thyssen portrait (see fig.23), but in the Leemput copy and in the many copies evidently made after the image in the wall-painting he is shown full-face, a commanding image with which Holbein was already experimenting in his portraits. In the cartoon itself the head is on a separate piece of paper, suggesting this was the subject of some experiment by Holbein. There was probably no need for another sitting with the King, however: Holbein would simply have adjusted the features to produce the powerful frontal image familiar from numerous copies of Holbein's portraits.

EXH: RA 1950–1 (204); *Erasmus enzijn Tijd*, Museum Boymans-van Beuningen, Rotterdam 1969 (159); *Sir Thomas More*, NPG 1977–8 (72); *Holbein and the Court of Henry VIII*, Queen's Gallery 1978 (81)
LIT: Millar 1963 (216); Rowlands 1985, cat.L14A, p.225

SF

HANS HOLBEIN THE YOUNGER

6 Edward, Prince of Wales *c.*1538

Oil on panel 56.8 × 44 (22⅜ × 17⅜)
Inscribed 'PARVVLE PATRISSA, PATRIÆ VIRTVTIS ET HÆRES | ESTO, NIHIL MAIVS MAXIMVS ORBIS HABET. | GNATVM VIX POSSVNT COELVM ET NATVRA DEDISSE, | HVIVS QVEM PATRIS, VICTVS HONORET HONOS. | ÆQVATO TANTVM, TANTI TV FACTA PARENTIS, | VOTA HOMINVM, VIX QVO PROGREDIANTVR, HABENT | VINCITO, VICISTI. QVOT REGES PRISCVS ADORAT | ORBIS, NEC TE QVI VINCERE POSSIT, ERIT. Ricard: morysini. car:' at the bottom
PROV: …; Arundel collection; …; Het Loo by 1711; …; Ernest Augustus, Duke of Cumberland and King of Hanover by 1844; by descent; purchased 1925 Andrew W. Mellon; passed to National Gallery of Art, Washington 1937
National Gallery of Art, Washington. Andrew W. Mellon Collection

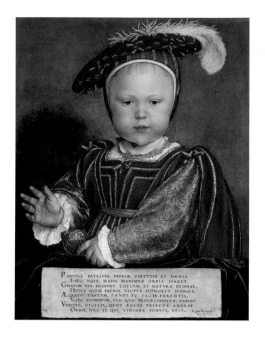

This is the earliest-known portrait of Henry VIII's heir Edward, Prince of Wales, and is the only surviving painting of him by Holbein. A portrait of Edward, Prince of Wales was given by Holbein as a New Year's gift to Henry VIII in 1539, and this portrait is usually assumed to be identical with the gift made by Holbein; the artist received a gold cup in return, the standard offering made by the King in return for such gifts. The face of the child in the portrait, which is based on a drawing which survives in the Royal Collection, could well be that of a child of fourteen months, although the pose is clearly deliberately that of an adult: Edward holds a royal child's gilt rattle as though it were the sceptre of an adult monarch.

Two portraits of Edward are listed in the royal inventories of 1542 and 1547, one a full-length portrait on cloth. Full-length versions of the Washington portrait type are known, and may possibly derive from the portrait listed in Henry VIII's collection. However, this is uncertain, and neither of Henry's portraits of Edward is otherwise described, making identification difficult. Henry VIII seems to have commissioned few portraits of his own family from Holbein, despite making the artist a salaried painter. The New Year's gift was offered after a busy period abroad taking portraits of potential brides for the King (see no.66). During that time he had also revisited Basel, where the town authorities were urging his return. This is the only recorded occasion on which Holbein gave the King a New

Year's gift (although many lists are lost) and it may be speculated that Holbein felt that such a specially flattering gift would be an assurance of his loyalty.

The Latin verses included on the portrait are praising Henry VIII, and in translation read: 'Little one, emulate thy father and be the heir of his virtue; the world contains nothing greater. Heaven and earth could scarcely produce a son whose glory would surpass that of a father. Do thou but equal the deeds of thy parent and men can ask no more. Shouldst thou surpass him, thou has outstript all, nor shall any surpass thee in ages to come'. They bear the name of Richard Morison, a protégé of Holbein's patron Thomas Cromwell, the King's Secretary and overseer of the English Reformation. Morison wrote works of propaganda under Cromwell's aegis, but he was also a humanist scholar of note. Such combinations of verse and portraiture were not unusual, as the Whitehall mural shows (no.5).

The painted portrait head is, unusually for Holbein, slightly larger than the drawing, indicating that he either did not transfer it directly, or, more probably, enlarged it after doing so. Alternatively it might have been used for another portrait of Edward. Interestingly, the imprimatura on which Holbein painted this portrait has been found to be a salmon pink colour, similar to the coloured grounds Holbein used for his own drawings in the 1530s and 1540s. The background has discoloured owing to the pigment used, smalt, a blue pigment which turns grey-brown. The effect of the original would therefore have been similar to many other Holbein portraits with their blue backgrounds overlaid with gold lettering.

LIT: Rowlands 1985 (70); *Paintings from England*, Mauritshuis, The Hague 1988–9, pp.117–18 (not exhibited); John Oliver Hand with Sally E. Mansfield, *German Paintings of the Fifteenth through Seventeenth Centuries in the collection of the National Gallery of Art: Systematic Catalogue*, Washington and Cambridge 1993, pp.83–91

SF

HANS HOLBEIN THE YOUNGER

7 An Unknown Man with a Hawk

Oil on panel 25 × 19 (9⅞ × 7½)
Inscribed '1542.ANNO.ETATIS. | .SUAE.XXVIII'
PROV: ...; James II; William III; Het Loo, Apeldoorn 1713; Kabinet of William V 1763–1795; Louvre, Paris 1795–1815; since 1816 at The Hague
Royal Cabinet of Paintings Mauritshuis, The Hague

This small, beautifully painted portrait is characteristic of the work that Holbein produced in the latter part of his career in England, just before his death in 1543. The manner in which the sitter is presented, with little surrounding background space, makes him appear particularly close to the viewer. Such compositions distinguish themselves from Holbein's earlier work, where the sitters are not only given greater background space, but are more frequently shown with backgrounds of curtains, leaves or objects, and sometimes tables in the foregrounds. Moreover, in Holbein's earliest portraits of English men and women the sitters are rarely shown facing the viewer, as here, adding to the impression of directness. The background is ambiguous, for although it might suggest the open space of the sky, the gold lettering reminds us of the presence of the picture surface, and in this way calls attention to the skill of the artist in the creation of this portrait. Such references to Holbein's powers as a portraitist were clearly appealing to his patrons: his portrait of Derich Born in the Royal Collection includes Latin verses on this theme.

The identity of this twenty-eight-year-old man remains undiscovered. He is probably an Englishman, rather than one of the foreigners – German merchants and French diplomats – who made up the minor part of Holbein's clientele, and whose portraits mostly proclaim their identities and include other distinctive characteristics. His hairstyle, beard and clothing can be compared to those in a number of Holbein's preparatory studies in the Royal Collection, for instance to those of Lord Vaux (see no.94) and Sir Thomas Wyatt, but his facial features are different from these sitters. There is no surviving preparatory drawing for this portrait, but it is likely that the painting is based on such a drawing, now lost.

A small number of Holbein's English portraits show the sitters with animals, probably because these animals were kept as pets (compare the squirrel in no.4). Holbein's portrait of Robert Cheseman of 1533, also at The Hague, depicts him with a falcon. The hawk with which this sitter has chosen to be portrayed is unlikely to indicate that the sitter held any official position relating to the hunting animals kept for Henry VIII, but he presumably enjoyed the pastime of hunting with hawks, which was extremely popular in sixteenth-century England. The hawk was added late in the composition.

EXH: *Paintings from England*, Mauritshuis, The Hague, 1988–9 (21)
LIT: Rowlands 1985, no.75

SF

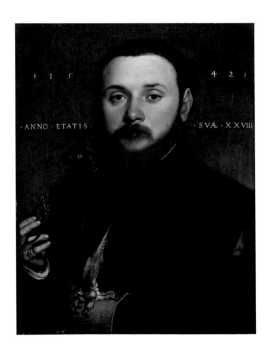

CIRCLE OF HANS HOLBEIN THE YOUNGER

8 Henry VIII *c.*1540

Oil on panel 88.2 × 75 (34¾ × 29½)
Inscribed ANNO ETATIS | SVAE XLIX
PROV: ...; Pallavicini, Milan; Duke Torlonia, 1892; Galleria Corsini
Galleria Nazionale d'Arte Antica, Rome

Despite Holbein's achievement in creating the likeness of the bulky King by which he is instantly recognisable, and which was so often repeated, there are remarkably few surviving depictions of Henry VIII which can be attributed to Holbein himself with complete certainty. Holbein's first depiction of the King may well be that in the miniature of 'Solomon and the Queen of Sheba' (The Royal Collection), in which King Solomon bears a striking resemblance to Henry VIII, but that likeness may not have resulted from a sitting with the King.

This image of Henry is based on the final version of the portrait of the King as he appeared in Holbein's wall-painting at Whitehall Palace (see no.5). He is shown completely frontally, rather than in three-quarter face, as Holbein had first planned in his cartoon in the National Portrait Gallery. Although there are a number of small differences in costume between this painting and the cartoon, notably the higher necked doublet here, the similarity in size is close enough for this portrait to give a very good idea of the impact of Holbein's formidable depiction of Henry VIII in his wall-painting. The proportions of the face in this portrait are sufficiently near to those of the cartoon to suggest that this painting may well have been produced from a pattern made from the finished head.

Many versions of the image of Henry derived from the Whitehall wall-painting survive, but this is certainly the highest in quality, and is extremely close to Holbein's manner of painting. The depiction of some details however fall short of Holbein's standard: some lack of control in the foreshortening of the embroidered patterns for instance, and other weaknesses in the delineation of parts of the costume, especially where they differ from the cartoon.

Most images of Henry show him full-face, following the Whitehall type. An exception that seems to have been derived from the three-quarter face cartoon for the Whitehall mural is the small, exquisitely painted portrait by Holbein in the Thyssen-Bornemisza collection in Madrid (fig.23).

The three-quarter view and the propor-

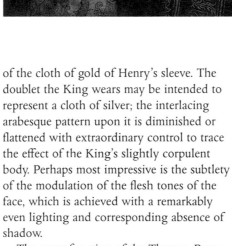

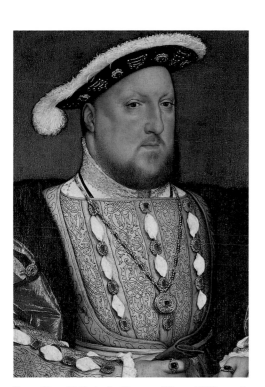

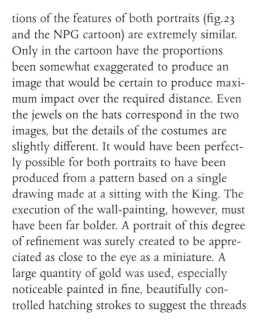

fig.23 Hans Holbein the Younger, 'Henry VIII' *c.*1536, oil on panel. *Fundación Colección Thyssen-Bornemisza, Madrid*

tions of the features of both portraits (fig.23 and the NPG cartoon) are extremely similar. Only in the cartoon have the proportions been somewhat exaggerated to produce an image that would be certain to produce maximum impact over the required distance. Even the jewels on the hats correspond in the two images, but the details of the costumes are slightly different. It would have been perfectly possible for both portraits to have been produced from a pattern based on a single drawing made at a sitting with the King. The execution of the wall-painting, however, must have been far bolder. A portrait of this degree of refinement was surely created to be appreciated as close to the eye as a miniature. A large quantity of gold was used, especially noticeable painted in fine, beautifully controlled hatching strokes to suggest the threads

of the cloth of gold of Henry's sleeve. The doublet the King wears may be intended to represent a cloth of silver; the interlacing arabesque pattern upon it is diminished or flattened with extraordinary control to trace the effect of the King's slightly corpulent body. Perhaps most impressive is the subtlety of the modulation of the flesh tones of the face, which is achieved with a remarkably even lighting and corresponding absence of shadow.

The exact function of the Thyssen-Bornemisza portrait is unknown, and it cannot be identified with any portrait in the inventories of Henry VIII. A diptych with portraits of Henry and Jane Seymour is mentioned in the inventory of 1542, and the size of this portrait is such as to make it suitable for a folding pair of portraits. However, the original frame has

long been lost and so it is impossible to know if the image was originally hinged. The back is unpainted, which might argue against the diptych form. The portrait has not apparently been cut down. It has sometimes been suggested that this picture was paired in such a diptych with the portrait of Jane Seymour at The Hague, but the quality of that portrait is not acceptable as an original work by Holbein. It has also been suggested that the portrait might have been paired with a portrait of Anne Boleyn, and this possibility cannot be excluded. A date of a little before or a little after 1536 would seem equally probable.

LIT: Rowlands 1985, L.14(c), p.226

SF

After Hans Holbein the Younger

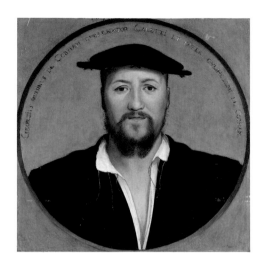

9 George Brooke, 9th Baron Cobham after 1544

Oil on panel, diameter 32 (12⅝)
Inscribed 'GEORGIVS DOMINVS DE COB-
HAM GUBERNATOR CALETTI ET PATER
GVLIHELLM DE COBHAM'
PROV: …; Sotheby's 25 June 1969 (36);
Rafael Valls whence purchased by the pre-
sent owner
Private Collection

Lord Cobham (*c*.1497–1559) succeeded his
father as 9th Baron Cobham in July 1529, in
his early thirties. The most dramatic events of
the reign of Henry VIII – the divorce from
Catherine of Aragon and the break with
Rome – followed soon afterwards, and Lord
Cobham was a staunch upholder of the new
policies, often reporting instances of disloyal-
ty to the King. An inscription on his tomb
pays tribute to his Protestant loyalty: he was
one of the supporters of Sir Thomas Wyatt's
rebellion against Queen Mary I, but was par-
doned. His most important official post under
Henry VIII was as Deputy or governor of
Calais, still under English rule, to which he
was appointed on 17 June 1544.

The inscription on this portrait refers to
that appointment, made in the year following
Holbein's death. It also mentions Cobham's
eldest son William, born in 1527. The portrait
is, however, based on a drawing by Holbein
in the Royal Collection (fig.8 on p.24). The
drawing shows Lord Cobham wearing an
open-necked shirt, rather than the more closely buttoned shirt and coat of the painting, but
is otherwise extremely similar. No other
painted version is known, although a small
portrait of Lord Cobham was noted by Vertue
in the possession of Dr Meade. Lord Cobham
is not shown wearing the Order of the Garter,
with which he was invested in 1549, and thus
this painted image probably originated before
that date.

Although the quality of the portrait does
not match that of Holbein's work, recent
examination has made clear how closely
dependent on the drawing the painting is.
The contours of the face and features in this
portrait were shown to match exactly with a
facsimile of the preparatory drawing by Holbein in the Royal Collection. Differences are
found only in the line of the hat and in the
costume. The painting must therefore be

based on a pattern taken from the drawing, or
from one made from a painting originating
with the drawing. In the latter case it may
closely reflect Holbein's lost original portrait
of Cobham.

The preparatory underdrawing revealed by
examination by infrared reflectography (fig.9
on p.24) gave no indication of the method of
transfer of the pattern, such as the dots indicating pouncing found in some other versions
of Holbein portraits, or of traced lines (see
pp.22–6). The visible drawing is freehand,
probably in black chalk, where Holbein
favoured a liquid medium, and there is some
hatching to indicate shading on the left-hand
side of the face and eyes. None of this is comparable to Holbein's own underdrawing,
where lines tend to be much bolder.

The brown background of the portrait is
misleading. Analysis of pigment samples by
Marika Spring has shown that under the lead-
tin-yellow lettering are traces of smalt, a blue
pigment used in sixteenth-century portraits,
which discolours to brown. An example of
such discolouration in Holbein's own work
occurs in the portrait of Edward, Prince of
Wales (no.6). Whether the whole of the original background remains, or whether it was
removed and repainted, cannot at present be
confirmed, but it must once have been blue.

LIT: J. Rowlands, '"Holbein and the Court of Henry
VIII" at the Queen's Gallery, Buckingham Palace',
Burlington Magazine, vol.121, 1979, p.54; Rowlands
1985; J. Roberts, *Drawings by Holbein from the Court of
Henry VIII*, exh. cat., Houston, Texas 1987 (48); J.
Roberts, *Holbein and the Court of Henry VIII*, exh. cat,
National Galleries of Scotland 1993 (22)

SF

2 Edward VI, Mary I and Continental Art

Following Holbein's death – probably of the plague – in London in 1543, Henry VIII's court had need of a new portrait painter. It is presumed that Holbein had used and therefore trained some local assistants but firm evidence on this is lacking. One likely candidate is John Bettes in whose portrait of an 'Unknown Man', dated 1545 (no.10) the influence of Holbein is clear. Less sophisticated is the 'John' who had portrayed Princess Mary the previous year (no.11).

Another German artist, who had settled in England by about 1545, was Gerlach Flicke from Osnabrück. Flicke died in London in 1558 but only three signed paintings survive. Little is known of his life here, including the reason for his imprisonment, recorded in his rediscovered miniature self-portrait with a fellow prisoner (no.67).

The most important artist of these years was the Netherlander Guillim Scrots who became Henry VIII's King's Painter at the enormous salary of £62 10s per annum. He must have been an exponent of the official portrait style of the Habsburg courts, for he had previously been official artist to Mary of Hungary, Regent of the Netherlands. A full-length type of Edward VI, four versions of which survive (fig.24; see the entry for no.13), whose official painter Scrots also became, is most likely to represent his work.

Holbein had used the full-length format for the portraits in the Whitehall Mural (no.5) as early as c.1537. An early use on the Continent of a standing full-length form for secular portraits had been by the German Lucas Cranach in 1514 and it was to become a favoured form for the Habsburg state portraits. The seated full-length portrait, meanwhile had been pioneered by Raphael (1483–1520). From the 1530s onwards, the Emperor Charles V patronised the Venetian, Titian (1477–?1576), in whose hands these formats were transformed into the two most favoured for regal portraiture.

The Netherlander Antonis Mor, working for Charles V and his son Philip II of Spain, built on Titian's work and used these formulae, allied to a precision of likeness, to record the images of many of the rulers of Europe and their spouses. In England he is best known for his image of Mary I as a Habsburg bride (no.16), resulting from his brief visit in 1554. Mor's pupil, Alonso Sánchez Coello recorded Mary's successor as wife of his patron Philip II, the French princess Isabel de Valois (no.17).

Back in the Netherlands, retired from Philip's court, Mor was sought out by English visitors (nos.18, 20) while the portrait formulae that he disseminated (e.g. no.21) were adapted by other artists across Europe (see fig.25) until at least the end of the century.

In the England of Mary I, meanwhile, the principal portraitist was the Flemish incomer, Hans Eworth, by whom a number of portraits of the Queen, from throughout her reign, survive.

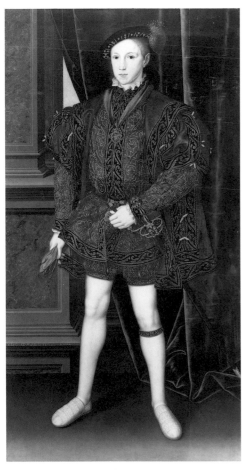

fig.24 Guillim Scrots, 'Edward VI' c.1550, oil on panel. *Musée du Louvre, Paris*

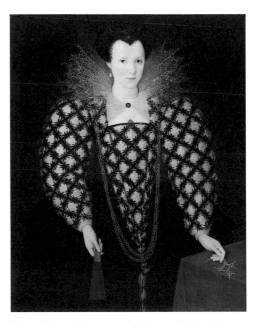

fig.25 Marcus Gheeraerts the Younger, 'Mary Rogers, Lady Harington' 1592, oil on panel. *Tate Gallery, London. Purchased with assistance from the National Art Collections Fund and subscribers 1974*

JOHN BETTES THE ELDER
active *c.*1531–1570

10 An Unknown Man in a Black Cap 1545

Oil on panel 47 × 41 (18½ × 16⅛)
Inscribed '[...]I . 1545.', left; '.ÆTATIS .
SV[...]' right; on the back of the panel
'faict par Johan Bettes | Anglois' above
'faict par Johan Bettes Anglois' ('made
by John Bettes, Englishman')
PROV: ...; 2nd Earl Cornwallis, Brome
Hall, Suffolk, by 1780; ...; sale of collection of Thomas Green of Ipswich and
Upper Wimpole Street, Christie's
20 March 1874 (22 or 23); George Richmond by 1875; his sale, 1 May 1897 (13)
as 'Portrait of Edmund Butts', bt Agnew
for the National Gallery; transferred to
the Tate Gallery 1949
Tate Gallery, London. Purchased 1897

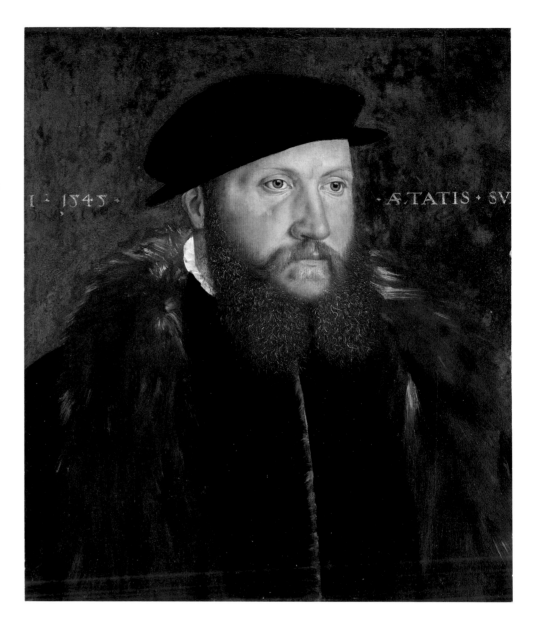

This subtle portrait is of especial importance
in the study of British art, as the artist's name
and nationality are recorded upon it. Signatures or inscriptions identifying the artist are
rare on British paintings of this period.

It is painted on an oak panel originally
composed of at least three boards of roughly
equal widths, placed vertically and glued
together with butt joints. At some time prior
to 1897 it was cut down along the sides and
bottom and now consists of the central board
flanked by two strips, each about 7.5cm wide.
The central board is 24.5cm across and contains the full width of the head and hat.
Assuming an original three-plank construction, the type most commonly found in this
period, the painting would formerly have
been about 69cm wide. A section containing
inscriptions naming the artist was evidently
retained when the painting was reduced in
size. It is now affixed to the back of the panel
(fig.26). The inscriptions are both in 'mixed
hands', that is, italic coupled with basic cur-
sive. Such scripts were in use roughly between
1525 and 1575; France was more advanced in
the introduction of italic (verbal communication, Dr Michelle Brown, British Library). It
is impossible to guess why the inscriptions are
in French; Calais at this period was, of course,
English territory.

On the front of the painting, the shadows
of duplicate inscriptions 'ANNO DNI 1545',
left, and 'XXVI' right, can be seen above and
below the present ones. The age given,
twenty-six, seems consistent with the appearance of the sitter. A suggestion by Sir George
Scharf that this may represent Edmund Butts
was first published in the 1897 sale catalogue.

For a technical study of this work, see
pp.231–5.

This portrait is very close to the work of
Holbein, who had died in London two years
previously, and Bettes probably received training with Holbein. William Musgrave recorded
this painting at Brome Hall in 1780, where he
was told it portrayed Henry VIII's physician,
William Butts (*c.*1485–1545). He transcribed
the upper of the two French inscriptions, presumably still part of the main panel and prior
to the cutting down. He also transcribed a
coat of arms which he saw in some connection with this portrait: 'Sable a Cheveron
between 3 Mullets Or. A mullet for difference'. These are not the arms of Dr Butts –
azure on a chevron between three estoiles or
as many lozenges gules – but are close

enough to suggest that poor light might have
led to an error. Butts and his wife had been
portrayed by Holbein himself (see pp.22–3).
Butts's eldest son William was painted by
John Bettes in *c.*1543, and the present sitter
could be Butts's third son, Edmund, a fore-
bear of the Lords Cornwallis. Edmund was
born after 1516, married by 1543 and died
1549/50, and thus could have been twenty-
six in 1545 (Old Style) – an important year for
him, in which he inherited property from his
father (advice from Timothy Duke, Chester
Herald).

John Bettes the Elder, portrait-painter,
miniaturist and wood-engraver, is first recorded as carrying out decorative work for King
Henry VIII at Whitehall Palace, London, in
1531–3. In the accounts of Queen Catherine

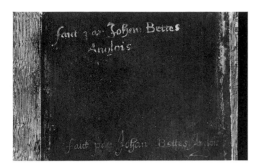

fig.26 Reverse, detail of the inscriptions

Parr for 1546/7, Bettes was paid a total of £3 for 'lymmyng' portraits of the King and of the Queen which were engraved by one 'Gyles', and for six other pictures; the word 'limning' suggests that these were miniatures. John Foxe attests that Bettes engraved a pedigree and vignette for Edward Halle's *Chronicle*, published 1550, and the engraved title-border in William Cunningham's *Cosmographical Glasse* (1559), signed IBF is also assumed to be by him. A court-case record indicates Bettes was living in Westminster in September 1556. Foxe notes that he was dead by 1570.

The most talented member of a dynasty of painters, Bettes has often in the past been confused with his portraitist son John Bettes the Younger, a pupil of Nicholas Hilliard, who died in 1616; references exist to Thomas Bettes, perhaps a brother of the latter, and a painter grandson, Edward Betts [sic], died 1661.

Bettes may have been the 'skilful Briton' who designed the woodcut portrait of the Saxon ambassador to England Franz Burchard, published in 1560. No extant miniatures have been satisfactorily identified as by his hand; Vertue records one of Sir John Godsalve (another Holbein client), now lost, with a later inscription: 'made by John Betts'.

EXH: RA 1875 (175, as 'Portrait of a Man'); RA 1880 (158, under same title); RA 1950–1 (31); Tate Gallery 1969–70 (21); *Dendrochronology*, NPG 1977 (no catalogue)
LIT: William Musgrave, Add.MS 5726.E.1. fol.4, British Museum; Martin Davies, *National Gallery Catalogue: British School*, 1946, pp.9–11; Erna Auerbach, 'Holbein's Followers in England', *Burlington Magazine*, vol.93, 1951, p.45; Strong 1969, p.66, no.1; Waterhouse 1978, pp.22–3

KH

ATTRIBUTED TO 'MASTER JOHN'

11 Mary I as Princess 1544

Oil on panel 71.2 × 50.8 (28 × 20)
Inscribed 'ANNO DŊI 1544 | LADI MARI DOVGHTER TO | THE MOST VERTVOVS PRINCE | KINGE HENRI THE EIGHT | THE AGE OF XXVIII YERES'
PROV: Brocas family, Beaurepaire, Hants; by descent to Blanche Brocas (died 1862); Beaurepaire Park estate sold 21 Aug. 1873 by Mr F. Ellen, the Auction Mart, Tokenhouse Yard, London; Christie's 10 June 1876 (165), bt Henry Graves & Co; bt by the National Portrait Gallery, London 1876
National Portrait Gallery, London

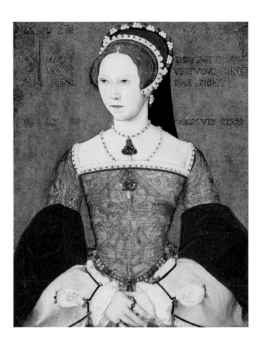

This depicts the future Mary I, eldest surviving daughter of Henry VIII, at the age of twenty-eight. It is generally assumed to be the portrait paid for in November 1544: 'Item, pd to one John that drue her grace in a table, v.li [£5]' (F.E. Madden, *The Privy Purse Expenses of the Princess Mary*, 1831, p.168). No other portrait of Mary at this date is now known, but it is not certain that this is the one referred to. The composition follows that used by Holbein for potential royal brides less than ten years earlier. It would later be reused, from 1553 onwards, with the eyes looking directly at the viewer, by Hans Eworth for Mary's portraits as Queen.

The portrait that Mary commissioned in 1544 reflected her newly regained position of honour. In that year, although still regarded as illegitimate, she was reinstated in the order of succession. Since Henry's marriage to Catherine Parr in July 1543, Mary had been 'retained to be with the queen' (cited Drey 1990, p.5) and was to remain at court until Henry's death. The family unity that Catherine worked to promote is given public expression in 'The Family of Henry VIII' *c*.1545 (The Royal Collection), where Mary is depicted with her father, half-sister Elizabeth, half-brother Edward and deceased stepmother Jane Seymour.

In the present portrait Mary is shown as befits a king's daughter. Her love of fine clothes and jewellery was remarked on throughout her life and, even in the years of financial privation when she was out of her father's favour, her surviving privy purse expenses clearly show her attempts to keep up with fashion. Here she wears a French gown with oversleeves folded back on to the elbow to display a rich facing of crimson velvet. The background is costly pigment, azurite.

The identity of 'John' the painter is not known. The maker of the present portrait is evidently less accomplished than John Bettes (no.10). However, it does appear to be by the same hand as a full-length of a richly dressed lady, at present identified as Lady Jane Grey, also in the National Portrait Gallery. The composition and the treatment of the costume are very similar. That work was first recorded, as a picture of Catherine Parr, in an early eighteenth-century sketch when it was at Glendon Hall, formerly the home of Catherine's kinswoman Maud Parr, Lady Lane (BL Add MS 32,467, see letter from Sir Gyles Isham of 28 May 1970, NPG files).

As Elizabeth Drey points out, Mary had spent much of her childhood in a betrothed state, which had called for exchanges of portraits. From 1521–6 she was affianced to the future Emperor Charles V, whose aunt, Margaret of Austria, in 1524 possessed two portraits of her. A miniature of Mary, wearing a jewel inscribed 'The Emp[er]our', attributed to Lucas Horenbout and evidently of this period, is on loan to the National Portrait Gallery from Brian Pilkington, Esq. In 1527, François I of France, negotiating for her hand for himself or one of his sons, was sent an image of her. Although she fell from favour following the annulment of her parents' marriage in 1533, Henry VIII had continued to negotiate marriages for her, but refused requests for her portrait. In 1541 when the French ambassador tried to obtain a portrait of her he was told that 'no painter dare attempt it without the King's command' (Drey 1990, p.3). Thus, any portraits that were made must have been done with the King's approval.

EXH: Tate Gallery 1969–70 (27); *After Holbein*, NPG, 1994 (no catalogue)
LIT: NPG 1969, I, pp.207–9; Alison J. Carter, 'Mary Tudor's Wardrobe', *Costume*, no.18, 1984, pp.9–28; Elizabeth Ann Drey, 'The Portraits of Mary I, Queen of England', MA report, Courtauld Institute, 1990; Rosalind K. Marshall, *Mary I*, 1993

KH

GERLACH FLICKE
active *c.*1545–1558

12 Archbishop Thomas Cranmer
1545 or 1546

Oil on panel 98.9 × 76.2 (38¾ × 30)
Inscribed 'Gerlacŭs flicŭs | Germanus | faciebat' t.l.; 'Anno etatj 57 Julij 20' on the strip of paper stuck with red wax above the sitter's right shoulder; '[Too the most Reverend | fathere in gode and my | singulare goode Lorde my | Lorde tharchbusshope off | Canturbury hys grace | be thes' on the letter at the left-hand side of the table; 'Epist | Paul' on the book in the sitter's hands; 'Au[…] de fide et | operib' on the book in the centre of the table; 'p[…]t[…] n | te' on the book to the right
PROV: …; in the collection of John Mitchell of Bayfield Hall, Norfolk; presented by him to the British Museum in 1776; transferred to the National Portrait Gallery, London in 1879
National Portrait Gallery, London

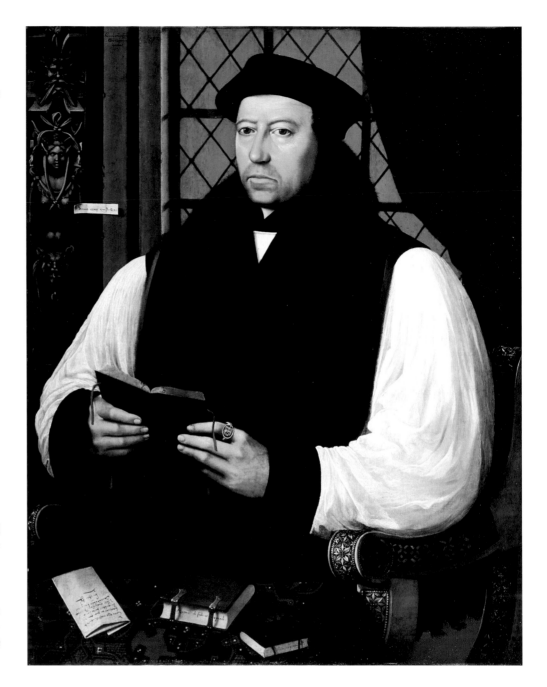

A rare signed painting by the German artist Flicke, the portrait of Archbishop Cranmer is also the earliest evidence for the artist's presence in this country. Assuming that the age given for the sitter is correct, the painting can be dated to either 1545 or 1546, depending on whether 'Anno etatj 57' is taken to mean that Cranmer was in his fifty-seventh year, or that he was fifty-seven years old; Cranmer was born on 2 July 1489. Flicke, a native of Osnabrück in Germany, lived for a period in the parish of St Mary Woolnoth in London; at the time of his death in 1558 he was resident in the parish of St Giles Cripplegate (see his self-portrait, no.67).

Flicke was working in London in the wake of Holbein's success in this country, and his portrait of Cranmer clearly reveals his awareness of Holbein's legacy in portraiture of this type. In a number of respects it closely follows the pattern established by Holbein's portrait of Cranmer's predecessor, Archbishop Warham (1527; see fig.12 on p.25), which is itself related to Holbein's earlier portrait of Erasmus (1523; on loan to the National Gallery, London). Both archbishops are shown seated behind a table or ledge, turned almost squarely towards the viewer. Both paintings include a damask curtain, rich carpet and books. Like Holbein, Flicke is clearly interested in the varied textures of the materials he depicts: the thick fur of Cranmer's collar, the fine fabric of his sleeves, the heavy satin of his tippet and the hard, chipped stone of the window casement behind him. However, the jewelled mitre and archiepiscopal cross which are so prominent in Warham's portrait are absent from Cranmer's, and the emphasis here is on the archbishop's scholarly, theological interests rather than on the rich trappings of ecclesiastical life. Cranmer's portrait in its turn provided a model for the portrait of

Archbishop Matthew Parker; this exists in a number of oil versions, but the original is probably the engraving by Remigius Hogenberg of 1572 (Andrew Moore et al., *Family and Friends*, Norwich Castle Museum, 1992, p.197; Ingamells 1981, pp.316–17).

Although clearly influenced by Holbein's portrait of twenty years earlier, Flicke locates his portrait of Cranmer firmly in the 1540s with the strip of grotesque carving to the left of the window. Anthony Wells-Cole has suggested likely sources for the various elements in this carving, and has generously made this information available in advance of the publication of his book, *Barbarous and Ungraceful Ornament*, forthcoming 1996. Two separate prints attributed to Jean Mignon after drawings probably by Luca Penni include a mask set against strapwork, and a female term figure almost identical to those of the carving. The mask appears to derive from the marginal decoration of a print showing 'The Creation of Eve' (Henri Zerner, *The School of Fontainebleau: Etchings and Engravings*, 1969, JM 56), and the female term from the margin of a print of 'The Metamorphosis of Actaeon' (Zerner 1969, JM 60). Mignon was active from c.1543–6, and Zerner dates both these prints to the latter part of this period. If Flicke's grotesque work does come from this source, it represents a remarkably rapid response to the most fashionable productions of the Fontainebleau School.

Allusions with more personal relevance to the sitter are made by the books in the portrait. The book in the centre of the table has been plausibly identified as St Augustine's treatise *De fide et operibus* (Of Faith and Works). C.B.L. Barr, Sub-Librarian of York Minster has pointed out that Cranmer himself wrote two sermons entitled 'Of the True, Lively, and Christian Faith', and 'Of Good Works', which were included in his *Certayne Sermons or Homilies* published in 1547 for use in all churches (note in NPG files). Also published at this date for the use of churches was an edition of Erasmus's *Paraphrase upon the New Testament*, for which Cranmer provided a translation in 1548–9; the second volume of the translation began with Paul's Epistles. However, if the date of 1545 or 1546 for this painting is correct, it is difficult to see how Cranmer's translation can be associated with the book in his hands. The identity of the book inscribed 'p[…]t[…]n | te' is also uncertain. What does appear certain, however, is that Cranmer wished the painting to convey a clear message about his belief in the importance of Christian teaching, and of faith

and good works, with the authority of both St Augustine and St Paul behind him.

Cranmer's personal iconography is completed by his signet ring, prominently displayed on the forefinger of his left hand. The coat of arms has previously been described as showing the arms of the see of Canterbury impaling those of Cranmer: three cranes between a chevron charged with three cinquefoils (NPG 1969, I, p.54; Todd 1831, p.xiii). In fact, close examination reveals that the arms shown are those of Cranmer, quartered with those of Cranmer impaled by the arms of Aslacton (another ancestral coat of arms of Cranmer's). The Cranmer coat of arms was changed from three cranes between a chevron to three pelicans between a chevron, at some point before 1539 (Morice 1859, pp.250–1), and the black birds on Cranmer's ring can be seen to have the distinctive arched necks of the heraldic pelican. Apparently Henry VIII ordered this change, intimating that Cranmer ought to be ready to shed his blood for the good of his flock; the pelican was believed to shed her own blood for the nourishment of her brood. Of course this was the fate that eventually befell Cranmer, when he was burned at the stake for heresy in 1556.

The significance of the three areas of broken glass in the leaded lights of the window is more difficult to explain. Recent conservation has removed a layer of overpaint from the entire window, which had been concealing the original blue sky as seen through the glass, as well as these three holes. The artist has carefully delineated the edge of the glass and cracks in the panes, and the sky which appears through the holes has been painted with expensive ultramarine pigment, unlike the rest of the sky, seen through the glass, for which he has used the more common azurite. Although it is tempting to assume that the broken window is in some sense symbolic, it is unclear what its symbolism might be.

Another revelation of the recent cleaning has been the colour note 'rot' (the German for 'red') visible through the thin red paint of Cranmer's chair cushion. Although such notes are to be found on a number of drawings of the period (including several of Holbein's drawings at Windsor), even with the help of infrared reflectography they have rarely been discovered on paintings. Never intended to be seen on the completed panel, it provides an unexpected note of informality in a portrait which is otherwise a carefully and formally arranged image of one of the most important men of his day.

EXH: British Institution, 1820 (128); Tate Gallery 1969–70 (8); *The King's Good Servant*, NPG, 1977–8 (210); *Cranmer Primate of all England*, British Library, 1989–90 (84)

LIT: H.J. Todd, *The Life of Archbishop Cranmer*, 1831, I, pp.xiii–xiv; Ralph Morice, 'Anecdotes and Character of Archbishop Cranmer', in John Gough Nichols (ed.), *Narratives of the Days of the Reformation*, 1859, pp.234–72; Mary S. Hervey, 'Notes on a Tudor Painter: Gerlach Flicke – I', *Burlington Magazine*, vol.17, 1910, pp.71–9; Auerbach 1954, pp.52, 87, 163; NPG 1969, I, pp.53–6 (repr. in col.); John Ingamells, *The English Episcopal Portrait 1559–1835: A Catalogue*, 1981, pp.9–10

CM

?FLEMISH SCHOOL

13 Edward VI c.1546

Oil on panel 107.2 × 82 (42¼ × 32¼)
Inscribed 'Edwardus Sextus Rex | Angliae' in same slightly later hand as no.32
PROV: See Millar 1963, p.64
Her Majesty The Queen

Portrayed by Holbein as a baby (no.6), Edward was the son of Henry VIII and his third wife, Jane Seymour. Despite his early death, the diverse range of his surviving portraits bears witness to intense contemporary interest in this male heir to the throne.

Edward here wears a russet satin gown with hanging sleeves, trimmed with velvet guards, embroidered with gold thread, and lined with lynx fur. His white satin doublet is embroidered and slashed, with puffs of linen shirt pulled through on the sleeves. With his right hand he grasps a betasselled dagger, while the position of his left hand draws attention to his codpiece, assuring the viewer of the future continuance of the dynasty.

As he also wears a jewel decorated with the crown and feathers of the Prince of Wales, the portrait is presumed to predate Edward's accession, and so may have been painted for his father. The classical interior includes a column whose base is carved with a roundel of a horseman inscribed 'MARCVS. CVRCIVS. ROMAN[VS]'. The window embrasure, through which can be seen a deer park with Hunsdon House in the distance, is also carved with 'antique work' including a helmeted head in profile. Edward was in residence at Hunsdon from May to July 1546 (Howard Colvin, 'Edward VI and Hunsdon House', *Burlington Magazine*, vol.113, 1971, p.210).

Another version of this image at Petworth House in Sussex is a full-length; it bears the date '1547', the year of Edward's coronation, omits the Prince of Wales's feathers and crown on the pendant jewel, and shows him before a royal cloth of estate. According to Vertue in 1734 (IV, pp.65–6) the present picture 'originally was only done to the knees, but since of late added at top something, and at bottom more to make the leggs & feet. but so ill and injudiciously drawn that he stands like a cripple'. These additions had disappeared by 1813, and Millar observes that the panel seems to have been cut on all sides.

Technically this portrait closely resembles no.32, the portrait of Edward's half-sister, Princess Elizabeth. Dendrochronological evidence has suggested that the widest board on each of the two panels may have come from the same tree. On both, moreover, the joins between the boards have been reinforced with narrow strips of canvas under the gesso. Both works currently have roughly the same dimensions. The same approach to modelling and meticulous attention to detail is evident in both.

It has been suggested that the painter of these two works was Guillim Scrots, previously court painter to the Habsburg Mary of Hungary at Brussels. He was employed by Henry VIII from at least Michaelmas 1545 on an extremely high salary, which he continued to receive when Edward ascended the throne. A payment to Scrots in March 1552 for three full-lengths – two of which depicted Edward and were to be sent to ambassadors abroad – seems to be associated with a particular type of which four versions survive. The version in the Louvre (see *d'Outre Manche*, Louvre 1994, p.92 no.50) and that acquired for the Royal Collection in 1882 are the best preserved, and their handling is consistent with that of two earlier portraits of about 1544, also attributed to Scrots, of Maximilian and Ferdinand, sons of the Emperor Ferdinand I (Kunsthistorisches Museum, Vienna, exhibited at Schloss Ambras, Innsbruck).

The present portrait and that of Princess Elizabeth, however, seem much softer in feeling, the lighting less harsh, the flesh less polished and the temper gentler than in the works described above. MacLeod (1990, p.58) wonders whether an irregular line running across Prince Edward's neck with differing flesh tones on either side might indicate the involvement of more than one artist.

EXH: *The King's Pictures*, RA 1946 (7); RA 1950–1 (17); Tate Gallery 1969–70 (2); *Masterpieces from Windsor Castle*, NPG 1979 (no cat.); *Kings and Queens*, Queen's Gallery 1982 (13)
LIT: Millar 1963, pp.64–5, no.44; Arnold 1988, p.253; Catharine MacLeod, 'Guillim Scrots in England', unpublished MA report, Courtauld Institute, 1990, pp.58–60

KH

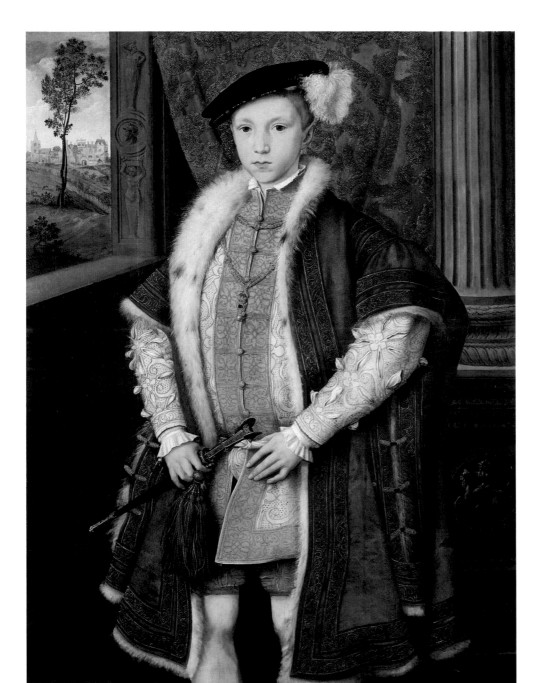

UNKNOWN ARTIST

14 Henry Howard, Earl of Surrey
*c.*1546

Oil on canvas 222.4 × 219.9
(87½ × 86½)
Inscribed 'H' top, held by putti; 'ANNO . DÑI . 1546 . ÆTATIS . SVE . 29', within arch; 'SAT | SVPER | EST' on base of column
PROV: …; noted by de Loigny in 1637 as with 14th Earl of Arundel and presumably the picture recorded in 1655 inventory of Arundel collection; Arundel sale, Stafford House, 1720 bt Sir Robert Walpole and presented to Duke of Norfolk; thence by descent; ceded to the nation in lieu of tax
National Portrait Gallery, London

Henry Howard (?1517–1547) was the eldest son of the 3rd Duke of Norfolk, the premier

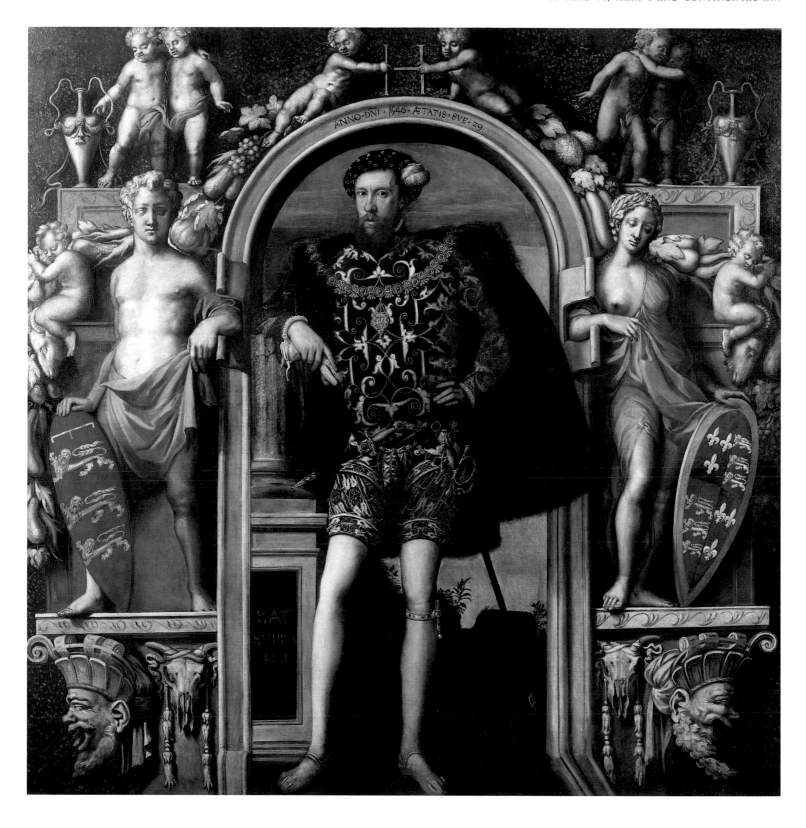

nobleman in England. He is principally remembered as a poet who, like his older contemporary Sir Thomas Wyatt, was the first to write in English following Italian models such as the sonnet. He was also the first poet to use blank verse, in his translation of part of Virgil's *Aeneid*.

Surrey was educated in classical and contemporary languages, spending from 1530 to 1532 at Windsor as the companion of Henry

VIII's illegitimate son the Duke of Richmond. In 1532, Surrey and Richmond accompanied the King to France to meet François I, and the boys spent the following eleven months at the French court, in the company of the French King's own sons. On their return to England, Richmond married Surrey's sister, but he died in 1536. Surrey paid subsequent visits to France on military missions. He was accused of behaving with inordinate pride in his

ancestry and was eventually beheaded for treason in January 1547 (1546 Old Style), just prior to the death of Henry VIII.

The date of this remarkable portrait has been the subject of much debate. Its innovatory nature, and the fact that it is painted on coarsely woven canvas (rather than panel, which was much more usual in mid-sixteenth-century England) have been said to indicate that it is a later copy of a lost original, perhaps commissioned by the sitter's grandson the 14th Earl of Arundel (see nos.140, 146) early the following century.

However, Anthony Wells-Cole's discovery that the grisaille surround is closely based on a print of the 1540s by an unknown artist of the School of Fontainebleau, 'Landscape in an Oval Surrounded by Genies' (see fig.27) strongly suggests that this work is contemporary with the date inscribed upon it. Anthony Griffiths, of the British Museum, kindly confirms that the fashion for these extremely distinctive prints was shortlived and that one would be unlikely to be used as a source seventy years later. While in France, Surrey would have seen the stucco and painted decorations that followed this form in François I's Galerie at Fontainebleau. In fact, inconsistencies in the shape of the arch in the present painting suggest that it, too, might have been intended for inclusion in a specifically designed setting. Surrey built a sumptuous, apparently Italianate, house in Norfolk called Mountsurrey, which was destroyed two years after his death.

X-ray studies confirm that portrait and grisaille surround were painted at the same time. The surround, however, is in a freer, more open technique and it is possible that, as MacLeod suggests, the work may have been a collaboration between two artists. The greenish areas in the grisaille represent later overpainting; infra-red studies show that the unclothed areas beneath follow the design of the engraving.

The painting has been associated with the following payment of 1551: 'To gwillm Strete the k. painter the som of l marks for recompense of iij great tables made by the sayd Gwillm whereof ij were the pictures of his highnes [i.e. Edward VI] sent to Sr Phillip hobby and Sr John Mason. The third was a picture of the late earle of Surrey attainted and by the counsailles comanndement fetched from the said Gwillms howse.' (BM. MS Royal 18 CXXIV fol.69v, transcribed MacLeod 1990, p.4). The painter here referred to, Guillim Strete or Scrots, was active at the English court from 1545–53, and was, on this and other evidence, Edward's official painter (see no.13). Susan Foister has demonstrated that a 'table' – formerly thought to signify a work on panel – can in fact be an image on almost any support, including linen or canvas. It is not clear, however, why the Privy Council decided to pay for and collect a portrait of Surrey four years after his execution.

Painters in England familiar with the Fontainebleau style included the Italians

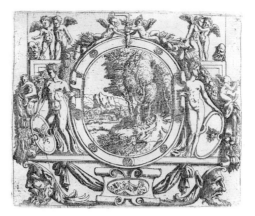

fig.27 School of Fontainebleau, 'Landscape in an Oval Surrounded by Genies' 1540s *Trustees of the British Museum*

Nicholas Bellin of Modena and Bartholomew Penn. Bellin had worked there before coming to England prior to 1540 and he may have painted the 'faire picture of the French King' which he was to give to Edward VI in 1552. Penn was the brother of Luca Penni, a designer of School of Fontainebleau prints.

Four less elaborately bordered later variants of the present portrait are known. One, which includes an arch, may be twentieth century; two others, also in English private collections, seem to be of the seventeenth and eighteenth centuries. A fourth, labelled as by Paris Bordone, recently appeared at auction in New York (Christie's, 14 Jan. 1993, 1) and has not been examined by the present writer.

A painting of some kind formed part of the case against Surrey. MacLeod transcribes various contemporary and later accounts, but concludes that few correlate and some, in fact, conflict. Van der Delft, the envoy of the Emperor Charles V, wrote, for instance, on 23 January 1547 (Cal. S.P. Spanish 1547–9, p.3) of a portrait of Surrey leaning against a broken pillar, which had been considered to be evidence against him. The not always reliable *Chronicle of King Henry VIII of England* (ed. M.A. Sharp Hume, 1889, pp.xiv–xiv) referred to a painting of a treasonable coat of arms concealed by 'another painted canvas' and quoted Surrey's comment that 'the painter is an Italian and has gone to his own country' (apparently referring to the painter of the other canvas). Surrey was certainly accused of illegally adopting the royal arms. In the present portrait, however, the male figure at left holds a shield with the Brotherton arms, and the female one with the arms of Thomas of Woodstock, both of which Surrey was entitled to bear as a descendant of Thomas Mowbray.

Surrey was also accused of wearing foreign dress, and Janet Arnold indicates that the costume in the present work is in the Italian fashion, but finds it puzzling that there is no opening down the centre of the doublet. A.V.B. Norman comments that the sword and dagger are convincingly represented – often not the case with a later copy of a painting. They are the height of fashion for 1546, and are decorated with painted grisaille enamels including classical heads. Thus they show not only Surrey's wealth but also his interest in antiquity and classical learning.

Surrey's son confirmed that he had indeed used the motto 'Sat Superest' (Enough survives), appropriate for one who left such a rich literary legacy (MacLeod 1990, pp.49–50).

The format of this portrait, from a period in which English full-lengths are extremely rare, is unique. The closest analogy is to the work of the northern Italian artist Moretto da Brescia, or, particularly, that of his pupil Moroni. The unknown sitter in a portrait by Moroni of 1554 (Bib. Ambrosiano, Milan), for instance, places his right elbow on the inscribed plinth of a broken column, grasping a pair of gloves in the same hand, amid battered classical ruins with sparse plants.

EXH: *Tudor Exhibition*, New Gallery 1890 (51); *Tudor Exhibition*, Manchester 1897 (81); *Between Renaissance and Baroque*, Manchester 1965 (221); Tate Gallery 1969–70 (25); *Patronage Preserved*, Christie's, 1991 (60) LIT: De Loigny, *Annales des choses les plus memorables ...* , Paris 1647, pp.284–5; R.A. de Vertot, *Ambassades de Messieurs de Noialles en Angleterre*, Leyden 1762, I, pp.87–9; E. Auerbach, 'Holbein's Followers in England', *Burlington Magazine*, vol.93, 1951, p.49; NPG 1969, I, pp.307–8; Roy Strong, 'Some Early Portraits at Arundel Castle', *Connoisseur*, vol.197, 1978, pp.198–201; Catharine MacLeod, 'Guillim Scrots in England', unpublished MA report, Courtauld Institute 1990, pp.31–50; Anthony Wells-Cole, *Barbarous and Ungraceful Ornament*, forthcoming

KH

BRITISH SCHOOL

15   A Lady in Black c.1550

Oil on panel 178.4 × 95 (70¼ × 37½)
PROV: ...; Huddleston family, Sawston
Hall, Cambridge by 1954; by descent
Collection of the Huddleston Family

English full-length portraits of this date are
exceptionally rare. The early history of this
portrait is unknown. The supposition that it
had 'always' been with the Huddleston family
of Sawston Hall (*British Portraits*, 1956–7)
remains to be proved, as does a recent family
alternative suggestion that it may have been
purchased at the start of the present century.

In 1956–7 it was exhibited as a portrait of
'Mary I', although the catalogue expressed
doubts about the likeness. The slender face
seen here does not tally with contemporary
comments such as those of the Venetian
ambassador Soranzo on 18 August 1554: 'She
is of low stature, with a red and white complexion, and very thin; her eyes are white and
large, and her hair reddish; her face is round,
with a nose rather low and wide' (CSP Venetian 1534–44, p.532). While Eworth's sequence
of portraits suggests that Mary's face did
become more gaunt with age, the fashion
worn here can be quite narrowly dated to
c.1550–4. Above all Mary was noted throughout her life for her love of fine clothes and
rich jewels. According to Soranzo (ibid., p.533)
'she ... makes great use of jewels, wearing
them both on her chaperon [headdress] and
round her neck, and as trimming for her
gowns, in which jewels she delights greatly'.
The austere lady portrayed here wears only a
simple brooch at her neck, a gold fillet in her
hair and a costly row of biliments, or hat jewels, in her hood.

However, the full-length format seems
at this date to have been used for only the
highest-born sitters, and this lady's all-black
French gown is of sumptuous fabric. Alison
Carter observes that Mary I's ladies followed
her formal style, and that they were frequently recorded as wearing French gowns. She
also notes that Mary gave such gowns to special companions. The present portrait shows
elements such as embroidered guards and a
black velvet partlet on a satin gown, which
are found on items in Mary's wardrobe
c.1550–4. These features are, for instance, also
seen in the portrait of 'Mary Dudley, Lady
Sidney' (Petworth House) of this date.

Mary I was a significant figure in the history of the Huddleston family. John Huddleston
had sheltered her at Sawston on the death of
her half-brother Edward VI, enabling her to

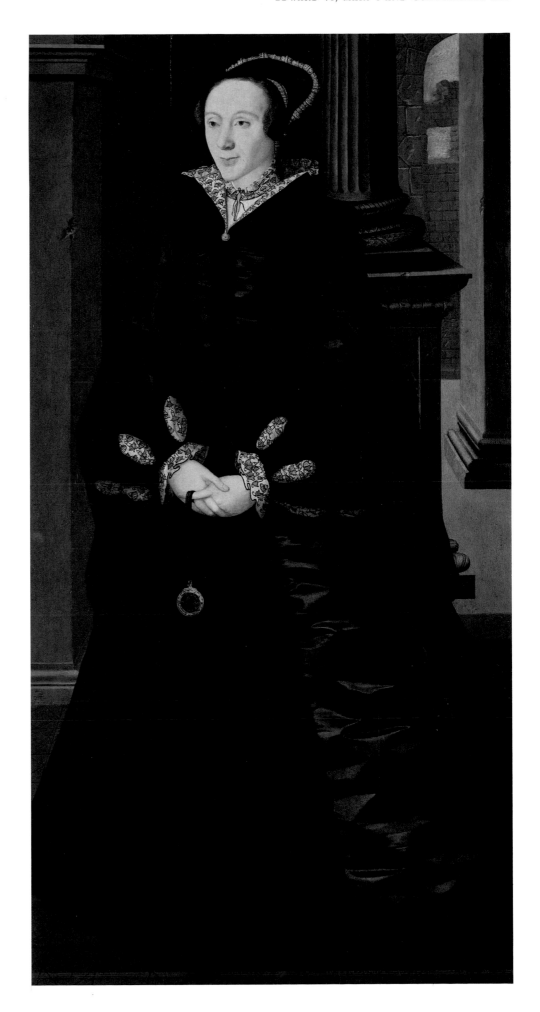

evade the Earl of Northumberland's supporters. The latter set the house ablaze, but on her accession, Mary rewarded Huddleston with a knighthood and appointed him vice chamberlain and chaplain of the guard to her husband, Philip of Spain, also granting him materials to rebuild Sawston.

The portrait has a powerful air of melancholy, which prompts the suggestion that the sitter may be in mourning. The enamelled object suspended from the black ribbon held in her clasped hands may be a mirror, a watch (often a symbol of the transience of life) or the case for a portrait miniature. Philippa Glanville observes (verbal communication) that the object is in the style of about 1520–50, and that the artist has carefully indicated that it has been damaged at the right-hand edge. The underdrawing revealed by infrared reflectography shows that the artist had difficulty with this area, placing the ribbon and pendant first to one side, then to the other, before settling on this central position.

There are no parallels for the background of chipped stone columns, with a ruinous brick wall beyond, in English paintings of this period. There is evidence of green pigment beneath the wall area but it is not clear whether this was always an underlayer or whether that area originally depicted vegetation. The background may, like that of no.14, the portrait of 'Henry Howard, Earl of Surrey', represent a response to the full-length portraits by the north Italian artist Moretto da Brescia (c.1498–1554).

In 1974, the late Dr John Fletcher measured three out of the four principal vertical boards of which it is constructed. In his view all three came from the same tree and had probably been used between 1545 and 1555. Additional strips of wood, each about an inch wide, are later additions at either side.

EXH: *British Portraits*, RA 1956–7 (10); Tate Gallery 1969–70 (26) (col. repr. p.19)
LIT: Strong 1969, no.9; Alison J. Carter, 'Mary Tudor's Wardrobe of Robes', unpublished MA report, Courtauld Institute 1982, pp.45–6

KH

ANTONIS MOR VAN DASHORST
between 1516 and 1521–c.1576

16 Mary I 1554

Oil on panel 114.4 × 83.9 (45 × 33)
Inscribed upper right: 'Antonius mor pinxit | 1554'
PROV: Possibly Philip II inventory 1598–1610 in the first room of the Wardrobe ('*Guardajoyas*' '*Pieza Primera*') of the Alcazar palace, Madrid (156) (F.J. Sanchez Canton, *Inventarios Reales* 1959, p.229 (3.958)); probably 1772, Madrid, Buen Retiro palace inventory (69) (Unpublished inventory, Prado Museum Library (14784)); presented (?by Isabella II of Spain) to the 2nd Lord Ashburton c.1855 (information kindly provided by Lord Northampton); bequeathed to Castle Ashby (one of the seats of the Marquis of Northampton) by Louisa, Lady Ashburton
The Marquess of Northampton, Castle Ashby, Northampton

On 25 July 1554 Mary I of England (1516–1558) became second wife to Philip of Spain, heir to the Habsburg Emperor Charles V. In the autumn of that year, the Utrecht-trained painter Antonis Mor, who had since 1549 been working for various members of the Habsburg family in Brussels, Portugal and Spain, obeyed an order from Charles V to go to London, where he portrayed the Queen. This remarkable image, which exists in two other full-scale variants (signed, Prado, Madrid); Isabella Stewart Gardner Museum, Boston) and innumerable bust-length versions, marks the transition between Mor's employment by the older generation of the Habsburg family, which was preparing to bow out of political life, and his appointment as principal painter to the ascending monarch, Philip II of Spain.

Mary herself seems to have had relatively little control over this definitive image and the format remained alien to English painting. The visual disempowerment engendered by Mary's foreign marriage may have been partly responsible for Elizabeth I's subsequent attempt to regulate her portrayal, and her concern to create a visual identity which utilised feminine exemplars to her personal advantage.

In 1604 Karel van Mander reported that although Mor was sent to London by Charles V, the Emperor was subsequently reluctant to accept an example of the image because, he said, 'I do not hold court, I have handed everything over to my son' (Miedema 1994, p.182). A *cedula* (letters patent) signed in Philip's name in London on 20 December 1554 confirms his assumption of responsibility, stating that 'I have commanded to take into my service for as long as is my will the painter Antonio Moro at an annual salary of three hundred *escudos*, from 1st November last when he left Brussels to come to my court, which will be paid when he is present and resident at my court and service, in addition to which salary he shall be paid extra for the works which he makes in my service in the form that I command.' (Archivo de Simancas, Contaduria Mayor de Cuentas, Primera Epoca, Legajo 1184, 1554, unfoliated).

The etiquette of court patronage, and van Mander's testimony, suggests that this appointment, together with a cash sum, was provided in reward for the portrait of Mary. Mor's image thus seems to have been created during the month between the painter's arrival in London in November 1554 and the signing of the *cedula* on 20 December.

The reconciliation of the English and Roman Catholic churches on 29 November, and the belief that Mary was pregnant, made this an exceptionally propitious moment from a Habsburg perspective. This perceived success perhaps motivated the commission and is claimed by attributes such as the diamond ring and pendant jewel, which represent betrothal gifts from Charles and Philip respectively. The red rose was a Marian symbol which could be read in terms of the love tendered by the Queen to her Habsburg partner, or the Church preferred back to Rome, as well as the Queen's Christian name and family emblem.

The broader iconography of the portrait also characterises the Queen as a Habsburg consort, rather than an English sovereign. In contrast to the contemporary full-length image by Hans Eworth (fig.29a on p.66), which works within English pictorial conventions, the type of seated format and aspects of the costume link no.16 with a visual 'genealogy' of Habsburg brides. This descends from two posthumous images of Charles V's wife Isabella of Portugal (died 1539) by Titian (Prado, Madrid, and a lost image of Isabella in black, one example of which was in Abraham van der Doort's inventory of the English royal

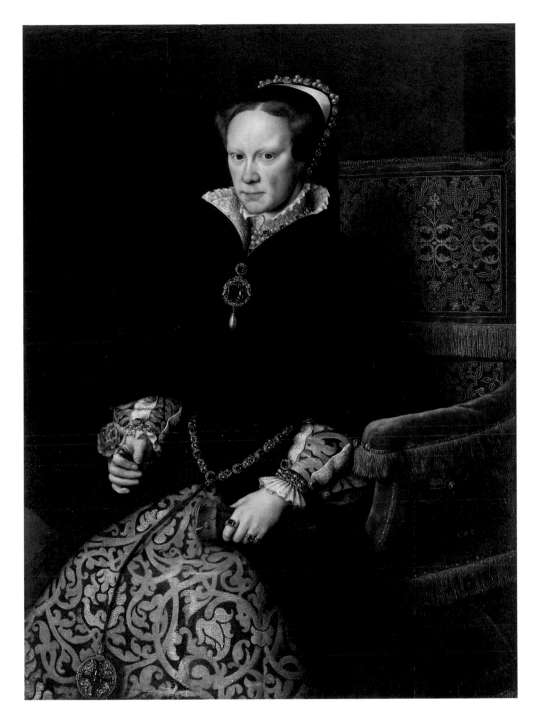

collection 1637–40) through Mor's own portrait of Philip's proposed fiancée, Maria of Portugal (Convento de las Descalzas Reales, Madrid), painted *c*.1551–2.

A prototype inspiring all of these images was Raphael's portrait of Joanna of Aragon (Louvre, Paris), a famous exemplar of beauty and virtue which deployed a repertoire of allusions to the Virgin and Venus. That within this idealising schema, no.16 seems uncompromising in its depiction of Mary's physiognomic particularities and slightly aging flesh may betray some tension between its two Habsburg patrons. While Charles V enthusiastically supported the marriage on dynastic and religious grounds, Philip resented a match arranged on his behalf with a woman whom he did not find attractive. He reportedly cursed Mary's previous portraitists and would thus have appreciated Mor's acute mimetic skills (see also no.17).

EXH: RA 1950–1 (200); Tate Gallery 1969–70 (35); Washington 1985–6 (19).
LIT: Strong 1969, pp.117–18 (65); A. Carter, 'Mary Tudor's Wardrobe of Robes' unpublished M.A. report, Courtauld Institute, 1982; J. Woodall, 'The Portraiture of Antonis Mor', unpublished Ph.D. thesis, Courtauld Institute, 1989, I, pp.238–74, II, pp.423–5; J. Woodall, 'An Exemplary Consort: Antonis Mor's Portrait of Mary Tudor', *Art History*, vol.14, June 1990, pp.192–224

JW

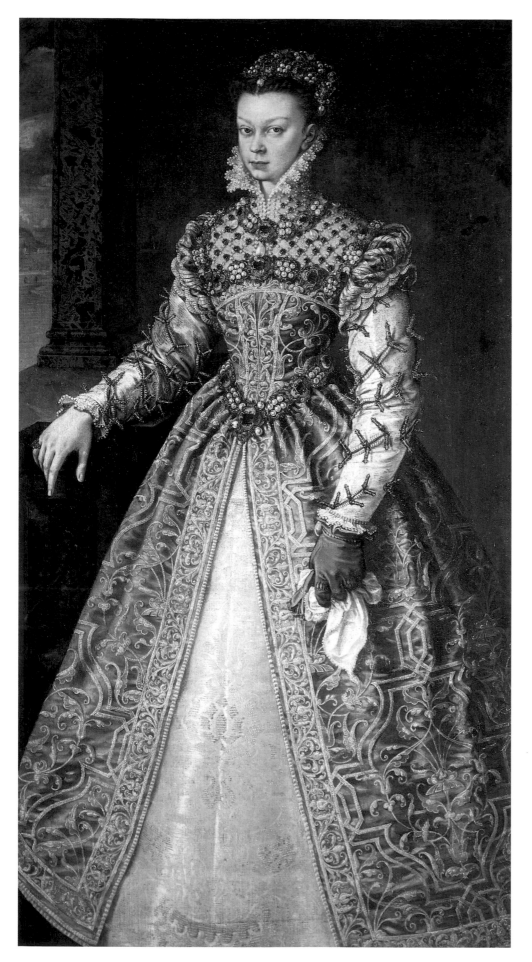

ALONSO SANCHEZ COELLO
1531/2–1588

17 Isabel de Valois ?1560

Oil on canvas 163 × 91.5 (64⅛ × 36)
PROV: The Habsburg imperial collections
Kunsthistorisches Museum, Vienna, Gemäldegalerie

This glorious painting represents the French princess Isabel de Valois (1546–1568), who became the third wife of Philip II of Spain after the death of Mary I in November 1558. The eldest daughter of Henry II of France and Catherine de'Medici, Isabel was married to Philip by proxy in Paris in June 1559 and in person in Guadalajara in February 1560. The picture was painted by Alonso Sánchez Coello (1531/2–1588), an artist of Portuguese background who, having spent a period working with Antonis Mor (cf. nos.16, 20, 21), was to succeed him as principal portrait painter to Philip II from about 1564.

The attribution of this unsigned work is not in question. It is stylistically compatible with secure works of the early 1560s, such as the signed 'Prince Don Carlos in Black and Yellow' of 1564 (Kunsthistorisches Museum, Vienna). As might be expected, the schema is quite similar to Mor's images of 'beauties' (cf. no.21), although the near full-length format is indicative of the sitter's very high status. The structure of the composition is, however, more relaxed and planar than in Mor's work, and 'painterly' qualities such as brushstroke are not suppressed to the same extent in favour of a transparent illusionism. These characteristics may have been encouraged by Sánchez Coello's experience of Titian's works in the Spanish royal collections. The greater resulting reliance upon the viewer to resolve and balance the figure produces a slightly less self-contained impression of the sitter than Mor's portraiture.

The identification as Isabel de Valois is based on comparison with documented portraits and on a gold monogram 'YF' visible in the hair jewel on the right. As Varez noted, this could be deciphered as either 'Ysabeau de France' or 'Ysabel Felipe'. The latter would be more appropriate, in that this was a Habsburg commission which characterises Isabel in terms of her marriage to Philip and identifies her with Spain. She is shown before a townscape which has been identified as Toledo, the city into which Isabel made her formal entry as queen on 17 February 1560 and where she lived until her departure to the new capital of Madrid in May 1561.

Isabel's relationship to Philip is articulated primarily through the striking device of the brilliant rose-pink dress. Wearing this colour, which is very unusual in a portrait, was a recognised sign of love (e.g. *Dialogo de M. Ludovico Dolce: Nel quale si Ragiona delle qualità, diversità e proprietà di i colori*, Venice 1565, fol 33r: *cornelio*). It was also employed for an image of Isabel by Antonis Mor, and Titian's posthumous portrait of her predecessor as Habsburg consort, Charles V's wife 'Isabella of Portugal' (Prado, Madrid). A romantic attachment between Philip and Isabel (which can be contrasted with his distaste for Mary I; cf. no.16) is reported in contemporary sources and the marriage certainly inaugurated a period of social and cultural vivacity at the Spanish court. Isabel herself, for example, learned portraiture from her lady-in-waiting, the Italian artist Sophonisba Anguissola, and Philip created a magnificent portrait gallery at his country palace at El Pardo (see no.21).

It is, however, difficult to separate personal emotions from political decorum during this period and no.17 would also have been understood in the context of the relationship between Spain and France. Intermittently at war through the preceding decades, these rival powers recommenced hostilities in 1556. Victories at St Quentin in 1557 and Gravelines in 1558 demonstrated Spanish military superiority and the Habsburgs' financial straits favoured longer-term peace. The resulting treaty of Cateau-Cambrésis, signed in April 1559, was sealed and guaranteed by the marriage between Philip and Isabel. Isabel was christened 'Isabel de la Paz' and taken to their hearts by the Spanish. Her portrait characterisation as young, beautiful, dressed in warm pink and laden with jewels similarly represented her as a kind of peace-trophy: the embodiment of optimism and love.

Because it refers to Isabel's marriage and her brief sojourn in Toledo, no.17 has been dated to 1560. However, portraits characterising sitters in relation to particular historical circumstances could be produced retrospectively and the existence of 'bridal' images of Isabel by Anguissola and Mor suggests that there may have been considerable competition to paint the new queen. As principal portraitists to Isabel and Philip respectively, both of these artists are likely to have taken precedence over the more junior Sánchez Coello. Mor's own portrait of Isabel in rose pink was almost certainly executed before he definitively left the Madrid court in autumn 1561 and the presence of Anguissola's 'Isabel with a

Miniature of Philip II' in the Spanish royal collections suggests that it was made earlier than no.17, which was sent to Philip's cousins in Vienna. It seems possible, therefore, that no.17 was painted around 1564, when the portrait of Don Carlos was sent to Vienna and Sanchez Coello was consolidating his position as Philip's new principal painter.

Besides providing a comparative example of female royal portraiture at the Habsburg court to set against Elizabethan imagery, no.17 indicates how the image of Philip's consort noticeably changed after Mor's portrait of Mary I (no.16). This was an exceptionally large shift, given that court portraiture of figures of similar role and status generally displayed the conservatism suitable to a world in which precedent was given enormous weight. Philip II's rejection of the seated format, together with Isabel I's concern to develop a mode of characterisation different from Mary, provides circumstantial evidence of the manifold tensions and dissatisfaction surrounding Mor's portrait of the English queen.

LIT: M.W. Freer, *Elizabeth de Valois and the Court of Philip II*, 1857; A.G. de Amezua y Mayo, *Isabel de Valois*, Madrid 1949; S. Breuer, 'Alonso Sanchez Coello', doctoral dissertation, Ludwig-Maximilians-Universität, Munich 1984, pp.108–12, 204–5; S. Breuer *et al.*, *Alonso Sanchez Coello y el Retrato en la Corte de Felipe II*, exh. cat., Museo del Prado, Madrid 1990; J.M. Varez, 'The Portraits of Elizabeth de Valois as Queen of Spain' unpublished M.A. report, Courtauld Institute, 1990

JW

ANTONIS MOR VAN DASHORST
between 1516 and 1521–*c*.1576

18 Presumed Portrait of Sir Thomas Gresham
late 1550s–1560s

Oil on panel 90 × 75.5 (35⅜ × 29¾)
PROV: Ann Compton, dowager Countess of Northampton, by 1792 (R.Thew engraving 1792, reissued 1823); …; probably collection of William Leveson Gower, Titsey Place by 1893 (Burgon 1839 and cf. exhibs. below); probably G. Watson Taylor and sold 1832 at the Erlestoke sale for £42 (Burgon 1839); by 1838 Hermitage, St Petersburg, with provenance wrongly given as Robert Walpole, Houghton Hall; sold to Rijksmuseum, Amsterdam 1931
Rijksmuseum, Amsterdam

This picture is one of a pair. Its pendant, which apparently depicts the sitter's wife Anne Fernely, is also in the Rijksmuseum.

Although neither picture is signed or documented, the attribution to the Utrecht-trained portrait specialist Antonis Mor dates from at least 1792 and is not doubted. The pictures can be assigned to the very late 1550s or 1560s on the basis of dress, and accord well with Mor's signed mature works in style and technique. An intense illusion of physical solidity and presence is achieved by means of convincing draftsmanship, precision of detail, extremely skilful differentiation of surface qualities and subtly rendered relationships between the edges of objects and their surrounding environment. The positioning and lighting of the head are characteristic, and the spatial manipulation whereby the right-hand side of the face is depicted more frontally than the left, was perfected by Mor. Also typical is the subdued yet rich palette of blacks, whites and neutral tones, set off by crimson, gold and green.

The identification as Sir Thomas Gresham (?1519–1579), mercantile capitalist, official royal financial agent in the Low Countries from 1551 and ambassador to the Regent of the Netherlands from 1559–61, seems probable. A tradition that Mor depicted Gresham dates back until at least 1744 and, although there are several candidates for the identification, no.18 has a good claim. A mezzotint by Robert Thew published in 1792 both attributes the image to Mor and identifies the sitter as Gresham. The likeness may also be compared with the best authenticated image of Gresham, an unattributed full-length portrait dated 1544 (the year of his marriage) in the

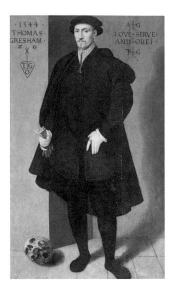

fig.28 Flemish School, 'Sir Thomas Gresham' 1544, oil on panel. *By courtesy of the Mercers' Company*

Mercers' Hall, London (fig.28). Features which would have remained relatively constant, such as the thin face with unusually broad cheekbones, the widely spaced eyes and the area of beard growth, are very similar. (It is noticeable, incidentally, that the sitter in no.18 apparently had very distinctive ears.)

Further evidence concerning the identification is circumstantial but suggestive. The depicted couple can be grouped together with two sets of similar pendants, producing a distinctive category within Mor's oeuvre, different in format and dress from the kinds of portrait he produced for the Spanish court. Since these aspects of visual characterisation were highly responsive to the social role and status of the sitters, it seems reasonable to conclude that the group depicted people who were not regarded primarily as court aristocrats and who had some kind of common social identity.

Although the names of none of the sitters is known for certain, there are some grounds for believing that they were English. They look northern European rather than Spanish and, in addition to the traditional identification of no.18 as Gresham, all the pictures have some English provenance. If the sitters were indeed English, it seems possible that they belonged to the English merchant community in Antwerp, of which Gresham was a leading member. In October 1564 it was reported that Mor was in Antwerp, making money from portraying 'les marchantz' (Piquard 1947–9, p.141). The use of the definite article here is notable in view of the fact that, unlike other 'nations' of foreign traders, the English merchants had formed the Company of Merchant Adventurers. Membership of this exclusive body may explain the strong corporate identity of the three pendant pairs.

Having visited England in 1554–5 to paint Mary I (see no.16) Mor perhaps subsequently maintained some connection with, and enjoyed renown and prestige among, an English clientele. He is, for example, known to have painted Sir Henry Lee (no.20) when Lee visited Antwerp in 1568 and it is noticeable that the format of the 'female' pendants corresponds quite closely to Mor's image of Mary Tudor.

This was formerly thought to have been the portrait of Gresham attributed to Mor and mentioned in the Common Parlour at Houghton in 1744 and 1752. This, however, was significantly smaller than no.18 and had no pendant. No.18 was in the Hermitage by 1838, whereas the Walpole Strawberry Hill sale did not take place until April–May 1842 (see further Woodall 1989, II, pp.388–93).

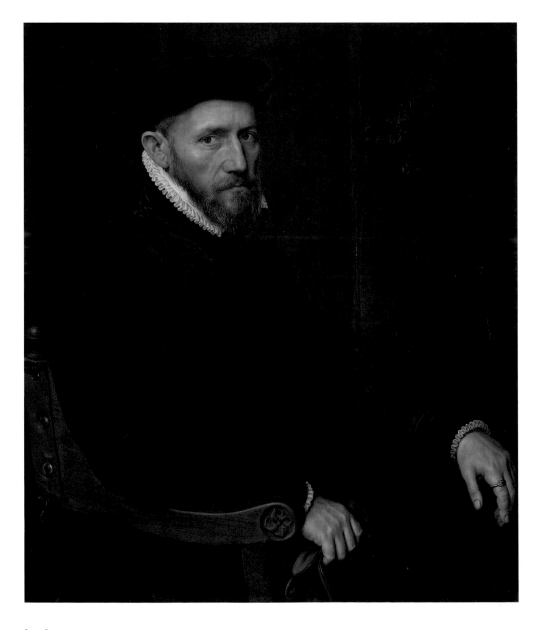

EXH: The picture in the Leveson Gower collection, Titsey Place, was exhibited at the Royal Academy in 1893; *Van Jeroen Bosch tot Rembrandt*, Brussels 1946 (69); *De Kogel door de Kerk,* Utrecht 1979; *Antwerp: Story of a Metropolis,* Hessenhuis, Antwerp 1993 (86)
LIT: J. Burgon, *The Life and Times of Thomas Gresham*, 1839, I, p.207 and *passim*; H. Hymans, *Antonio Moro, son oeuvre et son temps,* Brussels 1910, pp.132–4, 178; M. Piquard, 'Le Cardinal Granvelle, amateur de tapisseries', *Revue Belge d'Archéologie et d'Historie de l'Art,* vols.17–18, 1947–9, pp.133–47; NPG 1969, I, pp.129–33; J. Woodall, 'The Portraiture of Antonis Mor', unpublished Ph.D. thesis, Courtauld Institute 1989, II, pp.385 *et seq.*

JW

ALONSO SÁNCHEZ COELLO
1531/2–1588

19 Archduke Rudolf 1567

Oil on canvas 98.2 × 80.4 (38⅝ × 31⅝)
Inscribed 'RVDOLFVS.VNGARIÆ.PRIN-
CEPS. |.ANNO ÆTATIS SVÆ. XVI' t.l.;
'ALFONSVS.S.F. | .MADRITI 1567.' b.l.
PROV: Presumably commissioned by
Philip II of Spain; brought to France in
1808 for the collection of Louis
Philippe, and recorded in his Spanish
Gallery in the Louvre in 1838; bt Queen
Victoria at the sale of Louis Philippe's
pictures, Christie's 14 May 1853 (302a)
Her Majesty The Queen

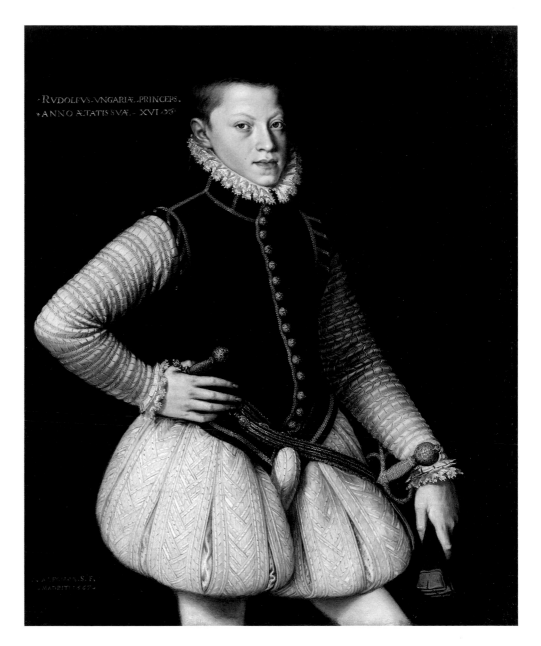

Rudolf (1552–1612) was the son of Emperor
Maximilian II, and was crowned King of
Hungary in 1572, and King of Bohemia in
1575. In 1576 he succeeded his father as
Emperor Rudolf II. He is depicted here as a
boy of sixteen, when he was living in Madrid
at the court of his uncle, Philip II of Spain.
Philip II presumably commissioned the por-
trait, together with its pair, Rudolf's brother
Archduke Ernst, also by Sánchez Coello (The
Royal Collection).

Sánchez Coello was appointed Philip II's
court artist sometime after 1560, on the
departure of Antonis Mor, although he was
already in Philip's service and had been in
Spain since 1555. He trained initially in Portugal, but met Mor, possibly in Lisbon in 1550,
and returned to Flanders to study under him.
He made copies of both Mor's and Titian's
portraits, and his resulting style – detailed
depiction of costume, but with a greater technical freedom than Mor, and the use of strong
chiaroscuro – is a synthesis of the two.

As Emperor, Rudolf became renowned
throughout Europe for his astonishing collection of works of art and curiosities. His passion for collecting, which included not only
the visual arts, but the natural and mechanical
sciences as well, and his use of art and symbolism to bolster the imperial image was
nothing new – for instance his uncle Archduke Ferdinand II of the Tyrol's fine collection at Schloss Ambras – but the scale of his
collecting and patronage was unsurpassed. At
the imperial capital, which he had moved
from Vienna to Prague in 1583, he gathered a
remarkable group of Italian, German and
Netherlandish artists around him, including
Giuseppe Arcimboldo who also designed
court festivals, Bartholomäus Spranger, Hans
von Aachen, Joris Hoefnagel, and Hans and
Paul Vredemann de Vries. Several of these
also acted as his agents, actively acquiring

works for the collection, particularly those by
Correggio, Parmigianino and Titian, and
above all Dürer, of whom the Emperor was
especially fond.

After his death, Rudolf's collection
remained in Prague until it was pillaged and
dispersed by the Swedish capture of the city
in 1648. It was the highlight of the Earl of
Arundel's embassy to the Emperor Ferdinand
in 1636. It must have made a great impact on
Arundel, although the nature of his own collection, and those of his English contemporaries, was less wide-ranging. It is possible
that the Keeper of Charles I's collection,
Abraham van der Doort, was formerly in the
Emperor's employ.

EXH: *Alonso Sánchez Coello y el Retrato en la Corte de
Felipe II*, Museo del Prado, Madrid 1990, p.148
LIT: Hugh Trevor Roper, *Princes and Patrons: Patronage
and Ideology at Four Habsburg Courts*, 1976, reprinted
1991, pp.79–115; Thomas DaCosta Kaufmann, *The
School of Prague: Painting at the Court of Rudolf II*, revised
ed. 1988

TB

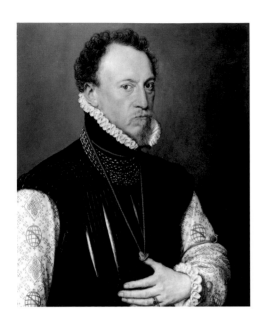

ANTONIS MOR VAN DASHORST
between 1516 and 1521–*c*.1576

20 Sir Henry Lee 1568

Oil on panel 64.2 × 53.3 (25¼ × 21)
Inscribed 'Antonius mor | pingebat aº
1568' lower right
PROV: Apparently by descent from Sir
Henry Lee; at the Lee family seat at
Ditchley Park, Oxfordshire, when given
to the National Portrait Gallery by Lord
Arthur, 17th Viscount Dillon, in 1925
National Portrait Gallery, London

This signed image provides an excellent
example of Mor's later manner and reveals
how he adapted his mode of characterisation
to accommodate an English court sitter. Born
and trained in Utrecht, Mor was appointed
principal court painter to Philip II of Spain in
London in December 1554 (see no.16). In 1561
he unexpectedly left the Madrid court and
returned to the Netherlands, working subsequently in Brussels, Utrecht and Antwerp.

Although the picture is not documented,
the identification of the sitter as Elizabeth I's
courtier Sir Henry Lee (1533–1619) is not in
doubt. It is justified by comparison with later
portraits of Lee by Marcus Gheeraerts the
Younger and the provenance of the picture
from the family home at Ditchley. In addition,
the armillary spheres (schematic representations of celestial orbits) which patterns the
sleeves, can be associated with Henry Lee. In
Lee's 'Ditchley Portrait' of Elizabeth I (no.45),
painted *c*.1592 by Gheeraerts, an armillary
sphere hangs by the Queen's ear. As Strong
pointed out, Lee is also known to have visited
Antwerp in June 1568, which would have provided the opportunity and occasion for him
to be portrayed by Mor.

The relatively small size of the picture
would have been practical given the necessity
of transporting a delicately painted panel
from Antwerp back to England. However, it
also places the image within a specifically
English tradition of half-length portraiture
deriving from Holbein. The slight shadow
cast on the relatively light, opaque background, which is unusual within Mor's
oeuvre, seems responsive to Holbein, who
had painted Lee's mother at a similar age
(Metropolitan Museum of Art, New York).

No.20 characterises Lee as a courtly lover.
The patterning of the sleeves incorporates
lovers' knots and the gold chains were a conventional gift from royal and noble patrons to
their clients, conveniently combining realis-

able monetary reward with connotations of
the binding relationship between the two parties. The surfeit of rings, suspended from the
neck on a scarlet cord and tied with similar
cords around the left arm, as well as adorning
the fingers, here connote special affection. A
contemporary report which mentions Mary,
Queen of Scots wearing a ring given to her
by Elizabeth I hanging at her breast from a
black and white cord implies that a ring could
be worn in this way to express its particular
significance to the wearer (Pepys MSS. Magdalene College, Cambridge, T. Randolph to
R. Dudley, 15.1.1563/4). In no.20 the use of
red, the colour of passion (cf. no.17), for both
the cord and the precious stone set into the
suspended ring, the deliberate way in which
this ring is indicated within the charged
ambience of a portrait, and the gesture of
heartfelt faithfulness produced by the placement of the hand, all set the figure within a
discourse of love.

It is tempting to think that the beloved
object constructed by the image may be Elizabeth I, for whom Lee acted as personal
champion in the Accession Day tilts, the neo-
chivalric tournaments which were held annually from at least 1571 in honour of the
Queen. Although no.20 is dated four years
earlier, it seems likely that Lee's important
role on these occasions evolved from less formal court festivities held previously in the
reign. Lee wears black and white, which were
the Queen's personal colours, and the rings,
worn like chivalric favours on the arm, speak
in favour of his characterisation as Elizabeth's
symbolic lover and representative. In addition,
the armillary sphere can be specifically connected with Lee's portrayed relationship with
the Queen. As a representation of the universal harmony of the sun and planets in orbit
around the earth, it might be seen in terms of
an ideal relationship between courtiers and
sovereign. Such a declaration of personal service and constancy would have been appropriate to Lee's political situation *vis-à-vis*
Elizabeth in 1568, when he was abroad, partly as an agent of the crown, during a period
of increasing tension between his two great
patrons, the Earl of Leicester and Sir William
Cecil.

However, if Elizabeth were the intended
recipient of the portrayed love, it might be
expected that she would have been the recipient of the portrait itself, and there is no evidence for this. Since Lee is later known to

have used lovers' knots in combination with the initials of his paramour Anne Vavasour for chivalric armour, the portrait was perhaps intended as a gift from abroad to a real lover, whether his mistress or his wife. The Ditchley provenance may suggest the latter, but the evidence that the portrait remained in Lee's possession also hints that the crucial concern was the creation of his *own* image as a lover, rather than the specific identity of the other. This ambiguity between actual and symbolic purpose parallels the way in which no.20 combines the mimetic illusionism for which Mor was renowned with the abstract, emblematic signifiers of identity which were to become defining characteristics of Elizabethan court culture.

This superb portrait seems likely to have impressed Lee's circle. A damaged picture of similar size and format depicts Edward, 3rd Lord Windsor, who accompanied Lee in Antwerp (Earl of Plymouth, Oakely Park) and the image of Lee's patron the Earl of Leicester attributed to Steven van de Meulen (Wallace Collection, London) displays some characteristics reminiscent of Mor's manner.

EXH: *Art Treasures Exhibition*, Manchester 1857 (500, as Sir Francis Drake); *National Portraits Ending with the Reign of James II*, South Kensington 1868 (663 as Drake); *The Royal House of Tudor*, New Gallery, London 1890 (268 as Lee); *Portraits of English Historical Personages who Died prior to the Year 1625*, Oxford 1904 (99); *British Portraits*, Royal Academy 1956–7 (25) LIT: F. Gordon Roe, 'The Last of Sir Henry Lee', *Connoisseur*, vol.110, 1942, pp.3–12; E.K. Chambers, *Sir Henry Lee*, Oxford 1936; NPG 1969, I, pp.129–30, 189–90; R. Strong, *The Cult of Elizabeth*, 1971, pp.129–61; J. Woodall, 'The Portraiture of Antonis Mor', unpublished Ph.D. thesis, Courtauld Institute, 1989, II, pp.488–92

JW

ANTONIS MOR VAN DASHORST

21 An Unknown Lady *c.*1560

Oil on canvas (95 × 76) (37⅜ × 29⅞)
Inscribed '268' (in white), '1717' (in red) lower left
PROV: Apparently entered the Spanish royal collection through Carlos IV (ruled 1788–1802); catalogued in the Prado collection 1823
Museo del Prado, Madrid

This picture, which is datable to *c.*1560 or later on grounds of style and dress, was painted by a Netherlandish artist of international repute who visited England in 1554–5 (see no.16) and appears to have retained English connections (see nos.18, 20). It may conceivably depict an English sitter and it exemplifies an international, generic portrait type in which aristocratic-looking women are apparently depicted primarily to signify feminine allure.

In 1908 Carl Justi identified the sitter as Jane Dormer (1538–1612), a lady-in-waiting to Mary I who married the Duke of Feria, Spanish ambassador to the Tudor court. In 1559, after Mary's death, Jane led six Catholic noblewomen into exile in Spain. Their royal entertainment during their journey, and official welcome on their arrival, suggest that they were recognised as symbols of Catholic virtue in the politico-religious posturing which greeted the accession of the protestant Elizabeth I.

Justi's hunch was based on sixteenth-century records of an image of Jane Dormer by Mor in Philip II of Spain's renowned portrait gallery at El Pardo, a country palace near Madrid. The sitter's colouring may indicate that she was from northern Europe, but the El Pardo picture was reportedly destroyed by fire in 1604 and the extremely high quality of no.21 perhaps mitigates against it being a replica of a lost primary image.

One might imagine, nevertheless, that the El Pardo portrait of Jane Dormer would have resembled no.21. It was three-quarter-length and displayed alongside three other similar portraits of foreign women, apparently connoting exotic, virtuous beauty, in Habsburg possession. No.21 can itself be linked with at least six other three-quarter-length portraits on canvas, all by or close to Mor, in which anonymous, attractive female sitters are shown in elaborate costumes, ornamented with distinctive jewels. Four of these figures face to their left, which suggests that they

were not intended to be paired with male partners, since the man was usually depicted on the more honoured, right-hand side. In a Spanish royal inventory of 1636 one of these portraits was 'said to be' Madame de Bourbon, principal French lady-in-waiting to Philip II's third wife, Isabel de Valois (see no.17). If this hearsay is true, the parallels which can be drawn with Jane Dormer suggest that some portraits of this type depicted ladies of the royal household.

However, no.21, which is qualitatively the best of the group and the touchstone for their association with Mor, is distinguished by the presence of the floral bracelet and scattered blooms. This unique feature in Mor's oeuvre may be compared with the insistent presence of flowers in early sixteenth-century, portrait-like images of attractive female figures by Palma Vecchio and Titian (who subsequently became Mor's predecessor as Habsburg court portraitist). The prevalence of flowers and the dishabille of these voluptuous Venetian sitters led Julius Held to link them with Flora, the beautiful goddess of spring and an exemplary courtesan.

No.21 is certainly very strait-laced by comparison, but considered within the austere context of Mor's oeuvre (which can be related to the stricter etiquette and more reticent – though by no means unswerving – sexual mores of the Spanish court), the half smile and glance become relatively provocative. It is also notable that in 1604 a source generally accurate in its information about Mor (van Mander, fol.231r; Miedema 1994, p.182) reported that the artist had painted all the 'concubines' of the Duke of Alva after the life.

The difficulty of dating these images renders it possible that no.21 actually represents not Jane Dormer but one of the 'four hundred courtesans … beautiful and worthy as princesses' (Brantome, I, p.106) who reputedly accompanied Alva when he arrived in the Netherlands as Governor in 1567. Van Luttervelt has also established that Mor painted a group of wives of leading Netherlandish aristocrats in the mid-1550s. While these are earlier in style than no.21, they are similar in format, aspect and the inclusion of distinctive, fashionable dresses. Such images seem to have been originally paired with military portraits of their husbands, but replicas and versions were subsequently incorporated into series of illustrious ladies or beauties, just as their spouses' images were included in series of famous generals.

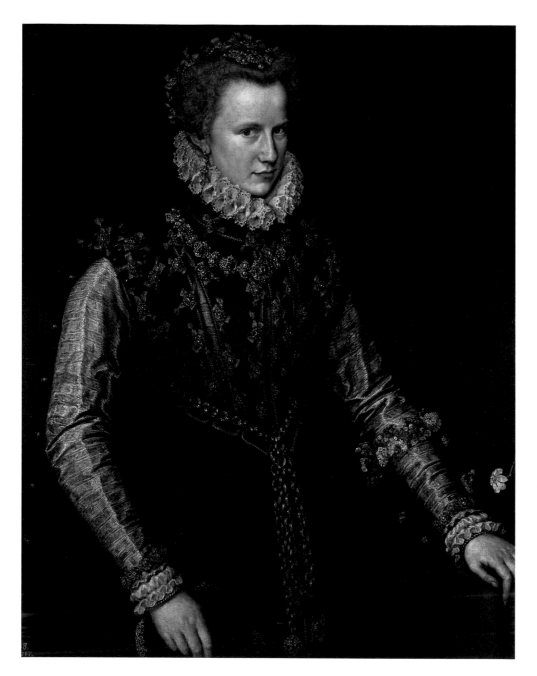

It is impossible to reconcile ideas of noble matrimony or Catholic virtue with the physical prostitution which ultimately defined the courtesan. The images of these different kinds of women could, however, apparently look very similar, and even be juxtaposed in series, when the sitters were represented not for their enacted character but as mannequins – signs or emblems of physical beauty. In a society structured around arranged marriage and the double standard, the symbolic aspect of pictorial possession allowed the interdependence of court lady and courtesan to become manifest in a single object of desire.

LIT: Pierre de Bourdeille, Seigneur de Brantome, *Oeuvres completes*, ed. L. Lalanne, Paris 1864–82, I, p.106; C. Justi, *Miscellanean aus drei Jahrhunderten Spanischen Kunstlebens*, Berlin 1908, I, p.13; H. Hymans, *Antonio Moro, son oeuvre et son temps*, Brussels 1910, pp.113, 175; R. van Luttervelt, 'Een schilderij van Anna van Buren en andere portretten uit haar omgeving', *Oud Holland*, vol.74, 1959, pp.183–202; J. Held, 'Flora, Goddess and Courtesan', in M. Meiss (ed.), *De artibus opuscula: Essays in Honour of Erwin Panofsky*, New York 1961, pp.201–8; J. Woodall, 'The Portraiture of Antonis Mor', unpublished Ph.D. thesis, Courtauld Institute of Art, 1989, I, pp.111–13, II, pp.547 et seq.; J. Woodall, '"His Majesty's Most Majestic Room": The Division of Sovereign Identity in Philip II's Lost Portrait Gallery at El Pardo', in *Nederlands Kunsthistorisch Jaarboek* (forthcoming 1995)

JW

3 Eworth and his Contemporaries

The artist known today as Hans Eworth is probably the most important figure for our understanding of painting in the period following the death of Holbein. Since Lionel Cust's identification of him as the monogrammist 'HE', now widely accepted, almost forty works by his hand have been identified.

Eworth's frequent use of the monogram signature 'HE' has alerted us to the extent of his oeuvre. The quality and comparative sophistication of his work, particularly evident where it has survived in good condition, makes it clear why he was able to sustain a career in Britain for almost thirty years.

Almost nothing is known of him prior to his life in London. A 'Jan Eeuwowts' became a freeman of the Guild of St Luke – the artists' guild – in Antwerp in 1540. In November 1544, Jan and Nicolas Ewouts, painter and mercer, were expelled from Antwerp for heresy. In October 1546 a Jan Ewouts in Amsterdam applied for permission to sell books, calling himself a 'figuersnijder ende boeckverkooper' (engraver in a booksellers) (J. Cuvelier, 'Le Graveur Corneille van den Bossche', *Bulletin de l'Institut Historique Belge de Rome*, vol.20, 1939, pp.13–15, 17). The Lumley Inventory (no.105) mentions a portrait 'Of Haward a Dutch Juello[r], drawne for a Maisters prize by his brother Haunce Eworth', which both confirms his Netherlandish origin, and his family links with the goldsmith's trade, which may help to account for the precision with which he depicts the jewellery worn by his sitters (see e.g. no.28).

During this period Antwerp was the commercial capital of the Spanish empire. It was a major banking centre and the focal point of various trade routes. It gave privileges to foreigners that enabled them to trade there, and for almost half the year international fairs would be in progress in the region. English merchants were based there and business with England was regular and frequent.

It is not known exactly when Eworth came to England. A Nycholas Ewotes is recorded in 1545, living in Southwark. From 1549 onwards Hans Eworth, his name undergoing many curious mutations, can be spotted at various addresses, initially in Southwark where he could practise outside the jurisdiction of the London guilds. 'John Euwoots',

'Maister Hans', 'John Ewottes', 'Jan Evertz', 'Haunce painter', 'Huet', and 'Suete' may all be references to him.

The first known work signed 'HE' is of 1549 (no.22). It is thought to relate to sketches which Eworth could have seen only in Antwerp. The portrait of 'Sir John Luttrell' (no.23) of the following year contains elements close not only to the Antwerp Mannerism of Frans Floris but also to the School of Fontainebleau.

Eworth was clearly determined to make his career in England, as in 1550 he was granted letters of denization. He was to continue working well into the reign of Elizabeth I. Throughout much of this period the Serjeant Painter, the official royal artist, was the French-born Nicholas Lizard. It is not known whether Lizard painted portraits, but he gave religious pictures as New Year gifts to Queen Mary: a 'table painted with the Maundy' in 1556 and a 'table painted of the history of Assuerus [Ahasuerus]' in 1558.

Almost all Eworth's surviving works are portraits, albeit occasionally with complex allegorical elements. The signed and dated 'Allegory of the Wise and Foolish Virgins' (see fig.35 on p.74) and the lost signed 'Mars and Venus' recorded in the eighteenth century (Waterhouse 1978, p.29) indicate that he produced religious and mythological works.

A further area of his oeuvre, of which nothing survives, was his work as a designer for the Office of the Revels. For a masque to be held at Whitehall before the Queen and the French ambassador in June 1572 he was appointed designer at the request of 'Mr Alphonse' (thought to be the musician Alfonso Ferrabosco), and a payment of £3 19s. is recorded to 'Haunce Eott[e]s for drawing and payting of dyvers & sundry patternes/viz/of the Chariott & mounte … wi[th] all the p[er]sonages apparell and Instruments & setting them owte in apte cool[our]s & such like s[er]vice by him doone in this office at this tyme' (see Varkonda-Bishop 1979, p.144).

Like Holbein, he could work at widely ranging scales, from full-length (e.g. the Holyroodhouse version of 'Henry, Lord Darnley and his Brother' 1562, The Royal Collection) down to the miniature, such as the portrait of 'Mary I' (fig.29b on p.66). This

queen, indeed, was his most important patron (see no.24). Because the surviving records are incomplete it is not clear whether he had official status as such, although the probability that he was given access to her jewellery suggests a high degree of trust. There is no evidence that he painted Queen Elizabeth, unless her portrait with the goddesses (see no.39) should prove to be by him.

Eworth frequently made use of compositions already introduced to English portraiture by Hans Holbein. Queen Mary is repeatedly portrayed according to a formula used by Holbein for 'Christina of Denmark' (see fig.43 on p.119); other ladies echo Holbein's 'Jane Seymour' (Kunsthistorischesmuseum, Vienna); while the double portraits of 'Henry, Lord Darnley and his Brother' (The Royal Collection) seem indebted to Scrots's images of Edward VI (see fig.24 on p.45).

Not surprisingly, Eworth's style altered during the course of his career. His early English portraits set the sitters outdoors within environments that convey additional information. As he assimilated the influence of Hans Holbein, his backgrounds become plainer, the sitter casting a shadow on one side. Finally the rich costumes of the 1560s take centre stage, in portraits preoccupied with pattern and with the attire, jewellery and heraldry that indicate wealth and high status.

Certain works seem to have some connection with Eworth, yet cannot be attributed to him with certainty. No.26 employs one of Eworth's formulae, yet the treatment seems softer and looser. 'Elizabeth I and the Three Goddesses' bears an HE monogram, but this differs from Eworth's characteristically upright HE. There are also differences in the handling of the paint, although the figures of the goddesses are in line with the work of the Antwerp Mannerists influenced by Frans Floris. The opportunity to examine this painting further in the context of a group of Eworth's securely identified works may reopen this debate. Finally, the painting known as 'The Allegory of Man' has much in common with the 'Allegory of the Wise and Foolish Virgins', Eworth's last known surviving work and one of remarkable refinement and delicacy (fig.35 on p.74).

HANS EWORTH
active 1540–1574

22 A Turk, possibly Süleyman the Magnificent, on Horseback
1549

Oil on panel 56.9 × 48.3 (22⅜ × 19)
Inscribed '1549 | HE' on rock, b.r.
PROV: ...; George René Aufrere of Chelsea (1715–1801); by descent through the marriage of his daughter Sophia to Charles Anderson Pelham
Private Collection

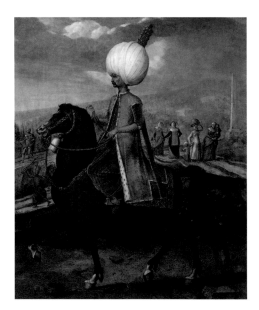

This is Eworth's earliest known work. It is signed in monogram and dated 1549, the year in which 'John Ewout' is recorded as resident in Southwark (Cust 1912–13, p.4). In subject, composition and treatment it is unparalleled in surviving English easel painting of the period.

The delicate colouring is not found in Eworth's subsequent portraiture. Much under-drawing is evident, and a pentiment indicates that the horse's head was originally to be in a higher position.

The subject seems to relate to a long, sequential woodcut by Eworth's Antwerp compatriot Pieter Coecke van Aelst (1502–1550). Coecke van Aelst had visited Constantinople (Istanbul) in 1533 on behalf of the Brussels tapestry weavers and, while there, had made sketches of life under the Turkish ruler Süleyman the Magnificent (1494–1566). The woodcut was entitled 'Les Moeurs et fachons de faire de Turcs avecq'les Regions y appartenantes ont este au vif contrefaictes par Pierre Coeck d'Alost, luy estant en Turquie, l'An de Jesuchrist M.D. 33' (Berlin 1989, no.8.1 and pp.240 et seq.). However, as it was not issued by Coecke's widow until 1553, four years after the date of Eworth's painting, Eworth is presumed to have had access in Antwerp to the original sketches on which it was based. The obelisk, the mountainous landscape, and figures similar but not identical to the turbanned rider, the male courtiers behind left, and the women with children behind right, appear therein. Eworth's horse-man is most like the central figure in the final section of the woodcut, identified as the Sul-tan Süleyman the Magnificent in procession in the At Meyden in Istanbul. It has been sug-gested that the four women represent the four wives allowed to a Muslim (Berlin 1989).

The face of Eworth's horseman resembles that of Süleyman in profile in a c.1530 head-and-shoulders engraving by Hieronymus Hopfer of Augsburg (Berlin 1989, p.700, no.7.33). This shows similarly fine-boned fea-tures with a strong chin and curved nose, clean-shaven with a drooping moustache, a slender neck and an air of elegant composure. The engraving is thought to share a common source, now lost, with Albrecht Dürer's draw-ing of Süleyman, dated 1526 (Musée Bonnat, Bayonne).

The composition, however, is closest to the profile portrait on horseback of Sultan Mehmet II (died 1481) on a medal by Con-stanzo da Ferrara (British Museum; see Berlin 1989, no.5.5, pp.630–1). Islamic law has been interpreted as banning representations of the human figure, but in the previous century Mehmet II had commissioned portraits from various artists, including, in 1480, Giovanni Bellini (National Gallery, London). It is evi-dent that, whatever his actual sources, Eworth was following a tradition of portraying Turk-ish figures, especially rulers, in profile and on horseback. In exaggerating the turban to immense proportions, he emphasises both the exoticism and the rather menacing elegance of his subject.

In the sixteenth century the Osmanli Turks were perceived as a very real threat to Christ-ian Europe. In 1521 they had captured Bel-grade, and in 1529 Süleyman's army had been encamped outside Vienna, returning in 1532, though eventually compelled to retreat. France's alliance with the Turks, made public in 1543, shocked and alarmed the other Euro-pean powers.

Eworth's picture should be seen in the con-text of the European fashion for collecting portraits of illustrious figures, such as foreign monarchs. Such collections included political enemies as well as allies, and figures of fear as well as those to be reverenced and admired. The 1516 inventory of the collection of Mar-garet of Austria listed 'Ung petit tableau de la pourtraicture du Grand-Turc' (I am grateful to Dr Dagmar Eichberger for this reference). In England, as early as 1546, the Duke of Nor-folk had a collection of twenty-eight portraits 'of divers noble persons'. Susan Foister notes that 'Sir Ralph Warren in 1554, John West in 1569 and Thomas Key in 1572 all owned pic-tures of the Sultan or Great Turk' (Foister 1981, p.278).

EXH: RA 1950–1 (137); *Hans Eworth*, NPG, London 1965 (1); *Europa und der Orient 800–1900*, Berliner Festspiele, Berlin 1989 (8.2, repr. p.259)
LIT: Cust 1912–13; R.W. Goulding, 'Notes on Addi-tional HE Portraits', *Walpole Society*, vol.3, 1914, p.118; Erna Auerbach, 'Holbein's Followers in England', *Burlington Magazine*, vol.93, 1951, p.50, repr. no.13; Strong 1969, p.85, no.20; Waterhouse 1978, pp.28–9; Varkonda-Bishop 1979, pp.41–3

KH

Hans Eworth

23 Sir John Luttrell 1550

Oil on panel 109.3 × 83.8 (43 × 33)
Inscribed 'MOR THE ROCK AMLODYS Y^e
RAGING SEAS | THE CONSTAT HEART
NO DAGER DREDDYS NOR FEARYS |
S.I.L. | 1550 | HE' on the rock, b.l., and
much restored; 'NEC FLEXIT LVCRVM' on
the right-hand bracelet; and 'NEC [FRE-
GIT DISCREMEN]' on the left
PROV: Possibly the portrait of Luttrell
recorded in the Lumley Inventory, 1590;
…; sold by the Bromley family, Bad-
mondisfield Hall, Suffolk, Christie's 22
July 1932 (8); presented to the Courtauld
Institute Galleries by Viscount Lee of
Fareham 1950
*Courtauld Institute Galleries, London
(Lee Bequest)*

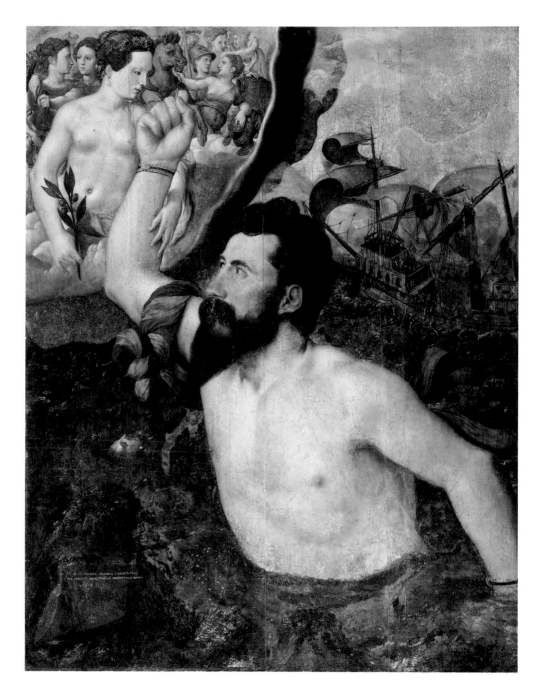

The complex allegorical allusions in this picture remained a puzzle until Frances Yates's
compelling explanation of them in 1967
(Yates 1967, pp.149–60). She argues that the
picture is an allegory of the Treaty of
Boulogne of 1550 (the date of the painting),
which brought to an end the war between
England and France. The peace treaty
annexed Boulogne, formerly in English
hands, to France, but in return the French
King was to pay to Edward VI a sum of
money in two instalments. This is shown in
the separate allegorical group in the sky,
where a female figure hands another a bag of
money, but reaches into her purse for more.
On the extreme right of this group Venus is
seen bridling the war horse. The central
female figure is Peace herself. She holds a
symbolic olive branch and gently touches
Luttrell's raised arm, which forms a compositional link with the rest of the picture, but
also alludes to the consequences of the peace
treaty on Luttrell's personal circumstances.
The Treaty also brought peace between
England and Scotland, where Luttrell
(?1518–1551) had fought at the Battle of
Pinkie-Musselborough in 1547, and Inchcolm
Island defending the Firth of Forth. He was
subsequently captured and imprisoned. The
sinking ship and floating drowned corpse
possibly allude to Pinkie-Musselborough, a
victory gained through the combined efforts
of land and sea forces, and the inscriptions on
Luttrell's bracelets (translated as 'neither
swayed by love of gain nor deterred by danger') and on the rock, refer to his steadfastness and courage.

Frances Yates has drawn a comparison
between Luttrell's extraordinary appearance,
wading in the sea naked to the waist with
raised arm and fist, and the Canning jewel,
datable to the second half of the sixteenth
century (Victoria and Albert Museum, London), which represents a Triton in a remarkably similar position, with bracelets about his
wrists which hide awkward links in the workmanship. She suggests that Luttrell must have
been aware of similar imagery, and intended
to be represented as a warlike water divinity.

The picture has suffered from poor condition and consequent restorations, which have
damaged several areas including the inscriptions, but its original appearance can be

gauged from a copy of the picture at Dunster Castle. This was made in 1591 for George Luttrell, Sir John's nephew and heir, and was for a long time believed to be the prime version until a technical comparison of the two was made in 1960. This concluded that in the Courtauld version a different hand had been responsible for the allegorical group in the sky. It was thought that such sophisticated Mannerist allegory, rare in England at this date, was strongly suggestive of the School of Fontainebleau. However, it is quite possible that Eworth was responsible for it himself. He is documented as having painted mythological pieces (an apparently signed 'Mars and Venus' was at Gunton Park, Norfolk, in the eighteenth century), and the figures are close enough in conception to those in 'Queen Elizabeth and the Three Goddesses' 1569 (no.29) attributed to him, and his 'Allegory of the Wise and Foolish Virgins' 1570 (fig.35 on p.74). His inspiration would presumably have been Flemish mythological pictures such as those by Frans Floris of Antwerp. However, so little is known of Eworth's life and travels, particularly before he came to England, that it is impossible to be certain of the influences to which he was exposed.

The picture is signed with Eworth's monogram HE and it is one of his earliest known pictures. It was painted in the same year as the portrait of his uncle Thomas Wyndham (private collection), and both pictures are listed in the Lumley Inventory of 1590 (see no.105). Curiously, however, neither are specifically mentioned as by Eworth, although three others are – among them a portrait of Edward Shelley. All three – Luttrell, Wyndham and Shelley – were involved with the campaigns in Scotland.

EXH: Leicester and London 1965–6 (p.2); Tate Gallery 1969–70 (29)
LIT: Cust 1912–13, pp.19–20; Cust 1917–18, p.24; Frances Yates, 'The Allegorical Portraits of Sir John Luttrell', in Fraser, Hibbard and Lewine (eds.), *Essays in the History of Art Presented to Rudolf Wittkower*, 1967, pp.149–60; Strong 1969, p.86; Waterhouse 1978, pp.29–30; Varkonda-Bishop 1979, pp.46–54

TB

HANS EWORTH

24 Mary I *c.*1555–8

Oil on panel 22 × 17.3 (8⅝ × 6¾)
PROV: …; Fitzpatrick (of Stamford?, see Steegman 1957) from whom bt *c.*1830–40 by a private collector
Private Collection

A number of portraits of Mary by Eworth have survived. Although they vary remarkably in size, the basic face pattern is the same for each. They can be dated according to the fashion of the costume depicted, and because Mary's features are seen slightly to age. The present portrait appears to be from the latter part of her reign. It is not clear whether Eworth held any official status as the Queen's painter, as the Exchequer accounts for this period have been lost.

The earliest, and most magnificently costumed version is inscribed 'HE | 1554' prior to restoration, apparently 'HF') (fig.29a). A half-length miniature, painted on copper (fig.29b) was recorded as by 'Hanc' or 'Manc Seward' – presumed to mean Hans Eworth – in the inventory of Charles I's collection (Millar 1958–60, p.110).

Figure 29a was presumably painted after Mary's marriage to Philip II, as she appears to wear jewels given by him on 20 June 1554, and it is possible that it predates Mor's image of her of the same year but which was not started until November (no.16). However, the heavy brocade and fur wrap indicate that it was done in winter. Eworth's image is far more traditionally English than Mor's. The pose, standing with head slightly to one side and with clasped hands, has several antecedants in English portraiture having been introduced first by Holbein, for example in his portraits of Christina of Denmark (fig.43 on p.119) and Anne of Cleves (see no.66). It was a pose that, for female sitters, strongly denoted rank and high status, and it had been used for Mary before by Master John in 1544 (see no.11). The pyramidal composition and strict symmetry is deliberate. Elizabeth Drey has shown how Eworth made slight departures from the underdrawing in order to achieve this, heightening Mary's forehead, extending her fingers, and ironing out the more characterising features of her face in

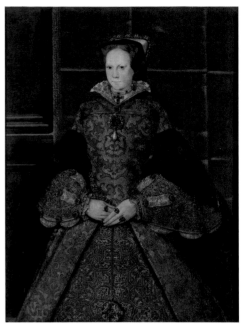

fig.29a Hans Eworth, 'Mary I' 1554, oil on panel. *Private Collection*

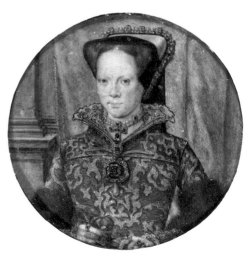

fig.29b Hans Eworth, 'Mary I' *c.*1555, oil on copper. *By permission of the Duke of Buccleuch and Queensberry KT*

order to create a more regal and imposing image. Eworth probably made her appear younger and prettier than in reality, as in 1554 Giacomo Soranzo, the Venetian ambassador, described her thus: 'She is of low stature, with a red and white complexion, and very thin; her eyes are white and her hair reddish; her face is round, with a nose rather low and wide, and were not her age on the decline, she might be called handsome rather than the contrary' (CSP Venetian, 1534–54, p.532). The royal status of the sitter is underlined by the rich cloth of state in the background. Eworth's precision suggests that he had direct access to her jewels. The great table diamond worn at her breast, also shown in Mor's portrait but in less detail, is possibly identifiable as one of the two great diamonds given to her by Philip II. The jewel suspended from her girdle could be the 'Tablet of Burbyon' listed in an inventory of Henry VIII's jewels, a reliquary decorated with the four Evangelists (see Drey 1990).

In the present portrait the cloth of estate behind the Queen is of green velvet. Her left hand rests on a table covered in rich fabric. In her right hand she holds a document. In 1890 the words 'The Supplicate ...' could be discerned on this. In a life-scale version of the present work by another hand (Leicester and London 1965–6, p.14, repr. pl.26b) the same document appears, there inscribed 'The Supplication of Thomas Hongad' (thought to refer to a courtier called Thomas Hungate); that version was engraved, in reverse, in the *Baziliωlogia* in 1618.

EXH: *Tudor Exhibition*, New Gallery 1890 (235); *Some Masterpieces from Welsh Houses*, Arts Council of Great Britain 1946–7 (1); *L'Art flamande dans les Collections Britanniques*, Bruges 1956 (50); *Between Renaissance and Baroque*, Manchester City Art Gallery 1965 (98); Leicester and London 1965–6 (26)
LIT: J. Steegman, *Portraits in Welsh Houses*, I, 1957, p.124; NPG 1969, I, pp.211–13; Strong 1969, p.105; Alison Carter, 'Mary Tudor's Wardrobe', *Costume*, no.18, 1984, pp.9–28; Elizabeth Ann Drey, 'The Portraits of Mary I, Queen of England', unpublished MA report, Courtauld Institute 1990, pp.33–50, pl.34

KH and TB

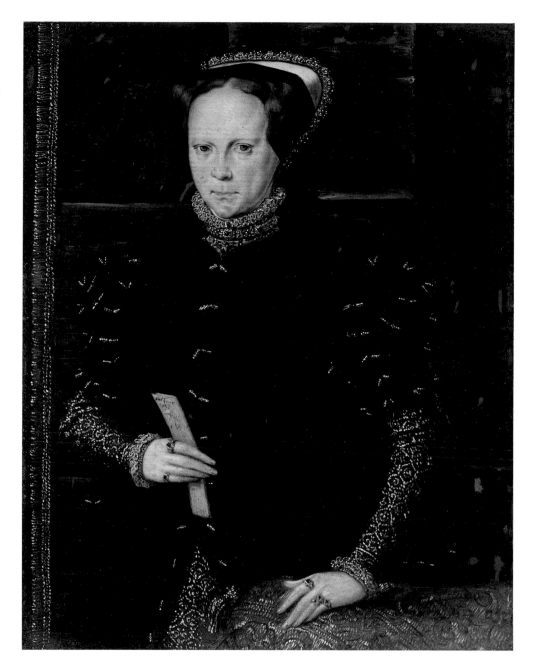

HANS EWORTH

25 Lady Mary Neville and her Son Gregory Fiennes, 10th Baron Dacre 1559

Oil on panel 50.2 × 71.4 (19¾ × 28⅛)
Inscribed 'ÆTATIS XXXVI.' t.l.; 'M.D.LIX.'
top centre; 'ÆTATIS XXI' and 'HE' t.r.
PROV: Noted by Vertue in sale of Mr
Collevous, Covent Garden, Feb. 1727 as
by Holbein; Earl of Oxford sale 8 March
1741 (11), bt Horace Walpole; Strawberry
Hill sale 17 May 1842 (37) as by de
Heere, bt by a private collector
Private Collection

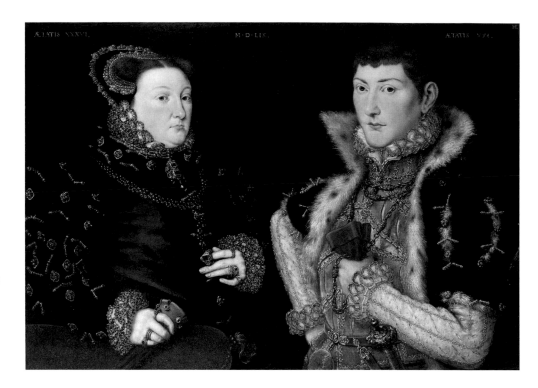

This powerful double portrait, in exceptionally good condition, is one of the finest works
to be painted in Britain in the mid-sixteenth
century. The identity of the sitters, however,
has only recently been ascertained.

Its history is not known prior to 1727,
when at the sale of Mr Collevous's pictures,
Vertue (II, p.23) noted that 'on the back of
this picture is wrote on a peice of paper pasted the Duches of Suffolk' and suggested that
the sitters must be Frances Brandon, Duchess
of Suffolk (1517–1559, see *Burke's Peerage*,
1916, IV, p.421) and her second husband, the
former groom Adrian Stokes (1535/6–
1585). This notion remained unchallenged
until 1986 when Susan Foister reidentified the
sitters and convincingly suggested the context
in which the work was painted.

Foister pointed out that the ages thirty-six
and twenty-one, inscribed above the sitters'
heads, do not correspond with those of
Stokes and his wife in the year 1559. The features of the female sitter, however, strongly
resemble those of the widowed Mary Neville,
whom Eworth had previously portrayed in
about 1555–8 (fig.30). In both portraits, moreover, the same distinctive ring is shown on
the fourth finger of the lady's left hand. Foister suggests that this double portrait, dated
1559, was painted to mark the restitution of
the Dacre family honours following the
accession of Queen Elizabeth I in the previous year, as the inscribed ages in fact fit both
Mary Neville and her son, Gregory Fiennes
(1539–1594).

On the night of 30 April 1541, Mary
Neville's first husband, Thomas, 9th Baron
Dacre was part of a poaching expedition into
a neighbouring estate, during which a keeper
was killed. Lord Dacre, though not directly
involved, was among those charged with mur-
der, and on 29 June 1541 he was executed at
Tyburn. His title and honours were consequently forfeited and his family disgraced.

In the earlier portrait in Ottawa, Eworth
shows a redoubtable Mary Neville seated at a
table with a book in her left hand and the
pen in her right raised as she pauses in the act
of writing. A tapestry hanging on the wall
behind her is similar to that seen at the outer
sides of Eworth's portraits of the Duke and
Duchess of Norfolk (no.27). Fixed to this, in a
rare depiction of the way in which portraits
were hung at this period, is an image of her
long-deceased young husband. It is in the
style of Hans Holbein, its frame inscribed
with Lord Dacre's age, twenty-four, and also
the date 1540, the year preceding his death.
This powerful view of Mary Neville, dressed
in austere but costly black garments, serves to
emphasise her determination to reverse the
injustice done to her husband, particularly as
it affected his children.

The double portrait does seem to mark the
restitution of those honours and the attain-
ment of his majority by Gregory Fiennes
(whose elder brother Thomas had died in
1553). Both sitters are extremely richly dressed
and bejewelled, the new Lord Dacre in a
gown lined with the ermine that only the
nobility were permitted to wear. As Elizabeth
Honig observes, the double depiction of a
mother and son is most unusual. In addition,
this painting breaks the convention generally
used for pendant male and female portraits
(compare nos.18, 27, 140, 141), certainly those
of betrothed or married couples, where the

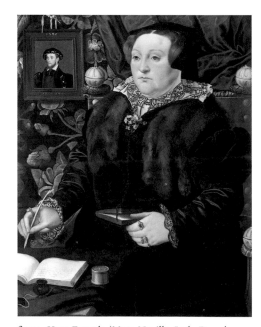

fig.30 Hans Eworth, 'Mary Neville, Lady Dacre'
c.1555–8, oil on panel. *National Gallery of Canada,
Ottawa*

male portrait is placed to the left of the female. Honig relates this convention, equally prevalent on the Continent, to the practice in heraldry under which 'the man is placed to the woman's right, in the more important position' (1990, p.252 n.32).

In fact, by 1559, Mary Neville had remarried twice, to Norfolk gentlemen named Wooton and then Thursby, and had given birth to at least six further children (Thomas Barrett Lennard, *An Account of the Families of Lennard and Barrett*, 1908, p.207). Her son was himself a married man, although as his wife Anne Sackville apparently complained, he remained under the influence of his mother (*Dictionary of National Biography*, 1909, XVII, p.428). None of these other family ties, however, is apparent from this portrait. Eworth depicts Mary Neville at a slight distance from the viewer, behind a wide red cushion. Her son, portrayed on a slightly larger scale, is to the fore and looks directly out at the viewer, though with a somewhat vacant gaze. His mother passes the tip of her forefinger through a large signet ring, the symbol of dynastic power. The unusually dominant, 'masculine' role adopted by Mary Neville in her two portraits might be explained by William Camden's comment that Gregory Fiennes was 'a little Crack-brain'd' (*The Life and Reign of Queen Elizabeth*, 1706, p.580).

With reference to the label noted by Vertue, in 1561–62 a 'Haunce the drawer', possibly Eworth, was recorded as in the service of Katherine, Duchess of Suffolk (1520–1580) (Auerbach 1954, p.162).

The portrait was engraved by George Vertue in 1748 (as of Duchess of Suffolk with Adrian Stokes and by de Heere).

LIT: Strong 1969, p.91, no.30; Varkonda-Bishop 1979, pp.77–80; Susan Foister, 'Nobility Reclaimed', *Antique Collector*, April 1986, pp.58–60; Elizabeth Honig, 'In Memory: Lady Dacre and Pairing', in Gent and Llewellyn 1990, pp.62–85

KH

ENGLISH SCHOOL

26 An Unknown Lady *c.*1557

Oil on panel 76 × 48 (30 × 18⅞)
Inscribed 'H.h.' on base of column, lower left; 'THE RIGHTFVL GOD SET ON IVGMENT GAINE TO IVGE:' round edge of pendant
PROV: ...; at Angers by 1885
Musée des Beaux Arts, Angers

This powerful portrait is unusual in bearing what appears to be a monogram signature 'H.h.' on the base of the column.

If these initials relate to the painter of the portrait (and were not added later to imply erroneously that this is a work by Hans Holbein), it has not so far proved possible to make an identification. It has, for instance, recently been demonstrated that the 'Hewe Hawarde' who received payment for portraits of Henry VIII and Catherine Parr in December 1547 was the Surveyor of the Queen's Stable, who had married Lucas Horenbout's widow Margaret. Thus the payments were probably for works painted by Horenbout himself before he died (Lorne Campbell and Susan Foister, 'Gerard, Lucas and Susanna Horenbout', *Burlington Magazine*, Oct. 1986, pp.724–5). Herman Harden and Humfrey Horsnaile (Auerbach 1954, pp.97, 166, 172) carried out decorative painting for the royal revels in the 1550s, but there is no reason to think either was a portraitist. A 'Hans Heywarde, pictur maker', who may or may not have been Hans Eworth, was recorded as a denizen at 30 March 1567 (Varkonda-Bishop 1979, p.143). In the 1580s there are various references to works, mainly portraits, by and payments to an artist called simply 'Hubbert[e]' or 'Hubbard' (see Strong 1969, p.185; also Clark 1981, pp.28, 54 n.10; J. Ashelford, *Dress in the Age of Elizabeth I*, 1988, p.36; and Alnwick MSS. U.I.1, the 'Accounts of Henry Percy, 3rd Earl of Northumberland', extracts transcribed in NPG Archive, London).

The style is very close to that of Hans Eworth, and may be compared with the latter's portrait of an 'Unknown Lady' of about the same date (Strong 1969, no.29, p.90). The artist has used the triangular, head-on composition, with the hands clasped in front at waist level, that derives from Holbein's portraits of 'Christina of Denmark' (fig.43 on p.119) and particularly 'Anne of Cleves' (no.66) and which had become the standard English portrait presentation for illustrious female subjects (see no.11).

The sitter wears an English variation of the

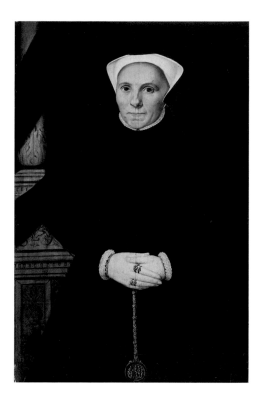

French hood with the velvet curtain turned up to lie flat on the top of the head. Arranged in this way, the edge projecting slightly over the forehead, it protected the complexion from the sun, and was known as a 'bongrace' (information, Jane Arnold).

The identity of the sitter is unknown. A clue may lie in the jewelled tablet suspended from her clasped hands; it bears a text in English, suggesting that the sitter is a Protestant. I am grateful to Diana Scarisbrick for her suggestion that the scene depicted thereon is that of the Judgement of Daniel, from the Apocryphal book of Susanna (the Book of Daniel in the Vulgate). In revenge for Susanna's refusal of their own advances, two elders who have been appointed as judges falsely accuse her of adultery. Susanna is about to be taken off for execution when the young Daniel appears from the crowd to challenge the elders' story. By questioning them separately he exposes inconsistencies that reveal them to be liars. In this depiction the boy Daniel stands on a dais, left, at the knee of a bearded, seated figure, presumably one of the elders. In the centre a soldier grasps Susanna, ready to lead her away, while the other elder, right, stoops slightly to hear Daniel's questions.

A pair of rectangular enamelled book-covers, apparently made in London *c.*1525–35 (British Museum Inv. no. M&LA, AF, 2852-3; *Princely Magnificence*, no.12) show both the

Judgement of Solomon and the Judgement of Daniel. The handling of these scenes somewhat resembles that depicted here. The British Museum Daniel is similarly surrounded by a text in black enamelled letters 'RED-ITE. IN. IVDITVM QVIA ISTI FALSUM IN ANC TESTIMONIVM. DIX. ERVNT' (Susanna, 49). A girdle book with a cover very like the latter appears in the portrait of Lady Speke by an unidentified artist (*Princely Magnificence*, p.106 no.P17) dated 1592, by which date it would

have seemed very old-fashioned but was perhaps included as a valuable heirloom.

The history of the painting prior to its entering the collection at Angers is unknown. I am grateful to Dominique Cordellier for drawing this work to my attention.

EXH: *Le Matin des peintres*, Musée des Beaux Arts, Angers 1993–4 (29)

KH

HANS EWORTH

27 Thomas Howard, 4th Duke of Norfolk 1563

Oil on panel 108.6 × 81.3 (42¾ × 32)
Inscribed (signed and dated) '[H]E 1563', and 'AETATIS 25' on the cross guard
PROV: Possibly by descent to Norfolk's sister, Jane, Countess of Westmorland; by descent in that family until bt *c*.1890 by a private collector
Private Collection

Thomas Howard (1536–1572), son of the poet Earl of Surrey who was executed in 1547 (see no.14), was Philip II's first gentleman of the bedchamber, and succeeded his grandfather as Duke of Norfolk and Earl Marshal in 1554. A Catholic, despite his Protestant upbringing under John Foxe, he was to pursue a scheme to marry Mary, Queen of Scots as his fourth wife, for which he was imprisoned in the Tower. He was executed in 1572 for his part in the Ridolfi Plot.

In 1558 he had married as his second wife Margaret (1540–1564), daughter of Thomas, Lord Audley. Their son Thomas (1561–1626) was created 1st Earl of Suffolk and 1st Baron Howard de Walden, and was the builder of Audley End.

Margaret's own portrait, signed in monogram by Eworth (fig.31), for which this one

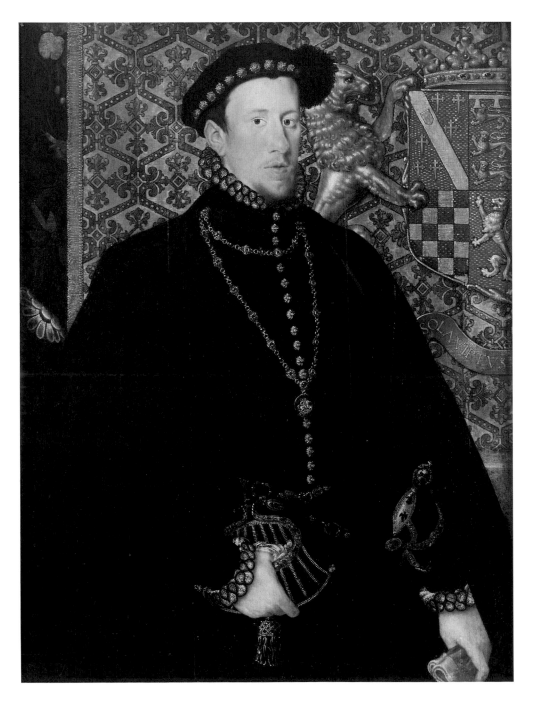

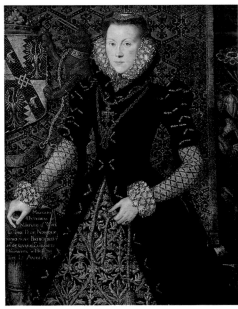

fig.31 Hans Eworth, 'Margaret Audley, Duchess of Norfolk' 1562, oil on panel. *Lord Braybrooke*

was presumably intended as a pair, is dated 1562, the previous year. The Norfolk coat of arms on the right in the present portrait corresponds with that of Audley on the left in the Duchess's portrait, a linking device used by Eworth again in a portrait of an unknown lady (Art Institute of Chicago), also dated 1563. The Duchess stands, in splendid costume befitting her rank, before a rich embroidered hanging which displays the Audley arms, supported by the 'Audley Beast', which corresponds with the arms of Howard supported by the Howard lion on her husband's portrait. On the right the edge of a tapestry of birds and flowers can be seen, which matches that on the left hand of her husband's portrait. In the early 1560s the Duke and Duchess lived in London, at Charterhouse, for which these two portraits were presumably painted. The Duchess died in childbirth in 1564.

Norfolk's appearance and pose are very similar to those in a miniature portrait of him, formerly attributed to Mor, dated 1562, from which most engraved images of him were taken, and which Eworth presumably also used. It is not impossible that Eworth was responsible for the miniature himself; a miniature of Mary I, c.1555 (fig.29b on p.66) is recorded as by him. Norfolk was perhaps influenced in his patronage of Eworth by Lord Lumley, his brother-in-law through his first marriage to Mary Fitzalan, daughter of the Earl of Arundel. Her sister Jane had married Lumley before 1552. He is known to have owned several portraits by Eworth which are listed in the 1590 Lumley Inventory (see no.105). These included one of Mary, Duchess of Norfolk, formerly identified as the portrait now at the Center for British Art, New Haven.

Another portrait of Norfolk, dated 1565 (private collection) was formerly attributed to Steven van der Meulen, also patronised by Lumley. A drawing of Norfolk, Wellesley sale, Sotheby's, 28 June 1920 (208), was attributed to Lucas de Heere (repr. Hervey 1921, pl.II, opp. p.2).

A portrait of Norfolk's political enemy, the Earl of Leicester, probably of the same date but by an unknown artist (no.49) uses the same accessories of handkerchief and purse.

EXH: Leicester and London 1965–6 (13)
LIT: Cust 1912–13, p.31; NPG 1969, I, p.233; Strong 1969, p.95

KH and TB

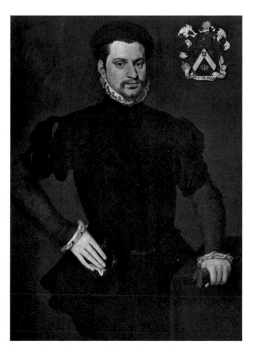

fig.32 Pieter Pourbus, 'Pierre Dominicle' 1558, oil on panel. *Private Collection*

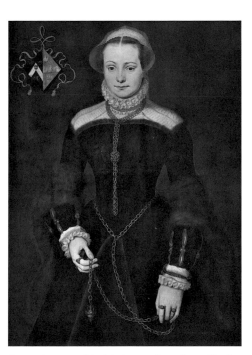

fig.33 Pieter Pourbus, 'Livina van der Beke, Wife of Pierre Dominicle' 1558, oil on panel. *Private Collection*

HANS EWORTH

28 An Unknown Lady c.1565–8

Oil on panel 99.8 × 61.9 (39¼ × 24¼)
Inscribed 'ÆTATIS x[...] | M.D.LXV [...]' t.r.
PROV: ...; Vernon-Wentworth family, Wentworth Castle, Barnsley, Yorkshire, by 1866; sold by Capt. B.C. Vernon-Wentworth, Christie's 13 Nov. 1919 (54 as 'Portrait of Lady Eleanor Brandon') bt F. Howard; sold to Marmaduke, 1st Viscount Furness; descended in the family until anon. sale, Sotheby's 15 July 1984 (256); purchased by the Tate Gallery
Tate Gallery, London. Purchased with assistance from the Friends of the Tate Gallery 1984

The identity of this sitter remains unclear, although her opulent attire and jewellery indicate that she is of extremely high rank. The large coat of arms was added perhaps as much as a century later, and cannot refer to the sitter herself. It had been borne by Henry Clifford, 2nd Earl of Cumberland and by his wife Eleanor Brandon, who accordingly was long thought to be the subject of the portrait. She, however, died in 1547, about twenty years before the date of this painting. Later it was thought that the sitter might be this couple's only child, Margaret Clifford (1540–1596) who married Henry Stanley, Lord Strange, later 4th Earl of Derby, in 1555. At some time prior to 1866, a 7.5 cm (3 in) strip was removed from the right-hand side of the painting and part of the inscription was consequently lost. So, while the truncated Roman numerals can refer only to 1565–8, the age of the sitter is now unknown. Margaret Clifford would have been aged twenty-five to twenty-eight during these years although, as a married lady, one would expect her to have used not her parents' arms but her own impaled with those of her husband. Lorne Campbell has, however, shown that in sixteenth- and early seventeenth-century English portraits, married women could often be represented by their maiden coat of arms, surmounted by helmet and crest ('Holbein's Miniature of "Mrs Pemberton"', *Burlington Magazine*, 1987, p.369). Eleanor Brandon was the daughter of Henry VIII's sister Mary, who had briefly been married to Louis XII of France. Her descendants thus had a claim to the English throne.

The Wentworth Castle collection contained, in addition to this picture, another portrait by Eworth of an unknown lady, aged twenty-four, dated 1563 and of similar size

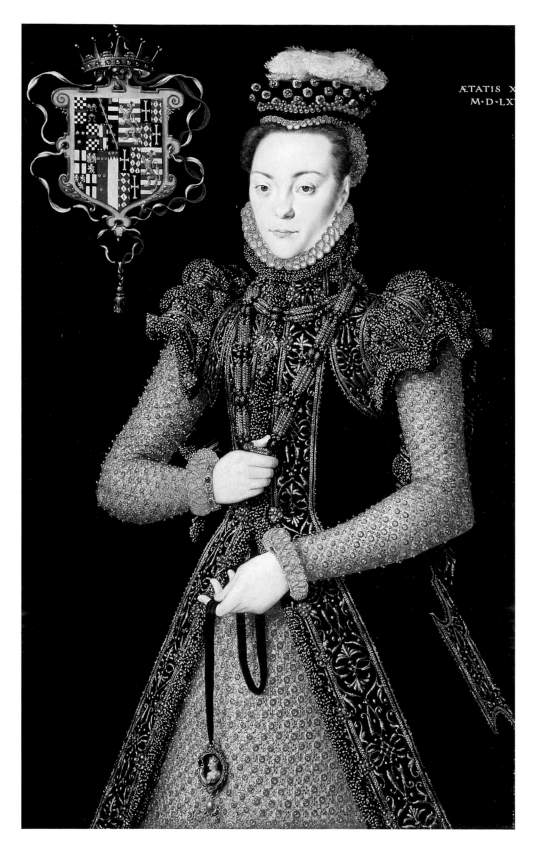

ÆTATIS X
M·D·LXI

(Art Institute of Chicago, see Strong 1969, p.96, no.38), with the Wentworth arms placed at the left-hand edge, as if to match those of a husband in a now-lost pendant portrait (compare Eworth's paired portraits of the Duke and Duchess of Norfolk of the same period, no.27). Sir Roy Strong (letter dated 7 January 1986) suggested that the ladies portrayed might be two of the three daughters of Thomas, 1st Baron Wentworth of Nettlestead (1501–1551): Jane (d. 1614), Margaret (d. 1587) and Dorothy. Each married advantageously more than once, although the exact wedding dates are not known.

The three-quarter-length composition in which a female sitter, her hands at waist-level, loops up a prized and valuable object on a chain or ribbon to present it to the viewer's gaze, was also popular in the Low Countries. Early examples include the 1558 'Portrait of Livina van der Beke' by the Bruges artist Pieter Pourbus, with a pendant portrait of her husband (figs.33, 32). Eworth used it for other portraits in the 1560s (see fig.31) and it is seen in various works of the same decade by his contemporary artists in England, many of whom are unidentified (e.g. Strong 1969, nos.56, 63–4, 67, 72, 75, 79, 81–2, 86). The sitter's remarkable open balloon 'wings' at the shoulders – a short-lived fashion of the late 1560s – appear as a fantastical Mannerist touch. The sitter's fine jewellery includes a pendant at her throat with a cabochon ruby, and one large lozenge and three table-cut diamonds in an enamelled gold setting with acanthus scrolls and classical figures and a pearl knop at its base (Dr Yvonne Hackenbroch suggests that this may be French). The double gold chain is made up of enamelled oblong links set with pearls, alternating with pomanders caged in gold. The lady's cap and dress are studded with jewelled buttons and pearls and she wears a pearl and ruby bracelet on each wrist.

Her most exceptional piece is the jewel hanging from the black ribbon at her waist, which is a chased gold and chalcedony commesso, or cameo, set in diamonds, representing Prudence holding a diamond or rock-crystal mirror. It is close in style and subject to an extant commesso, of Prudence dated 1550–60 and thought to be French (sold Sotheby's 1 Dec. 1983 (288)), and the theme was not uncommon in emblematic jewellery at this time (Hackenbroch 1979, pp.90–1; Diana Scarisbrick and Shirley Bury also helped to identify the jewellery).

The panel itself is made up from three vertical oak members, the right-hand one having

THE MONOGRAMMIST HE (?HANS EWORTH)

29 Elizabeth I and the Three Goddesses 1569

Oil on panel 70.8 × 84.5 (27⅞ × 33¼)
Inscribed '1569 | HE', lower right; 'IVNO
POTENS SCEPTRIS ET MENTIS ACVMINE
PALLAS | ET ROSEO VENERIS FVLGET
IN ORE DECVS | ADFVIT ELIZABETH
IVNO PERCVLSA REFVGIT OBSTVPVIT
PALLAS ERVBVITQ VENVS' on frame
PROV: Queen Elizabeth I (noted at
Whitehall Palace by Baron Waldstein in
1600); at Greenwich, when valued by
the Trustees for the sale of Charles I's
collection; sold to Hunt and Bass on 1
March 1653, but recovered for the royal
collection by the time of James II
Her Majesty The Queen

Queen Elizabeth, left, wearing her crown and
holding the orb and sceptre, impassively faces
three classical goddesses. They are: Juno who,
with her peacock behind her, spins round to
gaze at the Queen and loses her left shoe as
she turns; the helmeted Pallas, who raises her
hand in surprise; and the naked Venus who
sits with her arm round her disarmed son
Cupid, and her swan-drawn chariot on the
path behind. On the hill beyond Juno stands
Windsor Castle, one of the earliest painted
views of it. The interior from which the
Queen emerges has a frieze with the Tudor
arms and a canopy embroidered with her own
arms; the arch is decorated with her initials,
roses and fleurs-de-lis. Her dress is richly jewelled and embroidered with the Tudor rose as
a principal motif.

The inscription on the frame may be translated thus: 'Pallas was keen of brain, Juno was
queen of might, | The rosy face of Venus was
in beauty shining bright, | Elizabeth then
came. And, overwhelmed, Queen Juno took to
flight; | Pallas was silenced; Venus blushed
for shame' (Waldstein 1981, p.46).

The Queen here plays the role of Paris
who, according to classical legend, had to
judge which of these three goddesses was the
most beautiful. His choice, to whom he
awarded the golden apple, was Venus. Here,
however, Elizabeth seems to cause confusion
to the deities, and the conceit of this, the earliest known painted allegory involving the
Queen, is that, as both ruler and woman, she
combines the qualities of all three.

The Queen's possible marriage was a principal concern for much of her reign, and Juno,
the goddess of marriage, is the central figure
here.

In the same year, 1569, a woodcut allegory
in the quarto edition of the Bishops' Bible

---

been cut down as described above. The
approximate original proportions have been
reconstructed by placing a loose strip of
wood in the frame to represent the missing
section. An unfaded strip of paint protected
by the frame along the bottom shows that the
red of the pearl-studded dress was originally a
much deeper shade of rose madder. The background, on the other hand, was probably
originally lighter and seems to have been covered by a layer of dark brown paint quite
early in the painting's history. It appears that
a space for a coat of arms was reserved in the
background, where it can be seen as a smaller,
blank shield under the present elaborate cartouche.

When photographed for the 1866 exhibition, the portrait bore a painted label, bottom
left. Illegible in the photograph, all trace of
this had vanished by 1984.

EXH: *National Portraits*, South Kensington Museums,
1866 (198 as 'Portrait of Lady Eleanor Brandon' by
Lucas de Heere); *National Exhibition of Works of Art*,
Leeds 1868 (516); *Tudor Exhibition*, New Gallery 1890
(455); *Woman and Child in Art*, Grosvenor Gallery 1913
(XLII, repr.); *Meisterwerke englischer Malerei*, Galerie der
Secession, Vienna, Sept.–Oct. 1927
LIT: Cust 1913–14, p.34, pl.xviii(a); R. Strong, 'Hans
Eworth Reconsidered', *Burlington Magazine*, vol.108,
1966, p.229, fig.6; Strong 1969, pp.103, 342–5, no.48;
Y. Hackenbroch, *Rennaissance Jewellery*, 1979, p.91,
fig.232 (detail of cameo); Varkonda-Bishop 1979,
pp.93–5; *Illustrated Catalogue of Acquisitions 1984–86*,
Tate Gallery, pp.66–8; J. Ashelford, *Dress in the Age of
Elizabeth I*, 1988, pp.22, 24, pl.1 (col.)

KH

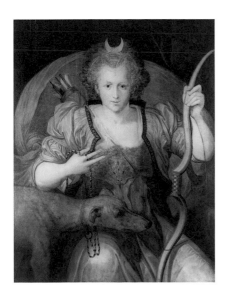

fig.34 Attributed to Frans Floris, 'Fragment of
a Composition of "Diana"' *c*.1560, oil on panel.
Courtesy of The Marquess of Salisbury

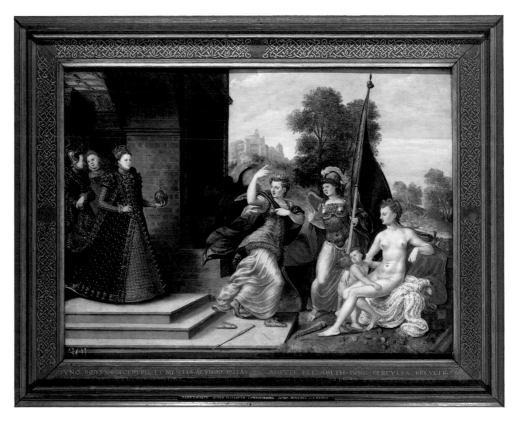

depicts Elizabeth enthroned, with orb and sceptre, among four classically attired Virtues, Fortitude, Prudence, Justice and Mercy, the last two holding the crown above her head. She thus appears as the summation of these four virtues (King 1989, p.233).

The monogram 'HE', bottom right, appears in a sloping form, slightly different from the upright one generally used by Hans Eworth. As well as Eworth, Lucas de Heere (see nos.35, 101) and Joris Hoefnagel (see no.62) have been suggested as the author of this painting, who was evidently Netherlandish trained and apparently familiar with the work of the influential Antwerp Mannerist Frans Floris (see fig.34). Photographs might suggest that the 'Allegory of the Wise and Foolish Virgins', dated 1570 and signed with the upright form of 'HE' (see fig.35) makes an interesting comparison with the present picture.

EXH: *National Portraits*, South Kensington Museums 1866 (219); *Elizabethan Exhibition*, Grosvenor Place 1933 (105), *The King's Pictures*, RA 1946–7 (13); RA 1950–1 (205); *Le Triomphe du Manerisme*, Rijksmuseum, Amsterdam 1955 (50); *British Portraits*, RA 1956–7 (22); *The Age of Shakespeare*, Whitworth Art Gallery, Manchester 1964 (3); *Hans Eworth*, NPG 1965–6 (37); *Kings and Queens*, Queen's Gallery 1982–3 (16); *The Queen's Pictures*, National Gallery 1991 (62)
LIT: Millar 1963, p.69; van Dorsten 1973, pp.54–5; Frances Yates, *Astraea: The Imperial Theme in the Sixteenth Century*, 1975, p.63; Louis Montrose, 'Gifts and Reasons: The Contexts of Peele's "Araygnement of Paris"', *English Literary History*, vol.47, 1980, pp.445–7; *The Diary of Baron Waldstein: A Traveller in Elizabethan England*, ed. G.W. Groos, 1981, pp.46–7; Strong 1987, pp.64–9; John N. King, *Tudor Royal Iconography*, 1989, p.233; David Evett, *Literature and the Visual Arts in Tudor England*, 1990, pp.117–19, fig.24

KH

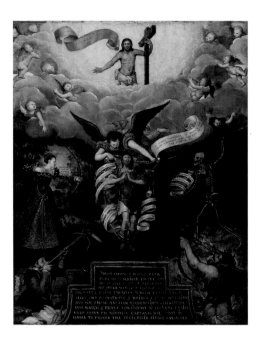

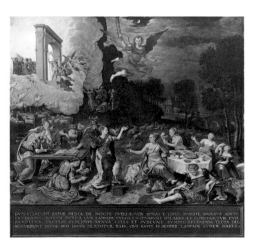

fig.35 Hans Eworth, 'Allegory of the Wise and Foolish Virgins' 1570, oil on panel. *Statens Museum for Kunst, Copenhagen*

ANGLO-FLEMISH SCHOOL (?HANS EWORTH)

30 An Allegory of Man *c.*1570

Oil on panel 57 × 51.4 (22½ × 20¼)
Inscribed 'O MAN THOW WRETCED CREA | TVRE HOW MAIEST THOVE DEL | ITE IN RICHES BEWTY STRENGTH | OR OTHER WORDLY THINGE. RE | MEMBRINGE THINE ENEMYES WHICH CONTINVALLY | SEEKE THEE TO DESTROYE & BRINGE THEE TO NOTHING | BVT SINE SHAME AND FYER EVERLASTINGE. THEREFORE | FAST WATCH & PRAYE CONTINVALY Wᵀᵀ FERVENT DESIER | VNTO IESVS THE MIGHTIE CAPTAYNE WHO ONLY IS | HABLE TO DEFEND THEE FROM THEIR FIERIE ASSAWLTS.' bottom cartouche; 'COVETVSNES' on miser's arrow, b.l.; 'GLOTONY', 'SLOWTH' and 'LECHERY' on lady's three arrows, centre left; 'GRATIA ME SVFICIT TIBIE, 2 COR[.] 12.' on scroll by Christ, top; 'BE SOBER THEREFORE & WATCH FOR | THOW KNOWEST NEITHER THE DAY NOR | THE HOWRE.' on scroll, centre right, above Death; 'BEHIND THEE Y STEALE | LIKE A THEIF THE TEM | PORAL LIFE TO DEVOWER' on shield (oval target) of Death the skeleton; 'PRYDE', 'WRATH' and 'ENVYE' on three arrows of devil, b. r.; 'TEMPORANS', 'GOOD REISINES', 'CHASTITY', 'ALMES DEEDS', 'AND COMPASSION', 'MEEKENES', 'CHARITY', 'PACIENS' on scroll encircling central figure of Man
PROV: …; Sir J.C. Robinson, Newton Manor, Swanage; his sale, 2–4 Sept. 1913 (131), bt D.L. Isaacs for Viscount Leverhulme; Leverhulme sale, Knight, Frank and Rutley, 15 June 1926 (166); …; anonymous sale, Robinson & Foster 1955, bt Derek Sherborn Esq, Fawns Manor by whom sold Sotheby's 18 Nov. 1987 (97, as by 'The Monogrammist HE'), bt Weiss Gallery, from whom purchased by the Patrons of British Art
Tate Gallery, London. Presented by the Patrons of British Art 1990

Surviving paintings on religious subjects of this period are extremely rare. Since the many inscriptions on this panel are in English there can be no doubt that it was painted for British consumption. This combination of images, labels and texts is more usually found in prints of this period.

At the bottom, the main inscription reminds the viewer of the vulnerability of the human soul to the dangers of the vanities of the world. The central figure – Man – wears classical military attire and the imagery is martial, suggesting that this may have been painted for an active soldier. Strong has also proposed that the theme of the angel investing Man with a shield of Christian Virtues (whose names are inscribed on the white scroll that spirals protectively about his figure) has been influenced by Erasmian concepts of the Christian knight. Strong points out the similarity of the allegory to that in Jodocus Hondius's engraved 'Christian Knight Map of the World' of 1596 (Strong 1969, p.41, fig.34). The features of Man and of the resurrected Christ above appear to be identical, and the direct relationship between the two, without intercessors, indicates that this must be a Protestant meditation.

The original purpose of the work is not known. It has been proposed that it might have been part of a domestic altarpiece. The trompe l'oeil framing of the cartouche containing the principal inscription is incomplete at the bottom, suggesting that this panel might have formed part of a larger structure, such as a funerary monument. The text of this inscription contains numerous ellisions of the letters 'HE'.

The work is full of painstaking detail, such as the office from which the broad arrow of covetousness is aimed from a sporting crossbow. On the desk lie piles of coins, open books and purses, one with a projecting handle. From nails in the panelled settle back (echoing the nails on Christ's cross above) hang a string of papers and a pencase and inkwell on a cord. The richly dressed lady above wears a jewel with an hourglass device suspended from her waist, presumably alluding to the time wasted by sloth. Her hair is pulled back from the face into a jewelled caul in 'the Italian fashion', and her attire is of c.1567–9 (information, Janet Arnold). The landscape beyond her was originally depicted in shades of bright green, produced by laying the pigment copper resinate over layers of azurite (blue). Discoloured by the action of light, copper resinate turns into the opaque brown film now seen. The path through this landscape is strewn with tiny pink blooms, and, beyond, minute figures can be seen embracing or sitting engaged in other actions – presumably representing the lechery and gluttony named on the lady's other two arrows.

The figure, standing in a pit of flames, bottom right, has the attributes of the Devil as depicted by Flemish artists (for instance in a print after Maerten van Heemskerck showing

'The Devil as a Painter', *Von Breughel bis Rubens*, Cologne 1992, no.146.1) – horns, pointed ears, a tail emerging from the naked flesh of his back, a fringe of hair along his arms, and wings. Such figures abound in 'The Fall of the Rebel Angels' by the Antwerp artist Frans Floris, of 1554 (Royal Museum of Fine Art, Antwerp). Above, the skeleton, representing Death aiming his dart, was particularly favoured in Protestant iconography (see Watt, *Cheap Print and Popular Piety*, 1994, pp.162–3).

The 'Allegory of the Wise and Foolish Virgins' of 1570, signed 'HE' (fig.35) was unfortunately too fragile to travel to the exhibition, but photographs of it suggest numerous similarities of composition with the present work. Apart from the most obvious ones these include the putti, quite crudely painted, some with their hands pressed together like little divers, the crisp depiction of minute still-life details, the landscape, the inclusion of texts (which use no contractions of the letters) in trompe l'oeil panels, of cast shadows and of similar female profiles.

This work is undoubtedly by a Netherlandish-trained artist, and one familiar with Antwerp work. Until recently it was assumed that Hans Eworth, the majority of whose known English patrons appear to have been Catholic, was himself of that faith, and thus that he would have been unlikely to have painted such an overtly Protestant work. It is now known that Eworth was expelled from Antwerp for heresy, although in any case there is no strong evidence that the personal faith of artists in England prevented them from working for patrons of another persuasion.

The painting is constructed of three vertical oak boards, to which was directly applied a priming layer of chalk in animal glue size. Unusually, over the lower non-celestial half of the panel only, a second layer (similarly composed but with the possible addition of white lead) was subsequently applied. No underdrawing is visible in the painting.

EXH: *The Age of Shakespeare*, Whitworth Art Gallery, Manchester 1964 (28); Leicester and London 1965–6 (38, as by 'The Monogrammist HE')
LIT: Strong 1969, pp.40–1, fig.33; David Piper, *The Genius of British Painting*, 1975, pp.109–10; *Tate Report 1988–90*, p.34

KH

ENGLISH SCHOOL

31 Edward VI and the Pope: An Allegory of the Reformation
c.1568–71

Oil on panel 62.2 × 90.8 (24½ × 35¾)
Inscribed 'THE | WORDE | OF THE | LORD | ENDVR | ETH | FOR | EVER' on open book centre left; 'IDOLATRY' AND 'SVPERSTIC[ION]' on infulae of pope's tiara; 'ALL FLESHE | IS GRASSE' across pope's breast; 'POPS' and 'FEYNED HOLINE[SS]' lower left
PROV: …; presumably Thomas Green of Ipswich and Upper Wimpole Street, London, by whose executors 'Edward VI and his Council: an allegory of the Reformation' sold Christie's 20 March 1874 (9); …; Capt. R.M. Colvile by 1953; bt in at Sotheby's, 18 Nov. 1959 (111); purchased by National Portrait Gallery 1960
National Portrait Gallery, London

Until very recently this picture was presumed to be almost contemporary with the events of 1547 that it depicts. The meticulous scholarship of Dr Margaret Aston has now, however, revealed conclusively that it dates from at least twenty years later, well into the reign of Queen Elizabeth I, and that it was thus intended to reinforce anti-papal attitudes in the Elizabethan church and state. The information that follows is based on her book *The King's Bedpost*, which is a full-scale study of this painting.

To the left, King Henry VIII lies in a scarlet-hung bed and points towards his son, Edward VI, who is enthroned on a dais, centre, beneath a cloth of estate. At Edward's feet, an open book, with a text from Isaiah that had long been a motto for reformers, falls on to the slumped figure of a pope who points a triple cross towards two monks, lower left, who pull on chains attached to the young king's dais. To the right of the latter stands a bearded man beyond whom seven further men are seated round a table, right. Above them is an inset scene of two soldiers bringing down a statue from a column and a further man smashing images, in front of collapsing buildings. There are also five rectangular blank spaces.

The main scene represents the handover of power from Henry VIII, at his death on 28 January 1547, to his nine-year-old son Edward, who is shown seated above eight of his Privy Councillors. Dr Aston has identified these as follows, from left going round the table: (standing) Edward Seymour, Duke of

Somerset, Lord Protector (?1506–1552);
Thomas Seymour, Baron Sudeley, Lord High
Admiral (?1508–1549); Thomas Cranmer,
Archbishop of Canterbury (1489–1556) (see
no.12); John Russell, Earl of Bedford, Lord
Privy Seal (?1486–1556) (see no.97); William,
Baron Paget of Beaudesert, Comptroller of
the King's Household (1505–63); William
Paulet, Lord St John, Great Master of the
King's Household (1485–1572); Cuthbert
Tunstall, Bishop of Durham (1474–1559) and,
in profile, Thomas Wriothesley, Earl of
Southampton (1505–1550), Lord Chancellor.
In most cases, surviving portraits help to sup-
port these identifications.

Dr Aston discovered that elements of the
painting have been borrowed by the
unknown artist from two engravings of Old
Testament subjects by the Haarlem artist
Maerten van Heemskerck. Henry VIII's reclining figure, gesturing arm and rich bed, with
the sphinx bedpost, are taken in reverse from
'King Ahasuerus Consulting the Records'
(fig.36); the still-surviving drawing for this is
dated 1563, and the print was published in
1564. In addition, most elements of the inset
scene of iconoclasm have been taken, in this
case the same way round, from 'Destruction
of the Tower of Babel', drawn in 1567 and
probably printed in 1568 and in 1569 (fig.37).
Thus the painting cannot have been made
before these dates.

During his reign Edward, who had imple-
mented iconoclastic policies, had frequently
been praised as 'the young Josiah' after the
youthful Old Testament king who was famed
for having destroyed idols. Contemporary
Protestants, citing the second Commandment,
were anxious to encourage the Queen to follow the example of her brother, not merely to
reverse the Catholic work of Queen Mary's
reign, but to push his reforms even further.
There was particular concern that the Queen
insisted on retaining a cross and candles in
her own chapel, for the practices of the
Roman church were by now seen as pagan-
ism.

In 1570, John Foxe's revised and expanded
ecclesiastical history *Actes and Monuments*
(popularly known as 'The Book of Martyrs')
included a long section praising Edward as
Josiah. The new illustration to this showed
Edward handing a Bible to his bishops beside
a church emptied of ornament, as a result of
iconoclasm depicted in a scene above.

Antipapal propaganda had always been a
feature of the English Reformation. Girolamo
da Treviso's 'Protestant Allegory', for
instance, painted for Henry VIII and showing

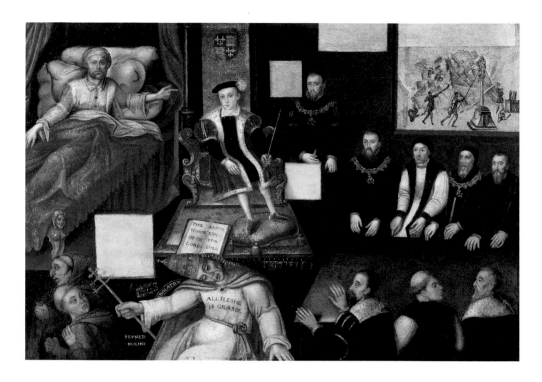

the Pope being stoned by the Four Evangelists – thus being toppled by God's Word –
was at Hampton Court by 1547 (C. Lloyd, *The
Queen's Pictures*, 1991, no.6). It reached a new
pitch, however, at the time that 'Edward VI
and the Pope' is thought to have been painted. The Northern Rebellion in summer 1569
was viewed by many as having been foment-
ed by the Pope. Then on 25 February 1570,
Pius V issued the bull excommunicating
Queen Elizabeth, and John Felton was
hanged in London that August for having
posted it up.

Dr Aston speculates that this painting may
have been intended either for the Queen, to
remind her of her princely duties, or for the
Duke of Norfolk (see no.27), to suggest how
his proposed marriage with Mary, Queen of
Scots threatened England with a relapse into
idolatry.

Whoever the patron, the intended recipient
and the artist may have been, it is interesting
to note how quickly these engravings had
reached England. They provide a direct link
with the iconoclasm that swept the Low
Countries in the 1560s, and which forced
some Netherlandish artists into exile in
Britain.

EXH: Tate Gallery 1969–70 (9)
LIT: Roy Strong, 'Edward VI and the Pope: A Tudor
Anti-papal Allegory and its Setting', *Journal of the War-
burg and Courtauld Institutes*, vol.23, 1960, pp.311–13;
Margaret Aston, *The King's Bedpost*, Cambridge 1993

KH

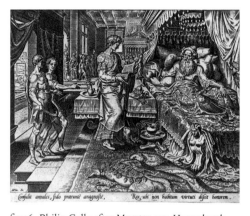

fig.36 Philip Galle after Maerten van Heemskerck,
'King Ahasuerus Consulting the Records', engraving
from *The History of Esther*, 1564, no.6. *Rijksmuseum,
Amsterdam*

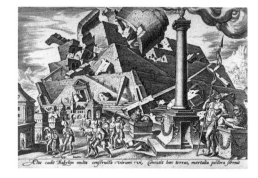

fig.37 Philip Galle after Maerten van Heemskerck,
'Destruction of the Tower of Babel', engraving from
Clades series, 1568–9, no.4. *Rijksmuseum, Amsterdam*

4 Elizabeth I

Elizabeth I (1533–1603) was the only surviving child of Henry VIII by his second wife, Anne Boleyn. At the age of three, following her father's remarriage to Jane Seymour, she was declared illegitimate. She was carefully educated under Roger Ascham, particularly in Greek and Latin, and grew up under the increasingly Protestant atmosphere of the court of Henry's final years, and that of her young half-brother, Edward VI. The political uncertainties of her childhood and adolescence made her insecure and cautious. She refused to be made a focus of plots against her Catholic half-sister following the accession of Mary in 1553, but was briefly imprisoned in the Tower of London in 1554.

She succeeded to the throne in November 1558 and set about reversing Mary's reintroduced Catholic practices, beginning with a proclamation that the litany should be read in English in the London churches. In 1563 the Thirty-nine Articles were issued and the range of the Oath of Supremacy extended.

Elizabeth refused offers of marriage from various European monarchs, including her brother-in-law Philip II of Spain. The exact nature of her relationship with her long-time favourite, Robert Dudley, Earl of Leicester, still remains unclear today. In 1568 Mary Queen of Scots fled south to England presenting Elizabeth with a problem, which she addressed by having Mary imprisoned.

In 1570 Elizabeth was excommunicated by Pope Pius V, and the Catholic rebellion that followed in 1571 was ruthlessly suppressed. Negotiations for a French marriage initiated in 1571 continued until 1584, latterly with François, duc d'Alençon. In 1572 an English force was sent to the Netherlands to assist in their struggle against Spain.

During the 1580s a series of plots to place Mary, Queen of Scots on the throne were revealed. Eventually in 1587, an unwilling Elizabeth signed Mary's death warrant, and recognised Mary's son as James VI of Scotland. Meanwhile, England had been drawn into a war with Spain which culminated in defeat of the Spanish Armada in 1588.

Her treasurer and principal adviser, William Cecil, Lord Burghley, died in 1598. Following a rebellion in Ireland she appointed her last favourite, the Earl of Essex, as governor-general there but his failure and subsequent attempted coup d'état compelled her to have him executed in 1601. She died at Richmond on 24 March 1603 and was buried the following month in Westminster Abbey.

There are surprisingly few contemporary descriptions of Elizabeth's appearance. In 1557 the Venetian envoy reported that 'her face is comely rather than handsome, but she is tall and well formed, with a good skin, although swarthy; she has fine eyes' (C.S.P. Venetian, 1556–7, p.1058). A number of contemporary references (Strong 1963, pp.18–19) indicated that she was proud of showing off her long slender hands. A description of her as an old woman by Paul Hentzner survives: 'her face oblong, fair but wrinkled, her eyes small, yet black and pleasant; her nose a little hooked, her lips narrow, topped with an auburn wig' (Rye 1865, p.104).

Henry VIII had been fully aware of the propaganda power of portraits, and of the need to exercise control over them. Portraits of Elizabeth dating from his reign are few, possibly because she had been proclaimed illegitimate. Portraits were much bound up with marriage negotiations, but Elizabeth's marital prospects then were uncertain. The earliest certain images of her are that in 'The Family of Henry VIII' by an unknown artist of c.1543–7 (The Royal Collection), and no.32 of c.1546.

Around the time of her succession, simple images of Elizabeth dressed in black appeared (Strong 1963, pp.54–6). These were followed by the well-known proclamation drafted by Cecil in 1563 – whether it was enacted is not known – intended to govern the production of images of the Queen. It forbade painters, printers and engravers from drawing the Queen's picture until 'some speciall conning payntor might be permitted by access to hir Ma^ty to take ye naturall representation of hir Matie wherof she hath bene allweise of hir owne [?riall] disposition very unwillyng' (transcribed Auerbach 1954, p.103). This special painter 'shall have first fynished a portraicture therof, after which fynished, hir Majesty will be content that all other payntors, or grauors … shall and maye at ther plesures follow the sayd pation [i.e. pattern] of first portraicture' (Strong 1963, p.5).

This is a useful insight into the proposed, and presumably the actual, way in which the monarch's public image was devised, fixed and then disseminated, by a number of artists working in different media, from one original design – like the establishment of a present-day corporate logo. Portrait patterns for other sitters (nos.98, 102) indicate the process.

This seems to have been the first of a number of attempts to regulate the quality and nature of images of the Queen, a procedure which seems to have had only partial success. A Privy Council order of July 1596 ordered that unsuitable portraits of her should be sought out and defaced and that subsequent portraits should be submitted to her Serjeant Painter, George Gower.

A series of face patterns have been discerned behind the portraits of Elizabeth in the course of her reign. Some survive in numerous examples – such as those employing the 'Darnley' pattern (so named after the National Portrait Gallery's portrait of c.1575, acquired from the Earls of Darnley) – others were less influential.

Apart from the portrait miniatures of the Queen, principally by Nicholas Hilliard, it is almost impossible to identify the actual artists who painted the portraits that have survived. A draft patent drawn up in 1584 would have given Gower a monopoly of her image in every format in large. Miniatures, however, were to be ceded to Hilliard. Yet no extant portraits can with certainty be assigned to Gower himself. Van Mander recorded that she was painted by Cornelis Ketel; a French court painter took her likeness in 1581. Payments for portraits of her are recorded to William Segar in 1597, Hilliard in 1599 and to an unnamed artist in 1572–6 (Strong 1987, pp.17–18). Until Metsys's signature on no.40 was revealed in 1988, the picture had been attributed to Ketel.

As the Queen aged, the portraits became more magnificent, culminating in the 'Ditchley' portrait by Gheeraerts the Younger (no.45). The final images depicted her as a beautiful young woman, in a 'Mask of Youth' pattern attributed to Hilliard by Strong. Its apotheosis is the 'Rainbow Portrait' (Hatfield House) in which the Queen grasps a rainbow and plays the role of the sun itself.

?FLEMISH SCHOOL

32 Elizabeth I when Princess
*c.*1546

Oil on panel 108.5 × 81.8 (42¾ × 32¼)
Inscribed 'Elizabetha | [?Filia or ?Soror]
Rex | Angliae', t.l., in same slightly later
hand as no.13
PROV: See Millar 1963, p.65
Her Majesty The Queen

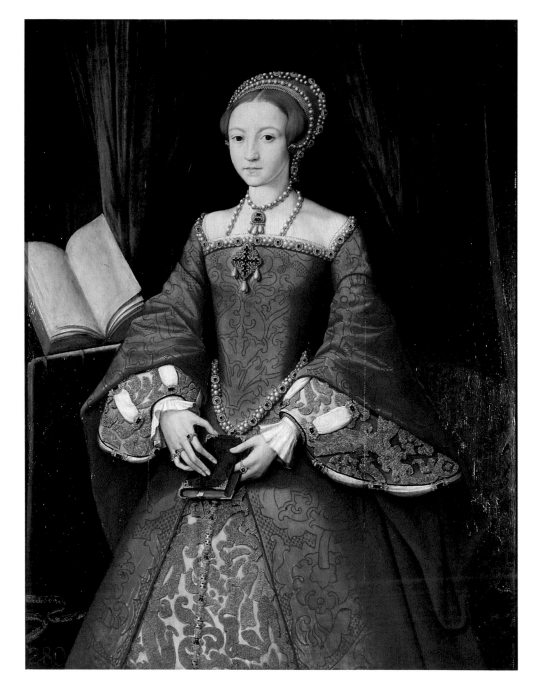

The earliest surviving individual portrait of
Elizabeth, this was probably painted for
Henry VIII. It is recorded in the collection of
her half-brother Edward VI in 1547 as 'a table
with the picture of the ladye Elizabeth her
grace with a booke in her hande her gowne
like crymsen clothe of golde withe workes'.
Millar has pointed out the technical similarities to the portrait of Edward as Prince of
Wales, presumably of similar date (no.13).

These two portraits may have been conceived as pendants, though both sitters face in
the same direction, which may argue against
this idea. The portrait of Edward predates the
death of their father in January 1547. Janet
Arnold (1981) has tentatively linked the present portrait with Elizabeth's letter from Hatfield to the young King, dated 15 May [1547]
which evidently accompanied a portrait of
herself, in response to an earlier request from
him. Whether or not this was the painting in
question, Elizabeth appears confident of the
likeness of the features, though aware of the
physical vulnerability of pictures: 'For the
face, I graunt, I might wel blusche to offer,
but the mynde I shal never be asshamed to
present. For thogh from the grace of the pictur the coulers may fade by time, may give by
wether may be spotted by chance, yet the
other nor time with her winges shal overtake,
nor the mistie cloudes with her loweringes
may darken, nor chance with her slipery fote
may overthrow … when you shal loke on my
pictur you wil witsafe to think that as you
have but the outwarde shadow of the body
afore you, so my inwarde minde wischeth that
the body it selfe were oftener in your presence'.

The picture was considerably altered during the course of painting. The paint has
become more transparent with time, revealing
changes to the fingers of the right hand and
to the position of the small book. There are
other alterations in the large book, and to the
wall above it, where there may originally have
been architectural features incorporating
carved rams' heads. The curtain has been
painted over a wall, the moulding on which

formerly continued above her head into a recess curving to the right.

John King describes how Hans Holbein established the definitive portrayal of Tudor Protestant royalism when he designed the title-page border of the 1535 Coverdale Bible to show Henry VIII wielding a sword and a book as an earthly manifestation of divine revelation (1989, p.54). 'In the text-centred Protestant kingdom, the Bible or symbolic Book often appeared as an autonomous symbol of royal authority' (ibid., p.56), and one that was to be much used in representations of Elizabeth following her accession. On entering London at the time of her coronation her dramatic gesture of kissing and embracing an English Bible publicly announced England's return to Protestant religious practices (ibid., p.104).

In a variant of no.13 (Haboldt & Co., Paris 1992–3, no.24) by a different hand, Edward grasps a sword, while the edges of two books in front of him (as here, one large and one small one) are labelled to represent the Old and New Testaments.

In the present portrait, Elizabeth is shown as a king's daughter, richly attired and wearing important jewellery. It is instructive to compare the sophisticated handling of this painting with that by 'one John' of her half-sister Mary (no.11).

The first certain surviving portrait of Elizabeth is her image in 'The Family of Henry VIII' (The Royal Collection) with those of her father, half-sister Mary, and Edward and his deceased mother Jane Seymour (as well as two servants passing through the garden behind). Painted perhaps a year or so before the present work it reflects Catherine Parr's efforts to reunite the King with all his children.

EXH: *The King's Pictures*, RA 1946–7 (24); RA 1950–1 (144); *Masterpieces from Windsor Castle*, NPG 1979 (no cat.); *Kings and Queens*, Queens Gallery 1982 (15) LIT: Millar 1963, no.46; Janet Arnold, 'The "Pictur" of Elizabeth I When Princess', *Burlington Magazine*, vol.123, 1981, pp.303–4; Strong 1987, pp.48–52; Arnold 1988, pp.1–19; John N. King, *Tudor Royal Iconography*, 1989, pp.211, 213; Catharine MacLeod, 'Guillim Scrots in England', unpublished MA report, Courtauld Institute 1990, pp.58–60; Piper 1992, p.46, repr. p.47

KH

BRITISH SCHOOL

33 Elizabeth I *c.*1565

Oil on panel 34 × 24.1 (13⅜ × 9½)
Inscr: 'CHRIST WAS THE WORD THAT SPAKE IT: | HE TOOK THE BREAD AND BRAKE IT: | AND WHAT HIS WORD DID MAKE IT: | THAT I BELIEVE AND TAKE IT:' in a later hand, on inner frame
PROV: … Christie's 14 July 1994 (9) bt present owner
Woollahra Trading Co. Ltd

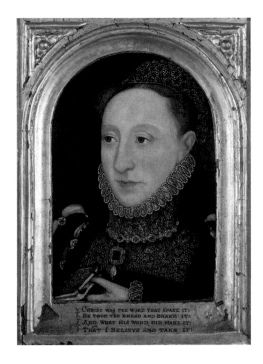

Until its appearance in the saleroom in 1994 this portrait was virtually unknown to art historians. It is of unusually archaic construction for its date, as the entire area of the image and the arched moulding with its two spandrels are fashioned out of a single piece of wood. Only the square-section battens nailed to the outside edges are later, as is the gilding over which the lettering has been added. Here and there on the bottom edge losses in this gilding reveal what may be the original gilding beneath.

In the first independent portrait of Elizabeth (no.32), she was depicted holding a book in which, as here, she marked a place with her finger. In the present portrait both the volume and her left hand have been introduced awkwardly, but deliberately, into the composition. Like its construction, the portrait itself harks back to a Netherlandish pre-Reformation devotional format (see Lord Berners's portrait, no.3) in which the sitter's gaze is averted from the viewer. These early examples were sometimes the right-hand panel of a diptych, attached by a hinge to a second panel depicting Christ, the Virgin Mary, or the sitter's particular saint. The sitter was thus portrayed looking across towards the adjoining sacred image.

Janet Arnold dates the costume of the present portrait to about 1565. Elizabeth's hair is pulled back from her face and held in a jewelled caul after the Italian fashion.

In 1963, Strong categorised the official portrait types of the Queen. The face in the present work conforms to what he called the 'Barrington Park' pattern, after a three-quarter-length in that collection. This type appears to have been introduced in the early 1560s to replace the initial basic type of *c.*1558 (Strong 1963, pp.54–9). In some examples of both these first types the Queen is shown with a small book, and John N. King (*Tudor Royal Iconography*, 1989, pp.107–110)

observes that she is thus portrayed as the ruler who had re-established the Protestant religious settlement of her half-brother Edward VI, and was committed to the dissemination of scripture in the vernacular. Books that survive from Elizabeth's personal library are bound in red velvet, and she possessed various small format editions of the scriptures and biblical prayers. Among these, a tiny sextodecimo volume (Bodleian Library Archive A.g.17) included *The Leteny*, published, according to its title page, in 1562.

The lettering on the frame was added with the present gilding. Richard Williams points out that a version of this text was attributed to Queen Elizabeth herself as early as 1650, in Samuel Clarke's *The Second Part of the Marrow of Ecclesiastical History*, I, p.220, as her reply to a question from a Marian priest on her view on Christ's presence in the Sacrament ('Twas God the word that spake it, | He took the Bread and brake it; | And what the word did make it; That I believe, and take it.'). The version on the frame is virtually identical to that cited in a nineteenth-century biography by Bishop Mandell Creighton (*Queen Elizabeth*, 1899, p.37).

EXH: *The Fine Art and Antiques Fair*, Olympia, 14–19 Feb. 1995

KH

ATTRIBUTED TO NICHOLAS HILLIARD 1546/7–1618

34 Elizabeth I ('The Phoenix Portrait') *c.*1575–6

Oil on panel 78.8 × 61 (31 × 24)
PROV: Perhaps bequeathed by Gabriel
Goodman (1529?–1601) to Christ's
Hospital, Ruthin, where first recorded
1839; with Colnaghi 1865, whence
acquired by NPG
*National Portrait Gallery, London. On long
loan to the Tate Gallery since 1965*

This portrait is named after the phoenix jewel
hanging at the Queen's breast. It is a reverse
image, in different attire, of that in the Walker
Art Gallery, Liverpool, in which Elizabeth
wears a pelican jewel and holds a pair of
gloves in her right hand rather than the red
rose shown here.

C.R. Beard first associated these two works
with the miniaturist Hilliard through comparison with no.69, his 1572 miniature of the
Queen. This attribution has since been
accepted by scholars with varying degrees of
conviction. A third portrait on panel is based
on the same face pattern (private collection); a
sophisticated work, it appears not to be by
the same hand and Arnold dates its costume
to *c.*1583–4. Also comparable are later miniatures of the Queen by Hilliard, such as one in
the Victoria and Albert Museum (no.4404-
1857).

No certainly identified portraits in large by
Hilliard have survived, but he is known to
have painted on that scale because in 1600 he
was commissioned by his own Company –
the Goldsmiths' – to paint 'a faire picture in
greate of her Ma[jes]tie'. Thornton and Cain
repeat this well-known reference (1992, p.24),
pointing out that Hilliard's advice on how to
paint pearls *in oils* (ibid. p.71) is further evidence that he worked in this medium, as well
as the water-based ones used for miniatures.

Arnold dates the costume of the present
portrait to *c.*1575–6, about a year later than
that of the 'Pelican Portrait', because the fashion is similar to that seen in Zuccaro's drawing (no.100). Elizabeth's white veil is pinched
into small pleats, with tiny silk tassels at its
edge. Across her shoulders lies a heavy jewelled collar of a type seen in portraits of
Henry VIII, and including large gold and
white enamelled roses set with single diamonds (Arnold 1988, p.23). The Queen holds
a red rose, traditionally symbolic of the Virgin
Mary and used by her half-sister Mary I (see
no.16), but also representing the Tudor rose.

Like the pelican, which traditionally drew

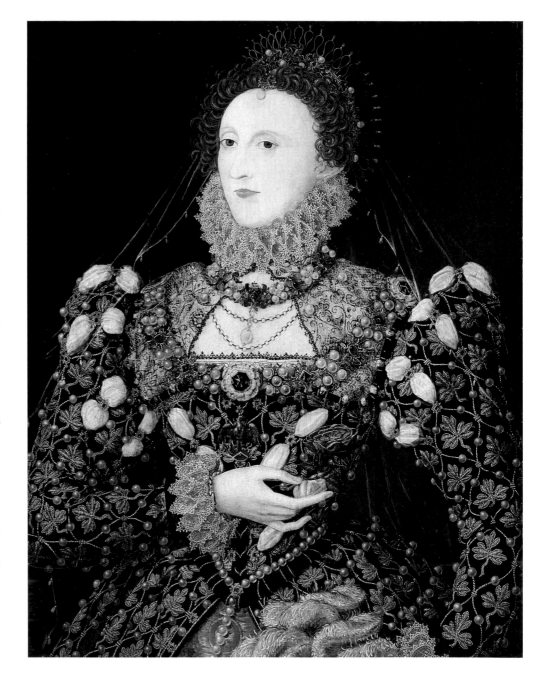

blood from its own breast to feed its young,
the phoenix came into use as a symbol of
Elizabeth in the 1570s. According to legend
this unique bird lived in the Arabian desert.
Every few hundred years it built a funeral
pyre and burnt itself to ashes from which it
would rise, once again young. It was a
symbol rich in meanings applicable to Elizabeth: unique, eternally youthful, celibate, yet
ever regenerating its dynasty. It had been one
of the *imprese*, or devices, published in Claude
Paradin's *Devises Héroiques* in 1557, appearing
in the English edition with the motto 'But

always one Phoenix in the world at once'
(Arnold 1988, p.74). It had been the *impresa* of
Mary of Guise, mother of Mary, Queen of
Scots.

A surviving 'Phoenix Jewel' (British Museum, see *Princely Magnificence*, p.59, no.35)
dates from *c.*1570–80. Within an enamelled
wreath of flowers is set a gold profile bust of
Elizabeth I, attired similarly to the present
portrait, with a phoenix in flames on the
reverse. In 1585 a phoenix jewel was recorded
as a New Year's gift to the Queen.

Infrared photography of the present portrait has shown that the features were originally drawn in different positions. For a technical study of this work, see pp.263–7.

EXH: *Coronation Exhibition*, Nottingham 1953 (38); Tate Gallery 1969–70 (73)
LIT: C.R. Beard, 'The "Pelican Portrait" of Queen Elizabeth', *Connoisseur*, vol.92, 1933, pp.263–4; NPG 1969, I, pp.101–2; Strong 1969, p.106; Strong 1987, pp.79–83; Arnold 1988, pp.22–4, 74; Simon Wilson, *Tate Gallery: An Illustrated Companion*, 1990, p.15; see also Nicholas Hilliard, *The Arte of Limning*, eds. R.K.R. Thornton and T.G.S. Cain, Manchester 1992

KH

ATTRIBUTED TO LUCAS DE HEERE 1534–1584

35 The Family of Henry VIII: An Allegory of the Tudor Succession *c.*1572

Oil on panel 131.2 × 184 (51⅝ × 72½) Inscribed 'THE. QVENE. TO. WALSINGHAM. THIS. TABLET. SENTE. MARKE. OF. HER. PEOPLES. AND. HER. OWNE. CONTENTE.' along the bottom; 'A FACE OF MVCHE NOBILLITYE LOE IN A LITLE ROOME. FOWR STATES WITH THEYR CONDITIONS HEARE SHADOWED IN | A SHOWE A FATHER MORE THEN VALYANT. A RARE AND VERTVOVS SOON. | A ZEALVS DAVGHTER IN HER KYND WHAT ELS THE WORLD DOTH KNOWE | AND LAST OF ALL A VYRGIN QVEEN TO ENGLANDS IOY WE SEE SVCCESSYVELY TO HOLD THE RIGHT, AND VERTVES OF THE THREE' around the frame

PROV: Walsingham family, Scadbury, Kent from whence bt by James West; James West sale 2 April 1773 (66), bt Sir Joshua Reynolds; …; bt Horace Walpole; Strawberry Hill sale 17 May 1842 (86), bt J.C. Dent; by family descent at Sudeley Castle
National Museum and Gallery, Cardiff 1991 (on loan to Sudeley Castle, Gloucestershire)

This blend of portraiture and allegory, in which Elizabeth appears in contemporary court dress alongside mythological figures, is paralleled only by the slightly earlier 'Elizabeth I and the Three Goddesses' of 1569 (no.29). Here the figures act as opposing symbols of Mary's Catholic, and Elizabeth's Protestant reigns. Henry VIII, the founder of the Church of England, appears in the centre enthroned under a canopy of state. His children are ranked on either side of him, with

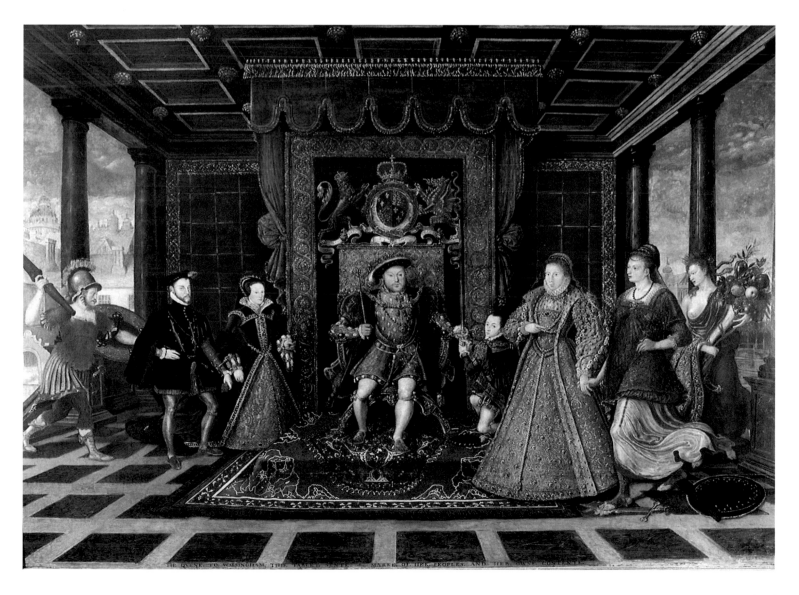

his immediate successor Edward VI kneeling by him receiving the sword of justice. Mary and Philip II are on the left with Mars, God of War close on their heels, symbolic of the course taken by their reign. In contrast, Elizabeth appears on the right accompanied by Peace, whom she grasps by the hand and who tramples on the sword of discord, closely followed by Plenty who bears her overflowing cornucopia. They act as flattering comments on Elizabeth's Protestant reign and its nurture of concord and harmony.

Strong attributed the picture to Lucas de Heere (see no.101) mainly on the strength of its compositional similarity to de Heere's signed and dated 'Solomon and the Queen of Sheba' of 1559, which also has a centrally placed throned figure on a dais, and a similarly patterned marble floor, and to his designs for the entry of the Duke of Anjou into Ghent in 1582 (Strong 1987, pp.72–3). However, as so few works by de Heere can be securely identified, particularly paintings in oil, the attribution should perhaps remain speculative.

Inherited pictures in Elizabeth's collection had also taken the Tudor succession for their theme – for example Holbein's 'Whitehall Mural' (see no.5), and 'The Family of Henry VIII' c.1545 (The Royal Collection) which has a similar composition and was perhaps the prototype work, with its pillared colonnade with glimpses of palace grounds in the background. The portrait likenesses are also ultimately based on known works. Henry is taken from his image by Holbein (fig.23 on p.43); Edward VI from that attributed to Guillim Scrots (see fig.24 on p.45); and Philip and Mary from portraits by Antonis Mor (see, e.g. no.16) or copies after them, such as the small double portrait at Woburn Abbey. Elizabeth does not appear to be based on any known portrait, although her appearance is similar, in reverse, to Hilliard's 1572 miniature (see e.g. no.69), and to her portrait by an unknown artist c.1571–5 (Reading Borough Council). The mythological figures, particularly Mars, may have their origins in engraved sources such as those of the School of Fontainebleau.

The inscription on the picture indicates that it was a gift from the Queen to her trusted servant, the zealous Protestant Sir Francis Walsingham (see no.118), possibly in gratitude for his negotiation of the Treaty of Blois, signed between England and France in 1572, while he was ambassador in Paris. The theme of the painting appears to have remained topical throughout Elizabeth's reign. Two updated versions of it were made, the first in oil c.1590–2 (Yale Center for British Art, New Haven) with Elizabeth in attire similar to that of the 'Ditchley' portrait (no.45), but with the jewelled and embroidered pattern of the 'Armada' (see no.43). In the second, an engraving by William Rogers of c.1592–5, Elizabeth wears a by-then fashionable drum-shaped farthingale (see Arnold 1988, p.34).

EXH: Leicester and London 1965–6 (39); Washington 1985–6 (2)
LIT: Strong 1987, pp.71–7; John N. King, *Tudor Royal Iconography*, 1989, pp.222–6; Christopher Lloyd and Simon Thurley, *Henry VIII: Images of a Tudor King*, 1990, p.40

TB

BRITISH SCHOOL

36 Henry VIII prior to 1590

Marble 67.5 × 70 × 37
(26⅝ × 27½ × 14½)
PROV: Made for John, Lord Lumley and
thence by descent
The Earl of Scarbrough

This is one of four sculptures of Tudor
monarchs made for John, Lord Lumley
(?1534–1609) for the hall at Lumley Castle.
They are recorded in the Lumley Inventory of
1590 (see no.105) as 'foure livelie statues all
wrought in white marble in memorie of K
Henry the 8, King Edward 6, Quene Marie
and Q. Elizabeth, in whose raignes his Lop
lived'. They are clearly recognisable in the
illustration in the Inventory (although there
are slight differences, which may be due to
the artist's interpretation) (see no.105), where
they are placed next to the Lumley Horseman,
described as 'a great statuarie on horseback,
as bigg as the life, wthin an arch of stone, in
memorie of King Edward the 3 in whose time
the most of this Castle was built'. They are
slightly smaller than life-size and are no
longer displayed on their scrolled stone bases,
which remain fixed to the walls of the hall of
Lumley Castle.

'The Horseman' (at present on loan to
Leeds Castle with the busts) is a life-size,
polychromed equestrian sculpture of Edward
III. It was the first equestrian statue to be
made in England and is clearly based on Italian examples, particularly the monuments to
Leonardo da Prato and Nicolo Orsini in SS.
Giovanni e Paolo, Venice. The Inventory also
notes a group of six smaller busts, now lost,
which are depicted below the Horseman and
are described as 'Wthin this arche … six
small pictures, in whyte marble in memorie of
his six sonnes, viz: Edward Prince of Wales,
Willm of Hatfield who died yung, Lyonell
Duke of Clarence, John of Gaunt, Duke of
Lancaster, Edmond of Langley, Duke of Yorke,
Thomas of Woodstock, Duke of Glocester'.

All of these objects were erected at Lumley
Castle around 1580 as part of an elaborate
programme that filled most of the public

spaces. This sought to emphasise the lengthy
ancestry and historical importance of the
Lumley family through reference to their
longevity and loyalty to the Crown. The busts
are a particular example of self-promotion; at
the time the Inventory was written Lumley
had lived under the reigns of four monarchs,
and he actually outlived the fourth one. As
well as proof of his longevity, the busts are
evidence of his loyalty to the Crown, whatever its religious persuasion and treatment of
him personally.

These four sculptures are unique; there are
no comparable contemporary free-standing
busts of the Tudor monarchs. It seems that
they are based on particular portrait-masks
that appear in pictures, medals and coins of
the period, although it is impossible to prove
absolutely the prototype for any of the busts.
It has been suggested that they were made for
Lord Lumley whilst he was in Florence in
1566–7 (M. Vickers, 'The Changing Face of
Henry VIII', *Country Life*, 24 April 1980,
pp.1248–9). However, it is certain that Lumley
did not go to Italy (see K. Barron, 'Classicism
and Antiquarianism in Elizabethan Patronage:
the Case of John, Lord Lumley', forthcoming
M. Litt, Oxford University 1995), and there is
little reason to suppose that the busts were
made outside England: they do not appear to
be the product of an Italian workshop,
although they are probably made of imported
Italian marble.

The quality of the carving of the four busts
is quite varied, that of Queen Mary being by
far the most competent of the four, whilst that
of Elizabeth is the most schematic. There is a
certain disparity in the amount of sculpted
detail, which confirms the theory that the
sculptor copied images in different media.
The possible existence of another bust in the
set (see no.39) could mean that a number of
busts were made of monarchs and other figures, of which Lord Lumley chose to buy four.

This bust of Henry VIII is clearly related to
a medal by the Dutch artist Steven van Herwijk, made in England in 1562, the best
example of which is in Vienna. A lead version
is also to be found in the British Museum

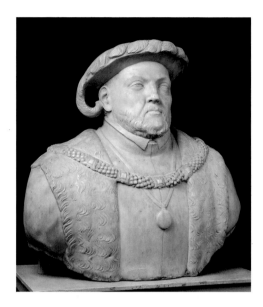

(*Medallic Illustrations*, 1904, pl.III, no.7).
Although the medal is very similar to the
bust, particularly in terms of the costume,
there is no evidence to suggest that Lumley
ever had a copy of this medal or came into
contact with it. It is possible that the bust was
taken from another image of Henry VIII, such
as the leaden box lid that was once in the collection of Sir Hans Sloane (British Museum).
It is clear that all of these images are in some
way related to Holbein's portraits of Henry
VIII, although the exact connection has not
yet been established.

There is a version of the bust of Henry VIII
in the Ashmolean Museum which came from
the Arundel Collection (Nicholas Penny, *Catalogue of European Sculpture in the Ashmolean
Museum*, Oxford 1992, III, p.195, no.599). It is
less well executed than the Lumley bust, but it
is unclear whether it is related to any of the
other copies of the busts (see nos.37, 39).

LIT: Cust 1917–18, pp.15–35

KB

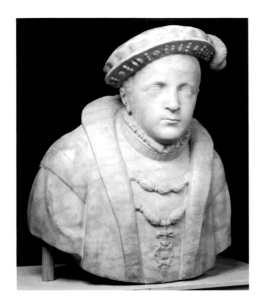

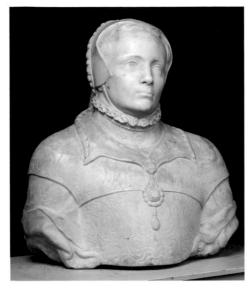

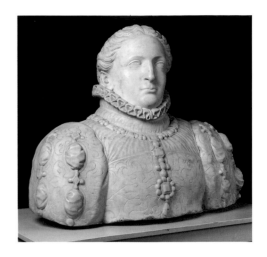

BRITISH SCHOOL

37 Edward VI prior to 1590

Marble 61 × 54 × 33 (24 × 21½ × 13)
PROV: Made for John, Lord Lumley and
thence by descent
The Earl of Scarbrough

This is the second of the four sculptures of
Tudor monarchs made for John, Lord Lumley
(see no.36). This bust of Edward VI is closely
related to the unique lead medal of 1547 in
the British Museum (*Medallic Illustrations*,
1904, pl.IV, no.1) but may equally well derive
from the portrait attributed to Scrots, now in
the Royal Collection, which belonged to Lord
Lumley.

A version of this bust was last recorded in
1966 as belonging to the Duke of Somerset at
Maiden Bradley, Wiltshire ('Portraits of
Edward VI', ed. N. Surry, 1966, unpublished
manuscript, NPG Archive). This version may
come from the same set as the busts of Elizabeth and Dudley in the National Portrait
Gallery (although it does not have the rounded base and inscribed plaque that differenti-
ates them from the Lumley busts) or it may
equally have come from a set which included
the bust of Henry VIII now in the Ashmolean
(see nos.36, 39).

LIT: Cust 1917–18, pp.15–35

KB

BRITISH SCHOOL

38 Mary I prior to 1590

Marble 59.5 × 53.5 × 32
(23⅜ × 21 × 12⅝)
PROV: Made for John, Lord Lumley and
thence by descent
The Earl of Scarbrough

This is the third of the four sculptures made
for John, Lord Lumley (see no.36). The most
probable medallic prototypes for the bust are
the three similar portrait medals of Mary
made for Philip II by Jacopo da Trezzo in
1555 (*Medallic Illustrations*, 1904, pl.IV, no.15;
pl.V, nos.1, 2).

Although all of the Lumley busts can be
linked to medals of the period, they may have
been made by an artist who was working
from painted portraits in Lumley's collection.
For instance this bust of Mary I is clearly
related to the portrait in the Chapter House
of Durham Cathedral, which may be by Gerlach Flicke (after Antonis Mor) and still bears
the Lumley cartellino, or painted label. Most
of the images of Mary, including medals of
her, derive ultimately from Mor's portrait and
it is therefore possible that the painting was a
prototype for the bust.

LIT: Cust 1917–18, pp.15–35

KB

BRITISH SCHOOL

39 Elizabeth I prior to 1590

Marble 49.5 × 59 × 25
(19½ × 23¼ × 9⅞)
PROV: Made for John, Lord Lumley and
thence by descent
The Earl of Scarbrough

The fourth sculpture made for John, Lord
Lumley (see no.36), this is the only one of the
set which can be definitely associated with a
specific prototype – a medal of the Queen by
Steven van Herwijk (National Portrait
Gallery), executed during one of the artist's
visits to England between c.1562 and 1567.
Specific similarities between the two portraits,
particularly in the details of the clothing, suggest that they are related.

Another version of this bust (National Portrait Gallery) came from Kimbolton Castle
with one of the Earl of Leicester which
appears to be from a series similar to Lumley's. Both busts have a rounded lower area
and a plaque on the base, inscribed with the
subject's name, but are otherwise similar to
the Lumley sculptures. The suggestion that
the bust of Leicester is a copy of a more competent work made for display with the Lumley set seems unlikely (Vickers, 'The Medal of
Robert Dudley, Earl of Leicester in the Bibliothèque Nationale', *Numismatic Chronicle*,
vol.141, 1981, pp.117–19). The Lumley Inventory (see no.105) makes it clear that the busts
were intended to represent the monarchs during whose lifetime Lumley had lived. Leicester, a prominent Protestant, had little in
common with Lumley, a staunch Catholic.

LIT: Cust 1917–18, pp.15–35

KB

QUENTIN METSYS THE YOUNGER ?1543–1589

40 Elizabeth I ('The Sieve Portrait') *c.*1583

Oil on canvas 124.5 × 91.5 (49 × 36)
Inscribed 'sta[n]cho | riposo | & ripo | sato | affa | nno' ('Weary, I rest and, having rested, still am weary'), below left; 'a terra ilben | al dimo- ra in sella' ('The good falls to the ground while the bad remains in the saddle') on the rim of the sieve; 'tvtto vedo et mo[lto mancha]' ('I see all and much is lacking') on globe; signed and dated: '1583. q. massys | ant.' on base of globe

PROV: ...; discovered rolled up in the attic of the Palazzo Reale, Siena 1895
Pinacoteca Nazionale, Siena

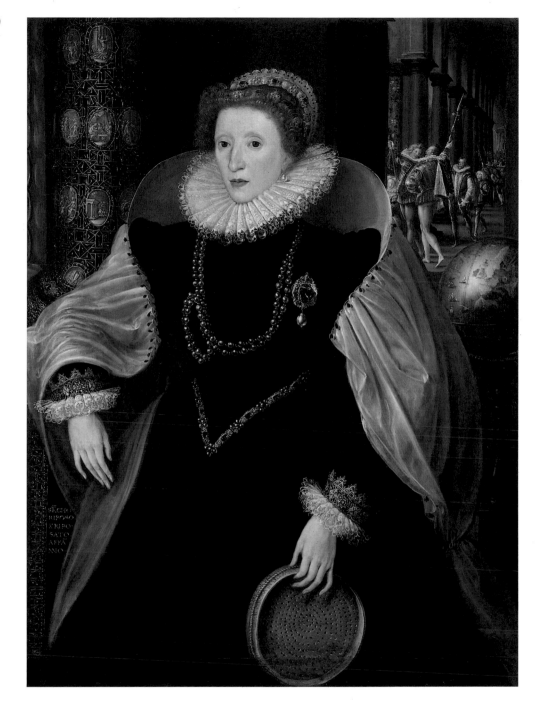

Queen Elizabeth is portrayed with a sieve, a symbol of chastity, in a number of portraits from as early as 1579 (see for example that illustrated in Strong 1987, p.94). The Siena version, dated 1583, is the most sophisticated, both stylistically and iconographically. Through an interlinking of Classical mythology and the imagery of Renaissance imperialism, Elizabeth appears as the chaste Virgin Queen who, by renouncing earthly love, has emerged as the powerful and wise figurehead of imperial Britain.

The sieve had appeared in Petrarch's *Triumph of Chastity*, in which the Roman Vestal Virgin Tuccia proved her purity by carrying water in a sieve without spilling a drop. As well as symbolising chastity it was also emblematic of wisdom and discernment, appearing thus in Whitney's *Choice of Emblemes* in 1586, and it is to this that the inscription on the rim which describes the sieving action refers. The implication is that Elizabeth's wise and good government is a direct result of her virgin state.

The richly jewelled column behind her is an adaptation of widespread imperial imagery – a column surmounted by a crown – but here the imperial crown appears in a roundel at the bottom. The other roundels, based on engravings of the 1560s by Marcantonio Raimondi, depict the story of Dido and Aeneas. Elizabeth, whom it was said had descended from the Trojan Brutus, is here compared to Aeneas, who having resisted the temptations of Dido, followed his true destiny, the founding of the Roman Empire. Like him, Elizabeth has resisted marriage, leaving her free to pursue her imperial aspirations. The latter are symbolised by the globe which depicts ships

heading westwards, presumably representing England's quest for maritime expansion in the New World. The scene in the upper right-hand side has been interpreted as an enactment of Elizabeth's refusal of Philip II's 1558 proposal of marriage (see Oakeshott and Jordan 1986). More plausibly the central figure has been identified as Sir Christopher Hatton whose white hind badge is discernible on his cloak. Hatton was a vociferous opponent of the proposed marriage of Elizabeth and the Duc d'Anjou, under discussion at this period, and was also an active supporter of Drake's

and Frobisher's voyages of exploration. To Schulting has pointed out that Hatton, if this commission were connected with him, could first have encountered the members of the Metsys (Massys) artistic dynasty on his visit to Antwerp in 1573 (verbal communication).

The occasion of this commission, and how it reached Siena, remains, however, unknown.

Only a handful of signed works survive by this artist, a grandson of the great Quentin Metsys (or Massys). These include an 'Allegory' dated 1570 (Galerie Fischer, Lucerne, 17–21 June 1958, no.2993) and an 'Allegorical

Painting' dated 1572 (private collection, Barcelona, see André de Bosque, *Quentin Metsys*, Brussels 1975, figs.29, 30). Metsys the Younger joined the Guild of St Luke in Antwerp in 1574, the year in which Federico Zuccaro (see nos.99, 100) visited Antwerp and is known to have met members of the Metsys family. 'ANT' in the inscription on the present portrait evidently alludes to this city. As dissenters, Metsys's painter father Jan and uncle Cornelis, had been forced to leave Antwerp at the same time as Hans Eworth, and so it was possibly for reasons of religion that Quentin Metsys the Younger is recorded living in London, in Langborne Ward, by c.1581 and in St Nicolas Lane c.1586 (*Proceedings of the Hugenot Society*, x, 2, pp.214, 402). In 1588 he left for Frankfurt, where he died the following year.

It is curious to note that in around 1577 Elizabeth I attempted to buy from the Carpenters' guild in Antwerp their great 'Burial of Christ' triptych by Quentin Metsys the Elder.

EXH: *Ritratto italiano...*, Florence 1911 (8); *Fontainebleau e la maniera italiana*, Naples 1952 (85); *British Portraits*, 1956–7 (19); *Shakespeare Exhibition*, The Hague 1958 (33); London and Belfast 1988–9 (3.22)
LIT: Mariana Jenkins, *The State Portrait*, 1947, pp.24-5, fig.46; Strong 1963, pp.66–9; Frances Yates, *Astraea: The Imperial Theme in the Sixteenth Century*, 1993 ed. (first published 1975), pp.114–20; Walter Oakeshott and Anson Jordan, 'The Siena Portrait of Queen Elizabeth I', *Apollo*, vol.124, Oct. 1986, pp.306–9; Strong 1987, pp.91–107; entry by Alessandro Bagnoli in *Restauri 1983/1988,* Soprintendenza per i Beni artistici e storici, Siena, pp.41–3

KH and TB

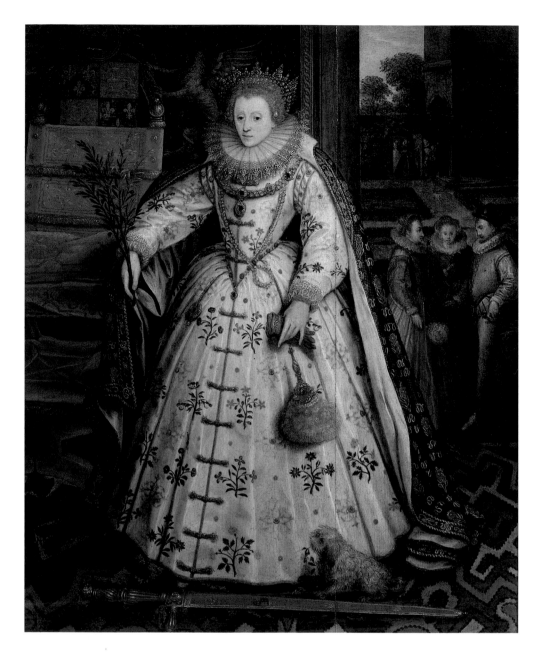

MARCUS GHEERAERTS THE ELDER *c.*1525–before 1591

41 Elizabeth I *c.*1580–5

Oil on panel 45.7 × 38.1 (18 × 15)
Signed 'MGF' on the chair support
PROV: ...; Matthew Prior, who bequeathed it in his will of 9 Aug. 1721 to Henrietta Cavendish-Holles, wife of the 2nd Earl of Oxford, and first recorded at her house in 1747; thence by descent
Private Collection

As in the 'Allegory of the Tudor Succession' (see no.35) Elizabeth appears again as the progenitor of Peace, but this time she holds the various distinguishing attributes herself, as opposed to being attended by allegorical personifications. In her left hand she holds an olive branch, and at her feet is a symbolically sheathed sword, which before the figure of Peace had trampled underfoot. The imagery is similar to that in the Ermine portrait of Elizabeth *c.*1585 (Hatfield House) in which she also holds an olive branch, and a sword, this time possibly the sword of Justice, is placed on a table on the right. The Queen's facial appearance is also very like that in the Ermine portrait, and she possibly wears the same jewelled headdress, collar and girdle. Also common to both is the 'Polish' style of her gown with its horizontal ornamental fastenings, or froggings.

No other portrait in oils by Marcus Gheeraerts the Elder is known, although in the *Returns of Aliens* he describes himself as a painter, not as an etcher or engraver, for which he is better known. On grounds of costume the portrait has been dated *c.*1580–5, and it is clearly signed 'MGF', which stands for 'Marcus Gheeraerts Fecit'. Karen Hearn observes that the form of the monogram is identical with that on two drawings by the elder Gheeraerts in the Rijksmuseum, Amsterdam (no.11.81, dated 1583, and no.19.47). The fact that Gheeraerts the Elder was resident in

Antwerp from 1577 to about 1586 is problematic. However, the dating is by no means secure and it could be either slightly earlier or later than thought, and it is recorded by van Mander that Gheeraerts signed with his initials his triptych of the Descent from the Cross for the church of the Recollets, Bruges. Hodnett draws parallels between passages in the portrait and Gheeraerts's etchings and drawings, particularly the small pet dog and the profile of the male courtier who stands in the foreground of the garden scene on the right.

Marcus Gheeraerts the Elder was a prominent member of the Protestant community in Bruges, but was forced to flee to London as a religious refugee in 1567/8, leaving his Roman Catholic wife behind. In 1571 he married Susanna de Critz, sister of the portrait painter John de Critz. It is thought that, with Lucas de Heere, he worked on the illustrations for Jan van der Noot's *Het Theatre*, the first etchings to be produced in England. Hodnett suggests that he possibly studied under Hieronymous Cock in Antwerp, where he would have known de Heere who was one of Cock's chief engravers. Gheeraerts certainly seems to have been a member of the circle of Antwerp refugees in London, which included De Heere and Hoefnagel, whose costume figures (see fig.42 on p.117) are very like those in the background of this portrait. Prominent in this circle was Emanuel van Meteren, leader of the Dutch merchants, who was Susanna de Critz's uncle. In August 1586, Gheeraerts was godfather to his thirteenth child, Nathaniel, in London. Along with de Heere, he contributed to van Meteren's *album amicorum* (see no.101).

Little survives from Gheeraerts's English period, but his well-known etching of the Procession of the Knights of the Garter, dated 1576 and corrected in pen to 1578, is in the British Museum. A painting, 'Queen Elizabeth and her Court at Kenilworth' 1575 (private collection) has been attributed to him in the past.

LIT: Edward Hodnett, *Marcus Gheeraerts the Elder*, Utrecht 1971; Mary Edmond, 'Limners and Picture-makers', *Walpole Society*, vol.47, 1978–80, pp.134–5, 150; Strong 1987, pp.113–15; Arnold 1988, pp.136–8

TB

FLEMISH SCHOOL

42 Queen Elizabeth I Feeds the Dutch Cow *c.*1586

Oil on panel 39.4 × 49.5 (15½ × 19½)
PROV: …; sold anonymously, Sotheby's 4 April 1962 (44, as by Adriaen van de Venne) bt Leger
Private Collection

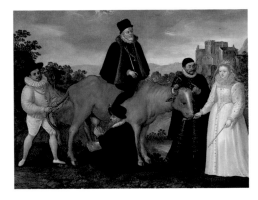

Satirical representations of the Netherlands as a cow being manhandled by various foreign powers were circulating in several versions from at least 1583 onwards. This picture represents Philip II of Spain attempting to ride the cow, drawing blood with his spurs. At the same time it is being pulled backwards by the Duke of Anjou, the Netherlands' much-disliked French ally and lord of the rebellious Northern Provinces until 1583. He is being spattered with cow-pat for his trouble, presumably in reference to his failed attempt to seize full power over the Netherlands in January 1583. Philip's agent, the Duke of Alva (or perhaps the Earl of Leicester, the luckless Governor-General of the United Provinces 1585–7) is milking it, while Prince William of Orange steadies it by the horns, allowing the Queen of England to feed it, in an allusion to his longstanding efforts to secure an alliance with England against Spain.

William was assassinated on 10 July 1584, and his successor Prince Maurice pleaded with the Queen to take the House of Orange under her protection. A related painting in the Rijksmuseum, now dated to around 1583, represents Prince William milking the cow, and was clearly inspired by opponents of the Franco–Dutch axis that William also pursued. This version could refer to the Anglo–Dutch treaty finally signed in August 1585 at Nonsuch (perhaps represented symbolically by the fortified castle between William and Elizabeth) in which Elizabeth undertook to support the Dutch United Provinces against Spanish rule with money and troops. Even posthumously, William would be regarded as the treaty's architect.

The later date of this panel can be surmised on the grounds that it uses an image of Philip II engraved in 1586 and one of the most widely known likenesses of William by Key. The figure of the Queen appears to be quite close to that by the elder Gheeraerts, dated to about 1585, where she is represented as the bringer of justice and peace (no.41). This was an image she was repeatedly given in pageants during the Earl of Leicester's progress through the Netherlands in 1586, following his appointment as its Governor-General after the Nonsuch treaty.

EXH: *Antique Dealers' Fair*, Grosvenor House, June 1962
LIT: Strong 1963, no.9, pl.XXIII; R.C. Strong and J.A. van Dorsten, *Leicester's Triumph*, 1964, p.77, pl.4, and fig.2 for related engraving; London and Belfast 1988–9, no.6.13, for Rijksmuseum version; Jan Van der Stock (ed.), *Antwerp: Story of a Metropolis*, exh. cat., Hessenhuis, Antwerp 1993, no.128, for Rijksmuseum version; *All the Paintings in the Rijksmuseum in Amsterdam*, 1976, no.A2684, repr., for full transcript of inscriptions on Rijksmuseum version

EE

British School

43 Elizabeth I ('The Armada Portrait') c.1588

Oil on panel 110.5 × 127 (43½ × 50)
PROV: Possibly commissioned by Sir
Francis Drake; by descent to his second
wife Elizabeth Sydenham, and after her
death to his godson Richard Drake of
Ash, whose descendants inherited
Shardeloes, where first recorded in 1775
Mr Tyrwhitt-Drake

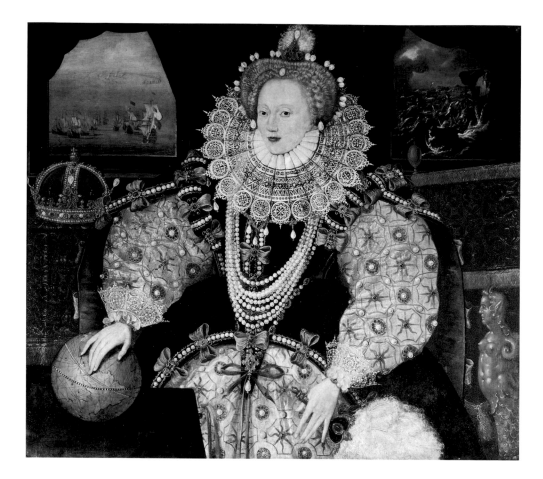

Elizabeth is celebrated here as a potent and
victorious monarch, the defender of her kingdom against Spanish aggression. The tableaux
in the background show episodes from the
defeat of the Spanish Armada, which sailed
into the English Channel in July 1588. On the
left English fire ships descend on the Spanish
fleet, and on the right the fleet is dashed to
pieces on the rocky coasts of Ireland and
Scotland. Directly below this, forming the
arm of the chair, is a carved Mannerist figure
of a mermaid, whose traditional function is to
lure seafarers to their doom, just as Spain had
been tempted by Elizabeth. Her left hand
rests on a globe, her fingers covering the
Americas, indicating England's dominion of
the seas and plans for imperialist expansion in
the New World.

Dr Margarita Russell (verbal communication) comments that although the ships do
not relate directly to extant drawings or
paintings they are well-observed and convincingly represented.

In terms of long-term damage to the Spanish the destruction of the Armada actually
achieved little, but at the time it was fêted
both by the English and the Dutch as a significant victory. Poems, pamphlets and
engravings extolled Elizabeth as the van-
quisher of the Catholic threat, and medals
and coins were struck to commemorate the
event. The 'Armada' portrait takes its place in
this outpouring of eulogistic material. The
Queen appears as an austere and authoritative
monarch, bedecked in jewels and rich embroidery as outward signs of her magnificence.
Her costume, with large ruff and voluminous
sleeves and skirt, both gives her presence and
reflects contemporary fashion, relating particularly to the images of her attributed to
Hilliard in the Mildmay and Ashburne Char-
ters (1584 and 1585). Hilliard's miniature of
her c.1588 (Mauritshuis, The Hague) and a
drawing attributed to him called 'Queen Eliz-

abeth' c.1588 (Victoria and Albert Museum)
show what is perhaps the same costume as
this, with slight differences, though all have
the characteristic bows.

This is one of three versions of the
'Armada' portrait, the handling of the features
in this being particularly sensitive. The other
two, by a different hand, are at Woburn
Abbey and in the National Portrait Gallery
(the latter has been cut down at the sides).
The facial image, pose and clothes of the
Queen were used as the basis for other depictions of her, for example the full-length portraits at Trinity College, Cambridge, and Jesus
College, Oxford, as well as for engravings of
her.

EXH: London and Belfast 1988–9 (16.1)
LIT: Strong 1987, pp.131–3; Arnold 1988, pp.33–40;
Andrew Belsey and Catherine Belsey, 'Icons of Divinity: Portraits of Elizabeth I', in Gent and Llewellyn
1990, pp.11–35

TB

BRITISH SCHOOL

44 The Spanish Armada c.1590

Oil on canvas 121.3 × 284.5 (47¾ × 112)
PROV: Bequeathed to the Society in
1846 by John Nuffey, Master of the Soci-
ety in 1833 and Apothecary in Ordinary
to George IV, William IV and Queen
Victoria
*The Worshipful Society of Apothecaries of
London*

The scene is a celebration of the defeat of the
Spanish Armada. It does not represent a specific episode, but is an amalgamation of
events. The fortified English coast, which is
exaggeratedly rocky and exotic, is possibly
intended as either Plymouth or Portland Bill,
and warning beacons can be seen prominently
against the sky. Queen Elizabeth appears on
the left among her troops, representing her
famous address to the army at Tilbury, but is
also present as the figurehead of England and
the defender of the Protestant faith. The ship
on the far right, flying the royal standard, is
Lord Howard of Effingham's flagship the *Ark
Royal*, and to its left a Spanish galleon is sinking. In the distance is the towering presence
of the rest of the fleet.

Dr Margarita Russell comments that inac-
curacies in the depiction of the ships indicate
that the artist was not a marine specialist.

Sea-pieces were rare in England at this date
although isolated examples do exist, for
example 'The Embarkation of Henry VIII'
*c.*1550 (The Royal Collection), thought to be
by a Netherlandish artist. The artist of this

picture must certainly have been aware of
Netherlandish works, particularly those of the
earlier sixteenth century, for example by
Joachim Patinir (*c.*1485–1524), although the
craggy landscape is reminiscent of contemporary etchings by Paul Brill. The composition,
and the representation of individual ships,
seems to be entirely independent of engravings produced to commemorate the victory,
and bears no relation to the famous Armada
tapestries (destroyed by fire but known
through Pine's eighteenth-century engravings
after them). They were commissioned by Lord
Howard and designed by Hendrick Vroom,
who also painted 'The Seventh Day of the
Battle of the Armada' (Tiroler Landesmuseum
Ferdinandeum, Innsbruck), and whose work
was represented in Henry, Prince of Wales's
collection by the early seventeenth century
(M. Russell, *Visions of the Sea: Hendrick C. Vroom
and the Origins of Dutch Marine Painting*, 1983,
pp.162–3). It is possible that the figure of the
Queen was adapted from an engraving or a
medal.

The picture has been traditionally ascribed
to Hilliard, possibly because Van der Doort
lists in the collection of Charles I 'the Spanish
fleete in liming of: 88:' done by him, but this
was a much smaller work (Millar 1958–60,
p.121).

EXH: London and Belfast 1988–9 (14.53)
LIT: Ernest Busby, letter to Collector's Questions,
Country Life, vol.103, March 1948, p.476

TB

MARCUS GHEERAERTS THE YOUNGER 1561/2–1636

45 Elizabeth I ('The Ditchley Portrait') c.1592

Oil on canvas 241.3 × 152.4 (95 × 60)
Inscribed with a partially legible sonnet
comparing the Queen's divine powers
with those of the natural elements. For a
full transcription, see NPG 1969
PROV: First recorded at Ditchley by
Vertue in 1718; by descent to the 17th
Viscount Dillon, by whom bequeathed
to the National Portrait Gallery, London
1932
National Portrait Gallery, London

This is one of the few full-length portraits of
Queen Elizabeth and is the largest. Originally
it was even bigger, but at some point was cut
down by about three inches on each side,
which explains the curtailment of the inscriptions on the right. It is likely to have been
commissioned by Sir Henry Lee, from whose
house, Ditchley, in Oxfordshire, it originally
came. In 1592 he staged a lavish private entertainment there in the Queen's honour which
this portrait may mark. Elizabeth, who stands
on top of a globe, and specifically a map of
England, rests her foot near Ditchley.

During the Ditchley Entertainment Elizabeth was led into a hall hung with allegorical
pictures, the meaning of which she had to
divine, and the Ditchley portrait would have
been intended to be read in such a manner.
The iconography was possibly devised by
Lee, who was also responsible for the com-

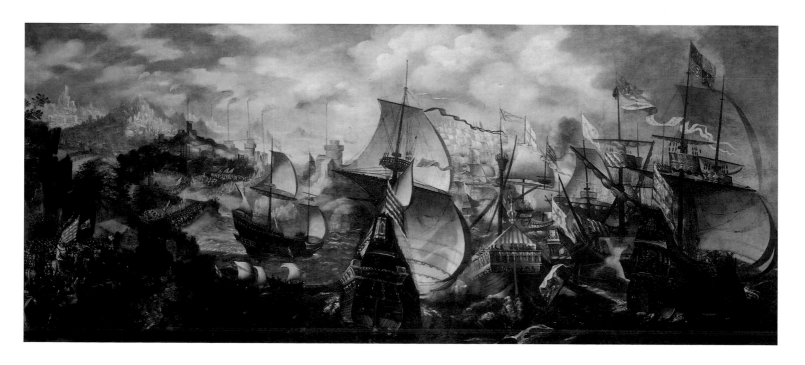

plex symbolism which surrounded the Queen at the annual Accession Day Tilts, which he had initiated and over which he presided as the Queen's Champion. Here Elizabeth is celebrated as a powerful and, indeed, divine monarch, standing astride the world, the sun, as the sonnet says, reflecting her glory and the thunder her power. From her right ear hangs an ornament in the shape of an armillary or celestial sphere. This is a symbolic reference to her as a divine power, but is also an emblem used in connection with the Accession Day Tilts. It was worn as an emblem by Sir Henry Lee, and can be seen embroidered on his sleeves, with lovers' knots, in his portrait by Antonis Mor (see no.20). The same combination appears on the Queen's gown in a portrait by an unknown artist c.1580–5 (illustrated Arnold 1988, p.343), and George Clifford, 3rd Earl of Cumberland, who succeeded Lee as Queen's Champion in 1590, wears spheres on his sleeves in his miniature by Hilliard (no.74).

This is one of the earliest portraits by Gheeraerts, dated by the costume c.1592–5 ('Mary Rogers, Lady Harington', fig.25, and 'An Unknown Lady', private collection, are both of 1592), and Sir Henry Lee appears to have been one of his first patrons. He was perhaps attracted to Gheeraerts's style through his experience of Continental art, seen on his travels in 1568 to Antwerp, where he sat to Mor, and through Germany to Italy. He was painted by Gheeraerts throughout the rest of his life, for example the three-quarter-length still at Ditchley dated c.1590 (Strong 1969), and the full-length in Garter robes c.1602 (Armourers and Braziers Company), and owned other works by him (see no.120). In 1602, he and his mistress Anne Vavasour were godparents to Gheeraerts's son, Henry, further evidence of the links between artist and patron.

Elizabeth's appearance is close to the German traveller Paul Hentzner's description of her at Greenwich in 1598: 'her Face oblong, fair, but wrinkled; her Eyes small, yet black and pleasant; her Nose a little hooked; her Lips narrow … she had in her Ears two pearls, with very rich drops; she wore false hair, and that red; upon her Head she had a small Crown … Her Bosom was uncovered, as all the English ladies have it, till they marry; and she had on a Necklace of exceeding fine jewels' (Rye 1865, p.104). It is not known if Gheeraerts was granted a sitting from the Queen, or if his image was adapted from another work, for example Crispin van de Passe's drawing of her c.1592–5 (C. White and C. Crawley, *Dutch Drawings at Windsor Castle*, Cambridge 1994, no.138) in which she

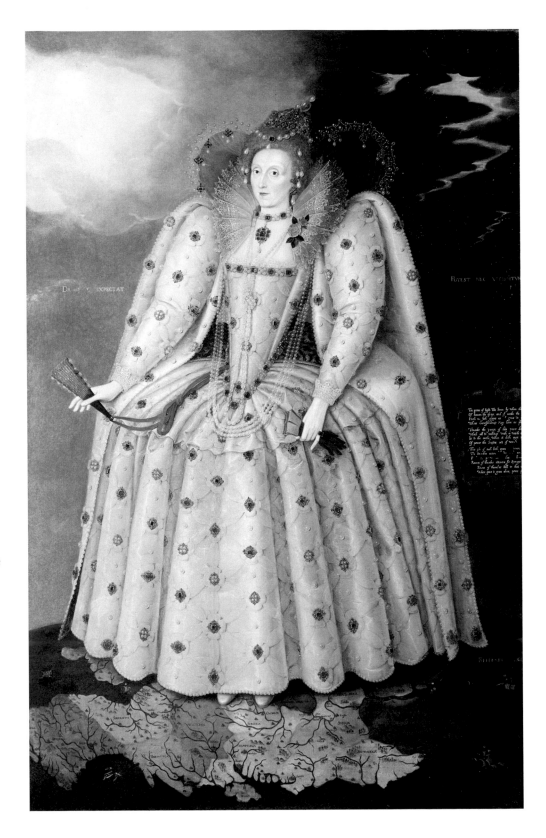

wears the same costume. Janet Arnold suggests that the costume and accessories were taken from life, and could have been assembled for Gheeraerts to paint but without the Queen present. The jewels, or buttons, sewn on to her gown, with rubies, diamonds or pearls set in enamelled gold, are possibly those mentioned in the 1587 inventory of her jewels, as is the girdle (Arnold 1988, p.43).

LIT: Roy Strong, 'Elizabethan Painting: An Approach through Inscriptions III: Marcus Gheeraerts the Younger', *Burlington Magazine*, vol.105, 1963, p.149–57; NPG 1969, 1, pp.104–7; Frances Yates, *Astraea: The Imperial Theme in the Sixteenth Century*, 1975, pp.10–17; Strong 1987, pp.135–41; Arnold 1988, pp.42–7; Susan Frye, *Elizabeth I*, New York and Oxford 1993, pp.114–15

TB

5 Elizabethan Painters and Patrons

The career of Hans Eworth continued beyond 1570. During the first decades of Elizabeth I's reign we know from documents the names of various artists who worked in England (see e.g. Auerbach 1963), some of whom may have produced easel paintings. Connecting extant works with names in documents is, however, once again extremely difficult. Where associated documentary evidence, or even more rarely a signature, identifies the artist of a specific painting, the work can act as a touchstone allowing a tentative identification of other works by the same hand as, for example, in the case of the English-born George Gower's self-portrait (no.57) and his documented images of the Kytsons (nos.53, 54). In other cases a common hand can be identified in portraits with similar characteristics, yet the artist's name remains unknown (no.51).

This exhibition has brought to light previously unknown works by the Dutch artist Cornelis Ketel (nos.58–61) and a clearer picture has emerged of his English oeuvre. Ketel, who arrived in 1573 was one of many artists and, indeed, craftsmen of all kinds, who left the Netherlands to come to England at about this time. Some came for economic reasons, others as religious exiles. Ketel, like the Bruges-born Protestant Marcus Gheeraerts the Elder, Lucas de Heere, and Joris Hoefnagel did not ultimately settle. All returned to the Low Countries to continue their careers there.

Immigrant craftsmen who came to work in England settled in particular parishes, and especially in Southwark, where they were beyond the jurisdiction of the London Painter-Stainers' Company. Members of this company continued to struggle against such foreign competition, as well as to protest at infringement by the plasterers and heralds of their monopoly of painted work .

In 1575 the Painter-Stainers petitioned the Queen, complaining of a decline in the quality of painting, which they related to their impotence to control the general output. In 1581 they were granted a charter of incorporation, which gave them some of the powers they sought. Nevertheless, foreign artists who worked principally for the court, were able to continue to ply their trade.

While the majority of the easel paintings produced in England were portraits, allegories and narrative paintings were also made. That many of these were based upon foreign engraved designs can be conjectured in some cases (no.50) and demonstrated in others (nos.52, 64). Allegorical elements also begin to appear in portraiture at about this time (no.56). Another development is the depiction of female sitters in an advanced stage of pregnancy (fig.38). In an age when the production of a healthy male heir was perhaps a woman's finest achievement, such an image was a record of anticipated dynastic success. Death in child-birth was common, however, and such a portrait provided a record of one whose death might be imminent.

A form of painting that cannot be represented here is the painted memorial panel, of which a handful of examples have survived. At least one is known from the hand of Melchior Salabosch – the Cornewall monument which is signed and dated 1588 (see figs.39, 40). From his name evidently another Netherlander, Salabosch revealed some of his techniques to the herald painter John Guillim who transcribed them into his working notebook (Murrell, *Walpole Society*, vol.57, 1995, pp.7–8, 18–22). This newly published text provides a rare insight into contemporary painting practice.

While herald painters were principally occupied with illustrating genealogies, some must also have ventured into portrait painting, like William Segar (died 1633) who rose to be Garter King of Arms. Although praised as an artist by Francis Meres in *Palladis Tamia* in 1598, and known to have portrayed the Earls of Leicester and Essex (see fig.44), Segar's works are difficult to identify with certainty or tend to have survived in poor condition.

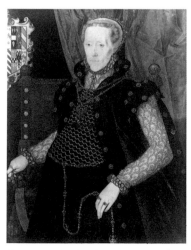

fig.38 British School, 'Mildred Cooke, Lady Burghley' 1562–3, oil on panel.
Courtesy of The Marquess of Salisbury

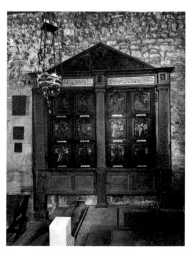

fig.39 Melchior Salabosch, Cornewall Family Monument (doors closed). *Private Collection*

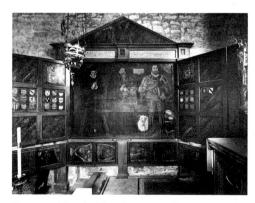

fig.40 Melchior Salabosch, Cornewall Family Monument (doors open). *Private Collection*

NETHERLANDISH SCHOOL

46 A Gentleman, traditionally called Vaughan of Tretower
1560

Oil on panel 98.4 × 72.4 (38¾ × 28½)
Inscribed 'REMEMBER THEM THAT
WACHE AND WARD FOR YOV THEIR
PRINCE AND REALME AND SVCHE AS
DOO WYTHE BLVDY SWETS OFTE
TYMES DESERVE TO GAYNE M.D.LX.'
around frame

PROV: …; a family descent has been
proposed from Gwyn Vaughan of Trebarried, whose daughter and heiress
Roach married John Harley, Bishop of
Hereford (died 1788); Edward Harley,
5th Earl of Oxford (1773–1848), whose
daughter Lady Frances Harcourt (died
1872) was the owner in 1866; by family
descent
Edward Harley Esq.

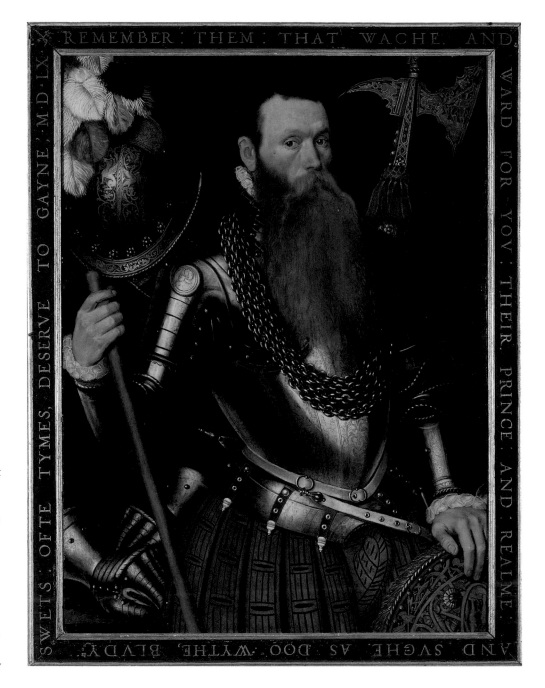

The sitter has traditionally been called
'Vaughan of Tretower, Warden of the
Marches'. According to Nevinson, the gold
chain and weapon identified the sitter as a
member of the royal bodyguard called the
Gentleman Pensioners, although the name
Vaughan does not appear on the surviving list
of Pensioners in 1560.

Recent research has merely deepened the
mystery. Mr A.V.B. Norman (letter of 7 March
1995) considers that nothing in the portrait
indicates that the sitter is a Gentleman Pensioner, as all the known depictions show
them carrying poleaxes, whereas the weapon
in the present portrait is a halberd. He also
observes that, with the exception of the arm-
pieces, gauntlets and the cuirass, which match
each other, each of the pieces is from a separate set of armour and each is quite differently
decorated. All are of north Italian manufacture or of north Italian style, and he wonders
whether some may be trophies, or gifts from
important patrons. The helmet is a 'comb
morion', while the sitter's left hand rests on a
round 'target' decorated in the north Italian
style of about 1550. The head of the halberd
is etched in relief and gilt against a blackened
ground. Intended for parade, rather than for
action, it is probably of German manufacture.
The red straps on the skirts are for attaching
the tassets or thigh defences; much of the
skirt area was once covered in overpainting,
and was revealed by cleaning in the mid-
1930s.

Dr David Robinson of CADW (Welsh Historic Monuments), who has been carrying out
research into Tretower Court, Powys, has

found no references to an official post of
'Warden of the Marches' (although Henry
Fitzroy had been made Warden-General of
the *Scottish* Marches in 1525). Information on
the Vaughans of Tretower at this date is scant,
but he notes that of the three sons of Sir
Thomas Vaughan – Roger, Henry (died 1561)
and Watkin – the first two inherited the
house successively. It then passed to Henry's
son Christopher, who was High Sheriff of
Brecknock in 1548/9 and died *c.*1573. It subsequently passed to his son William (dates
unknown), then to another William, High
Sheriff in 1591/2, who died in 1613. The
Vaughans had an important connection at

Queen Elizabeth's court. While a princess, her
steward had been Thomas Parry (or 'ap
Harry'), born *c.*1510, an illegitimate son of
Henry Vaughan of Tretower. At her accession
he was knighted, assuming, among other
honours, that of Controller of her household
in November 1558 until his death in December 1560 (see *Dictionary of National Biography*).

The sitter's heavy gold chain may have
been an official reward; its length and thickness indicate a very high value. This portrait
is of exceptional quality, but in the present
state of knowledge the artist remains unidentified. He or she was evidently Netherlandish-
trained, and demonstrates a preoccupation

with verisimilitude, right down to the wart on the cheek. As the sitter is also unidentified, there is some uncertainty as to whether the work was painted in England. The reproachful legend round the frame suggests an active military career that in 1560 the sitter considered to have been insufficiently rewarded.

A proposed provenance for the work is given above. In fact, the numerous branches of the Vaughan family frequently intermarried. The eventual heiress, in 1706, of the Vaughans of Hergest, Herefordshire, married into the Vaughans of Trebarried, 'descended from an illegitimate son of Sir Roger Vaughan of Tretower' (*Dictionary of Welsh Biography*, 1959, pp.996–7).

Cuthbert Vaughan, of the Hargest branch, became Edward VI's keeper of bulls, bears and dogs in 1553. Imprisoned briefly in the Tower under Mary I for marginal involvement in Sir Thomas Wyatt's Rebellion and for his staunch Protestantism, he was a distinguished soldier whose troops spent early 1559 in Berwick whence he wrote regularly complaining to William Cecil that he had spent the majority of his time in the wars but had not been rewarded by any gifts or lands. In 1560 he was leading twelve hundred English and five hundred Scots soldiers in the successful siege of the French at Leith in Scotland. Surviving correspondence also indicates that he was responsible for the care of a great deal of armour and weaponry for his company. Cuthbert Vaughan died in 1563 on active service in the expedition to hold Protestant Le Havre. A portrait of his widow, Elizabeth Royden, by Hans Eworth is in the Tate Gallery's permanent collection.

EXH: South Kensington Museum 1866 (306), *Art Treasures of the Midlands*, Birmingham 1934 (70, as 'Portrait of – Vaughan of Tretower, possibly Warden of the Marches'); *Exhibition of Treasures from Midland Houses*, Birmingham 1938 (49, as by Anthonis Mor); *British Portraits*, RA 1956–7 (16, as 'Vaughan of Tretower Warden of the Marches'); *Between Renaissance and Baroque*, City Art Gallery, Manchester 1965 (8, as 'Anglo-Flemish School, Vaughan of Tretower, Warden of the Marches')
LIT: Cust 1912–13, p.29, repr. (as 'Colonel Harry Vaughan' by Eworth); J.L. Nevinson, 'Portraits of Gentlemen Pensioners before 1625', *Walpole Society*, vol.34, 1952–4, pp.7–8, 12, pl.IIIA; David M. Robinson, *Tretower Court and Castle* (forthcoming)

KH

ATTRIBUTED TO STEVEN VAN DER MEULEN died 1563/4

47 Erik XIV of Sweden 1561

Oil on canvas 186 × 104 (73¼ × 41)
PROV: Presumed to have been presented to Queen Elizabeth I in 1561; …; Standish Collection, Marwell Hall, Winchester from whence bt in 1932 by Cecil Partridge, Duke Street, London; presented by D. Nasiell to Swedish National Collection 1932
Nationalmuseum, Stockholm. Gripsholm Castle Collection

Erik XIV (1535–1577) was the son of King Gustav Vasa of Sweden, whom he succeeded in 1560, at the age of twenty-seven. He was extravagant and capricious, but also highly educated, well-read and musical, and could himself paint and draw (Washington 1988, p.18).

In the summer of 1557, before either of them had succeeded to their thrones, he had been proposed as a husband for the English Princess Elizabeth (Perry 1990, pp.114–15). At the beginning of her reign he was again one of a number of foreign potential husbands under consideration. The others included Emanuel Philibert of Savoy and the Habsburg Archdukes Charles and Ferdinand. The latter's envoy in London, Baron Breuner, wrote back on 6 May 1559 'I have also learned that the Swedes have brought a likeness of their young King with them and shown it to the Queen, who praised the portrait highly' (*Queen Elizabeth and some Foreigners*, ed. Victor von Klarwill, 1928, pp.112–13). Strömbom suggests that Erik was painted by the Netherlander Domenicus ver Wilt in that year. Erik wrote passionate letters in Latin to Elizabeth. In the summer of 1560, and again in 1561, he was reported to be on the point of leaving for England, where his younger half-brother, Johan of Finland, had already been sent to plead Erik's case.

Early in 1561, the English merchant John Dymocke (c.1493–1585) travelled to Sweden. A wealthy cloth-exporter and ship-owner, he had been employed as a royal agent under Henry VIII and Edward, and was described as 'the queen's servant' (T.S. Willan, *The Muscovy Merchants of 1555*, 1953, p.94). He brought with him a 'holländsk Konterfegare' (Dutch painter) called Master Staffan who was granted a sitting by the King in March. Erik was so pleased with the resultant portrait that he gave the painter the considerable sum of 100 daler. Two Swedish envoys, Nils Sture and Nils Gyllenstierna, took the painting back to

England, where they presented it to Elizabeth in June 1561. She is said to have responded that if the King was as handsome as the portrait no one could resist him (Constable 1935, p.136).

In Gyllenstierna's accounts for the English journey there are several entries concerning royal portraits: for instance on 3 February 1561 he paid £6 for three 'portraits of the Queen' (presumably Elizabeth) (Strömbom 1933, pp.42–4).

On 13 September 1561, Bishop Quadra wrote from England to his master, the King of Spain, that Elizabeth was only encouraging Erik to prevent him from marrying Mary, Queen of Scots, mentioning that Dymocke had recently been in Sweden to sell jewels to the King (C.S.P. Spanish, *Elizabeth I*, pp.212–13; information from Diana Scarisbrick).

A smaller version of the present work, on panel and measuring 58 × 31 cm, thought by Cavalli-Björkman to be contemporary with it and also by van der Meulen, has been at Gripsholm since at least 1755. An eighteenth-century note on the back states that it was made in connection with Erik's proposal of marriage to a princess of Hessen-Cassel. It thus appears that Erik may have employed van der Meulen to make replicas for potential brides, the size depending on the importance of the match.

The present work, in the mainstream of Continental court portraiture, would have been an appropriate vehicle for promoting Erik as a suitable consort for the English Queen. His rich red and gold costume is in the Spanish fashion, as was customary for Swedish court dress. His majesty is indicated by his chain, sword and the crown, lying on a table covered in opulent green velvet embroidered with crowns and lions. Constable pointed out how the handling of the nose, eyes, beard and hands corresponds with that of the same features in the portrait of 'Lord Lumley', documented as being by 'Steven' in the Lumley Inventory (no.105).

A slightly more youthful, three-quarter-length portrait of Erik is in the Slottsgalleriet, Meiningen (Strömbom 1933, p.29, fig.26). It echoes the composition used by Antonis Mor for his portraits of Philip II of Spain, and re-used by 'Steven' in his documented portraits of 'Lord Lumley' and 'Lord Arundel'.

Erik was deposed and imprisoned in 1568 by his half-brother Johan, who had him put to death in 1577.

Little is known of van der Meulen's life,

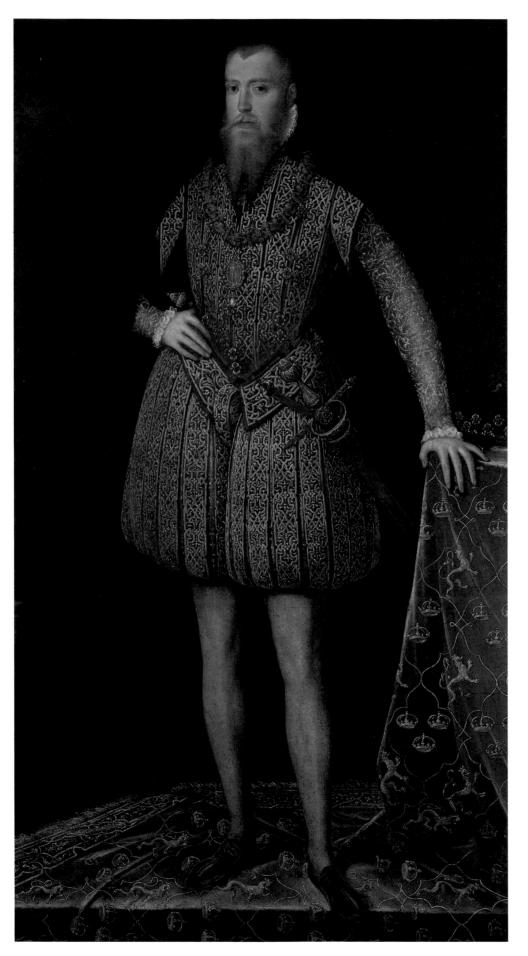

although Elizabeth Drey's recent discovery of his will, written on 5 October 1563 during a plague epidemic and proved on 20 January 1564, means that the oeuvre proposed for him (Strong 1969, pp.119–34) must be reduced. The first mention of him is as a pupil of Willem van Cleve in 1543 in Antwerp where he was admitted to the Guild of St Luke in 1552. By September 1560 he was in London, where on 22 June 1561 he is named in a list of members of the Dutch church. On 4 February 1562 he was naturalised, indicating that he was intending to make a career in England, and his will shows that his wife and children were living with him. Hill (1923, p.31) identi-fied him as 'the famous paynter Steven' whose portraits of Lord and Lady Lumley (private collection) bear the precise date 8 May 1563. Vertue apparently saw 'receipts of this Stevens' for these pictures and recorded that the painter's name 'Stephens' was inscribed on the portrait of Lord Lumley. This cannot now be seen, but both portraits have suffered from the vagaries of time. Lumley also owned portraits by 'Steven' of 'the last Earl of Arun-dell drawn twise' (one could be that now in the National Portrait Gallery, though it bears the date 21 December 1565) and of the Count of Egmont.

The handful of surviving portraits have in common a noticeably softened handling, and a rounded quality to the features, which are modelled with dark shadows. Similar charac-teristics are seen in the portrait of 'Catherine Carey, later Lady Knollys, Aged 38', which is dated 1562 (Yale Center for British Art, New Haven).

EXH: Tate Gallery 1969–70 (37); *Masterpieces from Gripsholm Castle: The Swedish National Portrait Collection*, National Gallery of Art, Washington, and travelling, 1988 (3)
LIT: G.F. Hill, 'Two Netherlandish Artists in England: Steven van Herwijk and Steven van der Meulen', *Walpole Society*, vol.11, 1923, pp.29–32; Sixten Strömbom, 'Erik XIV:s porträtt', *Nationalmusei årsbok*, 1933, pp.12–48; K.E. Steneberg, *Vasarenässansens porträttkonst*, Stockholm, 1935, pp.25–9; W.G. Constable, 'A New Work by "The Famous Paynter Steven"', *Burlington Magazine*, vol.67, 1935, pp.135–6; Strong 1969, no.68; Boo von Malmborg, *Svensk porträttkonst under fem århundraden* (Nationalmusei skriftserie nr.18), Malmö 1978, pp.29–30; Görel Cavalli-Björkman, *Dutch and Flemish Paintings, I, c.1400–c.1600*, Stockholm 1986, no.39; Maria Perry, *The Word of a Prince*, 1990, pp.152 (repr.), 154; Elizabeth Drey, *The Will of Steven van der Meulen* (forthcoming)

KH

BRITISH SCHOOL

48 Frances Sidney, Countess of Sussex 1570–5

Oil on panel 193 × 111.1 (76 × 43¾)
Prov: At the College by 1639 in the
Master's Lodge ('The foundresse's pic-
ture at large', inventory of 5 July 1639,
MR.31D f.6)
*The Master, Fellows and Scholars of Sidney
Sussex College, Cambridge*

Lady Frances Sidney (1531–1589) was the
daughter of Sir William Sidney, Edward VI's
Chamberlain, and aunt of the famous Sir
Philip Sidney. In 1555 she married, as his second wife, Thomas Radcliffe, subsequently 3rd
Earl of Sussex (?1526–83). A respected servant
of Queen Elizabeth, Radcliffe was Lord Lieutenant of Ireland from 1560 to 1564, Lord
President of the Council of the North, and
adversary of Elizabeth's favourite, Leicester.
Although individual members of the powerful
Sidney family were important literary and
artistic patrons, little is known of Lady
Frances or her activities in these fields. In her
will she left £5,000, together with some plate
and other goods, for the foundation of 'a
newe Colledge in the Universitie of Cambridge, to be called the Ladie ffrauncis Sidncy
Sussex Colledge'. This need not reflect any
particular scholarship on her part, but more a
desire to promote the particular branch of
Puritanism that the Sidney family, and others
at court, supported.

It has been suggested that the portrait,
dated *c.*1575 on grounds of costume, may have
been reduced on either side, which would
explain the slightly awkward placement of
the figure within the picture space. Lady
Frances was one of the Queen's Ladies of the
Bedchamber, and the black velvet French kir-
tle she wears, with the fur-lined trained gown
over it, was the height of fashion at court.
Such rich fabrics were often given by the
Queen as gifts to her servants. An elaborately
jewelled chain hangs down the front of her
skirt, terminating in a pomander, and she
holds a 'flea cravat' or 'tippett' made of sable
with a jewelled animal's head, intended to
attract the offending vermin. The picture has
been attributed to Steven van der Meulen
(Strong 1969, p.133) (see no.47), but is too late
to fit into his oeuvre, and does not compare
convincingly with the rather softer handling
of the two, badly damaged, portraits securely
given to him, 'Lord Lumley' and 'Lady Lumley' of 1563 (see no.47 and Strong 1969,
p.121). It is by a sophisticated Anglo-Nether-
landish painter, and the ambitious full-length

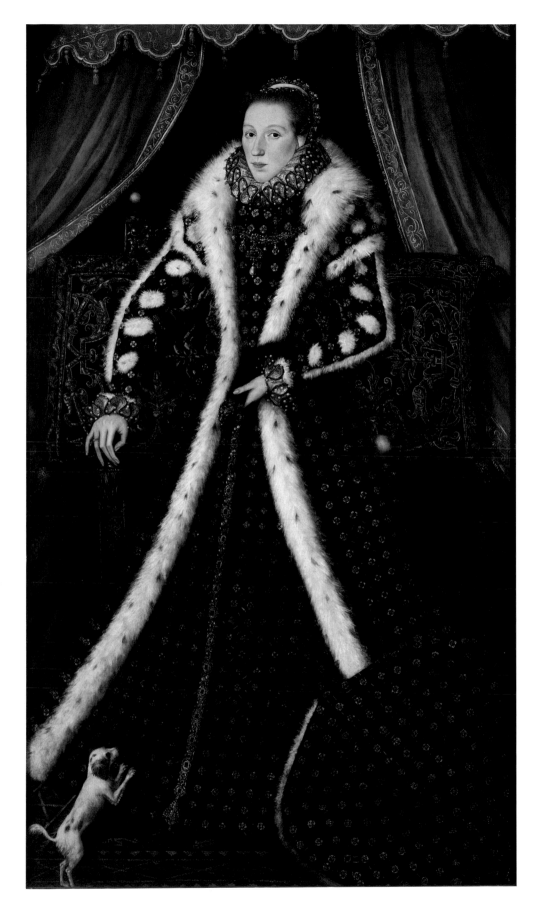

BRITISH SCHOOL

50 A Riddle c.1565–70

Oil on panel 40.5 × 61 (16 × 24)
Inscribed 'My faire Lady, I pray yove tell
Me | What And of whens, be yonder
thre | That cometh ovt of the castell, in
svch degre | And of ther dyscent, And
Natyvity' on a tablet in the tree, upper
left; 'Syr. the one ys My brother, of My
fathers syede the Trewthe, you to show
| The other by My Mothers syede. ys
My brother also | The thyred ys my
own sonne lawfully begat | And all be
sonnes to My husband That sleepes here
on my Lappe | Without hurt of lynnege
in any degre | Showe Me by Reason
how that May be', lower centre; the coat
of arms of William Cecil, later Lord
Burghley, top centre, below which is a
cartouche now illegible but on which
Gibson records the following inscription
'This Ryddle is dyvotyd to the | Right
honorable Syr Wylliam | Cecyll,
Knyght, Principall Secreatry to Her
Ma.t.ie (?)'
PROV: …; perhaps 1st Earl of Clarendon
(1609–1674); recorded under the title 'A
Riddle', in Lord Hyde's inventory of
1750, as in the Back Parlour at Corn-
bury, Oxon; thereafter by family descent
The Earl of Clarendon

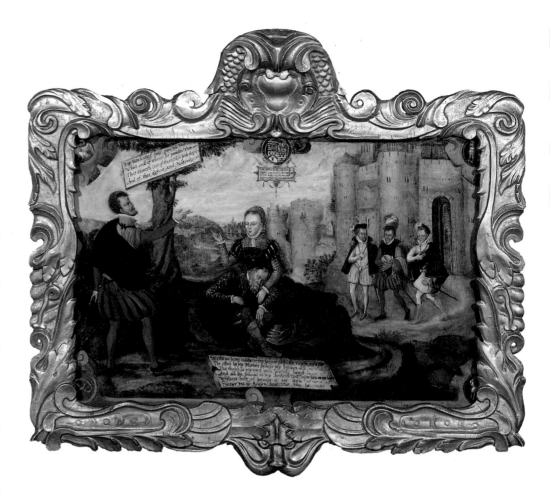

Three paintings on this subject survive, each
by a different hand, indicating the fascination
that it held for contemporaries. Whether it
was an abstracted puzzle, however, or based
on an actual family situation remains to be
resolved. In its combination of image and
texts – indeed the meaning lies primarily in
the words – it resembles contemporary prints,
and it is possible that a related print may in
due course be found.

This rare instance of a narrative image –
rather than a portrait – seems to be by one of
the Netherlandish painters working in Britain
at this period. It is perhaps closest to 'The
Return of Ulysses to Penelope' (see no.52,
here attributed to John Balechouse).

The man at the left gestures towards a seated lady in the centre, in whose lap sleeps an
old, bearded man. To the right three men, the
right-hand one much younger than the others, have emerged from a fortified building. A
painted strapwork border includes an emblem
in each corner: a pelican, top left; a gryphon,
top right; a unicorn, bottom right; and a knot
bottom left. Gibson, following Lewis, may be
correct in relating the subject to 'the Elizabethan fondness for puzzles and allegories'

and in answering the riddle as follows: 'The
lady's two half-brothers must have married
the daughters of her husband by a former
marriage, which made them sons (i.e. sons-in-
law) to her husband and brothers to the son
of her sister.'

The two other versions are later in date.
The one in the Fogg Art Museum, Cambridge, Massachusetts, datable by the costumes to the 1570s, includes a crude trompe
l'oeil architectural surround. The other, at
Knole, Kent, has figures wearing the fashions
of the late 1620s. All three versions include
the same two main texts with small variations,
and six figures – five men and a woman –
within a landscape, while fortified walls with
turrets, varying in design in each case, are
seen behind on the right.

As Gibson notes, the top centre inscription
dedicating this, the earliest version, to 'Sir
William Cecil', means that the work must predate Cecil's creation as Baron Burghley in
1571. While there is no clear reference to it in
early inventories at Hatfield House, it seems
likely that the painting must once have
belonged to him or to a member of his family.
The figures resemble less sophisticated ver-

sions of those seen in Joris Hoefnagel's 'Fête
at Bermondsey' of approximately the same
date (see no.62, possibly first recorded in
Robert Cecil, Lord Salisbury's collection at
Hatfield House as early as 1611). The border
with emblems is also a format used by Hoefnagel in the 'Allegory including a View of
Windsor' of 1571 (private collection), a highly
accomplished work, where the four corner
images represent the ages of Man.

A label on the back of the Fogg version
gives the following specific names for the six
figures: 'SIR THOMAS CAVE. KNT. of Stanford
co Northampton. [died 1558] 1st husband
(man reclining) = ELIZABETH DANVERS dau.
& coheir of Sir John Danvers of Waterstock
co. Oxon. [died 1572] (Lady seated) = JAMES
SKEFFINGTON (son of William Skeffington of
Fisherwick co. Staff. by Joanna Leveson)
(brother to Lady Cave's son in law)'; 'ROGER
CAVE of Stanford co. Northampton [died
1586] (one of the three men) = Margaret
Cecil married 1562. (sister of William, Lord
Burghley, Lord Treasurer of England); 'Mary
Cave, married to WILLIAM SKEFFINGTON of
Skeffington (son of Thomas Skeffington by
Mary Stanley) (one of the three men)'; 'Alice

Cave, married circa 1570 JOHN. SKEFFING-
TON of Fisherwick. co. Stafford [died 1604]
(son of William Skeffington by Joanna
Levesen) (one of the three men)'.

As this indicates, Lady Cave's second husband was the brother of the husband of one
of her daughters, and close kin to the husband of her other daughter. Unfortunately,
however, these complex relationships do not
fit the texts on the paintings, although the
family connection with William Cecil should
be noted.

The Fogg version can at present be traced
no further back than its sale in England in
1928, and it is not known when the third version entered the Knole collection. It is thus
not clear which is the picture 'on the same
subject' formerly at an inn at Epping Place
with the tradition 'that the strange relationship described … had occurred in the house
of Copt Hall, situated in that neighbourhood'
(see Lewis 1852, III, p.286). Again no such
links have so far been found in the family of
Sir Thomas Heneage, owner of Copped Hall
from 1564 to his death in 1595 (*Victoria County
History of Essex*, v, p.122, and see also no.122).

The frame is of the 'Sunderland' type,
which was used on many of the paintings
owned by the 1st Earl of Clarendon.

LIT: Lady Theresa Lewis, *Lives of the Friends and Contemporaries of Lord Chancellor Clarendon … 1852, III,
p.286; Robin Gibson, *The Clarendon Collection*, 1977,
pp.131–2, repr. no.145.

KH

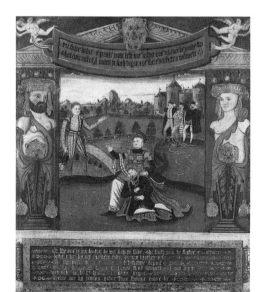

fig.41 British School, 'Allegory of a Fair Lady'
oil on panel. *The Fogg Art Museum, Harvard University
Art Museums, Gift of Robert Rantoul Endicott*

BRITISH SCHOOL

51 William Brooke, 10th Lord Cobham and his Family 1567

Oil on panel 91.7 × 120 (36⅛ × 47¼)
Inscribed 'AE 2, AETA I, AETA 6, AETATIS
SVAE 5 GEMELLI, AETA 4', the ages of the
children, above their heads; 'Nobilis.
hinc. pater. est. illinc. est optima. mater |
Circumfusa sedet. digna. parente. cohors
| Talis. erat. quondam. patriarchæ.
mensa. Iacobi | Mensa. fuit. Iobo. sic.
cumulata. pio. | Fac. Deus. ut. multos.
hæc. gignat. mensa. Iosephos. | Ger-
minet. ut. Iobi. stirps. renovata. fuit. |
Fercula. praeclaro. donasti. læta. Cob-
hamo. | Hæc. habeant. longos. gaudia.
tanta. dies. | Ano. DN. 1567' on the cen-
tral cartouche
PROV: possibly the 'piktur of my Lord
Cobham' in the 'great dyninge Cham-
ber' at Longleat in 1594; recorded there,
in the 'Blew Parlor', in 1718 ('Lord Cob-
ham a family Piece', inventory of 26
Feb. 1718, Thynne Papers LXXVII f.142r);
by family descent
*The Marquess of Bath, Longleat House,
Warminster, Wiltshire*

William Brooke, 10th Lord Cobham
(1527 1596) was Lord Warden of the Cinque
Ports, Lord Chamberlain of the Queen's
Household and Lord Lieutenant of Kent
1558–96. He is shown here with his second
wife Frances, daughter of Sir John Newton,
whom he married in 1559/60. The lady seated on the far left is usually identified as Lady
Cobham's sister Johanna, an inscription near
the figure (visible in 1913 but no longer
apparent) identifying her as such (Cust
1912–13). Frances held an important post at
court, as one of Queen Elizabeth's Ladies of
the Bedchamber. Her duties including making
up the Queen's clothes and advising, among
others, the formidable Bess of Hardwick (see
no.52) on suitable New Year's gifts for the
Queen (see index references to Lady Cobham
in Arnold 1988). The Queen was entertained
twice at Cobham Hall, in 1559 and 1573, and
the architecture in the background of the picture possibly reflects the style that the owners
adopted for the enlargement and improvement of the house.

Lady Cobham's several pregnancies neces-
sitated frequent absences from court, and her
six children, with their exotic pets, are shown
here – from left to right Henry, William,
Maximilian, Elizabeth (who married Sir
Robert Cecil – see no.119), her twin Frances,
and Margaret. A second version of the picture

(Devonshire Collection) includes another son,
George, born in 1568, but depicted not as an
infant but as a grown boy, with a tiny dog.

Wilson (p.366) observes that this image of
parents supervising children at mealtime corresponds with Erasmus's recommendations on
education – a meal was the occasion for a les-
son in manners and courtesy. A family meal
was the image of harmony and rightful order.
The animals have their own significance. Pup-
pies stand for Christian aptitude, and the
goldfinch is associated with the Christ child.
The parrot refers to a child's capacity for imitation and the monkey – which is being
restrained – to the mischief and sin inherent
in the human child.

The format of the picture – the children
seated round a table – is similar to works such
as 'Pierre Moucheron and his Wife, Isabeau
de Berbier with their Children in Antwerp',
attributed to Cornelis de Zeeuw and dated
1563 (Rijksmuseum, Amsterdam), although
that work is on a grander scale, with eighteen
children. Like the Cobham group, the table is
laid with pewter dishes and fruit, with the
family gathered rather stiffly and awkwardly
around; the ages of the children are inscribed
above them; and the daughters wear identical
jewellery. In the Cobham group each has a
gold jewel set with a ruby and a pendant
pearl, fixed at the neck. The jewel worn by
Lady Cobham, in the form of a ship, was a
favourite sixteenth-century design and Queen
Elizabeth had several in her collection. This
included one inherited from Catherine
Howard (BL Stowe MSS. 559 f.59b) which
was still in the Queen's possession in 1587
(see Arnold 1988, p.76).

Little is known of the artist of the picture –
for the moment called 'The Master of the
Countess of Warwick' on account of the portrait of that lady which is by a distinctive but
as yet unidentified hand. Several portraits are
stylistically similar to it, and all date from the
1560s. Common features include the angle of
the head, which is almost always presented in
the same way, a fresh, unsophisticated handling, and a lack of interest in the rules of perspective. A number of portrait groups, quite
rare in England at this date, have been attributed to the artist, most convincingly 'Edward,
3rd Baron Windsor and his Family', 1568
(Bute Collection), where instead of eating
fruit, the children are seated at a table playing
chess and cards.

The Latin inscription on the central cartouche can be translated as follows: 'See here
the noble father, here the most excellent
mother. Seated around them spreads a throng

worthy of their parents. Such was once the family of the patriarch Jacob, such the progeny gathered about the pious Job. God grant that the line of Cobham beget many offspring such as Joseph, and flourish like the seed of Job restored. Much has been given to the noble race of Cobham. Long may their joys endure.' (translation, Dr Keith Cunliffe, St Edmundsbury Council Museums). In fact the second son and heir, Henry (1564–1619), brought the family into disgrace through his arrest in 1603 on suspicion of involvement in a plot against the King. He was attainted and the peerage forfeited.

EXH: Leicester and London 1965–6, p.21–2; V&A 1980 (P9); Washington 1985–6 (25)
LIT: Cust 1912–13, p.35; R. Edwards, *Early Conversation Pictures*, 1954, pp.155–6; Strong 1969, p.110; Jean Wilson, 'The Noble Imp…', *Antiquaries Journal*, vol.70, Pt.II, 1990, pp.360–79; Susan E. James, 'A New Perspective on the Portrait of the Family of William Brooke, 10th Lord Cobham at Longleat House', unpublished article

KH and TB

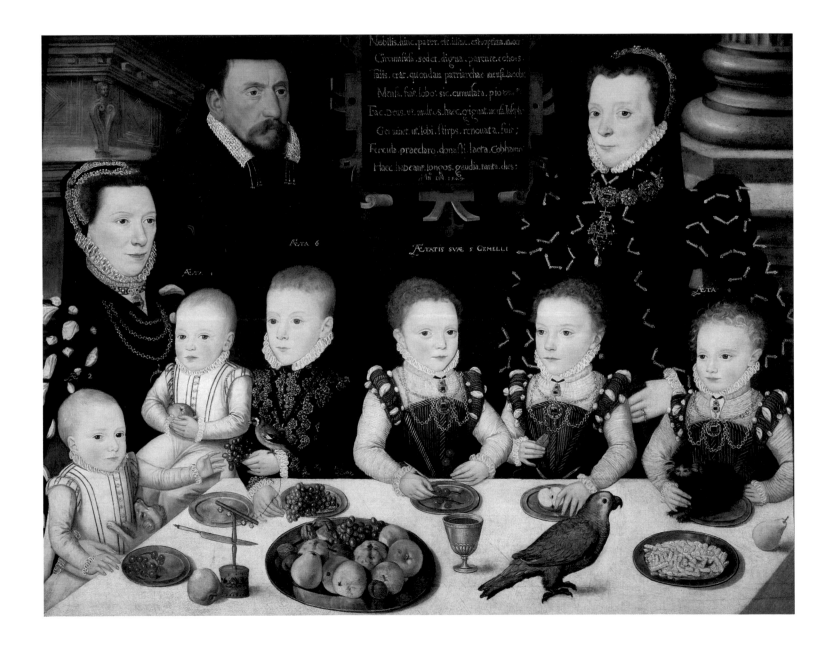

ATTRIBUTED TO JOHN BALECHOUSE died *c.*1618

52 The Return of Ulysses to Penelope 1570

Oil on canvas 85 × 103 (33½ × 40½)
Dated 1570 on entablature, upper left
PROV: Elizabeth, Countess of Shrews-
bury (Bess of Hardwick), thence by
descent
*Hardwick Hall, The Devonshire Collection
(The National Trust)*

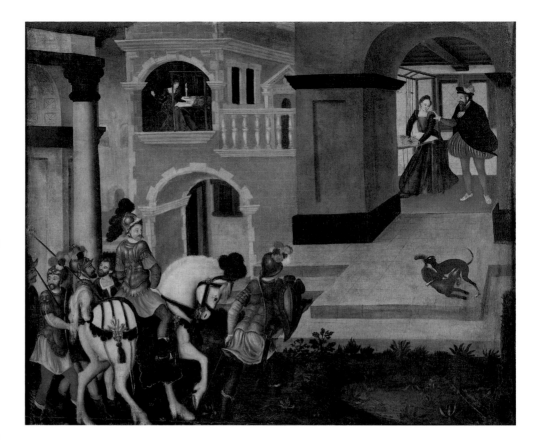

The subject of this painting has been the
source of endless speculation. In the 1601
Inventory of Hardwick Hall (compiled during
the lifetimes of its first owner and the possible
painter) it was probably the picture described
as 'Ulisses and Penelope', but subsequently it
was 'said to be the Earl of Shrewsbury coming to court Elizabeth of Hardwicke' (Walpole 1760), 'A painting of an Historical
Subject not known – date upon it 1570'
(Inventory 1792), and 'Domestic incident,
during the confinement of Mary Queen of
Scots at Hardwick' (Inventory 1811). Lord
Hawkesbury (1903) revived Penelope as the
possible subject and has been followed by
Girouard (*Hardwick Hall*, 1976, p.93) who suggested that Bess identified herself with Penelope, the faithful wife sometimes depicted
putting off potential suitors until her husband
Ulysses returned from the Trojan War. Most
recently, Alastair Laing (who kindly supplied
details from St John Gore's National Trust
catalogue card, together with his own additions) has pointed out that the supposed
Ulysses is shown not as a beggar but as a gentleman with a train of companions (the suitors
would have been inside the parlour), and that
the lady of the house and her maid are weaving by night (when Penelope *unravelled* her
work). He concludes that the subject is actually 'Tarquinius Collatinus Returning to Lucretia' (Livy, 1:57) and indicates that Bess had
already begun by 1570 to represent herself to
the frequently absent Earl of Shrewsbury as
the virtuous wife diligently working at her
embroideries. Significantly, Lucretia was the
subject of an appliqué wallhanging which still
survives at Hardwick. Bess named her
youngest daughter after the heroine.

The authorship of the picture has also been
disputed. Waterhouse suggested Hans Eworth,
Strong and Girouard an unknown Flemish
artist. The picture is newly attributed here to
John Balechouse, a painter of hitherto uncertain origin who worked for the Shrewsbury
family at Chatsworth from no later than 1578
until after the death of Bess of Hardwick in

1608. The grounds for this attribution are as
follows. The painting is not an original composition but represents the careful amalgamation of two woodcuts designed by Jost
Amman for a Lutheran Bible published in
Frankfurt in 1564: the arched structure on the
extreme left and the group of soldiers were
copied from Amman's illustration of the Triumph of Mordecai (Esther 6), while the rest
of the architecture including the stepped
plinth and the brawling dogs were lifted from
Amman's Nebuchadnezzar's Dreams (Daniel
2). Although Continental prints were widely
used in the decoration and furnishing of Elizabethan Chatsworth and Hardwick (see
Anthony Wells-Cole, *Barbarous and Ungraceful
Ornament: The Use of Continental Prints in Elizabethan and Jacobean England*, forthcoming) –
the combination of more than one print in a
single composition is characteristic of work
generally ascribed to Balechouse, particularly
the painted cloths still in the Chapel at Hardwick.

John Balechouse first appeared in the
Chatsworth accounts in May 1578 and at
Hardwick in 1589 (D. Durant and P. Riden,
The Building of Hardwick Hall, 1984, p.lxviii).
Despite his unusual Flemish-sounding sur-
name – he was more generally known in the

accounts as John Painter – Balechouse was
almost certainly French and may be identical
with the painter 'Jehan Baleschoux' recorded
in Tours in 1557. He perhaps arrived in England during the 1560s although how he came
to be employed by the Earl and Countess of
Shrewsbury remains a mystery.

LIT: Mentioned in manuscript inventories or lists in
1601, 1792, 1811, 1815 and 1933; also Walpole 1760,
p.30 (Paget Toynbee (ed.), 'Horace Walpole's Journals
of Visits to Country Seats, etc.', *Walpole Society*, vol.16,
1927–8); Duke of Devonshire 1845, p.213; Lord
Hawkesbury, 'Catalogue of the Pictures at Hardwick
Hall', *Derbyshire Archaeological Society Journal*, vol.25,
1903, no.269; F. Brodhurst, *Notes on Hardwick Hall*,
1903, p.95; C. Hussey, 'Hardwick Hall, Derbyshire –
III – The Seat of the Duke of Devonshire', *Country
Life*, 22 Dec. 1928, p.910; Waterhouse 1978, p.32; E.
Mercer, *English Art 1553–1625*, 1962, p.145; Strong
1969, p.41, fig.35; L. Boynton and P. Thornton, 'The
Hardwick Hall Inventory of 1601', *Furniture History*,
1971, VII, p.27; M. Girouard, *Hardwick Hall, Derbyshire:
A History and a Guide*, 1976, p.93 (illus.); M. Girouard,
Hardwick Hall, 1989, pp.70–1 (illus.)

AW-C

GEORGE GOWER died 1596

53 Sir Thomas Kytson 1573

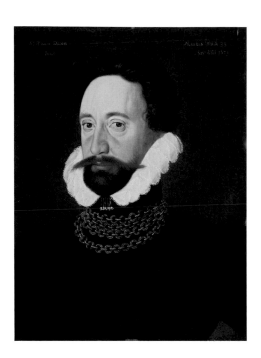

Oil on panel 52.7 × 40 (20¾ × 15¾)
Inscribed 'Ano dni 1573' t.l.; 'Ætatis
[s]uæ. 33' t.r.; 'S^R Tho-' left; 'Kitson |
Juner' right; both in a later hand copying earlier inscriptions
PROV: By descent with Hengrave Hall
through the sitter's daughter Mary,
Countess Rivers, and possibly recorded
in inventory of her goods dated 28 June
1644 (HMC Earl of Verulam, 1906,
p.42); noted at Hengrave c.1797 (BM
Add. MS 6391.f.191); Lady Rokewood
Gage, from whose estate bt with Hen-
grave Hall in 1887 by Mr Lysart; pur-
chased with Hengrave Hall by Sir John
Wood Bart 1897; Hengrave Hall sale,
Knight, Frank & Rutley and Arthur Rut-
ter Sons & Co, 23 Sept. 1952 (1648) bt
Tate Gallery
Tate Gallery, London. Purchased 1952

A payment in Kytson's surviving accounts for
1573 indicates that this and its companion
(no.54) were painted by George Gower (Gage
1822, p.200). Together with the self-portrait
(no.57), they form a nucleus upon which further attributions to Gower have been based.
In both cases, however, the subject faces in
the same direction, which suggests that the
pictures were not conceived as a pendant pair.
They may originally have been the same size,
but that of Sir Thomas has been cut down
subsequently.

The sitter (1541–1602) was the posthumous
son, by his father's second wife Margaret
Donington, of Sir Thomas Kytson 'the Merchant', who was a member of the Mercers'
Company and Sheriff of London in 1533, and
who had begun building at Hengrave,
Suffolk, in 1525. Kytson 'the Merchant'
amassed a sizeable fortune through trading in
cloth with the Low Countries. For his funeral
in 1540 payments to a painter called Thomas
Parys include 4s 4d apiece for decorating four
banners with respectively the Trinity, the Virgin Mary, St George and St Thomas (Gage
1822, p.114). His widow subsequently remarried, first Sir Richard Long, Gentleman of the
Privy Chamber to Henry VIII, and then the
Earl of Bath, kinsman to Mary I. Thus, the
fortune established by the elder Kytson
enabled his family to rise up the social ladder,
so that when the younger Thomas Kytson
inherited Hengrave Hall and other estates in

1561, he was able to live in some style. Following the death of his first wife, Jane Paget,
he married in 1560 Elizabeth Cornwallis, who
was in service to her godmother Margaret,
Duchess of Norfolk (see fig.31 on p.70). As a
result of his association with the Duke of
Norfolk, Kytson would later briefly suffer
imprisonment and both he and his wife were
listed at various times as recusants. In a letter
to the Duke in the 1560s (Gage 1822, p.176)
Kytson writes of his regular suffering with
'colic and the stone'.

The accounts kept by Kytson's steward for
'forren charges' in 1573 record an eventful
summer visit to the family's house in Cole-
man Street in London. In April, 2s 6d was
spent on painting the couple's coat of arms
upon their coach; in May 30s 4d was paid
'For the fascioning of my mr. and mres. armes
upon two basons and ewers', while the keeper
of the gardens at the Palace of Whitehall was
tipped 10s when Elizabeth Kytson visited. In
June there were medical expenses when she
fell 'sicke of the measells'. In August the well-
known payment of £6 5s 'To Gower, of London, painter, for v. pictures' is recorded (Gage
1822, pp.196–200).

Apart from the pair exhibited here, the
remaining three pictures commissioned from
Gower have not been identified; according to
the accounts the couple's young daughters
Margaret and Mary, and Elizabeth Kytson's
sister Mary Cornwallis, were with them in
London, but surviving portraits of these sitters are all later in date and only the one of
Mary Cornwallis (Manchester City Art Galleries) seems definitely to be attributable to
Gower.

In August 1578 the Kytsons entertained
Queen Elizabeth twice at Hengrave (Gage
1822, p.180) where, according to Thomas
Churchyard, 'the fare and banquet did so
exceed a number of other places, that it is
worthy the mention. A show representing the
fayries, as well as might be, was there seene;
in the which show a riche jewell was presented to the Queen's Highness' (cited Gage 1822,
p.180). The Queen knighted Kytson during
her visit.

Music was an important part of life at Hengrave. There was a permanent band of musicians, and the names of the composers
Edward Johnson and, later, John Wilbye,
appear in the Hengrave papers (David C.
Price, *Patrons and Musicians of the English Renaissance*, Cambridge 1981, pp.71–83). So, too, do

numerous records of the purchase and repair of instruments, many of which are specifically listed in an inventory of the Hall dated 29 March 1603 (Gage 1822, pp.23–5). Both Sir Thomas and his wife evidently played the lute, and their children were taught to sing and play various instruments.

Kytson died on 28 January 1602 at Hengrave, where his spectacular freestanding canopied monument shows him dressed in armour between the effigies of his two wives.

EXH: Tate Gallery 1969–70 (95)
LIT: John Gage, *The History and Antiquities of Hengrave*, 1822, p.40 as 'Sir Thomas Kytson the younger, three quarters, on pannel, 1573.'; E. Farrer, *Portraits in Suffolk Houses (West)*, 1908, p.178, no.26, repr.; J.W. Goodison, 'George Gower', *Burlington Magazine*, vol.90, 1948, pp.261–4, pl.22; Mary Chamot, *British School: Concise Catalogue,* Tate Gallery 1953, p.86; Strong 1969, no.111; Waterhouse 1988, p.109

KH

GEORGE GOWER

54 Elizabeth Cornwallis, Lady Kytson 1573

Oil on panel 67.9 × 52.1 (26¾ × 20½)
Inscribed 'ANᵒ ÐNI 1573 | ætatis suæ 26' t.l.; 'LADY KITSON' upper left, in a later hand
PROV: As for no.53 (1649 in Hengrave sale of 1952)
Tate Gallery, London. Purchased 1952

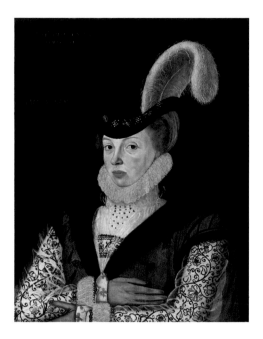

Elizabeth Kytson, born c.1547 according to the inscription on her portrait, was the daughter of Sir Thomas Cornwallis of Brome Hall, Suffolk. Her godmother was the Duchess of Norfolk, from whose house at Kenninghall, Norfolk she was married on 15 January 1560 to Thomas Kytson (Gage 1822, p.175), becoming his second wife (see no.53).

Of their three children, a son, John, died in infancy in 1562. Their elder daughter Margaret married Sir Charles Cavendish of Welbeck, a son of Bess of Hardwick (see no.52), in 1582 but died in childbed the same year. In 1583 their younger daughter, and eventual heiress, wed Thomas Darcy of Chich, later Earl Rivers, although this unhappily married couple separated in 1594.

With her husband, the steadfastly Catholic Lady Kytson was indicted for recusancy in 1588, and a decade later seems for some time to have been imprisoned for her religion (Gage 1822, pp.183–4). She died on 2 August 1628 and is buried at Hengrave with Sir Thomas. A fine head-and-shoulders portrait dating from about ten years before her death (Sotheby's 21 July 1943 (84)) shows her wearing a cross-shaped jewel, her expression as formidable as that captured by Gower.

In her portrait by Gower, Lady Kytson wears the bright colours that began to become fashionable at the end of the 1560s. Her sleeves, beneath gauze oversleeves, are embroidered with popular floral motifs: roses, honeysuckle and carnations. As she is wearing rather than carrying her gloves, she is presumably dressed for outdoors, as indicated also by her tall, masculine hat with its jewelled band and linen undercap. Recent cleaning has revealed its true shape, as well as Gower's subtle depiction of the fur collar of her sleeveless red gown.

EXH: Tate Gallery 1969–70 (112); V&A 1983 (62)
LIT: John Gage, *The History and Antiquities of Hengrave*, 1822, p.40 where inaccurately identified as of Thomas Kytson's first wife 'three quarters, on pannel aetatis suae 26'; E. Farrer, *Portraits in Suffolk Houses (West)*, 1908, no.24; J.W. Goodison, 'George Gower', *Burlington Magazine*, vol.90, 1948, pp.261–4; Mary Chamot, *British School: Concise Catalogue*, Tate Gallery, 1953, p.86; Jane Ashelford, *Dress in the Age of Elizabeth I*, 1988, pp.24–5; Arnold 1988, pp.201–2

KH

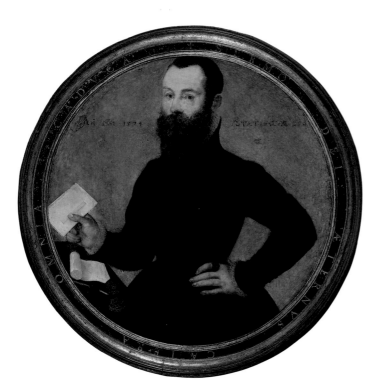
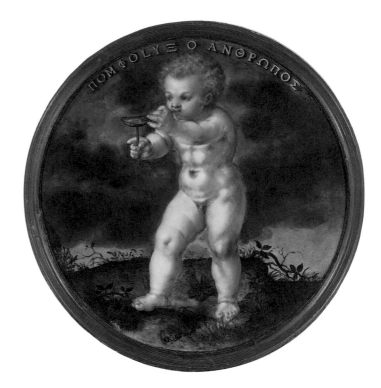

CORNELIS KETEL 1548–1616

55 A Man of the Wachendorff Family 1574

Oil on panel (both sides) diameter 43 (16½)
Inscribed on front 'AN° DNI 1574' and 'AETATIS SVAE 35 | CK' at either side of head, and 'SERMO DEI AETERNVS CAETERNA OMNIA CADVCA [The Word of God is eternal, all else is fleeting]' around frame; on reverse 'ΠΟΜΦΟLYE O ANOPΩπOE' [Man's life is like a bubble] and 'CK Inv.et.pin.' bottom centre
PROV: …; bt from unnamed art dealer by Zacharias Hackenbroch, Frankfurt am Main; Adolf Lapp Rottmann, Frankfurt am Main; Mr and Mrs de Bruyn-Van der Leeuw, Muri (Berne) 1929, by whom bequeathed to the Rijksmuseum, Amsterdam, 1961
Rijksmuseum, Amsterdam

Born in Gouda, Ketel trained there with his uncle, working in 1565 with Anthonie Blocklant in Delft. He completed his training in Paris and at Fontainebleau, but was prevented from going on to Italy by a French decree of 1567 that forced all visitors from Spanish territories to return home. In 1573 he arrived in London, initially staying with a friend of his uncle, the sculptor William Cure.

Ketel's friend and biographer Karel van Mander records that Ketel's first clients in England were the merchants of the German Steelyard, and the arms shown on the lid of the watch on the tabletop reveal that the sitter is a member of the Wachendorff family (arms distinguished by Dr Hessel Miedema, and their identity confirmed by Timothy Duke, Chester Herald). A letter of 22 September 1575 from Adam Wachendorff and bearing the same seal has been found by To Schultung in the Hanse Archive, Cologne (Kölner Inventar no.3, A.106.26). The Steelyard in Upper Thames St was the London trading centre of the merchants of the Hanseatic League. They had special trading privileges and kept apart from Londoners, maintaining their own lifestyle behind its walls, where women were not allowed. Forty years earlier, Holbein had portrayed clients in the Steelyard, many of whom had come from Cologne. The German traveller Lupold von Wedel recorded finding his interpreter, 'John Wachendorff born in Cologne' at the Steelyard in 1584. A Constantyne Wachendorff is recorded in London in 1598–9.

The Secretary of the Steelyard was Adam Wachendorff and his will dated 27 February 1591 suggests that he could be the individual portrayed (PRO PROB 11 77/28, information Timothy Duke). A bequest to his laundress indicates that he had been living in London for at least fifteen years. His remaining property was to be divided between his brothers: three-quarters to Constantyne, his executor, and a quarter to John. The only other beneficiary was his servant Henry [?D]amstorffen, to whom he left his books 'for that his brethren have no use for them', which implies that Adam was the only scholar.

The circular portrait – a form also employed by Holbein – may perhaps have been favoured by German clients. They seem to have been the painted equivalent of the medal, arising originally out of an Italian humanist interest in the portraiture on antique coins. Rowlands (1985, p.78) points out that the earliest examples are a pair of roundels by Lucas Cranach of Martin Luther and his wife, which survive in a number of versions of 1525–6. Holbein painted a roundel portrait of Erasmus, and a larger circular image, on a square panel, of Erasmus's 'Terminus' device which had previously appeared on the reverse of Quentin Metsys's Erasmus medal.

The present, double-sided portrait is evidently in the same tradition, and the inscriptions, in Latin and Greek, suggest that Wachendorff was a man of learning. His own portrait includes in modest form some of the accessories of a man of business also included in Holbein's Steelyard portraits, such as that of 'Georg Gisze' (fig.21 on p.35) – letters, pen, inkwell, signet ring and watch. The watch is a reminder of the transience of life, which is also the theme of the image on the reverse side. There, before a stormy sky, a naked putto on a sparsely planted rock prepares to blow a bubble out of a mussel shell on a stick. This side is painted in a considerably looser style than the other. Ketel has chosen to sign each side in monogram. Stechow traces the origins of the theme 'man's life is like a bubble' back through Lucian to Marcus Terentius Varro in *De re rustica*, 36 BC, and identifies the author responsible for its revival in the Renaissance as Erasmus, in his *Adagia*, published in 1500.

To Shultung observes that the painting has a double frame, the profiles of which are different for each face and also wonders whether the reverse of the painting, painted in such a free manner, may be of a later date. Ketel's earliest English portraits show the influence of Holbein, his later ones are freer in style.

She adds that Ketel was unable to find patronage in England for his allegorical paintings, (no.61), and in 1581 left for Amsterdam, perhaps because his painterly style did not really suit English taste. In Holland he introduced the life-size, full-length portrait form for wealthy middle-class sitters, an iconographic novelty that suited their aristocratic pretensions. This burgher-elite was receptive to his complex allegories accompanied by poems, none of which has survived. Around 1600 he experimented with painting without brushes. Although many of his works are lost, Ketel played an important part in the development of Dutch portrait painting. He lived in Amsterdam, but had close connections with the artistic and literary circle around Karel van Mander in Haarlem, which influenced his work. He was paralysed by a stroke in 1613.

EXH: *Ausstellung von Meisterwerken alter Malerei aus Privatbesitz. Vorläufiges Verzeichnis*, Frankfurt am Main 1925 (119); *Dutch Art 1450–1900*, RA 1929 (43); *Katalog Ausstellung*, Kunstmuseum, Bern 1943, pp.49–50 (43); *Drie Eeuwen Portret in Nederland 1500–1800*, Rijksmuseum, Amsterdam 1952 (75); *Kunst Voor de Beeldenstorm*, Rijksmuseum, Amsterdam 1986 (338)
LIT: W. Stechow, 'Cornelis Ketels Einzelbildnisse', *Zeitschrift für bildende Kunst*, vol.63, 1929–30, p.202; Wolfgang Stechow, 'Homo Bulla', *Art Bulletin*, vol.20, no.2, June 1938, pp.227–8; R. Wittkower, 'Death and Resurrection in a Picture by Marten de Vos', in *Miscellanea Leo van Puyvelde*, Brussels 1949, p.118; *Bulletin of the Rijksmuseum*, 1961, nos.2–3, pp.47, 64–5; E. de Jongh, *Zinne- en minnebeelden in de schilderkunst van de zeventiende eeuw*, 1967, p.81–2; B. Haak, 'De vergankelijkssymboliek in de 16° eeuwse portretten en 17° eeuwse stillevens in Holland', in *Antiek*, vol.1, no.7, Feb. 1967, p.30; Strong 1969, no.98; *All the Paintings of the Rijksmuseum*, 1976, no.A4046. On Ketel: B.A. Heezen-Stoll, *Cornelis Ketel, uytnemende schilder, van der Goude ...*, Delft 1987, pp.7–12, reviewed by To Schulting, *Oud Holland*, vol.103, 1989, p.54; Miedema 1994, pp.357–78; To Schulting 'Cornelis Ketel en zijn familie: een revisie', *Oud Holland*, vol.108, 1994, no.4, pp.171–207

KH and TS

BRITISH SCHOOL

56 A Gentleman of the Delves Family, Aged 40, probably Sir George Delves 1577

Oil on panel 218 × 133.8 (85⅞ × 52⅝)
Inscribed 'ALTRO NO[?N] MI VAGLIA. CHE, A[MOR], | [?E] FAMA.' [that is, 'I prize only love and fame'] t.l.; 'TH[E].COVRT.WHOES.OVTWRD.SHOES | SET[S].FORH.A.WORLD.OF.IOYES | HA[E]TH.FLATTRED.ME.TO.LONG | TH[A]T WANDRED.IN.HER.TOYES | W[H]EAR.SHOVLD.THE THIRSTI DRINK | BVT.WHEAR.THE.FOVNTAIN.RON | THE HOEP OF SVCH RELEEF | H[A]ETH ALMOST ME.VNDON' upper right; 'THE.WARS.HAETH.WAST.MI.WEALT[H] | AND.BROGH.MI.YOVTH.IN.CAER | AND.TIME.CONSVEMD.BY STEALTH | AS.TROETH.CAN.WEL.DECLAER | WHEARIN.I.SOGHT.FOR.FAEM | OR.AT.THE LEAST.SOM.GAYN | IN.FINE.MY.HOEL.REWARD | WAS NOGHT BVT WOE AND PA [IN]' bottom centre; 'ANNO DNI | 1577' and 'AEtatis Suae | 40' lower left; 'DEFY FORTVNE' on pennant on helmet
PROV: Presumably by descent in the Delves (latterly Delves Broughton) family, Doddington Hall, Cheshire, from whence purchased (in the 1950s?) by Mr Langley, bookseller, 32 Watergate, Chester; bt Walker Art Gallery, Liverpool 1956
Trustees of the National Museums and Galleries on Merseyside (Walker Art Gallery, Liverpool)

This previously unpublished, and newly conserved, portrait is of exceptional quality. Surviving English full-length portraits of this date are rare. Cornelis Ketel is one of the few artists known to have been working here on this large scale (e.g. 'Sir Martin Frobisher', Bodleian Library), but the technique used in the present picture differs significantly from that noted in his other English works (see no.55, and pp.108–12).

Although the picture appears to have been trimmed by about one and a quarter inches at either side, the male figure was always placed at the centre. Among the pieces of armour at his feet is a pennant which bears the arms and motto of the Delves family of Doddington, Cheshire. Surviving records of this family are extremely incomplete and when the painting was acquired it was assumed that the subject was the head of the family in 1577, Henry Delves. While Henry's year of birth is

unknown, evidence now suggests that he was younger than the inscribed age of forty at the time this painting was executed.

A more likely candidate is Henry's uncle, George Delves. While his birthdate, too, is unknown, his career both at Queen Elizabeth's court and as a long-serving soldier could connect him with the inscriptions, which express a weariness both of court life and of war, both of which have failed to give reward.

George Delves was serving in Ireland perhaps as early as 1557 and captained a troop in 1561, by which date he had been appointed a Gentleman Pensioner to Queen Elizabeth. The role of this band of gentlemen, refounded by Henry VIII in 1539, was to guard the monarch. Delves's father had served the Earl of Rutland and the link was maintained, with Delves sending accounts of court gossip and parliamentary business back to the 3rd Earl in 1571. Delves's return as a member of parliament for the Nottinghamshire seat of East Retford in 1572 was presumably due to the Earl. George Delves acquired lands and a castle, Shyan, in Ireland. Much of his time seems to have been spent in Ireland, where, in 1591, he was knighted by Sir William Fitzwilliam, the Lord Deputy and his former brother-in-law. Delves died in 1604 and was buried on 24 September in St Dunstan-in-the-West (see P.W. Hasler (ed.), *The History of Parliament: The House of Commons 1558–1603*, II, 1981, p.29).

In the present portrait the remarkable garden in the background is thought to be imaginary. It has not proved possible to relate it to surviving evidence of an early garden at Doddington, and no such gardens are recorded at this date in Ireland. The arrangement of rectangular compartments divided into beds, often based upon French models, was becoming standard in England at this date. The cloistered boundaries are probably wooden pergolas and such timber constructions are shown in J.A. du Cerceau's *Les Plus Excellents Bastiments de France* (1575–9). There were a number of parallels for the maze, including one at Nonsuch Palace by the 1540s (information from Christopher Taylor). Infrared reflectography reveals that the perspective and layout of the garden was laid down on to the ground layer in ruled lines and freehand sketching; apart from some observed in the facial features, this was the only underdrawing found in the picture.

The armour piled at Delves's feet is a feature found in earlier Venetian portraits, and can also be seen in Zuccaro's full-length sketch of the Earl of Leicester (no.99) made

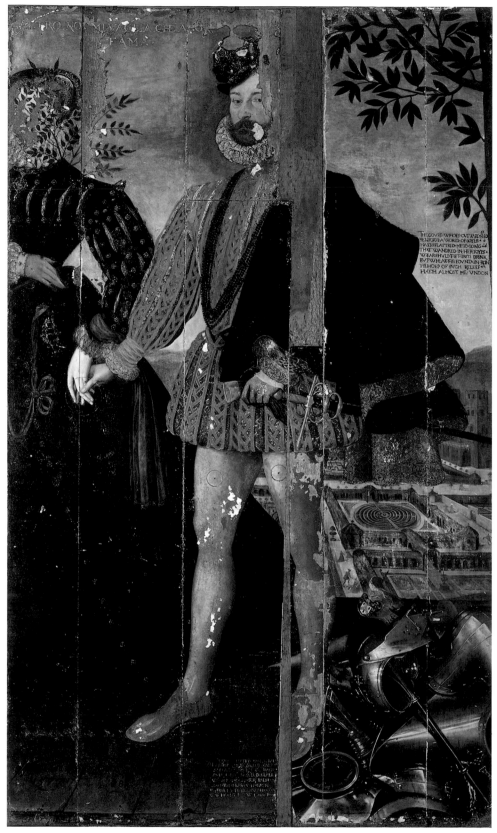

[Illustration shows the work before restoration was completed]

two years earlier. It is perhaps intended to appear to have been discarded as the sitter, dressed in civilian attire, repudiates an unrewarding military life. It includes a close-helmet for the tilt, a gorget, a left pauldron, a breast-plate with tassets and two gauntlets, all from a 'white' (that is, undecorated) suit of armour made in the Royal Workshop at Greenwich. The accompanying mace has a flanged head and steel shaft, with a plaited wrist cord. The little banner projecting from the helmet and showing the sitter's arms is unparalleled (information from A.V.B. Norman). There is also a broken lance.

Delves's costume is the height of fashion for the date, although Janet Arnold observes that the four strings of beads – apparently of glass and each bead tipped at the ends with gold – are most unusual wear for a man. Attached to his left wrist by a plaited cord is an enamelled ring with the legend 'NON DAPO[C…]' engraved within, perhaps a token of remembrance.

The leaves to the right are laurel (bay), while those on the branch held by the lady to conceal her face appear to be myrtle (information from Dr John Edmondson) which is an attribute of Venus and symbolises everlasting love, particularly conjugal fidelity. Thus Delves stands between the love and fame of the Italian inscription above.

The significance and identity of the female figure is not at present clear. George Delves's first wife was Christian, daughter of Sir William Fitzwilliam of Milton, Northants, and the widow of Sir Richard Wingfield who had died by June 1559. Neither the date of their marriage nor of her death are known but in March 1583 Delves, described as 'of Westminster', married again, to Anne Isley who brought him an estate at Bredgar, Kent. It is hard to decide whether Christian may have had any connection with the lady shown here in black with her face concealed. The figure wears a French hood, slightly old-fashioned by 1577, and a gown in the Italian style, its skirt primarily supported by a cone-shaped Spanish farthingale. She wears very specifically delineated jewels, including a pendant set with a cameo of a woman with a snake twined round each arm, who has been identified as either the goddess Ceres or the figure of Prudence (compare the jewel in no.28). Another jewel, attached to her skirt, is set with three large diamonds; Cupid with his bow is shown at the left and Psyche on the right (information on costume and jewellery from Janet Arnold).

The technical study made by Katherine Stainer-Hutchins shows that the work is constructed of six vertical boards (with three narrow later vertical interpolations), with a seventh – on which is painted Delves's head and collar – inserted above the third panel from the left. The difference in the preparation of the seventh panel is evident in X-radiographs: it has two ground layers. It is possible that the face was painted separately first, either because this enabled the artist to do it *ad vivum* more conveniently, or because the commission was subsequently rethought on a much more ambitious scale. The armour was among the last main features to have been put in; it is painted over finished flagstones and parts of the garden. A contemporary alteration was made to the sitter's age, which was originally given as thirty-eight.

LIT: Unpublished draft catalogue entry by Mark Evans and Alex Kidson, Walker Art Gallery, Liverpool; unpublished technical report, Katherine Stainer-Hutchins, MNGM Conservation file, Feb. 1995

KH

GEORGE GOWER died 1596

57 Self-Portrait 1579

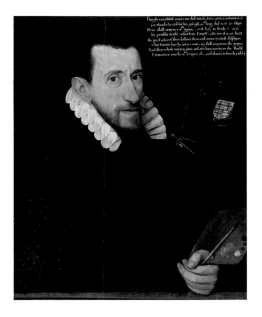

Oil on panel 56.4 × 49.6 (23¾ × 19½)
Inscribed 'Thogh yovthfull wayes me did intyse, From armes and uertew e[ke] | yet thanckt be God for his god gift, wch long did rest as slepe | Now skill reuyues wth gayne, and lyfe to leade in rest | by pensils trade, wherfore I must, esteme of it as best | The proof wherof thies ballance show, and armes my birth displayes | what Parents bare by iust re[n]owme, my skill mayntenes the prayes | And them whose vertew, fame and acts, haue won for me this shield | I reuerence muche wth seruyce eke, and thanks to them do yield' t.r.; and 'Ano dni 1579' on top edge of palette
PROV: …; recorded by Vertue c.1721 in the collection of John, 2nd Earl Fitzwilliam; thence by descent
Private Collection

This work is unique, for it is the only known surviving self-portrait in large by a British sixteenth-century artist. In their own self-portraits in miniature, neither Nicholas Hilliard in 1577 (see no.73), nor Isaac Oliver, c.1590–5 (see no.77), portrays himself with the tools of his artistic trade, and indeed Hilliard presents himself in a fashion hardly distinguishable from his aristocratic sitters. Gower, however, proclaims his status as an artist to be greater than his status as a gentleman by birth, a startling claim in England where a painter was still viewed as little more than an artisan. Like Gerlach Flicke (no.67), he depicts himself holding a brush and palette charged with paint in the left hand, while above, in the pans of a beautifully described metal balance, a pair of dividers is shown outweighing his family coat of arms. Above this allegorical device, an eight-line verse attests to Gower's personal pride in his professional skill, which he considers comparable to the military feats that had won his forefathers their status as gentlemen. 'Pensil' was the contemporary term for a brush.

George Gower was a grandson of Sir John Gower of Stettenham, Yorks. Neither his date of birth nor the circumstances of his training are known. His earliest extant works are the documented portraits of 'Sir Thomas Kytson' and 'Lady Kytson' of 1573 (see nos.53 and 54), painted in London. Those two and the present work have been used as the basis for reconstructing a wider oeuvre for Gower.

Gower portrays himself, austerely dressed in black and standing behind a ledge, holding a palette on which colours have been laid out in preparation for painting flesh tones. From the top these are: black, dark red (perhaps lake?), dark ochre, white, bright red (vermilion?) and a mixture of white and bright red. These largely echo the colours of his coat of arms above. A shrewd, rather careworn face returns directly the gaze of the viewer.

First mentioned by Vertue as 'a picture of Gower on bord. small picture with Armes & inscriptions', it is not known how or when the painting entered the Fitzwilliam collection, but when in 1948 Waterhouse identified fully the quarterings in the coat of arms, he suggested that the similarity of the fourth quartering to the Fitzwilliams' own arms might have led to its acquisition under the misapprehension that Gower was a family connection.

In 1581 Gower was appointed Serjeant Painter to the Queen, and his name appears in the royal accounts in connection with decorative and heraldic painting from 1581 to 1596. The Serjeant Painter's duties were generally of a decorative nature: Gower's official commissions included painting an astronomical clock (1584–5) and the lost great fountain topped with the figure of Justice (1591–2), both at Hampton Court, and decorating coaches and furniture for the Queen. As Auerbach points out, he was the first artist known to specialise in portraiture to be appointed to the Serjeant Painter's post, and there is no evidence that portrait-painting had been any part of his predecessors' duties.

A surviving draft patent of 1584 granted

Gower the monopoly of all painted and engraved portraits of the Queen, while allowing Nicholas Hilliard the monopoly of her portraits in miniature; Gower was also given exclusive rights in the purveying of art materials as part of his function as Serjeant Painter. In spite of this, it has not proved possible to identify with confidence any portraits of the Queen painted by him. However, a patent of 1589, under which she granted him various properties, indicates that she certainly considered he merited special reward. From 1585 until his death in August 1596, Gower lived in the London parish of St Clement Danes.

EXH: *Late Elizabethan Art*, BFAC 1926 (12); *Between Renaissance and Baroque*, Manchester City Art Gallery 1965 (125); Tate Gallery 1969–70 (100)
LIT: Vertue II, p.78; Kennett Gibson, *History of Castor*, compiled 1769, publ. by R. Gough and J. Nichols, 1800, with their own additions; *Gentleman's Magazine*, vol.72, 1802, p.59; ibid., vol.77, 1807, p.511; J.W. Goodison, 'George Gower, Serjeant Painter to Queen Elizabeth', *Burlington Magazine*, vol.90, 1948, p.263; E.K. Waterhouse, 'A Note on George Gower's *Selfportrait* at Milton Park', *Burlington Magazine*, vol.90, 1948, p.267; Auerbach 1954, p.108; NPG 1969, I, pp.167, 170, II, no.113 (illus.)

KH

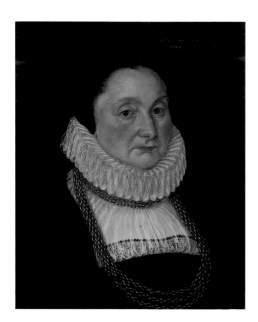

CORNELIS KETEL 1548–1616

58 Alice Smythe, née Judde
1579/80

Oil on panel 46.8 × 39 (18½ × 15⅜)
Inscribed 'Ao DNI 1579 | AETATIS 46', t.r.
PROV: Thomas Smythe; and from him by family descent to the Lords Strangford, Henry James Baillie PC MP, and Sir Charles Grant KCSI; by family descent
Private Collection

This and the following two paintings are from a previously unknown set of portraits painted by Ketel in England. The sitters are the family of Thomas 'Customer' Smythe (1522–91), the collector of customs duties in the Port of London, and one of the leading commercial figures of his day. No comparable contemporary group of English paintings, of such extent and quality and by a securely identified artist, has survived.

Although none of them is signed, Ketel's characteristic technique is evident (see pp.238–9). The attribution to Ketel was first suggested by Dr Malcolm Rogers, who noted that the inscriptions began with the artist's very individual serpentine 'A'.

Smythe evidently commissioned head-and-shoulders portraits of himself (now known only through a later copy), his wife Alice, and a number of their children, twelve of whom lived to adulthood. Portraits of their sons Thomas (born 1558), Richard (bapt. 1 December 1563) and Robert (see no.59) and their daughters Ursula (bapt. 27 May 1555), Joan (see no.60), and Alice (bapt. 21 December 1564) remain in the collection of their descendants. Portraits of their eldest son John (bapt. 15 September 1557) (Yale Center for British Art, New Haven) and daughter Mary (bapt. 20 June 1554) (private collection) have recently also been identified.

The couple's firstborn son Andrew, born 1556, had died young; it is not known whether the remaining children, Henry (born 1559/60 or 1562/3), Katherine (born 1561), Simon (born 1570), or Elizabeth (born 1572), were ever portrayed.

Each portrait bears the date 1579 and the age of the sitter. 'Aetatis 46' can mean either 'aged forty-six' or 'in her forty-sixth year'. Comparing the ages with the known dates of birth suggests that the portraits were made at the very end of the old legal year of 1579 (that is, up to 24 March 1580).

The able son of a Wiltshire clothier and

mill-owner, Smythe's career was much advanced by his marriage in about 1554 to Alice, daughter of the great Sir Andrew Judde (c.1495–1558) by his first wife Mary Mirfyn. Lord Mayor of London in 1550, Judde was Master of the Skinners' Company six times, a founder of the Muscovy Company and of Tonbridge School. Smythe was able to develop his contacts within Judde's business circle which included trade with Spain, Russia and the Guinea coast of Africa. When Judde died in 1558, Alice inherited an extensive fortune and a number of properties, particularly in Kent.

In the same year Smythe became collector of the subsidy of tonnage and poundage on all wares brought into the Port of London. From 1575–82 he built a great new stone house at Corsham, Wiltshire, but his principal country home was Ostenhanger (now Westenhanger) in Kent. Smythe was an investor in overseas trading ventures and in mining enterprises. Indeed the Latin inscription on his ambitious monument in St Mary's Church, Ashford, Kent, singles out his 'cherishing those who professed the true religion, promoting literature and, for the advantage of the State fitting out ships for long voyages, discovering new countries, and opening copper mines'.

Smythe might have encountered Ketel in any of a number of ways: possibly through his twenty-year business connection with Judde's friend Sir Thomas Gresham (see no.18) whose cousin William also sat to Ketel in 1579, the year of his death (see Strong 1969, no.101). Moreover, the two were neighbours, since Ketel owned property in Bishopsgate Street near Smythe's mansion, which extended from Gracechurch Street to Philpot Lane. They may well have met when in 1577 Ketel carried out a major commission for nineteen portraits for the Cathay Company, portraying, among others, Sir Martin Frobisher (Bodleian Library) and the two Eskimos that he had brought back from his expedition in search of a north-west passage to China (these portraits are now lost). Records for this commission show that Ketel was charging £5 for a full-length and £1 for a head (see *Proceedings of His Majesty's Commissioners on the Public Records of the Kingdom, June 1832–August 1833*, ed. C.P. Cooper, 1833, pp.75 and 560). Smythe was associated with many of the Cathay Company members. According to van Mander (Miedema 1994, p.358) Ketel was commissioned to paint the Queen the following year, 1578, a portrait that apparently has not survived; he would thus no doubt have appealed to an ambitious City man like Smythe.

The head-and-shoulder images of the Smythes fill and in some cases burst from the picture area, the faces richly modelled with pearly highlights over a dark grey ground, more animated, more three-dimensional than those in contemporary English portraits. The close-cropped composition with the head tilted back seems to have been originated by Antonis Mor (see no.18), and to have been developed by the Antwerp-based Adrien Thomaszoon Key (active 1568–89). More than Ketel's other English works, they presage the portraits he would produce on his return to the Netherlands (e.g. 'Dirck Barendszoon', 1590, Rijksmuseum, Amsterdam) where, his friend van Mander notes, his works were considered 'good likenesses'.

The Smythes' son Thomas, knighted in 1603, was, like his father and grandfather, much involved with overseas trade. He was appointed the first Governor of the East India Company and in 1604 travelled to Russia as special ambassador to the Tsar. He promoted voyages in search of the North-West Passage, and gave his name to 'Smith's Sound'; in 1609 he obtained the charter for the Virginia Company.

Although no private family papers remain, Thomas and Alice Smythe's married life seems to have been harmonious. The respect in which she was held by her family is surely indicated by how many of her children – seven – named their daughters after her. Alice is depicted wearing a heavy gold chain which will have been of great value; matching chains are worn also by her adult daughters Mary, Joan and Ursula. On her death in 1592 she bequeathed to Mary her best chain (see her will, PCC 42 Lewin).

Copies of this portrait and of that of her husband, both extended to three-quarter-length, and considerably later in date, also remain in the collection of their descendants. Alice Smythe was a major benefactor to her father's old Company, the Skinners', which owns a twentieth-century Ketel-derived portrait of her.

LIT: L.L.S. Lowe, 'Mr Customer Smythe', unpublished B.Litt diss, Bodleian Library, 1948; Karen Hearn, 'A Newly Identified English Commission for Cornelis Ketel' (forthcoming)

KH

CORNELIS KETEL

59 Robert Smythe 1579/80

Oil on panel 46.8 × 39 (18½ × 15⅜)
Inscribed 'Ao DNI 1579 | AETATIS 12'
t.r.
PROV: As for no.58
Private Collection

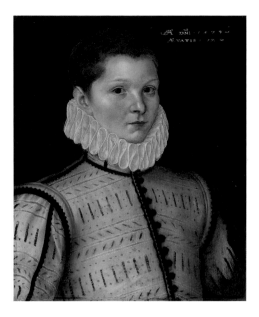

With nos.58 and 60, this is one of the Smythe family portraits painted by Ketel in 1579/80. Once again, Ketel's typical form of inscription, with its swirling capital 'A', is evident.

Van Mander recorded that in England Ketel portrayed 'great lords of the nobility, with wives and children' (Miedema 1994, p.358). Though never ennobled, Robert's father Thomas Smythe was at the height of his wealth and influence at the end of the 1570s; his commission for portraits of the members of a family was evidently of a kind familiar to Ketel. Another of Ketel's surviving English portraits is also of a teenaged boy, the three-quarter-length portrait of an 'Unknown Youth', signed and dated 1576 (Parham Park). The surface of the latter is rather abraded, but the influence of Hans Eworth, still a leading portraitist at the time of Ketel's arrival in England, is clearly seen. Three years later, in the Smythe portraits, Ketel uses a more direct observation and imparts greater animation to the features. The effect is one of vivid realism when compared with the shadowless icons of contemporary painters in England.

Little is known about Robert, the fifth son of Alice and Thomas Smythe. Like most of his siblings, he was baptised at Allhallows, Lombard Street, on 7 October 1567; he was dead by 1629 when his sister Elizabeth made her will. He married Ann, daughter and heiress of William Lynford, and lived in Highgate, at

that time a village north of the Cities of London and Westminster. Two children, John and Alice, are known. On the death of his mother, he supervised the disposal of the money that she left for charitable bequests including assistance for scholars at Oxford and Cambridge Universities, and for the provision of preachers.

A handwritten label on the back of the panel identifies the sitter as Richard Smythe. Richard was, however, sixteen in 1579 and his true portrait, inscribed with his correct age, has also survived in the family collection.

LIT: As for no.58

KH

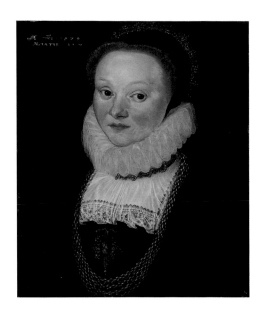

CORNELIS KETEL

60 Joan Fanshawe, née Smythe 1579/80

Oil on panel 46.8 × 39 (18½ × 15⅜)
Inscribed 'Ao DNI 1579 | AETATIS 19'
and in a later hand 'Johanna, Wife of
Tho. Fanshaw Esq.', t.l.
PROV: As for no.58
Private Collection

Baptised at Allhallows, Lombard Street, on 15
October 1560, the sitter was the third daugh-
ter of Alice Judde (see no.58) and Thomas
'Customer' Smythe, and the sister of Robert
Smythe (see no.59).

On 22 December 1578, the year before her
portrait was painted by Ketel, Joan had married as his second wife the lawyer and
Queen's Remembrancer Thomas Fanshawe
(1533–1600), of Ware Park, Hertfordshire.
Joan's stepson, Henry Fanshawe (1569–1616),
a scholar, lawyer, horticulturalist and later a
member of the circle of Henry, Prince of
Wales, was subsequently to marry her
younger sister Elizabeth (1572–1631). On the
death of his father he provided a home for
Joan, her daughters and stepdaughters. Joan
was the mother of eight children, of whom
only Thomas, William, Alice, Katherine and
Margaret lived to adulthood. She was buried
at Ware, Hertfordshire, on 30 May 1622.

Joan is portrayed, like her mother and sisters, in expensive black attire. Beneath a gauze
partlet can be seen the edge of her smock,
embroidered with a pattern of flowers and
stems in blackwork. In addition to the band
of gold biliments in her hood, a pearl and
gold necklace and her heavy multi-stranded
gold chain, she wears at her breast a remarkable jewel, perhaps a gift from her much-
older husband, composed of a cameo of a
helmeted head in profile set in enamelled
gold amid diamonds and rubies, from which
hangs a large pearl.

Ketel's animated and naturalistic portrayal
extends to the inclusion of a cyst or mole on
the lower lid of her right eye.

LIT: As for no.58

KH

CORNELIS KETEL

61 Fragment of an Allegory 1580

Oil on canvas 190.5 × 137.2 (75 × 54)
Inscribed 'CK. INVĒTOR | . ET . F 1580'
b.r.
PROV: Possibly the same as recorded by
van Mander in 1604 as bt in London by
Pieter Hachten, who presented it to Sir
Christopher Hatton; ...; bt at Butterfield
and Butterfield's, San Francisco, 25 July
1986 (4018, as School Hans von Aachen)
by Maxwell Galleries, San Francisco;
Sotheby's, New York 15 Jan. 1987 (23),
not sold
Delman Collection, San Francisco

This fragment, which was recently discovered,
today forms, together with the reverse of
no.55, the sole remnant of Ketel's rich production of painted allegories, described in detail
by van Mander in his *Schilder-Boeck* of 1604
(Miedema 1994).

There are various indications that this was
originally a larger work: the absence of cusp-
ing, or undulating threads in the tissue along
the borders, which is an after-effect of stretching it with nails on a frame; incomplete figures, caused by the cutting-down of the
canvas; the direction of the gaze of some figures, focused sideways on persons or objects
outside the present format. The work has
recently been restored, but some details of the
darkened background are hard to identify.

On the right is depicted a woman in a
white dress, holding a serpent, which is an
attribute of Prudence, in her right hand. She
is being bestowed with branches of laurel, the
symbol of victory, by a winged putto flying
above her. In front of her is a group of three
kneeling or crouching men, all nude, apparently bereft of their armour, which surrounds
them. This armour must be taken in the sense
of *spolia*, indicating their submission; armour
stands for the strength or force of the body.
The main male figure, heavily muscular, forms
a sharp contrast to the delicate Prudence. Sitting straddled as a victor on a second man, he
stands for Force, here in the more negative
sense of brute, uncontrolled strength, distant-
ly related to rage. In his turn Force has fallen
victim to Prudence, who is tying his hands
behind his back. The second man is trying to
protect his head with his hand or is making a
gesture of despair. To the left a third man is
kneeling, his hands crossed and bound, which
is also an attitude of submission.

The subject – virtue victorious – and the
year 1580 (not 1586 as recorded in the 1987
sales catalogue) agree very well with a passage

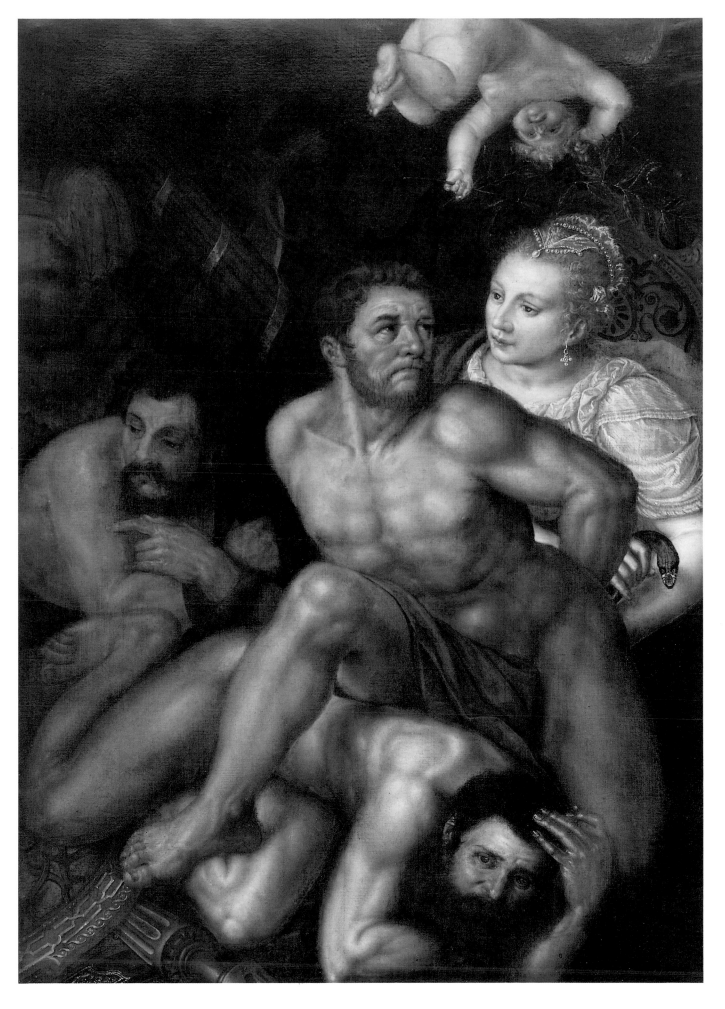

in Ketel's biography by van Mander: '[in England] he obtained many portrait commissions but none for histories towards which his spirit still ever inclined. Therefore he made a piece on canvas with more than life-sized figures with the symbolic representation of how Power is overcome by Wisdom and Prudence, that was bought from him by a respectable young man, an English merchant called Mr Pieter Hachten, who presented it to 'Sir Christoffel Hatten, who died as High Chancellor' (Miedema 1994, pp.358–9). Wisdom (and possibly other figures) is not represented here, but this may be due to the above-mentioned reduction of the canvas.

It is tempting to identify this painting with a work by Ketel on the same subject that is listed in two inventories of the collection of George Villiers, the 1st Duke of Buckingham, drawn up seven and twenty years respectively after his death. Unfortunately there is one drawback: the Duke's painting is given a smaller size, mentioned only in the list of 1648, a manuscript once in the possession of Brian Fairfax: 'Length 4 feet 6 inch, Breadth 7 feet' (137.2 × 213 cm). This given 'length' means that the figures cannot possibly be of life-size, as is related by van Mander. Two possibilities may be considered: either the Duke was the owner of a smaller copy, or Fairfax, or his editor W. Bathoe, a century later, misread the measurements in the original manuscript. The subject of the Buckingham painting seems to be the same as the one in no.61; the description of 1635 reads: 'A great Piece of divers men and women, being the virtues overcoming vice'; the 1648 version has: 'A large piece representing the virtues and vices, wherein there are several large figures'. This painting, which according to Fairfax was part of the collection brought over in 1648 to Antwerp to be sold there to sustain the young 2nd Duke in his exile, has left no traces in the notarial records of Antwerp that deal with this collection (Duverger 1991, 1992).

Stylistic characteristics of the Antwerp painter Frans Floris are easily distinguished in the headdress of Prudence. However, this influence was indirectly effected, by various channels. In the first place, Ketel's teacher Anthonie Blocklant was trained by Frans Floris. Secondly, Ketel spent some months at Fontainebleau, in company with three other pupils of Floris, and lastly, he saw prints after works by this painter. The muscular nudes ultimately derive from antique sculptures, such as the famous 'Laocoön', of which there was a bronze copy at Fontainebleau. This

style would also have reached Ketel by way of prints, for he never travelled to Italy. Italian prints or engravings after Maerten van Heemskerck, who had visited Italy, might have served as a source of inspiration. From records in the City Archive of Gouda, Holland, we know that Ketel had on loan from his uncle and first teacher an unspecified collection of prints. As usual with Ketel, the prints are never exactly copied, but always applied with slight alterations, conforming to theoretical principles, such as *varietas* and *emulatio*. The subject, unusual as it is, had nevertheless been painted before, in the picture by Frans Floris that was recently discovered in an Italian private collection (*Fiamminghi a Roma 1508–1608*, Palais des Beaux-Arts, Brussels 1995, no.89). Though the composition is different, it is further proof of Floris's influence on Ketel.

Ketel was unable to find patronage in England for his allegorical paintings, and in 1581 left for Amsterdam, perhaps because his painterly style did not really suit English taste.

LIT: Randall Davies, 'An Inventory of the Duke of Buckingham's Pictures etc., at York House in 1635, 11 May', *Burlington Magazine,* vol.10, 1906–7, p.380; Brian Fairfax, *A Catalogue of the Curious Collection of Pictures of George Villiers, Duke of Buckingham* … 1758, p.19; Vertue IV, p.69; Erik Duverger, *Antwerpse Kunstinventarissen uit de zeventende eeuw*, vols.5, 6, Brussels 1991, 1992; Miedema 1994, I, pp.358–9

TS

JORIS HOEFNAGEL 1542–1600

62 A Fête at Bermondsey
*c.*1569–70

Oil on panel 73.8 × 99 (29 × 39)
Signed and inscribed b.l. but only the signature legible
PROV: Possibly the picture 'of the solemnities of a marriage' first recorded in the 1611 inventory of pictures at Hatfield House, and mentioned in subsequent inventories; by descent in the family
Courtesy of The Marquess of Salisbury
[Not exhibited]

The scene of Hoefnagel's only known large-scale oil painting is Bermondsey, with the Tower of London visible on the opposite bank of the Thames. The church on the right is possibly St Mary Magdalene. It is not entirely certain what the subject of the picture is. Traditionally it has been called a marriage feast, which accords with early references to a picture of such a subject at Hatfield, which otherwise cannot be accounted for. The processsion of people on the right appears to be coming from the church, preceded by four figures carrying large cakes wrapped in white cloths, and a man holding a cup aloft, filled with bay or rosemary and decorated with coloured streamers. These details correspond with a nearly contemporary account of a bridal procession, where a silver cup 'wherein was a goodly braunch of Rosemarie gilded very faire, hung about with silken Ribonds of all colours' was carried before the bride, who was followed by 'the chiefest maydens of the Countrie, some bearing great Bride Cakes' (Thomas Deloney, *The Pleasant History of John Winchcomb,* 9th ed. 1633, probably first printed *c.*1597; cited Auerbach and Adams 1971, p.54). However, the aristocratic lady heading the procession makes an unlikely bride, dressed in black, as are the others. Merrymaking of some sort is certainly in progress, with genteel company arriving on horseback for the laid-out feast, as villagers dance and look on.

Hoefnagel, an Antwerp artist, was in England *c.*1568–70, presumably when this was painted. The composition, with details seen from a slight aerial perspective with the river and surrounding panorama in the distance, and the crowd of small figures in the foreground, is very much in the manner of the Flemish topographical school with which he was closely associated. The format is similar to that of panoramic views of Spain and France he produced *c.*1560–7 for Braun and Hogenberg's *Civitates Orbis Terrarum*, a survey of European cities illustrated with maps and engraved views, incorporating figures wearing local costume, published over a number of years from 1572–1618. This view of Bermondsey was not connected with the project, although several of his English views were, including his one of Nonsuch (Washington 1985–6, no.342) which appeared in volume 5 with a series of female costume figures appended to the bottom. Interestingly, one of these figures is recognisable as one of the ladies in the group on the extreme left of the Bermondsey view. Other figures in the picture are close to watercolour costume sketches made by the Flemish artist Lucas de Heere for his *Der Beschriving der Britsche Eilanden* (see fig.42 on p.117), a treatise on the geography, customs and manners of the British Isles, which illustrated British costumes of all classes of society, and also to his survey of costumes of the world, the *Theatre* (Ghent University Library), *c.*1573–7. De Heere and Hoefnagel were in England at the same time, and de Heere dedicated a drawing to Hoefnagel (see no.101), but it is not clear who was the originator of the costume designs.

Both artists were Flemish and can be associated with a close-knit group of humanist exiles from Antwerp, living in London. It included Jan Radermacher and Emanuel van Meteren, a historian and relative of Abraham Ortelius – a friend of Hoefnagel and a distinguished cartographer who was responsible for the atlas *Theatrum Orbis Terrarum*, a forerunner of the *Civitates*, in which he also had an interest. Van Meteren kept an *album amicorum* in which his friends signed their names, wrote poems or drew their devices, which is preserved in the Bodleian Library, and both Hoefnagel and de Heere appear in it. Hoefnagel was a close friend of Radermacher (his painting 'Allegory of Friendship between Hoefnagel and Johannes Radermacher' is in the Museum Boymans van Beuningen) and dedicated his manuscript 'Patentia' – a collection of political emblems and poems dating from his London years – to him. It has been suggested that Hoefnagel has included himself and his Antwerp friends in the Bermondsey scene, under the tree on the far right, the artist leaning against it: it is possible that the picture is a pictorial record of the group and commemorates, through its format and precise depiction of costume, the topographical and geographical interests of its members.

It is not known who commissioned the picture, or how it came to Hatfield, but this type of topographical landscape in oil was highly unusual in England at this date.

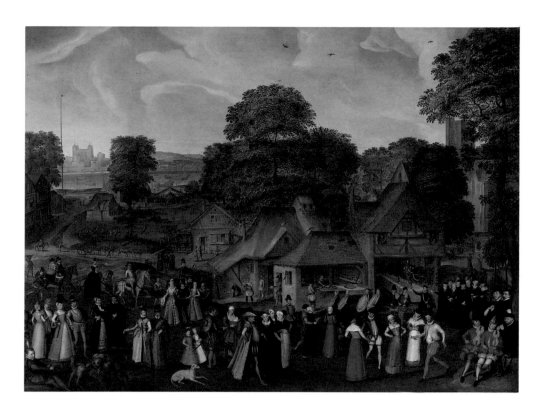

LIT: Strong 1969, p.48; Erna Auerbach and C. Kingsley Adams, *Paintings and Sculpture at Hatfield House*, 1971, pp.53–5; Frances Yates, *The Valois Tapestries*, 1975 (2nd ed.), particularly pp.22–7; Thomas DaCosta Kaufmann, 'The Nature of Imitation; Hoefnagel on Dürer', *Jahrbuch der Kunsthistorischen Sammlungen in Wien*, no.82/3, 1986/7, pp.163–77 (for the links between Hoefnagel, Radermacher and Ortelius); M.L. Hendrix, *Joris Hoefnagel and the 'Four Elements': A Study in Sixteenth-century Nature Painting*, D.Phil, Princeton University 1984, printed Ann Arbor 1989, pp.46–8; Miedema 1994, pp.306–13

TB

HIERONIMO CUSTODIS
active 1589–1593

63 Elizabeth Brydges, later Lady Kennedy 1589

Oil on canvas transferred from panel
92 × 69.8 (36¼ × 27½)
Inscribed 'ÆTATIS SVÆ. 14 | ANNO DÑI.
1589' t.r.; below, a painted cartellino
inscribed in later handwriting: 'Elizabeth
Bruges daughter | to the Lord Giles
Chandos'; below this, in black: 'Hieroni-
mo Custodis. Antverpiensis | Fecit. 8,ᵃ
July 1589'
PROV: Presumably inherited by Elizabeth Brydges's sister Catherine, who
married Francis, 4th Earl of Bedford in
1608/9; by family descent
*By kind permission of the Marquess of
Tavistock and Trustees of the Bedford Estate*
[Not exhibited]

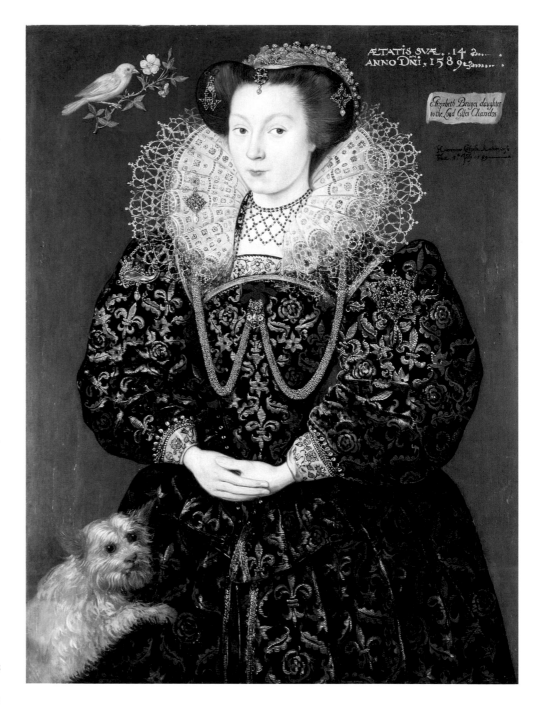

Elizabeth Brydges, or Bruges, was the eldest
daughter and co-heiress with her sister
Katherine to Giles, 3rd Lord Chandos, of
Sudeley Castle. She was a Maid of Honour to
Queen Elizabeth, and is said to have had the
Earl of Essex as a suitor. In 1603, with a
dowry of £16,500, she made a disastrous marriage to Sir John Kennedy, one of James I's
favourite Scottish courtiers, who was subsequently rumoured to have a wife already. In
1609 she fled from him to her cousin Elizabeth Gorges, 'in hir night gear, in great fright
and starved with cold' (letter from Sir Arthur
Gorges to Robert Cecil, 4 September 1609),
and lived until her early death in 1617 on the
charity of her relatives.

Little is known of Custodis. A native of
Antwerp, he came to England possibly as a
religious refugee. The first definite record of
him here is 1589, when he signed and dated
three portraits, of which this is one, the others
being Sir John Parker (The Royal Collection)
and Elizabeth Brydges's father, Lord Chandos
(Woburn Abbey). A portrait of her mother
Frances Clinton, Lady Chandos, also at
Woburn and similarly dated, although not
signed, can be taken to be by Custodis as
well. A portrait of Sir Henry Bromley with an
earlier dating of 1587 is attributed to him
(Strong 1969, p.198). In 1590/1 he is recorded as living in the London parish of St
Botolph-without-Aldgate, where on 2 March
'Jacobus the son of Ieromye Custodis A Paynter' was baptised. He was dead by 1593, when
his widow remarried at the Dutch Reformed
Church, Austin Friars. On the basis of inscriptions, Strong has assembled a number of portraits attributable to him, but they are of varying quality (Strong 1969, pp.195–206).

As in the portrait of Frances Clinton, great
attention is paid to the depiction of textile
patterns and surface ornament. Her dress,
embroidered with a pattern of roses and
fleurs-de-lis, has pinned to it several magnificent jewels, including a vase of flowers at her
breast, and a curious design of a sea monster,
its body a large baroque pearl, with a goat's
head and a frog or toad riding on its back. It
is not clear what the significance of this is.

Toads, and goats, could be symbolic of lust,
although this conflicts with the age and inno-
cence of the girl, with her pet dog leaping up
at her skirt, and the spray of eglantine in the
top left-hand corner, symbolic of chastity.
Eglantine reappears in her hair and is embroidered on her cuffs and across her chest.

The jewelled monogram HW in her hair is
also a mystery, as no one sufficiently closely
associated with Elizabeth Brydges with these
initials can be identified. The inscription giving her age as fourteen in 1589 is also prob-

lematic as it conflicts with *G.E.C. Complete Peerage* which says she was fourteen in 1593/4. However, her facial appearance is sufficiently close to other portraits said to be of her at Woburn, which would indicate that the identification is correct. These portraits include a full-length (a pair to one of her sister Catherine) with a garden with courtly figures in the background (Woburn Abbey); a three-quarter length, attributed to Marcus Gheeraerts the Younger (Woburn Abbey); and a miniature by Isaac Oliver (private collection).

EXH: Tate Gallery 1969–70 (116)
LIT: J.H. Wiffen, *Historical Memoirs of the House of Russell*, 1833; George Scharf, *Catalogue of the Pictures at Woburn Abbey*, 1890, pp.49–50; Adeline Marie Tavistock and Ela M.S. Russell, *Catalogue of the Pictures at Woburn Abbey*, 1890, II, pp.318–21; Vertue II, p.41; Roy Strong, 'Elizabethan Painting: An Approach through Inscriptions – II: Hieronimo Custodis', *Burlington Magazine*, vol.105, 1963, p.107; Strong 1969, p.197p; Diana Scarisbrick, 'Symbols of Rank and Riches: Jewellery in the portraits at Woburn', *Country Life*, Jan. 1986, pp.254–6; Jane Ashelford, *Dress in the Age of Elizabeth I*, 1988, p.34

TB

BRITISH SCHOOL

64 Jephthah's Daughter

Oil on panel 41.9 × 185.7 (16½ × 73⅛)
PROV: …; Sotheby's 2 June 1954 (60); …; bt Her Majesty The Queen 1955
Her Majesty The Queen

The history of this work prior to its appearance in the saleroom in 1954 is unknown.

The main section of the Old Testament story of Jephthah (Judges XI: 29–40) is told sequentially across the panel, reading from left to right. Jephthah and his forces defeat the Ammonites and he returns to his home at Mizpeh. Before the campaign he had vowed that he would sacrifice to God whatever emerged first from the door at his homecoming; to his horror, it is his daughter who greets him with musical instruments. She insists that the vow must be fulfilled, requesting only that she may first spend two months in the mountains, mourning the fact that she will die a virgin. On her return she is sacrificed. Jephthah subsequently became a judge of Israel.

It has recently been discovered (by Richard Williams, Courtauld Institute), that this painting is closely based on three out of a set of four engravings of the story of Jephthah by Gerard de Jode after Hans Bol (1534–93) (formerly in the Kupferstichkabinett, Berlin, but lost in the Second World War; photographs in Warburg Institute archive, London). The present artist has, however, omitted Bol's third subject, the daughter's sojourn in the mountains. He or she has also removed the Mannerist contrapposto from the figures, straightened them up and attired a number in English costume, set the action in the English countryside and added a view of Windsor Castle, top left, seen from the south.

A handful of drawings and woodcuts of early views of Windsor survive (see Margaret

Aston, *The King's Bedpost*, 1993, pp.172–5). Unfortunately direct comparison with the rendering of the castle in these images is not possible because they depict it from the north. They are: the etching of the procession of the Knights of the Garter by Marcus Gheeraerts the Elder, 1576 (which like the present painting also includes a windmill); a woodcut illustrating the 1583 edition of Foxe's *Actes and Monuments*; and drawings of *c*.1568 by Joris Hoefnagel, used as a basis for the engraving of Windsor in Braun and Hogenberg's *Civitates Orbis Terrarum*, published in Cologne from 1572, and for a miniature painted in Antwerp in 1571 (see *Dutch and Flemish Drawings from the Royal Library, Windsor Castle*, North Carolina Museum of Art, Raleigh 1994, pp.36–8). The structure shown here on top of the Round Tower is a puzzle, as it does not appear in the above views, nor in Norden's aerial view of the castle in his 1607 survey of Windsor and its park (British Library, Harleian MS.3749; I am grateful for this specific reference to Professor Howard Colvin, who also suggests that the buildings on the right may represent one of the various lodges in Windsor Great Park, all of which had been rebuilt by the eighteenth century).

The battle, seen left, can be related to elements in earlier military panoramas, such as 'The Battle of the Spurs' (fig.20 on p.35).

The date of this painting is extremely hard to determine, as is the reason for its commission. According to A.V.B. Norman, the armour depicted, with its long breastplates, is of 1580 onwards. The manner of painting the brick wall to the right and its moulding, and the plumes on the helmets of Jephthah and his mounted men at arms, is strongly reminiscent of that found in Robert Peake's 'Henry, Prince of Wales on Horseback', of *c*.1611 (fig.51 on p.188). Analysis of the pigments indicates the use of azurite, an expensive blue,

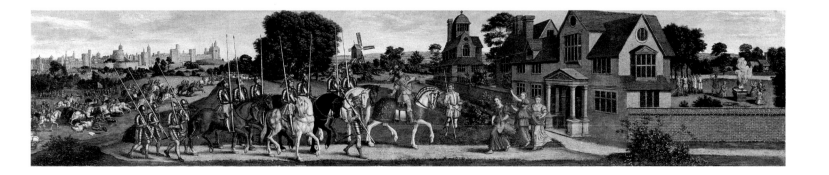

in the sky area, and of lead tin yellow, a pigment commonly used in the sixteenth and seventeenth centuries.

The subject is rarely encountered in the visual arts at this period, although a set of five hangings on this story, now lost, was inventoried in the 'Great Chamber' at Lacock House in 1575 (Thelma E. Vernon 'Inventory of Sir Henry Sharington', *Wiltshire Archaeological Society Magazine*, vol.63, 1968, p.75; information from Dr Maurice Howard). The medieval view, represented by Thomas Aquinas, had condemned Jephthah as mistaken while admiring the strength of his piety. The story was subsequently the subject of a new play in Latin, published in Paris in 1554, by the humanist scholar George Buchanan, later tutor to James VI of Scotland (information from Claire Gapper). Buchanan's interest in the Greek playwright Euripedes may have led him to this biblical parallel with the story of Iphigenia. When he was writing *Jephthes*, in the 1540s, the question of vows – including monastic ones – was topical and both Catholic and Protestant writers were discussing their validity. The traditional opinion was that a vow must be fulfilled, but other writers argued that it depended on whether the vow was an acceptable one. Jephthah's sacrifice of his daughter was also a parallel with God's sacrifice of his Son (George Buchanan, *Tragedies*, ed. P. Sharratt and P.G. Walsh, Edinburgh 1983, pp.13–19).

Williams notes that the Bishops' Bible of 1568 includes an engraving of the story, quite unlike the present image. It shows the moment that the daughter emerges from the house as Jephthah approaches. The summary at the chapter opening glosses the story as 'He maketh a rashe vowe'. This suggests that the story was understood to signify not an exemplary adherence to a covenant made with God, but a foolish error.

According to Dr Nicholas Cranfield, the earliest literary treatment of it in English is in the puritan preacher R. Rogers's A Commentary upon the Whole Book of Judges Preached First and Delivered in Sundrie Lectures (London 1615). Dr Cranfield notes that among these 103 sermons, Rogers gave two to the story (ibid., nos.67, 68, pp.564–88), speaking with particular enthusiasm of the daughter's honour in returning to her death, as an example of submission. The omission by the present artist of the daughter's vigil in the mountains specifically throws the emphasis on to Jephthah and his own dilemma and not on to her personal submission.

It is exceptionally rare to find an English painting on walnut and the panel may once have formed part of a piece of furniture. It could, for instance, have been the inside of the lid of a chest: a chest discovered in the barber-surgeon's cabin on the ship the *Mary Rose* (David Knell, *English Country Furniture*, 1992, p.38, fig.25) was, for example, constructed of walnut, pine, and poplar. This suggestion is supported by three triangular repairs, each with two filled holes, along the bottom edge of the panel, where there might formerly have been hinges. A 2 × 8 cm rectangular fill, its upper edge 3 cm from the top edge of the panel, perhaps replaced a handle. If it were indeed the inside of a lid, this could also account for the good condition of the painting itself. The panel is made up of two horizontal boards, 30.6 cm and 11 cm wide respectively. Its back has been cradled at some time in the past.

LIT: Millar 1963, no.60; John Harris, *The Artist and the Country House*, 2nd ed., 1979, no.6

KH

6 The Private Image

So far this exhibition has focused on painting in large. This period, however, saw the introduction, development and flowering of the portrait miniature.

It is uncertain whether the form first arose in England or in France – or even in both simultaneously and independently – but the earliest exponent in England appears to have been Lucas Horenbout from Ghent (no.65). A highly paid contemporary of Holbein at Henry VIII's court, he is said to have there taught 'limning', or miniature-painting to Holbein (no.66).

A female exponent of the art was the Netherlander Levina Teerlinc (no.68) who became a waiting-gentlewoman to Mary I and Elizabeth I.

The career of the English limner Nicholas Hilliard is charted in the following pages. Apart from the shadowy John Bettes, Hilliard is the earliest securely identified *English*-born artist of stature in this period. His practical treatise *The Arte of Limning*, written *c.*1598–1603, is one of the most important documents in the history of English art. In it, Hilliard argued that painting in miniature was a suitable practice for a gentleman, a contention that would probably have been met with incomprehension by many of his clients.

As well as his own son Laurence, Hilliard trained Rowland Lockey (no.76) who also painted works in large. The French-born Isaac Oliver spent some time in Hilliard's studio, before visiting Italy in around 1596. The 1590s saw the introduction of the larger, rectangular limning or 'cabinet miniature' (nos.74, 76, 81, 86, 104).

After 1603, the new king and queen diverged in their patronage of limners. James retained Hilliard, while Anne made Oliver her official miniaturist in 1605. In due course their heir, Prince Henry also favoured Oliver.

Oliver's range is demonstrated by the figurative and narrative drawings which he prized enough to mention specifically in his will in

1617, and which he left to his artist son Peter. The recently rediscovered 'Entombment' (no.104), left unfinished at Isaac's death was later completed by his heir.

After the remarkable portrait drawings by Hans Holbein (nos.93–7), whose purpose is discussed by Susan Foister on pp.21–6, nothing of comparable quality survived until Rubens's portrayal of the Duke of Buckingham of 1625, almost a century later.

A group of diverse surviving patterns on paper (nos.98, 102) indicate that such material was used in the manufacture of repetitions of portraits.

The sketches of the Earl of Leicester and Elizabeth I made by Federigo Zuccaro on his

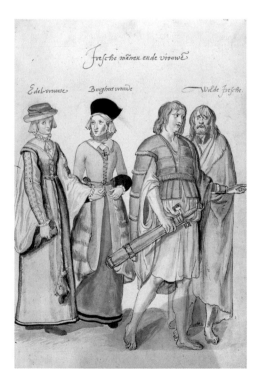

fig.42 Lucas de Heere, 'Irish Costumes' *c.*1567–76 from *Der Beschrijving der Britsche Eilanden. The British Library*

brief visit to England in 1575 are survivals from an enterprise that seems to have proved abortive (nos.99, 100)

Drawings remain from the Netherlander Lucas de Heere's time in England (*c.*1567–77), including embellishments to his own verses in the emblematic tradition (no.101) and the watercolour sketches illustrating his treatise on the geography, institutions, manners, customs and history of the British Isles, *Beschrijving der Britsche Eilanden* (see fig.42) compiled between 1573 and 1575. Additional costume sketches from de Heere's English visit may be found in his manuscript 'Theatre de tous les peuples …' (Ghent University Library MS 2466). The watercolour drawings by John White (active 1585–93) relating to his experiences in the New World seem to be in the tradition established by de Heere.

The Lumley Inventory, a unique document for our understanding of art and collecting at the end of the sixteenth century, is embellished with watercolours (no.105). These record objects such as sculpture, furniture and fountains in the possession of John, Lord Lumley, as well as funerary monuments commissioned by him.

The position alters as the century closes and two significant draughtsmen emerge in Isaac Oliver and Inigo Jones (nos.106–12).

The early life of Francis Cleyn is obscure. Perhaps trained in the Netherlands, he spent a number of years in Italy before moving to Denmark to produce decorative painting for the royal palaces. On a visit to London in 1623 he impressed James I, but his duties in Denmark prevented him from settling in England until 1625 where he was immediately employed by the new king, Charles I, to make various designs. He became principal designer to the Mortlake tapestry factory (see no.116), as well as painting decorative panels for country houses, and was latterly a prolific illustrator of books, preparatory sketches for which still survive.

Lucas Horenbout
*c.*1490/5–1544

65 Henry VIII *c.*1525–7

Watercolour on vellum on card 5.3 × 4.8
(2⅛ × 1⅞)
Inscribed 'HR | VIII' centre left; 'AN⁰ |
XXXV' centre right; and 'HK' top centre
and bottom centre
PROV: …; ?Horace Walpole, Strawberry
Hill; …; by 1862 Hollingsworth Magni-
ac, sold Christie's 4 July 1892 (183), bt
Colnaghi; Duke of Buccleuch, from
whom bt by lender 1949
*Syndics of the Fitzwilliam Museum,
Cambridge*

This is probably the earliest individual portrait miniature to be produced in England. Its
exact date is not known, because it depends
on how the inscription 'AN⁰ XXXV' is interpreted. It could mean that the King is in his
thirty-fifth year (between 28 June 1525 and 27
June 1526) or that he is thirty-five (between
28 June 1526 and 27 June 1527).

He is shown beardless, against a deep blue
background separated by a thin gold line
from the red border. Angels in each corner

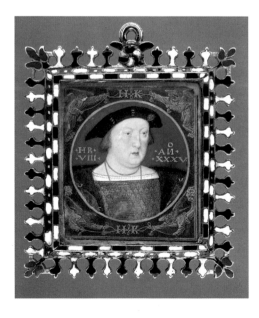

hold golden cords that entwine with the initials of 'HK', for Henry and his queen,
Catherine (or Katherine) of Aragon.

Three similar contemporary but less elaborate miniatures of Henry, as well as some later
ones and miniatures of other members of
Henry's family also survive. They have been
plausibly attributed to Lucas Horenbout,
assumed to be the 'famous master' Lucas who
taught Holbein miniature painting (see van
Mander, ed. Miedema 1994, p.149). A similar
image of the King by the same hand appears
in the initial H of a manuscript bestowing letters patent of 28 April 1524 (sold Sotheby's 11
July 1983 (25)), which indicates that Horenbout was already painting portraits of the
King by that date.

Lucas was the son of the Ghent manuscript
illuminator Gerard Horenbout, painter to the
Habsburg Margaret of Austria, who was
working for Henry VIII by the end of the
1520s; Lucas's sister Susanna, also a painter,
married an Englishman in the 1520s. In England the name is sometimes spelt
'Hornebolte'.

There has been much debate as to whether
the portrait miniature as an independent
object – that is, emancipated from a manuscript page – first appeared in England or in
France. Madame d'Alençon sent lockets containing portraits of her brother François I and
his two sons, at that time prisoners of Charles
V following the defeat of Pavia, to Henry
VIII late in 1526. They are thought to have
been by a Netherlandish painter at the French
court, Jean Clouet. Early in 1527, Henry reciprocated with portraits, probably miniatures,
of himself and his small daughter Mary. A
previously unknown miniature of Henry by
Horenbout, with a French provenance, was
recently acquired by the Louvre in Paris.
Whether the form initially arose in France or
in England, it clearly derived from manuscript
illumination, which often included portrait
likenesses, and images in circular form.

Holbein's later portrait-type of Henry VIII
(see no.8) was so successful, and has thus
become so familiar, that Horenbout's earlier,
youthful depiction – evidently satisfactory to

the King as many versions of it are known –
surprises with its subtlety. As Reynolds points
out, Horenbout fixed what was to remain the
format of miniatures in England for decades
to come: circular, with a blue background and
gold script, showing only the head and
shoulders, the figure placed three-quarters on
and facing either right or left, and the rather
flat features only lightly modelled.

The first salary payment to 'Lewke
Hornebaud pictor maker' in the Chamber
accounts of Henry VIII was made in September 1525 (B.L. MS Egerton 2604 fol.lv,
Campbell and Foister 1986, p.721 n.37) and
payments continue in the surviving accounts
up to the artist's death in 1544. At £33 6s a
year, he received slightly more than Hans
Holbein at £30. On 22 June 1534 Horenbout
was granted the office of King's Painter,
became a denizen, was granted a tenement at
Charing Cross and was licensed to employ
four foreign journeymen. When his grant of
office was renewed in 1544, the patent specifically mentioned the King's long personal
acquaintance with the artist's skills.

The enamelled blue and white frame is
modern.

EXH: As in Bayne-Powell 1985, plus *Treasures from the
Fitzwilliam*, National Gallery of Art, Washington, Kim-
bell Art Museum, Fort Worth, National Academy of
Design, New York, High Museum of Art, Atlanta, and
Los Angeles County Museum 1989–90 (50)
LIT: As in Bayne-Powell 1985, pp.129–30, to which
should be added: J.C. Robinson, *Notice of the Principal
Works of Art in the Collection of Hollingsworth Magniac,*
1862, no.193; Susan Foister, 'Tudor Miniaturists at the
V.&A.', *Burlington Magazine*, vol.125, 1983, p.635;
Reynolds 1988, p.4; Janet Backhouse, 'Illuminated
Manuscripts and the Development of the Portrait
Miniature', in *Henry VIII: A European Court in England*,
1991, p.89. On Horenbout: Campbell 1985, pp.xv–xvi,
xx; Lorne Campbell and Susan Foister, 'Gerard, Lucas
and Susanna Horenbout', *Burlington Magazine*, vol.128,
1986, pp.719–27

KH

HANS HOLBEIN THE YOUNGER
1497/8–1543

66 Anne of Cleves 1539

Vellum on playing card,
diameter 4.5 (1¾)
PROV: ...; Vertue 1720, records it, apparently in the collection of Mr Alexander;
...; Col..James Seymour 1732 ; ...;
Thomas Barrett, by descent; sold 1826;
resold and bt Francis Douce; by descent
to Miss Eleanor Davies, by whom sold to
George Salting; bequeathed to Victoria
and Albert Museum 1910
*Board of Trustees of the Victoria and Albert
Museum, London*

This is one of two very similar portraits of
Anne of Cleves by Holbein. The other, full-size, portrait is in the Louvre, and extends to
half-length. Anne of Cleves was Henry VIII's
fourth wife: he married her in 1539 and
divorced her shortly afterwards. The death of
Jane Seymour in 1537 following the birth of
Prince Edward prompted an extensive search
for a new bride, and Holbein was given the
important task of taking portraits of potential
marriage candidates which could then be
shown to Henry VIII. In order to do so he
travelled extensively in 1538 and 1539, taking
the portraits of at least six women, including
in 1538 Christina of Denmark (fig.43), but
there was no marriage.

In June 1539 Holbein was sent to Düren to
take the portrait of Anne of Cleves and her
sister Amelia, daughters of the Protestant
ruler of Jülich-Cleves. The portraits which
had been sent to England were regarded as
unsatisfactory by the English ambasssadors
since 'under such a monstruouse habyte and
apparell, was no syght, neither of theyr faces
nor of theyr persones'. Holbein's unobstructed, fully frontal image was presumably
intended to rectify this deficiency. The marriage treaty was speedily concluded and Anne
was sent to England (accompanied by the
artist Susanna Horenbout, sister of Lucas; see
no.65). The marriage took place on 6 January
1540, but was shortlived. Henry ended the
marriage in July of the same year, and with it
the political alliance with Protestant Germany
which inspired it.

Anne of Cleves is shown in Flemish dress
in this portrait and in the otherwise identical
full-size version. There is therefore every reason to believe that this is the image that Holbein produced of Anne from his sitting with
her in 1539. It is probable that Holbein made
one or several drawings of Anne, as was his
usual practice, and then worked up the painted versions back in London. This seems certain in the case of the portrait of Christina, as
the panel for this full-length portrait would
have been large and unwieldy. The miniature
however is small and eminently portable. The
Louvre painting is on parchment, also easily
portable (although at some stage it has been
attached to a panel support). However, it is
now clear that this painting could not have
been begun by Holbein at his sitting with
Anne, since it is pounced, that is, made from a
cartoon. Although it is just conceivable that
Holbein made or began the miniature on the
spot, he would have needed to take notes of
the foreign costume to work up the Louvre
portrait, and it seems much more probable
that he made drawings from which at least
two portraits were made, including this
miniature. It is perhaps not too fanciful to
imagine Henry VIII keeping this by him in
anticipation of his marriage. The turned ivory
box setting in the form of a Tudor rose is of
the Tudor period but the miniature has apparently been trimmed to fit it.

Holbein is said by Karel van Mander in
1604 to have learned the miniature technique
from Lucas Horenbout. We do not know
whether he normally made miniature portraits
from full-size drawings rather than painting
directly onto vellum at a sitting; the surviving
miniature and drawing (no.96) of Lady
Audley, as well as our knowledge of how the
Louvre portrait of Anne of Cleves was made,
suggests this might sometimes have been the
case, but whether this was his usual practice is
far from certain.

EXH: V&A 1983 (30)
LIT: Murdoch et al. 1981, p.37; Strong 1983, p.47;
Rowlands 1985, no.M.6; Reynolds 1988, p.7

SF

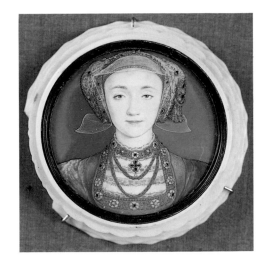

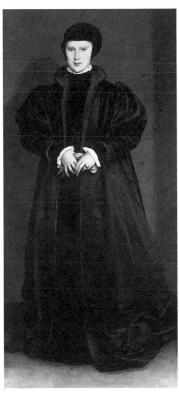

fig.43 Hans Holbein the Younger,
'Christina of Denmark' 1538, oil on panel.
Trustees of the National Gallery, London

GERLACH FLICKE
active c.1545–died 1558

67 Self-Portrait with Henry Strangwish 1554/5

Oil on paper or vellum laid on panel
8.8 × 11.9 (3½ × 4¾)
Inscribed 'Talis erat facie Gerlachus Flic-ci°: ipsa Londonia quândo Pictor Vrbe fuit | Hancis ex speculo p charis pîxit amici. Post obitû possint quo meminisse sui.', t.l.; 'Strangwish, thus strangely, depictedis One prisoner, for thother, hath done this | Gerlin, hath garnisht, for his delight This woorck whiche you se, before youre sight', t.r.; 'ANNO 1554', twice, at either side of sitters' heads
PROV: …; recorded by Horace Walpole as in the collection of Dr Thomas Monkhouse (died 1793), Queen's College, Oxford (the remains of an old label inscribed '… Monkhouse' are still on the back); possibly by family descent through Monkhouse's niece or great-niece Mrs Layton to the Smorthit family, from whom bt by James Frankes 1915 (but George Scharf's notes, SSB 102, NPG archive, record it as bt in at the sale of Robert de Ruffières' pictures, Christie's 27 July 1881); …; anon. sale, Sotheby's 9 July 1975 (16)
Railways Pension Fund

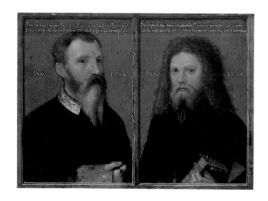

This important work – an example of a portrait in miniature by an artist known otherwise for his paintings 'in large' – seems never to have been publicly exhibited before.

The Latin inscription may be translated as 'Such was the face of Gerlach Flicke when he was a painter in the City of London. This he himself painted from a looking-glass for his dear friends. That they might have something by which to remember him after his death.' The English inscription reveals that his companion is a man called Strangwish and that the two men are prisoners.

The auburn-haired 'Strangwish' is thought to be a gentleman privateer, Henry Strangwish, or Strangways, a member of a distinguished West Country family. He is first recorded in 1552, attacking part of the Biscayan fleet, and in 1553 is reported by the pursuing authorities to be successively in Ireland, France, back in the Channel and (precise date unknown) accused in the court of the Admiralty of piracy. In February 1555 he had escaped to Suffolk, but during March he was in the Tower of London; in November 1555 he was moved to the Marshalsea prison. This account may help to pinpoint exactly when the present painting was made, as, under the Old Style calendar in use in England at this period, the year '1554' inscribed here ran from 25 March 1554 to 24 March 1555 – the latter being the month in which Strangwish is known to have been incarcerated.

Flicke states that he has used a mirror to record his own image. He gazes out at the viewers, 'his dear friends', holding the palette which defines his profession and with which he is painting this very picture. The pigments shown upon it – the red lake, white, two mixed shades of pink, and the brown – have been used to paint the flesh we see before us, while azurite (an expensive blue) has been used, mixed with lead white, for the background. If Flicke represents the sense of sight, his friend who holds – and seems to be playing – a lute, personifies sound. The trompe l'oeil frame, the central element of which serves to separate the two men, has been added last; it runs over the completed image, although it appears to be contemporary.

Flicke wears a fine blackwork collar, now a little rubbed, and a signet ring with a device on it, too small to distinguish. His skin has

the pallor of the elderly and he could certainly be approaching sixty, which would fit a proposed date of birth of c.1495. Little is known of the artist, although he was probably born at Osnabrück in Germany. He was in England by 1545/6 when he painted Archbishop Cranmer (no.12), which, like the 'Portrait of an Unknown Nobleman' (National Gallery of Scotland, Edinburgh) is signed and inscribed with his nationality: German. Flicke died in London early in 1558 and his will, which describes him as a 'Drawer', indicates that he still owned property in Osnabrück and had a wife in England (Hervey 1910, p.71). His will names him '*Garlick* Flicke', and he has been accepted as being the painter of three portraits listed as by 'Garlicke' in Lord Lumley's inventory (no.105): of Queen Mary, of Thomas 3rd Duke of Norfolk, and a 'Statuary', or full-length, of Thomas, 1st Lord Darcy of Chiche. Only the first, identified by its Lumley cartellino is known to have survived (Durham Cathedral Library). A recent suggestion that he may have been responsible for certain small roundel portraits formerly attributed to Holbein (Rowlands 1985, p.234) awaits substantiation.

Strangwish was to continue his piratical career. He was sentenced to death in late 1559, but execution was stayed and like other privateers of good family, such as the Killigrews and the Carews, he entered Queen Elizabeth's service. He died of injuries sustained in the English attack on Rouen in October 1562 (information on Strangwish, Susan Bracken).

LIT: Mary F.S. Hervey, 'Notes on a Tudor Painter: Gerlach Flicke – I', *Burlington Magazine*, vol.17, 1910, pp.71–9; Sotheby sale catalogue 9 July 1975 (16) (but details on Strangwish have been superseded), pp.19–20; Waterhouse 1978, p.27

KH

ATTRIBUTED TO LEVINA TEERLINC c.1510/20–1576

68 An Elizabethan Maundy Ceremony c.1560

Vellum on playing card, oval 7 × 5.7
(2¾ × 2¼)
PROV: …; probably acquired before
1863, from an unknown source; by
descent
Trustees of the late Countess Beauchamp

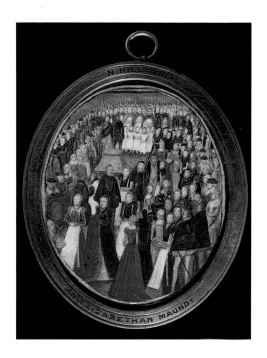

This miniature, originally straight-edged, and either square or rectangular, but now cut down into an oval, is very likely to be a surviving work by Levina Teerlinc, the daughter of Simon Benninck (c.1483–1561), the internationally distinguished illuminator who had settled in Bruges in 1519.

Late in 1546, Levina, by then married to George Teerlinc of Blanckenberg, entered the service of Henry VIII as a painter. In England she is always described as a 'gentlewoman', and was awarded an annuity of £40 a year, even higher than the generous salary enjoyed by Horenbout; her husband was appointed a Gentleman Pensioner. She was employed by Edward VI and in 1553 she presented Queen Mary with 'a smale picture of the Trynite'. Between 1559 and 1576 she is recorded as presenting to Queen Elizabeth nine New Year's gifts of pictures (references transcribed Strong 1983, p.55 and Campbell 1985, p.xxviii), either portraits of the Queen alone or with 'many other personages'.

This miniature, which may be one of these gifts, shows the Queen, dressed in purplish blue, participating in the Maundy Thursday ceremony at which the monarch washed the feet of a group of poor people, their number being the same as the age of the sovereign, before presenting them with money, food (loaves, fishes and wine) and clothing.

The ceremony, in imitation of Christ's washing of the feet of His disciples before the Last Supper, was part of the Easter vigil and dated back at least to the reign of Edward II. In spite of the breach with Rome, Edward VI had continued the ceremony, as, naturally, had Mary I. For Elizabeth it was one of the spectacles through which the monarchy could demonstrate its prestige.

The poor folk are shown sitting in two rows extending from the front to the back, each with a gentlewoman standing behind. At the back, in the centre, stand the almonry

children, the gentlemen of the Chapel Royal wearing copes, and behind them the Gentlemen Pensioners holding their poleaxes. The Queen, attended by her retinue of ladies, some of whom hold basins of warm water sprinkled with flowers, moves to the front left. Like others, she wears a long white apron (in 1567, four ells, that is, five yards, of fine cambric were purchased to make an apron and towel for her 'to were at our Maundy'). Her train is held by an older lady in black. The elderly man whose face is now at the centre of the picture holds a white staff of office, and may be the Lord Chamberlain of the Household (V&A 1983), or the Treasurer of the Chamber (in 1573 this was Sir Thomas Heneage, who officiated at that year's Maundy; see Robinson 1992, p.33).

The costumes depicted are of about 1560 (Arnold 1988, p.67). Two accounts survive of the ceremony that year, which took place at Whitehall. Both give the number of recipients of the Maundy as only twenty, although the age of the Queen was then twenty-six. The number of recipients shown here is not clear; it seems to be about twenty, but additional figures could have been lost when the work was trimmed to an oval. In 1563 and 1564, the Queen did not participate in person, because of epidemics of plague.

Before the Queen's arrival the recipients' feet were, in fact, carefully washed by her Yeomen of the Laundry. Nevertheless, during the ceremony the Queen would kneel before each one, wash one foot, wipe it and, before kissing it, make the sign of the cross over it. The Spanish ambassador Canon Guzman de Silva was delighted to report this aspect of the ceremony in 1565 (Aston 1993, pp.103–4) but Elizabeth's enthusiasm for the cross here horrified her Protestant subjects.

Teerlinc may not have been the first to present a New Year's picture on this subject to the monarch. In 1556 Queen Mary had received two: one 'a table painted with the Maundy' from 'Nicholas Luzer' (i.e. Lizarde, the painter), while a gentleman called Curtes gave 'a table of nedleworke of the Maundy' (John Nichols, *Illustrations of the Manners and Expences of Antient Times in England …*, 1797, section 3, pp.11, 14). It should however be noted that the word 'Maundy' was also used to refer to the Last Supper.

EXH: *Exposition de la miniature*, Hôtel Goffinet, Brussels 1912 (181); V&A 1983 (42); London and Belfast 1988–9 (3.10)
LIT: Basil Long, *British Miniaturists*, 1929, p.211; Auerbach 1961, pp.53–4, 287–8; Murdoch et al. 1981, p.45; Jim Murrell, *The Way Howe to Lymne*, 1983, p.27; Strong 1983, pp.57, 60; Susan Foister, 'Tudor Miniaturists at the V. & A.', *Burlington Magazine*, vol.125, 1983, p.635; Strong 1987, pp.54–5; Arnold 1988, pp.67–8; Reynolds 1988, p.9; Carole Levin, '"Would I Could Give You Help and Succour": Elizabeth I and the Politics of Touch', *Albion*, vol.21, no.2, 1989, p.201; Brian Robinson, *Silver Pennies and Linen Towels*, 1992, p.31; Margaret Aston, *The King's Bedpost*, 1993, pp.103–4, col. pl.VI

KH

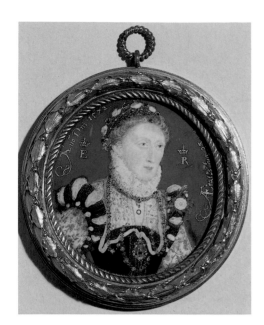

NICHOLAS HILLIARD
1546/7–1618

69 Elizabeth I 1572

Vellum on playing card, with part of a
queen showing on verso 5.1 × 4.8
(2 × 1⅞)
Inscribed 'E | R crowned; Ano
Dni.1572. | Ætatis suae 38' on either
side of the head
PROV: …; bt in 1860 from Mrs Sarah
Mallet of St Helier, Jersey, via C.B. Hue
National Portrait Gallery, London

In 1572, the year this miniature was painted,
Elizabeth I was under pressure from the claim
to the English throne by the Catholic Mary,
Queen of Scots, and from news of the St
Bartholomew's Day massacres of Protestants
in France. She considered marriage to a
French prince to produce an heir and counter
Mary's claims, but ultimately rejected
marriage as politically hazardous. Elizabeth
died childless in 1603, nominating Mary's son
James VI of Scotland to succeed her as James
I of England, first of the Stuart dynasty of
Great Britain.

This miniature is thought to be one of
Hilliard's earliest, and the first he painted of
Queen Elizabeth. In his treatise on miniature
painting, *The Arte of Limning*, he wrote that
Elizabeth chose to sit outdoors in the sun-
shine 'in the open ally of a goodly garden,
where no tree was near, nor anye shadow at
all', rather than in a studio (Hilliard, *A Treatise
Concerning the Arte of Limning*, 1992 ed., p.66).
He commented that strong shading was not
as necessary in a miniature, which would normally be held in the hand, as in a painting
intended for viewing from a distance.

Hilliard's technique differed from Holbein's: instead of beginning with a drawing
and scaling it down, Hilliard made a graphite
drawing on the painting surface, and then
painted one-off miniatures from life (he later
supplied replica portraits, repeating the faces
but varying hair, jewels and dress). He applied
opaque carnation over the hair and face,
defined the facial features, and painted a
background of azurite. The ruff, in transparent grey on a white ground, was finished with
thick white paint in embossed 'lace'. In this
miniature, according to V.J. Murrell, the jewels
were painted on in opaque paint rather than
built up with resin in the technique which
Hilliard used from *c.*1576.

The miniature has undergone alteration:
the face and ruff have been repainted. Ultra-
violet light has revealed stronger, more linear
drawing of Elizabeth's features, comparable
with the life-scale 'Phoenix' and 'Pelican'
portraits of Elizabeth which have been attributed to Hilliard (see no.34).

Hilliard trained as a goldsmith, producing
jewels as well as miniatures for Elizabeth (see
no.73). His hatched brushstrokes – which he
considered the 'true order and principall
Secret in Limning' – resemble those used by
engravers. He recommended practising by
copying engravings by Albrecht Dürer, using
the point of the brush.

Hilliard was not on the court payroll, but
in 1573 was rewarded by Elizabeth for his
'good, true and loyal service' with a reversion
of the lease of a Somerset rectory and church.

EXH: V&A 1947 (6); V&A 1983 (182); *Master Drawings
from the NPG,* NPG 1993 (1)
LIT: Hilliard, pp.66–7, p.81; F.M. O'Donoghue, *A
Description and Classified Catalogue of Portraits of Queen
Elizabeth*, 1894, no.3; C.R. Beard, 'The "Pelican Portrait" of Queen Elizabeth', *Connoisseur*, vol.92, 1933,
pp.263–4; Auerbach 1961, pp.63–4; Strong 1963, p.89,
no.3; NPG 1969, I, p.101; V&A 1983, pp.117–8,
no.182, and pp.15–16; Campbell 1990, p.142, fig.163

AT

NICHOLAS HILLIARD

70 An Unknown Man 1574

Vellum on playing card with two spades
on the reverse, diameter 4.1 (1¾)
Inscribed in gold, on either side of sit-
ter's head, 'Anō Dni 1574' at left, 'Aetatis
Sue 37' at right
PROV: …; bt by the 5th Duke of Buc-
cleuch in 1811; thence by descent until bt
by the lender 1949 (Leverton Harris
Fund)
*Syndics of the Fitzwilliam Museum,
Cambridge*

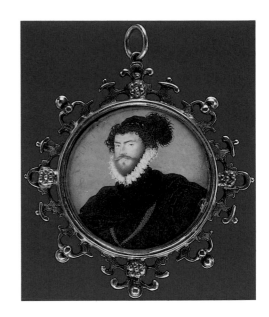

This was formerly called a self-portrait of
Nicholas Hilliard.

The sitter's identity is unknown, but he
bears some resemblance to Robert Dudley,
Earl of Leicester (?1532–1588), Queen Eliza-
beth's favourite, and an important patron of
Hilliard during the early 1570s. In 1571
Hilliard painted a 'booke of portraitures' for
Leicester. Hilliard gave many of his children
names from the Dudley family.

Other miniatures by Hilliard of Leicester
exist. One, dated 1576, depicting him at
forty-four, is in the National Portrait Gallery,
London. There the Earl is depicted wearing a
black doublet with lace ruff, a black bonnet
with a jewelled hatband and black feather,
and a gold chain (of a design differing from
that in the Fitzwilliam miniature, which sup-
ports a medallion). The eyes of the sitter in
the National Portrait Gallery miniature are
brown, his beard and moustache brown, and
his hair grey-brown. Unfortunately, the
Fitzwilliam miniature is slightly faded, so the
original colours of the sitter's eyes are uncertain.

Roy Strong has pointed out that a fourth
portrait is mentioned as a Hilliard family heirloom in the 1640 will of Hilliard's son Laurence Hilliard: 'the Earl of Lestars picture in a
yet [?jet] box draune in his Cloake with a Cap
and Fethar' (cited in Auerbach 1961, p.227).

The inscription on the present portrait has
been tampered with: the sitter's age has been
changed to thirty-seven to correspond with
the date of Hilliard's birth, which was once
thought to be 1537. The miniature was also
given a later frame with a Latin inscription on
the reverse, 'NICVSHILLYARDAVRIFABER-
SCVLPTORETCOELEBRISILLVMINATORREGI-
NAESERENISSIMAEELIZABETHAE', to imply
that the sitter is indeed Hilliard.

Whether or not the sitter is Leicester himself, the miniature is among a group by
Hilliard from the early 1570s, when the artist,
who had finished his goldsmith's apprentice-
ship in 1569, was establishing himself as a
miniaturist (see no.73). The miniature is in the
traditional circular format, but the green
background is an innovation, as is the calli-
graphic inscription, with flourishes playing an
integral part in the composition.

The elegance and delicate handling of
details of hair and costume reflect the influence of Continental court portraiture, particularly French – although in 1574 Nicholas
Hilliard had not yet visited France (see no.73).

EXH: *Loan Exhibition of Miniatures from the Collection of
the Duke of Buccleuch*, Victoria and Albert Museum
1916–17, Case B, no.9, pl.8 (as a self-portrait by
Hilliard); V&A 1947 (11), pl.III; *Treasures of Cambridge*,
Goldsmith's Hall 1959 (328)
LIT: Bayne-Powell 1985, p.110

AT

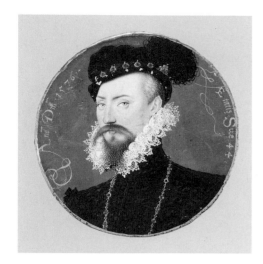

NICHOLAS HILLIARD

71 Robert Dudley, Earl of Leicester 1576

Vellum on playing card, with part of an unidentified picture card verso, painted over with black watercolour, diameter 4.4 (1¾)
Inscribed 'Anō.Dñi.1576 Ætatis Sue 44.'
PROV: …; A. Staal, Amsterdam; sold anonymously (Bernard Stadel); bt at Christie's 21 Feb. 1961 (90)
National Portrait Gallery, London

The handsome looks of Robert Dudley, first Earl of Leicester (?1532–1588), son of John Dudley, first Duke of Northumberland, were important to his career. He became a favourite of Elizabeth's on her accession in 1558, although the death of his wife Amy Robsart in 1560 in suspicious circumstances rendered their marriage impossible. He concealed two subsequent marriages from Elizabeth, and promoted his own interests by attempts to marry his son into the Stuart dynasty. In 1585 he commanded Elizabeth's armies fighting against the Spanish in the Netherlands, became absolute ruler there in 1586 (against the Queen's wishes) and was recalled in 1587 for incompetence and arrogance, resigning in 1588. Leicester's sudden death in 1588 brought rumours – reflecting his unpopularity – that he had been poisoned, and that he had himself poisoned the former husbands of his second and third wives.

In this miniature Leicester wears the type of gold chain which would have supported the medallion badge of the Order of the Garter, which Leicester received from Elizabeth in 1559. The portrait was painted the year after Leicester had entertained Elizabeth at Kenilworth with a spectacular entertainment, the 'Princely Pleasures of Kenilworth'.

Leicester was interested in arts and letters, and was one of Hilliard's most important patrons, intervening for him at court and probably standing godfather to some of the artist's seven children (several bore names in honour of Leicester's family). In 1571 Hilliard had made a 'booke of portraitures' for the Earl.

This miniature was probably painted from life. The facial features are unfaded.

EXH: V&A 1983 (68)
LIT: NPG 1969, I, p.194; Roy Strong, 'The Leicester House Miniatures: Robert Sidney, 1st Early of Leicester and his Circle', *Burlington Magazine*, vol.127, 1985, pp.694–701

AT

ATTRIBUTED TO FRANÇOIS CLOUET c.1515–1572

72 Catherine de'Medici c.1555

Vellum on card, oval 6 × 4 (2⅜ × 1¾)
PROV: …; H.E. Backer, from whom acquired by lender 1954
Board of Trustees of the Victoria and Albert Museum, London

Catherine de'Medici (1519–1589), of the famous Medici dynasty of Florence, married the future Henri II of France in 1533. She became Queen in 1547, and Regent at the death of her husband in 1559. She was the mother of the last three Valois kings: François II (the husband of Mary, Queen of Scots), Charles IX, and Henri III.

This is a rare portrait of Catherine before she was widowed in 1559, when she adopted the veil and severely plain dress of a widow. Here, her black dress is elegantly cut and trimmed with white fur. She wears magnificent jewels, a jewelled French hood, and holds a feather fan.

The miniature is one of a group attributed to François Clouet, who was appointed by François I in 1541 to succeed his father Jean Clouet as court portraitist. His portrait miniatures meticulously record the fine details of Valois court dress. He executed chalk portrait drawings, and oil paintings as well.

Although the French royal family employed Italian artists to bring Italian influence to royal architecture, sculpture and interior decoration, they valued the naturalistic observation found in French portraiture. Clouet here renders Catherine's face with tiny brushstrokes. The result is more three-dimensional in appearance than Holbein's more linear portraits. The illusion is heightened by the way in which Catherine's fingers extend over the gold border, a pictorial trick typical of northern Renaissance portraits.

The miniature of Catherine is probably based on a drawing, since Clouet, like Holbein, began his miniature portraits with drawings. It may be related to a version of a drawing of Catherine in the British Museum, which has been attributed to Clouet. French court portraits were known to Holbein and Hilliard, who both visited the Valois court, Holbein in the 1520s, when he adopted the Clouet practice of drawing with coloured chalks, and Hilliard in 1576–8.

The black-stained wooden box which frames the portrait is seventeenth-century; the other half contains a portrait of James I by John Hoskins.

EXH: V&A 1983 (70)
LIT: For the British Museum drawing, *Le Portrait en France à la cour des Valois: Crayons français du XVIe siècle conservès dans la collection de M.G. Salting à Londres* (ed. E. Moreau-Nélaton), pl.xxxii

AT

NICHOLAS HILLIARD
1546/7–1618

73 Self-Portrait 1577

Vellum on card, diameter 4.1 (1⅝)
Inscribed 'Anno Dni. | 1577; Ætatis Suæ | 30' on either side of the head; monogram NH (damaged) above the left shoulder. On the back of the frame, an inscription by the Hon. Mrs Thomas Liddell: 'Hilliard the son | painted by | himself – se the Father | These pictures were given | to me by Mrs Clavering | who had them originally from Sir Robt Rich | 1843 C E Liddell.'
PROV: Laurence Hilliard (mentioned, possibly with the companion miniature of Nicholas Hilliard's father, in Laurence's will of 21 Feb. 1640); by descent to Laurence's son Thomas; …; in 1706 in the possession of Simon Fanshaw, Esq., according to Roger de Piles, *The Art of Painting*, 3rd ed., 1754, p.384 (See also Vertue II, p.129); acquired by John Sidney, 6th Earl of Leicester (1680–1737) and in 1735 seen by George Vertue at Leicester House; inherited 1737 by John's brother, Jocelyn Sidney, 7th and last Earl of Leicester (died 1743); by him given to Field-Marshal Sir Robert Rich, Bt (1685–1785); by descent to his son Lt-Gen. Sir Robert Rich, 5th Bt (1714–1785); passed to Mrs Clavering; given by her to her niece Caroline Elizabeth (died 1890), eldest daughter of George, 5th Viscount Barrington on her marriage to the Hon. Thomas Liddell; by her given to her niece, Mary Frances (died 1913) (Mrs Alfred Sartoris), daughter of William, 6th Viscount Barrington; sold by her at Christie's 27 June 1906 (76), bt Hodgkins; acquired by George Salting and bequeathed by him with his collection to the Victoria and Albert Museum 1910
Board of Trustees of the Victoria and Albert Museum, London
[Not exhibited]

Nicholas Hilliard was born in about 1547, the son of the Exeter goldsmith Richard Hilliard. He was apprenticed in 1562 to Elizabeth I's goldsmith, Robert Brandon, became a freeman of the Goldsmiths' Company in 1569, and married Brandon's daughter Alice in 1576. From 1571 Hilliard produced miniature portraits, as well as working for the Queen as a goldsmith and jeweller. After visiting France in 1576–8/9, he returned to England, where he continued to work for the Queen (he made

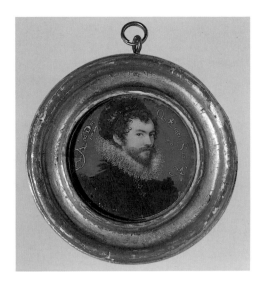

her Second Great Seal in 1584). Hilliard depended on commissions for his income (he did not obtain a monopoly of royal portraiture until 1617) and experienced financial difficulties: he and Alice had seven children. As a result, Hilliard extended his practice of miniature-painting beyond court circles. He died in 1619, leaving his son Laurence to continue his business.

This self-portrait of Hilliard was formerly the companion to a miniature of Hilliard's father, Richard Hilliard (1518/9–1594), now also in the Victoria and Albert Museum. They were formerly in identical frames, which were removed by 1735 but which bore inscriptions which have been recorded.

The self-portrait frame was inscribed 'Nicholas Hilliard Aurifaber, Sculptor, & celebris Illuminator Serenissimae Reginae Elisabethae, Anno 1577. Aetatis suae 30' ('Nicholas Hilliard Goldsmith, Sculptor, and famous Illuminator of the most Serene Queen Elizabeth, in the Year 1577 and the 30th of his Age').

By July 1577, Nicholas Hilliard had left for France in the train of Queen Elizabeth's ambassador, Sir Amyas Paulet. During Hilliard's time in France, negotiations were underway for the marriage of Elizabeth with François, duc d'Anjou (1554–1584), fourth son of Catherine de'Medici (see no.72). Hilliard painted miniatures of d'Anjou (Musée Condé, Chantilly, and Kunsthistorisches Museum, Vienna) and illuminated a prayer book (now lost) for him. The duc gave Hilliard the post of *valet de chambre* in his household.

Hilliard also visited the court of Anjou's sister, Marguerite de Valois, at Béarn, and stayed with the court painter to Louise, the French Queen of Lorraine. He had plenty of opportunity to see the French palaces decorated by artists of the Italianate School of Fontainebleau, and to meet French court artists, who enjoyed high status at the sophisticated, art-loving Valois court. He stayed with the French Mannerist sculptor, Germain Pilon (c.1531–1590), and probably saw his portrait medallions. Although François Clouet was dead, Hilliard probably saw miniatures by him (see no.72). During Hilliard's time in France he moved towards the oval format used by French artists for miniatures. He returned to London in late 1578, or in 1579.

In his self-portrait, still in the English circular format, Hilliard depicts himself as youthful (he was in his early thirties) and exquisitely dressed: a gentleman rather than a working artist. The miniature of his wife Alice Brandon, Mrs Hilliard (Victoria and Albert Museum, London), which he painted in 1578, shows her equally well dressed, with a costly lace ruff. Both miniatures have an elegance and refinement which may reflect Hilliard's French experience.

The miniature has been damaged and the beard, ruff and right cheek have been repainted.

EXH: V&A 1947 (14); V&A 1983 (49)
LIT: Roger De Piles, *Art of Painting*, 1754, ed. B. Buckeridge, p.431; Vertue IV, p.80; Horace Walpole, *Anecdotes of Painting in England*, 1782 ed., I, p.257n.; Carl Winter, *Elizabethan Miniatures*, 1943, pl.III (a), no.14; Auerbach 1961, pp.30, 70–1, pl.30, p.292, no.29; Strong 1975, pl.I; Murdoch et al. 1981, p.53, col. pl.3(a)

AT

NICHOLAS HILLIARD

74 George Clifford, 3rd Earl of Cumberland ?1590

Vellum on panel 25.7 × 17.8 (10⅛ × 7)
PROV: …; Duke of Buccleuch
Inscribed 'Hasta quan[do]' on shield, upper right
National Maritime Museum, Greenwich

George Clifford, 3rd Earl of Cumberland (1558–1605), courtier, gambler, and seaman, succeeded as Earl in 1570. He inherited large estates in the north of England, commanded a ship against the Armada in 1588, and became a Knight of the Garter in 1592. During his lifetime Cumberland spent a fortune on unsuccessful privateering expeditions against the Spanish bullion fleet. He died in 1605.

The miniature commemorates Cumberland's role as Queen's Champion, pledged to defend her honour against all comers in the tilting-yard at Whitehall Palace in the Accession Day tilts. By the early 1580s, these annual pageants held in the Queen's honour on 17 November, the anniversary of her accession to the throne, were the most important Elizabethan festivals. The combats were accompanied by allegorical plots with patriotic, Protestant themes. The combatant knights and their attendants wore fancy dress, featuring the emblems and devices which were part of Renaissance court culture.

Cumberland first attended Accession Day tilts in 1583, and in 1590 became Queen's Champion. In the miniature he is shown holding his tilting lance, in the costume of the Knight of Pendragon Castle (one of his castles in Westmorland). As the Knight, he entered the tilting-yard riding a dragon laden with booty.

The Earl often wore this star-patterned Greenwich armour for Accession Day tilts, and is also shown wearing it in 'The Great Picture of Lady Anne Clifford', the portrait triptych of 1646 commissioned by his daughter, now attributed to Jan van Belcamp (Abbot Hall Art Gallery, Kendal, on loan at Appleby Castle, Westmorland).

His gold-braided, jewelled surcoat and his hat are embroidered with armillary spheres, branches of olive and *caducei* (the Roman god Mercury's serpent-encircled wand). Armillary spheres were symbols associated with the Queen and her champions: they also appear in the 1568 portrait by Antonis Mor of Cumberland's predecessor as Queen's Champion, Sir Henry Lee, and in 'The Ditchley Portrait' of Queen Elizabeth c.1592 (nos.20, 45). The Queen's jewelled glove has been sewn onto

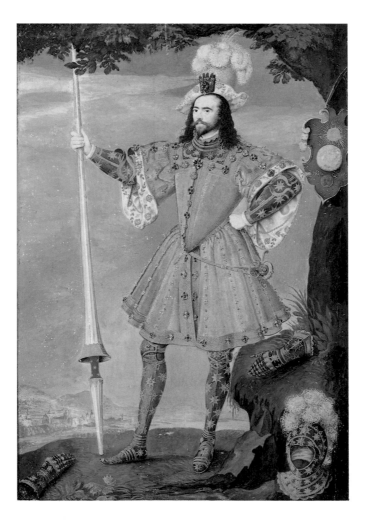

his hat; his helmet and gauntlets are displayed, as in other tournament portraits of knights.

At left is a view across the Thames towards Whitehall Palace and the tilting-yard. At right, Cumberland's emblematic shield hangs from the tree. It would be hung in the Shield Gallery of the palace after the tournament. The shield's motto 'Hasta quan[do]' proclaims that Cumberland will wield his lance (hasta) as Queen's Champion until the sun, moon and earth are eclipsed.

The miniature is one of a group of large-scale, mostly rectangular miniatures painted *c.*1585–95 by Hilliard for wealthy sitters, who are shown full-length. He based the composition of the Cumberland portrait on a 1582 engraving of a pike-bearer by the Netherlandish artist Hendrick Goltzius (1558–1617).

The miniature suffers from fading and from blackening through oxidisation.

EXH: V&A 1947 (54); V&A 1983 (216); London and Belfast (13.28)
LIT: H.A. Kennedy, 'Early English Portrait Miniatures in the Collection of the Duke of Buccleuch', ed. C. Holmes, *Studio*, vol.69, 1917, pl.17; Carl Winter, *Elizabethan Miniatures*, 1943, pl.5; John Pope-Hennessy, *A Lecture on Nicholas Hilliard*, 1949, pl.31; Auerbach 1961, pp.112–13, pl.89; 302 (87); NPG 1969, I, p.57; Roy Strong, *The Cult of Elizabeth: Elizabethan Portraiture and Pageantry*, 1977, p.156; Murdoch et al. 1981, pp.54, 72, col. pl.8; Sheila O'Connell, *William Larkin and the 3rd Earl of Dorset: A Portrait in Focus*, exh. cat., Ranger's House, Blackheath 1989; Graham Parry, 'The Great Picture of Lady Anne Clifford', in Howarth 1993, pp.206–7

AT

NICHOLAS HILLIARD

75 Leonard Darr 1591

Watercolour on vellum on playing card, clipped at the top edge, oval
7 × 5.7 (2¾ × 2¼)
Inscribed 'Anō. Ætatis. Leonardi.Darr.' and 'Anō.Dnī. 1591', on either side of the head
PROV: …; sold May 1726 from the collection of Mr Halstead or Halsted, when recorded by Vertue (Vertue II, p.13); Edward Harley, 2nd Earl of Oxford (1689–1741) when recorded *c.*1731 by Vertue (Vertue IV, p.41); thence by descent
Private Collection

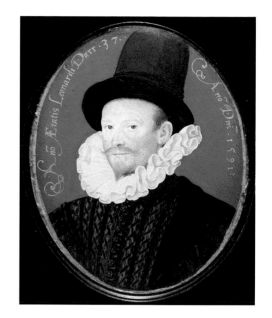

Little is known about the sitter. It was suggested by Goulding that he was the Tavistock merchant Leonard Dare, who received a licence in October 1585 to ship fifty-four tons of pilchards and conger in the *Trudeler*, bound for St Malo in France. The sitter's clothing suggests that Leonard Darr, whoever he was, was prosperous, but not of high social rank.

Nicholas Hilliard was obliged to accept sitters from circles beyond the court, because at this time he was still not on the court payroll, and lived by commissions. In the process he helped to extend the portrait miniature beyond an exclusive court clientele. At the time that he painted Leonard Darr, Hilliard was also producing costly, large miniatures for the richest courtiers: his miniature of George Clifford, 3rd Earl of Cumberland in tilting armour (no.74) dates from only a year earlier than Leonard Darr.

The miniature is in mint condition, its colours unfaded. Hilliard's bright red hatching brushstrokes are still visible in the face.

EXH: V&A 1947 (53); V&A 1983 (91)
LIT: R.W. Goulding, 'The Welbeck Abbey Miniatures', *Walpole Society*, vol.4, 1914–15; Auerbach 1961, pp.134, 306, no.109, pl.109

AT

ROWLAND LOCKEY c.1565–1616

76 The More Family, Household and Descendants 1593–4

Vellum on card 24.6 × 29.4 (9⅝ × 11⅝)
Inscribed: The family are identified by gold letters painted on their clothing, which correspond to those in the inscription painted in gold along the upper edge: 'A. Johannes Morus eques auratus et iudex B. Tho. Mors eques aur. Dns. Canc. Angl. et fil. et haer. dti. Johannis C. Joh. More Ar. fil. et haer. Dti. Tho D. Anna sola fil. et haer. Ed. Cresacre Ar. Vxor Joh Mor Ar. E. Tho. More Arm. fil. et haer. Dictor. Joh. Mor. Ar. et An VX. eius F. Maria fil. Joh. Scroope Ar. frat. Henrici Dni. Scroope G. Duo filii dictorum Tho. Mor. et Mar. VX. eius H. Tres filiae Tho. Mori Dni. Cancellarij Angliae'
(In translation: 'A. John More distinguished knight and judge B. Thomas More distinguished knight and Lord Chancellor of England and son and heir of the said John C. John More son and heir of the said Thomas D. Anne only daughter and heir of Edward Cresacre Knight wife of John More Knight E. Thomas More [the Younger] Knight son and heir of the said John More Knight and Anne his Wife F. Mary daughter of John Scroope Knight brother of Henry Lord Scroope G. Two sons of the said Thomas More and Mary his Wife [i.e John More and Cresacre More] H. Three daughters of Thomas More Lord Chancellor of England [i.e. Cicely Heron, Elizabeth Dauncey and Margaret Roper]'). A label lettered in gold in the lower left corner reads: 'Thomas Morus Londini | An.Do.1480. est natus | Scaccarij primu.tum. A.D. | 1529. totius Angliae | Cancellarius est tactus [factus ?]. | Henrici.8.iussu decollatus | interijt A.D.1535. 6 non.Jul.' ('Thomas More of London was born in the Year of our Lord 1480 […] first [made] Chancellor of all England in 1529 A.D. died beheaded by order of Henry the Eighth on 6 July 1535')

PROV: …; Lady Gerrard, a descendant of the More Family, from whom bt 1705 by James Sotheby; by descent at Ecton Hall, where seen by Vertue in 1742 (Vertue v, pp.10–11); Sotheby's 11 Oct. 1955, bt by the Revd James Edmund Strickland; bequeathed by his widow Anne Louise Strickland to the lender in 1973
Board of Trustees of the Victoria and Albert Museum, London

Sir Thomas More (1478–1535), Catholic humanist and reformer, and author of the book *Utopia* (c.1516), was appointed Chancellor of England by Henry VIII in 1529. He was beheaded in 1535 after refusing to take an oath which involved repudiating papal authority. In 1935 he was canonised as a martyr by the Roman Catholic Church.

The miniature is a family group portrait and a commemoration of a dynastic connection with Sir Thomas More. It was probably commissioned by More's grandson Thomas More the Younger, himself imprisoned for his Catholicism.

The sitters are identified by gold letters on their clothing. From left to right, they are:
A. Sir John More (1451–1530), father of Sir Thomas More, Serjeant at Law (1503), Judge of the Court of Common Pleas (1518) and of King's Bench (1523)
B. Sir Thomas More (1477/8–1535)
C. John More (?1509–1547), only son of Sir Thomas More
D. Anne Cresacre (1511–1577), ward of Sir Thomas More. She was the daughter and heiress of Edward Cresacre of Barnborough, Yorkshire, and married John More in 1529
E. Thomas More the Younger (1531–1606), son of Anne Cresacre and John More
F. Mary Scrope (1534–1607): wife of Thomas More the Younger, niece of Lord Scrope of Bolton
G. The two sons of Thomas More the Younger and Mary Scrope: John More (1557–?1599) and Cresacre More
H. The three daughters of Sir Thomas More: Cicely Heron (born 1507), Elizabeth Dauncey (born 1506), and Margaret Roper (1505–1544)
The miniature has long been attributed to Rowland Lockey. It is related to the lost painting of 'The Family of Sir Thomas More', by Hans Holbein, and to other group paintings of the More family by Rowland Lockey.

Hans Holbein painted a group portrait of the More family when he stayed with them during his first visit to England, c.1527. That

portrait is lost (probably burned in the eighteenth century), but Holbein's drawing for it survives in the Kupferstichkabinett, Basel, where he probably took it to show Erasmus in 1528.

The lost Holbein painting was owned in the 1590s by Sir Thomas More's descendants, who commissioned two life-scale oil paintings based on the Holbein group portrait. One, signed by Rowland Lockey and dated 1592 (collection Lord St Oswald), is believed to be a copy of the lost Holbein painting.

The other, attributed to Lockey and dated 1593, alters the Holbein composition by adding the next generation of More's family to the Holbein sitters. It was probably commissioned by Thomas More the Younger, belonged to his son Cresacre More, and is now in the National Portrait Gallery.

Thomas More the Younger is also thought to have commissioned this miniature from Lockey. It was probably painted in 1594, since Thomas More the Younger's son Cresacre More appears cleanshaven in the large painting of 1593, but had grown a slight beard and moustache by the time the miniature was painted.

Rowland Lockey, presumably acting on instructions from his patron, looks at the Holbein composition from the point of view of the Elizabethan descendants. Dynasty is emphasised: the people of Sir Thomas More's household who appeared in the Holbein picture, but who were not related by blood to the Elizabethan Mores, were left out of the new painting, and the miniature. Sir Thomas More's wife Alice, his foster daughter Margaret Giggs, and his secretary John Harris are all missing. An exception was made for Henry Patenson, Sir Thomas More's jester, who appears in the Holbein drawing and in this miniature, but not in Lockey's large oil painting. The woman in front of Patenson is More's daughter Elizabeth Dauncey (no.93).

Sir Thomas More's ward Anne Cresacre was included by Lockey, since she married More's son John and was the mother of Thomas More the Younger. In the Lockey oil she appears twice: as the young woman painted by Holbein, and as an older woman in a portrait hanging at the back of Lockey's composition. In the miniature, she is second from left, but the portrait-within-a-portrait of her has been replaced by a view of a Tudor garden, with 'knots' of low-clipped hedge, and a banqueting house. According to the eighteenth-century antiquarian George Vertue, it is a view of Sir Thomas More's garden at Chelsea. Beyond it is a view of London, with

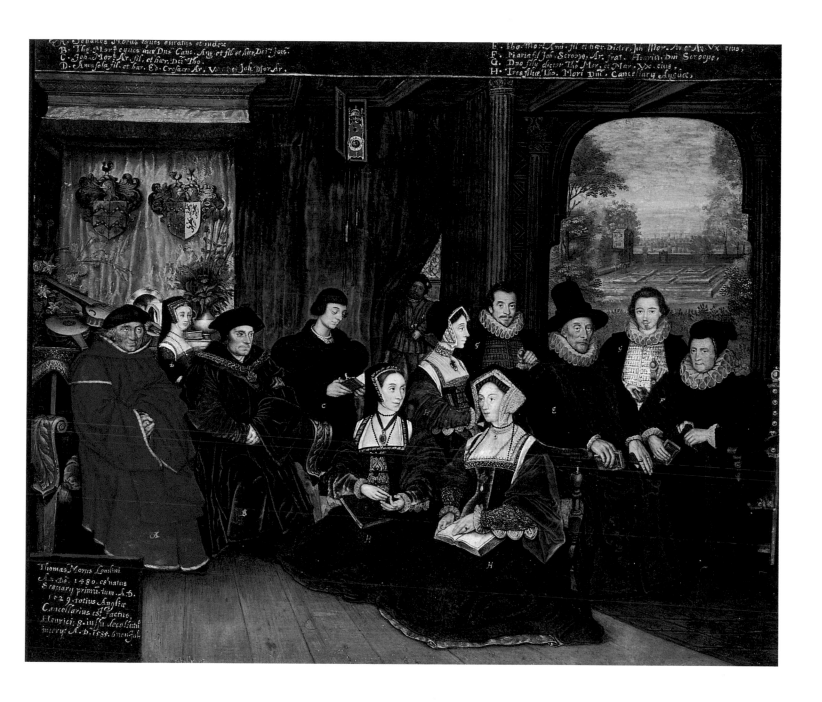

old St Paul's Cathedral. To the left are the escutcheons of the More and Cresacre families.

Rowland Lockey was a pupil of Hilliard, and worked closely with him in the early 1590s. The miniature preserves the brighter colours of a Hilliard miniature of the 1580s. It demonstrates the versatility of an Elizabethan portrait artist: Lockey's larger version of this composition, in the National Portrait Gallery, is over seven feet long (227.4 × 330.2 (89½ × 130)).

The facial features in the miniature have been restored after flaking, and the silver has oxidised.

EXH: *Royal House of Tudor*, The New Gallery 1890; *'The King's Good Servant': Sir Thomas More 1477/8–1535*, NPG 1977 (170, repr. in col, p.90); V&A 1983 (267)
LIT: Vertue V, pp.10–11; Horace Walpole, *Anecdotes of Painting in England*, ed. James Dallaway and R.N. Wornum, 1849, I, pp.145–46; O. Kurz, 'Rowland Lockey', *Burlington Magazine*, vol.99, 1957, p.15; Auerbach 1961, no.262; S. Morison and N. Barker, *The Likeness of Thomas More*, 1963, pp.18 et seq., no.405; NPG 1969, I, pp.345–51; Murdoch et al. 1981, p.61, col. pl.16; Campbell 1990, pp.142–3

AT

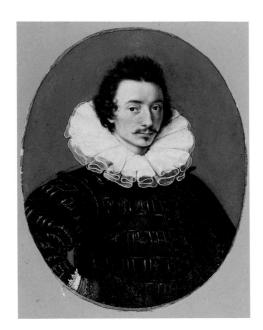

ISAAC OLIVER c.1560/5–1617

77 Self-Portrait c.1590

Vellum on plain card, oval 6.3 × 5
(2½ × 2)
PROV: …; c.1726–7 in collection of Col.
James Seymour (?1658–1739), when
recorded by George Vertue (II, p.47); bt
by Thomas Barrett of Lee Priory, Kent
(1698–1757); bt by Horace Walpole
(Lord Orford), Strawberry Hill (*Description of the Villa … at Strawberry Hill*, 1774,
p.84); Strawberry Hill sale 9 May 1842
(13th day) (85) bt by the 13th Earl of
Derby; Christie's 8 June 1971 (79) bt by
National Portrait Gallery
National Portrait Gallery, London

Isaac Oliver came to England as a child in
1568, brought from France by his father, a
Huguenot goldsmith, to escape religious persecution, and trained as a limner (miniature
painter) with Hilliard. He visited Venice in
1596, and possibly the Netherlands in 1588.
In 1602 Oliver married the sister of the leading portrait-painter Marcus Gheeraerts the
Younger, and in 1605 was appointed limner to
Queen Anne of Denmark, wife to James I. In
1606 he became a denizen of England. Later,
Oliver was limner to Henry, Prince of Wales
(died 1612). He died in 1617, bequeathing his
drawings and limned pictures (including histories and stories) to his son Peter Oliver.

This miniature, in excellent condition, is
one of two self-portraits by Oliver (another is
in the Royal Collection) which reflect Netherlandish portrait styles of the late sixteenth
century. Oliver's exposure to Flemish influences reflects his position in a Huguenot community (his second marriage, into the
Gheeraerts family, can only have increased his
contacts).

If, as has been thought, Oliver was a fully-
trained artist before he went to Nicholas
Hilliard to learn the technique of miniature
painting (his first known miniature is dated
1587), he may have trained on the Continent:
an early familiarity with Flemish portrait
painting on the scale of life may help to
explain the difference between Oliver's and
Hilliard's miniatures. Oliver's portraits are
painted rather than drawn. His oval compositions resemble the portrait engravings of the
Netherlandish artist Hendrick Goltzius
(1558–1617). From the late 1580s his miniatures featured highly finished faces, modelled
with shadows, in the manner of his Flemish
contemporary Frans Pourbus the Younger.
The effect is more three-dimensional than in
the miniatures of Nicholas Hilliard.

Horace Walpole, who once owned Oliver's
self-portrait, remarked on its naturalism: 'This
picture alone would justify all I have said of
him. The art of the master and the imitation
of nature are so great in it that the largest
magnifying-glass only calls out new beauties.'
(Horace Walpole, *Anecdotes of Painting in England*, ed. James Dallaway and R.N. Wornum,
1849, I, p.178).

EXH: V&A 1947 (135); Tate Gallery 1969–70 (149);
V&A 1983 (133); *Master Drawings from the NPG*, NPG
1993 (3)
LIT: George Scharf, *A Catalogue of the Collection of
Pictures at Knowsley Hall*, 1875, Supplt., p.229

AT

ISAAC OLIVER

78 An Allegorical Scene *c.*1590–5

Watercolour and gouache on vellum on card 11.3 × 17 (4½ × 6¾)
Signed with monogram followed by 'in' (invenit), b.l.
PROV: Possibly identifiable as the miniature 'May Day' in the collection of Backer, a Leyden lawyer, 1622 (A. Staring, *Kunsthistorische Verkenningen*, 1948, p.3); sold Justitsraad Geheimearkivar Chr. Eberhard Voss sale, Copenhagen 23 May 1791 (43), probably bt by Count Holstein; by descent in the Holstein family, Ledreborg, to Countess Louise Christina Holstein by whom sold to the Statens Museum 1976
Den Kongelige Maleri- og Skulptursamling, Statens Museum for Kunst, Copenhagen

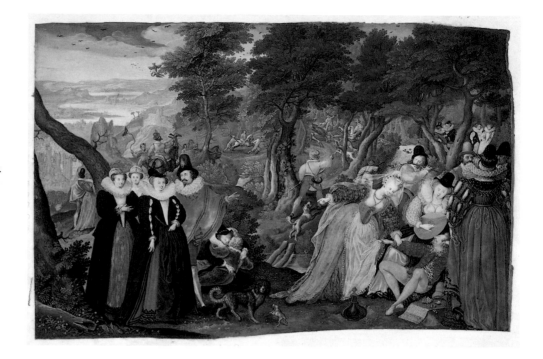

This miniature is probably an allegory on conjugal love. The scene of strolling and merry-making figures can be read as a moralising comment on different types of love, particularly the married and unmarried states, represented by two distinct groups on either side of the picture. Comparison between them is invited by the dignified man on the left who gestures, in a rather stern way, towards the merry goings-on on the right, and the gold-clad female of that group who points with amusement towards the sedate woman on the left. The left represents true love and felicity and the figures, dressed soberly and with restrained deportment, walk along the path of righteousness. The embracing couple on the ground, below the gentleman's outstretched hand, may be a mother and son who represent maternal love. In contrast to this, the gaudy pleasure-seeking group sprawled on the ground on the right is an illustration of misguided wantonness, transient amusement and moral laxity. The young man, in an undignified posture, is surrounded by symbols of decadence – wine, grapes, and women in revealing attire, and is perhaps supposed to be reminiscent of the Prodigal Son among the harlots, a popular theme in Netherlandish art of the late sixteenth and early seventeenth centuries. The dogs in the centre foreground of the picture continue the theme of confrontation. Both are presumably allied to their appropriate party, the one on the left representing fidelity, the small one,

leaping up at the other, being a fashionable and frivolous pet belonging to the right-hand group. As Finsten notes, the idea for this narrative possibly derived from Sir Thomas Hoby's *The Book of the Courtier* (1561, reprinted 1577 and 1588), a translation of Castiglione's book on courtly manners, which dwells on the differences between the 'vertuous or vitious' kinds of love, and which was extremely popular in courtly circles at this date.

This mixture of allegory, landscape and genre painting is unique in Oliver's oeuvre, and is a blend of various types of Netherlandish painting that seem to have been known to him at least through prints. As a direct source Finsten cites a Flemish woodcut by P. Huys, made for Jan van der Noot's *Lofsang van Brabant* (1580), in which the artist is showing his betrothed the way for a good and honest life. The couple stand in a similar position to the sober couple in Oliver's miniature, the man gesturing towards two seated women, one playing a musical instrument and the other paying attentions to a young man at her feet (Finsten 1981, II, pp.22–6, illus. R28). The hunting scene in the background does not seem to have a specific source but broadly draws on Netherlandish works, a 'Boar Hunt' by Hans Bol (Munich Residenz) being particularly cited (Colding and Andersen 1950,

pp.326–7). The landscape background, totally un-English in topography and character, is also an adaptation of Netherlandish examples, for example the work of Gillis van Coninxloo.

Outdoor scenes of merry-making, with figures in contemporary dress, were rare in English painting at this date, although parallels can be found in embroidery and tapestry, and also in prints, for example the woodcuts of Queen Elizabeth's hunting parties in George Turbervile's *The Noble Art of Venerie* and *The Book of Faulconrie* (both 1575). The figures in Hoefnagel's 'Fête at Bermondsey' (see no.62) are quite close in feel.

EXH: *A Kind of Gentle Painting*, Scottish Arts Council, 1977 (54); *Christian IV and Europe*, 19th Council of Europe Exhibition, Denmark 1988 (1071)
LIT: Torben Holck Colding and Jorgen Andersen, 'An Elizabethan Love Theme', *Burlington Magazine*, vol.92, 1950, pp.326–7; Finsten 1981, I, pp.102–4, II, pp.22–6; Strong 1983, pp.155–7; Reynolds 1988, p.22

TB

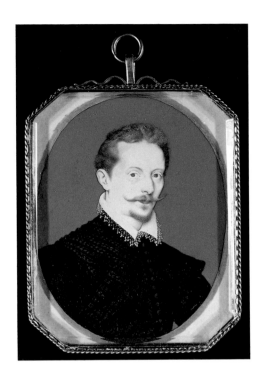

79 Called 'Sir Arundel Talbot'

*c.*1596

Vellum on playing card, an ace of hearts verso 7 × 5.4 (2¾ × 2⅛)
Inscribed on the front 'Anno Domini 1595 | Aetatis M. Isacq Oliviero | Francese 10 [in monogram] V.14 | da e8' on either side of head. Inscribed on the back by the artist; 'adi. i3 Magio. 1596. In Venetia. Fecit m.Isacq oliuiero Francese I O v̄. i4. da L 8' (i.e. 'May 13th, 1596, made by Isaac Oliver the Frenchman in Venice'); 'Viva & vera effigies | Arundelli Talbot | Equitis Aurati' below in a later hand
PROV: ...; W.G. Eden, London, from whom bt 12 Feb. 1909 by Messrs Durlacher; ...; H.P. Pfungst collection, sold Christie's 14 June 1917 (57); acquired by the lender under the Capt. H.B. Murray Bequest
Board of Trustees of the Victoria and Albert Museum, London

Nothing is known of a 'Sir Arundel Talbot'. His name, if genuine, suggests that he might have been related to the Earls of Shrewsbury, and that he might have had as godparent a member of the Howard family.

The inscription on the back of the miniature indicates that on 13 May 1596 Oliver was in Venice. He may have travelled there with a kinsman of the Earl of Shrewsbury, Roger Manners, 5th Earl of Rutland, who was in Venice in the spring of 1596 as part of a trip which also took in Heidelberg and Paris. An association with Rutland is suggested by the fact that, once back in England, Oliver painted some of the Earl's associates: George Clifford, 3rd Earl of Cumberland (see no.74), Robert Devereux, 2nd Earl of Essex (see no.80), and Vice-Admiral Sir Richard Leveson (Wallace Collection, London).

In Venice, Oliver must have seen portraits by Titian, and is known to have painted a copy of a Veronese, afterwards in Charles I's collection.

The inscription also describes Oliver as 'francese', a Frenchman, from London. Oliver had come as a child to London in 1568, brought from Rouen by his father Pierre Oliver, a Huguenot goldsmith escaping religious persecution. Isaac did not become an English denizen until 1606.

The miniature itself appears to be unfinished, with little hatching-in of facial features, and almost no shadowed modelling. The gold border has been added, but the miniature has not been clipped to its final shape.

EXH: *Exposition de le miniature*, Hôtel Goffinet, Brussels 1912 (254), p.v (col.), 21, p.19 (inscription on verso); V&A 1947 (149); Tate Gallery 1969–70; V&A 1983 (152)
LIT: B.S. Long, *British Miniaturists 1520–1860*, 1929, p.318; *Miniatures Catalogue*, Victoria and Albert Museum 1930, p.51; Carl Winter, *Elizabethan Miniatures*, 1943, p.28, col. pl.xi(b); Auerbach 1961, p.244, pl.209; no.244; Finsten 1981, II, pp.40–2; Murdoch et al. 1981, p.63, col. pl.12a

AT

ISAAC OLIVER

80 Earl of Essex *c.*1596

Vellum on plain card, oval 5 × 4.1
(2 × 1⅝)
PROV: ...; sold by E.J. Clark, Sotheby's
26 Nov. 1973 (96)
National Portrait Gallery, London

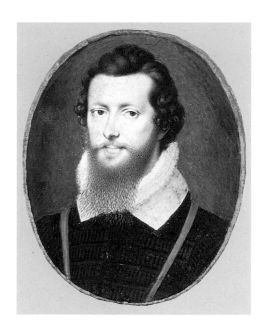

Robert Devereux, second Earl of Essex
(1566–1601), stepson of the Earl of Leicester
(no.71), was Elizabeth I's court favourite in her
old age. Essex was a military commander
strongly opposed to Spain, and a patron of
letters. He was appointed Master of the Horse
in 1587, and made a Knight of the Garter in
1588. In 1599 Essex was appointed commander of the army sent to quell revolt in Ireland,
but was dismissed from the post of Governor-
General there when he returned to England.
His 1601 rising against Elizabeth failed to
attract the support of London citizens, who
remained loyal to the Queen; he was arrested
and executed.

The miniature is closely related to a life-
scale painting of 1596 by Marcus Gheeraerts
the Younger (1561/2–1636) commemorating
the Earl's return from his successful military
expedition against Cadiz (Woburn Abbey).
Essex grew his beard on this expedition.

Essex's career as a courtier was at its peak
when this miniature was made. He had
regained Elizabeth's favour after losing it by
his secret marriage in 1590, and had uncovered a Spanish plot to poison her in 1594.
Unsuccessful campaigns against the Spanish
treasure fleet, and his Irish command, still lay
in the future.

In 1602 Oliver married Marcus Gheeraerts's sister Sara, as his second wife. Essex's
choice of Oliver and Gheeraerts – rather than
Nicholas Hilliard and William Segar, previously his portrait-painters (see fig.44) – was a
fashionable one. Oliver depicts Essex as a
mature, soberly dressed man (he had been
appointed to Elizabeth's Privy Council in
1593). The Earl wears the ribbon of the Order
of the Garter. The grey background is an
innovation.

This is an autograph repetition by Oliver;
other versions include miniatures at Burghley
House, Chatsworth, and in the Royal Collection. The prime version is probably the full-
length formerly owned by Charles I.

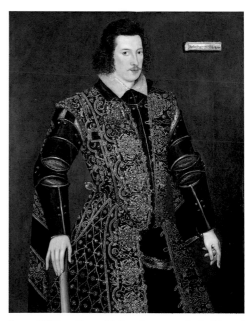

fig.44 William Segar, 'Robert Devereux, Earl of Essex'
1590, oil on panel. *National Gallery of Ireland*

EXH: V&A 1983 (155)
LIT: G.C. Williamson, *Catalogue of the Miniatures in the
Possession of J. Pierpont Morgan*, 1906, I, no.51; Millar
1960, p.108, no.23; NPG 1969, I, pp.116–17

AT

ISAAC OLIVER

81 The Browne Brothers 1598

Gouache and watercolour on vellum on card 24.1 × 26 (9½ × 10¼)
Inscribed in gold 'Ano Dom. 1598', t.l.; 'FIGVRÆ CONFORMIS AFFECTVS', top centre; and, from left to right near the sitters, their ages: 'Ætatis.21.; Ætatis 24; Ætatis.18.; Ætatis.21.'. Signed with monogram on the central decorated pilaster
PROV: First recorded by Vertue at Cowdray, seat of the Brownes, Viscounts Montague, c.1730 (Vertue II, p.82); by family descent at Cowdray to Elizabeth Poyntz, sister and heir of the 8th Viscount Montague; passed into the collection at Burghley House, presumably through her daughter Isabella, who married Brownlow, 2nd Marquess of Exeter in 1824, where recorded by 1847
Burghley House Collection

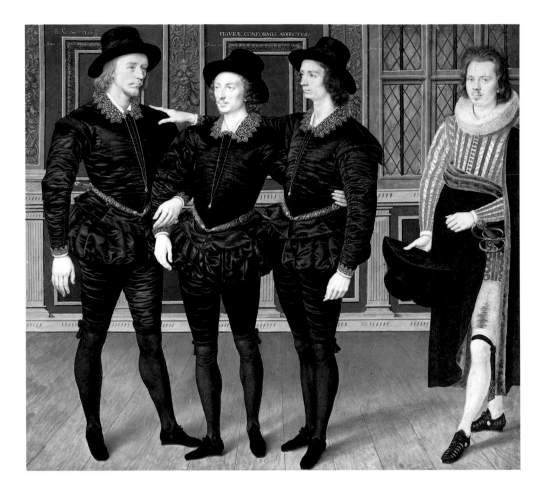

The three identically dressed young men are brothers, grandsons of Anthony Browne, 1st Viscount Montague. The central figure is Anthony Maria Browne (1573/4–1629) who succeeded his grandfather as 2nd Viscount in 1592. His younger brothers, John and William, stand on either side of him. The architecture in the background is possibly a true representation of one of the two long galleries at Cowdray, the family seat, which was largely destroyed by fire in 1793. The identity of the figure on the far right, at a distance and dressed differently from those in the main group, is not known. Like the three brothers, his age is given. He is either an unknown companion, or possibly one of the fourteen gentlemen servants employed by Anthony Maria, which is suggested by the deferential removal of his hat.

The Brownes were staunch Catholics, and Cowdray a known Catholic centre. Anthony Browne, 1st Viscount, although a loyal servant of Queen Elizabeth, was implicated in the Ridolfi Plot of 1571. Anthony Maria, in whose house Guy Fawkes had been a servant, was suspected of complicity in the Gunpowder Plot and was imprisoned in the Tower in 1605. It has been suggested that Oliver's miniature is a comment on the brothers' unity in their faith (V&A 1983, no.272), which is underlined by their identical clothing, their interlinked arms, which perhaps is an allusion to groups of the Three Graces and therefore to harmony and concord, and the motto 'Figuræ conformis affectus'. This can be translated either as 'Alike in character and in face' or as

'The heart matches the outward form' (translation Dr Keith Cunliffe, St Edmundsbury Council Museums). On the other hand it could simply represent fraternal affection and loyalty, something which Anthony Maria was keen to promote at Cowdray. In 1595 he compiled a 'Booke of orders and rules' (Cowdray MS.18. See *Sussex Archæological Collections*, VII, 1854, pp.173–212) by which his household and family should be governed, which he intended should be read out to them annually. In it he requires that 'all my people of what sorte soever that they studiously ymbrace unitye, peace, and goode agreemente amonge themselves as the only means whereby they shall procure quiett and commendacon to themselves and much honor and comforte to me'.

Oliver has once again used an engraving as a source for the composition, 'Les Frères Coligny' by Du Val, 1579 (a preparatory drawing is in the Bibliothèque Nationale, Paris), the similarity of which was noticed by Vertue c.1730 ('there is a print at whole lenght Collignæ Fratres. Odetus. Gaspar. Franciscus. Three standing together. Perhaps from hence Oliver might have taken his thought', Vertue

IV, p.54). Informal full-length group portraiture became more frequent in England in the early seventeenth century, Eworth's 'Henry Stuart, Lord Darnley and his Brother' 1563 (The Royal Collection) being a rare previous example. Gheeraerts's 'Barbara Gamage, Countess of Leicester and her Children' 1596 (private collection) takes what would become another chosen form, that of a mother being represented with her children.

The costumes of the figures are painted with great precision, and the whole is in monochrome colouring enlivened with silver and gold.

EXH: V&A 1983 (272); Washington 1985–6 (43)
LIT: Revd W.H. Charlton, *Burghley*, 1847, no.81; Mrs Charles Roundell, *Cowdray: The History of a Great English House*, 1884, pp.45–7; Vertue IV, p.54; Finsten 1981, II, pp.59–62; Strong 1983, p.169

TB

ISAAC OLIVER

82 A Lady in a Masque Costume
*c.*1610

Vellum on playing card, oval 5.4 × 4.1
(2⅛ × 1⅝)
PROV: ...; recorded 1815–21 in Dutch
Royal Collection
*Royal Cabinet of Paintings Mauritshuis (on
loan from the Rijksmuseum, Amsterdam)*

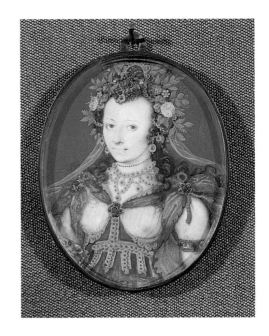

The sitter in this miniature, which was formerly considered a portrait by Hilliard of
Queen Elizabeth, has not been identified.

It is thought that she wears a costume for a
court masque. In 1605 Isaac Oliver was
appointed 'painter for the Art of limning' to
James I's queen, Anne of Denmark, an important patron of masques – the allegorical entertainments which featured dances by members
of the court, wearing magnificent clothes and
headdresses.

The pink roses and pansies in her hair suggest an association with Flora, goddess of
flowers, or with summertime. The sitter wears
a high-waisted dress of grey, shot with silver.
It is cut to expose her breasts, under transparent fabric – a style typical of early masque
designs by Inigo Jones (see Orgel and Strong
1973, I, nos.5–6, 22, 32, 75). She also wears a
veil and mantle.

The latest masque of ladies took place in
1613. Two other Isaac Oliver miniatures of
women in costumes probably relating to
masques are known. One, in the collection of
the Victoria and Albert Museum, may depict a
performer in the *Masque of Queens* by Ben Jonson, which was danced in 1609 by Anne of
Denmark and a group of lady masquers. Not
all the costume designs and descriptions for
this survive. The other portrays Anne herself
in a costume possibly either for *The Masque of
Beauty* (1608) or for *Love Freed from Ignorance
and Folly* (1611) (see fig.53 on p.192). It cannot
be more precisely identified, as the costumes
for the sixteen dancers in the former, on 10
January 1608, were not fully described.

The miniature is in good condition, though
faded.

EXH: V&A 1947 (181); V&A 1983 (223)
LIT: L. de Vries, *Spiegel Hist.*, vol.4, 1969, p.166, fig.7;
other refs. to sources considering the sitter as Queen
Elizabeth I by Hilliard; P.J.J. Van Thiel et al., *All the
Paintings of the Rijksmuseum in Amsterdam*, Amsterdam
and Maarssen 1976, no.A4347: 'Portrait of a Woman as
Flora'; Ellen Chirelstein, 'Lady Elizabeth Pope: The
Heraldic Body', in Gent and Llewellyn 1990, p.58

AT

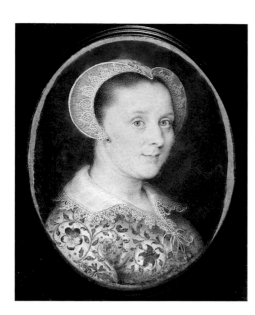

ISAAC OLIVER

83 Elizabeth Harding, Mrs Oliver
1610–15

Watercolour on vellum on playing card, three clubs verso, oval 5.2 × 4.2 (2 × 1⅝)
Inscribed 'Mrs. Oliver wife of Is. Oliver, Limner' on verso in the hand of Bernard Lens
PROV: …; Edward Harley, Earl of Oxford (1689–1741); thence by descent
Private Collection

Elizabeth Harding or Harden was born in 1589, the daughter of James Harding, a court musician of French ancestry. She married Isaac Oliver in 1606 as his third wife and bore him six children. Aged seventeen at the time of her marriage, Elizabeth was much younger than her husband; her younger sister Anne married Isaac Oliver's son by his first marriage, Peter Oliver. After Isaac's death in 1617, Elizabeth married a mercer, Pierce Morgan. She died some time between 1628 and 1640.

Elizabeth's pose and smiling expression are unusual and suggest that this is indeed an intimate family portrait. It has been compared with the relaxed, friendly atmosphere of Netherlandish family portraits of this period, notably Rubens's portraits of his first wife, Isabella Brant. Oliver would have been familiar with Netherlandish portraits and portrait prints, and had been related through his second marriage to the Flemish portraitists, Marcus Gheeraerts and John de Critz.

The embroidered Jacobean jacket Elizabeth wears in the miniature was fashionable in *c.*1615. Oliver painted another portrait of his wife (now lost), in which she was shown wearing a ruff, according to its description in the inventory of Charles II's collection.

The miniature is in a pearwood frame by Bernard Lens. The sitter's features are somewhat faded, the silver oxidised and the lead whites blackened.

EXH: Manchester 1857; Grafton Gallery 1894; BFAC 1926, p.558, pl.XXII, II.8; *Elizabethan Art*, Grosvenor Gallery 1933 (46); Royal Academy 1934 (940); V&A 1947 (154); V&A 1983 (173)
LIT: George Vertue, *Catalogue of the Portland Collection*, 1743, no.81a; Horace Walpole, *Anecdotes of Painting in England*, ed. James Dallaway and R.N. Wornum, 1849, I, pp.222–3, as by Peter Oliver; Amelia B. Edwards, *Historical Portrait Gallery*, 1964, I, pl.XXVIII, as 'Mrs Hoskins'; J.J. Foster, *Miniature Painters*, 1903, I, pl.XVI; Daphne Foskett, *A Dictionary of Miniature Painters*, 1972, I, p.15 (6) and pl.2 (6); repr. in col. on cover, vol.I; Edmond 1980, pp.74–6; Finsten 1981, II, pp.110–11, and fig.71

AT

ISAAC OLIVER

84 Henry, Prince of Wales 1610–11

Vellum on card, oval 5.1 × 4.1 (2 × 1⅝)
Signed with monogram 'I O' in gold,
centre right
PROV: …; Duke of Buccleuch; bt 1942
by the Fitzwilliam Museum, Cambridge,
with a grant from the National Art Collections Fund
*Syndics of the Fitzwilliam Museum,
Cambridge*

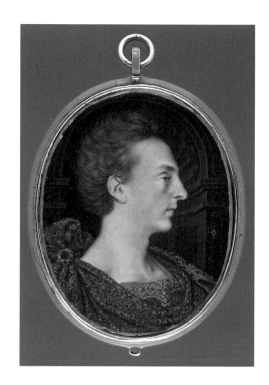

Henry Frederick, Prince of Wales (1594–
1612), eldest son of James VI of Scotland and
his wife Anne of Denmark, was born at
Stirling and came to England when James
acceded to the English throne in 1603. He
was created Prince of Wales in 1610, with his
own court at St James's Palace, and it was
hoped by some that he would assert the
Protestant cause more militantly in Europe
than his pacifist father had done. The prince
died of typhoid fever on 5 November 1612,
aged eighteen, leaving his younger brother
Charles to inherit the throne.

The design, with its classical and martial
allusions, pays homage to the prince as a
model of antique virtue and heroism, while
echoing the profile portraits of Henry V,
another 'warrior prince'. Prince Henry was an
expert horseman, interested in military and
naval matters. He is shown here bare-headed,
and in profile to the right, 'all'antica', i.e.
wearing a Jacobean version of ancient Roman
armour and drapery. The architectural background is a grey shell-shaped niche of classical design. Other portraits of British courtiers
survive from the same period, with similar
costumes or backgrounds: Renaissance classicism was fashionable in Prince Henry's circle,
as evidenced by the court entertainments
devised for the Prince by Inigo Jones and Ben
Jonson.

Prince Henry enjoyed tilting and
masquing, and starred in the court entertainment for New Year's Day 1611, *Oberon, the
Fairy Prince*. He wore the costume of a Roman
Emperor, although not the dress shown here
(see no.109). The art-loving prince also

owned a valuable collection of classical antiquities, acquired from Abraham Gorlaeus
(1549–1609) of Delft, which included antique
medals with profile portraits of Roman
emperors. In 1610 an engraved portrait of
Prince Henry in imperial profile was published as preface to *Poly-Olbion*, the patriotic
poem about Britain by one of the Prince's
poets, Michael Drayton (1563–1631).

This may be the miniature of the Prince
which was inventoried in Charles I's collection about 1640 by Abraham van der Doort
(*c*.1575/80–1640) as a 'Picture of Prince
Henry side faced with a naked neck and a
redd scarff after the old Roman … fashion',
'Don by the life by Isack Olliver'. At that
time, the miniature was in a black ebony
turned box, with a crystal over it to protect it.

The survival of replicas and copies in the
Victoria and Albert Museum, the National
Portrait Gallery and the Rijksmuseum, Amsterdam (on loan to the Mauritshuis), suggests
that the image Oliver created of Henry was a
popular one. In 1611/2 Oliver used the profile
for a large miniature, Prince Henry fighting at
the Barriers, now lost, which depicted Henry
in modern armour, exercising with the pike. It
was the basis of portrait engravings by
William Hole and Simon van de Passe.

Oliver not only replaced Hilliard as the
Prince's portraitist, but collected art for him.
He may have been supplanted as 'lymner' to
Prince Henry following a wager pitting Oliv-
er's skills against those of one Mr Bilford
(*Letters of John Chamberlain*, ed. N.E. McClure,
Philadelphia 1939, I, p.312). In 1612 Oliver
walked in Prince Henry's funeral cortège as
his 'paynter', Mark Bilford, by whom no sur-
viving works are known, as his 'lymner'.

EXH: V&A 1947 (180); *Treasures of Cambridge*, Goldsmiths' Hall 1959 (336); Arts Council 1973 (57)
LIT: Auerbach 1961, p.249; Strong 1969, p.55, fig.48;
Murdoch et al. 1981, p.67, fig.79; Finsten 1981, II,
p.104–5 and passim, fig.66; Strong 1983, p.171,
fig.224; V&A 1983, no.230; Bayne-Powell 1985,
pp.166–7, no.3903, pl.III; Strong 1986, pp.98, 118,
157–8

AT

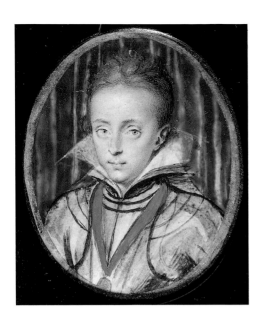

ISAAC OLIVER

85 Prince Charles *c.*1615–6

Vellum on plain card, oval 5.1 × 4.1
(2 × 1⅝)
PROV: …; recorded *c.*1732 by Vertue in
the collection of Edward Harley, Earl of
Oxford (1689–1741); thence by descent
Private Collection

Prince Charles, the second son of James VI of
Scotland and his wife Anne of Denmark, was
born in 1600 at Dunfermline, Scotland. He
succeeded his older brother Henry (no.84) as
heir to the throne on the latter's death in
1612, and in 1625 acceded to the throne as
Charles I. He married Princess Henrietta
Maria of France in the same year. From 1629
until 1640 he ruled without Parliament; Civil
War between King and Parliament broke out
in 1642. Charles was defeated, and executed
in 1649. He was a major collector and patron
of the arts, particularly favouring Anthony
Van Dyck (1599–1641).

This is an early portrait of Charles I, as the
new Prince of Wales. He wears armour and
the ribbon of the Order of the Garter, just as
Prince Henry had done in the miniature portraits which Isaac Oliver had painted five
years earlier, but this portrait presents the new
heir to the throne as a far less robust figure
than Prince Henry.

'Charles I as Prince of Wales' was probably
painted from life, and served as a pattern for
replica portraits. In another version, in the
Nationalmuseum, Stockholm, the head is by
Isaac Oliver but the doublet may have been
painted by his son Peter Oliver. From about
1612 Peter Oliver participated in the production of images of Prince Henry and the other
royal children, and in 1617 inherited Isaac's
business.

Although in excellent condition, the miniature is unfinished, the bare vellum showing
through in areas. The facial features have been
more highly worked than the collar, armour
and Garter ribbon, which remain incomplete.

EXH: V&A 1983 (260; see also 261)
LIT: Vertue IV, p.41; Murdoch et al. 1981, p.94

AT

ISAAC OLIVER

86 Edward Herbert, 1st Baron Herbert of Cherbury c.1613–14

Vellum on card 18.1 × 22.7 (7⅛ × 9)
PROV: By family descent to 4th Lord
Herbert; 1691 inherited by his sister and
co-heir, Florentia, wife of Richard
Herbert of Oakley Park, Montgomery,
whose grandson became 1st Earl of
Powis; by descent in the family
The Rt Hon. the Earl of Powis

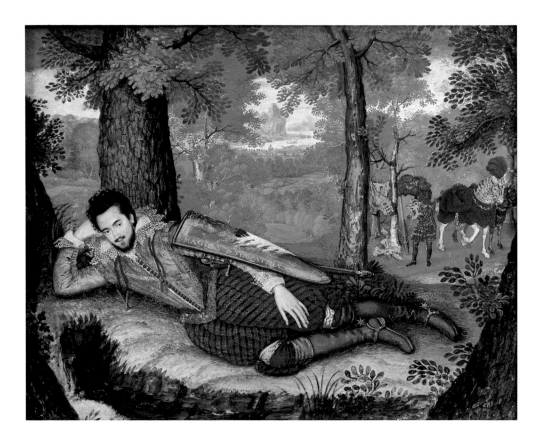

Lord Herbert of Cherbury (1583–1648),
brother of the poet George Herbert, was a
philosopher, a diplomat and an important
metaphysical poet. In his *Autobiography*, which
covers his life up to 1624, he recounts with a
high degree of vanity his Continental travels,
his passion for duelling and his favour at
court, and also records several portraits of
himself including one by Larkin (see no.133).
He seems to have been obsessed with his self-
image, and to judge from the surviving portraits of him, probably kept a tight control
over the various ways in which he was represented. Unfortunately this, one of Oliver's
most magnificent cabinet miniatures, is not
mentioned by him.

Oliver presents Herbert in the dual role of
chivalrous knight and poet/philosopher. He
rests on the ground before a tilting match
holding his shield, with his armour, plumed
helmet, lance and horse depicted in the background. However, his meditative pose, which
imitates that of Hilliard's 'Earl of Northumberland' of c.1590–5 (Rijksmuseum, Amsterdam), is the epitome of the Jacobean
melancholic, a state of mind at the height of
fashion at the time. Coupled with the shady
tree and the trickling brook, contemporaries
would immediately have recognised his attitude as that of the poet-philosopher. The
motto on his shield, 'Magica Sympathia'
(referring to the doctrine of sympathetic
magic discussed in his philosophical treatise
De Veritate) and the *impresa* – a heart emerging
from wings or flames with sparks rising from
it – continues the theme. Its meaning is presumably similar to that of a device in Wither's
Emblemes (1635) of a winged heart resting on a
book, onto which divine rays shine and from
which smoke issues (Strong 1983, p.184). It

signifies 'those Desires, By which, the Rea-
sonable-soul, aspires ... and, attempts to
clime to Mysteries and Knowledge, more sub-
lime'. The smoke, or sparks, represent 'those
Perturbations' apparent until 'Heavenly wise-
dome' has been attained. This divine aid in
the creative process, whereby a poet's or
philosopher's thoughts are raised above the
pedestrian, is alluded to in another portrait of
Herbert (Powis Castle), where his head is surrounded by clouds (George Chapman also
appears in this manner on the frontispiece to
his translation of *The Whole Works of Homer*,
1616, reproduced in Hind, *Engraving in England*, II, 1955, pl.197).

The costume dates the miniature to
c.1613–14, but the style and dependence on
interpretative emblems are archaic and refer
back to the 1580s and 1590s and to Nicholas
Hilliard. This traditionalism may reflect the
attitudes of Oliver's medieval-minded patron,
but it is offset by the innovatory and Dutch-
inspired realism of the landscape setting.

EXH: V&A 1983 (273); Washington 1985 (42)
LIT: John Pope-Hennessy, *A Lecture on Nicholas
Hilliard*, 1949, pp.27–8; David Piper, *Catalogue of Seventeenth Century Portraits in the National Portrait Gallery*,
1963, pp.164–5; Roy Strong, 'The Elizabethan Mala-
dy: Melancholy in Elizabethan and Jacobean Portraiture', *Apollo*, vol.79, 1964, pp.264–9; Strong 1969,
pp.3–6; David Piper, *The Image of the Poet: British Poets
and their Portraits*, 1982, p.24; Strong 1983, pp.180–4;
Alastair Laing, 'Lord Herbert of Cherbury', *National
Art Collections Fund Review*, 1991, pp.147–51

TB

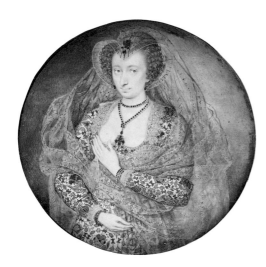

ISAAC OLIVER

87 A Lady, possibly Lucy Harington, Countess of Bedford

Bodycolour and watercolour on vellum on card, diameter 12.7 (5)
Inscribed: signed with initials 'IO' in gold, lower left
PROV: See Bayne-Powell 1985
Syndics of the Fitzwilliam Museum, Cambridge

The sitter for this, one of Oliver's most ambitious and beautiful works, has traditionally been identified as Lucy Harington, Countess of Bedford (1581–1627), friend and Lady in Waiting to Queen Anne of Denmark. A major figure in the cultural life of the court, she directed and performed in masques and was the dedicatee of many literary works.

Bayne-Powell, dating the hairstyle and costume to about 1605, with which Janet Arnold concurs, has argued against the identification, finding little physical resemblance between this sitter and the full-length portrait of Lady Bedford of c.1606 at Woburn Abbey.

However, examples of the wired gauze veil (e.g. no.132) and embroidered décolleté bodice seen here are also found later, and Strong dates this work to c.1615. Moreover, there is a definite likeness to the plumper, profile representation of Lady Bedford on the unpublished silver medal by Nicholas Briot of 1625 (private collection; repr. Hearn 1990, pls.XVIa, b). The only physical description of Lady Bedford is that of John Chamberlain who in 1619 wrote of her as 'thin & leane' (PRO SPDom. 14/109 fol.251). Her portraits, however, consistently depict a long, uneven nose, narrow face, fairly rounded eyes, upward-turning mouth with a thin upper lip and fuller lower one, and a pointed chin emerging from slightly plump jowls. These features can also be seen in the present work.

Finsten suggests that the pose derives from classical sculpture of the *Venus pudica* type. Strong has identified the source of this composition as Venetian, citing as an example Veronese's 'Portrait of an Unknown Lady', 1560 (Louvre, Paris). This would not be inapposite for the Italian-speaking Lady Bedford, tutored by John Florio, who, in a surviving letter, expresses admiration for Italian painting. It is certainly likely that she would have sat to Oliver, official limner to her mistress, the Queen.

The silver used to render much of the detail has oxidised and something of the original sparkling effect has been lost. The background has been damaged by an attempt in the past to clean it.

The format and presentation recall those used by Oliver for the portrait of an unknown lady, formerly called 'Frances Howard, Countess of Somerset' (Victoria and Albert Museum, London), which has been dated, again on grounds of costume, to 1596–1600 (V&A 1983, no.271).

A rectangular drawing, also in the Fitzwilliam Museum, is related to the present miniature. Both Bayne-Powell and Strong consider it likely to be a preparatory sketch. The features in the sketch are considerably sweeter, and younger, leading John Woodward to suggest that it was not taken from the life, but was a study for pose and costume (*Tudor and Stuart Drawings*, 1949, p.19). Graham Reynolds, however, has argued that it is a later sketch of an existing portrait (*Apollo*, Nov. 1985, p.402).

A monochrome version of this miniature, of the same diameter, was recorded in the Pierpont Morgan Collection (see Dr G.C. Williamson, 'Mr J. Pierpont Morgan's Pictures', *Connoisseur*, vol.16, 1906, p.207, repr. p.205).

EXH: See Bayne-Powell 1985; plus *Treasures from the Fitzwilliam*, National Gallery of Washington etc., 1989 (55)
LIT: See Bayne-Powell 1985; plus Hearn 1990, p.18

KH

NICHOLAS HILLIARD
1546/7–1618

88 An Unknown Lady c.1615

Watercolour on vellum on playing card,
two clubs verso, oval 6.3 × 5.2
(2½ × 2)
Inscribed 'VIRTUTE AMORE' on front at
the top; on reverse 'Nics: Hillard/fecit'
(probably by Bernard Lens)
PROV: …; recorded c.1732 by George
Vertue in the collection of Edward
Harley, Earl of Oxford (1689–1741)
(Vertue IV, p.41); thence by family
descent
Private Collection

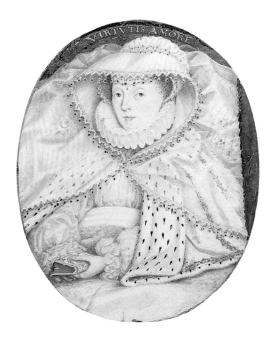

The sitter is a mature woman, of high social
rank: she wears an ermine cape, a wired headdress, and a pearl-edged veil. She reclines in a
state bed (the bed-curtain is at right). The
oval format of the miniature has given the
artist room to include the sitter's hands; she
holds a book, presumably devotional.

In the eighteenth century George Vertue
recorded that the sitter was 'Qu. Scots in
White' (Vertue IV, p.41), an identification
doubted by Roy Strong. It has, however, been
accepted by Graham Reynolds, who suggested that the inscription 'VIRTUTIS AMORE'
yielded an anagram of the name, 'Marie
Stouart'. On the grounds of style and
costume, he identified the miniature as a
memorial portrait made after her execution in
1587. Roy Strong pointed out that the ochre
border of the miniature, with 'pearls' and
sapphire, emerald and ruby 'jewels', is of a
type used by Nicholas Hilliard c.1610–15.
Regardless of the identity of the sitter, if the
miniature dates from c.1610–15, it demonstrates that even at a time when Hilliard was
producing run-of-the-mill multiple images of
James I and Anne of Denmark, he could
produce superb, individualised portraits.

The limited, white-and-silver colour range
is more typical of Isaac Oliver than of
Hilliard, who is usually associated with
brighter colours than those favoured by his
pupil. In 1616, though, Oliver proved himself
capable of painting miniatures as brilliantly
coloured as Hilliard's, with his 'Richard

Sackville, 3rd Earl of Dorset' (Victoria and
Albert Museum, London), thereby demonstrating the danger of assumptions about
these two artists.

The pearwood frame is of the type made
by Bernard Lens (1682–1740).

EXH: V&A 1947 (32); V&A 1983 (120)
LIT: L. Cust and K. Martin, 'The Portraits of Mary
Queen of Scots', *Burlington Magazine*, vol.10, 1906,
p.40; Auerbach 1961, p.98, pl.72, no.69; Graham
Reynolds, 'The English Miniature of the Renaissance:
A "Rediscovery" Examined', *Apollo*, vol.118, 1983,
pp.308–11, at p.310; Murdoch et al. 1981, p.59, fig.70,
as 'Unknown Woman'

AT

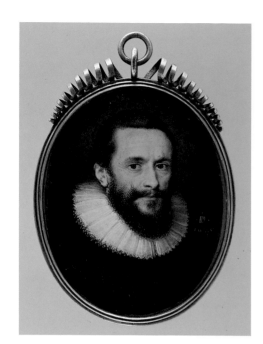

Peter Oliver c.1594–1647

89 An Unknown Man 1620

Vellum on card, oval 6.1 × 4.9 (2½ × 2)
Dated and signed with initials 'PO |
1620' in gold at right
PROV: …; L.D. Cunliffe, by whom
bequeathed to the Fitzwilliam Museum
in 1937
*Syndics of the Fitzwilliam Museum,
Cambridge*

Nothing is known about the sitter in this
miniature by Isaac Oliver's son Peter, who was
also a court artist. Most of Peter Oliver's portrait miniatures date from before 1630. Later,
as court limner, he concentrated on producing
miniature copies of the Old Master paintings
in Charles I's collection, especially works by
or attributed to Titian. He also taught
miniaturists, among them Alexander Cooper
(1609–1660), younger brother of the miniaturist Samuel Cooper (Sandrart, *Acadamia
Nobilissimae Artis Pictoriae* (1683)).

Peter Oliver was Isaac's eldest son, from his
first marriage. The boy spent his teenage years
in his father's house in Blackfriars, the London parish which was home to many artists,
including several miniaturists.

Peter was named after his French grandfather Pierre Oliver, and continued the family's French links. He evidently spent some
time in France, where in 1611 he was paid by
Queen Marie de'Medici for seven portraits at
forty-five livres each, receiving a further payment in 1613 of 6,000 livres (Louis Batiffol,
La Vie intime d'une reine de France, Paris [1906],
pp.435, 521–2; cited Eugenia McGrath, 'The
Court Portraits of Frans Pourbus the Younger',
unpublished MA report, Courtauld Instutute
1986). Before 1 May 1626, Peter married his
father's sister-in-law Anne Harding, who
came from a family of French immigrant
musicians employed at court. Peter's portrait
drawings of himself and his wife, formerly
owned by the English engraver and antiquary
George Vertue (1684–1756), survive in the
National Portrait Gallery, London.

He would have been familiar with his
father's work for the court, and himself

attended the funeral of Queen Anne in 1619.
In the accounts for King James I's funeral in
1625, Peter was listed as a member of Charles
I's household, appearing as Charles's court
'limner' in the Lord Chamberlain's books for
1628–34 (PRO L.C. 5/132, p.37).

Isaac (died 1617) had bequeathed to Peter
all his drawings, as well as his unfinished
limning pictures, including narrative paintings
(Will of Isaac Oliver, registered copy: PRO
P.C.C. 93 Weldon, Prob. 11/130/93, orig.
Prob. 10/346). Among these was Isaac's 'The
Entombment', completed by Peter and presented by him to Charles I (see no.104). In
1636, Peter was awarded a pension of £200
annually in consideration of the gift of 'The
Entombment', and of limnings to be made in
the future by Peter. The onset of the Civil
War put an end to this pension. He made
many portraits of Frederick, King of
Bohemia, Elector Palatine (1596–1632), husband of King James's daughter Princess Elizabeth.

Peter died at Isleworth, Middlesex and was
buried at St Anne's, Blackfriars, on 22 December 1647. He had already erected a monument
there to his father, with a marble bust of Isaac.
The monument was destroyed in the Great
Fire of 1666.

LIT: See Bayne-Powell 1985. For Peter Oliver, see M.
Edmond, *Hilliard and Oliver: The Lives and Works of
Two Great Miniaturists*, 1983

AT

JOHN HOSKINS *c.*1595–1665

90 Catherine Howard, Countess of Salisbury *c.*1620

Watercolour on vellum 5.4 × 4.8
(2⅛ × 1⅞)
Signed with monogram, in gold, above her shoulder on the right; inscribed on the reverse 'Mary Countess of Pembroke | Wife of Earl Henry and | Sister of Sir Phillip Sydney | by John Hoskins | the Elder', in a later hand
PROV: ...; probably acquired before 1863, from an unknown source; by descent
Trustees of the late Countess Beauchamp

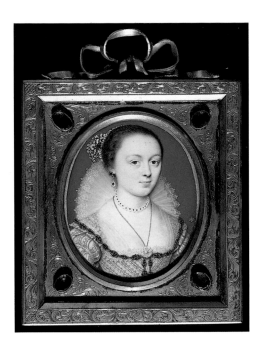

Catherine Howard (died 1672/3) was the youngest daughter of Thomas Howard, 1st Earl of Suffolk and Catherine Knyvett, widow of Lord Rich, and members of her family appear in the magnificent set of portraits at Ranger's House (see nos.135, 136). In 1608 she married William, Viscount Cranborne, later 2nd Earl of Salisbury, who set out almost immediately on a European tour to France, possibly with Inigo Jones, and on to Italy, leaving his bride behind. The marriage was apparently an attempt to mend the bad relationship between the Cecils and the Howards, but by 25 July 1610 William Trumbull records that Cranborne already 'begins to look sour upon his wife' (*HMC Downshire MSS*, vol.11, p.328).

Although this miniature is inscribed on the reverse 'Mary, Countess of Pembroke', another version of it (Duke of Rutland) is known as Catherine Howard, and the family links that existed in the seventeenth century between the Howard, Cecil and Manners families would explain its presence there. The identity of the sitter is not certain and she could be Catherine's notorious sister Frances, Countess of Essex and later Countess of Somerset. Robert Carr, Earl of Somerset was also painted in miniature by Hoskins (The Royal Collection). Both sisters appear to have been very similar in looks and their iconographies have probably become muddled, although Catherine's appearance in her portrait of 1626 by George Geldorp (Hatfield House) is very different to this miniature.

Hoskins was the most important miniaturist working in the period between the death of Isaac Oliver and the emergence of Samuel Cooper, who was his nephew. His earliest miniatures, for example that of an unknown lady *c.*1615 (The Royal Collection) are much in the tradition of Hilliard and Oliver, to either of whom he may have been apprenticed at some stage. This miniature is also from early in his career, but already displays a knowledge of contemporary portraiture 'in large', a discipline in which it is said he was initially trained, particularly of the work of Marcus Gheeraerts the Younger and of Hoskins's friend and contemporary, Cornelius Johnson.

EXH: *British Portrait Miniatures*, Scottish Arts Council 1965 (64); Tate Gallery 1972 (191)
LIT: John Murdoch, '"Hoskins" and Crosses: Work in Progress', *Burlington Magazine*, vol.120, 1978, pp.284–8

TB

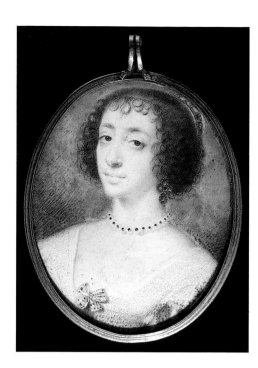

JOHN HOSKINS

91 Queen Henrietta Maria
*c.*1630–2

Vellum on card, oval 5.1 × 4.2 (2 × 1⅝)
PROV: …; probably acquired before 1863, from an unknown source; by descent
Trustees of the late Countess Beauchamp

Henrietta Maria was born on 26 November 1609, the youngest daughter of Henri IV of France and his queen, Marie de'Medici. A Catholic, she married Charles I by papal dispensation on 1 May 1625; the marriage was at first unhappy but in the 1630s was celebrated in art and court entertainments as a love match. Their first surviving child, the future Charles II, was born in 1630. During the 1630s Henrietta Maria was an active patron of the arts and the inspiration for some of Van Dyck's most beautiful portraits; she also participated with her husband in court masques. Her attempts to improve the status of Catholicism in England were a political embarrassment for Charles but involved renewed contact with the Vatican, and the completion of a Catholic chapel at Somerset House. During the Civil War, Henrietta Maria went abroad and sought to raise support for the royalist cause. She returned to England in 1662 as Queen Dowager, to live briefly in the Queen's House at Greenwich, which she had begun to decorate before the Civil War, but retired to her native France and died there in 1669.

The Queen is seen here from much the same angle as in Van Dyck's portrait of her now in the Royal Collection, painted *c.*1637–8. That portrait may have been painted to be sent to the Italian sculptor Gianlorenzo Bernini, to enable him to sculpt a portrait bust of the Queen, as he had already done of Charles I.

However, Hoskins has interpreted Henrietta Maria's facial features as being heavier than in her portraits by Van Dyck, although not quite as heavy as in Daniel Mytens's 'Charles I and Henrietta Maria' of *c.*1630–2 (The Royal Collection). Rather than relying on a Van Dyck prototype, Hoskins may have painted the Queen directly from life for the miniature. He is known to have painted Henrietta Maria from life as well as from large-scale portraits by other artists. The treatment of face and hair, softer than one might expect in Jacobean miniatures, matches the development of life-scale Stuart court portraiture, away from the precision of the Jacobean William Larkin to the more atmospheric Van Dyck. Hoskins provided miniature copies of Van Dyck portraits for patrons seeking an intimate, portable – even wearable – version of their favourite images. In response to the influence of Van Dyck's female portraits, Hoskins developed large-scale miniatures of ladies, sometimes with landscape backgrounds.

The head of the sitter now appears rather high in the composition, with the top of her head missing. The miniature may have been trimmed to fit a frame.

LIT: Murdoch et al. 1981, p.100, fig.113

AT

JOHN HOSKINS

92 Charles I *c.*1630–2

Vellum on card, oval 5.1 × 4.2 (2 × 1⅝)
PROV: ...; probably acquired before
1863, from and unknown source; by
descent
Trustees of the late Countess Beauchamp

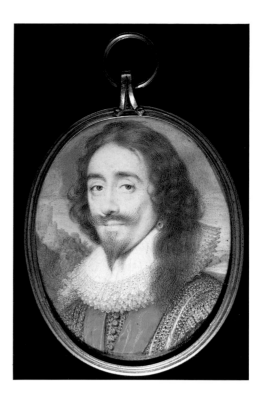

Charles I was one of the earliest large-scale
collectors of miniatures, making a collection
of about eighty at Whitehall. As well as portrait limnings, Charles commissioned miniature copies of large-scale paintings in his
collection.

Charles is shown here as a mature man,
rather than as the boy depicted by Isaac Oliver in no.85. The King wears the blue ribbon
of the Order of the Garter, the chivalric order
which he promoted.

The miniature is an example of the close
relationship which developed at the Stuart
court between miniature and life-scale portraits. In the late 1620s and early 1630s, John
Hoskins, principal court limner, produced a
group of miniatures based on life-scale portraits by the Dutch-born Daniel Mytens
(*c.*1590–1647), the King's painter. Charles's
clothing here closely resembles that in a portrait attributed to Daniel Mytens, 'Charles I
and Henrietta Maria', *c.*1630–2 (The Royal
Collection).

The treatment used to depict the King's
hair, however, is quite different from Mytens's
style; it looks much as it does in Van Dyck's
portraits. Hoskins was familiar with Van
Dyck's life-scale royal portraits, as he was
commissioned to copy them, and became
associated with Van Dyck in the eyes of his
customers. Hoskins's miniatures were in keeping with the taste of the Stuart court in life-
scale portraits, with softer handling and more
natural lighting than in Hilliard's Elizabethan
miniatures. The facial features are painted in a
blended stipple of pink, yellow and grey.
Clearly, in the 1630s Hoskins's miniatures
were sufficiently in demand for him to use
assistants in his studio in Covent Garden, as
there are variations in style of handling
between different versions of portraits of the
same sitter. In 1640 Charles granted him an
annuity of £200 on condition that he did not
work for any other patron without permission. The annuity was paid only once, since
the King soon left London, and Hoskins produced little in the 1640s. His claim at the
Restoration for £4,000 in back payments of
the annuity failed, and he died in poverty in
1664/5.

The King's head is viewed from a different
angle from that used by Mytens and Van
Dyck for their versions of Charles I and Henrietta Maria. Hoskins may have painted
Charles from life, as in his large miniature of
the King, dated 1632 (private collection).

LIT: J. Murdoch, '"Hoskins" and Crosses: Work in
Progress', *Burlington Magazine*, vol.120, 1978, p.287;
Murdoch et al. 1981, p.98, fig.105

AT

Hans Holbein the Younger
1497/8–1543

93 Elizabeth Dauncey 1526–8

Black and coloured chalks on paper
36.7 × 25.9 (14½ × 10¼)
Inscribed 'The Lady Barkley', and
annotated 'rot' (red)
PROV: ...; Edward VI; ...; Lumley
Inventory 1590, according to which from
the collection of Edward VI; ...; Charles
I; Earl of Arundel; ...; James II and by
descent in the royal collection
Her Majesty The Queen

Despite the erroneous inscription misidentify-
ing the sitter this drawing is one of several
surviving studies for Holbein's great lost
portrait of the family of Sir Thomas More,
a painting on cloth (see no.76). Elizabeth
Dauncey was the second of More's three
daughters, and married William Dauncey,
Knight of the Body and Privy Councillor to
Henry VIII, in 1525.

Holbein's preparatory sketch for the More
family group (Kupferstichkabinett, Basel), and
copies of the painting (see no.76), show Elizabeth Dauncey depicted standing on the left of
the group composition. However, it is clear
that these figures did not necessarily pose for
Holbein exactly as they would ultimately be
portrayed: Anne Cresacre, More's daughter-
in-law, is shown with her back against a chair
in Holbein's study of her, but she is standing
in the finished composition. It is characteristic
of Holbein's skill in the making of large-scale
compositions that a study such as this, ostensibly an individual portrait, and certainly
originating as such, could have been so fluently incorporated into the family group. The
technique of this drawing, using coloured
chalks alone on an unprimed paper, is characteristic of Holbein's earlier drawings, particularly of the period of his first visit to England
in 1526–8.

EXH: *Holbein and the Court of Henry VIII*, Queen's
Gallery 1977–8 (10); *Drawings by Holbein from the Court
of Henry VIII*, Museum of Fine Arts, Houston 1987 (5)
LIT: Parker 1983, no.4; S. Foister, *Drawings by Holbein
from the Royal Library, Windsor Castle*, New York 1983,
no.4

SF

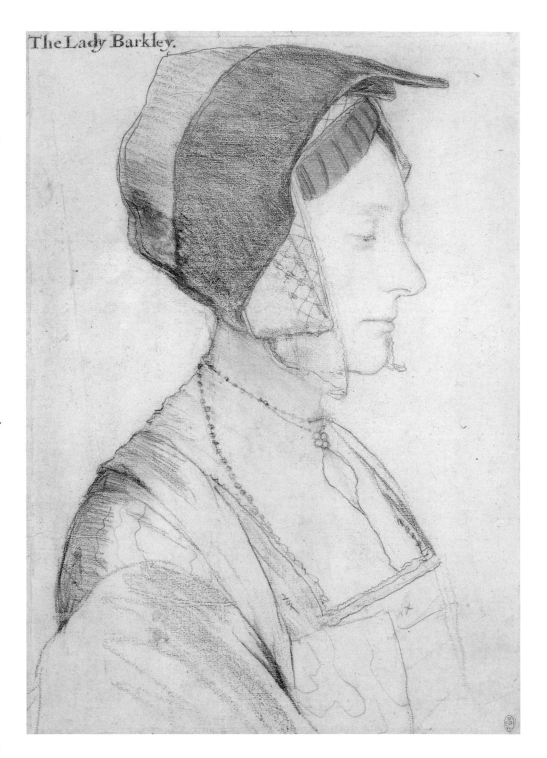

The Lady Barkley.

HANS HOLBEIN THE YOUNGER

94 Thomas, 2nd Baron Vaux
early 1530s

Black and coloured chalks, white body-colour, black ink and metalpoint on pink prepared paper 27.8 × 29.3 (11 × 11½)
Inscribed '[…][u]x'; annotated by the artist 'silbe' (silver) twice; 'w.sam' (for weiss sammet, white velvet); 'Gl' (gold); 'karmin' (carmine)
PROV: As no.93
Her Majesty The Queen

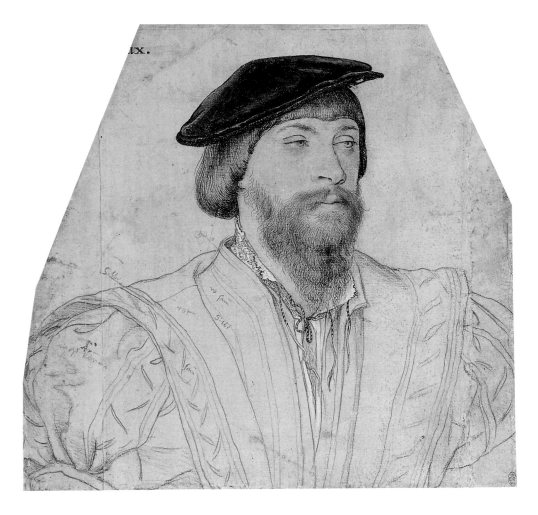

Lord Vaux (1510–1556) was a poet as well as one of Henry VIII's courtiers. Several poems of an elegiac nature were published after his death from the plague in 1556, some in *Tottel's Miscellany* of the following year. Lord Vaux succeeded his father in 1523 at the age of thirteen, by which time he was already married to Elizabeth Cheney. He was a first cousin of the influential Sir Henry Guildford and led the conventional life of a courtier to Henry VIII over the next few years, travelling to France in official embassies in 1527 and 1532, and in 1532 being made a Knight of the Bath. From January to August 1536 he held the appointment of Governor of the Isle of Jersey. After that date he seems to have retired from the court to his Northamptonshire estates, probably because he held strongly Roman Catholic beliefs and disliked the increasing tide of Protestantism.

Two drawings by Holbein labelled 'Lord Vaux' survive in the Royal Collection, and appear to show the same sitter. The differences in style are such as to suggest that Lord Vaux sat for two different portraits, rather than that these drawings were alternatives for one. In this drawing he wears the hairstyle covering the ears that was usual in the 1520s and early 1530s, but in the other drawing his hair has been cropped, as has that of 'Henry VIII' (fig.23 on p.43) and he has grown his beard.

A drawing by Holbein also exists showing Lady Vaux, and painted versions of this are presumably based on a lost original by Holbein. No painted versions are known after either drawing of Lord Vaux. In the drawing of Lady Vaux she is turned slightly to the left, suggesting that her portrait was to be paired with one of those of Lord Vaux. Of the two

this is perhaps the closer in style and technique and more likely to have made up the pair. Both drawings probably date from before 1536, the year in which Lord Vaux retired from public life.

The drawing shows Holbein's characteristic process of annotating for colours and fabrics, one which he had used from his earliest surviving portraits. Lord Vaux was to have worn a white velvet doublet trimmed with silver, under a red coat also adorned with silver. Most of the Holbein drawings in the Royal Collection, including this one, have been trimmed; this one has also been cropped at the upper edges, thus losing most of the identifying inscription. The inscriptions were probably copied onto the drawings late in their history from identifications made when they were bound together in a book in the sixteenth century.

EXH: *Holbein and the Court of Henry VIII*, Queen's Gallery 1977–8 (56); *Holbein and the Court of Henry VIII*, Pierpont Morgan Library 1983 (41); *Drawings by Holbein from the Court of Henry VIII*, Museum of Fine Arts, Houston 1987 (15)
LIT: Parker 1983, no.24; S. Foister, *Drawings by Holbein from the Royal Library, Windsor Castle*, New York 1983, no.24

SF

Hans Holbein the Younger

95 An Unknown Lady 1530s–40s

Black, red, brown chalks with black ink
and white body colour on pink primed
paper 26.8 × 16.6 (10½ × 6½)
Annotated 'Samat' (velvet); 'Damast'
(damask)
PROV: …; Jonathan Richardson; Dr
Richard Mead; Walter Chetwynd;
Benjamin Way by whom presented to
the royal collection in the reign of
George III
Her Majesty The Queen

This is one of the most exquisite of Holbein's
English drawings. It is one of a small number
that at some point became detached from the
main collection, held in the 'great booke'
which passed in and out of the royal collection in the seventeenth century, to return by
the end of that century. This drawing was
purchased in the late eighteenth century, but a
handful of similar ones remained outside the
royal collection. The drawing has been cut
around the outlines of the head, thus losing
any inscriptions or notes which may have
been on the original sheet, and which might
have identified the sitter.

The frontal pose of the sitter is uncompromising, but as this drawing and others
demonstrate, it was not reserved for male sitters such as Henry VIII (see no.8). The pose is
close to Holbein's portrait of Anne of Cleves
(no.66), a resemblance which accounts for an
old but unjustified identification of this sitter
as her sister Amelia. The use of coloured
chalks and pen and ink on a paper already
primed to give the flesh tones is characteristic
of Holbein's English drawings of the 1530s
and 1540s. This example is both extensively
worked over in ink and exceptionally well
preserved. The delineation of the feathery
eyebrows and the thick eyelashes is particularly delicate and beautiful, as is the drawing
of the line of the mouth. The costume is
inscribed with notes on the fabrics but not
the colours, which may have been black in
such cases. With characteristic economy only
one of the motifs of the blackwork embroidery at the sitter's neck has been drawn by
Holbein; the others could be repeated when
he made the painted version of the portrait.

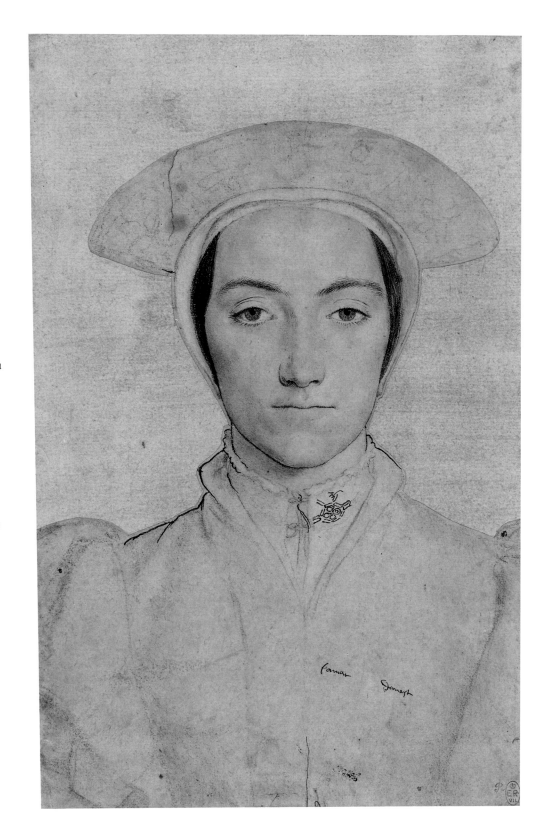

EXH: *Holbein and the Court of Henry VIII*, Queen's
Gallery 1977–8 (43); *Drawings by Holbein from the Court
of Henry VIII*, Museum of Fine Arts, Houston 1987
(50)

LIT: Parker 1983, no.47; S. Foister, *Drawings by Holbein
from the Royal Library, Windsor Castle*, New York 1983,
no.47

SF

HANS HOLBEIN THE YOUNGER

96 Lady Audley *c.*1538

Black and coloured chalks with metalpoint on pink prepared paper
29.3 × 20.8 (11½ × 8⅛)
Inscribed 'The Lady Audley' and annotated 'samet' (velvet); 'rot damast' (red
damask); 'rot' (red); 'w' (weiss, white);
'Gl' (gold)
PROV: As no.93
Her Majesty The Queen

Lady Audley may be the daughter of Sir
Brian Tuke, himself a patron of Holbein, who
married George Touchet, who succeeded as
Baron Audley in 1557. But she is more plausibly the daughter of the Marquess of Dorset
(whose wife was portrayed by Holbein), and
second wife of one of the most important
political figures of the latter part of the reign
of Henry VIII, Sir Thomas Audley, created
Baron Audley of Walden in 1538, the year of
his marriage. The marriage may have provided
the occasion for the portrait, which would
appear to date from this period. Audley succeeded Sir Thomas More as Lord Chancellor
in 1532. He died in 1544 and Lady Audley
married Sir George Norton in 1549; she died
in 1564.

This portrait drawing is notable for the
detailed depiction and annotation of the jewels Lady Audley wears. A small heart-shaped
note indicates the colour green, and other
colours are noted in German. The colours of
these jewels are matched precisely by those
which are seen in the portrait miniature of
Lady Audley by Holbein in the Royal Collection. She wears a dress of red damask, as
noted in the drawing, and the only major
difference between drawing and miniature is
the addition of arms and hands in the painted
version. It would appear that Holbein used
his preparatory drawing in the making of a
portrait miniature rather than painting from
the life (see no.66). However, although no
full-size painted portrait survives, it is possible
that the drawing was made in preparation for
such a portrait, and the miniature was subsequently produced as a reduced version of the
portrait.

EXH: *Holbein and the Court of Henry VIII*, Queen's
Gallery 1977–8 (44); *Holbein and the Court of Henry
VIII*, Pierpont Morgan Library 1983 (47); *Drawings by
Holbein from the Court of Henry VIII*, Museum of Fine
Arts, Houston 1987 (40)
LIT: Parker 1983, no.58; S. Foister, *Drawings by Holbein
from the Royal Library, Windsor Castle*, New York 1983,
no.58

SF

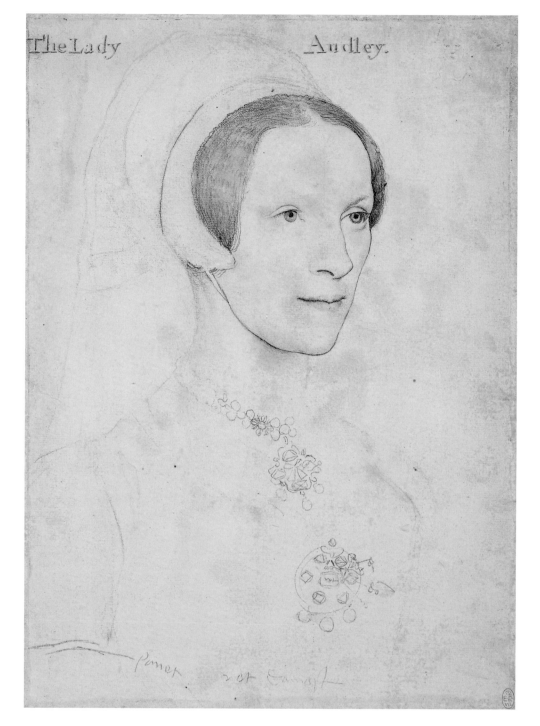

HANS HOLBEIN THE YOUNGER

97 John Russell, 1st Earl of Bedford late 1530s

Black, white and coloured chalks on
pink prepared paper 34.9 × 29.2
(13¾ × 11½)
Inscribed 'I Russell Ld Privy Seale. with
one Eye'
PROV: As no.93
Her Majesty The Queen

John Russell, 1st Earl of Bedford (?1486–1555)
was one of the most powerful political figures
of the reign of Henry VIII. He was appointed
a Gentleman of the Privy Chamber in 1526,
and held in the late 1530s and early 1540s the
offices of Comptroller of the Royal Household, Lord Privy Seal and Lord High Admiral. In 1539 he was created Baron Russell of
Chenies and elected to the Order of the
Garter. He was an executor of Henry VIII's
will and an important member of the Privy
Council which ruled after Henry VIII's death
when the boy Edward VI became king (see
no.31). He was created Earl of Bedford in 1550
and died in 1555.

Bedford had lost an eye at the battle of
Morlaix in 1526, and it may be for this reason
that Holbein portrayed him in three-quarter
view with the unseeing eye further from the
viewer, although this was a pose that Holbein
often used for his sitters. An eighteenth-
century copy of this drawing seems to show a
blanker, more unseeing eye, and it is therefore
possible that this drawing has been altered by
a later hand to expunge the sense of blind-
ness.

No painted versions of this portrait by
Holbein himself survive, but one at Woburn,
the seat of the Earl's descendants, shows a
portrait similar to the drawing, but with the
addition of the collar of the Order of the
Garter. The drawing probably dates from late
in Holbein's English career.

EXH: *Holbein and the Court of Henry VIII,* Queen's
Gallery 1977–8 (27); *Holbein and the Court of Henry
VIII,* Pierpont Morgan Library 1983 (37); *Drawings by
Holbein from the Court of Henry VIII,* Museum of Fine
Arts, Houston 1987 (41)
LIT: Parker 1983 (69); S. Foister, *Drawings by Holbein
from the Royal Library, Windsor Castle,* New York 1983
(69)

SF

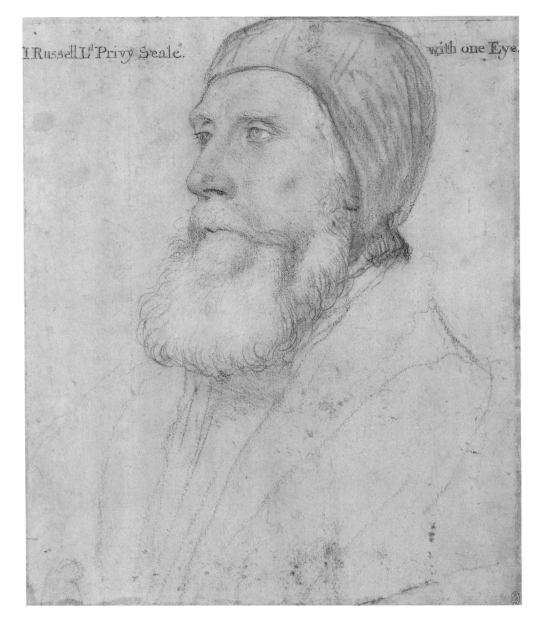

UNKNOWN ENGLISH
WORKSHOP AFTER HANS
HOLBEIN THE YOUNGER

98 Bishop John Fisher
16th century

Oil on paper 21 × 19 (8¼ × 7½)
PROV: ...; seen by Vertue in 1734, col-
lection unrecorded; ...; according to the
account of his grandson in 1892, said to
have been acquired by the Rev. Thomas
Bancroft in 1795 from the Librarian to
George III, John Chamberlaine; ...; sold
Sotheby's 1 April 1936 (6)
National Portrait Gallery, London

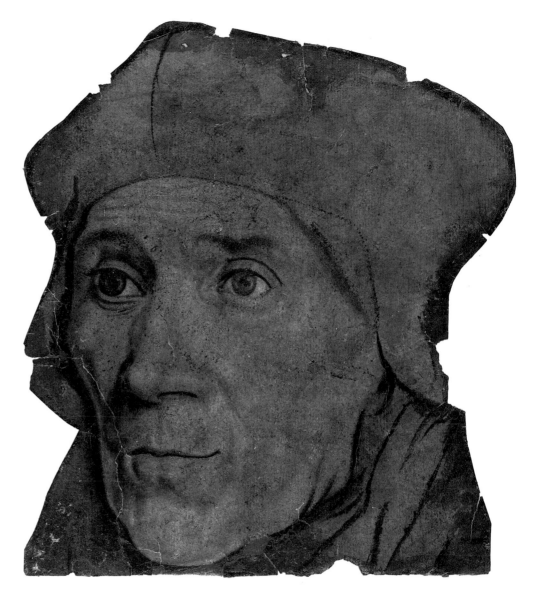

Sixteenth-century portraits frequently exist in
multiple versions and it is likely that workshops often made such versions to satisfy
demand for a particular likeness. In order to
reproduce such portraits patterns must have
been kept which could be re-used as needed.
This portrait is evidently one such pattern.

The subject portrayed is John Fisher,
Bishop of Rochester (1459–1535). Fisher was
the first Lady Margaret Professor of Divinity
at Cambridge University in 1503 and Chancellor from 1504. He took a leading part in
the foundation of both Christ's College and
St John's College, acting on behalf of Margaret, Countess of Richmond. He was responsible for the appointment of Erasmus as
Professor of Greek at Cambridge in 1511. As a
result of his opposition to Henry VIII's
divorce from Catherine of Aragon and the
legislation under which Henry VIII declared
himself head of the Church in England, he
was imprisoned along with Sir Thomas More
and in 1535 he was executed. He was canonised as a saint in 1935. Although this martyr-
dom might be thought to have limited the
appeal of Fisher's image to Protestants later in
the century, there seems to have been some
interest in his image, possibly especially for
his association with the University of Cambridge, where various portraits survive. A portrait of Fisher was recorded in the Lumley
collection at the end of the sixteenth century.

This image of Bishop Fisher is clearly
based on the Holbein drawing in the Royal
Collection at Windsor. No painted portrait
after the drawing is known, though it can be
assumed that the drawing was made in order
to serve as the basis for a painting. The
National Portrait Gallery image is usually
described as a pattern which has been pricked
along the outlines so that it could be used as
a cartoon in the production of painted portrait images of Fisher. It has recently been
established, however, from a close examina-

tion of the image under the microscope, that
the dots which were previously described as
pricked holes are actually the result of pouncing. That is, the dotted lines were produced
by the intervention of another pattern, which
must itself have been pricked. The first,
pricked pattern would have been superim-
posed over this one, and charcoal dust shaken
through the holes would have left the characteristic small dots now visible. These dots are
evident along the outlines of the hat, including the central crease. The presence of thick
black outlines around the features makes the
dots difficult to discern, but some indications
of charcoal dots can be seen in the eyebrows
under the microscope. However, when the
portrait was removed from its backing during
its recent conservation, and held up to the

light, many more dots were visible along the
outlines. The line of the mouth can be seen in
raking light to show a line of small raised
bumps, as though an attempt has been made
to transfer this line from the reverse of the
paper. On the reverse of the pattern thick
brown lines, apparently executed in paint,
cover the outlines of the pattern; the purpose
of these lines is obscure.

The image has a demonstrably close relationship to the Holbein drawing which it
resembles in size and detail. When a tracing
of the National Portrait Gallery pattern was
placed over a facsimile of the Holbein
drawing, the match between the two was
extremely close, although there were some
discrepancies at the outer edges, in the con-
tour of the hat, particularly at the left and top

edge, where the Holbein drawing shows a slightly larger hat, and a little on the right where the undercap is smaller in the drawing, and at the collar on the right shoulder. The facial shadows and the line of the fur form a very exact match. There is a very slight mismatch between the positions of the eyes and the mouth, of the kind which might have occurred if the pattern had shifted a little during the process of tracing.

The comparison shows beyond any doubt that the pattern of Fisher was itself taken from a tracing made from or, more probably, after the Holbein drawing. A drawing in the British Museum copies the drawing, and other such copies may well have existed. However, none of the surviving painted portraits of Fisher appears to be sufficiently close to suggest that the present pattern was used in its creation.

EXH: *After Holbein*, NPG 1992 (no cat.)
LIT: NPG 1969, I, pp.119–21

SF

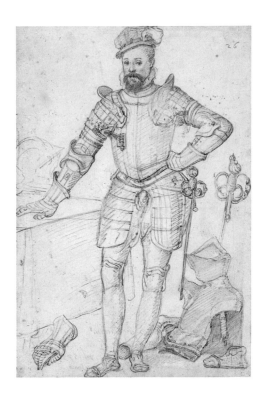

FEDERICO ZUCCARO
1540/1–1609

99 Robert Dudley, Earl of Leicester
1575

Black and red chalk on paper 37.8 × 27.5 (14⅞ × 10⅞)
PROV: See Gere and Pouncey 1983, no.30
Trustees of the British Museum

The drawing is inscribed on the back (now covered) in the artist's hand 'Il Conte Roberto de leicestre | Milord lestre favorito de la | Reina d'Ingiltera nel 1575 | londra fedco Zucharo'.

Zuccaro, who trained in Rome under his brother Taddeo, was a leading Mannerist painter of allegorical decorative schemes and worked principally within Italy. After working in France (for the Cardinal of Lorraine) and the Netherlands, Zuccaro came to England briefly in 1575. This was apparently at the invitation of Leicester and in order to paint his portrait and that of the Queen (see no.100). He must have arrived soon after 15 March 1575, which is the date of a letter of recommendation written in Antwerp by the Marquis of Cetona, presumably to Leicester himself. He was back in Antwerp in August the same year (Gere and Pouncey 1983, p.192). His contemporary, Raffaello Borghini, stated in 1584 that Zuccaro had made whole-length, life-sized portraits of Queen Elizabeth and of 'Milord Lostre' (ibid.) in England. There is no other evidence that Zuccaro painted a full-length portrait of the Queen. However, a large full-length on panel depicting Leicester standing in the manner of this drawing with pieces of armour at his feet did exist, but is now thought to have been destroyed during the Second World War (repr. NPG 1969, II, pl.383). In this painting he was shown wearing a different suit of armour, made at Greenwich and owned by Leicester himself. This is now in the Royal Armouries. Examination of the surviving photograph of the painting suggests that the armour shown was painted over an original suit resembling that in Zuccaro's sketch; indeed the pieces lying on the floor appear to be from the same suit as that shown in the drawing.

I am grateful to A.V.B. Norman for identifying the set in the drawing as the purple and gilt armour for field, tilt and tourney course

made for the Earl early in Elizabeth's reign at the Royal Workshop at Greenwich when the Master Workman was John Kelte. It is recorded in the fifth and sixth drawings in the late sixteenth-century *Almain Armourer's Album* (Victoria and Albert Museum). In the painting the Earl's hands were shown uncovered, and he was wearing hose with the Garter on his left leg rather than the leg-armour depicted by Zuccaro. Presumably Leicester, the owner of both sets of armour, instigated this repainting. From the photographic evidence alone, it is now difficult to be certain whether the overpainted and destroyed portrait was by Zuccaro himself, or was a copy made after his original.

Jane Clark notes that in 1583 at Kenilworth Leicester kept 'Two great Tables of the Queen's Majestie's Pictures, with one curtaine changeable silke. Two great Pictures of my Lord in whole proportion: the one in Armour, the other in a sute of russett sattin. With one curtaine to them.' In 1588, the year of his death, a picture 'of therle of Leyscester, whole proportion in armour' was recorded as being at Leicester House.

Leicester owned one of the largest picture collections for which records survive and it included a number of Italian (particularly Venetian) works (Clark 1981, pp.36–7). It seems that Leicester may have made an earlier attempt to bring over an artist from Italy. Clark (p.53 n.3) refers to the letter of 3 January 1565 from an Italian banker, Baroncelli, addressed to Leicester, implying that he should expect the arrival of an artist from Florence; the outcome is not known. This letter may have been linked to the search for 'some special conning painter' to convey the Queen's official image (Clark 1981, pp.27, 54 nn.2, 3). In 1574, Leicester's nephew, Sir Philip Sidney, had been in Venice, and sat for his (now lost) portrait by Veronese.

Zuccaro has often been credited with reviving the fashion for full-length portraits in England, on the basis of these drawings. The full-length portrait of 'Sir Henry Sidney', however, by 'Arnold' (presumed to be Arnold Bronckorst; see fig.45, on p.155) is dated 1573, two years earlier, while Cornelis Ketel, who made a number of full-length portraits, was also already in London. It is in fact possible that Zuccaro encountered this as existing practice on his arrival in London. Van Mander recorded (Miedema 1994, pp.149–50) Zuccaro's admiration for Holbein's English works and that he told Goltzius of seeing Holbein's 'portrait of a Countess, full-length and life-sized, dressed in black satin' (evidently 'Christina of Denmark', fig.43 on p.119, and perhaps a prototype for his drawing of Elizabeth I). The sketches Zuccaro made in the Steelyard Hall after Holbein's lost paintings there, the 'Triumph of Riches' and the 'Triumph of Poverty', still survive (Berlin-Dahlem Print Room; see Rowlands 1985, p.224).

Until it was realised how short Zuccaro's English visit had been, many Elizabethan portraits were erroneously attributed to him. James Mundy (letter of 4 April 1995) comments that, as full portrait studies of important individuals, these drawings of Leicester and Elizabeth are without real analogies in Zuccaro's Continental oeuvre. In 1575 Zuccaro was also busy on the cupola of the Duomo in Florence. That fresco includes many portraits and he was evidently 'in portrait mode' as numerous related studies survive. Mundy adds that Zuccaro tended to use chalks, as here, when he was rendering; when he was inventing, he used pen and ink.

A handful of other drawings survive from the notebook Zuccaro used in and on his way to England (see e.g. Christie's 4 July 1995 (19–21)).

EXH: Tate Gallery 1969–70 (91)
LIT: Jane Clark, 'The Buildings and Art Collection of Robert Dudley, Earl of Leicester', unpublished MA report, Courtauld Institute, 1981, p.27, pls.xxvi, xxvii(a); John A. Gere and Philip Pouncey, with Rosalind Wood, *Italian Drawings in the Department of Prints and Drawings in the British Museum: Artists Working in Rome, c.1550–c.1660*, I, 1983, no.301; Strong 1987, pp.85–6; Jacob Voorthuis, 'Portraits of Leicester', *The Dutch in Crisis 1583–88: People and Politics in Leicester's Time*, Leiden 1988, pp.60–6, pl.9; E. James Mundy, *Renaissance Into Baroque*, Milwaukee Art Museum 1990, p.20; Susan Frye, *Elizabeth I*, 1993, New York and Oxford, pp.58–60

KH

FEDERICO ZUCCARO

100 Elizabeth I 1575

Black and red chalk on paper
36.5 × 27.5 (14⅜ × 10⅞)
PROV: See Gere and Pouncey 1983, no.300
Trustees of the British Museum

Inscribed 'La Rigina Elisabeta de ingiltera | in londra magio 1575' ('Queen Elizabeth of England in London May 1575') on the back by the artist. Strong suggests that this must have been made before 23 May when the court set off from London on a five-month progress (1987, p.85).

This appears to be a companion to the portrait drawing of the Earl of Leicester (see no.99), but as both subjects are shown facing in the same direction – very slightly to their right – they could not be said to be pendants. In any case, it would not have been appropriate for the Queen to be depicted publicly as paired with the Earl.

An analogous pair of very small miniatures by Nicholas Hilliard of the same sitters facing in the same direction, similarly attired and of about the same date (V&A 1983, nos.185, 186), were probably also commissioned by Leicester, perhaps to be inserted together into a jewel. In this more intimate format, the representation of the Earl as Elizabeth's consort *manqué* could be more overt.

The Mannerist Zuccaro has sketched in allegorical attributes for the Queen – an early example of this in the canon of her portraiture. On the right is a column, symbolising fortitude and constancy – an accessory found in European and English portraiture since at least the 1540s. This is encircled by snakes, representing prudence, while on the top sit a dog, for fidelity, and a creature that is thought to be an ermine. This would stand for purity and is certainly found in the Queen's later portrait in black of 1585 (repr. Auerbach and Adams, *Paintings and Sculpture at Hatfield House*, 1971, col. pl.iv). The motifs on the left are unclear. They are perhaps flowers on a ledge,

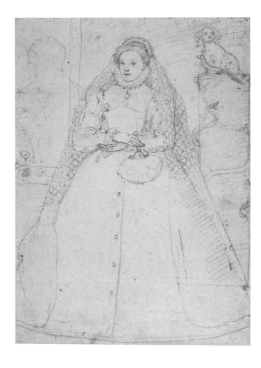

before an object with a shell-shaped finial. The conical composition, with hands joined at waist-level, could derive from Holbein's 'Christina of Denmark', which Zuccaro admired while in London (see no.99).

Nicholas Hilliard recorded the Queen's awareness of, and apparent liking for, the work of 'Italian' painters, which she expressed on the first occasion that she sat to him, presumed to be in 1572 (see no.69): 'she noted great difference of shadowing in the works, and the diversity of drawers of sundry nations, and that the Italians, who had the name to be cunningest and to draw best, shadowed not' (*The Arte of Limning*, pp.66–7).

EXH: Tate Gallery 1969–70 (74)
LIT: See no.99: Clark 1981, p.27; Gere and Pouncey 1983, no.300; Strong 1987, pp.85–9; Voorthuis 1988, pl.8; Mundy 1990, p.20

KH

LUCAS DE HEERE 1534–1584

101 A Siren Luring Seafarers to their Doom 1576

Pen and brown ink and blue wash on paper 32.9 × 44.2 (13 × 17⅜)
Inscribed with a fourteen-line 'SONNET' in Dutch on the story of Ulysses, in pen and ink, in the top centre of the painted broken surround, incorporating the words 'SCHADE LEER V' in gold letters in the last line, with the line 'DAMNA DOCENT' underneath. Also 'DAMNA DOCENT | D.GEORGIO HOEFNAGHEL PICTORI ET | POETAE CLARIS, IN VERAE ET PER | PETVAE AMICITIAE TESTIMONIVM HEC | DEPINXIT LVCAS D'HEERE GANDA | LONDINI 2. AVGVSTI 1576' in a rectangular block in the bottom centre of the painted surround
PROV: …; J.A.G. Weigel of Leipzig, sold by Gutekunst, Stuttgart 15 May 1883 (424); …; Adalbert Baron von Lanna of Prague, sold by Gutekunst, Stuttgart 6–11 May 1910 (290); …; purchased by Rijksmuseum 1911
Rijksmuseum, Amsterdam

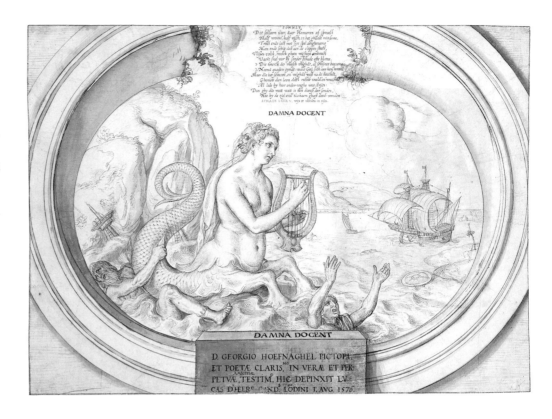

Lucas de Heere, a man of considerable learning and refinement, as well as a painter and poet, adopted as his personal motto 'Schade leer u', an anagram of his name which translates from the Dutch roughly as 'Misfortune teaches you'. This he frequently incorporated in his poetry, as he does here, also adding its Latin version 'Damna Docent'. The image shows the singing Siren, surrounded by shipwrecked and drowning men, and is the most handsome of at least three related versions of a device that de Heere seems to have favoured when contributing to the friendship books of fellow exiles of the Flemish community in London. It is also of special documentary importance for its dedication to the artist Joris or George Hoefnagel (see no.62), and proves that de Heere was still in London in 1576: 'Lucas d'Heere of Ghent painted this as proof of his true and enduring friendship for the celebrated poet and painter D. Georgius Hoefnaghel. London 2nd August 1576' (translation supplied by Dr Keith Cunliffe, St Edmundsbury Council Museums).

In Homer's *Odyssey* the Sirens' song led seafarers to founder on rocks, where they either drowned or starved to death. However, Ulysses' previous near-fatal adventure with the witch Circe had taught him to avoid the danger by stopping his men's ears with wax, demonstrating that one can learn from adversity. Sirens are traditionally represented as half

bird, half woman, but Homer does not describe them, which allows de Heere to use some artistic licence. His sea-monster is more representative of the dangers of the sea, such as the terrible Scylla and Charybdis which Ulysses had to face next, an image not inappropriate for a political refugee buffeted by strife and persecution.

De Heere himself joined the community of Flemish Protestant exiles in London in about 1567, when the Duke of Alva's persecution of non-Catholics in the Netherlands began in earnest. Other examples of de Heere's device and poems are known from the friendship books of several prominent Flemish exiles in London, like the Antwerp merchant and historian Emanuel van Meteren (Bodleian Library, Oxford), or Abraham Ortelius (Pembroke College, Cambridge), and the merchant Jan Radermacher, or Rotarius (Ghent University Library), who had close contacts with Thomas Gresham, founder of the Royal Exchange and principal English agent for business transactions with merchants in Antwerp (see no.18). De Heere's name has been proposed for the painter of 'The Family of Henry VIII' (no.35). While he was in London he is known to have taught John de Critz the Elder, and other artists of the next generation may also have received training from him.

Lucas was born in Ghent and was trained

first by his sculptor father (his mother was a miniaturist) and then by Frans Floris in Antwerp. He subsequently worked for Queen Catherine de'Medici at Fontainebleau, and spent about ten years in London as a religious exile, before returning to the city of his birth after the Pacification of Ghent in 1576. Though celebrated as a portraitist, very few certain works by him survive. A large painting in oil on canvas, 'The Liberal Arts Sleeping in Time of War', which has been attributed to de Heere (Galleria Sabauda, Turin) was seen in 1995 in the exhibition *Fiamminghi a Roma* (119), in Brussels and Rome.

The main source of information about de Heere is his pupil Karel van Mander (Miedema 1994, pp.278–85) who relates that while in England he painted a gallery of the costumes of different nations for 'the Admiral' (Edward Clinton, Earl of Lincoln). Lucas also produced an illustrated manuscript description of Britain, *Der Beschrijving der Britsche Eilanden* (see fig.42 on p.117; British Library, MS 28330; this was published in Antwerp, 1937, eds. T.M. Chotzen and A.M.E. Draak).

LIT: L. Cust, 'Foreign Artists of the Reformed Religion Working in London from about 1560 to 1660', *Proceedings of the Huguenot Society*, vol.7 (1901–4), 1905, pp.45–51, fig. facing p.45 for repr. of Bodleian Library version; L. Cust, 'Notice of the Life and Works of Lucas D'Heere', *Archaeologia*, vol.54, 1954, pp.59–80, pl.VII for Bodleian Library version; Jean Puraye et al.,

'Abraham Ortelius Album Amicorum, édition facsimile avec notes et traduction', *De Gulden Passer: Bulletin van de Vereeniging der Antwerpsche Bibiliophielen*, 45e Jaargang, 1967, repr. p.29 for Pembroke College version, and 46e Jaargang, 1968, p.31 for translation of text; F. Yates, *The Valois Tapestries*, 2nd ed. 1975, pp.27–8, pl.18b; K.G. Boon, *Netherlandish Drawings of the Fifteenth and Sixteenth Centuries*, The Hague 1978, pp.111–22, fig.316

KH and EE

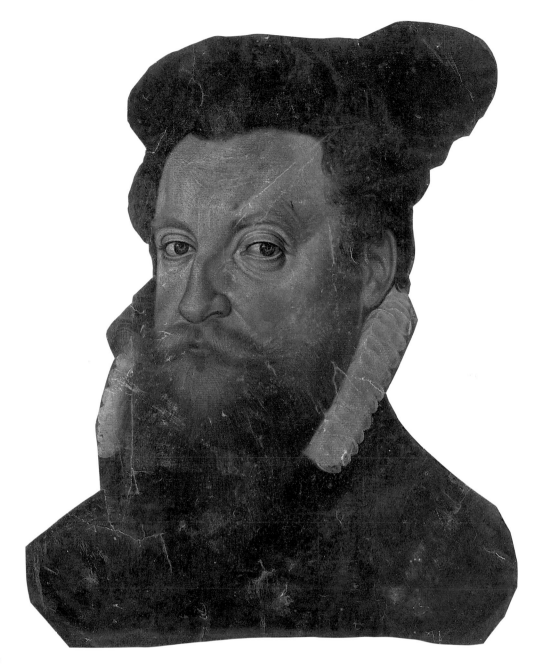

Unknown English Sixteenth-century Workshop

102 Sir Henry Sidney

Varnished oil on paper 30.5 × 27.9
(12 × 11)
PROV: As for no.98
National Portrait Gallery, London

Sir Henry Sidney (1529–1586), was the brother of Frances Sidney, Countess of Sussex (no.48). He grew up at Henry VIII's court as the companion of Prince Edward. Knighted by Edward in 1550, he managed to retain his position under Queen Mary, whose husband Philip II was godfather to Sidney's eldest son, the future poet Sir Philip Sidney. Much of Sir Henry's public career was concerned with Ireland, of which he was three times Lord Deputy.

Like no.98 this comes from a set of drawings and paintings on paper that appear to have come down as a group until their dispersal at auction in 1936. Vertue saw them together in 1734 'in a large book of prints pasted in', although he did not record where (Vertue IV, p.65). They may be the remains of the working material of an artist's workshop.

Such drawings and patterns were of great professional value to artists. On 23 February 1571, for instance, the wife of John Rutlingen promised to deliver 'vnto Thomas Clerke a booke of portraitures wthin this sennyght wholle and perfett, wch is now in the handes of Nichas Helliard' (Auerbach 1961, pp.6–7). The engraver Rutlingen was also, like Hilliard, a goldsmith, but the exact nature of the book's contents is entirely unknown. Elizabeth Drey notes that Myles Bygland, also a goldsmith, had a book of 'portraitures' while he was an apprentice, and that sixteenth-century painters can be found bequeathing their

'patrons' or patterns (e.g. Volpe in 1536). Later on 'prints' are bequeathed as well; Rowland Lockey handed down Italian prints.

Patterns of this kind will have enabled a workshop to produce the multiple versions of portraits frequently encountered (see for instance that of Robert Cecil, no.119). Repeat orders could be produced by assistants or even, perhaps, a different workshop. They also account for the difficulty there can be in identifying the hand and style of an individual artist in portraits of this period.

Surviving portraits of Sidney are all based on a single original. The most important image is the full-length portrait on panel at Petworth, dated 1573 (fig.45). The present work relates very closely to it, including, for

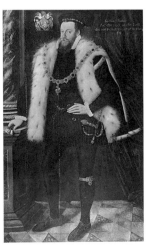

fig.45 'Arnold', 'Sir Henry Sidney' 1573, oil on panel. *Petworth House (The National Trust)*

instance, the scar by Sidney's left eyebrow. A payment to the painter 'Arnold' made in the same year would seem to be linked to this full-length (*HMC Penshurst*, I, p.248). The same painter had been paid for an earlier picture of Sidney (no longer known) in 1565–6.

'Arnold' is thought to be Arnold Bronckorst, a Netherlandish artist who was subsequently professionally involved with Nicholas Hilliard and another painter, his kinsman Cornelis de Vos, in a gold-prospecting enterprise in Scotland. A signed portrait of 1578, of 'Oliver, 1st Baron St John of Bletso' (private collection) survives. From 1580–3 he worked at the court in Scotland (Duncan Thomson, *The Life and Art of George Jamesone*, 1974, pp.44–9), and a group of Scottish portraits are convincingly attributed to him. 'Arnolde' is mentioned among the significant painters in England by Francis Meres in 1598.

Strong (NPG 1969) lists references to other versions of Sidney's portrait, some now lost. This painting on paper might have played some role in their manufacture.

LIT: C.F. Bell, 'On Some "Holbein" Questions', *Burlington Magazine*, vol.88, 1945, pp.190–1; John Woodward, *Tudor and Stuart Drawings*, 1951, pp.13, 44; NPG 1969, I, pp.120, 289–90

KH

ISAAC OLIVER *c.*1560/5–1617

103 Lamentation over the Dead Christ ?1584/6

Pen and black ink with watercolour and bodycolour on paper 21 × 28 (8¼ × 11)
Inscribed 'I. Olliverus | In[vent]? | Tuarnic[um]? | 15[?8][?6]' b.r.
PROV: ...; bt in Lisbon in 1940 by Sr. José Casimiro Serrao Franco; sold Sotheby's 20 November 1957 (66); Fitzwilliam Museum, Cambridge
Syndics of the Fitzwilliam Museum, Cambridge

This is an early working of the subject to which Oliver returned for his miniature dated 1616 now in the Musée des Beaux-Arts, Angers (see no.104). Its date is a matter of some dispute: even under ultra-violet lighting the inscription is difficult to read, being interpreted by Cordellier as 1584, Strong as 1586, and such an early dating being totally rejected by Reynolds. If done in 1584–6 it makes it the earliest dated work by Oliver, although Strong suggests that 'Moses Striking the Rock' (The Royal Collection) was executed prior to this.

The style and attire of the figures and the compositional crowding suggest a familiarity with Flemish or French Mannerism, particularly the work of Frans Floris or the School of Fontainebleau. On the other hand, the attitude of Christ suggests Italian work, particularly that of Michelangelo, although this could have come down to Oliver in a distilled version through pictures or engravings by either Flemish, French or Italian artists influenced by him. Several sources have been suggested, for instance van der Weyden through the engravings of Cornelis Cort, Germain Pilon or Luca Penni (Cordellier 1983), or Taddeo Zuccaro or Toussaint Debreuil (Finsten 1981). No single source seems to have been specifically used, Oliver preferring to develop his own composition while referring to passages from other artists.

This eclecticism in his choice of sources is perhaps responsible for the confusion apparent in his understanding of his subject. The exact occasion depicted is uncertain, being a cross between a Descent from the Cross, with Christ supported by Joseph of Arimathaea, and a Pietà, with Christ surrounded by weeping holy women, with the Virgin swooning on the right. On the left a male figure stands near an open sarcophagus with welcoming arms, suggesting an Entombment. The following catalogue entry (no.104) shows that by 1616 Oliver appears to have addressed these problems.

EXH: V&A 1983 (136); Stainton and White 1987, pp.51–2
LIT: Finsten 1981, I, pp.151–3, II, pp.222–4; Dominique Cordellier, 'La Mise au tombeau d'Isaac Oliver au museé d'Angers', *La Revue de Louvre*, no.3, 1983, pp.178–87; Strong 1983, pp.146–7; Reynolds 1988, pp.21–2

TB

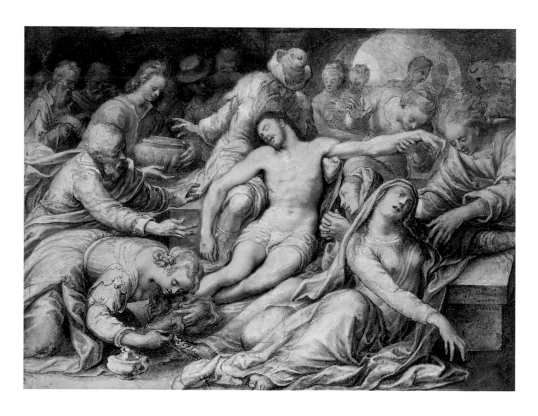

Isaac Oliver *c.*1560/5–1617
and Peter Oliver *c.*1594–1647

104 **The Entombment**
  1616, completed by 1636

Bodycolour on vellum laid on panel
28.5 × 39 (11¼ × 15⅜)
Signed, dated and inscribed, ?by Peter
Oliver, 'Incepit. | IO | 1616'
PROV: Inherited by Isaac Oliver's son
Peter 1617; in Charles I's collection by
1639; bt by Hunt and Bass at the Commonwealth Sale of 1 March 1652/3;
said to be in the possession of
Endymion Porter 1658; back in the
royal collection by 1688, and last mentioned there, at Kensington Palace,
1760–70; entered the collection of the
Museé des Beaux-Arts, Angers, by 1801
Museé des Beaux-Arts, Angers

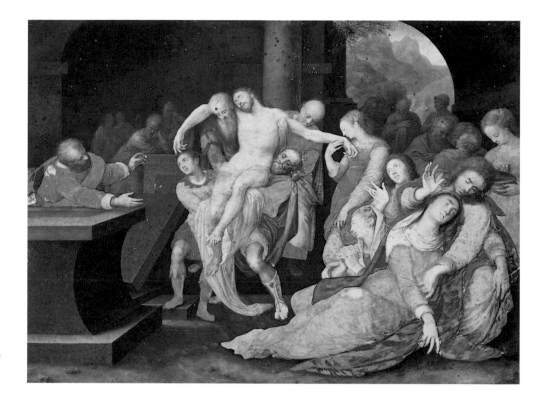

This is undoubtedly the much-prized cabinet
miniature described by Van der Doort in the
inventories of the collection of Charles I (Millar 1958–60, p.103). It was left unfinished at
Oliver's death in 1617, and was completed by
his son Peter on the request of the King, who
awarded him an annual pension of £200. In
March 1636/7 it is recorded that this was to
be paid in quarterly instalments, beginning in
December 1636 for the completed miniature,
and for all other limnings to be done in the
future (Mary Edmond, *Hilliard and Oliver*,
1983, p.174). A drawing by Isaac Oliver in the
British Museum is very close to it, and is
believed to be a preliminary sketch for it.

The subject is a reworking of his earlier
miniature on the same theme at the
Fitzwilliam Museum (no.103), but there are
significant differences. The same three compositional groups remain – the central figure
of Christ, with heavy limbs in the attitude of
the Crucifixion; the swooning Virgin on the
right; and the figure with outstretched arms
on the left – but they are more balanced and
isolated. More important is Oliver's introduction of the four disciples who support Christ.
This firmly establishes the scene as an
Entombment, as opposed to the indecisive
nature of the subject matter in the Fitzwilliam
work, and demonstrates Oliver's greater
clarity of purpose.

These changes indicate a familiarity with
Italian art. Oliver is known to have visited
Venice in 1596 (his so-called 'Sir Arundel Talbot' is inscribed on the reverse '… 1596. In
Venetia …', see no.79). Possibly he also made
a trip to Rome *c.*1610, to judge by sketches he
made after works by Guido Reni known to
have been there at that time (Finsten 1981, II,
p.228). On these journeys he would, of
course, have been exposed to Italian art, but
he could also have built up a knowledge of
the work of Italian masters through studying
pictures and drawings in English private collections. Cordellier sees Michelangelo as the
initial inspiration for the treatment of the subject here, drawing attention particularly to a
drawing by a follower whose treatment of
Christ with the four disciples is strikingly
similar (illustrated in Cordellier 1983, p.182,
fig.7). In the seventeenth century this was in
the collection of the court musician and connoisseur Nicholas Lanier, where Oliver could
well have seen it.

Two children, or putti, appear at the foot
of the sarcophagus in the British Museum
drawing, but have been omitted from the
miniature. This could illustrate the incomplete
state in which Oliver left it rather than an
alteration in his intention.

EXH: Stainton and White 1987, pp.51–2; *D'Outre
Manche: l'art britannique dans les collections publiques
françaises*, Museé du Louvre, 1994 (173)
LIT: Vertue I, p.130; Millar 1958–60, p.103; E. Croft
Murray and P. Hulton, *Catalogue of British Drawings
(British Museum), I: XVI and XVII Centuries*, 1960, p.23;
Finsten 1981, II, pp.222–9; Dominique Cordellier, 'La
Mise au tombeau d'Isaac Oliver au museé d'Angers',
La Revue du Louvre, no.3, 1983, pp.178–87; Strong
1983, pp.146–7; Reynolds 1988, p.24

TB

105 The Lumley Inventory 1590

Ink and watercolour on vellum, folio,
41 × 29.5 (16⅛ × 11⅝)
Inscribed 'A certyficate of … all his Lo:
monumentes of Marbles, Pictures and
tables in Paynture with other his Lord-
shippes Howseholde stuffe, and
Regester of Bookes. Anno 1590 … and
A sumarye of certayne stuffe within
your Lo: houses,etc …'
PROV: Made for John, 12th Lord
Lumley and thence by descent
*Trustees of the Earl of Scarbrough's
Children's Settlement*

The Lumley Inventory, an account of works of
art and property owned by the Elizabethan
Catholic John, Lord Lumley (?1534–1609), is
probably the single most important document
for the study of the cultural history of the
Elizabethan era. Also known as the 'Red Velvet Book' (on account of its binding) it was
made for Lumley in 1590 when he moved out
of the royal apartments of Nonsuch Palace,
which he had been forced to cede to Elizabeth I in order to defray the huge debts that
he had inherited from his father-in-law,
Henry Fitzalan, 12th Earl of Arundel
(?1511–1580). The inventory contains a list of
all Lumley's paintings and sculptures as well
as his household goods, excepting his huge
library which was separately catalogued in
1596 (S. Jayne and F.R. Johnson, *The Lumley
Library*, 1956). It also includes a series of illustrations by an unknown artist, as well as a
description of Lumley Castle and various
genealogical devices. The text is credited to
John Lampton, Lumley's steward.

The manuscript begins with a written and
pictorial description of Lumley Castle
(Chester-le-Street, Co. Durham) which he
refurbished and improved in the years after
his second marriage to Elizabeth D'Arcy in
1582. Sheer richness was an important quality
of the castle's decoration, but the desire to
commemorate and publicise Lumley's distinguished lineage was its main single theme.

Many of the features described remain visible today, for instance the sculpted reliefs in
the courtyard (illustrated on the page opening; see large illustration, opposite), described
as 'a faire scutchion of whyte marble with my
Lord Lumleys Armes. On each side a table
picture, cutt in whyte marble, the one repre-

senting the memorie of Sir Robert Lumley,
the other of Sir Marmaduke Lumley … who
were the begynners, and laid the foundacon
of this Castle'. The importance of the Lumley
pedigree was emphasised with increasing
force as the visitor progressed through the
castle from the courtyard to the Hall, where
the message was proclaimed in a variety of
media including 'The Statuaryes of xv^ien
Auncestors of yor Lo: lyneally descending
from the Conquest unto yor self'. The hall
also incorporated four marble busts of the
Tudor monarchs (see nos.36–9) and the 'Lumley Horseman', all of which are shown on the
page opening.

The Inventory continues with a series of
heraldic devices and coloured illustrations of
objects, including the fountain in the courtyard of Lumley Castle, various pieces of furniture, such as marble-topped tables, and some
of the sculptures erected in the garden of the
Palace of Nonsuch, which Arundel purchased
from Mary I in 1557. The majority of the garden ornaments depicted in the Inventory –
fountains, columns and a large monumental
marble obelisk – were made for the Privy
Garden of the Palace in the early years of
Elizabeth I's reign (John Speed, *Theatre of the
Empire of Greate Britaine*, 1611, Bk 1, chap.VI,
p.11). The fountain of Diana (seen opposite,
top right) is also visible in Speed's illustration
of the garden, which it shows flanked by
columns. This type of candelabra fountain
was based on Italian examples such as the figure of Ceres by Bartolomeo Ammannati,
made for the Sala del Gran Consiglio in the
Palazzo Vecchio, Florence, around 1556.
Many of the objects are decorated with
popinjays, or parrots, a motif taken from the
Lumley coat of arms. Elizabeth's visit to Nonsuch of 1559 would have provided a reason
for changing the statuary and heraldry of the
garden from that of Henry VIII (for whom the
Palace had been built) to Arundel and Lumley's own.

The Inventory also contains designs for the
tombs of Lumley and his two wives (in St
Dunstan's, Cheam), which were prepared in
advance of Lumley's death. The illustration
opposite (bottom right) shows the tomb of
Jane, Lumley's first wife, which carries three
alabaster panels, depicting her and her three
dead children in classical surroundings which
may refer to the architecture of Nonsuch.

The famous list of paintings and sculptures

occupies the last part of the inventory. Lumley
inherited certain works from Arundel such as
the 'great booke of Pictures doone by Haunce
Holbyne of certyn Lordes, Ladyes, gentlemen
and gentlewomen in King Henry the 8: his
tyme' (The Royal Collection; see nos.93–7).
Although the majority of Lumley's pictures
were dispersed in sales in 1785 and 1807,
many of the works described can still be identified through the distinctive Lumley cartellino. This is a scrap of paper, painted in a
highly illusionistic style, bearing an inscription describing the name and status of the sitter, added to the corner of the painting (D.
Piper, 'The 1590 Lumley Inventory: Hilliard,
Segar and the Earl of Essex', *Burlington Magazine*, vol.99, 1957, pp.224–31, 299–303).

The vast majority of the pictures listed in
the inventory are portraits, both of the Lumleys and other aristocratic families, and of
important figures from history and contempo-
rary politics such as 'The Statuary of the
Duches of Myllayne, afterwards Duches of
Lorreyn daughter to [Christierne] king of
Denmarke doone by Haunce Holbyn' (fig.43
on p.119; cartellino removed, National Gallery,
London). The inventory has been of great
importance in identifying individual artists,
particularly Hans Eworth and Steven van der
Meulen (Cust 1912–13, pp.1–45; Hill, 'Two
Netherlandish Artists in England: Steven van
Herwijk and Steven van der Meulen', *Walpole
Society*, vol.11, 1922, pp.30–2). Lumley's choice
of portraiture as the predominant subject matter of his picture collection has often been
considered indicative of the minimal value
that he placed on the artist and the work of
art as an aesthetic object. However, there is a
great range of subject matter mentioned in the
Inventory ranging from 'a great large table in
folds of the Passion, very auncient and
notable' to 'the 9: worthies in roundels
enealed'.

EXH: *British Heraldic Art*, BFAC 1916 (37); Washington
1985 (346)
LIT: Cust 1917–18, pp.15–35; M. Hervey, 'A Lumley
Inventory of 1609', *Walpole Society*, vol.6, 1918,
pp.36–50

KB

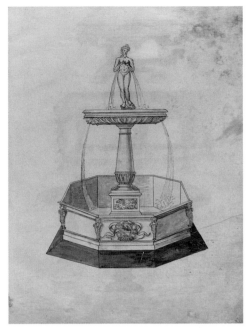

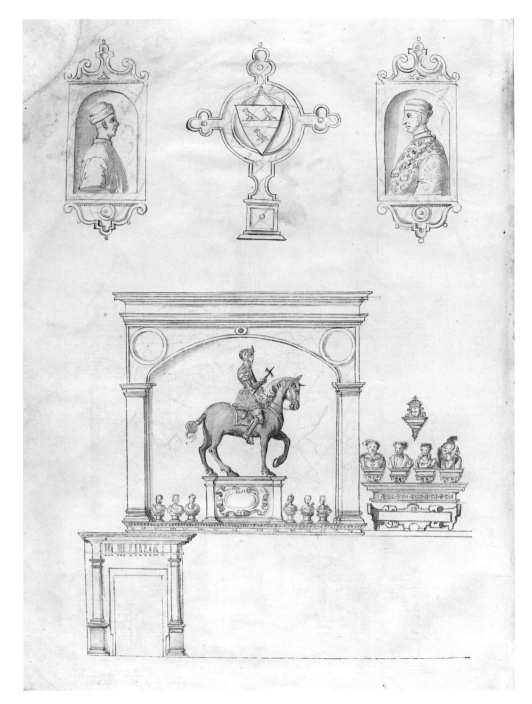

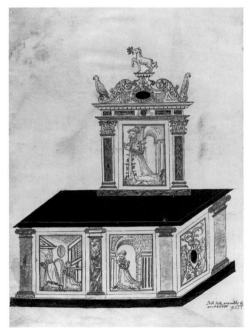

INIGO JONES 1573–1652

Designs for Court Masques

Before Inigo Jones became Surveyor of the Office of Works in 1615 he was employed at the Stuart court mainly as a designer of court masques. The latter were theatrical entertainments, the magnificence and symbolism of which were intended as a reflection of the sophistication and status of the monarch and the court. Leading poets such as Ben Jonson were responsible for the texts, which were acted out by royalty and courtiers in assumed allegorical or mythological guise.

Allegorical entertainments had been a staple ingredient of the Elizabethan court, but Jones's costumes and scenery, and his use of mechanical devices for special effects, were innovatory introductions to England. They were conceived in the spirit of European court festivals, which by the early seventeenth century deployed a common language, ultimately based on the repertory of Italian Renaissance *intermezzi*, which continued to be used by Bernardo Buontalenti at the Medici court, by Rosso and Primaticcio and the Fontainebleau School for the French court, and at the Habsburg courts. Jones would have had access to these designs through festival books and prints that were in circulation, which he adjusted and made relevant to the Stuart court.

His sources for more specific details were numerous. For costume designs they included costume manuals such as Cesare Vecellio's *Habiti antichi et moderni di tutto il mondo* (1598), encyclopedias of classical iconography such as Cesare Ripa's *Iconologia* (1603), as well as prints after artists such as those by Marcantonio Raimondi after Raphael, and ones after Parmigianino and Schiavone, the latter's work being particularly admired and collected by Jones. For architectural elements in his scenery designs Jones relied on architectural books and treatises, for example those of Serlio and Palladio.

In 1605 Jones was described as 'a great Traveller', which suggests that he had a familiarity with Continental Europe before his well-documented trip to Italy with the Earl of Arundel in 1613–14. It is possible that he travelled in France, Germany and Italy with Lord Roos from 1589, and in 1603 it is recorded that he was in Denmark with the Earl of Rutland for the presentation of the Order of the Garter to Christian IV, serving him presumably in the capacity of festival designer. In 1609 he travelled to France, where he had the opportunity to study buildings in Paris and classical architecture, for instance the Maison Carré in Nîmes. His masque designs certainly show the influence of Italian and French designs and techniques before 1613–14, but it is not clear to what extent he was relying on books and prints, as opposed to applying to his work what he had studied at first hand abroad.

Jones's masque costume designs display a rapid development in his figurative drawing technique, from a stiff immobility to a liveliness and freedom of style, and a confident use of light and shade, which demonstrate a close study of Italian drawing, either directly or through manuals and engravings. He owned a copy of Vasari's *Lives*, in which Vasari advocates the primacy of figurative drawing, and the need to copy the best in order to learn good draughtsmanship. In the margin next to this Jones wrote 'gudd manner coms by Copiinge ye fayrest thinges' (John Peacock, 'Inigo Jones as a Figurative Artist', in *Renaissance Bodies*, 1990, pp.154–79), which, like his near contemporary Isaac Oliver, was a policy he followed, his designs often a hybrid compilation of elements from varying sources.

TB

INIGO JONES

106 Winged Masquer c.1605

Pen and ink and watercolour heightened with gold and silver on paper 27.6 × 18 (10⅞ × 7⅛)
PROV: Inherited after Jones's death in 1652 by John Webb; sold soon after his death in 1672 by his daughter-in-law to John Oliver, a city surveyor and master in the Office of Works, by whom sold to William Talman before 1701; inherited by Talman's son John, by whom sold to the collector Elihu Yale (1648–1721); purchased by Lord Burlington 1723, after whose death inherited by his daughter Charlotte, wife of the 4th Duke of Devonshire; thence by descent
The Duke of Devonshire and the Chatsworth Settlement Trustees

This is one of the earliest of Jones's costume designs, although the masque for which it was intended has not been identified. It is quite stylised and stiff and has much in common with earlier drawing techniques, such as the costume drawings of John White (active 1585–1593) and those by Lucas de Heere, in England c.1567–76. The design bears some relation to the fancy dress worn by ladies in three full-length portraits attributed to John de Critz, who also painted stage scenery for masques. One version is that at Woburn Abbey, said to be of Lucy Harington, Countess of Bedford, in the costume she wore in the masque *Hymenaei*. The latter was designed by Jones and performed at Whitehall in 1606 in celebration of the marriage of Frances Howard to the Earl of Essex. Common features include the horizontal banding, the two-tier skirt (shown in both no.129 and the Berkeley Castle version of the portrait) and the gauze mantle, which in the portraits is wired. However, no designs by Jones for *Hymenaei* are known. The headdress has been compared with that worn by Vecellio's 'Lady of Caramanica' (Orgel and Strong 1973, p.101, fig.4), and is also similar to those seen in Buontalenti's sketch for the mountain of the Hamadryads, for the second Florentine *intermezzo* of 1589 (A.M. Nagler, *Theatre Festivals of the Medici 1539–1637*, 1964, fig.49).

EXH: Arts Council 1973 (41); John Harris and Gordon Higgott, *Inigo Jones: Complete Architectural Drawings*, RA 1990 (2)
LIT: Orgel and Strong 1973, I, p.101

TB

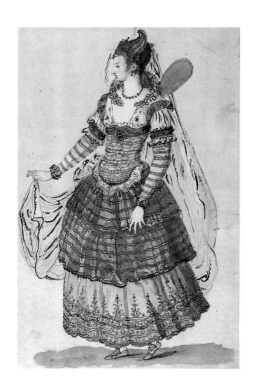

INIGO JONES

107 Atalanta 1609

Pen and brown ink and grey wash on paper 27.7 × 15.4 (10⅞ × 6⅛)
Inscribed 'The Countess of Arundell | Attalanta Q of the Ætolyans', in ink across the top and 'Crimson | yelow | whit' to the right of this
PROV: As no.106
The Duke of Devonshire and the Chatsworth Settlement Trustees

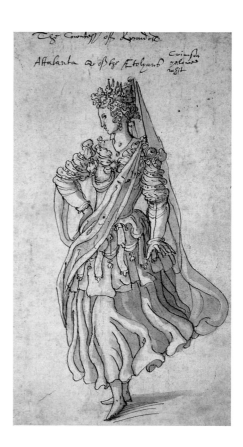

Several designs exist for the *Masque of Queenes*, Queen Anne's Christmas masque performed at Whitehall in February 1609/10, of which this is one. It was Jones's most magnificent masque yet staged, expenses running in excess of £3,000, and was one of the first to use a *machina versatilis*, a revolving stage set, which was lit by coloured lights, said to glitter like emeralds and rubies. The Queen was among the performers, appearing as Bel-Anna, Queen of the Ocean, as was Alatheia Talbot, Countess of Arundel (see no.141), who took the part of Atalanta, and whose costume design this is.

Among the surviving designs are ones for extravagant headdresses, of which Atalanta's is perhaps one of the less exuberant. Jones adapted them, along with the severe profile faces, from Réné Boyvin's engravings after Rosso Fiorentino's headdress designs for French court festivals (Peacock 1984). The same source appears to have been used by Giuseppe Arcimboldo for headdress designs for imperial festivals in Vienna and Prague (Uffizi, Gabinetto dei Disegni: for illustrations see DaCosta Kaufmann, *Variations on the Imperial Theme in the Age of Maximilian II and Rudolf II*, 1978, and Andreas Beyer, *Giuseppe Arcimboldo Figurinen: Kostüme und Entwürfe für Höfische Feste*, Frankfurt am Main 1983), which emphasises the universality of pageant costume.

Queen Anne was a keen dancer and a lover of pageantry and splendour, and was responsible for commissioning Jones's first court masque, *The Masque of Blacknesse* (1604/5), in which, in the manner of the French *Cour de Ballet*, she and the ladies of her court were the principal participants. Jones designed several other masques for her, including *The Masque of Beauty* (1608) and *Love Freed from Ignorance and Folly* (1611), and she appears in masquing costume in a miniature by Isaac Oliver (fig.53 on p.192). The profile image and headdress are close to Jones's designs, but the rest of her costume cannot be related to a specific masque, and the image was perhaps not intended as a record of a particular event.

LIT: Orgel and Strong 1973, I, pp.139–53; John Peacock, 'The French Element in Inigo Jones's Masque Designs', in David Lindley (ed.), *The Court Masque*, 1984, p.149–50

TB

INIGO JONES

108 Oberon's Palace 1611

Pen and brown and black inks and grey
wash on paper
33.3 × 39.3 (13⅛ × 15½)
Inscribed '2 sceane K: oberons Pallace',
in ink by John Webb, b.r.
PROV: As no.106
*The Duke of Devonshire and the Chatsworth
Settlement Trustees*

Jones was appointed Surveyor to Henry,
Prince of Wales on 9 May 1610, but in fact
undertook no major architectural project for
him. He was principally engaged in designing
masques and pageants, including *Oberon, the
Fairy Prince*, performed in January 1611, for
which this is a set design. The part of
Oberon, based on Spenser's *Faerie Queene*,
whose role was to restore virtue and order to
his kingdom, was taken by Henry himself,
attired as a Roman Emperor.

Like the theme of the masque, the design
for Oberon's palace is a curious blend of classical and medieval styles, which reflects Prince
Henry's preferences and the character of his
court. On the one hand Henry was a young

connoisseur and virtuoso, promoting fashionable tastes and a classical aesthetic more or
less new to England. He wished his court to
match the cosmopolitanism and sophistication
of that of the Medici in Florence, with its use
of classical forms in court festivals, and its
gardens with dramatic waterworks. To this
end he employed foreigners such as Constantino de'Servi, who was sent over by Cosimo
II, as his architect and garden designer, and
the French Huguenot Salomon de Caus, a
hydraulic engineer who also claimed to have
taught Henry the art of perspective. On the
other hand he was intensely interested in
martial arts and medieval chivalry, for which
he drew on native traditions of chivalric
knighthood, but which was probably also
inspired by his reverence of the heroic qualities of Henri IV of France, who in 1607 presented Henry with a gilded suit of armour.

This is Jones's second design for Oberon's
Palace. The first, apparently not used, was
pointedly French in its sources, reflecting his
visit to that country in 1609. It was derived
mainly from Philibert de l'Orme's design for
the chateau of Anet, and fountain designs by
Salomon de Caus. The second design is more

eclectic, an amalgam of various sources which
he has adapted to suit his purpose. The main
inspiration – a chateau rising from rock, with
a rusticated basement – is still French, but the
windows, pediment and the dome are based
on Serlio (Bramante's *Tempietto*); the battle-
ments and the crenellations on Stephen Harri-
son's illustrations of the triumphal arches
erected in London for James I's entry in 1604;
and the terms supporting the pediment on du
Cerçeau (Vredeman de Vries's *Chateau de
Madrid* in *Les Plus Excellents Bastiments de
France*, 1576–9).

EXH: Arts Council 1973 (64); John Harris and Gordon
Higgott, *Inigo Jones: Complete Architectural Drawings*,
RA 1990 (8)
LIT: Orgel and Strong 1973, I, p.216; Graham Parry,
The Golden Age Restor'd, 1981, pp.64–94; John Peacock,
'Inigo Jones's Stage Architecture and its Sources', *Art
Bulletin*, vol.64, 1982, pp.199–205; John Peacock, 'The
French Element in Inigo Jones's Masque Designs', in
David Lindley (ed.), *The Court Masque*, 1984, pp.150–3;
Strong 1986, pp.86–113, 138–83

TB

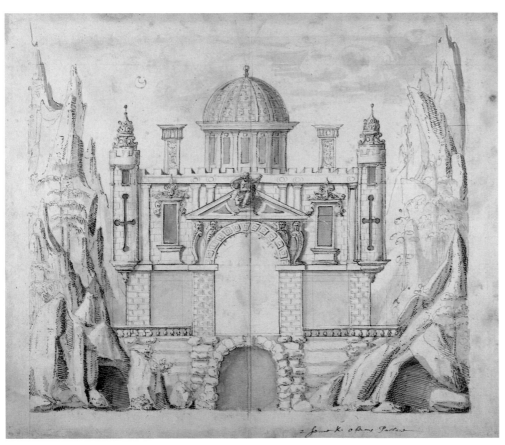

108

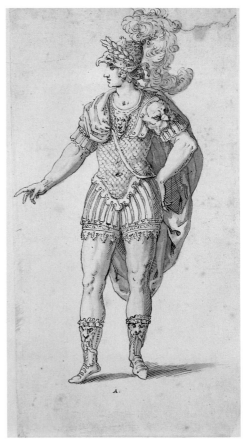

109

INIGO JONES

109 Oberon 1611

Pen and brown and black inks and grey
wash on paper 29.5 × 14.9 (11⅝ × 5⅞)
Inscribed 'A' bottom centre
PROV: As no.106
*The Duke of Devonshire and the Chatsworth
Settlement Trustees*

William Trumbull, who was a witness to the
performance of *Oberon, the Fairy Prince*,
declared that the masquers appeared 'as
Roman emperors are represented'. This was
true only to a certain extent because Jones, as
he had done with the scenery, designed the
costumes in a blended classical-medieval style.
The design for Oberon is the most Roman in
appearance, others having short tunics,
slashed sleeves or flat caps reminiscent of
medieval or early Tudor costume, with
Roman headdresses. No specific source seems
to have been used for the designs. They are
closest in feeling to those by Giorgio Vasari
in 1566 for the Medici court (see illustrations
in A.M. Nagler, *Theatre Festivals of the Medici,
1539–1637*, 1964), which Jones could have
known through engravings. Prince Henry was
interested in procuring information on the
Florentine festivals, Sir John Harington writing to him from Italy in 1608 apologising for
the non-arrival of a book he had dispatched
describing the wedding celebrations of Cosimo de Medici (John Peacock, 'Ben Jonson
and the Italian Festival Books', in J.R. Mul-
ryne and Margaret Shewring (eds.), *Italian
Renaissance Festivals and their European Influence*,
1992, p.276). It is quite possible that designs
and engravings after them found their way to
England through this method.

The classicising spirit at Prince Henry's
court is further emphasised by the various
depictions of him, and others attached to his
court, *à l'antique*, for example Isaac Oliver's
miniature of him in a toga and in profile, in
imitation of a Roman cameo or coin, of which
he had several in his collection (see no.84).

EXH: Arts Council 1973 (65)
LIT: Orgel and Strong 1973, I, p.220

TB

INIGO JONES

110 A Star 1613

Pen, ink and watercolour heightened
with gold and silver, on paper
31.5 × 17.7 (12⅜ × 7)
PROV: As no.106
*The Duke of Devonshire and the Chatsworth
Settlement Trustees*

The Lords' Masque, written by Thomas Campion and designed by Jones, was performed at
Whitehall on 14 February 1613 in celebration
of the marriage of Princess Elizabeth to Frederick of the Palatinate. Soon afterwards the
couple set out for their castle at Heidelberg,
escorted by the Earl and Countess of Arundel
and Lord and Lady Harington, with Jones in
the train, where they were met with similar
allegorical pageantry. From there Arundel and
Jones continued to Italy to make their celebrated tour.

The costume designs for this masque are
among Jones's finest and most finished. They
display a marked Italian influence, and owe a
debt particularly to the designs for the Florentine *intermezzi* of 1589. Campion's idea of
the Lords appearing from the heavens as stars
seems to have been taken from Giovanni
de'Bardi's 1589 text, and the costumes, of
cloth of silver with flaming headdresses, are
remarkably close in conception and technique
to Bernardo Buontalenti's designs, particularly
to the headdresses worn by his Celestial
Sirens. Jones has used Buontalenti as his initial inspiration, and has followed his fluid
drawing and use of wash, although the
hatched lines may indicate he has been using
an engraving, among other sources. The
composition for the legs of this masquer have
been taken from Thomas de Leu's engraving
of Servius Tullius in Blaise de Vigenère's *Les
Decades qui se trouve de tite live …*, 1583 (Peacock 1986).

Jones and Campion must have had access
to the text and designs for the 1589 intermezzi, or at least to printed accounts of the
festivities, for example Bastiano de'Rossi's
description of the costumes. It is known that
Constantino de'Servi made at least two applications to the Florentine court for designs to

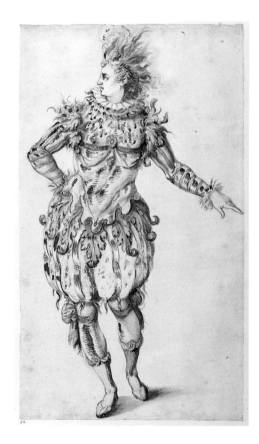

be sent to him. In 1611 he requested 'a number of the sketches of the different designs
formerly made by Bernardo delle Girandole
[Buontalenti], or by others, either for
masques, barriers, or intermedii from the time
of the Grand Duke Francesco up to now',
which he wished to use for designs for 'bal-
letti' requested by Prince Henry and in 1612
he requested designs again, in anticipation of
a commission to design the 1613 wedding festivities (Strong 1986, pp.92, 95). It is not
known whether the designs were dispatched,
but Jones must have got hold of them through
this or other means.

EXH: Arts Council 1973 (75)
LIT: Orgel and Strong 1973, I, no.80; John Peacock,
'Inigo Jones and the Florentine Court Theater', *John
Donne Journal*, vol.5, 1986, pp.201–34

TB

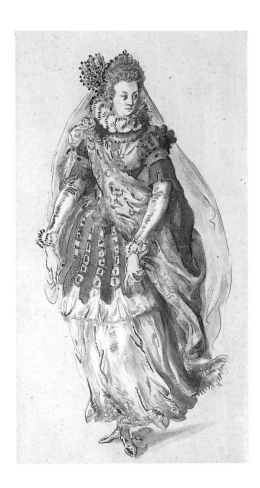

INIGO JONES

III Lady Masquer: A Transformed Statue 1613

Pen, ink and watercolour heightened
with gold and silver on paper
27.5 × 14.8 (10⅞ × 5⅞)
PROV: As no.106
The Duke of Devonshire and the Chatsworth Settlement Trustees

This design is also associated with *The Lords' Masque* but, although loosely based on Italianate intermezzo costume design, it also relates very closely to contemporary court fashions. The flowing mantle and placement of the headdress is consistent with the attire of the period and the placement of coronets, and the knotted cloak also appears frequently in portraiture of the period – for instance in the magnificent costume pieces attributed to William Larkin (English Heritage, Ranger's House). The costume is also similar to that in two portraits *c.*1615 by the same, unidentified, hand, called 'Lady Elizabeth Tanfield' (Tate Gallery) and an 'Unknown Lady' (Bristol City Art Gallery) who appear in what has been traditionally accepted as masque attire, but is not necessarily so.

The extreme décolletage of ladies in Italian festival designs was presumably not thought appropriate or applicable to the noble status of female masquers at the Stuart court. However, miniatures by Isaac Oliver *c.*1605 (Victoria and Albert Museum) and cat.no.82 show unknown ladies with bared breasts in just such costumes, directly inspired by the designs of Vasari or Buontalenti. They do not, however, appear to relate to any known performed masque.

LIT: Orgel and Strong 1973, I, no.82

TB

INIGO JONES

II2 Proscenium and Hunt Scene 1621

Pen and brown and black inks, black
lead and brown wash on paper
44.5 × 46.2 (17½ × 18⅛)
PROV: As no.106
The Duke of Devonshire and the Chatsworth Settlement Trustees

This has been associated with the lost masque of 1621, performed on Twelfth Night, possibly in the Hall at Whitehall while Jones's Banqueting House was under construction.

As well as being one of his largest and most accomplished drawings, it also reveals his development in stage design, based on that perfected in sixteenth-century Italy. This is possibly his first design to show a full perspective picture scene, giving an illusion of reality, framed by a proscenium arch. It was constructed by means of a series of side wings and painted shutters, giving a sense of recession, which could slide back and forth to change the scenery, which Jones first used in a limited way in '*Oberon, the Fairy Prince*' (see no.108).

The freely handled landscape drawing is remarkable in England at this date, and is similar in technique to his Arcadian designs for the 1620 masque *Pan's Anniversary or the Shepherd's Holiday*. Like them, elements of it are probably based on engravings. Sources such as Antonio Tempesta, Hieronymus Cock after Bruegel and Hendrick Goudt after Elsheimer have been identified for his scenic views for later masques (Stainton and White 1987, nos.20–4), as well as engravings by Jacques Callot for the French court theatre.

EXH: Arts Council 1973 (230); John Harris and Gordon Higgott, *Inigo Jones: Complete Architectural Drawings*, RA 1990 (93) and pp.270–1
LIT: Orgel and Strong 1973, I, p.322

TB

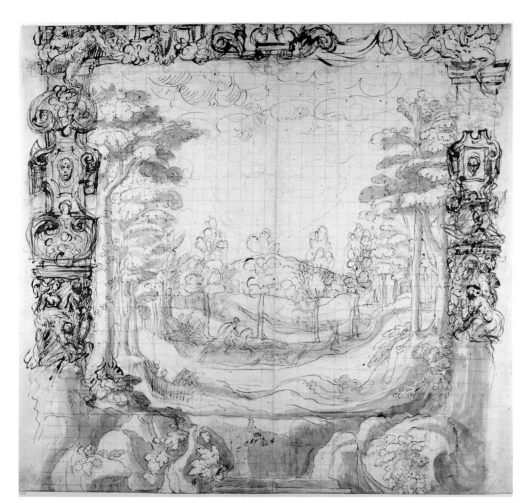

112

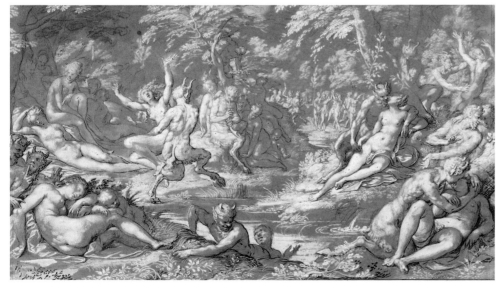

113

ISAAC OLIVER *c.*1560/5–1617

113 Nymphs and Satyrs *c.*1610

Black and white chalk and black ink on paper 20.5 × 35.2 (8⅛ × 13⅞)
Signed 'Ollivier' lower right
PROV: Recorded in collection of James II 'By Isaac Oliver. A drawing in black and white of satyrs and women sporting' (W. Bathoe, *A Catalogue of the Pictures &c Belonging to King James the Second* [and] *in the Closet of the Late Queen Caroline*, 1758, pp.55–6)
Her Majesty The Queen

As with all Oliver's drawings the date is uncertain, although Strong puts it relatively late, *c.*1610, due to its distinctive quality and the confidence of the draughtsmanship. The subject matter and concentration on the nude is unparalleled in English art of comparable date, and again underlines Oliver's dependence on Continental sources. In this case the main influence is Flemish, particularly the artists of Haarlem, who in the 1580s and 1590s were producing mythological scenes such as this, based on Ovid. They were in turn influenced by Italian Mannerist art, and the erotic interpretation of it by Rudolf II's court artist in Prague, Bartholomäus Spranger (1546–1611). Strong draws particular attention to the influence of Cornelis van Haarlem (1562–1638), for example 'The Marriage of Peleus and Thetis' 1593 (Frans Hals Museum, Haarlem). Finsten argues that Oliver must have been familiar with the work of Joachim Wtewael (*c.*1566–1638), whose manner and disposition of figures he follows closely (for example 'The Judgment of Paris', Fitzwilliam Museum, Cambridge). She also points to similarities with other artists such as Goltzius, whose work Oliver knew through engravings (see his self-portrait, no.77) and draws a parallel with the sleeping nymph on the far left and the School of Fontainebleau 'Domestication of Cupid' (Palace of the Legion of Honor, California).

The polished Mannerist style of the drawing and composition has made it one of Oliver's most highly regarded works. He produced it at a time when the notion of drawings as works of art in their own right was only just beginning to be formed, and it is not known if this particular work was produced for his own pleasure, or as a commission. In 1605 he had secured the patronage of the artistically sophisticated Anne of Denmark, who may well have owned it and others on a similar theme, which Vertue, but not van der Doort, records in the royal collection: 'a large lymning Venus a Cupid & Satyrs', 'a naked Venus a sleepe and satyrs by her', and 'Satyrs and venus sporting' (Vertue IV, pp.91, 93). It is possible that his composition with nude figures (Yale Center for British Art, New Haven) is a preliminary idea for this, and that the drawing of the reclining Antiope (British Museum) was executed at around the same time.

EXH: V&A 1983 (180); Jane Roberts, *Master Drawings in the Royal Collection*, Queen's Gallery 1986, p.97; Stainton and White 1987, pp.49–51
LIT: A.P. Oppé, *English Drawings – Stuart and Georgian Periods – in the collection of His Majesty the King*, 1950, p.79, no.460; Finsten 1981, II, pp.139, 216–219; Strong 1983, p.150; MacGregor 1989, p.118

TB

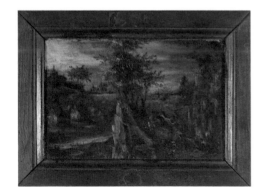

SIR NATHANIEL BACON
1585–1627

114 Landscape 1620s

Oil on copper 7.1 × 10.7 (2¾ × 4¼)
Inscribed 'NB' upper centre, in tree
PROV: Tradescant family; Elias Ashmole (1617–1692), by whom presented to the Ashmolean Museum
Visitors of the Ashmolean Museum, Oxford

This is thought to be the earliest pure landscape painting by an English-born artist.

This status is dependent on its being the work mentioned in the 1656 published catalogue of the Tradescant Collection as 'A small Landskip drawn by Sir Nath. Bacon' (p.40). If so, it is one of only two paintings now in the Ashmolean Museum identified as having survived from that list. In a manuscript inventory of 1685, two years after the opening of the Museum (Ashmolean Library AMS 8), it appears as 'Pictura Prospectûs elegantissimi margine ex Ebeno insignita'.

Freely painted in a range of impastoed greens, browns and greys, it shows a tree-topped rock at the centre up which ascend a tiny horseman and a figure on foot. Buildings are seen to the right, cottages to the left and a church behind, with another on the horizon. The monogram 'NB' in the tree (centre) may identify the artist. The composition is possibly intended to represent the Flight into Egypt, but the figures are too small in scale to establish this with certainty.

The horticulturalist John Tradescant the Elder (died 1638) may have acquired the painting from the artist himself. The Bacon family were closely related by marriage to Tradescant's first patron, Robert Cecil, Earl of Salisbury (see no.119). Sir Nathaniel's surviving correspondence indicates his own interest in gardening, and his monument in the church at Culford calls him 'well skilled in the history of plants, and in delineating them with his pencil' (MacGregor 1983, p.28). This tribute, suggesting that he and Tradescant had interests in common, is demonstrated on a spectacular scale in Bacon's newly identified 'Cookmaid with Still Life of Vegetables and Fruit' (no.148).

No signature has been found on any of his other surviving works, none of which are so small in scale, nor on copper nor painted in such a free manner. The 'Cookmaid' paintings, however, show that Bacon ventured into genres unexplored by his British contempo-

raries, but which his frequent travels to the Low Countries would have enabled him to study at first hand.

In *The Gentleman's Exercise* of 1622, Henry Peacham names Bacon as the prime example of an upper-class Englishman who could paint: no one 'deserveth more respect and admiration for his skill and practice herein … not inferiour in my judgement to our skilfullest Masters' (p.126). Elsewhere, Peacham devotes a chapter to the painting of landscape, a genre previously practised in Britain, for topographical purposes only, by Netherlandish artists. As Millar and Whinney 1958 (pp.260–1) observed, for Edward Norgate, the contemporary of Peacham and Bacon, this was 'an Art soe new in England, and soe lately come a shore, as all the Language within our fower Seas cannot find it a Name, but a borrowed one … from … the Duch' (that is, *landschap*, the Dutch word for landscape). Norgate commended the work of Adam Elsheimer and Paul Brill, examples of whose small paintings on copper were owned by the great English collectors such as the Earl of Arundel and Charles I.

In this little picture, Bacon clearly owes a technical debt to Paul Brill (1554–1626). Both composition and execution are, however, closer to the work of Pieter Steevens (c.1567–after 1624), born in Mechlin, probably trained in Antwerp and by 1594 a court painter to Rudolf II (see no.19) in Prague (I am grateful to Gregory Rubinstein for this suggestion). Steevens's work, loose in handling, and with vertical features that rise immediately from the foreground, was disseminated in engravings by Aegidius Sadeler and Hendrik Hondius.

The ebony frame appears to be original to the work. A similar frame can be seen round the little painting of Minerva depicted on the wall in Bacon's self-portrait (no.149).

EXH: *The Origins of Landscape Painting in England*, Kenwood 1967 (1)
LIT: *Musaeum Tradescantianum*, 1656, p.40; Colonel M.H. Grant, *Old English Landscape Painters*, rev. ed. 1957, Leigh-on-Sea, I, pp.33–4, pl.2; John Hayes, 'British Patrons and Landscape Painting', *Apollo*, vol.82, 1965, p.40; Waterhouse 1978, p.66; *Tradescant's Rarities*, ed. Arthur MacGregor, Oxford 1983, pp.291, 298, no.254

KH

Sir Peter Paul Rubens
1577–1640

115 George Villiers, 1st Duke of Buckingham 1625

Black, red and white chalk and ink on paper 38.3 × 26.7 (15⅛ × 10½)
Inscribed 'Hertoeg van Bochengem P.P.Rubbens f.' in red chalk across the top, in a hand which appears on several Rubens drawings in the Albertina
PROV: …; Duke Albert of Sachsen-Teschen (died 1822); by family descent at the Albertina, Vienna until handed over to the State in 1918
Graphische Sammlung Albertina, Vienna

George Villiers (1592–1628) was the favourite of both James I and Charles I, and was created Duke of Buckingham and Lord High Admiral in 1623. Through his meteoric rise to power, becoming chief minister in all but name in the 1620s, he generated not only the jealousy of his contemporaries, but also great wealth, with which he was able to build up one of the largest and most important art collections in England. His bungled diplomatic dealings with foreign powers, which led the country into war, caused him extreme unpopularity and led to his assassination in Portsmouth in 1628, which was followed by national rejoicing.

Rubens was the pre-eminent artist in Europe and his full-blooded Northern Baroque works were greatly sought after. He was courted by English collectors from at least 1612, including the Earl of Arundel (see no.146) and Sir Henry Danvers on behalf of Charles I, then Prince of Wales, but did not visit England until 1629–30, and then only briefly, when, as a mark of his great distinction, he was knighted. His influence on his former studio assistant Sir Anthony Van Dyck had profound implications for the course of English painting when the latter settled in London in 1632 – not only stylistically, but also in studio practice. Rubens, and also Van Dyck, put emphasis on the preparatory sketch, of which this is an example. The sketches themselves were not intended as works of art in their own right, but came to be regarded so as the status of drawings in English collections increased.

This portrait sketch is the first instance of Buckingham's patronage of Rubens. It was presumably done in Paris in 1625, where they met briefly in May when Rubens was completing the Marie de' Medici cycle of paintings for the Palais du Luxembourg, and where Buckingham arrived on the 14th to escort

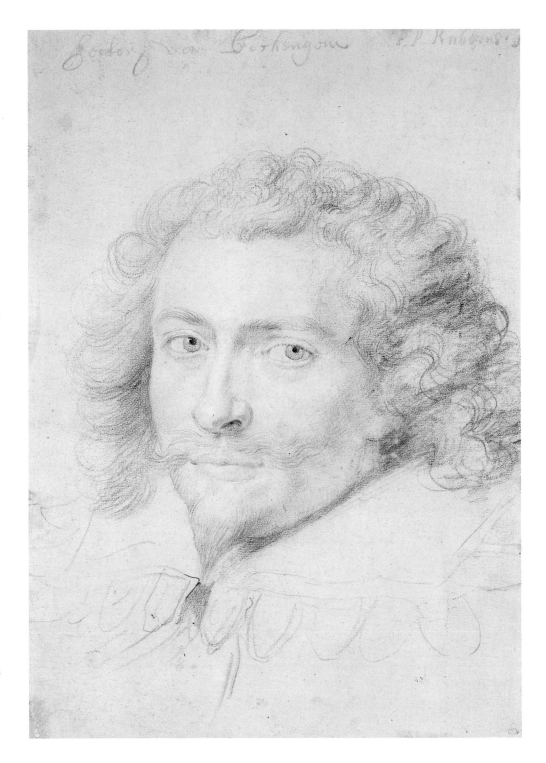

Charles I's new queen, Henrietta Maria, back to England. Buckingham eagerly commissioned a head-and-shoulders portrait (a copy of which is in the Pitti Palace, Florence; whereabouts of the original unknown) and an ambitious equestrian portrait for which he paid £500 in advance (destroyed by fire 1949, Osterley Park; oil sketch in the Kimbell Art Museum, Texas). The latter commission was possibly inspired by Titian's equestrian portrait of Charles V which Buckingham had seen in Madrid in 1623, and which he had had copied for the Great Hall of his London residence, York House. The portraits were painted later, but this preliminary sketch served as the basis for the likeness of the Duke in both.

Buckingham remained in contact with Rubens (who had no illusions about his patron, referring to his 'caprice and arrogance') for the rest of his life, and made further commissions: most importantly an allegorical ceiling painting for his closet at York House, showing him being borne up to the Temple of Virtue, assisted by Fame (also destroyed by fire in 1949; oil sketch in the National Gallery, London), which was in place well before the Banqueting House ceiling – a coup of which Buckingham would have been only too well aware; and a portrait of the Countess of Buckingham (Dulwich Picture Gallery), a sketch for which is also in the Albertina, presumably done in England in 1629–30. In 1627 he purchased from Rubens his famous collection of antique sculptures, as well as a great number of pictures by him, which in the 1635 inventory of York House numbered thirty – the largest collection of the artist's works in England.

EXH: Tate Gallery 1972 (11); *Die Rubenszeichnungen der Albertina*, Albertina, Vienna 1977 (39–40)
LIT: C.R. Cammell, *The Great Duke of Buckingham*, 1939, p.374–7; C.R. Cammell, 'George Villiers, First Duke of Buckingham: Portraits of a Great Connoisseur', *Connoisseur*, vol.98, 1936, pp.127–132; Julius S. Held, 'Rubens's Sketch of Buckingham Rediscovered', *Burlington Magazine*, vol.118, 1976, pp.547–51; Graham Parry, *The Golden Age Restor'd*, 1981, pp.140–3; Julius S. Held, *Rubens: Selected Drawings*, revised ed. 1986, pp.133–4; Hans Vlieghe, *Corpus Rubenianum Ludwig Burchard, Portraits II*, XIX, 1987, pp.62–7

TB

116 'Perseus and Andromeda'
from a set of tapestries known as
'The Horses'
Mortlake Manufactory, from a design by Francis Cleyn
(c.1580s–1657) c.1635–1642

Wool, silk and gilt metallic thread
304.8 × 322.5 (120 × 127)
PROV: …; recorded at Wentworth Castle in 1904; sold Christie, Manson & Woods, 20 Nov. 1919 (104), along with a companion panel; bt by Stair and Andrew; …; James R. Herbert Boon Collection, sold Sotheby's, New York, 22 Nov. 1988 (302); bt by S. Franses Ltd on behalf of the Victoria and Albert Museum
Board of Trustees of the Victoria and Albert Museum, London

Lacking its original border but otherwise complete, the 'Perseus and Andromeda' tapestry is the only known survivor of a set of six to eight pieces woven at the Mortlake manufactory sometime between 1635 and 1642. The series illustrated scenes from Ovid's *Metamorphoses* but was referred to as 'The Horses' during the seventeenth century on account of the equestrian figures which each tapestry featured. The rest of the subjects are known from mid-seventeenth-century weavings (Standen 1985, II, pp.700–1). They included 'The Destruction of Niobe's Children', 'Meleager with the Head of the Calydonian Boar', 'Ajax Carrying off Cassandra at the Sack of Troy', 'Picus and Circe' and 'Scylla and Minos' (Hefford 1990, pp.97–102).

Stylistically, the design reflects the hand of Francis Cleyn, chief designer of the Mortlake manufactory from the mid 1620s till his death in 1657 (Campbell 1987). His authorship is confirmed by Sir Sackville Crow, a former administrator of the works, who wrote in 1670 that 'the Horses, also, are by Clyne, the figures noble enough, but the rest of the designe not soe excellent'. The date of conception is not documented but it must have been after 1633 as one of the horses in the 'Ajax and Cassandra' design is copied from Van Dyck's portrait of Charles I on horseback painted for the Long Gallery at St James's in that year (The Royal Collection). A *terminus ante quem* is provided by Charles's debt for five pieces of this subject in June 1637. Assuming that these would have taken twelve to eighteen months to weave it seems reasonable to date the preparation of the cartoons around 1634–5. Cleyn drew freely on a number of

sources besides Van Dyck. The body of the winged horse in this design combines two plates from Tempesta's *Horses from Different Lands* (1590), while that of Andromeda appears to derive from a Bernard Salomon woodcut in Jean de Tournes's *La Métamorphose d'Ovide figurée* (Lyon, 1557). This plate, or a derivation, may also have inspired the depiction of Perseus on Pegasus, a departure from Ovid's text. Generally speaking, the dynamic compositions and vigorous figures reflect Cleyn's response to the influence of Rubens.

The provenance of this tapestry is unknown before it was recorded at Wentworth Castle in 1904 (C. Latham 1904, I, p.188). At this date it was accompanied by a companion panel whose border appears in a 1913 photograph of the stairway (National Monuments Record Photograph Archive). This was identical to the border on sets of 'Hero and Leander' woven in the mid 1630s (Thomson 1914, figs.19, 20). When the tapestries were sold at Christie's in 1919 the companion panel was described as 'woven with an Amazon on horseback, in border of Amorini and strapwork'. It was bought for 157gns. 10s by Nachemsohn, the Stockholm and London based dealer, but its current location is unknown.

The quality of the surviving tapestry is equal to that of sets of the 'Acts of the Apostles' and 'Hero and Leander' woven for Charles during the 1630s (now belonging to the French state and Swedish crown respectively) and the lavish use of gilt metallic thread indicates that it originated from a royal commission. The loss of the Mortlake records prevents any precise statement of the number of times that high-quality sets of this design were woven before the Civil War but, in view of the cost of such tapestry, it may not have been more than the two occasions of which incidental documentation survives. The first has already been mentioned. Purchased by Charles in 1637 at a cost of £1,204, the five completed pieces were subsequently given to Monsieur St Terre, the French Ambassador, along with a promise of a sixth piece when it had been completed (Campbell 1987, p.38 n.52; Loomie 1987, p.143). A second set of eight hangings was recorded among Charles I's possessions at Whitehall in the Commonwealth sale inventories. This was valued at £1,701 and purchased by a Mr Jackson. Its fate is unknown but it may well have been the set from which the Wentworth pieces derived. A set which some commentators have adduced from a sale reference to a 'Rape of Helen' tapestry with the arms of the Prince of

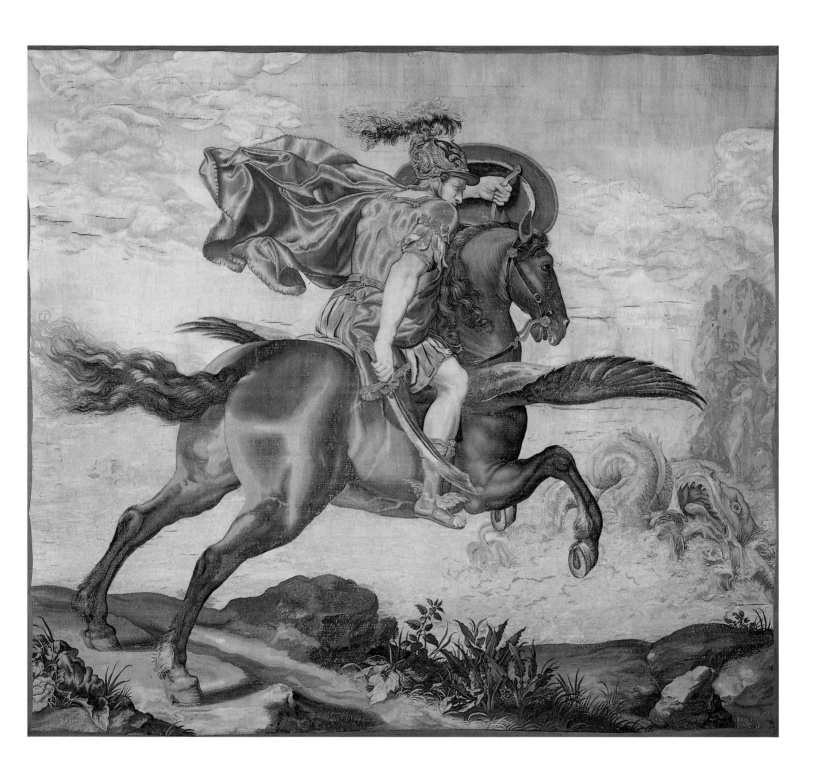

Wales (Standen 1985, ii, p.701) can be discounted as the panel in question derived from a set of 'Vulcan and Venus' (Hunter 1912, pl.107).

Along with the borders for the royal 'Acts of the Apostles' set and the 'Hero and Leander' series, the designs for the 'Horses' were the most ambitious which Cleyn undertook for the Mortlake works. Judgement of their success has been hampered in the past as they were known only through mid-seventeenth-century reweavings of moderate quality. The rediscovery of this panel provides striking evidence of the quality of the lost royal set and of the success of the collaboration between Cleyn and the Mortlake manufactory when his designs were executed by skilled weavers in fine materials.

Born in Rostock in the 1580s, Cleyn claimed to have travelled in Italy before settling at the Danish court in the 1610s where he worked for James I's brother-in-law, Christian IV. The exact nature of his introduction to Charles is unclear, but he travelled to England some time during the first part of 1623 and he probably returned early in 1624. Following Charles's accession Cleyn was granted an annual pension of £100 and the esteem in which he was held is indicated by the variety of tasks in which he was engaged. A bill dated March 1626 included charges for designs for a triumphal arch produced in cooperation with Inigo Jones, an altarpiece for the chapel in St James's, designs for a new great seal and an allegorical painting at Somerset House. Most importantly, it charged for the preparation of new working cartoons from the Raphael 'Acts of the Apostles' which Charles had recently acquired, and for new border designs to accompany them. The success of these led to Cleyn's appointment as full-time designer to the Mortlake works where he was resident from late 1626 until the outbreak of the Civil War. During this time he was involved in the continuing preparation of new cartoons from old designs and in the development of a number of entirely new series.

LIT: C. Latham, *In English Homes*, 1904, I, p.188; E. Standen, *European Post-Medieval Tapestries and Related Hangings in the Metropolitan Museum of Art*, New York 1985, II, pp.700–7; W. Hefford, 'Cleyn's Noble Horses', *National Art Collections Fund Review*, 1990, pp.97–102. For general background: G. Leland Hunter, *Tapestries: Their Origin, History and Renaissance*, New York 1912; W. Thomson, *Tapestry Weaving in England from the Earliest Times to the end of the XVIIIth Century*, 1914; T. Campbell, 'A Consideration of the Career and Work of Francis Clein', unpublished MA report, Courtauld Institute 1987; A. Loomie, *Ceremonies of Charles I. The Note Books of John Finet, 1628–1641*, New York 1987

TC

7 The Turn of the Sixteenth Century

From the beginning of the 1590s the nature of portraiture began to change and the full-length image became a favoured form. While on the Continent it continued largely to be reserved for the royal families alone, in England it was adopted for less exalted sitters (see no.120). Whereas previously, easel paintings had been on wooden panel, canvas now became the favoured support enabling paintings to become ever larger as well as more portable. With size came an increase in the magnificence and ostentatiousness of the image (see no.45) and, as in Mannerist portraiture throughout Europe, figures became excessively lengthened and etiolated, and thus more imposing. There are parallels between these paintings and the spectacular 'prodigy' homes built by courtiers to impress the monarch, and in which galleries were now incorporated to house and display collections of portraits.

Such large images must have called for the organisation of workshops, where painters could collaborate on their production.

The principal artists were John de Critz the Elder and Marcus Gheeraerts the Younger, both brought to London in about 1568 as children by their Netherlandish parents – de Critz at the age of about thirteen, Gheeraerts younger, after the Duke of Alva's persecutions of Protestants. De Critz was trained in London by another Netherlander, Lucas de Heere, and then travelled in France (and perhaps Italy), but little is known of Gheeraerts's training, though presumably it was at least partly at the hands of his father (see no.41).

Gheeraerts, a protegé of Sir Henry Lee, Elizabeth I's principal public image creator, came to the fore in the 1590s, adding a new element to contemporary portraiture by depicting the full-length figure out-of-doors in a fairly naturalistic setting. Thus Captain Lee (1594) stands in an Irish landscape, while the Earl of Essex (1596) was portrayed with his successful attack on Cadiz in the distance beyond him. The full-scale figure with an allusion-filled background, partly echoing the illustrations to the increasingly fashionable emblem books, is matched in contemporary miniature form by Hilliard (see no.74) and Oliver.

Gheeraerts, who was related by marriage to the limner Oliver, began, initially in his male portraits and those of older women, to introduce a closer observation of the features, that conveys something of the character of the sitter, rather than the mere display of status. Such works have a direct quality quite unmatched in English painting at this period. Technically too in their use of grey flesh tones they are highly idiosyncratic.

With the accession of James I came a multiplicity of royal patronage – the King favouring de Critz, and the Queen later turning to Gheeraerts. As Prince Henry grew to assert his own independence he employed the English-born Robert Peake, who also regularly produced images of the Prince's siblings, Elizabeth and Charles. Another indigenous English artist who enjoyed top level patronage was William Larkin (see no.133). The new monarch's accession also meant an influx of portraits of overseas rulers (see no.124), which must in turn have had an impact on the portraits commissioned by English patrons. The links of blood and of marriage between the painters in large, the miniaturists, the sculptors, the goldsmiths and other specialist craftsmen who served the court at this period have been outlined in the Introduction (pp.11–12).

James I's outward-looking policies, following the Somerset House Treaty of 1604, and after England's comparative isolation in Elizabeth I's final years, allowed more Britons to travel. Foreign works of art had previously been imported – apparently via the Netherlands – by certain sixteenth-century collectors, most notably the Earl of Leicester, Lord Lumley and Robert Cecil. The early seventeenth-century, however, saw an unprecedented English enthusiasm for collecting works of art and antiquities, which came to be seen as the mark of a cultivated and politically aware person. Henry, Prince of Wales's advisers inculcated in him a ready enthusiasm for Continental art. Collections were also formed by Anne of Denmark, the Earl and Countess of Arundel (see nos.140, 141), James I's early favourite Robert Kerr, the Countess of Bedford, the 2nd Marquis of Hamilton and, famously, the King's last favourite, James Villiers, subsequently Duke of Buckingham, among others.

English painting itself was still mainly confined to portraiture. Robert Cecil's commission to Rowland Buckett (active 1599–1639), a member of the Painter-Stainers' Company, for religious paintings for the Hatfield House chapel c.1611–12, was unusual (fig.46).

The masque, a traditional form of court entertainment, gained new impetus on James's accession. In the hands of the poet Ben Jonson and the designer Inigo Jones, both looking to Continental models, it rose to a remarkable level of sophistication. Staggering sums of money were spent on this ephemeral medium, of which only a few visual and textual fragments remain (see nos.106–12, 129).

The deaths in 1619 of the English court artists Nicholas Hilliard, William Larkin and Robert Peake – in the same year as the art patron Anne of Denmark – left the field open for a new group of incoming Netherlanders. While Gheeraerts continued to paint on until at least 1629, his sitters were no longer the grand and fashionable.

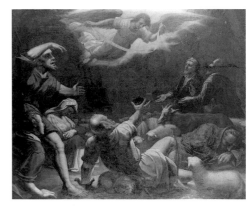

fig.46 Rowland Buckett, 'The Angel Appearing to the Shepherds'. *Courtesy of The Marquess of Salisbury*

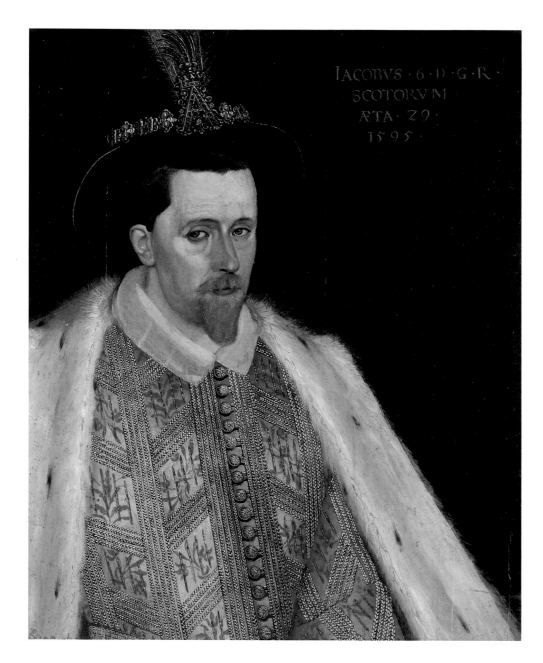

ADRIAN VANSON
active 1581–1602

117 James VI of Scotland, later James I of England 1595

Oil on panel 72.9 × 62.3 (28⅝ × 24½)
Inscribed 'IACOBVS. 6. D.G.R. |
SCOTORVM | ÆTA. 29. | 1595.' t.r.
PROV: ...; J. Whitford MacKenzie, from
whose effects purchased by the lender
1886
*Scottish National Portrait Gallery,
Edinburgh*

James (1566–1625) became King of Scotland
in 1568 when he was only thirteen months
old, on the abdication of his Roman Catholic
mother Mary, Queen of Scots. He grew up at
Stirling Castle in the household of the Earl
of Mar, one of a succession of Protestant
Regents, and had as his tutors the distinguished humanist, poet and historian George
Buchanan, and the Calvinist Peter Young.
Through their teachings he became an able
scholar and theologian, with an aversion to
his mother's faith.

Of the artists recorded as working in Scotland during James's reign, most appear to be
foreign, and of Netherlandish origin in particular, as opposed to Scotland's French orienta-
tion earlier in the century. Adrian Vanson
from Breda became the King's official painter
some time before 1584, taking over the post
from the Dutchman Arnold Bronckorst, and
remained in his service until 1602. He is first
recorded in Scotland in 1582 when he
received payment for two portraits (of John
Knox and George Buchanan) which had
been sent to Geneva to be engraved for
Theodore Beza's *Icones*, an iconography of the
Reformation. From then on there are regular
references to him in the royal accounts, for
carrying out decorative painting for pageants,
and for portraits. In 1594 the King gave him a
medal, referring to him as 'our painter'. Other
portraits have been attributed to him on
stylistic grounds, the most impressive being
the 1592 full-length of Sir Thomas Kennedy
of Culzean (Culzean Castle, National Trust
for Scotland). The will of his cousin Peter
Matheus, also a painter, who worked in London with Isaac Oliver and died in 1588, gives
further information on the Vanson family
(Campbell 1985, p.xxxiii).

This is the most important image of James
before his accession to the English throne in
1603, although Vanson had painted him
before in 1586 (Scottish National Portrait

Gallery). It is not known when this way of presenting the King, looking to the right, in a tall sugar-loaf hat, doublet and cloak, was first devised, or whether Vanson was originally responsible for it, but it is how James appears on a medal struck in 1590 to commemorate his marriage with Anne of Denmark, and is not dissimilar to the profile image on coins, first dating from 1591, described then as having 'his heines portrat according to the painteris draucht'. A miniature of James attributed to Vanson, also dated 1595, is obviously taken from this portrait and has as its pair one of Anne of Denmark.

The portrait has been cut down at the sides, and probably at the top and bottom as well, which makes the image less authoritative than it would once have been. Originally the figure would have been centrally placed and the pose would have appeared more striking, with hand on hip, the other possibly grasping a sword hilt, although stylistically there remains a certain awkwardness and lack of sophistication. Duncan Thomson sees this as typical of the 'Anglo/Scoto-Netherlandish' manner of Bronckorst and Vanson.

The large jewelled A on James's hat refers to his wife, Anne of Denmark.

EXH: Duncan Thomson, *Painting in Scotland 1570–1650*, Scottish National Portrait Gallery, Edinburgh 1975, pp.25–31
LIT: Duncan Thomson, *The Life and Art of George Jamesone*, 1974, pp.45–8; Duncan MacMillan, *Scottish Art 1460–1990*, 1990, pp.42–6

TB

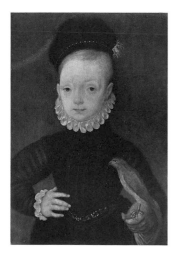

fig.47 Arnold Bronckorst, 'James I as a Boy' c.1580, oil on panel. *Scottish National Portrait Gallery, Edinburgh*

ATTRIBUTED TO JOHN DE CRITZ THE ELDER
c.1551/2–1642

118 Sir Francis Walsingham c.1587

Oil on panel 76.2 × 63.5 (30 × 25)
PROV: …; 2nd Earl of Hardwick, Wrest Park, by 1782 (Pennant, *Chester*, 1, p.392) and by descent; sold Christie's 16 Nov. 1917 (94), bt National Portrait Gallery
National Portrait Gallery, London

Only one portrait-type of Walsingham is known. It survives in numerous versions, two of which bear the dates 1587 and 1589. Surviving letters indicate that de Critz worked for Walsingham during the 1580s and it is probable that this image, of which the present work is the finest example, originated with him.

Walsingham (?1530–1590) was the son of a London lawyer. A zealous Protestant, he left England on the accession of Mary I and during the following five years gained a knowledge of foreign affairs that was to stand him in good stead on his return when Elizabeth came to the throne. He organised and funded a secret service that garnered information, initially for the Lord Treasurer, William Cecil, both in Britain and abroad. Sent to France on a number of diplomatic missions, he signed the Treaty of Blois between France and Eng-

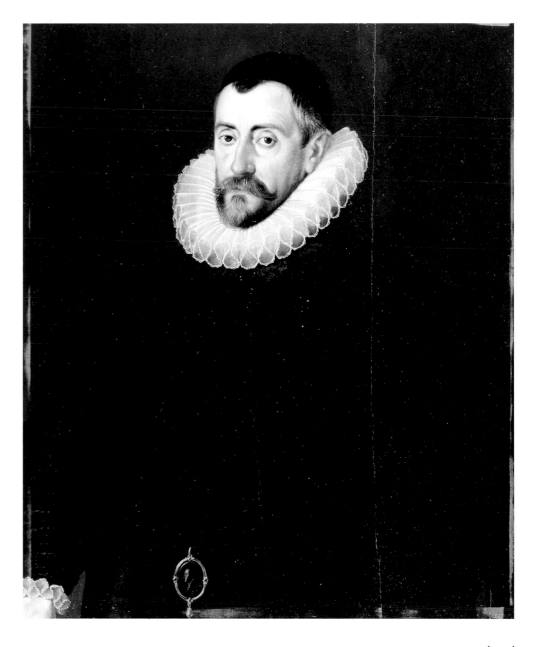

land on the Queen's behalf on 19 April 1572 (see no.35). In December 1573 he was appointed Secretary of State, a post he retained until his death, and repeatedly endeavoured to persuade the Queen openly to support the Protestant opponents of Spain in the Low Countries. His network of informants enabled him to uncover a series of Catholic conspiracies. These included the Babington Plot in 1586 which led to the conviction for treason of Mary, Queen of Scots later that year by a Commission that included Walsingham. She was executed the following year. The financial strain of paying for his intelligence network increased with the death in 1586 of Walsingham's son-in-law Sir Philip Sidney for whose debts he became responsible. Through a decade of growing financial anxiety, Walsingham entertained the Queen at his house at Barn Elms, near London, in 1585, 1588 and 1589, though he failed to persuade her to reward him. His intelligence kept him informed early of the Spanish preparations for the Armada in 1588, but he was unable to influence the Queen to act decisively in this matter.

The present portrait, presumably cut down at the bottom, presents Walsingham as a rather austere, remote figure. His principal adornment is a fine cameo of the Queen in profile, emphasising the patriotism which he may have felt was unrewarded. Examples of such profile jewels of Elizabeth still survive (see *Princely Magnificence*, 1981, pp.58–62). Walsingham was an enthusiastic patron of writers, including those of a Puritan tendency, and a supporter of overseas exploration.

The painter de Critz was brought to England from Antwerp as a baby. From about 1567 he was apprenticed in London to the Flemish painter and poet Lucas de Heere (no.101). From 1582 to 1588 he worked for Walsingham, visiting Paris, presumably on secret service business, from whence he sent back paintings by his own hand and by others; these included one of 'St John' and another of 'Neptune and Coenis' (Edmond 1978–80, p.144; Lane Poole 1912–13, p.47). He probably visited Fontainebleau and perhaps Italy. In 1603 he was appointed Serjeant-Painter, an office shared from 1607 with Robert Peake, with whom he may also have shared a studio in Holborn Conduit. De Critz seems increasingly to have acted as an organiser of decorative work and to have employed a large workshop to carry this out. He

received a number of payments for work for Robert Cecil (see no.119) who had succeeded Walsingham as Secretary of State.

The present image is attributed to de Critz because of his known connection with Walsingham, and the early annotation 'from Jo: de Critz' to an engraving of it in Henry Holland's *Herωologia*, 1620. It thus dates from comparatively early in de Critz's career. The modelling of the features is not dissimilar to that seen subsequently in the work of Marcus Gheeraerts the Younger, the stepson of de Critz's eldest sister Susanna and future husband of his younger sister Magdalena. In addition one of Susanna's daughters, Sara, was to become the second wife of the miniaturist Isaac Oliver in 1602, so de Critz's familial and professional network took in many of his more distinguished confrères. Three of de Critz's own sons are also recorded as painters.

EXH: Tate Gallery 1969–70 (170); London and Belfast 1988–9 (3.4)
LIT: Mrs Rachael Lane Poole, 'An Outline of the History of the de Critz Family of Painters', *Walpole Society*, vol.2, 1912–13, pp.46–68; NPG 1969, I, pp.320–2; Edmond 1978–80, pp.140–62, on the de Critz family

KH

ATTRIBUTED TO JOHN DE CRITZ THE ELDER

119 Robert Cecil, 1st Earl of Salisbury c.1602

Oil on panel 90.2 × 73.4 (35½ × 28⅞)
Inscribed 'SERO, SED SERIO' ('late but in earnest') t.l.; '1602' t.r.; 'To the right honorable Sir | Robert Cecil Knight principal | secretary to her Matie […] of the Courte of Wardes & Live | ries & one of her highnes most | honorable privie Councell' on the letter
PROV: …; presented by David Laing, of Edinburgh, to the National Portrait Gallery 1860
National Portrait Gallery, London

Although John de Critz the Elder was a leading artist of the period and Serjeant Painter from 1603 until his death, few works can with confidence be credited to him. Documentary evidence, however, suggests that the original version of this portrait of Robert Cecil (1563–1612) is one of them.

The attribution is based on the surviving bill of ' Mr. John de Creett; s[erjeant] painter', dated 16 October 1607, for making a number of portraits, each charged at £4. These included Cecil's own 'for the Embassador of Venice'. The English ambassador to Venice was Sir Henry Wotton, whose own letter to Cecil of 4 April 1608 reveals that he was arranging to have the picture of Cecil in Garter robes copied in Venice in mosaic. This mosaic, bearing the date 1608, now forms part of a chimney-piece at Hatfield House (Auerbach and Adams 1971, pp.72–5) and relates closely to this painting.

A unique commission at the time, it was originally hung as a gallery picture. Another payment to 'de Creet' was made on 25 March 1610, for a portrait of Cecil at £5.

All the surviving portraits of Cecil conform to this single face pattern, although the dress and accessories vary. There are four contemporary versions of this three-quarter-length portrait, of which the earliest is dated 1599; one has an inscription in Greek. In the present portrait, free underdrawing is evident in the face and hands, but not the dots left by the 'pouncing' method of pattern transfer.

Cecil was the only surviving son of Lord Burghley by his second wife, Mildred Cooke; his elder half-brother became 1st Earl of Exeter. Cecil openly began to seek high office in 1594 when he deputised for Burghley as host to the Queen at Theobalds; he had been knighted on a similar occasion in 1591. His political career began with his appointment in 1596 as Principal Secretary, alluded to in this picture by the seal bag on the table. By 1602 he was involved in the dangerous secret negotiations which would bring James VI of Scotland to the throne of England. He was subsequently to rise further, being made Viscount Cranborne in 1604, Earl of Salisbury in 1605, a Knight of the Garter in 1606 and Lord Treasurer in 1608.

He was to become the most extravagant architectural patron of his day. In 1602 he was building a new house south of the Strand in London, of which he considered himself the architect (he described his love of architecture as a 'vice … it hath almost undone me'). Cecil's estate at Theobalds was exchanged with James I for the royal one at Hatfield, where Cecil built his architectural master-piece. Cecil employed Inigo Jones as designer for a number of lavish entertainments (several with texts by Ben Jonson), Cecil's accounts also reveal a tantalising payment of £10 to the future Royal Surveyor for 'drawinge of some architecture' at Hatfield, although this has not been convincingly identified (Hatfield House MSS, 28 Feb. 1610).

Of small stature, and referred to by James I as 'my littil beagill', he may indeed have been sensitive about his appearance and was sub-jected to some cruel jokes. Despite this, he had something of a reputation where women were concerned, about which even the King teased him. Following the death of his wife Elizabeth Brooke in 1597 he remained a widower. His prominence as a statesman ensured that portraits frequently were required and of the four painted by de Critz in 1607, three were diplomatic gifts.

Cecil, one of the keenest art patrons, had an extensive collection of paintings (of those recorded, only Lord Lumley's was larger), many of which can no longer be traced. There were no portraits of him at either Salis-bury House or Hatfield in his lifetime, although two were at another residence, Cranborne House. The rest of the collection varied widely, but contemporary letters record his taste for 'Auncient Master peeces of paintinge'. Whereas other collections consist-ed principally of portraits, Cecil's was unusual in the number of religious and mythological paintings; he also owned two landscapes. His position ensured the presence of portraits of foreign rulers and statesmen and these far

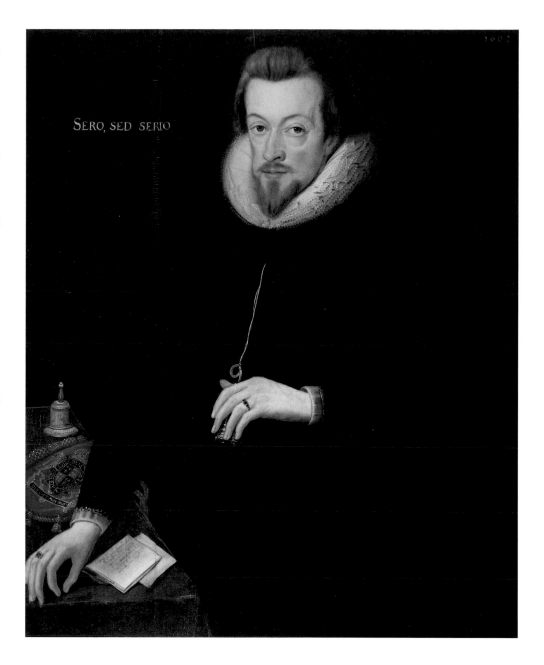

outnumbered family portraits. The collection was most typical in containing a series of paintings of English kings. Henry, Prince of Wales, who became a noted collector, took an interest in Cecil's paintings and special arrangements were made for the Prince to view the latest acquisitions in 1609.

Cecil's death in 1612, as political and per-sonal crises loomed, put a premature end to the activities of one of the most important patrons of the early seventeenth century.

SB

EXH: Manchester 1857 (340; as 'artist unknown'); Tate Gallery 1969–70 (171); Arts Council 1973 (27)
LIT: J. Maclean, ed. 'Letters from Sir Robert Cecil to Sir George Carew', *Camden Society*, 1864; Cust 1917–18, pp.15–35; Strong 1969; Auerbach and Adams, 1971; *Calendar of the Manuscripts in the Possession of the Most Hon. the Marquis of Salisbury, K.G.*, Historic Manuscripts Commission, 24 vols., 1883–1976; Susan Bracken, 'The Patronage of Robert Cecil, 1st Earl of Salisbury 1591–1612', unpublished MA report, Courtauld Institute 1993

MARCUS GHEERAERTS THE YOUNGER 1561/2–1636

120 Captain Thomas Lee 1594

Oil on canvas 230.5 × 150.8
(90¾ × 59⅜)
Inscribed 'Ætatis suæ 43 | An° D°
1594' in yellow paint upper right centre
and 'Facere et pati Fortia' in yellow
paint in tree upper left, 'S.ͬ Henry Lee
of Ireland' b.l., in later script
PROV: Presumably painted for Sir
Henry Lee and always in the Lee-
Dillon collections; first recorded at
Ditchley by Vertue in 1725; Dillon sale,
Sotheby's 24 May 1933 (46 repr.) bt
Francis Howard; Loel Guinness, by
whom lent to the Tate Gallery from
1953 until purchased 1980
*Tate Gallery, London. Purchased with
assistance from the Friends of the Tate
Gallery, the National Art Collections Fund
and the Pilgrim Trust 1980*

Thomas Lee (1552 or 1553–1601), the misfit
scion of minor Oxfordshire gentry, was in
many ways typical of the army officers who
sought to make their fortune in the rough
theatre of border warfare that was part of
English endeavours to colonise Ireland. Lee's
distinction lay in his friendship from childhood with the native chief of Ulster and eventual archtraitor Hugh O'Neill, 2nd Earl of
Tyrone, and in being a cousin of the influential courtier Sir Henry Lee, the Queen's champion of the tilt. From about 1593 onwards
Thomas tried to use these connections to set
himself up as the chief peace negotiator
between the Crown and the rebellious Irish
lords. Being rash, impulsive and of a disposition which earned him alternately commenda-
tions for bravery and censure for banditry,
this rough fighting man was hardly cut out
for diplomatic success. His petitions and
political tracts accusing the Crown's officials
of corruption earned him powerful enemies,
while his open and often brutally implement-
ed ambitions for land and status did little to
win the trust of the local clans and land-
owners. It is hardly suprising, therefore, that
both the ruthless power-play of Anglo-Irish
politics and his own lack of judgment
ultimately led him, in the wake of the
attempted *coup d'etat* by his master, the Earl
of Essex, to a traitor's death on the scaffold
at Tyburn on 13 February 1601.

This picture was painted in 1594, during
one of his periodic visits to England, and
marks the point at which Thomas seriously

upped his stakes in his attempt to become the
Crown's chief negotiator in Ireland. The bare
legs and the open shirt of his costume present
him in the guise of an Irish foot soldier or
kerne (see e.g. fig.42 on p.117), while the
exquisitely embroidered shirt and expensive
armour and weaponry leave one in no doubt
about his status as a gentleman of noble birth.
Morgan (1993) suggests that one of the aims
of the picture could be to advertise Thomas
on the marriage market following the recent
death of his wife. Be that as it may, the main
import of the portrait, however, is political.
Thomas stands in the shelter (or lee) of an
oak in reference to his kinsman Sir Henry
whose motto was 'Fide et constantia'. The
landscape alludes to his service in Ireland,
and, in view of the group of armed men in
the wood by the water on the right, probably
to his exploits at the battle of Erne ford the
previous year in particular. Most significant,
however, is the Latin quotation in the tree
beside him. This comes from Livy's *History of
Rome*, and translates roughly as 'both to act
and to suffer with fortitude is a Roman's part'.
These words were uttered by Gaius Mucius
Scaevola after being captured in the camp of
Estruscan rebels. He had entered it in an
attempt to kill their leader Porsena, wearing,
with the approval of the Roman Senate, Et-
ruscan disguise. On being apprehended,
Scaevola demonstrated Roman bravery by
thrusting his right hand into a sacrificial fire,
an act which so impressed Porsena that he
there and then decided to conclude a lasting
peace with Rome. This is exactly the role that
Lee envisaged for himself as negotiator of a
peace between the Crown and the Irish
rebels. Like Scaevola, who was granted lands
by a grateful Senate, Lee also expected to be
handsomely rewarded for this service. His
'Irish' disguise (i.e. his friendship with
Tyrone) was not to be seen as in any way
treasonable, but as something assumed in the
service of the Crown. In the event, Lee's mission failed, and he returned to Ireland not as
a plenipotentiary of the Queen, but to resume
his turbulent and doomed career as captain of
a troop of horse.

Sir Henry Lee was one of the foremost
patrons of the Flemish painter Marcus Gheeraerts the Younger, and his experience as
organiser of the Queen's court spectacles can
be suspected behind the elaborate programme
of this portait of his kinsman, whom he loyal-
ly supported to the end.

The portrait resembles images in the
emblem books popular with contemporary
readers, such as Alciati's *Emblemata* (published
1550), where a single figure, placed in a landscape, is accompanied by text. Such
figures, often holding a weapon, tend to be
positioned by a symbolic tree. In Claude
Paradin's *Devises Heroiques* (published 1557)
Scaevola himself is shown with the legend
'Agere & pati fortia' (p.120).

The portrait has been cleaned for this exhibition, which has shed light on the drooping
gesture of Lee's left wrist. Gheeraerts painted
a scar running horizontally across the base of
the hand, which suggests that Lee had
received an injury that affected his use of that
hand. His gesture displays the scar and ampli-
fies the comparison with Scaevola, whose
own hand had been permanently damaged by
his brave act in the name of Rome.

The portrait was later extended on all four
sides, probably in the nineteenth century;
with the recent cleaning, the extensions at the
bottom and vertical sides were removed.

EXH: Tate Gallery 1969–70 (155)
LIT: *Dictionary of National Biography*, 1909, under
Thomas Lee; Cust 1913–1914, p.35, repr. pl.XII (b);
E.K. Chambers, *Sir Henry Lee*, 1936, pp.31, 185–203,
218, 230–1, pl.IV; Frances A. Yates, 'Boissard's Cos-
tume Book and Two Portraits', *Journal of the Warburg
and Courtauld Institute*, vol.23, 1959, p.366, no.5; Roy
Strong, 'Elizabethan Painting: An Approach through
Inscriptions III: Marcus Gheeraerts the Younger',
Burlington Magazine, vol.105, 1963, pp.149, 571 fig.17;
Strong 1969, p.279, fig.267; Janet Arnold, 'Eliza-
bethan and Jacobean Smocks and Shirts', *Waffen- und
Kostümkunde*, (Munich) vol.19, 1977, pp.103–4; *Tate
Gallery Illustrated Catalogue of Acquisitions 1978–80*,
1981, pp.24–6; B. de Breffny, 'An Elizabethan Political
Painting', *Irish Arts Review*, vol.1, no.1, 1984, pp.39–41,
repr. also on cover; Hiram Morgan, 'Tom Lee: The
Posing Peacemaker', *Representing Ireland: Literature and
the Origins of Conflict 1534–1660*, ed. B. Bradshaw,
A. Hadfield and W. Morley, 1993, pp.132–65

EE and KH

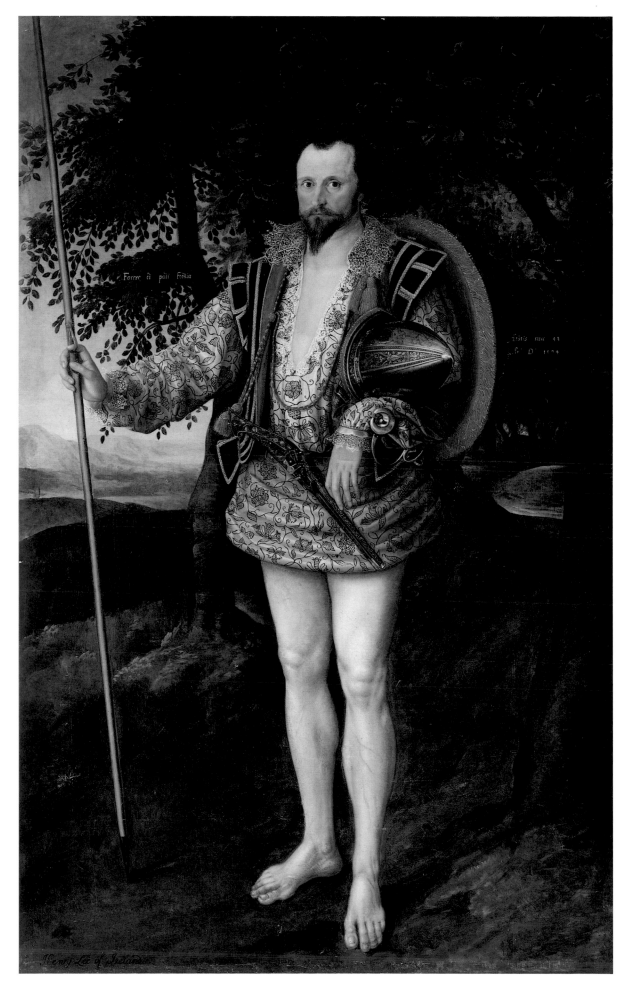

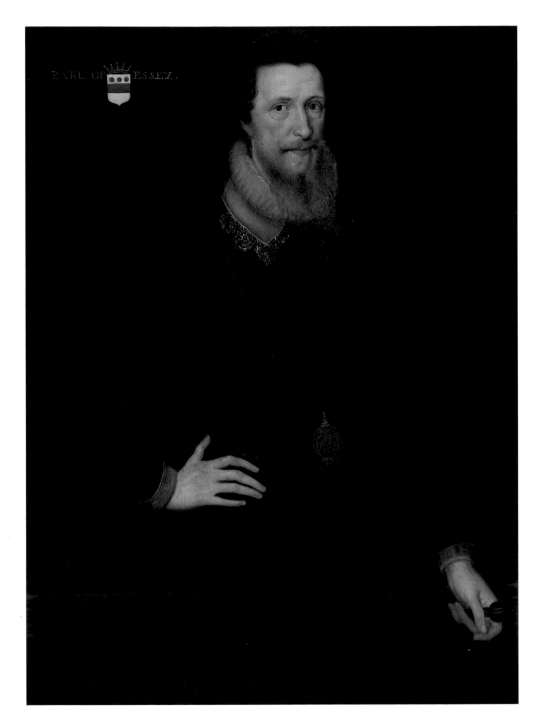

MARCUS GHEERAERTS THE YOUNGER

121 Robert Devereux, 2nd Earl of Essex *c*.1596–9

Oil on panel 110 × 80.5 (43 × 31¾)
Inscribed, '1601 Ætat.34' t.l. in a later
hand, commemorating the date and age
of Essex (1566–1601) at his death, with
'EARL OF ESSEX' on either side of the
coat of arms, below; 'Ex dono
Rob:Moxon Armig: 1756' b.l.
PROV: Presented by Robert Moxon to
Trinity College 1756
*The Master, Fellows and Scholars of Trinity
College, Cambridge*

Gheeraerts appears to have been responsible
for all large-scale portraits of Essex as a
mature man, as opposed to Essex's former
choice of William Segar, who had painted
him as a beardless youth (see fig.44, on p.133).
The Gheeraerts portraits almost all deploy the
same face pattern which was presumably first
created for the ambitious full-length at
Woburn Abbey, in which Essex appears before
an open landscape with Cadiz burning in the
background. Contemporaries described him
as 'fair-skinned, tall but wiry' (see D. Piper,
Burlington Magazine, vol.99, 1957, p.300 n.14)
with dark hair and a red beard, and thus he
appears in this portrait. He first began to
grow his beard on his famous Cadiz expedition of 1596, so Gheeraerts's portraits, which
show him wearing it, must have been painted
after that date.

The Trinity portrait is one of Gheeraerts's
standard three-quarter-length formulas for
men, unlike that at Woburn Abbey, or the
full-length in Garter-robes (National Portrait
Gallery). Essex's appearance is slightly older
and his face more angular than in his other
portraits, although the face pattern is basically
the same. It is possible that the differences
could be the result of a fresh sitting. The face
pattern and the costume are very similar to
Isaac Oliver's depictions of Essex, although in
reverse (see no.80), and also to the full-length
cabinet miniature of him (private collection)
attributed to Nicholas Hilliard. In the latter
Essex appears in the white costume of the
Woburn image, but with the combination ruff
and collar shown here and also by Oliver. It is
difficult to say if there was any collaboration
between Gheeraerts and Oliver, or borrowing
of patterns, although a preliminary drawing
of Essex by the latter (Yale Center for British
Art, New Haven) is thought to have been kept

in his studio as a pattern (see Stainton and White, 1989, p.48). It is relevant to note that in 1602 Gheeraerts's sister Sara married Oliver.

Essex's switch in the mid-1590s from employing the old-school Segar and Hilliard (the latter perhaps introduced to him by his stepfather the Earl of Leicester), to that of the more fashionable Gheeraerts and Oliver is significant. In this he seems to have been followed by his adherents, including the important patron the Earl of Southampton.

LIT: J.W. Goodison, 'Cambridge Portraits – I', *Connoisseur*, vol.139, 1957, p.217; David Piper, 'The 1590 Lumley Inventory: Hilliard, Segar and the Earl of Essex – II', *Burlington Magazine*, vol.99, 1957, pp.299–303; Roy Strong, 'Elizabethan Painting: An Approach through Inscriptions III: Marcus Gheeraerts the Younger, *Burlington Magazine*, vol.105, 1963, p.154; Strong 1969, pp.217, 220, 297; NPG 1969, I, pp.116–7; Mary Edmond, *Hilliard and Oliver*, 1983, see index references to Essex; Strong 1983, pp.10, 112, 161–2; Spike Bucklow, 'The Examination and Treatment of a Portrait of Robert Devereux, 2nd Earl of Essex', unpublished conservation report, Hamilton Kerr Institute, University of Cambridge 1993

TB

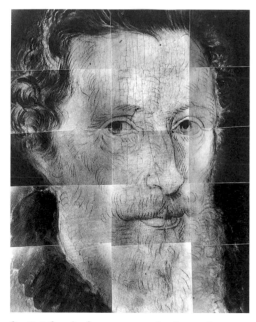

fig.48 Infrared reflectogram mosaic of no.121 by Spike Bucklow, Hamilton Kerr Institute

MARCUS GHEERAERTS THE YOUNGER

122 Elizabeth Finch, Countess of Winchilsea 1600

Oil on panel 111.8 × 88.9 (44½ × 35)
Inscribed 'Dame Elizabeth Finch Ætatis suæ 43. An° 1600.' t.r.
PROV: ...; said to have been in the collection of William Lenthall, Speaker of the House of Commons (died 1622), at Burford Priory, although this or another version recorded 1726 by Vertue in the collection of 'Mr. Stephens at Edmonton' as 'Lady Winchelsea. half len. a ruff. jewels. &c. Æta 43. 1600. painted on board. very well, cleanly colour'd, & well drawn, in the best manner of that date I have seen'; ...; sold Lenthall sale, Christie's 21 May 1808 (as by C. Janssens); by descent *Private Collection*

Elizabeth Finch (?1552–1633/4) was the daughter and sole heiress of Sir Thomas Heneage, one of Queen Elizabeth's most trusted servants, successor to Sir Christopher Hatton as Vice-Chamberlain of the Household, and Chancellor of the Duchy of Lancaster. In 1572 she was married to Sir Moyle Finch, heir and co-heir, through his mother, to the Finch and Moyle fortunes respectively. On his death in 1614 she was therefore an heiress of considerable account, and in a letter of 18 April 1615 to Sir Thomas Roe, Lord Carew tells us that she was 'pressed with suters, being, as I take it, the richest widdow in present estate, both in ioynture, moveables, and inheritances of her owne, that is in England' (John Maclean (ed.), 'Letters from George Lord Carew to Sir Thomas Roe', *Camden Society*, o.s., vol.76, 1860, pp.1–2). There is evidence that as early as 1618 she was in pursuit of a peerage in her own right, no doubt intended for the aggrandisement of her children, and perhaps spurred on by the precedent set by the Countess of Buckingham. In 1623 she was created Viscountess Maidstone, an honour conferred in remembrance of the good services of her father, but in fact a title for which she paid a tall price by transferring her family seat, Copped Hall, in Essex, to the Lord Treasurer, Sir Lionel Cranfield. In 1628 she was created Countess of Winchilsea, her second son Sir Thomas succeeding her as 2nd Earl in 1633.

This portrait is inscribed with the date 1600, which accords with the dating of the costume, and is therefore prior to her husband's death and her acquisition of titles. Her father died in 1595, so by this time she would have inherited the Heneage estates. She wears very elaborate and rich costume, with intricate embroidery which incorporates symbolic emblems in its design, intended as flattering reflections on her status and personality. The use of symbolic embroidery was increasingly fashionable from the 1580s and is common in portraiture of the period, and surviving inventories and wills show that such costumes were actually made, and were not fanciful emblematic creations of the artist. Her bodice is covered with ivy, which, as an evergreen, is symbolic of immortality. Owls, symbols of wisdom, perch among it on her sleeves. Her skirt is embroidered with a pattern of intertwined snakes, each one holding its tail in its mouth, symbolic of eternity; and her lace ruff is covered with rabbits, presumably representative of fertility. The snake design is very close to that in Thomas Trevelyon's *Miscellany*, a book of embroidery patterns published in 1608 (Folger Shakespeare Library, Washington. For an illustration of the design see Arnold 1988, p.300), and the other emblems are likely to have been taken from sources such as this, rather than emblem books of the period. The exact intention behind the reading of the emblems, other than generally complimenting the sitter, is unclear but could possibly allude to her status as the Heneage heiress, and that it would be through her and her progeny that the ancient line would continue. It is worth noting the pearl band she wears across her chest, at either end of which are jewels encrusted with rubies and diamonds in the shape of the Greek alpha and omega, with the sacred Chi-Rho monogram in the centre: it is recorded that Sir Thomas Heneage presented a similarly shaped jewel to Queen Elizabeth as a New Year's gift in 1588/9.

Although the portrait is not signed, the handling of the face is entirely consistent with the work of Marcus Gheeraerts the Younger, who in 1600 was one of the most fashionable and successful court painters. The slightly stiff three-quarter-length pose is one of his standard ones, particularly for female sitters. Elizabeth Finch was portrayed several times by various artists: in full-length by an unknown artist (private collection); and in full-length, and three-quarters when older, both formerly at Burley-on-the-Hill. A costly monument to her and her husband, attributed to Nicholas Stone, was erected during her lifetime at Eastwell, Kent, but is now in the Victoria and Albert Museum.

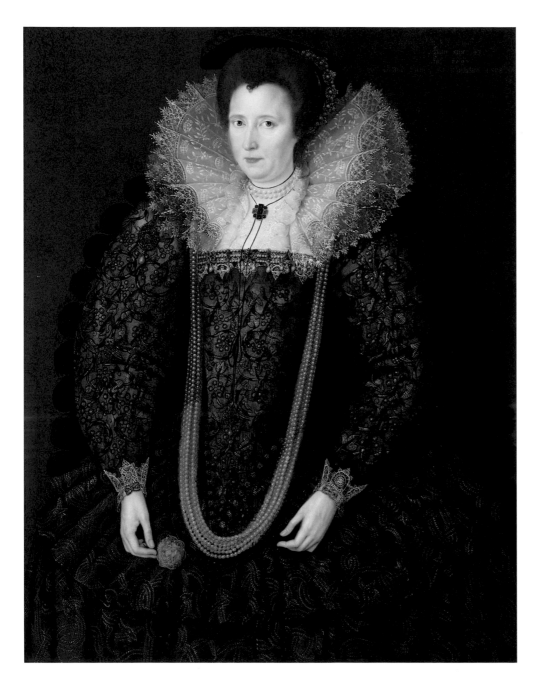

LIT: Cust 1913–14, p.44; Vertue II, p.14

TB

BRITISH SCHOOL

123 Mr Symonds of Norfolk
c.1595–1600

Oil on panel 76 × 96.5 (29⅞ × 38)
Inscribed 'SYMONDS of | C°. Norfolk.'
in a later hand, lower left
PROV: …; bt in Norfolk by Walter Rye
1898; bt Prince Frederick Duleep
Singh, by whom bequeathed to the
Mayor and Corporation, Thetford 1926
*Norfolk Museums Service (The Ancient
House Museum, Thetford)*

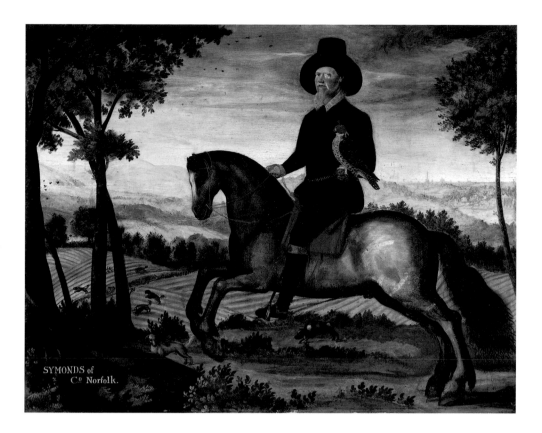

SYMONDS of
C°. Norfolk.

The identification of the sitter rests solely on
the later inscription, particularly since the earlier provenance of the painting is unknown.
The city shown in the distance clearly represents Norwich, with its cathedral and castle.
As the Norwich Castle Museum catalogue
notes, Symonds was a common Norfolk sur-
name, particularly so in Norwich itself, where
the name is frequently found in records for
the Tombland and Queen Street area. It is
possible that this horseman may be identified
with a gentleman called John Symonds who
was buried in St George's, Tombland, on 15
February 1609; he is commemorated, with his
wife Olive, by a wall-tomb which shows him
kneeling, wearing a goatee beard similar to
the one depicted here. A number of benefac-
tions to the church and parish by John
Symonds, freeman of Norwich, are recorded.

As hawking was the prerogative of a gentleman, the sitter's status is very clearly
defined by the hooded falcon on his gloved
left hand. There is also a presumption that he
is the owner of the ploughed fields behind, in
which his game-dogs sport. For coursing and
hawking, a gentleman would choose his stal-
lion for endurance and comfort, rather than
for speed, and as much dismounting and
remounting would be required, one that was
not too high. In the traditional form of non-
military equitation known as 'snaffle-riding',
stirrups were unknown. Thus the animal,
called a palfrey, was trained to give a very
smooth ride: it 'paced' instead of trotting, and
never galloped (I am grateful to Mr Anthony
Dent for the above information).

The painter of this remarkable portrait was
presumably a local artist, provincially trained.
It is unusual to find such an extensive representation of a landscape, particularly a specifically identified one, in a provincial work of
this date. Moreover, the equestrian format,
available in imported engravings, was confined to images of monarchs and important
military figures. It is likely that the artist, or
more probably the patron, had access to such
material or to illustrations in contemporary
hunting manuals.

EXH: *Family and Friends*, Norwich Castle Museum 1992
(15)
LIT: W. Rye, *An Autobiography of an Ancient Athlete and
Antiquary*, 1916, p.105; E. Farrer, *Catalogue of Norfolk
and Suffolk Portraits etc. …*, 1927, no.63; 'The Norfolk
Archaeological Society Excursion to Thetford and
Fersfield', *Norfolk Archaeology*, vol.24, Sept. 1929, p.xx

KH

?Frans Pourbus the Younger 1570–1622, or ?Otto van Veen 1556–1629, or ?Gysbrecht van Veen c.1562–1628

124 Archduchess Isabella Clara Eugenia and her Dwarf *c.*1599

Oil on canvas 217.2 × 130.2
(85½ × 51¼)
PROV: Presented to James I in 1603; apparently unsold at the Restoration and at Kensington Palace by early nineteenth century, where called 'Catherine of Aragon'; transferred to Hampton Court, identity re-established by Mrs Jameson in 1842
Her Majesty The Queen

This sumptuous portrait of the favourite daughter of Philip II of Spain and his third wife, Isabel de Valois (no.17) came to England in 1603 as a diplomatic gift to James I.

Isabella (1566–1633) was married in 1598 to her cousin Albert of Austria, with whom she governed the Southern Netherlands. This portrait, of which a number of versions in varying formats survive, may have been painted to mark their marriage, as there are also full-length pendant versions of her husband.

Following Isabella's arrival in Brussels in 1599 it is known that she was painted by Frans Pourbus the Younger, as in June 1600, just before he left for Italy to serve as court painter in Mantua, he was paid 620 livres for portraits of her and her husband.

In 1604, however, Karel van Mander wrote that Otto van Veen had painted two portraits of the Archdukes (as they are sometimes called) 'which were sent to the King of England, James the Second' [*sic*] (Miedema 1994, p.438). On 27 August 1604, though, Otto's brother Gysbrecht acknowledged receipt of 750 livres 'pour aultres deux grandz pourtraictz des personnes de Leur Altezes envoyez de Leur part au Roy d'Angleterre, l'an seize cens trois' ('for two other large portraits of their Highnesses, sent on their behalf to the King of England in 1603') (Marcel De Maeyer, *Albrecht et Isabella en de Schilderkunst*, Brussels 1955, pp.276–7, cited Millar 1963, p.14).

In composition, the present portrait is closer to the work of Pourbus than that known by either of the van Veens. It was first attributed to Pourbus by Waagen in 1854. An almost identical full-length version, in the collection of the Monasterio de las Descalzas Reales, Madrid, is also given to Pourbus (repr. p.103 in *Alonso Sanchez Coello*, exh. cat., Prado,

Madrid 1990). So, too, is the version now cut down to three-quarter length in the collection of Williams College (Williamstown, Mass.); this is said to have had as a pendant the portrait of Albert with his own dwarf before the palace at Brussels, which is now in the Royal Armouries. McGrath, however, considers that the present work was probably painted by Otto van Veen.

In September 1603, a few months after his accession, and after keeping the Flemish Ambassador waiting for forty days, James I accepted a pair of portraits of the Archduke and Archduchess. Lady Arbella Stuart wrote on 16 September 1603 that 'Count Arimberg was heere w[ith]in these few days and presented to the Queene [Anne] the Archduke and Infanta's portraits, most excellently drawne' (John Nichols, *The Progresses … of King James the First*, 1828, 1, pp.263–5).

The Archdukes were childless. The poignant inclusion in (presumably both) the portraits of the favoured Habsburg court dwarfs perhaps coloured Queen Anne's reaction to them. The Venetian envoy reported that 'the Queen being called, there was some conversation about [the portraits] in the course of which [she] expressed her pity that so great a lady should endure the sorrow of not enjoying the sweet name of mother' (C.S.P. Ven. 1603–7, x, no.136).

Indeed, the Queen may have actively disliked the portraits, as a letter of 13 February 1605 from her secretary William Fouler suggests that she was considering giving them away: they were 'verie fayre Large & costlie. And above xiij Florens paid for the workmanship' (Auerbach and Adams 1971, pp.70–1). They were, however, named among the 'whole-length Portraits, beautifully and artistically painted' seen at Whitehall in 1613 by the Duke of Saxe-Weimar (Rye 1865, p.161).

Apparently not listed in van der Doort's pre-1640 catalogue of Charles I's collection (which dealt mainly with the items at Whitehall), the present portrait remained unsold at the dispersal of the King's goods, when it was inventoried in the Crosse Gallery at Somerset House and valued at £20 (see Millar 1970–2, p.319). The portrait of her husband was sold, with two full-lengths of the Spanish King and Queen, for a total of £15 (ibid.).

This type of spectacular Habsburg state portrait must surely have influenced the

designer (thought to be William Larkin) of the Ranger's House full-length portraits (see no.136). Isabella is depicted in a magnificent pearl-encrusted gown lined with fur and embroidered with linked rings, fleurs-de-lys, anemones and pansies – the height of Spanish fashion. In 1613 the present portrait and its pendant were on view at Whitehall alongside full-lengths of the other principal rulers of Europe: Henri IV of France, painted by Bunel, Philip III of Spain and his queen, both by Pantoja de la Cruz (Millar 1963, pp.14–15). James I in turn sent versions of his own state portrait (see no.125) and other images of his family abroad.

After Albert's death in 1621 Isabella was to adopt the habit of the Poor Clares. It is in that plain black, white and grey attire that she was portrayed c.1628 by her court painter Van Dyck. She and her husband were also major patrons of Rubens. Many versions of the Van Dyck composition survive which were evidently, like the present work, used in diplomatic exchanges.

LIT: D. Lysons, *Environs of London*, III, 1795, p.183 n.69 (at Kensington Palace, as Catherine of Aragon and her dwarf by Holbein); Mrs Jameson, *Handbook to the Public Galleries of Art*, 1842, II, p.405; G. F. Waagen, *Treasures of Art in Great Britain*, 1854, II, p.367; W.B. Rye, *England as Seen by Foreigners*, 1865, p.161; E. Law, *A Historical Catalogue of the Pictures in the Royal Collection at Hampton Court*, 1881, no.343; Louise Roblot Delondre, *Portraits d'Infantes*, Paris and Brussels 1913, pp.141–3; Millar 1963, pp.14–15; Auerbach and Adams 1971, pp.70–1; Millar 1970–2, p.319; Eugenia McGrath, 'The Court Portraits of Frans Pourbus the Younger', unpublished M.A. report, Courtauld Institute 1986, p.9; *Fundáçion Carlos de Amberes 1594–1989*, Madrid 1989, pp.87–8

KH

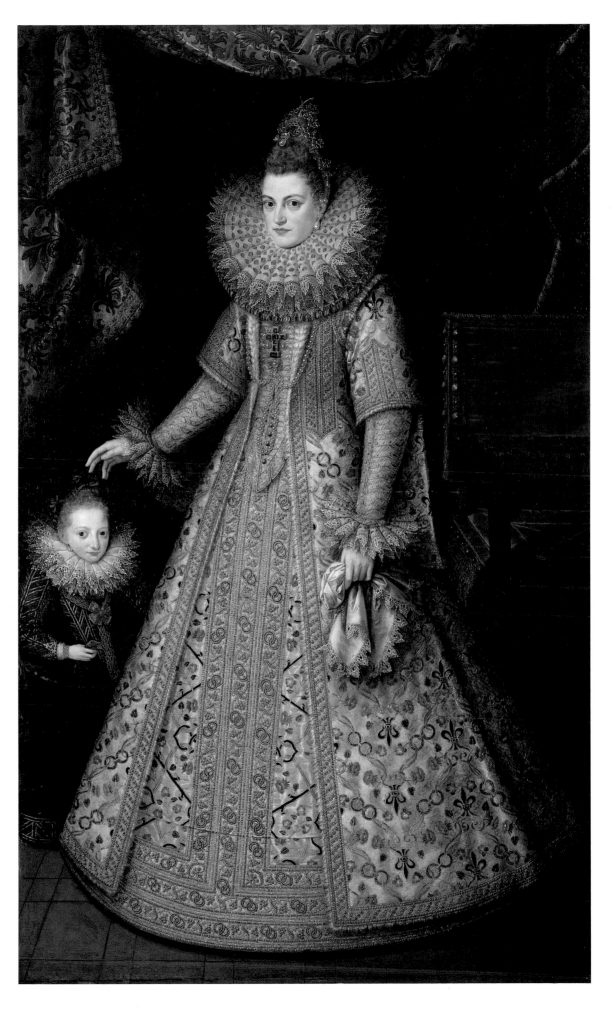

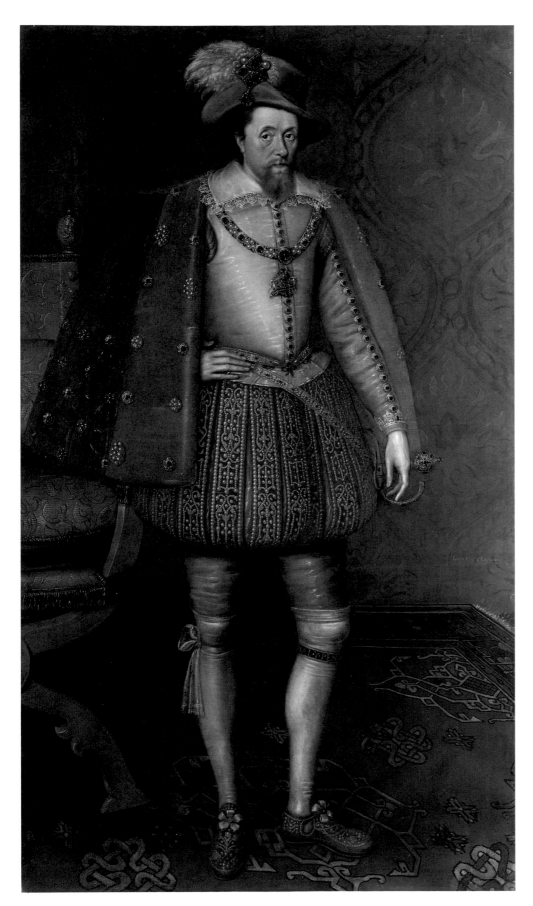

ATTRIBUTED TO JOHN DE CRITZ THE ELDER
*c.*1551/2–1642

125 James I *c.*1606

Oil on canvas 203 × 116 (80 × 45¾)
Inscribed: 'James King of England' in a
later hand, lower centre right
PROV: ...; 1st Earl of Ellesmere and by
descent to John Sutherland-Egerton,
5th Earl of Ellesmere (later 6th Duke of
Sutherland), sold Christie's 18 Oct.
1946 (152); ...; Mr M. Braham, from
whom bt Lane Fine Art *c.*1977; Mr and
Mrs Goldberg, USA, by whom sold
Phillips, New York, 6 June 1987 (394)
bt Lane Fine Art; sold Sotheby's 9 Jan
1988 (24) to present owner
Private Collection

James I succeeded Elizabeth I in 1603 and the
need arose for an official portrait of the new
King. He seems to have been an unwilling sitter and many versions of a single portrait type
survive from the earliest years of his English
reign. In these the face mask is very similar,
while the attire, accessories and the placing of
the arms and hands vary. The present portrait
is probably the finest and most sumptuously
dressed example of this type.

On 11 May 1605, John de Critz the Elder
was appointed Serjeant-Painter to the King,
jointly with the shadowy figure of Leonard
Fryer. In August 1606 de Critz was paid for a
full-length of the King, with two others of
the Queen and of 'the Prince' to be sent to
the Archduke of Austria (see Mrs Rachael
Lane Poole, 'An Outline of the History of the
de Critz Family of Painters', *Walpole Society*,
vol.2, 1912–13, p.48). In October 1607 de
Critz billed Robert Cecil (see no.119) for a
painting of the king (see Auerbach and
Adams 1971, pp.72–3). De Critz is therefore
presumed to be the originator of the type and
his workshop responsible for most of the versions. Later payments for portraits of the King
are also recorded, in 1611 and 1618, to de
Critz's brother-in-law, and possible collabora-
tor, Marcus Gheeraerts the Younger, who was
primarily the Queen's favoured painter.

Among other surviving full-length versions
similar to the present portrait are those at
Dulwich College, Loseley Park (see Tate
Gallery 1969–70, no.174), and in the Prado,
Madrid. Three-quarter-length versions
include that in the National Maritime Museum, Greenwich; the many surviving head-
and-shoulders examples include one in the
National Portrait Gallery. The large number of
these images bears witness to the immense

ROBERT PEAKE c.1551–1619

126 Princess Elizabeth, later Elizabeth of Bohemia 1603

Oil on canvas 134.6 × 95.3 (53 × 37½)
Inscribed 'AE7' on fan handle; '1603' on bridge

PROV: Probably commissioned by 1st Baron Harington of Exton (died 1613); perhaps by descent via his great-niece Anne Dudley, *née* Montagu, wife of 4th Lord North, whose son Francis acquired Wroxton Abbey in 1680 through his marriage to co-heiress Frances Downe; presumably by descent at Wroxton Abbey to William, 11th Lord North, from whom bt Agnew's, Oct. 1914; bt Henry P. Davidson 14 Oct. 1916; by descent; Christie's, 17 Nov. 1989 (39) bt the Weiss Gallery from whom bt Trustees of the National Maritime Museum 1990
National Maritime Museum, Greenwich

demand for the King's portrait both in Britain and as diplomatic gifts to be sent abroad.

In 1618 James evidently agreed to sit for Paul van Somer and a new full-length portrait type was created (Millar 1963, pp.80–1). Following van Somer's death, Adam de Colone, the son of Adrian Vanson, James's painter in Scotland (see no.117), appears to have been paid in 1623 for two full-lengths related to the van Somer type (see Duncan Thomson, *The Life and Art of George Jamesone*, 1974, pp.56–7). However, before this date the King had already sat to another Netherlandish immigrant painter, Daniel Mytens, whose remarkable 1621 portrait of James seated in Garter robes is both powerful and poignant, depicting him as sick, elderly and bereaved (National Portrait Gallery).

In the present portrait the King wears in his hat a major piece of jewellery. Known as the 'Mirror of Great Britain', it had been specially made in 1604 to mark the union of England and Scotland. It included a table-cut ruby, three large diamonds, two circular pearls and the famous Sancy diamond as a pendant.

The portrait was recorded in the display of paintings at Bridgewater House, in London. This comprised a collection formed mainly in the latter part of the eighteenth century by the last Duke of Bridgewater, who bequeathed it to the 1st Earl of Ellesmere. Paintings added by the latter are asterisked in the Bridgewater House catalogue. The present painting is not, although it has been suggested that it had descended to Ellesmere through the Sutherland family.

LIT: *Catalogue of the Bridgewater and Ellesmere Collections of Pictures at Bridgewater House*, 1897 (341, as by 'Paul van Somers'); NPG 1969, I, p.179

KH

Princess Elizabeth, the daughter of James VI of Scotland and Anne of Denmark, was born at Falkland Castle on 19 August 1596, and christened Elizabeth, after her godmother, the Queen of England. Following her father's accession to the English throne in 1603 she was brought to England where in the same August she was entrusted to the care of Lord and Lady Harington of Exton. She lived with them at Combe Abbey, near Coventry until 1608.

This is thought to be the earliest portrait of the Princess and it appears to be a pendent to that, also by Peake, of her elder brother Henry with Sir John Harington, also dated 1603 (see fig.49). In that portrait, the two boys are identified by heraldic shields painted above their heads and by their inscribed ages. Both portraits came from the collection at Wroxton Abbey (the double portrait is first recorded there by Vertue in a notebook of 1741; see Vertue IV, pp.191–2).

Since no payments for either portrait have been found in the royal accounts it is likely that the commission came from the Haringtons. It would have marked both their official charge of the Princess and the beginning of the close and lifelong friendship between their only son and the new heir to the throne.

The Harington family was under something of a cloud at the end of Elizabeth I's reign through the involvement of their son-in-law, the 3rd Earl of Bedford, in the rebellion of the Earl of Essex in 1601. Immediately after Elizabeth's death they had been able to make capital of their distant kinship to James

I and as a consequence their fortunes rose dramatically. They entertained James at Burley-on-the-Hill, Rutland, shortly after he arrived in England from Scotland. Subsequently, they received Queen Anne, Prince Henry and Princess Elizabeth at Combe Abbey, and it has been suggested that Peake's two portraits may refer specifically to this visit.

The Haringtons were to devote the rest of their lives to the service of Princess Elizabeth. At her wedding to Frederick, the Elector Palatine on 14 February 1613, Lady Harington was honoured with a seat on the dais. They subsequently escorted the couple out to their palace at Heidelberg; Lord Harington died at Worms on the return journey. In 1616, Lady Harington settled in Heidelberg to attend the Princess, remaining there almost until her death in 1618.

Frederick and Elizabeth's brief reign as King and Queen of Bohemia ended in 1621, and the rest of Elizabeth's life was largely spent in exile at The Hague. From thence she dispatched numerous portraits of herself and her family, by Miereveld and his studio, to potential allies and supporters. At the Restoration of her nephew Charles II in 1660 she was at last able to return to England, where she died the following year. Known to contemporaries as the 'Winter Queen' or the 'Queen of Hearts', it was through her line that the House of Hanover inherited the English throne. Her grandson became George I.

In the double portrait of the two boys, Harington kneels while the Prince draws or sheathes his sword, having perhaps exercised his royal prerogative of making an incision in the neck of the dead stag before them. They are attended by a groom who leads the Prince's horse, and by a white hunting dog.

In the present portrait of the Princess, corresponding figures can be seen engaged in the chase in the deer-park beyond the canal or river, in the background on the right. In the left background, two ladies sit in a garden building on an artificial mound. They may be intended to represent ladies of the Harington family. Such mounds were a fashionable element of contemporary garden design. Surviving examples built for Thomas Tresham (c.1597) with as here, adjoining waterways, can still be seen today at Lieveden New Bield, Northamptonshire.

In using an outdoor location for full-scale portraits, Peake was adopting Marcus Gheeraerts the Younger's innovation of the previous decade (see 'Captain Thomas Lee', no.120), which was paralleled in Hilliard's miniature of

'George Clifford, 3rd Earl of Cumberland' of c.1590 (no.74).

Peake came of a Lincolnshire family and, like Hilliard, trained as a goldsmith. He was apprenticed in London in 1565, becoming a freeman in 1576, the year in which he first worked for the office of revels. Various portraits have been attributed to him on the basis of a common form of inscription. The portrait of an 'Unknown Military Commander' 1593 (fig.50) bears the following inscription on the back of the panel, 'M.BY.RO. | PEAKE', and seems the likeliest guide to his early style. The three-quarter-length composition, baton of command held diagonally in the right hand, the left resting on the sword or, as in this case, the hip, was by now entirely traditional. Parallels could be found in the work of Mor or Coello, going back in England to the Holbein-related 'Sir Nicholas Carew' (Collection of the Duke of Buccleuch). From 1607 Peake shared the office of Serjeant Painter with John de Critz, and Mary Edmond suggests that the two, who were neighbours in the London parish of St Sepulchre, may have shared a studio. Peake was official painter to Prince Henry, numerous portraits of whom survive. In 1611 Peake dedicated a translation which he had commissioned of Sebastiano Serlio's *The Firste Booke of Architecture* to the Prince. Peake died in October 1619. His son William (c.1580–1639) and grandson Robert (c.1605–1667) were also painters, though, again, trained as goldsmiths.

LIT: Cust 1913–14, p.45, pl.xxv(b); Strong 1969, no.209; Karen Hearn, 'Lucy Harington, Countess of Bedford', unpublished MA report, Courtauld Institute 1990, pp.11–13; Mark Weiss, 'Elizabeth of Bohemia by Robert Peake', *Apollo*, vol.132, 1990, pp.407–10; Roger Quarm, 'Robert Peake's Portrait of Elizabeth of Bohemia', *NACF Review*, 1991, pp.102–7

KH

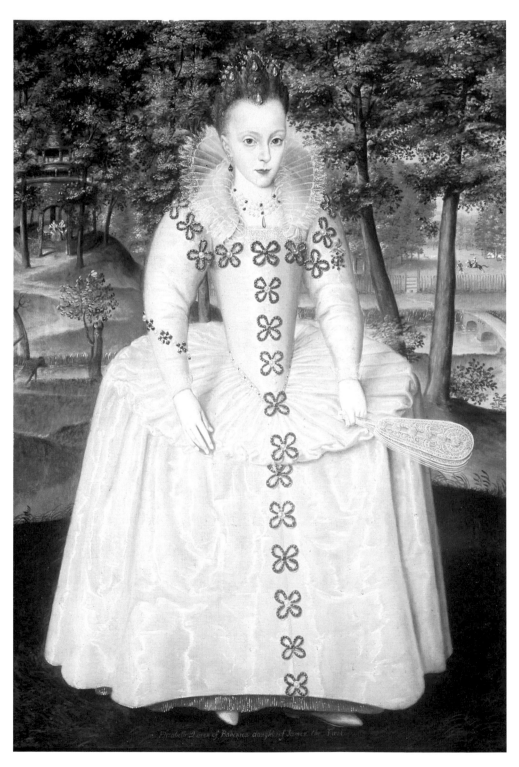

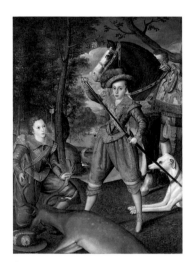

fig.49 Robert Peake, 'Henry, Prince of Wales with Sir John Harington' 1603, oil on canvas. *The Metropolitan Museum of Art, Purchase, Joseph Pulitzer Bequest, 1944*

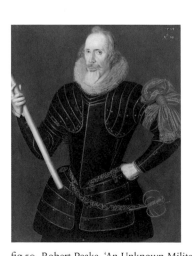

fig.50 Robert Peake, 'An Unknown Military Commander, Aged 60' 1593, oil on panel. *Yale Center for British Art, Paul Mellon Fund*

ROBERT PEAKE

127 Henry, Prince of Wales c.1610

Oil on canvas 133 × 90 (52⅜ × 35½)
Inscribed 'ICH DIEN' on shield; '[M]AL
Y PENS[E]' on garter
PROV: Presumed to be a gift to Duke
Charles Emanuel I of Savoy, and by
descent; …; first recorded as inv.
no.1099 in the 1879 inventory of works
of art given by the Crown (King Victor
Emanuel II of Italy) in the Royal
Palaces, Turin
Palazzo Reale, Turin

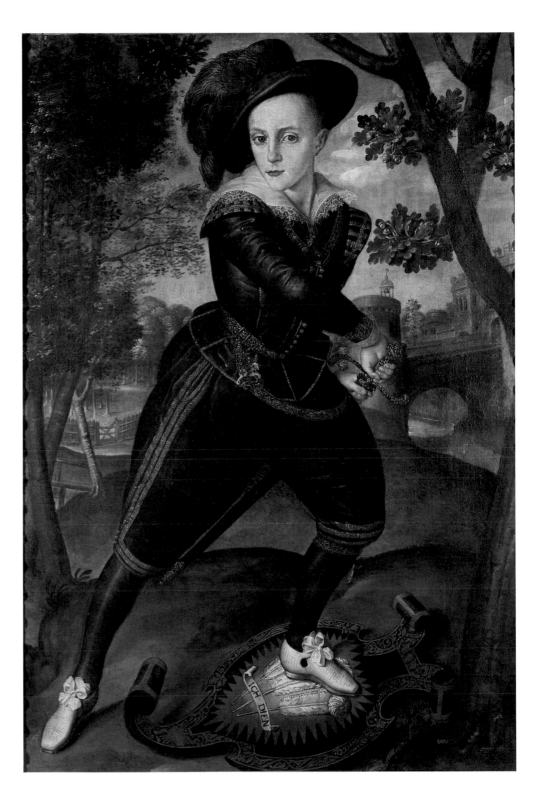

The eldest son of James I, Henry was born in
1594 and died of typhoid fever in 1612. As
official 'Paynter' in large to Henry, the heir to
the throne, Peake was required to produce
numerous portraits of him, some of which are
remarkably innovatory.

It is presumed that Peake had first come to
Henry's notice when the Harington family
commissioned two portraits in 1603, one of
Princess Elizabeth (no.126) and the other of
Prince Henry with their son (fig.49). These
two paintings share an outdoors setting in a
landscape traversed by a canal or river and
including a deer park.

For the present portrait, Peake retained a
similar setting, but this time included a building incorporating a substantial bridge, right.
This work is hard to date precisely, as the
Prince's features and physique seem only a
little more mature than in the portrait of 1603.
His foot, however, is set on a tournament
shield bearing the motto and three feathers
device of the Prince of Wales, a title not conferred on him until June 1610. Six months
earlier, this event had been prefaced by his
first bearing of arms, marked by the festivities
in the Whitehall Banqueting House known as
Prince Henry's Barriers. The parade shield
depicted here is of the type made of paste-
board and carried (but not, of course, used) at
such events (information courtesy of A.V.B.
Norman).

As in the double portrait of 1603, Henry is
shown as a young man of action, in the act of
drawing his sword. The weapon is encrusted
with precious metal and is of a military type,
with a small side-ring mounted on the centre
of the quillons (crossguards). Strong has identified a source for Henry's gesture in an
engraving by Hendrik Goltzius of *c*.1586,
'Manlius Torquatus' from *The Roman Heroes*
(Strong 1986, p.114 and fig.43). This is highly
appropriate, given the classicising form taken
by the *Barriers* and by Inigo Jones's designs
for the masque *Oberon*, performed in January
1611 (see nos.108–9).

This portrait must have been sent to Savoy
when a marriage, first proposed in January
1611, between Henry and the Infanta Maria
(1594–1656), daughter of Duke Charles
Emanuel I of Savoy, was under negotiation.
Initially it was also suggested that Princess
Elizabeth should marry the Duke's heir, the
Prince of Piedmont. A full-length portrait of
her, in a composition almost identical to that
used by Gheeraerts for his Woburn portrait of
her mother (no.130) is also now in Turin
(fig.52; see Cesare Bertana, 'Un ritratto di
Elisabetta Stuart di Marcus Gheeraerts nelle
collezioni sabaude', *Studi Piemontesi*, vol.20,
1991, pp.387–9).

Whenever a marriage between reigning
houses was proposed, the family of each party
would expect to be able to study an image of
the prospective spouse. James I was at the
same time considering for Henry potential

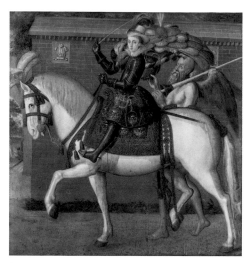

fig.51 Robert Peake, 'Henry, Prince of Wales on Horseback' c.1611, oil on canvas. *By kind permission of The Executors of Mrs P.A. Tritton, from the Collection at Parham Park, West Sussex*

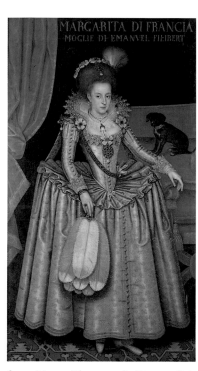

fig.52 Marcus Gheeraerts the Younger, 'Princess Elizabeth' c.1611, oil on canvas.. *Castello di Racconigi, Turin*

brides from Florence, Spain and France. As Wilks shows, by this date Henry was commissioning his own portraits, from Peake, for the various exchanges with foreign courts. In 1611–12 Peake was paid £50 for 'twoe great Pictures of the Prince in Armes at length sent beyond the seas' (Strong 1986, p.114).

Robert Oresko points out (letter of 21 April 1995) that through their mother the Duke's children bore the title Infante or Infanta of Spain, and that both King James and Queen Anne favoured the Savoy match as an opportunity to break into the great Catholic dynastic networks. Henry himself was deeply opposed to marrying a Catholic. The substantial dowry offered seems to have persuaded James and on 2 November 1612 the banker Gabaleone, the Duke's negotiator in London, wrote back to Savoy that matters were on the point of conclusion (Bertana 1983, p.425). On 6 November, however, Prince Henry died. Maria never married. She entered a Franciscan convent in 1629, subsequently playing a major role as a leader of the pro-Habsburg party in the civil wars of 1638–42.

Among Peake's final portraits of the Prince his most remarkable one was the immense equestrian image, a spectacular embodiment of confidence and hope for the future, but which was in fact to be so cruelly dashed (see fig.51). A few years ago, cleaning revealed that this painting also included the elderly, naked, winged figure of Time, being drawn along by the forelock by the youthful prince (see Ian McClure, 'Henry, Prince of Wales on Horseback' in *The Art of the Conservator*, ed. Andrew Oddy, 1992, pp.59–72).

LIT: Cesare Bertana, 'Il ritratto di uno Stuart alla corte dei Savoia', *Studi Piemontesi*, vol.22, no.2, Nov. 1983, pp.423–6; Roy Strong, *Henry, Prince of Wales*, 1986, p.114, repr. cover and fig.42; Timothy V. Wilks, 'The Court Culture of Prince Henry and his Circle 1603–1613', unpublished D.Phil diss., Oxford University 1987, pp.86–99 on Henry's patronage of Robert Peake; Ellen Chirelstein, 'Lady Elizabeth Pope: the Heraldic Body' in Gent and Llewellyn 1990, pp.51, repr. p.54; John Peacock, 'The Politics of Portraiture', Sharpe and Lake 1994, pp.213–15

KH

ROBERT PEAKE

128 Prince Charles, as Duke of York 1613

Oil on canvas 154.9 × 86.4 (61 × 34)
Inscribed 'CAROLE, TE MVSAE NAM TV DIGNATVS VTRVMQ | CEPIMVS HOSPI-TIO, PINXIMVS, OBSEQVIO | Academi-am inuisens A° Regni Paterni | Angliae 10°, die Martij 4°, cooptatus est | in ordinem Magistrorum, admissusq | hoc in Senatu, per Valentinum | Carey Pro-cancellarium.' on trompe l'oeil piece of paper, upper left
PROV: Commissioned for the University of Cambridge 1613
University of Cambridge

This magnificent portrait of the future Charles I commemorates his visit to Cambridge in March 1613. This occurred two weeks after the marriage of his sister Princess Elizabeth, and only four months after the sudden death of his elder brother Henry. Charles was now the heir to the throne and the most important youth in the land. Created Duke of York in 1605, he was not to be given the title of Prince of Wales until 1616.

The portrait shows a stylistic retreat from the innovation of outdoor settings for the portraits of his siblings (nos.126, 127) to the frozen grandeur of mainstream Continental court portraiture. Charles, wearing the Garter and Lesser George of the Order, stands beneath spectacular, looped-up cloth-of-gold curtains, his hat, with its jewelled hatband, on the table at his side. Both the table and the matted floor are covered in green velvet, fringed and decorated with gold. The presentation is not so very different from that of 'Erik XIV of Sweden', fifty years or so earlier (no.47).

The specific context of this commission is set out in the Latin inscription on the paper pinned to the curtain: its folds, shadows and pin add up to a virtuoso display of naturalistic painting. Goodison translates it as: 'Charles, we the Muses, since you deigned to agree to both, have both welcomed you as our guest and painted you in humble duty. Visiting the University in the 10th year of his father's reign over England, on 4 March, he was enrolled in the ranks of the Masters and admitted in this Senate House by Valentine Carey Vice-Chancellor.'

During recent cleaning the conservators at the Hamilton-Kerr Institute found that this portrait had been painted over another apparently well-advanced portrait. It was not clear whether Peake had re-used a previously painted canvas, or whether he had been required to rework the present commission extensively. In raking light the impasto of decoration on the tablecloth and of highlights on the curtains can be seen in different places from those elements in the present picture. An X-radiograph of the head area revealed another head beneath, slightly lower down and larger in scale. A pentiment visible to the naked eye suggests that the right hand may first have been positioned on the waist.

Robert Peake's receipt for £13 6s 8d from Vice-Chancellor Carew (or Carey) 'in full satisfaction for Prince Charles his picture' and dated 10 July 1613 survives (Finberg 1920–1, p.90).

Peake, the Serjeant-Painter and Prince Henry's chosen portraitist, had already painted Charles as a boy, and was evidently retained throughout the Prince's teenage years.

EXH: *Exhibition of Portraits*, Cambridge Antiquarian Society 1885 (34); Tate Gallery 1969–70 (113)
LIT: A.J. Finberg, 'An Authentic Portrait by Robert Peake', *Walpole Society*, vol.9, 1920–1, pp.89–95; Margaret Toynbee, 'Some Early Portraits of Charles I', *Burlington Magazine*, vol.91, 1949, p.6; J.W. Goodison, *Catalogue of Cambridge Portraits*, Cambridge 1955, 1, pp.16–17; Strong 1969, no.189; *The Hamilton Kerr Institute Bulletin*, vol.1, 1988, p.117

KH

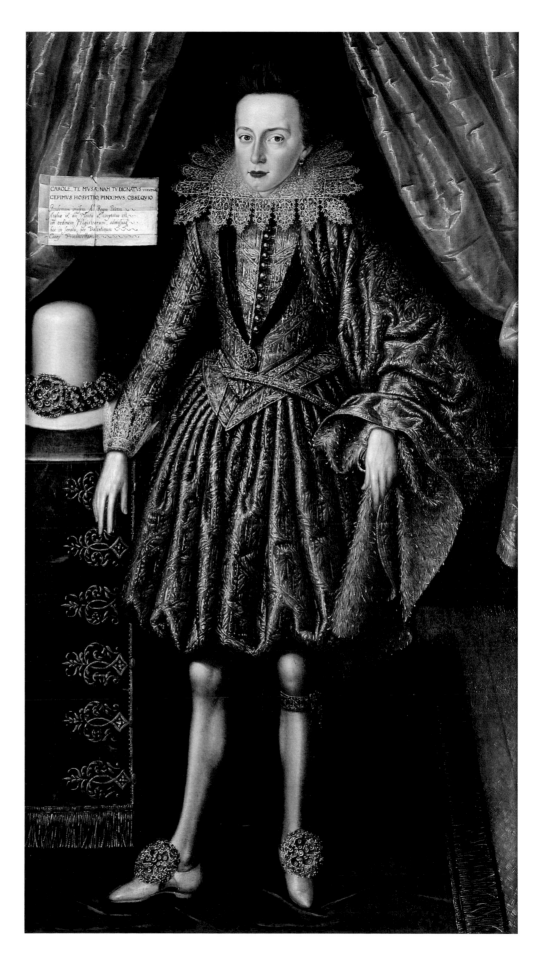

JOHN DE CRITZ THE ELDER
c.1551/2–1642 AND STUDIO

129 Lady in Masque Costume as a 'Power of Juno' 1606

Oil on canvas 203.8 × 122 (80¼ × 48)
Inscribed 'Lucy Harrington Css of Bedford' lower left, in a later hand
PROV: …; presumed to be 'A Turkish Lady', noted at Titchfield House, seat of the Wriothesley family, Earls of Southampton 1731 (Goulding and Adams 1936, p.xxv); inherited by Elizabeth Noel, Duchess of Portland and noted at Bulstrode after 1740 by Vertue (as 'Lady Turkish habit', ibid., p.xxvi), in 1762 by Sir William Musgrave (as 'Ann Carr Css of Bedford. In a Masquerade Dress, Crown & Turkish Feathr, Red Waistecoat & Blue petticoat Richly Laced. Red Stockings & Blue shoes.', ibid., p.xxvii) and by Thomas Pennant (as 'Lucy Css of Bedford', ibid. p.xxviii); by descent
Private Collection

On 5 January 1606, the masque *Hymenaei*, written by Ben Jonson and designed by Inigo Jones, was performed, probably in the earlier Banqueting House at Whitehall, to mark the marriage of Frances Howard, daughter of the Earl of Suffolk, to Robert Devereux, 2nd Earl of Essex. The masque celebrated not only the union of men and women, but also the symbolic marriage of the kingdoms of Scotland and England effected by James I's creation of Great Britain. Jones and Jonson had first collaborated on the *Masque of Blacknesse*, commissioned by James's Queen, Anne of Denmark in 1605.

Jones's designs for *Hymenaei* do not survive, although a similar female costume can be seen in no.106. While the speaking parts were performed by actors, favoured members of the court participated in the resolution of the masque, gorgeously attired in special costumes. In the final scene Juno, goddess of marriage, was revealed among clouds on the upper part of the stage, with two groups of four ladies at either side representing her 'Powers', who were lowered on to the stage in 'two concave clouds'.

Jonson describes their attire in his text: 'the upper part of white cloth of silver wrought with Juno's birds and fruits; a loose under garment, full gathered, of carnation [rosy pink], striped with silver and parted with a golden zone [a belt, or any encircling band]; beneath that another flowing garment of watchet

[light blue] cloth of silver, laced with gold … their haire being carelessly … bound under the circle of a rare and rich Coronet, adorn'd with all variety and choise of jewels; from the top of which, flow'd a transparent veile, down to the ground; whose verge, returning up, was fastened to either side in most sprightly manner. Their shoos were azure, and gold, set with rubies and diamonds; so were all their garments; and every part abounding in ornament.'

The present portrait is one of three full-lengths that appear to depict the masque costume described. One, identical in composition to this, and also including the cloud background described by Jonson, is at Berkeley Castle. The other, with the subject facing to the right, with both hands moving freely, and with the 'carnation' skirt at full-length rather than the original two-tier one shown here, is at Woburn Abbey, identified by a late-seventeenth century inscription and by her coat of arms, as of Lucy Harington, Countess of Bedford (1581–1627). That portrait has been attributed to de Critz through comparison with the portraits of Robert Cecil (see no.119) and with two portraits of the '1st Earl of Southampton' (Duke of Buccleuch and private collection) apparently by the same hand as Cecil's image.

The eight ladies who played the 'Powers' were the Countesses of Bedford (Lucy Harington), Montgomery (Mary Vere, 1587–1629) and Rutland (Elizabeth Sidney, 1585–1612), the Ladies Knollys (1586–1658), Berkeley (1576–1635), Dorothy Hastings (1579–before 1622) and Blanche Somerset (*c*.1585–1649) and Mistress Cecily Sackville. The accounts for Lady Rutland's costume survive at Belvoir Castle (repr. Orgel and Strong 1973, p.105).

Vertue noted with regret that the identities of some of the Wriothesley portraits were lost when they were moved from Titchfield (Goulding and Adams 1936, p.xxiii). Both the present portrait and that at Berkeley Castle have been called Lady Bedford, although in all three there are differences in the headdresses and each jacket has quite different embroidery. On the other hand, the facial features, the blue-grey eyes and brown hair in the present portrait do in fact correspond with other known portraits of Lucy Harington, who was the Queen's most favoured Lady of the Privy Chamber. It has the same long nose in a long face with a pointed chin emerging from slender but loose jowls. A patron of Jonson and of other writers, recipi-

ent of an exceptionally large number of literary dedications, she was a major shaper of court cultural life, and an organiser as well as a performer in masques.

The costumes of this and of the Woburn portrait are clearly painted using the same technique; the two heads, however, are quite different in their respective treatment and seem to have been painted by different hands.

This portrait evidently marks the sitter's participation in an event of exceptional importance in the life of the court. In a letter John Pory described *Hymenaei* thus: 'The men were clad in Crimson, and the women in white. They had every one a white plume of the richest Herons fethers, and were so rich in jewels upon their heades as was most glorious. I think they hired and borrowed all the principal jewels and ropes of perle both in court or citty' (*Jonson*, x, p.466).

EXH: Manchester 1857 (23); *Past Treasures*, The Harley Gallery 1995 (26)
LIT: C. Fairfax Murray, *Catalogue of the Pictures … at Welbeck Abbey, and in London*, 1894, no.334; C.H. Collins Baker, *Lely and the Stuart Portrait Painters*, 1912, p.28; Cust 1913–14, pp.30–1, pl.ix; R.W. Goulding and C.K. Adams, *Catalogue of the Pictures … at Welbeck Abbey*, 1936, no.334; *Ben Jonson*, eds. C.H. Herford and E. Simpson, Oxford 1941, VII, pp.xv–xix; Orgel and Strong 1973, I, no.10; B.K. Lewalski, *Writing Women in Jacobean England*, Cambridge, Mass. and London 1993, p.337 n.76

KH

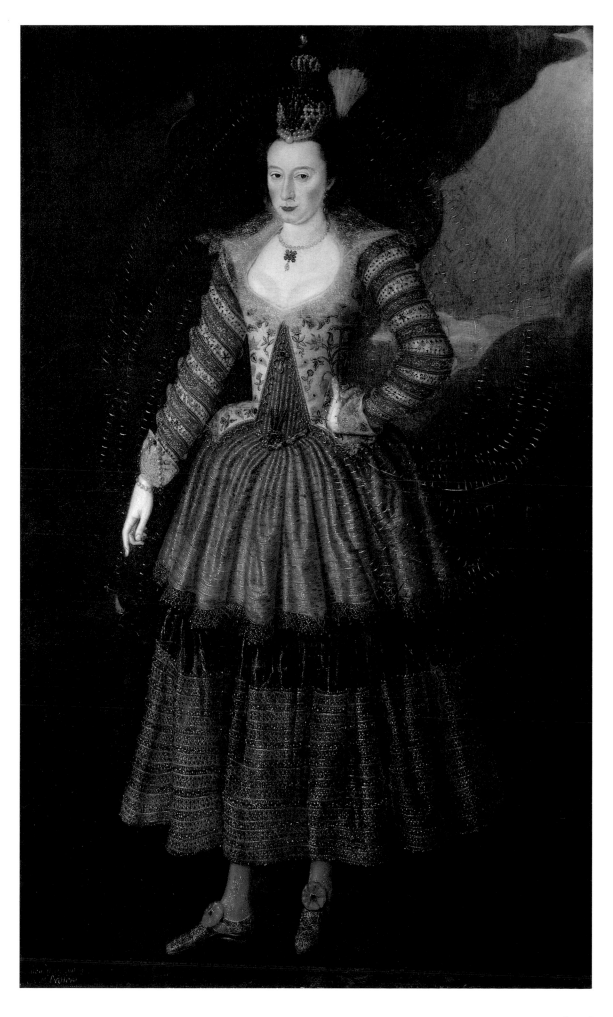

MARCUS GHEERAERTS THE YOUNGER 1561/2–1636

130 Anne of Denmark *c.*1611–14

Oil on canvas 221 × 131 (87 × 51⅝)
Inscribed 'La mia grandezza dal eccel-
so.', upper right; and 'fundamentum
meum', lower right; 'ANNE OF DEN-
MARK | wife of K, James I' on later
cartellino, b.l.
PROV: Possibly given to the sitter's
Lady of the Privy Chamber, Lucy Har-
ington, Countess of Bedford
(1581–1628), though not mentioned in
Charles Tough's list of paintings at
Woburn in 1727 (Vertue II, pp.40–1);
Dukes of Bedford, at Woburn by 1890;
by descent
*By kind permission of the Marquess of
Tavistock and the Trustees of the Bedford
Estate*

Anne (1574–1619) was the daughter of Frederick II of Denmark. In 1589, aged fifteen, she
married James VI of Scotland, with whom she
was to have seven children. Of these only
Henry (nos.84, 127), Elizabeth (no.126) and
Charles (nos.85, 92, 128, 142, 150) survived
childhood. Anne was carefully educated by a
formidable mother, and came from a cultured
court.

Following her husband's accession to the
English throne in 1603 Anne came down to
London. She became a patron of poets and
musicians and, above all, of the elaborate
court masques of Ben Jonson and Inigo Jones,
in which she also performed. She enjoyed
hunting and travelling and later became an
avid collector of paintings.

In the present portrait, Anne wears a dress
embroidered with flowered sprigs and with
peacock feathers. These were appropriate
symbols for the Queen, as this bird was
sacred to Juno, wife of the King of the Roman
gods, Jupiter. In Scotland James had written a
poem to Anne as 'Our earthlie Juno and our
Gratious Queen' (*King James VI & I*, Royal
Scottish Museum, Edinburgh 1975, p.7). The
low neckline was a style favoured by Anne,
who was proud of her white breast. The dress
is supported by a wheel farthingale of the
fashion which she had inherited from
Elizabeth I. A comparison with 'The Ditchley
Portrait' (no.45), also by Gheeraerts, shows
how Anne is here exploiting Elizabeth's visual
legacy (Wood 1981, p.50).

As in 'The Rainbow Portrait' of Elizabeth
(Hatfield House), the Queen is portrayed
standing within a classical archway. Behind,
to the left, is a formal garden, perhaps of the

kind that Anne commissioned for her residence at Somerset House.

Anne holds an enormous feather fan. As
well as her multiple ropes of costly pearls, she
wears some specifically identifiable jewellery.
Pinned to her collar is a crowned 'S', referring to her mother, Sophie of Mecklenburg.
The crowned 'C4' monogram jewel was given
to her by her beloved brother Christian IV in
about June 1611. Indeed, Wood suggests tentatively that the portrait may have been commissioned to mark the acquisition of these
jewels. The Venetian envoy to London, Fos-
carini, reported in 1611 of an audience in
which 'the Queen talked mostly about her
mother, her brother, the greatness of her
house, her debt to God for so many favours'.
Anne here also wears a large double cross,
which might be that described in her 1606
jewellery inventory (Scarisbrick 1991, p.208).

The inscription, which can be translated as
'My greatness comes from God', was the Italian motto that Anne had adopted for herself
(see also the 1616 engraving of her by Simon
de Passe, and no.139). In a letter of 1618 Fos-
carini explained why: 'she is daughter, sister
and wife of a king, which cannot today be
said of any other. She claims that her greatness comes not from the King but from God
alone, and her motto runs "La mia grandezza
dal eccelso"' (Wood 1981, p.51).

The present portrait, like the later one by
van Somer (no.139), places the Queen to the
left, turning towards the right. It is thus
unlikely to have been designed as a pendant
to one of the King. Its design, as well as the
motto inscribed upon it, appears to assert her
independence of her husband.

Lucy Wood has charted how the English
portraits of Anne begin with the curiously
characterless pendants to those of her husband, attributed to the de Critz studio. She
speculates that Anne may not have granted a
new sitting but that the de Critz type may be
based on images made earlier in Scotland.
Almost from the start of their reign, however,
Anne used Isaac Oliver for her miniatures,
whereas James employed the older Nicholas
Hilliard. Oliver was appointed her official
limner in 1605; his most spectacular miniature
of her is that in profile of *c.*1610, in what
appears to be masque costume (fig.53).

While James continued to commission versions of de Critz's formal full-scale images
(no.125), Anne's increasing independence, as
the couple grew distant from one another –
they ceased cohabiting in 1607 – was demonstrated by her patronage of Marcus Gheeraerts

the Younger. Gheeraerts thus successfully
made the transition between the successive
reigns, remaining in the forefront of fashion.
As in the portraits of the Earl of Essex
(nos.80, 121) there are close similarities
between the portraits in large of Anne by
Gheeraerts and many of the miniatures of her
by his brother-in-law Oliver.

On 4 July 1611 Gheeraerts was paid for
portraits of James, Anne and Princess Elizabeth to be sent to the Margrave of Branden-
burg (Wood 1981, p.36). A half-length version
on panel of the present portrait (probably cut
down) bears the date '1614' (The Royal
Collection). Another full-length (formerly in
Major George Burns's collection) seems to be
a later copy. A head-and-shoulders portrait by
Gheeraerts in the National Portrait Gallery is
thought to show Anne in mourning for
Prince Henry and thus to date from the
winter of 1612–13.

EXH: Tate Gallery 1969–70 (160); *Christian IV and
Europe*, 19th Council of Europe Exhibition, Denmark
1988 (302)
LIT: G. Scharf, *A ... Catalogue of the Pictures at Woburn
Abbey*, 1890, no.58; Oliver Millar, 'Marcus Gheeraerts
the Younger: A Sequel through Inscriptions',
Burlington Magazine, vol.105, 1963, p.534; NPG 1969, I,
p.9; Strong 1969, p.299; Lucy Wood, 'The Portraits
of Anne of Denmark', unpublished MA report,
Courtauld Institute 1981, p.14; Diana Scarisbrick,
'Anne of Denmark's Jewellery', *Apollo*, vol.122, 1986,
pp.228–36; see also Leeds Barroll, 'The Court of the
First Stuart Queen', *The Mental World of the Jacobean
Court*, ed. Linda Levy Peck, Cambridge 1991; Diana
Scarisbrick, 'Anne of Denmark's Jewellery Inventory',
Archaeologia, vol.109, 1991, p.208

KH

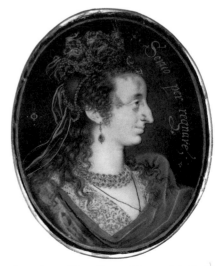

fig.53 Isaac Oliver, 'Anne of Denmark in Profile'
*c.*1610, *The Royal Collection, Her Majesty The Queen*

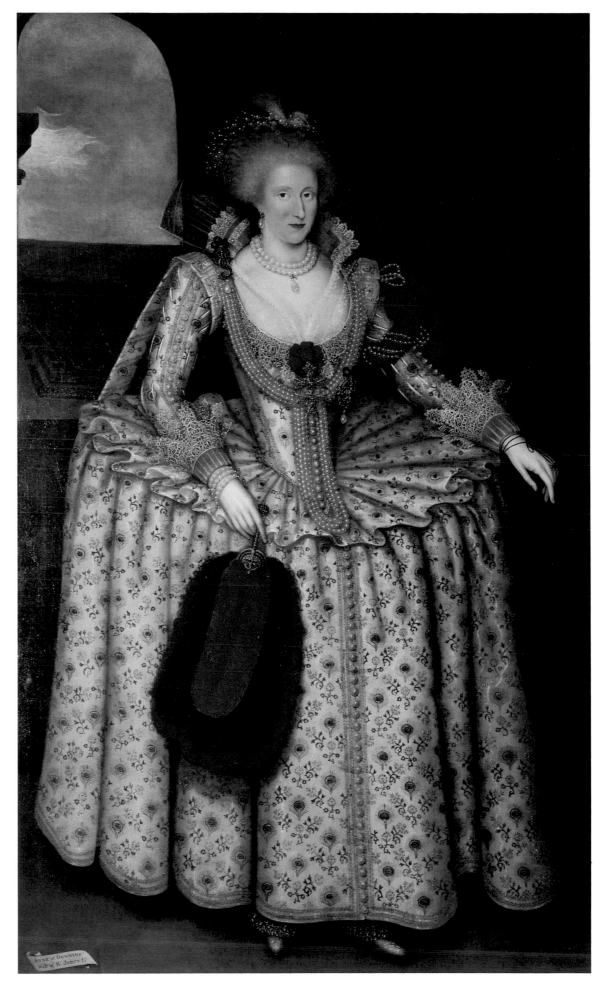

MARCUS GHEERAERTS THE YOUNGER

131 Tom Durie 1614

Oil on panel 71.4 × 57.9 (28⅛ × 22¾)
Inscribed '1614' t.l.
PROV: …; King Charles I; …; 18 June
1859 sale by T. Nisbet, 11 Hanover
Street, Edinburgh, which included part
of the collection of the late Col. Fergu-
son (101, as 'David Murray' 'by
Mytens'); …; Rt Hon. John Inglis, 30
Abercrombie Place, Edinburgh by 1884;
bequeathed by A. W. Inglis to the Scot-
tish National Portrait Gallery
*Scottish National Portrait Gallery,
Edinburgh*

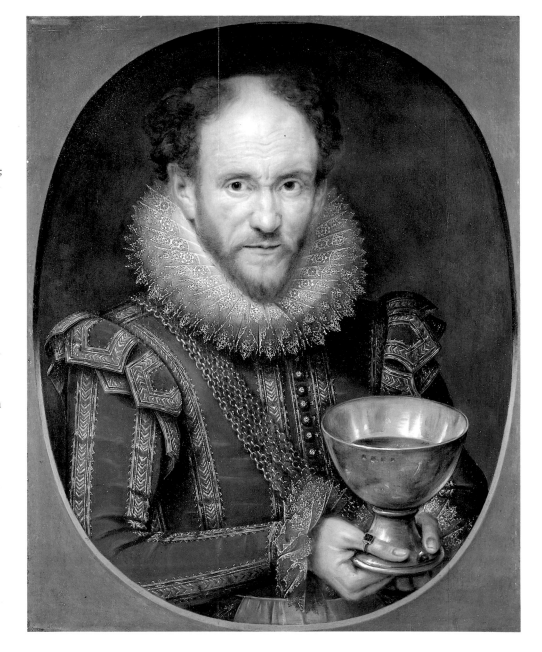

This portrait on panel bears Charles I's
crowned 'CR' brand on the back, indicating
that it was once in the King's collection.

The sitter was long thought to be Sir
David Murray of Gospertie, Viscount Stormont and cupbearer to James I, but the royal
brandmark led Sir Oliver Millar to re-identify
him, convincingly, as Tom Durie or Derry,
Anne of Denmark's jester. The portrait is of
the same dimensions as the work described in
van der Doort's inventory of Charles I's pictures as 'itm opan de raeht lijeht de pitur auff
tom duri qin ans vul holding a silffer bol Wit
bod his hands Werin rd Wijn in 2-4 1-10'
('item upon the right light the picture of Tom
Durie, Queen Anne's fool, holding a silver
bowl with both his hands wherein red wine
in 2 ft 4 in by 1ft 10 in') (Millar 1958–60,
p.197).

Almost nothing is known about Tom
Durie, here portrayed by the Queen's
favourite painter Gheeraerts in 1614, but she
evidently commissioned a further image of
him from her final artist, van Somer, which
appeared as '280: Tome Derey at Length. by
Van Somer' valued at £6 by the trustees for
the sale of Charles I's collection (Millar
1970–2, p.316). The present portrait is presumably that valued by the trustees at £1
(ibid., p.67). One of the portraits, probably
the present one, is recorded in the inventories
of Anne's own collection at Oatlands, as 'picture of Tom Duryes' (East Sussex Record
Office, GLY 319)

It was almost unprecedented in England
for such a figure to be the subject of a serious
portrait, although Lord Lumley (no.105) had
owned a picture 'Of Willm Somer, K[ing]:
H[enry]: 8: notable foole'. In the following
reign, in 1630, Mytens was paid £40 for the
full-length portrait of Queen Henrietta
Maria's dwarf Jeffery Hudson (The Royal
Collection).

According to Sandra Billington (*The Social
History of the Fool*, 1984) a fool was often
shown in illustrations to Psalm 13 'carrying a
round shape. If not the globe of the earth it
was a bladder football, bread, cake or pud-
ding'. Some satirical allusion might also be
intended: in August 1614, the Queen's husband met a handsome youth called George
Villiers (see no.115). The King was very taken
with Villiers, who was subsequently appointed his cupbearer (Robert Ashton, *James I by his
Contemporaries*, 1969, pp.168–9).

Durie wears a thick gold chain and a fine
ring on his thumb, presumably gifts from the
Queen. These are combined with the apron

that he wears to protect his suit from the wine
in the immense silver bowl he carries. The
bowl bears a large hallmark, but the individual marks, while suggesting that the bowl is
English, cannot be distinguished or identified.
Philippa Glanville comments that the bowl
cannot be being proffered for the Queen's
use, since she would have used only gilt ves-
sels. Its form, and its lack of a cover, would be
archaic at this date. References to Tom Durie
occur in the correspondence of King James
and of others with Robert Cecil, Earl of
Salisbury (see no.119), but no clear picture of
his activities emerges. According to Enid
Welsford (*The Fool*, 1935, p.179) 'he was a real

MARCUS GHEERAERTS THE YOUNGER

simpleton and no account of his personality or wit has survived'. More is known about James's own fool, Archie Armstrong, who lived on to serve Charles I, until he was discharged in 1637 for insulting Archbishop Laud.

EXH: *Exhibition of Scottish National Portraits*, 1884; *King James VI & I*, Royal Scottish Museum, Edinburgh 1975 (22, as 'Viscount Stormont')
LIT: The Concise Catalogue of the Scottish National Portrait Gallery, 1990, p.86, repr. p.89

KH

132 Catherine Killigrew, Lady Jermyn 1614

Oil on panel 78 × 58.5 (30¾ × 23)
Inscribed 'Ætatis Suæ 35 | Annᵒ: 1614' t.r.
PROV: Presumably by descent at Rushbrook Park, Suffolk; sold Knight, Frank and Rutley, 10–11 Dec. 1919 (105); ...; sold Christie's 22 Nov. 1963 (39), bt P. & D. Colnaghi; Mr and Mrs Paul Mellon 1965 by whom presented to Yale Center for British Art
Yale Center for British Art, Paul Mellon Collection

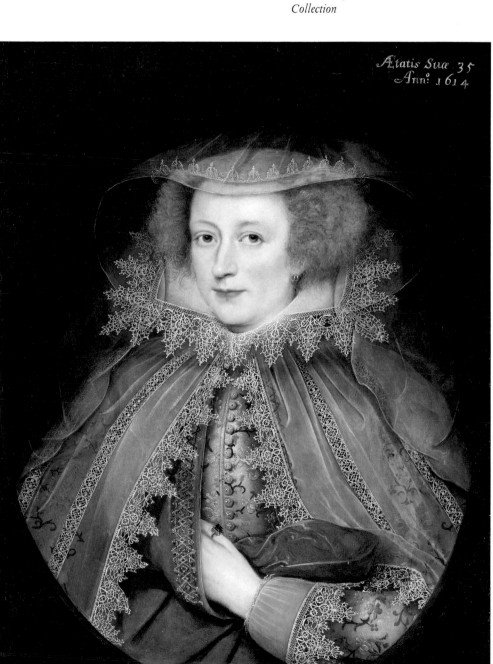

The sitter is probably Catherine Killigrew (?1579–1640), who married Sir Thomas Jermyn of Rushbrook (1572–1644) in 1599. Her father William Killigrew, from a Cornish family, was Groom of the Privy Chamber to Queen Elizabeth I, who granted him the right to farm the profits of the seals of the Queen's Bench and Common Pleas. He entertained the Queen at his estate at Hanworth in the years 1596, 1600 and 1601, and represented various Cornish seats successively in Parliament. In May 1603 he was knighted by James I, and was appointed Chamberlain of the Exchequer for 1605–6. He died in 1622.

Catherine had three surviving sons, Robert (1601–1623), Thomas (c.1602–1659) and Henry (c.1604–1684). Henry was to have a distinguished court career, becoming Vice-chamberlain to Queen Henrietta Maria in 1628, and later accompanying her into exile in France.

Catherine's husband came from an East Anglian Puritan family, had served under the Earl of Essex in campaigns to France, Spain and Ireland, and also held several seats as a Member of Parliament. In 1614, the date inscribed on this portrait, he inherited Rushbrook from his father. This led Hervey to suggest that Sir Thomas might have marked the event by commissioning this sumptuous portrait of his wife.

This work is one of the earliest examples of a portrait in a feigned oval – a trompe l'oeil stone or marble aperture through which the subject is seen. This form became increasingly popular in England in the ensuing decade, especially through the work of Cornelius Johnson. It may derive partly from the characteristic circular, or particularly, oval form of miniature portraits, and it carries with it something of the intimacy of presentation found in these. Lady Jermyn's gesture, her hand below her breast, can also be paralleled in miniatures such as no.87. Gheeraerts used it in a number of contemporary female portraits, such as that of 'Lady Scudamore' 1614–15 (National Portrait Gallery, London) where it seems to relate to the expectation of a new beginning occasioned by the wedding of the sitter's son – the inscription reads 'No Spring till now'.

This portrait of Lady Jermyn is one of Gheeraerts's finest and most sensitive works, and is particularly characteristic of the middle period of his career. The flesh is softly modelled in light blue-grey tones while the gauze and lace are a virtuoso display of fine and detailed painting. While her embroidered jacket, and particularly her lace, are very cost-ly items, Lady Jermyn wears little jewellery: two plain gold rings in her ear and a single ring, apparently set with a large diamond, on her left thumb. This may be her wedding ring, for at this date such rings were not worn on one specific finger.

Another portrait traditionally of Catherine Killigrew, and dating from the late 1590s before her marriage, is at Christchurch Mansion, Ipswich. The sitter, who has dark brown hair, is in court attire, and festooned with jewellery. Numerous pearls, an indication at this period of considerable wealth, are not only sewn on to her costume but are also seen in her elaborate silver wire headdress. The composition is a three-quarter-length version of that used in the 'Ditchley' portrait of Queen Elizabeth (no.45), and is close to the delicate, spindly form of female portraits attributed to Gheeraerts in the 1590s.

LIT: *Rushbrook Parish Registers 1567–1880*, ed. Revd H.S.A. Hervey, Woodbridge 1903, p.434 (as hanging 'near the great staircase' at Rushbrook Park); Revd E. Farrer, *Portraits in Suffolk Houses (West)*, [1908], pp.297–8; Oliver Millar, 'Marcus Gheeraerts the Younger: A Sequel through Inscriptions', *Burlington Magazine*, vol.105, 1963, p.534, repr. pl.12; Strong 1969, no.278; Malcolm Cormack, *A Concise Catalogue of Paintings in the Yale Center for British Art*, New Haven 1985, p.102, repr. p.103

KH

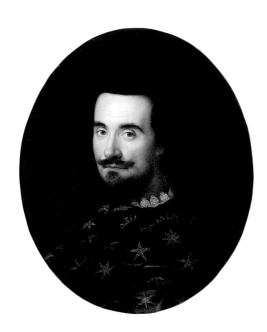

WILLIAM LARKIN 1580s–1619

133 Edward Herbert, 1st Baron Herbert of Cherbury
c.1609–10

Oil on panel, oval 55.9 × 45.8 (22 × 18)
Inscribed: during cleaning indistinct traces of an inscription were discovered, indicating that the picture was original-ly rectangular
PROV: Given to Sir Thomas Lucy by the sitter; by descent in the Lucy family at Charlecote Park
Charlecote Park, The Fairfax-Lucy Collection (The National Trust)

In his autobiography Lord Herbert recounts an incident concerning a portrait of himself by Larkin. He was in Dorset House being shown pictures by Lord Dorset, he tells us, when 'hee at last brought mee to a Frame covered in greene Taffita and asked mee who I thought was there and therewithall present-ly drawing the Courtaine shewed mee my owne Picture whervpon demaunding how his Lordship came to have it, he answered that he had heard soe many brave things of mee, that he gott a Coppy of a Picture which one Larkin a Painter drew for mee, the Originall whereof I intended before my departure to the Low Countrey for Sir Thomas Lucy'. The link between this and the portrait at Charlecote, first made by James Lees-Milne in 1952, seems very plausible as Charlecote Park is the Lucy family seat and the portrait there of Lord Herbert has as its pair one of Sir Thomas Lucy. Herbert had saved Sir Thomas from a shipwreck on his return from the Con-tinent in February 1609, and presented his portrait presumably to commemorate the event. It must have been painted some time between February 1609 and July 1610, when Lord Herbert set out for the Low Countries.

The date coincides with that of other por-traits, both in large and in miniature, which are similar in conception, including Isaac Oliver's miniature of Henry, Prince of Wales *à l'antique*, in profile against a classical shell niche (see no.84). All are in bust format, oval, with the sitters in vaguely classical costume, although this is less apparent with Lord Her-bert. The others have their cloaks knotted over the shoulder as Roman togas. They have been associated with the masque *Prince Henry's Barriers*, performed at Whitehall on Twelfth Night 1610, in which Prince Henry took the part of Meliades, a figure from Arthurian romance, whose task was to restore chivalry to Great Britain. The stage sets and costumes, by Inigo Jones, were strongly classical in

design as it was the contemporary belief that King Arthur and the great age of chivalry coincided with Roman Britain. It is not known if Lord Herbert took part in these fes-tivities, but this classical–chivalrous notion would certainly have appealed to him, strong-ly inclined as he was towards the pursuits of a courtly knight, such as jousting and tilting.

Herbert mentions two versions of the por-trait – one procured by Queen Anne (possibly the one now at University College, Oxford), and a version in miniature copied by Isaac Oliver for Lady Ayres, whose husband fell into a jealous rage on discovery of it.

William Larkin was a British-born artist, almost certainly the son of William Larkin, freeman of the Bakers' Company (Edmond 1978–80, p.127). He lived in the Holborn parish of St Sepulchre-without-Newgate, and later St Anne Blackfriars, both much inhabit-ed by artists. The first reference to him so far discovered is in 1606, when it is recorded that he became a freeman of the Painter-Stainers' Company on the request of Lady Arbella Stuart and the Earl of Hertford – indicating that by this stage he enjoyed noble patronage. However, until the attribution of this portrait and its pair no works by Larkin had been identified, although a few documents record payments for portraits (Rutland Papers for 1617 and 1619, Lady Anne Clifford's *Diary* for 1619) and a seventeenth-century inventory of pictures at Claydon lists pictures by him. It was through comparison with this portrait that in 1969 Sir Roy Strong attributed to him the magnificent series of Suffolk full-lengths (see nos.135, 136) and others similar to them, and reconstructed an oeuvre for Larkin. A subsequent technical analysis of the pictures (Cove 1985) concluded that, with only a cou-ple of exceptions, they were by the same hand, and that the technique employed was very similar to that of miniature painting but on a grand scale – which makes the past attri-bution of this portrait to Isaac Oliver under-standable (C.H. Collins Baker, *Lely and the Stuart Portrait Painters*, 1912, I, p.19). However, more than one hand seems evident in the full-length portraits, suggesting that they may be products of a workshop rather than of a single individual.

EXH: Sheila O'Connell, *William Larkin and the 3rd Earl of Dorset: A Portrait in Focus*, English Heritage, Ranger's House 1989 (2)
LIT: James Lees-Milne, 'Two Portraits at Charlecote Park by William Larkin', *Burlington Magazine*, vol.94, 1952, pp.352–6; David Piper, *Catalogue of Seventeenth Century Portraits in the National Portrait Gallery*, 1963, pp.164–5; Strong 1969, no.325; J.M. Shuttleworth

(ed.), *The Life of Edward, First Lord Herbert of Cherbury Written by Himself*, 1976, pp.60–1; Mary Edmond, *Hilliard and Oliver*, 1983, pp.169–70; Edmond 1978–80, pp.127–9; *Tate Gallery Illustrated Catalogue of Acquisitions*, 1982–4, pp.22–4; Sarah Cove, 'The Materials and Techniques of Painting Attributed to William Larkin 1610–20', Dip. Conservation of Paintings, Courtauld Institute 1985; Roy Strong, 'The Surface of Reality: William Larkin', *F.M.R.*, vol.61, 1993, pp.66–82

TB

BRITISH SCHOOL

134 A Lady, probably Mrs Clement Edmondes *c.*1605–10

Oil on canvas 232.5 × 133.5
(91½ × 52½)
Inscribed [...] | UPO[...] C[...]SARS | COMEN[...]ARIES | [medallion of Caesar] | BY CLEMENT EDMUNDES | REMEMBRANCER OF THE CITTIE | OF LOND...N
PROV: ...; Hollingsworth Magniac sale, Christie's 4th July 1892 (97); ...; Edward Brook, sold 1929; bt Saumarez Collection, Shrubland Hall, from whence sold 1964; with Sabin Galleries
Mrs Drue Heinz

The sitter was formerly identified as Queen Elizabeth I, by Zuccaro, or as Queen Elizabeth of Bohemia. It has also been suggested that she might be a member of the family of Sir Julius Caesar (1558–1636), who was Master of the Rolls from 1614 to 1636, but no one of suitable age and relationship to Sir Julius has been traced.

The inscription on the book she holds, which refers to Clement Edmondes's translation of *Caesar's Commentaries*, makes a connection with his family likely. Clement Edmondes (?1564–1622) was Remembrancer of the City of London from 1605 to 1609 and then became a Clerk of the Privy Council and was knighted by James I in 1617. His own family does not appear to have been distinguished and it has been suggested that he owed his advancement to his wife's court connections (*Dictionary of National Biography*, 1920–1, pp.389–91).

Edmondes married, on 15 February 1598, Mary Clerke 'attendant upon the Lady Stafford ... dau. of Robert Clerke, of Grafton, co. Northton, Gent ... Mr. John Johnson, one

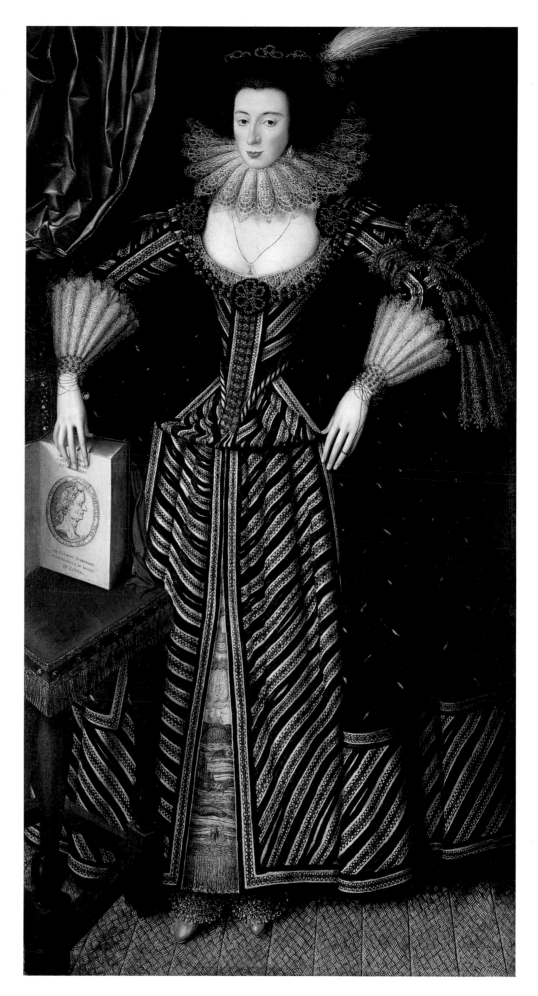

of her Majesty's Chaplains, & kinsman of sd Mary Clerk, attests consent of her parents' at St Alphage Church, in the City of London (*Harleian Society*, vol.25, 1887, p.247). Lady Stafford was Dorothy Stafford, who served Queen Elizabeth for forty years. She is recorded in a document of *c*.1589 as a Gentle-woman of the Privy Chamber and as having been with the Queen since the first year of her reign (Arnold 1988, p.101). Her husband, Sir William Stafford, died when she was twenty-seven (as recorded on her memorial in St Margaret's, Westminster; the inscription, now badly worn, appears in Hunter 1819, p.92). This was presumably, therefore, in 1553. She remained a widow for the rest of her life.

Mary Clerke's date of birth is not known. If she married at approximately twenty-one, she would have been in her late thirties when the portrait was painted. Both she and their son and two daughters survived Sir Clement. The dates of birth of the daughters, Elizabeth and Mary, are not known either, but the tombstone of the son, Charles, in Preston, Northamptonshire, records his death at the age of forty-nine in 1652.

The inscription on the title-page of the book depicted does not appear in any surviving edition of Edmondes's translations of *Caesar's Commentaries* (there were editions in 1600, 1604 and 1609; the surviving copies may be composite editions put together subsequently, rather than being in the precise condition in which they originally appeared). The medallion portrait of Caesar does appear in most. It seems likely that this title-page may have been especially composed for the purposes of the portrait. As it contains no reference to Henry, Prince of Wales, to whom the 1609 edition was dedicated, with a medallion portrait of the Prince on the title-page, it may be that this portrait predates that edition, whilst postdating Edmondes's appointment as Remembrancer of the City of London.

Many items of clothing were given away by Queen Elizabeth and a number of her gowns were inherited by Anne of Denmark and may have been given away subsequently (Arnold 1988, pp.87–9). Mary Edmondes's elaborate attire may represent just such a gown; figures 146 and 155 in Arnold 1988 illustrate fabrics with similar motifs to those which appear on this petticoat, with its waves, fish, sea-monsters, buildings and the sun. Black and white may have been associated with grief but there were not, as yet, strictly established rules for the wearing of mourning,

and they were colours greatly, although not exclusively, favoured by Elizabeth.

An early example of the Ranger's House type of full-length (see no.136), this is similar in composition to, for instance, the portrait of Elizabeth Howard, Duchess of Newcastle (*c*.1615) there, while differing in handling, especially of the face, hands and chair, as well as in the bodily proportions. The suggestion that these grand full-lengths were the products of a number of hands and came from more than one workshop, may account for this.

LIT: *Allegations for Marriage Licences Issued by the Bishop of London 1520–1610*; Will of Sir Clement Edmondes, 28 Oct. 1622, PRO, 92, Savile; J. Bridges, *History and Antiquities of Northamptonshire*, 1791, pp.382–3; J. Hunter, *Hallamshire*, 1819; *Harleian Society*, vol.25, 1887; *Dictionary of National Biography*, reprinted 1921–2. For general background: Arnold 1988; P. Cunnington and C. Lucas, *Costume for Births, Marriages and Deaths*, 1972; J. Arnold, *Lost from Her Majestie's Back*, 1980; L. Taylor, *Mourning Dress*, 1983; C. Gittings, *Death, Burial and the Individual in Early Modern England*, 1984

SB

ATTRIBUTED TO WILLIAM LARKIN 1580s–1619

135 Richard Sackville, 3rd Earl of Dorset 1613

Oil on canvas 206.4 × 122.3 (81¼ × 48⅛)
Inscribed '1613 Ætis suæ 24' and in another possibly contemporary hand 'Aut nunquam tentes: aut perfic.' t.l.; 'Sʳ Edward Sackvill Brother | to Richᵈ Earle of Dorset | who Succeeded him in ye Earledom' b.r., in a later hand and inaccurately
PROV: Possibly one of the full-lengths recorded in the 1697 schedule of pictures at Charlton Park, seat of the Earls of Suffolk; first recorded there 1774 (James Granger, *A Supplement … to a Biographical History of England*, 1774, p.481); by descent in the Suffolk family until 1974 when presented to Ranger's House
English Heritage (Ranger's House, The Suffolk Collection)

Although inscribed as depicting Edward Sackville, this is undoubtedly a portrait of Edward's elder brother Richard, who succeeded their father as 3rd Earl of Dorset in 1609. It is one of nine full-length portraits (see also no.136), formerly in the family collection of the Earls of Suffolk at Charlton Park, Wiltshire, which stylistically form a distinctive group and in the past have been attributed to the 'Curtain Master' because of the fantastically swagged curtains which appear in the background of each picture. In 1969 Sir Roy Strong attributed the series to Larkin (Strong 1969, p.20) and a subsequent technical analysis of the pictures, in comparison with the portrait of Lord Herbert of Cherbury which is believed to be documented as by Larkin (see no.133), has corroborated this judgment.

The 3rd Earl of Dorset, nephew to Thomas Howard, 1st Earl of Suffolk, was born in 1589 and matriculated from Christ Church, Oxford, in 1605. An intelligent man and a patron of poets including John Donne, he was also denounced by Clarendon as 'a licentious spendthrift'. He took as his mistress Venetia Stanley, later Lady Digby, by whom he had children, and had to mortgage the Sackville family seat, Knole, in order to support his extravagant lifestyle. His wife, the celebrated thwarted heiress Lady Anne Clifford, was at pains to defend him, beseeching her mother to 'have a better opinion of him', but had to admit that his love of 'noble ways at court' such as masqueing and tilting did much to diminish the family fortune (V. Sackville-West, *Knole and the Sackvilles*, 1922). Chief amongst his extravagances must have been his wardrobe, several items of which he deemed valuable enough to bequeath in his will to his brother Edward. It has been suggested that the preposterously elaborate costume he appears in here is the one that he wore on the occasion of the marriage of Princess Elizabeth to the Elector Palatine on 14 February 1613, the date of the portrait. A witness to the event was Sir John Finet, Master of Ceremonies, who reported that, among others, the splendour of the dress of Lord Dorset 'dazzled the eyes of all who saw'. Whatever the occasion, we can be certain that the suit of clothes really existed. An inventory of Lord Dorset's clothing survives and from the items listed we can identify several that he wears in this portrait, such as his 'Cloake of uncutt velvett blacke laced with seven embroidered laces of gold and black silke … and lyned with shagg of black silver and gold', and his 'doublett of Cloth of silver embroadered all over in slips of sattin black and gold'.

The artist's exaggeratedly stiff and one-dimensional style, akin to that of miniature painting on a grand scale, was eminently suited to the depiction of Lord Dorset's costume. In contrast to the more life-like modelled face, the completely flat surface area allows for the painstaking recreation of expensive fabric textures and elaborate patterns of lace and embroidery, with brushstrokes imitating individual stitches. The superb richness in colour, much loved by Jacobeans, would originally have been far more intense. During cleaning, large areas of restoration and pigment deterioration were discovered, particularly in the curtains and the carpet, which can never be returned to their original appearance.

Dorset and his wife are mentioned twice in documents relating to the patronage of Larkin. In his autobiography, Lord Herbert of Cherbury describes the occasion when he was shown a copy of his own portrait by Larkin which Lord Dorset had had done (see no.133); and on 16 January 1619 Lady Anne Clifford recorded in her diary that she 'sent my Coz. Hall of Gletford a letter and my picture with it which Larkinge drew this summer at Knole' (V. Sackville-West, *The Diary of Lady Anne Clifford*, 1923), of which the head-and-shoulders portrait of her there today may be a version. Two other full-lengths at Knole have

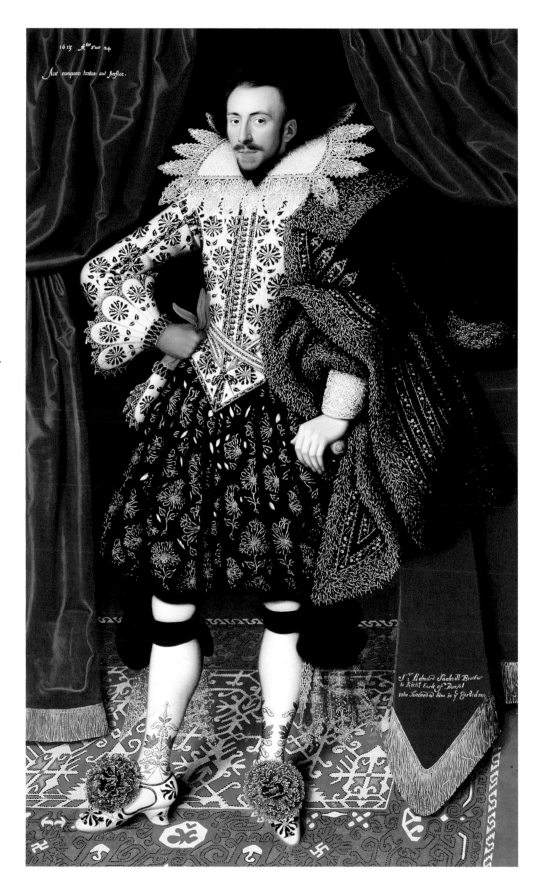

been attributed to Larkin. That of Lord
Dorset is now believed to be a studio copy,
and that of Lady Anne Clifford has been reidentified as Mary Curzon, wife of Edward,
4th Earl of Dorset (whose portrait attributed
to Larkin at Ranger's House is likely to be a
pair to that of the 3rd Earl). Lord Dorset was
also painted in miniature by Isaac Oliver (full-
length, Victoria and Albert Museum, London;
head-and-shoulders, Fitzwilliam Museum,
Cambridge).

EXH: Tate Gallery 1969–70 (131a); *William Larkin and
the 3rd Earl of Dorset: A Portrait in Focus*, Ranger's House
1989
LIT: Strong 1969, no.341; John Jacob and Jacob
Simon, *The Suffolk Collection: Catalogue of Paintings*,
1974, no.3; Peter and Ann MacTaggart, 'The Rich
Wearing Apparel of Richard, 3rd Earl of Dorset', *Cos-
tume*, vol.14, 1980, pp.41–55; V&A 1983, no.277; Alan
Cummings, unpublished Conservation Report on the
portrait of the 3rd Earl of Dorset at Ranger's House,
English Heritage 1983; Sarah Cove, 'The Materials
and Techniques of Painting Attributed to William
Larkin 1610–1620', Dip. Conservation of Paintings,
Courtauld Institute 1985; Roy Strong, 'The Surface of
Reality: William Larkin', *F.M.R.*, vol.61, 1993,
pp.66–82

TB

ATTRIBUTED TO WILLIAM LARKIN

136 Diana Cecil, Countess of Oxford *c.*1614–18

Oil on canvas 205.8 × 120 (81 × 47¼)
Inscribed 'Countes of Oxford:' t.r., by a
later hand
PROV: Possibly one of the unidentified
full-lengths recorded in the 1697
schedule of pictures at Charlton Park,
seat of the Earls of Suffolk; first recorded there 1801 (Richard Warner, *Excur-
sions from Bath, 1801*, pp.232–41); by
descent in the Suffolk family until
presented to lender 1974
*English Heritage (Ranger's House, The
Suffolk Collection)*

This is one of the nine portraits attributed to
Larkin in the Suffolk Collection, Ranger's
House (see also no.135), of which seven are of
females. It has been suggested that these
seven were specially commissioned, possibly
by Katherine Knyvett, Countess of Suffolk,
who owned Charlton, to commemorate the
dynastic alliance between the Howard and
Cecil families that came about through the
marriage in 1614 of Thomas Howard, son of
the 1st Earl of Suffolk, and Elizabeth Cecil,
daughter of William Cecil, 2nd Earl of Exeter
(Strong 1969, p.20). Diana Cecil was Elizabeth's sister which explains her inclusion in
the 'marriage set', along with her twin sister
Anne and her mother Elizabeth Drury (both
portraits also at Ranger's House). It is strange,
however, that the bride herself, and other sisters who could have been represented, are
missing from the series. It is perhaps best to
view the pictures simply as an accumulated
family collection rather than a single commission. The Howard and Cecil families were
frequent patrons of the workshop associated
with Larkin, as is witnessed by portraits of
other members of the family that were never
at Charlton, for example 'Frances Manners,
Countess of Rutland', sister of the Countess
of Suffolk (private collection, information
from Alastair Laing) and the two portraits of
the Sackville brothers (see no.135) which form
part of the Suffolk collection but which have
never been regarded as part of the so-called
marriage set.

Diana Cecil (*c.*1603–1654) was 'one of the
greatest fortunes and most celebrated beauties
of the period'. The exact date of the portrait
is not known, but her appearance is similar to
that in her portrait by the 'Comet Master'

dated 1618 (Savernake). She was unmarried at
the time of being painted, but later married
firstly, in 1624, Henry Vere, 18th Earl of
Oxford, who died at the siege of Breda the
following year, and secondly, in 1629,
Thomas Bruce, created Earl of Elgin in 1633.
Her pose and extraordinary costume, an
extreme and short-lived style of court dress, is
almost identical to that in the portrait of her
twin sister Anne, which is possibly a pair to
this one. They stand on identical carpets,
which are of the same pattern, although in
different colours, to that in the portrait of
their mother; and they both stand with
x-frame chairs to the left, a familiar prop in
portraits attributed to Larkin.

Cleaning has revealed that this portrait is
in a far better state of preservation than that
of Anne. Her face, hands, fan and lace are in
almost perfect condition, and fine details have
been revealed such as the frayed edges to the
slashed silk. The carpet and curtains have
fared less well, owing to past restorations and
general pigment deterioration. Originally the
background of the carpet would have been
bright crimson, and the colours throughout
the portrait brighter and stronger.

Diana was depicted again by the same
artist, full-length before a portcullised archway (versions at Savernake, Hardwick Hall,
and private collection).

EXH: Tate Gallery 1969–70 (134)
LIT: A. Finberg, 'Four Jacobean Portraits at Charlton
Park', *The Times Woman's Supplement* Dec. 1920,
pp.55–8; Strong 1969, no.331; John Jacob and Jacob
Simon, *The Suffolk Collection: Catalogue of Paintings*,
1974, no.10; Sarah Cove, 'The Materials and
Techniques of Painting Attributed to William Larkin
1610–20', Dip. Conservation of Paintings, Courtauld
Institute, 1985; Alan Cummings, unpublished Conser-
vation Report on Diana and Anne Cecil, English
Heritage 1987; Roy Strong, 'The Surface of Reality:
William Larkin', *F.M.R.*, vol.61, 1993, pp.66–82

TB

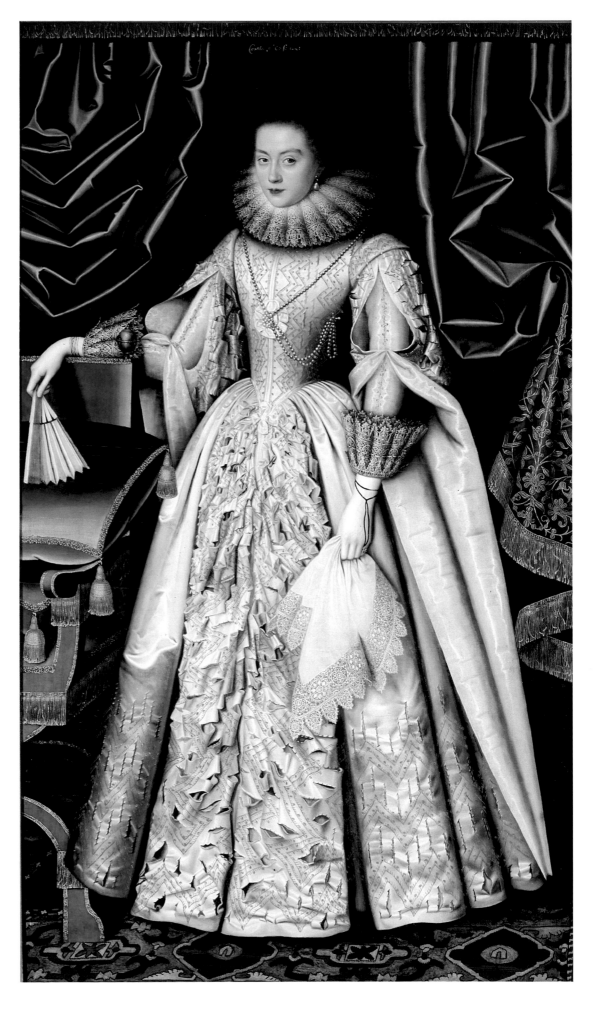

8 The New Netherlanders

Towards the end of the second decade of the seventeenth-century a new group of artists reached England from the Netherlands. They brought a style of sober grandeur, a greater naturalism, moulded by shadow. The first to arrive was Paul van Somer, born in Antwerp c.1576 and in London by December 1616. During his five-year career in England he became the favoured image-maker, first for Queen Anne and soon after for James I. Thus, he apparently supplanted Gheeraerts and John de Critz without effort. In total, his surviving oeuvre is small, although further works by him were listed as present in the collection of Charles I.

Concerning Abraham van Blijenberch, who worked in London from 1617 to 1622, little is known. Of his few surviving English portraits, one is of the poet Ben Jonson and others of particularly discerning court collectors: William, 3rd Earl of Pembroke (no.138), Robert Kerr, 1st Earl of Ancram and Prince Charles.

The most prolific, and long-staying, of this immigrant group of portraitists was Daniel Mytens. He was born in Delft about 1590 into a family of artists and entered the Guild of St Luke at the Hague in 1610. He could thus well have been a pupil either of Miereveld (no.137) or van Ravesteyn, or of both. Mytens had reached London by August 1618, when he was working for the great connoisseurs the Earl and Countess of Arundel (nos.140, 141).

Their seated portraits are probably Mytens's earliest known full-length portraits – presumably made in response to the English taste for portraits on this scale. Mytens first portrayed James I in 1621, and in 1624 he was granted an annual royal pension. On his accession in 1625 , Charles I appointed Mytens his 'picture-drawer' for life, and thereafter there are regular payments for portraits for official use. Mytens made some remarkable portraits during the 1620s – of 'The Duke of Buckingham' 1626, and the '1st Lord Baltimore' 1627 (private collections), and the future 1st Duke of Hamilton in 1623 (no.147) and 1629 – and is a much finer artist than is generally suggested. It was his misfortune to be supplanted by the international superstar Anthony Van Dyck. Van Dyck's brief visit to England in 1620–1 had resulted in a handful

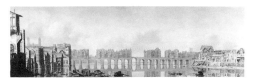
fig.54 Claude de Jongh, 'London Bridge' 1630, oil on panel. *Kenwood House*

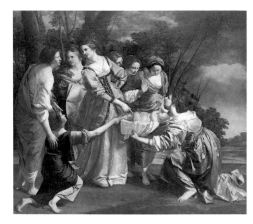
fig.55 Orazio Gentileschi, 'The Finding of Moses', oil on canvas. *Museo del Prado, Madrid*

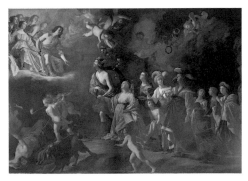
fig.56 Gerrit van Honthorst, 'Apollo and Diana' 1628, oil on canvas. *The Royal Collection, Her Majesty The Queen*

of works (no.146), but on his return in 1632, at the invitation of Charles I himself, he easily gained ascendency over Mytens.

The rival connoisseurs of Charles I's court attracted various other foreign artists and were by now collecting, and commissioning, a broad range of subjects. Some artists came on their own initiative, others by invitation. Hendrick van Steenwijck the Younger was in London by 1617, where he remained for the next twenty years. He specialised in architectural scenes, frequently darkly lit, and often ostensibly illustrating religious stories (no.143). The Dutch topographical painter Claude de Jongh (c.1600–1663) made brief visits to London (fig.54) and produced some astonishingly evocative depictions of it, although they are not entirely accurate in detail.

In 1626 the Pisan-born Orazio Gentileschi (fig.55), a painter of major international reputation, came to London, probably at the invitation of the Duke of Buckingham, and remained, working on history paintings for the monarch, until his death in 1639. A briefer visitor, during 1628, was the Caravaggist from Utrecht, Gerrit van Honthorst (1590–1656) (fig.56). From May 1629 to March 1630, Rubens was in Britain as a diplomatic envoy for the Archduchess Isabella of the Spanish Netherlands and her nephew Philip IV of Spain.

Meanwhile, two English-born artists who travelled to the Netherlands were greatly influenced by what they saw there. Cornelius Jonson was born in London to German/Dutch immigrant parents. Judging from his style, he must have received some of his training in the Low Countries. His earliest works are head-and-shoulders portraits (no.145) which in due course develop, under the influence of Mytens with whom he may sometimes have collaborated, to more powerful three-quarter-lengths (no.152).

Finally the gentleman amateur, Sir Nathaniel Bacon, ploughed his own furrow in artistic terms – working in his East Anglian country house, he produced self-portraits and enormous 'kitchen paintings' or 'market scenes' using Dutch themes, unparalleled in English art, and handled with astonishing individuality.

MICHIEL JANSZ. VAN MIEREVELD 1567–1641

137 Sir Edward Cecil, later Viscount Wimbledon *c.*1610

Oil on panel 113.4 × 85 (44⅝ × 33½)
Inscribed 'Chi non puol quel che vuol che puol' on baton
PROV: …; Douglas family, Bothwell Castle, Lanarkshire, by 1852, when called portrait of Sir Walter Raleigh; Douglas sale, Christie's 20 June 1919 (147), bt Agnew; …; by 1921 Lord Brassey, Apethorpe Hall; Apethorpe Hall sale, Oct. 1947 (1373), bt Wheeler; Arthur Tooth, from whom bt by lender 1947
Trustees of the National Museums and Galleries on Merseyside (Walker Art Gallery, Liverpool)

This portrait of the soldier Sir Edward Cecil (1572–1658), a member of Henry, Prince of Wales's inner circle, is by the Dutch artist, Miereveld. Miereveld, who spent his entire career in Delft, never visited England, but his work was known and admired there and in 1611–12 a serious attempt was made to bring him over to work for the Prince.

Miereveld was one of the most successful portraitists of his day. In 1604 his contemporary van Mander praised the quality of his likenesses and stated that the Archduke Albert had unavailingly invited him to work for him in Brussels (Miedema 1994, pp.381–5). After 1607, when Miereveld painted Prince Maurice of Nassau, he became the favoured artist of the House of Orange-Nassau at The Hague, a short journey from Delft. He had a large workshop which enabled him to produce multiple copies and repeat orders; Joachim Sandrart credited him with a total output of more than ten thousand portraits. Many of these were engraved by his son-in-law Willem Delff (1580–1638) and thus achieved wide circulation. His work can sometimes be confused with that of his contemporary, Jan Anthonis van Ravesteyn, of The Hague.

A head-and-shoulders portrait of Cecil in armour by Miereveld is dated 1610 (once owned by Charles I, now in a private collection and on loan to the National Portrait Gallary). The present portrait probably resulted from the same sitting, although the features seem slightly more mature. Cecil is here portrayed in civilian attire and wears a hat. Nevertheless his military status is evident from the plumed helmet on the table at his side and the baton of command that he

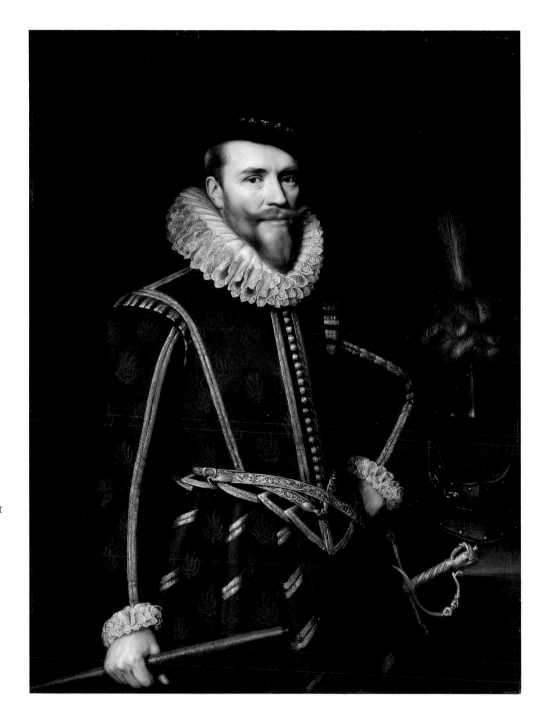

grasps. The motto on the baton has been translated as: 'Let that man that cannot do what he wants to do want to do what he can do' (Liverpool 1977, p.127, where it is identified as a misquotation from Giambattista Guarini's *Il Pastor Fido*, 1590).

In March 1610, Cecil was appointed commander of the four thousand English troops sent to the Netherlands during the disputes over the succession to the Duke of Cleves. Cecil's letters home to the Prince as his forces were besieging Julich, or Juliers (which surrendered in August 1611) survive (Thomas Birch, *The Life of Henry Prince of Wales*, 1760, pp.198–9, 201).

A nephew of Robert Cecil (no.119), Edward had served in the Netherlands periodically since 1598, and was to be Treasurer to Princess Elizabeth and her husband in 1613. He led the unsuccessful expedition against Spain in 1625 under Buckingham and was created Viscount Wimbledon the following year. He commanded in Holland again from 1627 to 1631 and was Governor of Portsmouth from 1630 until his death in 1638.

Cecil was widely travelled and a discerning patron of art. For his portraits he was to return time and again to the Miereveld studio. Simon van de Passe's English engraving after Miereveld, dated 1618, shows Cecil in armour once more, looking a little older than in the present painting. (The original for the print may have been the portrait in the collection of The Hon. Robert Marsham Townsend of Frognal, Kent, sold Knight, Frank and Rutley, 7 June 1915 (14), photo NPG archive, present location unknown.) In 1631 the elderly Cecil was once more portrayed by Miereveld (National Portrait Gallery).

Cecil seems to have been the earliest of the various English visitors to commission portraits from Miereveld. Prince Henry's own interest may have been prompted by Cecil, or by seeing Miereveld's full-length portrait of Maurice of Nassau which probably reached him early in 1610 (on Maurice's portraits, see *The Dawn of the Golden Age*, exh. cat., Rijksmuseum, Amsterdam 1993, no.265). Negotiations to persuade Miereveld to work for Henry were well under way by the end of January 1611 (Wilks 1987, p.90). Cecil was one of the negotiating team, led by Sir Edward Conway, the Governor of Brill. Miereveld was willing to spend no more than three months in England, as his letter of 11 February from Delft makes clear (Vertue v, pp.83–4, cited by Wilks 1987, p.94). The failure of this initiative, which petered out in February 1612, was, in

Wilks's view, the result of the inexperience of Henry's advisers, and above all of Conway, in dealing with an artist of Miereveld's stature.

The motto on the present painting is consistent with Cecil's Italian interests. In September 1594 he had received a licence to travel abroad with his brother, and in November 1595 they were in Florence, where the Grand Duke treated them with particular favour. It is thus not surprising that in March 1611 Cecil was involved in the negotiations for a Medici bride for the Prince. He was friendly with Henry's Florentine architect and painter Constantino de'Servi, and in May 1612 was with the Prince when he first viewed the Grand Duke's gift of Florentine bronzes. He commissioned work from Inigo Jones for his house in the Strand (*Inigo Jones*, exh. cat., Royal Academy 1990, nos.23, 24).

Although the initiative to bring Miereveld to England failed, his meticulously factual, slightly stiff style was imported less than a decade later by Daniel Mytens (see nos.140, 141, 147) who was probably his pupil.

LIT: *Foreign Catalogue*, Walker Art Gallery, Liverpool 1977, text vol., pp.127–8; Christopher White, *The Dutch Pictures in the Collection of Her Majesty The Queen*, Cambridge 1982, p.xxii; Malcolm Rogers, unpublished notes, NPG archive. On the project to bring Miereveld to England, Timothy V. Wilks, 'The Court Culture of Prince Henry and his Circle 1603–1613', unpublished D.Phil., Oxford University 1987, pp.86–7, 90–7

KH

ABRAHAM VAN BLIJENBERCH
active in England 1617–1621

138 William Herbert, 3rd Earl of Pembroke 1617

Oil on panel 111.8 × 78.7 (44 × 31)
Inscribed 'ÆTA 37' t.l.; 'ANNO DOMI.1617' t.r.; 'Abraham | van Blijenb | erch fecit' lower left
PROV: …; Earls of Powis, Powis Castle by 1948
Powis Castle, The Powis Collection (The National Trust)

This is one of only two known works signed by van Blijenberch, who is recorded as in England between 1617 and 1621. Little is known about this artist, whose patronage in London was of the very highest level. With van Somer and Mytens, he was one of the Netherlandish portraitists who arrived at this time and worked for the most discriminating and advanced collectors at Whitehall.

Van Blijenberch is known to have painted Charles I as Prince of Wales (perhaps the picture in the National Portrait Gallery, on loan to Montacute House) and his signed portrait of the connoisseur 'Robert Kerr, 1st Earl of Ancram' (Lothian Trustees) is dated 1618. His portrait of the poet and playwright Ben Jonson was recorded in the 1635 inventory of the Duke of Buckingham's collection (probably NPG 2752, engraved by Robert Vaughan by 1627). Van Blijenberch also worked on designs for tapestries to be woven at Mortlake (see no.116), and a subject painting by 'Blenberch', 'Jacob and Esau' (now lost) was sold from the royal collection in 1650 (see Millar 1963, p.83). He resided in the parish of St Martin-in-the-Fields, as did Dr Mayerne, who transcribed van Blijenberch's recipe for painting in distemper and for restoring works painted in this medium on canvas (Kirby Talley, pp.84–8). By 1622, however, the artist was in Antwerp, where he appears in guild lists taking Theodor van Thulden as his pupil.

Van Blijenberch's works are reminiscent of those of Frans Pourbus the Younger. He uses a harsh chiaroscuro and a hotter flesh tone than van Somer and Mytens, with short, staccato brushstrokes, and particularly bright light falling on to unusually heavy, shiny purposeful hands.

William Herbert, 3rd Earl of Pembroke (1580–1630) was one of the foremost figures of the age, and is portrayed wearing the ribbon and pendant badge, known as the Lesser George, of the Order of the Garter, to which he had been appointed in 1603. He holds the white staff denoting his office as Lord Chamberlain, and his key of office hangs on a ribbon (probably originally green) from his belt.

Pembroke was born at Wilton, near Salisbury, and his mother was the celebrated Mary Sidney, writer and patron of writers, and sister of Sir Philip Sidney. He matriculated from New College, Oxford, in 1592, and was later banished from Elizabeth I's court, and briefly imprisoned, for his affair with Mary Fitton, a Lady-in-Waiting. In 1604 he married Mary, daughter and co-heiress of the wealthy 7th Earl of Shrewsbury, whose formidable sisters were Lady Arundel (portrayed by Mytens in 1618, see no.141) and Lady Kent (portrayed by van Somer c.1619, Tate Gallery). A later love affair with his cousin, the writer Lady Mary Wroth, apparently produced two children but his legitimate offspring died young and he was succeeded by his brother Philip, who was to be a major patron of Van Dyck.

Pembroke was involved in many overseas ventures: he joined the Council of the Virginia Company in 1609, the North-West Passage Company in 1612, the East India Company in 1614 and the Bermudas Company in 1615. He had an interest in Barbados, and in 1620 became a member of the Council for New England, and an incorporator of the Guiana Company in 1627. He was also a poet, and followed his family's tradition in being a patron of writers. Aubrey called him 'the greatest Mæcenas to learned men of any peer of his time or since' (cited *Dictionary of National Biography*, 1908, IX, p.678). The First Folio of Shakespeare's works was dedicated to him and his brother in 1623 as 'the incomparable pair of brethren'. Inigo Jones stated that Pembroke financed his early travels to Europe, including Italy, (Finsten, II, p.130). He was among the picture-collectors named by Henry Peacham in his *Graphice* of 1612: the others were Henry, Prince of Wales and the Earls of Arundel, Salisbury, Southampton, Worcester, Suffolk and Northampton.

He appeared 'the very picture and viva effigies of nobility … His person was rather majestic than elegant, his presence full of stately gravity' (Wood, *Fasti Oxon.*, 1815 ed., p.313), although he was also described as 'immoderately given up to women' and enjoyed 'pleasures of all kinds almost in all excesses' (Clarendon's *History*, cited *Dictionary of National Biography*, 1908, IX, p.678).

In his late thirties, Pembroke became particularly interested in his own image and commissioned a series of portraits from various Netherlandish artists newly arrived in London. This may have been initiated to

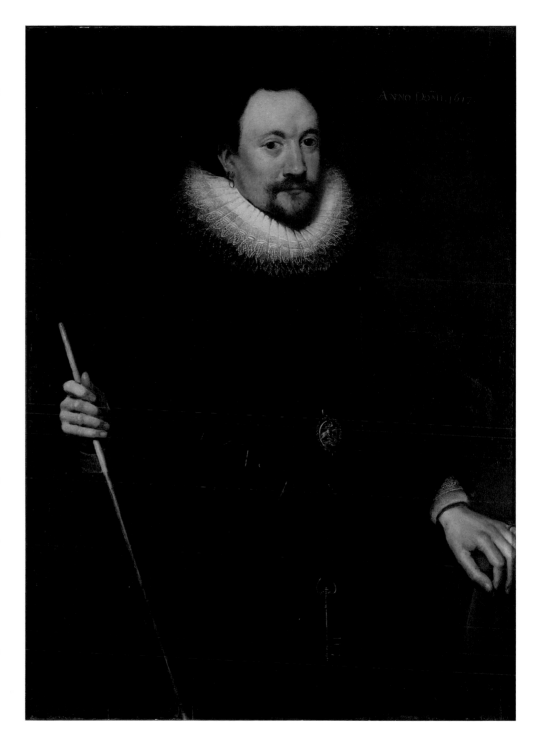

mark his appointment on 23 December 1615 as Lord Chamberlain, since in each he is shown with his staff and key of office. He became Chancellor of Oxford University in January 1617.

Van Blijenberch's portrait is dated 1617, as is another signed by van Somer (The Royal Collection). The van Somer portrait was chosen to be engraved by Simon van der Passe, and issued the same year. Subsequently, however, Pembroke was also portrayed by Daniel Mytens who seems to have found most favour, as a succession of portraits of Pembroke by him or his studio survive from the 1620s (a late one being engraved by Vorsterman in 1633). A letter from Lucy Harington, Countess of Bedford, of 5 Nov. 1621 (PRO SP84/103 f213, see Hearn 1990, p.39) reveals that Mytens was then working on a portrait of Pembroke, apparently commissioned by the Countess, who compares his work favourably with that of Miereveld. If, as Sir Oliver Millar and Dr Malcolm Rogers have suggested, Mytens's earliest image of Pembroke is the portrait belonging to the Pennington Mellor Charity Trust, it may be Lady Bedford's picture. In it, just as in van Blijenberch's and van Somer's portraits, Pembroke, attired in black, is shown at three-quarter length with his instruments of office. It thus appears that each Netherlandish artist was tested out in turn.

The only known earlier images of Pembroke are a miniature by Isaac Oliver of 1616 (Finsten II, p.130) and a probable head-and-shoulders portrait by Marcus Gheeraerts the Younger of c.1610 (Stanford University Museum of Art) whose pendant (Tate Gallery) is thought to represent his brother Philip. The Stanford sitter wears a distinctive annulet, or hoop, earring, and a similar earring, often with an extra loop or a black ribbon, is seen in the later portraits of Pembroke.

Pembroke died of apoplexy at his London house, Baynard's Castle, in 1630.

EXH: *Portraits from Welsh Houses*, National Museum of Wales 1948 (6); *Eeuw van Shakespeare*, The Hague 1958 (60); *Shakespeare Exhibition*, Stratford-on-Avon 1964; Tate Gallery 1969–70 (187)
LIT: John Steegman, *A Survey of Portraits in Welsh Houses*, 1957, I, p.262, no.8 pl.42c; E.K. Waterhouse, 'Portraits from Welsh Houses' review, *Burlington Magazine*, vol.90, 1948, p.204; Roy Strong, 'Shakespeare's Patrons', *Apollo*, vol.79, April 1964, p.294; Strong 1969, p.27, fig.20; Waterhouse 1988, p.28; *Powis Castle*, The National Trust 1994, no.9

KH

PAUL VAN SOMER c.1576–1622 AND STUDIO

139 Anne of Denmark

Oil on canvas 259 × 117 (104 × 46⅛)
Inscribed 'LA MIA GRANDEZZA DAL ECCELSO' on scroll above head
PROV: …; Sir Thomas Isham, Lamport Hall, Northamptonshire by 1676; by descent
Trustees of Lamport Hall

This is a nearly contemporary replica of that in the Royal Collection signed 'P.van somer | A° 1617' (see Millar 1963, no.105) which was inventoried at the Queen's house at Oatlands on 7 October 1617.

The two paintings are extremely similar, except that the present work shows additional wall and landscape to the right. The Queen, dressed for hunting, stands before her palace at Oatlands, accompanied by a liveried black attendant who holds her horse. Millar identifies the five black and white dogs, whose collars bear her initials 'AR' ('Anna Regina' – that is, 'Queen Anne') as Italian greyhounds. The Queen had an intense interest in all things Italian. She could speak the language and had adopted the motto seen in the scroll here above her head, as well as on her earlier portrait by Gheeraerts (no.130). To the left is an oak tree, a symbol of steadfastness, on which is perched an owl, an attribute of Minerva representing wisdom.

The classical gateway seen in the wall behind is the one designed for the Queen by Inigo Jones and erected in June–July 1617 (the architectural drawing is reproduced and discussed in *Inigo Jones*, RA 1989–90 (17), pp.76–7, 124–5). Combining elements taken from Serlio and Palladio, it formed the entrance to the vineyard from the Oatlands hunting park. Contemporary accounts indicate that the Queen was an enthusiastic collector of paintings, and surviving successive inventories for Oatlands reveal that many of these were on religious subjects.

The portrait owes an evident debt to Peake's earlier representation of Anne's late son, Prince Henry, in the hunting field (fig.51 on p.188).

Born in Antwerp, van Somer had settled in London by December 1616, later becoming a neighbour of Abraham van Blijenberch and Daniel Mytens in St Martin's Lane. Royal portrait commissions followed almost immediately. He created the final images in large of the Queen, and was evidently employed by members of her court in particular, such as William Herbert, Earl of Pembroke in 1618, and in c.1619 Elizabeth Talbot, Countess of Kent. After Anne's death he was paid in 1620 the immense sum of £170 'for diverse pictures by him made for the late Queenes Ma^ty' (PRO E.351/544, f117v, cited by Wood 1981, p.71). He also produced a number of full-length portraits of James I, reinventing James's public representation in the same way as he had done Anne's. Like Gheeraerts's image of the Queen, however, the present portrait places her on the left hand side and thus cannot be seen as a pendant to any of those of her husband.

The handful of surviving English works by van Somer, who had died by 5 January 1622, are all portraits. Little is known of his previous career, but in 1604 he was recorded in Amsterdam as a history painter as well as a portraitist. In 1612 and 1614 he was in Leyden, at the Hague in 1615 and in Brussels in 1616, a progression that would have exposed him to a wide range of Netherlandish influences.

William Musgrave recorded another version or copy of this image at Brome Hall, Suffolk, in 1780 (BL Add. MS 5761.E.I. fol.4).

EXH: Tate Gallery 1969–70 (186)
LIT: Gyles Isham, *A Catalogue of the Pictures at Lamport Hall, Northants*, c.1935, no.41; Millar 1963, p.81; Lucy Wood, 'The Portraits of Anne of Denmark', unpublished M.A. report, Courtauld Institute 1981, p.17 (royal version discussed on p.48)

KH

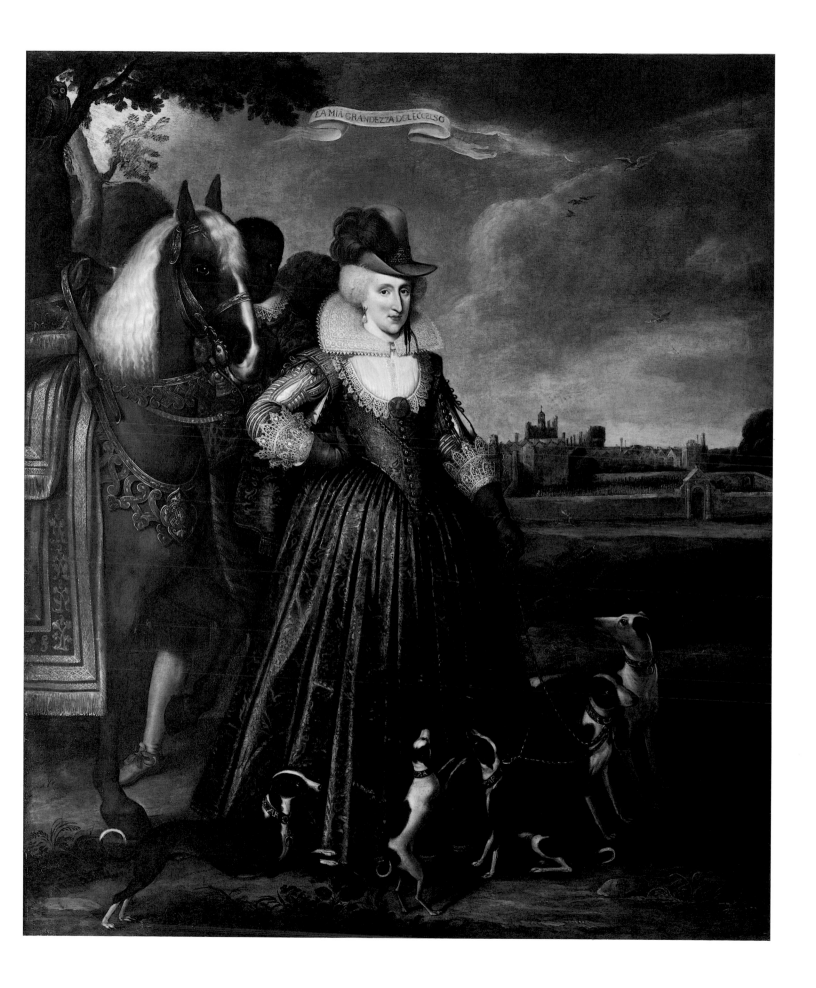

DANIEL MYTENS c.1590–1647

140 Thomas Howard, 14th Earl of Arundel c.1618

Oil on canvas 207 × 127 (81½ × 50)
PROV: Possibly commissioned by Sir
Dudley Carleton; Thomas Howard,
14th Earl of Arundel; by descent to
16th Duke of Norfolk and probably
always in the possession of the sitters'
descendants; among a group of portraits at Arundel Castle given to the
nation in lieu of death duties in 1980,
but allowed to remain at Arundel Castle, as property of the National Portrait
Gallery
National Portrait Gallery, London

This portrait and its pendant (no.141) have
traditionally been dated to 1618 on the basis
of a letter from the artist, Daniel Mytens, to
Sir Dudley Carleton of 18 August that year. It
referred to a small double portrait of Arundel
and his wife which Mytens was sending to
Carleton instead of larger pictures: 'I have
donne my indeaver to perswaide his Lordship
to send your Honnor those great pictures,
butt he is not willinge to parte from them bij
reason they doe leijcke his honr so well, that
he will keep them, and he willed me to make
these in a smaller forme' (ter Kuile 1969,
p.25).

In the present portrait, Arundel is shown
holding a staff of office, usually presumed to
refer his post as Earl Marshal. The staff is not
a later addition to the painting. Arundel was
associated with this office, traditionally held
by his family, by 1618 but was granted the
full appointment only in 1621. The presumably contemporary pendant portrait of the
Countess is unlikely to have been painted
between 1620 and 1622, at which time she
was in Italy.

Although wearing the austere black for
which he was well known, the Earl is expensively dressed, his robe lined with fur against
the cold. He wears the blue ribbon, Lesser
George and garter of the Order of the Garter.

His feet rest on an Eastern carpet on a
stone-tiled floor. Beyond the threshold
behind him is an idealised version of the
sculpture gallery at his chief London
residence, Arundel House on the Strand,
overlooking the Thames (the river is visible
through the doorway at the far end). Here
Arundel assembled the first major collection
of classical antiquities in London. The gallery
depicted is probably more modern than the
actual sculpture gallery at Arundel House,
although Arundel employed Inigo Jones to
update his London residences with new clas-
sical-style fireplaces and gateways.

The sculpture collection is an important
element of the portrait: it testifies to Arundel's
wealth, his connoisseurship, and his social
standing. His art collection was the visible
mark of a true aristocrat.

Thomas Howard, Earl of Arundel
(1590–1646) would have inherited the only
surviving English dukedom but for the attain-
der for treason of both his father, the Catholic
convert St Philip Howard, and his grandfather, the 4th Duke of Norfolk (see no.27). He
became the premier earl in England when he
was restored to the earldoms of Arundel and
Surrey by James I.

In 1606 he married the heiress Alatheia
Talbot, whose wealth enabled him to regain
family lands and assemble an art collection
which brought him international prestige.

As a Catholic, Arundel travelled in the Low
Countries, Italy, Germany and France from
1612 to 1615, before returning to London
where he became an Anglican. In 1615–18 he
employed Inigo Jones, who had travelled with
him in Italy, as a designer at his London
houses. Arundel also patronised Rubens, Van
Dyck, and the sculptors François Dieussart
and Francesco Fanelli.

During the 1620s Arundel's opposition to
the Duke of Buckingham (no.115), the royal
favourite, affected his relations with James I
and Charles I. In 1626 he was sent to the
Tower after his son secretly married a
kinswoman of Charles I against the King's
wishes. The fines imposed on Arundel by
Charles crippled him financially, but his
standing with the King improved after Buckingham was assassinated in 1628. During the
1630s Arundel visited the Netherlands, Vienna
and Prague as Charles's ambassador, taking
the artist Wenceslaus Hollar into his service in
1636 while on embassy to the Emperor Ferdinand II at Vienna.

In the late 1630s Arundel proved a poor
military commander but assembled a superb
collection of Old Master drawings and prints.
He acquired the library of the Renaissance
humanist Pirckheimer in 1636, and the collection of gems, coins and medals of the Venetian merchant Daniel Nys in 1638.

Arundel left England in 1642 to escort
Princess Mary to her new husband, William
of Orange, and spent his final years separated
from his wife, living as a Royalist exile first in
Antwerp and then in Italy. Recent research by
Edward Chaney suggests that Arundel died a
Catholic. His heart is buried in the cloister
wall of the Sant' Antonio in Padua (D. Jaffé,

'The Barberini Circle …', *Journal of the History
of Collecting*, vol.1, no.2, 1989, pp.119–47, p.35
n.162).

Collecting classical antiquities was a highly
prestigious activity in early seventeenth-century Europe, as Arundel would have known
from his Italian travels. His host in Rome in
1614 was the Marchese Vincenzo Giustiniani,
himself a collector of busts, statues, inscriptions, and reliefs (Howarth 1985, p.46). Giustiniani had arranged for Arundel to excavate
in the Forum at Rome – and probably planted
the antiquities Arundel unearthed there. Arundel also bought antique statues in the city,
and commissioned statues of Romans in
armour and togas by the modern sculptor
Egidio Moretti. These holdings were aug-
mented in 1616 by a shipment of statues from
Italy given to Arundel by William Cecil, Lord
Roos, on the eve of Roos's departure for
Spain.

Arundel's collection ultimately included
busts, architectural fragments and inscriptions.
Most of his statues were Hellenistic, or
Roman copies of Hellenistic works, restored
for him by modern sculptors, who added
missing heads, arms or legs. The tallest statue
on the right in the present portrait was
restored as a figure of Homer (its trunk survives in the Ashmolean Museum, Oxford). It
was the first major ancient sculpture bought
by Arundel.

Arundel supported the spread of knowledge about ancient culture through books,
such as *De Pictura Veterum* by his librarian
Franciscus Junius, and prints. He made efforts
to preserve his collections for viewing after
his death. In a will drafted in 1617, he
requested his heirs to treat politely 'all gentlemen of virtue or Artistes wch are honest' who
came to see the antiquities. Ultimately he
bequeathed the collections to Alatheia. They
were dispersed after her death, the largest
portion of the sculptures were given to
Oxford University by his grandson and are
now in the Ashmolean Museum.

EXH: with no.141: London RA 1938 (8, 28); London
RA 1960 (3, 25); Tate Gallery 1972 (1, 2); *Treasure
Houses of Britain*, National Gallery of Art, Washington
1985 (49); *Patronage Preserved*, Christie's 1991 (7, 8)
LIT: Hervey 1921, pp.143; O. ter Kuile, 'Daniel
Mijtens', *Nederlands Kunsthistorisch Jaarboek*, vol.20,
1969, pp.1–106, nos.2–3, pp.43–5, nos.1, 2; Water-
house 1978, p.54; *The Earl and Countess of Arundel:
Renaissance Collectors*, J. Paul Getty Museum, Malibu
1995, pp.6, 7, 9; see also J. Martin Robinson, *The
Dukes of Norfolk*, 1982, pp.97–116; Howarth 1985;
Thomas Howard Earl of Arundel, Ashmolean Museum,
Oxford 1985–6

AT

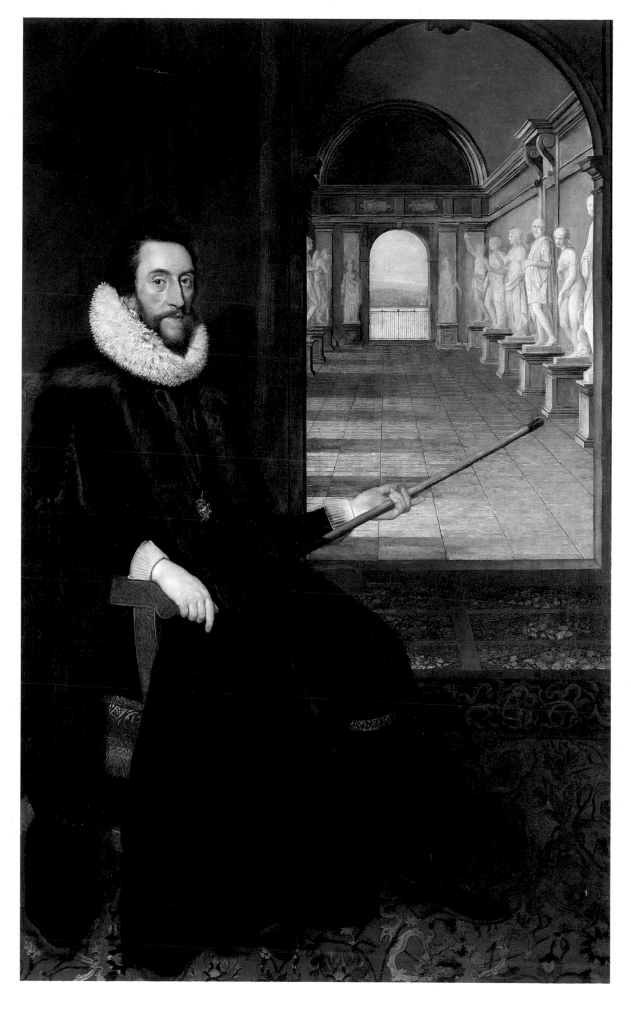

DANIEL MYTENS

141 Alatheia Talbot, Countess of Arundel c.1618

Oil on canvas 207 × 127
(81½ × 50)
PROV: As for no.140
National Portrait Gallery, London

Alatheia Talbot (c.1590–1654) was the third daughter of Gilbert, 7th Earl of Shrewsbury, who owned large estates in Yorkshire, Derbyshire, and Nottinghamshire. By birth she was the greatest lady among James I's courtiers, and one of the richest heiresses in England. In 1606 she married Thomas Howard, Earl of Arundel, whom she bore six sons. Alatheia was an attendant of Anne of Denmark and performed in court masques (see no.107).

Lady Arundel's portrait is a counterpart to her husband's (no.140). The Earl is shown with the marks of political power appropriate to an aristocratic man, backed by the Arundel sculpture collection. Lady Arundel displays instead the signs of piety and wealth appropriate for an aristocratic lady, against a background of Arundel paintings.

She wears sober black but, like her husband, is expensively dressed, with costly lace (even her handkerchief has a deep border of lace) and magnificent jewels. The most remarkable of these is her diamond brooch, forming the letters IHS, which she was also to be depicted wearing by Van Dyck in the 'Madagascar Portrait' (Kunsthistorisches Museum, Vienna). The letters IHS are an abbreviation of the name of Jesus. This brooch, so prominent in her portrait, is in keeping with her avowed Catholicism. Unlike her husband, she never became an Anglican, and embarrassed him by expressing her hopes for the reconversion of England to Catholicism.

The background may be intended to represent a gallery in Arundel House, idealised in the same way as the sculpture gallery in the portrait of Lord Arundel. The ceiling lacks decorative painting.

Alatheia is portrayed with the same Eastern carpet under her feet as her husband. The pattern of tiles under the carpet, however, is different, and the levels at which the carpet edges and the thresholds behind are seen have been carefully differentiated in the two portraits, giving the effect of raising up the Earl.

On the gallery wall at left are large paintings in uniform dark frames with gilt sight edges, while smaller paintings hang within

the embrasures by the window, where the light would be stronger. Some of the portraits may have come from Arundel's Lumley (see no.105) and Fitzalan relatives. Arundel's collection was celebrated not only for its sculptures, but for its paintings, which included Italian and northern European Renaissance works, particularly ones by Holbein. At Lord Lumley's death in 1609, Arundel had inherited some of his Holbein paintings, including the 'Christina of Denmark' (fig.43 on p.119) and portrait drawings (nos.93–7). Later, Lady Arundel's own house would also contain a number of portraits, recorded in a 1640 inventory, among them those of Elizabeth I (Lady Arundel's godmother), Edward VI, the 'Archduchess', the Queen of Spain, the Earl of Pembroke, and a man wearing the insignia of the Golden Fleece – all sitters important enough to be the subjects of full-length portraits.

The Arundels may have been aware that, as their librarian Franciscus Junius wrote in *De Pictura Veterum* (translated in 1638 on Lady Arundel's orders as *Of the Painting of the Ancients*) the ancients placed ancestral portraits in their halls to inspire their descendants to perform noble deeds (Bk 2, chap.VIII). However, the identities of the sitters, even in the contemporary rectangular portraits flanking the doors here, cannot be discerned.

A garden is visible through the classical doorway, with a tree-lined walk, a small fountain, and a pergola covered with greenery. Arundel House had a garden especially suitable for the display of classical statuary, of which Arundel and Inigo Jones would have seen examples in Italy in 1614. Another, non-autograph version of the present portrait, which shows the gallery empty of paintings, survives in a private collection.

In 1613–14 the Countess had travelled in Italy with her husband, using her time there to educate herself (she stayed in a Sienese monastery to learn Italian). Her courtly behaviour impressed the Italians and French, and Queen Marie de'Medici granted her etiquette privileges normally reserved for French duchesses.

The death of Alatheia's father in 1616 enabled the Arundels to develop their collections and art patronage. Her grandmother was Bess of Hardwick, the builder of Hardwick Hall and Alatheia herself designed buildings.

In c.1620 Alatheia took her sons to Venice for their education. En route, she sat with her attendants, dog and (probably) Sir Dudley Carleton for a group portrait by Peter Paul Rubens (fig.57), who considered the Earl of

Arundel 'one of the four evangelists, and a supporter of our art' (Rubens's letter of 1620, cited Hervey 1921, p.176 n.2). The Arundels had been among Rubens's first English patrons; in 1618 Rubens wrote to Sir Dudley Carleton about supplying some drawings for Arundel (Howarth 1985, p.231, nn.38, 152).

In Venice, where Alatheia lived in a fine palace on the Grand Canal, she was joined by Van Dyck, who shared with the Arundels a taste for the work of Titian. In 1622 a biography of Titian, *Breve compendio della vita del fam.Titano Vecelli di Cadore*, was dedicated to her as a liberal patron of the art of learning by its author Tizianello.

Alatheia planned to go on from Italy to Spain, but James I thought it 'not very good that a lady of such quality should go thus wandering through the world' (Amerigo Salvetti, Florentine agent in London, letter of 20 March 1623 to the Grand Duke of Tuscany; see Howarth 1985, p.230 n.55). Instead Alatheia returned to London in 1622, with treasures including a gondola for the Thames and 'prodigious edible snails'.

Her Venetian contacts included the dealer-merchant Daniel Nys, whose collections were later purchased by her husband and by Charles I. It was through Alatheia that in 1623 the Grand Chancellor of Mantua made approaches to Charles I regarding the King's possible purchase of the Mantuan art collection.

Alatheia appeared with her husband in Van Dyck's double portrait of 1639, which celebrated the Earl of Arundel's plans to colonise Madagascar. The couple separated, however, and she moved out of Arundel House in the

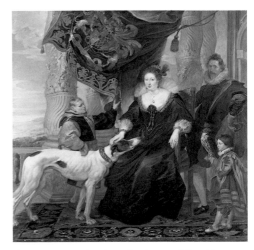

fig.57 Peter Paul Rubens, 'Lady Arundel and her Entourage' 1620, oil on panel. *Alte Pinakothek, Munich*

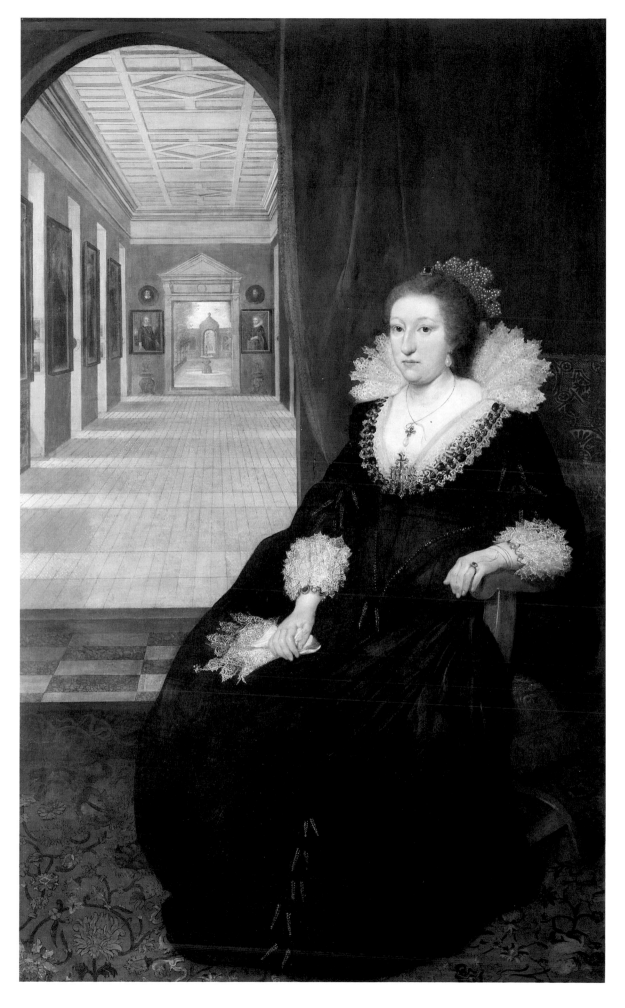

HENDRICK VAN STEENWIJK
THE YOUNGER *c.*1580–1649
AND OTHERS

late 1630s to Tart Hall in St James's Park, remodelled for her by George Gage (died 1639). In 1641 the Arundels escorted back to the Continent Marie de'Medici, who had been visiting her daughter Queen Henrietta Maria (Hervey 1921, pp.424–35). Lady Arundel travelled separately from her husband, visiting Rome in 1641 before establishing herself first in Antwerp, and later in Holland. Arundel rejoined her in 1642, but retired to Padua.

In Holland Alatheia lived at Alkmaar, then Amersfoort, and finally settled in Amsterdam. She inherited the Arundel collections in 1646. Following her death in Amsterdam in 1654 the collection became a source of contention among the Arundel heirs and was divided. Indeed, it was already split, as the sculpture had remained at Arundel House despite the exile of the Royalist Arundels.

EXH: As no.140
LIT: As no.140

AT

142 Charles I as Prince of Wales
*c.*1620

Oil on canvas 219.5 × 174.5
(86⅜ × 68¾)
PROV: Possibly given to the sitter's uncle, Christian IV of Denmark, and perhaps listed in inventories of Frederiksborg Castle in 1650 and 1677; transferred from Frederiksborg to the Royal Picture Gallery at Christiansborg 1827
Den Kongelige Maleri- og Skulptursamling, Statens Museum for Kunst, Copenhagen

This portrait appears to be the work of two, or probably three, collaborating artists. The architectural perspective, thought to be imaginary, must be by Hendrick van Steenwijk (see no.143) who arrived in London in November 1617. He seems to have provided architectural backgrounds in various portraits by other artists, although this seems to be the earliest such example. The best-known is the full-length standing portrait of Charles I (Galleria Sabauda, Turin), in which van Steenwijk signed and dated the architectural element in 1626, and Daniel Mytens signed and dated the figure in 1627.

Mytens has also been suggested as the portraitist in the present picture (Copenhagen 1988); he painted James I in 1621, and his earliest known portrait of Charles depicts him with the moustache that he first grew on his return from Spain late in 1623. An earlier attribution was to Paul van Somer (see no.139). A third possibility, however, is Abraham van Blijenberch (see no.138), who is known to have portrayed the young Prince at exactly this period, in a full-length generally identified as NPG 1112 (at Montacute), the handling of which is not inconsistent with the present work. A further comparison is 'The Earl of Monmouth and his Family' of *c.*1617 (National Portrait Gallery, also at Montacute) at present attributed to van Somer, and probably also by the same hand.

The interior and its accessories are likely to be by a third artist. The spectacular Mannerist throne seems to echo the sphinx or mermaid chairpost of Elizabeth I's 'Armada' portraits (see no.43). The Prince wears the ermine-lined robes of the Order of the Garter, with the Garter and the George. Behind him is a cloth of estate with elements of the royal coat of arms, while on the table is a reading-desk bearing on its side 'CP' (for 'Carolus Princeps'). A box containing an open watch-case rests on a sheet of paper showing a military groundplan. Charles holds a staff of office, which may allude to his appointment as Great Steward of Scotland (Toynbee 1939, p.122). He is accompanied by a small dog, a symbol of loyalty, but also perhaps one of the spaniels that he kept throughout his life (one called Rogue is said to have walked with him to his execution).

This grand portrait of the future king is thought to have been a gift to another king, Christian IV of Denmark, his mother's brother. The Queen herself died on 2 March 1619. A half-length version of this portrait, without the architectural perspective, is in the Claydon House collection (National Trust).

EXH: *Christian IV and Europe*, 19th Council of Europe Exhibtion, Denmark 1988 (1067)
LIT: F.M. Kelly, 'Mytens and his Portraits of Charles I', *Burlington Magazine*, vol.37, 1920, pp.84–9; Margaret R. Toynbee, 'A Portrait Called Henry, Prince of Wales by Daniel Mytens', *Burlington Magazine*, vol.74, March 1939, p.116; Charlotte Christensen 'From Elsinore to London' *Apollo*, vol.127, 1988, pp.112, 115; John Peacock, 'The Politics of Portraiture' in Sharpe and Lake 1994, p.213

KH

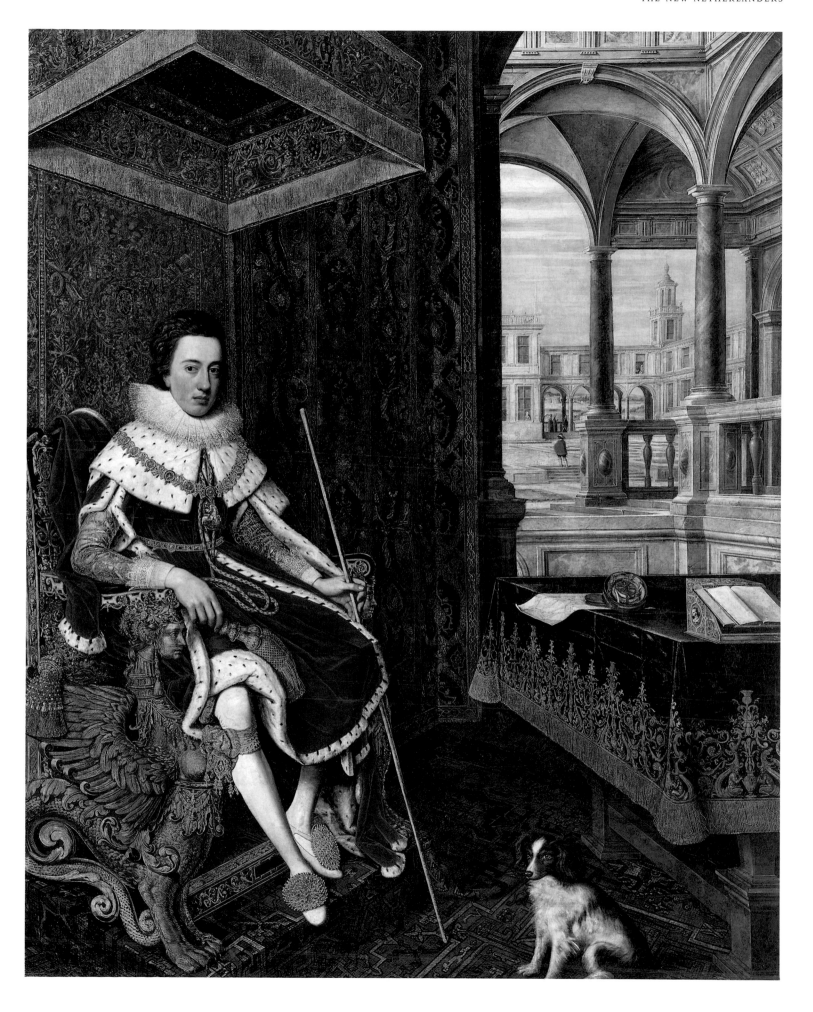

HENDRICK VAN STEENWIJK
THE YOUNGER

143 The Liberation of St Peter
1619

Oil on copper 48.4 × 65.4 (19 × 25¾)
Inscribed '1619' on block above angel's
wing; 'HENRI. V. STEINICK' on second
step at right
PROV: ...; George III and by descent
Her Majesty The Queen

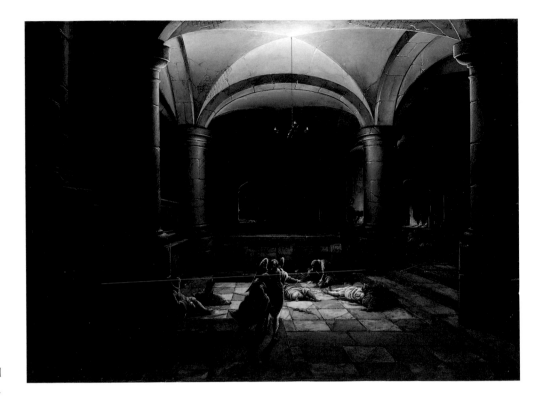

Van Steenwijk was in London by November
1617 where he remained until 1637. He specialised in small architectural scenes, usually
of religious subjects, and in perspective views
of interiors, often depicted by night.

The delivery of St Peter from prison was a
theme to which he returned repeatedly. It
enabled him to display his skill at painting
dark, vaulted interiors lit by specific sources
of artificial light. Numerous versions by him
are known, based on the account in the Acts
of The Apostles 12: 5–10 in which St Peter,
imprisoned by order of Herod, was asleep and
chained between two soldiers, when the angel
of the Lord appeared, accompanied by a light.
The chains fell away and the angel, telling
Peter to dress himself, led him to freedom.

These works seem to have been admired by
connoisseurs in London less for their religious
subject matter than for their intricate detail
and visual sophistication. Such a picture tended to be described in contemporary inventories as a 'prospective' [i.e. 'perspective'] rather
than by its title. At his death early in 1624,
for instance, the 2nd Marquis of Hamilton
owned 'A prospective of Steinwick'. Charles I
possessed twenty-six perspectives, twelve of
which were listed as by van Steenwijk (see
MacGregor 1989, p.416). The present Royal
Collection now has six variants on this
subject, at least two of which were originally
in Charles I's collection.

Van Steenwijk's father, Hendrick the Elder,
was one of the earliest artists to specialise in
paintings of architecture, a genre which first
emerged in Antwerp in the late sixteenth

century. The themes were often taken from
the prints of Jan Vredeman de Vries
(1527–c.1604), whose architectural fantasies in
the widely copied *Perspective* (1604–5) were
particularly influential.

Hendrick the Younger, who was born
either in Antwerp or Frankfurt, was a pupil of
his father. Many of his small works are painted, as here, on metal. The figures were sometimes done by another hand and van
Steenwijk also collaborated with other artists
on much larger works, painting impressive
and fantastical architectural backgrounds to
full-length portraits (see no.142). He usually
signed and dated his work meticulously.

EXH: Tate Gallery, 1972 (137); *The Queen's Pictures*,
National Gallery, 1991 (11)

KH

JOHN HOSKINS *c.*1595–1665

144 Alice, Lady Le Strange 1617

Oil on panel 57.5 × 44 (22⅝ × 16½)
Inscribed 'Alice Stubbs, wife | Sir
H.L'Estrange' t.r.
PROV: Private collection
Private Collection

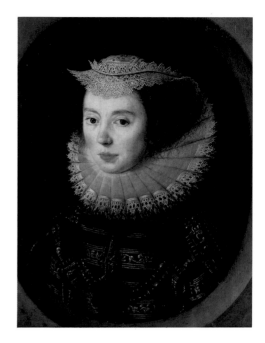

This and its pendant portrait of the sitter's
husband Sir Hamon Le Strange (1583–1654)
are among the earliest surviving works by
John Hoskins (see also nos.90, 91 and 92).

According to an eighteenth-century biography 'he was bred a Face Painter in Oil, but
afterwards taking to Miniature, far exceeded
what he had done'. Apart from the Le Strange
family portraits, no further paintings in large
by him are known.

Dame Alice's Household Account Book
records in 1617 the relevant payment to 'Mr
Horskins' (Norfolk Record Office, Le Strange
Papers, P7, repr. *Family and Friends*, p.85). He
was paid £4 'for drawing 2 pictures'. In addition, 1s 7d was paid 'For a Case and a Cord
for 2 picktures', 2s 6d for transporting them
to a boat, and 1s 9d for bringing them 'from
London to Linn', i.e. King's Lynn.

The portraits remain in their original
frames, which retain hooks at the top which
once supported individual protective curtains.
The use of such curtains was a widespread
and longstanding practice both in Britain and
on the Continent. Examples can occasionally
be seen in 'paintings-within-paintings' (e.g. in
the portrait of 'Sir John Kennedy' by Marcus
Gheeraerts the Younger, Woburn Abbey), and
this feature is frequently alluded to in six-
teenth- and seventeenth-century inventories.

Alice Stubbs of Sedgeford, Norfolk, married in 1602 Hamon Le Strange, who came
from a distinguished family in neighbouring
Hunstanton. He had been educated in London, and may have taken part in one of the
journeys in search of the North-East Passage.
It was Le Strange who, with his friend Sir
Robert Carey, carried the news of Queen

Elizabeth's death at Richmond up to James VI
in Scotland in March 1603, and was subsequently knighted at the latter's coronation as
James I of England. He became Sheriff for
Norfolk in 1609, was elected to three
Parliaments, and added to the grandeur of
Hunstanton Hall by successive building
enterprises. Lady Le Strange's meticulous and
detailed household accounts remain in
Norfolk Record Office. Of the eight children
born to the couple, four died young. At the
time of the Civil War, the family were active
Royalists and suffered financially as a
consequence.

EXH: *Family and Friends*, Norwich Castle Museum
1992, (19)
LIT: Prince F. Duleep Singh, *Portraits in Norfolk Houses*
(ed. E. Farrer), [1927], II, no.15; Waterhouse 1988,
p.133

KH

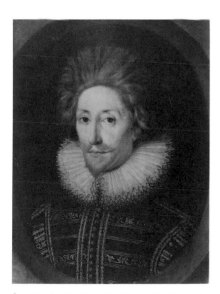

fig.58 John Hoskins, 'Sir Hamon le Strange'
1617, oil on panel. *Private Collection*

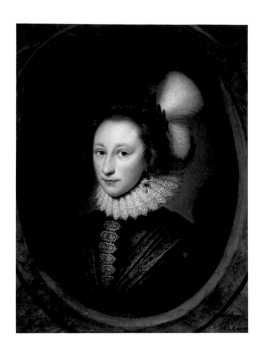

CORNELIUS JOHNSON
1593–1661

145 Susanna Temple, later Lady Lister 1620

Oil on panel 67.9 × 51.8 (26¾ × 20⅜)
Inscribed 'C.J. | fecit. | 1620' b.r.
PROV: Apparently by descent through the sitter's daughter Susanna who married George Gregory of Harlaxton, Lincs in 1664; almost certainly at Harlaxton by 1888; Thomas Sherwin Pearson-Gregory Esq. of Harlaxton Manor; his executor's sale, Christie's 18 June 1937 (27) as 'A Lady of the De Ligne Family', bt Vicars; ...; R.H. Leon sale, White House, Denham, 9–10 May 1961 (57); Mrs Wrighton of Fulmer House, Fulmer, Bucks, by 1978; Sotheby's, 13 Dec. 1978 (201, repr.) as 'A Lady, probably Elizabeth Petre'; Sotheby's 18 March 1981 (27) as 'Portrait of Elizabeth Petre', bt Thos Agnew & Sons Ltd, from whom purchased by the Tate Gallery 1981
Tate Gallery, London. Purchased 1981

This is one of Johnson's earliest surviving portraits and exemplifies the delicacy and reticence of his initial style.

Susanna Temple was the only daughter of Sir Alexander Temple (1583–1629), who owned property in Essex, Kent and Sussex. Her brother James was later one of the signatories of Charles I's death warrant (see *Dictionary of National Biography*, 1909, XIX, p.513). Her own date of birth is not recorded, but in 1627 she married Sir Gifford Thornhurst of Agnes Court, Kent, who died two months later. Their daughter Frances was subsequently the mother of Sarah, 1st Duchess of Marlborough. In 1633 Susanna married Sir Martin Lister of Thorpe Arnold, Leicestershire, by whom she had five daughters and five sons. Her second son, the zoologist Martin (born *c.*1638), later became physician to Queen Anne (see *Dictionary of National Biography*, 1909, XI, p.1229). Susanna was buried at Burwell, Lincolnshire on 28 November 1669.

She is depicted wearing a drop earring, of which the central element is a martlet; this bird is part of the Temple coat of arms. The portrait was among a group of De Ligne and Lister family portraits by Cornelius Johnson noted at Harlaxton by Dallaway by 1888, although he erroneously identified a different portrait as being of Susanna Temple. The painting had earlier, however, been engraved by Robert White (1645–1703), inscribed with the correct name and titles of the sitter. A

family tradition that she was a Lady-in-Waiting to Queen Anne of Denmark (died 1619, see nos.130, 139) does not appear to be substantiated.

A portrait of Susanna's father, also dated 1620, is in the collection of Viscount Cobham at Hagley Hall, with a replica, formerly in the Northwick Park collection, now at the Center for British Art, New Haven. Both paintings give Temple's age as thirty-seven, in an italic script. A number of early head-and-shoulders portraits on panel, signed by Johnson, bear inscriptions in this script, such as the 'Young Man aged 22', also dated 1620, in the Holburne of Menstrie Museum, Bath (kindly pointed out by Dr F.G. Meijr), and the 'Unknown Lady, Aged 50', dated 1619 (Lamport Hall). It is conceivable that they may all have formed part of a Temple family commission. The similarity of handling in the Lamport portrait to that of John Hoskins's 'Alice, Lady Le Strange' (no.144) may permit the speculation that Hoskins and Johnson received training from some common source, perhaps Marcus Gheeraerts the Younger. The enamelled surfaces of the portraits of Susanna Temple and her father, on the other hand, suggest a period of study in the Netherlands.

All Johnson's surviving works are portraits and his earliest, up to the mid-1620s, are head-and-shoulders portraits within a trompe-l'oeil oval. This format may derive from the shape favoured for contemporary portrait miniatures, or from the oval-within-a-rectangle form of portrait engravings, found from the end of the late-sixteenth century onwards both in Britain and the Low Countries (see also nos.131, 132). Johnson also painted portrait miniatures.

LIT: H. Walpole, *Anecdotes of Painting in England*, ed. R.N. Wornum, notes by Dalloway, 1888, I, p.212 n.4; Revd H.L.L. Denny, *Memorials of an Ancient House*, Edinburgh 1913, p.215; A.J. Finberg, 'A Chronological List of Paintings by Cornelius Johnson', *Walpole Society*, vol.10, 1922, p.8; J.A. Temple, *The Temple Memoirs*, 1925, p.49 and repr. facing page; Waterhouse 1978, p.61; *Tate Gallery Illustrated Catalogue of Acquisitions 1980-82*, 1984, pp.25–6

KH

ANTHONY VAN DYCK
1599–1641

146 Thomas Howard, 14th Earl of Arundel 1620–1

Oil on canvas 102.8 × 79.4
(40½ × 31¼)

PROV: First recorded in 1727 in the collection of Philippe, duc d'Orléans (the Regent); by descent to Philippe, duc d'Orléans (Philippe Egalité) 1792; Citoyen Robit sale, Paris, 11 May 1801 (36); Michael Bryan sale 6 Nov. 1801–31, May 1802 (92), bt 3rd Duke of Bridgewater; by descent to 1st Duke of Sutherland before 1913; ...; Daniel Guggenheim, New York 1929; Robert Guggenheim, Washington 1950; Mr and Mrs Francis Lenyon, Washington 1980; John A. Logan, Washington 1980; Mrs Rebecca Pollard Logan, sold Christie's, 8 July 1983 (92); Jamie Ortiz Patino, Switzerland, by whom sold, through Messrs Agnew, to the J. Paul Getty Museum 1986

J. Paul Getty Museum, Malibu, California

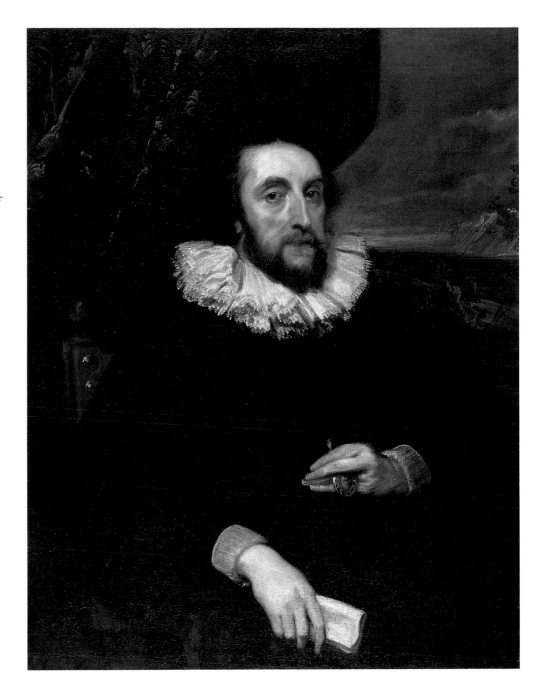

Depicted three-quarter length, the Earl, soberly dressed in black, is seated, holding the jewel of the Lesser George, the badge of the Garter, in his left hand. In company with Charles, then Duke of York, Arundel had been created a Knight of the Garter in 1611. The portrait accords well with a contemporary description of the sitter: 'his Countenance was Majestical and grave, his Visage long, his Eyes large, black and piercing'. Described by Horace Walpole as 'the father of *virtù* in England', Arundel (1585–1646) was one of the greatest and most discerning of collectors of paintings, drawings, prints, books and antiquities that England has known.

Although undocumented, the portrait was almost certainly painted during Van Dyck's first visit to England, which lasted from October 1620 until February 1621. There is conflicting evidence as to whether Arundel or Buckingham, at that time a marquess, was responsible for inducing the artist to come to London, where he was employed by both patrons, as well as by James I (for unspecified services).

One of the first of Van Dyck's mature portraits, this study conveys a sense of lifelike vitality, combined with elegance and sophistication. Unlike the artist's earlier portraits set against a plain background, the sitter, following Venetian Renaissance tradition, is placed before a richly patterned curtain on one side and a sparkling and spacious landscape on the other. The richer colouring reflects Van Dyck's increasing admiration for Titian. Compared with the unbending image of the Earl in his sculpture gallery by Daniel Mytens (no.140) painted two years earlier, this relaxed and fluently painted work must have made a considerable impression on English patrons. It gave a vivid foretaste of what he was to achieve during his second much longer stay in England in the 1630s, when, inter alia, he was to produce a series of dynastic portraits of Arundel and his family.

EXH: *The Young Van Dyck*, National Gallery of Canada, Ottawa 1980 (65); *Van Dyck in England*, NPG 1982 (2); *The Earl and Countess of Arundel; Renaissance Collectors*, J. Paul Getty Museum 1995
LIT: Hervey 1921, pp.187–8; G. Glück, *Van Dyck, des Meisters Gemälde*, Klassiker der Kunst, Stuttgart and Berlin 1931, pp.125, 533; C. Brown, *Van Dyck*, Oxford 1982, pp.55–6; E. Larsen, *The Paintings of Anthony van Dyck*, Freren 1988, II, no.38; C. White, *Anthony van Dyck: Thomas Howard, The Earl of Arundel*, Malibu 1995

CW

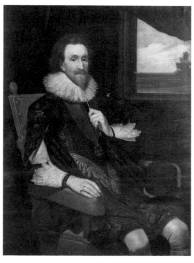

fig.59 Daniel Mytens, 'Philip Herbert, 4th Earl of Pembroke' *c*.1625, oil canvas. *Courtesy of The Marquess of Salisbury* This portrait was clearly influenced by no.146.

DANIEL MYTENS *c*.1590–1647

147 James Hamilton, Earl of Arran, later 1st Duke of Hamilton
1623

Oil on canvas 200.7 × 125.1 (79 × 49¼)
Inscribed 'DM Mijtens.f..e 1623', between knees
PROV: Presumably by descent (first recorded Hamilton Palace *c*.1700); Duke of Hamilton sale Christie 6 Nov. 1919 (17) (as of Lord John Hamilton, 1st Marquis of Hamilton, by Marcus Gheeraerts the Younger) bt Agnew; presented to National Gallery by Colin Agnew and Charles Romer Williams 1919; transferred to Tate Gallery 1954
Tate Gallery, London. Presented by Colin Agnew and Romer Williams 1919

The sitter's identity had been lost by the nineteenth century, but there is no doubt that he is the seventeen-year-old son of the 2nd Marquis of Hamilton. This is confirmed by the reference of *c*.1700 in M4/41, Hamilton Archives, to 'James Duke of Hamilton's Picture in Black with red stockings, a full length, by Vandike' which hung in the 'Great Dining Roome' at Hamilton Palace (information from Dr Rosalind K.Marshall). Moreover, the facial features agree with those in Mytens's full-length portrait of the same subject in a silver suit, dated 1629 (Scottish National Portrait Gallery).

The Hamiltons were next in line to the Scottish throne after the Stuarts, and had immense landholdings. Arran's father was among the most powerful of the Scottish nobles who joined James I's court in England.

Born on 19 July 1606 at Hamilton Palace near Glasgow, Arran grew up in Scotland. In 1620 he was unwillingly married to Lady Mary Feilding, niece of the future Duke of Buckingham.

Daniel Mytens first painted the King in 1621 (National Portrait Gallery), and was the leading court portraitist when he portrayed the sitter's nine-year-old wife in 1622. Subsequently, he painted Arran's father, the 2nd Marquis of Hamilton, holding his staff of office as Steward of the Household, to which he was appointed in 1624 (ter Kuile 1969, pp.67–9): Mytens must have employed considerable studio assistance, for at least twenty-two versions or derivatives of that image are known. These indicate both the success of Mytens's portrayal and the extent of Hamilton's power network. Hamilton himself was a picture collector of some stature (see Hearn

1990; and Philip McEvansoneya, 'An Unpublished Inventory of the Hamilton Collection in the 1620s and the Duke of Buckingham's Pictures', *Burlington Magazine*, vol.134, 1992, pp.524–6).

The present portrait is dated 1623, which under the Old Style calendar used in England until 1751, ran from 25 March 1623 to 24 March 1624. During that year Prince Charles visited Spain in a vain attempt to conclude a marriage with the Infanta Maria, sister of the seventeen-year-old King Philip IV. Setting off initially in secret with Buckingham on 17 February 1623, he arrived in Madrid on 7 March. The visit became Arran's first foray into public affairs as he set off for Spain with his father-in-law on 13 March to join the Prince (*Acts of the Privy Council of England 1621–1623*, 1932, p.440). His mother wrote 'My eldest soune Jhamis is gon post efter [the Prince]. He, albeit young, is now on the staig [stage] to play his part' (Scottish Record Office, Breadalbane Muniments, GD112/39/33/4; I am indebted to Dr Marshall for both references).

The months Charles spent in Spain with Philip IV were to have a profound effect upon him, opening his eyes to the work of major European artists such as Titian and to the uses of art as a political tool.

In the summer of 1623, another young man, the painter Diego Velásquez visited the Spanish court for the first time. Before 30 August he had painted the Spanish King. In addition on 8 September he was paid 110 reales by Charles's staff 'for drawing the Prince's Picture' (a *bosquejo* – possibly an oil sketch). Neither portrait has survived.

The examples of Velásquez's work that he had seen in Madrid may have influenced how Arran chose to be represented in the present portrait, made after his return to England. The composition is remarkably similar to a full-length of the Prince, with the small moustache he is said to have worn on his return from Spain (probably Parham Park Collection, see ter Kuile 1969, no.19). This is thought to be the full-length of Charles, for delivery to the Spanish Ambassador, for which Mytens was paid £30 on 9 October 1623. The portrait of Arran is the more powerful of the two, since the setting is uncluttered by carpet and curtain, and the sitter has been given a solidity and a presence absent from that of the Prince.

Arran's sombre attire may reflect the Spanish fashion for black, a result of Philip IV's dress reform laws, introduced in March 1623, banning the wearing of rich materials and ornaments. The only physical description of the sitter dates from *c.*1625; according to Sir Philip Warwick 'the 2nd Marquis had two sons, James and William, neither of them so graceful persons as himself, and both of some hard visage, the elder of a neater shape and gracefuller motion … The air of his countenance had such a cloud on it'.

This portrait may have been commissioned to mark Arran's appointment as a Gentleman of the Prince's Bedchamber, in which capacity he served until Charles's accession, when he carried the sword at the coronation. During the 1630s his intimacy with the King was marked by mutual gifts of paintings, and Hamilton became one of the principal English collectors. Though it has recently been suggested that he was more a politic follower of the fashion for collecting than a connoisseur, he was to amass a collection of about six hundred works, more than half of them Venetian. His particular triumph was the acquisition of the collection of Bartolomeo della Nave from Venice in 1639. The core of his collection eventually found its way into the Kunsthistorisches Museum, Vienna.

Charles entrusted Hamilton, because of his Scottish birth and influence, with the implementation of his policies there, conferring a dukedom on him in 1643. Hamilton was as poor a politician as he was later to prove a general. One of Charles's principal advisers during the Civil War, he eventually led a Scottish army into England to intervene on behalf of the royalists but was comprehensively beaten by Cromwell at the Battle of Preston. He was executed in March 1649, a few weeks after the King. His military ambitions are evident in his portrait in armour by Van Dyck, of *c.*1640 (*Anthony van Dyck*, National Gallery of Art, Washington 1990 (87)).

EXH: Edinburgh 1883 (226); *Childhood in 17th-Century Scotland*, Scottish National Portrait Gallery, Edinburgh 1976 (134)
LIT: H. Avray Tipping, 'The Hamilton Palace Collection of Pictures – 1', *Country Life*, 18 Oct. 1919, pp.481–3 (as William, 2nd Duke of Hamilton, by Marcus Gheeraerts); C.H. Collins Baker, 'Een portret van Daniel Mijtens', *Onze Kunst*, Jan.–March 1922, pp.27–8; H. Isherwood Kay, 'A Portrait by Daniel Mytens in the National Gallery', *Connoisseur*, vol.56, 1920, pp.77 repr., 111; *National Gallery: Illustrations to the Catalogue. British School*, 1936, p.69 repr.; M. Davies *National Gallery Catalogues. British School*, 1946, p.103; *Tate Gallery Report: Transfers from the National Gallery 1954–5*, p.33; O. ter Kuile, 'Daniel Mijtens', *Nederlands Kunsthistorisch Jaarboek*, vol.20, 1969, pp.1–106; Valerie Cumming, *A Visual History of Costume in the Seventeenth Century*, 1984, p.42, fig.34

KH

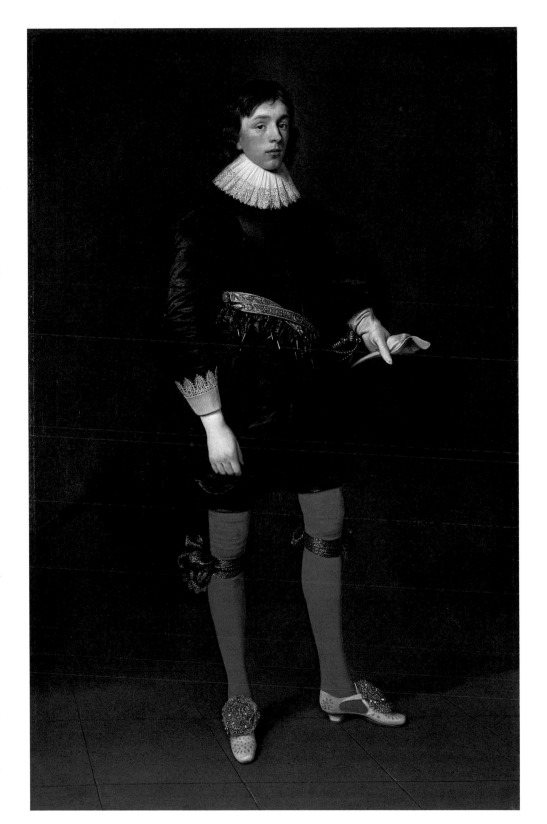

SIR NATHANIEL BACON
1585–1627

148 Cookmaid with Still Life of Vegetables and Fruit *c.*1620–5

Oil on canvas 151 × 246.7 (59½ × 97⅛)
PROV: …; sold Christie's 26 Oct. 1973
(104, as by Adriaen van Utrecht); …;
sold Christie's 9 July 1993 (9, as by
Nicholaes van Heussen), bt Mr Ronald
Lee by whom sold to the Tate Gallery
1995
*Tate Gallery, London. Purchased with
assistance from the National Art Collections
Fund 1995*

Modern still-life painting originated in the
Low Countries when such artists as Joachim
Beuckalaer and his pupil Pieter Aertsen
(*c.*1533–*c.*1573) combined a contemporary
foreground kitchen scene with a New Testament episode in a distant room beyond. For
this the story of Martha and Mary (Luke x,
38–42) was generally preferred. By the beginning of the seventeenth century these had
evolved into 'Cookmaid' and market scenes,
in which a lavish array of produce was displayed, attended by low-life figures.

The only English artist of this period
known to have painted such works was Sir
Nathaniel Bacon. Surviving letters indicate
that he travelled regularly to the Low Countries from his home in East Anglia. Late in
1613 he set off specifically for Antwerp, and
the content, though not the handling, of the
present work very much recalls the work of
the Antwerp artist Frans Snijders (1579–1657),
for instance, 'Still Life of Vegetables'
(Staatliche Kunsthalle, Karlsruhe).

An inventory of 1659 linked to the will
of Bacon's wife lists 'Ten great peeces in
wainscote of fish and fowle done by Sir Nath.
Bacon' (Herts County Record Office,
Gorhambury papers). It is presumed that a
'Cookmaid with Still Life of Birds' which is
still in the possession of the artist's descendants is one of these, as is a 'Cookmaid with
Still Life of Game', acquired by the family in
the 1950s, and evidently by the same hand.

The present recently rediscovered work is
perhaps a third survivor from this group as,
although each is of a different length, all are
59–60 inches high. Such a set might sometimes depict the produce of the four seasons,
or the twelve months of the year. The present
painting, however, combines vegetables and
fruit that would have matured at differing

times, though every item shown was grown in
England at this date (information from Royal
Horticultural Society, Wisley, 31 Aug. 1993). In
fact, a surviving letter dated 19 June [1626]
indicates that Sir Nathaniel himself was growing melons at Brome, the East Anglian estate
where he resided, and painted (*The Private
Correspondence of Jane Lady Cornwallis*, ed. Lord
Braybrooke, 1842, p.164). Other letters make
clear his interest in horticulture.

George Vertue particularly admired the
paintings he saw by Bacon, commenting in
1739 that 'many of his workes remain being
fruits flowers fowls &c'. He also noted 'two
large pictures at Redgrave Hall in Suffolke [a
Bacon estate]. by Nath Bacon. one Ceres with
fruit & flowers. the other Hercules & Hydra
overcom.' The whereabouts of these are now
unknown.

The resonance between the maid's cleavage
and the opened melon on the table to the left
is evident. In the Netherlands at least such
paintings often had erotic connotations, and
the gesture of a woman holding a fowl, seen
in the other two 'Cookmaids' attributed to
Bacon, was considered to have sexual implications.

Bacon's professional contemporaries
praised him as the inventor of a particular
type of 'pink', by which they meant yellow, a
colour used lavishly in the present work (see
no.149).

Although no English examples of this
genre other than Bacon's have survived, such
works were evidently prized by English collectors. By 1590 Lord Lumley had owned 'A
table of Cookerye' and 'A great table of a
Dutche woman selling of fruyte'. By 1616
Anne of Denmark, to whom Bacon's wife had
been a Lady of the Bedchamber, displayed in
the Garden Stone Gallery at Oatlands House
'A lesser picture of a gardener wth his sonne
& daughter selling in ye market mellons,
Cabbages, & other hearbes & fruite'
(Campbell 1985, pp.xxxiv–v).

KH

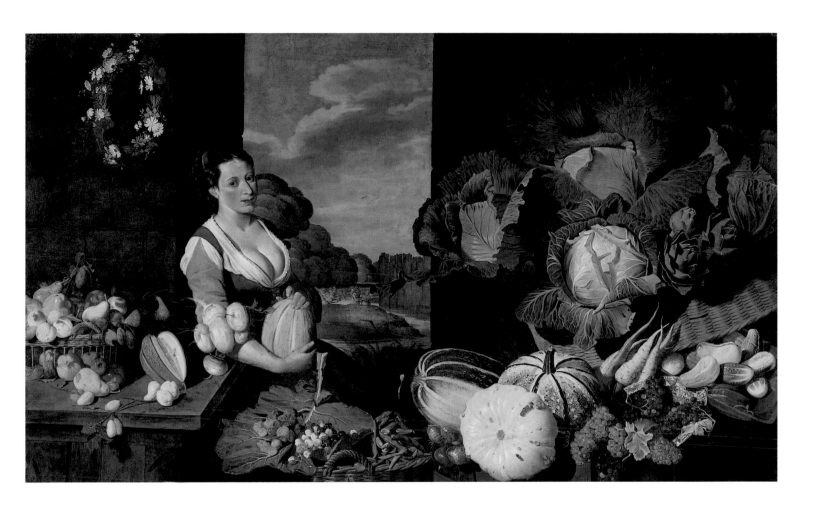

SIR NATHANIEL BACON

149 Self-Portrait *c.*1620

Oil on canvas 206.4 × 153.7
(81¼ × 60½)
PROV: By descent through the artist's
daughter, Anne
Private Collection

The Bacon dynasty was founded by the
artist's grandfather, Sir Nicholas, Lord Keeper
under Queen Elizabeth. Sir Nathaniel was a
kinsman of the politician and philosopher, Sir
Francis Bacon, and was appointed a Knight of
the Bath early in 1626.

In 1614, Nathaniel married Jane Meautys,
wealthy widow of Sir William Cornwallis of
Brome in Suffolk, and a Lady of the Bedchamber to James I's queen, Anne of Denmark. A half-length profile portrait, thought
to be his portrait of her has, like the present
work, remained in the possession of their
descendants. While his wife made regular visits to London, surviving correspondence suggests that Bacon largely remained in Suffolk
at Culford or at Brome, or made journeys to
the Low Countries.

Sir Oliver Millar has called Bacon 'the
most accomplished amateur painter of the
century' (Washington 1985). Fewer than a
dozen extant works can at present be attributed to him (see nos.114, 148). The reference
to 'Ten Great peeces' by him in the inventory
with his wife's 1659 will, and by George
Vertue to other named works now lost, attest,
however, to Bacon's artistic industry. He also
experimented with varnishes and pigments,
such as the 'Pinke' (that is, yellow) credited as
his invention by Edward Norgate (for the
recipe, see *Miniatura*, pp.69–70).

The present painting is Bacon's only
known full-length self-portrait, though a
handful of half-lengths also remain. Like his
other works it is extremely Netherlandish in
content, being for example close in spirit to a
smaller and slightly later work by the Amsterdam artist Thomas de Keyser, 'Constantijn
Huygens and his Secretary' 1627 (National
Gallery, London). De Keyser's English
brother-in-law, the sculptor Nicholas Stone,
had worked for the Bacon family.

On the wall above the table, along with a
shelf of antiquities, hang Bacon's two principal defining attributes: his sword, indicating
his gentlemanly status, and his painter's
palette with pigments set out upon it. A pair
of palettes as well as his family arms are also

to be found on his monument in Culford
church, made in 1628, the year after his early
death, probably from tuberculosis. Bacon
depicts himself holding a drawing, while on
the table lie a perspective diagram, writing
implements, and a beautifully composed still
life of books, the top one open to display a
map of northern Europe, including East
Anglia and the sea separating it from the Low
Countries. The framed painting of Minerva on
the wall is reminiscent of a Parmigianinesque
drawing by Peter Oliver (see no.89) in the
Ashmolean Museum, Oxford (acc. no.195).
Norgate records that Oliver thought so highly
of a version of Bacon's yellow pigment that
he 'used none other to his dyeing day'
(*Miniatura*, p.14)

There are few specific allusions in his own
surviving letters to Bacon's artistic activities,
apart from requests for 'coullers' to be sent
from London. His wife's close friend, Lucy
Harington, Countess of Bedford (see nos.87,
129), valued his artistic judgement and consulted him about the acquisition of paintings.
He seems also to have painted at least one
work for her as on 6 February [1614] he
wrote to his betrothed, who was staying with
Lady Bedford, 'tell her that the weather hath
bin very vnfauorable to the proceedinges of
her picture' (*Cornwallis Correspondence*, p.20).

EXH: *British Portraits*, RA 1956–7 (41); Tate Gallery
1972 (27); *The Treasure Houses of Britain*, National
Gallery of Art, Washington 1985 (65)
LIT: Vertue II, pp.15, 43; Whinney and Millar 1957,
pp.82–3; Waterhouse 1978, pp.65–6; N. King, *The
Grimstons of Gorhambury*, Southampton 1983, pp.158–9

KH

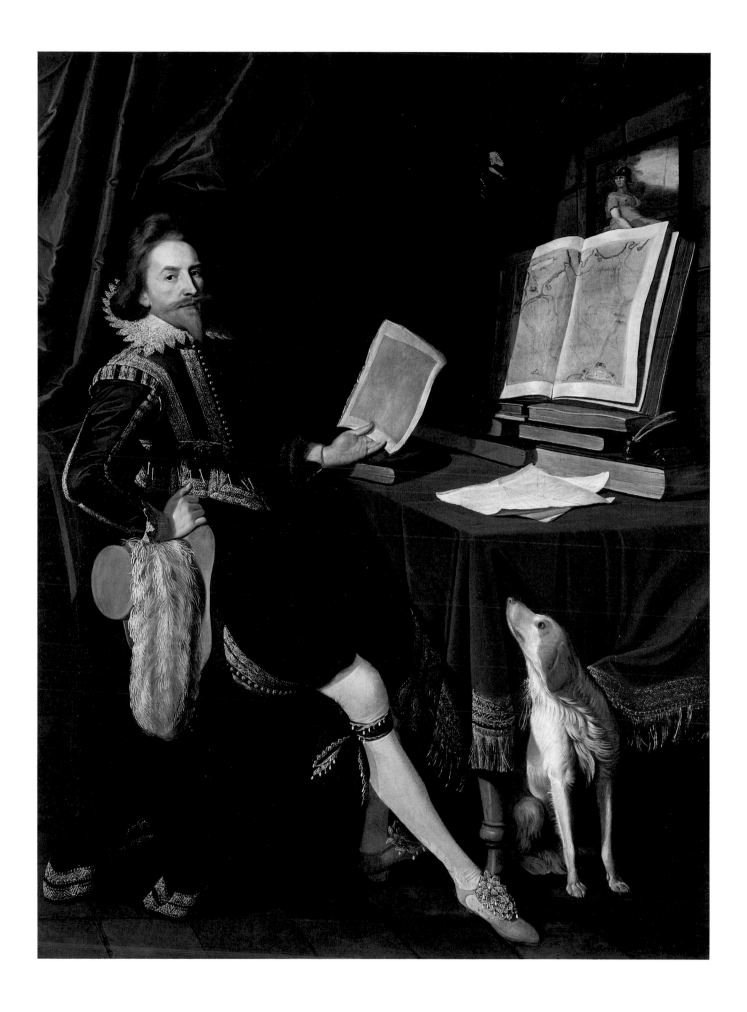

ATTRIBUTED TO JACOB VAN DOORDT died 1629

150 Charles I c.1624–5

Oil on canvas 219.2 × 136 (86¼ × 53½)
PROV: …; possibly the painting at York
House in 1635; …; possibly at Cobham
Hall by 1672, and by descent there; sale
of Cobham Hall pictures, Christie's 1
May 1925 (54), presumably bt in;
Sotheby's 23 July 1957 (368), where bt
by the lender
Her Majesty The Queen

This may have been painted very shortly
before Charles succeeded to the English
throne on 27 March 1625. The falling ruff is a
fashion of the early to mid-1620s. Millar
argues that the costume is very close to that
worn in Daniel Mytens's dated portraits of
Charles of 1624 now in Ottawa and Copenhagen (ter Kuile 1969, nos.22, 23). He also
points out that if Charles were already king,
this dramatically formal portrait would
include the regalia, rather than the plain dark
hat on the table. The features, on the other
hand, with their powerful but icy dignity,
seem older than the Prince's twenty-four
years.

A 1672 inventory of the contents of Cobham Hall, Kent, from whence this picture was
acquired in 1957, included a portrait of King
Charles I. Millar (1962, p.325) traces a convincing line of inheritance from that date
back to the Duchess of Buckingham, among
whose pictures at York House in 1635 was
'Abra: Dorts Bro: A Picture of King Charles at
length'. 'Abra: Dort' was clearly Abraham van
der Doort (died 1640), medallist and keeper
of Charles I's collections, of which he was to
compile an invaluable catalogue (Millar
1958–60). He had originally served Prince
Henry who, before his death, had promised
him the post of Keeper of his cabinet and
medals.

The brother referred to is thought to be
Jacob van Doordt, Doort, or Dort, who painted portraits in large and in miniature. Based
in Hamburg, he travelled extensively, working
for various northern courts, including in 1609
that of the Duke of Brunswick, whose wife
Elizabeth was the sister of James I's queen,
and of Christian IV of Denmark. A group of
attributed full-length portraits of the Duchess
and of her children Elizabeth, Dorothea,

Hedwig, Rudolf and ?Christian – cousins of
Prince Charles – are still in the British royal
collection, to which they were probably dispatched soon after completion.

By 1611 van Doordt was in Denmark,
where on 16 January 1612 he was paid for
three full-length portraits, of which only that
of 'Christian IV' himself survives (*Christian IV
and Europe*, no.151). In 1623 van Doordt signed
a portrait of Christian's wife Kirsten Munk
and her children (ibid., no.113). The following
year Christian IV wrote two letters in Latin to
James I and to Charles, recommending
'Jacobus de Dort'. The first, dated 3 July 1624,
describes him as a skilful painter of portraits,
the second, written from Copenhagen on 10
August, names van Doordt, 'a man of Hamburg', as the bearer of the letter (Millar 1962,
p.326). The present portrait was perhaps
painted soon after the letter was delivered,
and subsequently given to Buckingham.

While the international court full-length
formula, with looped-up curtains and the hat
resting on luxurious fabric on a table at the
side, was by now somewhat old-fashioned,
the artist has invested the Prince with an
unexpectedly dramatic elegance. Millar points
out that the portrait seems to have had a profound influence on England's principal court
painter at the time, Mytens, and on the expec-
tations of his patrons. Mytens adopts almost
the identical composition for his portrait of
Buckingham in a pale suit, dated 1626
(Euston Hall; ter Kuile 1969, no.11). Buckingham may by then, of course, already have
owned this portrait of Charles in black. Moreover, Mytens used a similar composition, with
something of the swagger, anchored by the
right hand pressed firmly on the stick, for his
own portraits of Charles as king, from 1627
(Turin; ter Kuile 1969, no.24) onwards.

It is not known how long van Doordt
stayed in England. He died in Stockholm in
1629.

EXH: *Christian IV and Europe*, Copenhagen 1988 (174)
LIT: Oliver Millar, 'Some Painters and Charles I',
Burlington Magazine, vol.104, 1962, pp.325–6; Millar
1963, no.113; O. ter Kuile, 'Daniel Mijtens', *Nederlands
Kunsthistorisch Jaarboek*, vol.20, 1969, pp.1–106; Steffen
Heiberg, 'Engelske Christian IV-portraetter', *Carlsberg-
fondets Årsskrift* 1986, Copenhagen, 1986, pp.97–8

KH

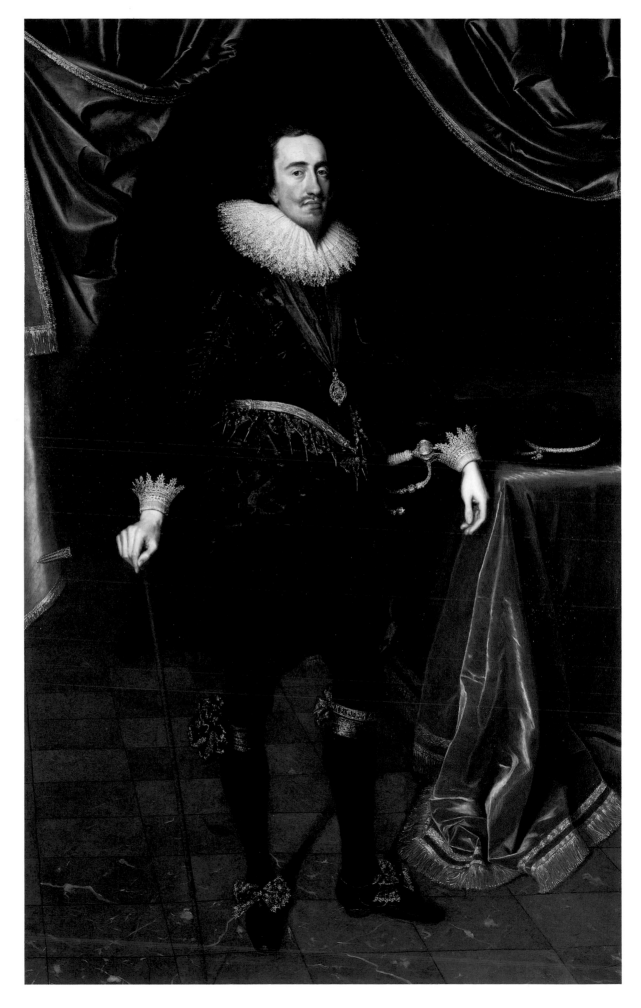

SIR PETER PAUL RUBENS
1577–1640

151 The Apotheosis of James I, Surrounded by Six other Sketches for the Ceiling Decoration of the Banqueting House 1629–30

Oil on panel 95 × 63.1 (37⅜ × 24⅞)
PROV: …; Nathaniel Bayly (= Thomas Trevor, afterwards Hampden, 2nd Viscount Hampden (1746–1824)), sale, Christie's, 31 May 1799 (102) bt in; thence by descent; on loan to the National Gallery from 1985
Private Collection on loan to the National Gallery, London

This complex sketch, executed by Rubens in grisaille and thus for his own reference, is the key to the development of the ceiling decoration of the Banqueting House. The building, all that remains of the Palace of Whitehall, consists of a vaulted semi-basement and the great assembly room above. Designed by the cultural demiurge of the early Stuart courts, Inigo Jones, and quickly erected c.1620, it was used for the performance of masques (until the decorations were in place), Order of the Garter ceremonies, and for the reception of ambassadors.

The fifteen or so years' hiatus between the first approach to Rubens about the ceiling in 1621 and the installation of the paintings was primarily due to Rubens taking his services elsewhere and to the collapse of Anglo–Spanish relations. Rubens, a stalwart for peace and officially involved for much of the troubled 1620s, was the Spanish King's emissary sent in 1629 to the Stuart court to arrange an exchange of ambassadors.

Rubens's sojourn in London in 1629–30 was propitious for his triumphant artistic career as difficulties were already in prospect over the Medicis' commission that had earlier diverted him. Although there is no external evidence, it was probably during this time, and presumably after the completion of his diplomatic brief, that it was at last agreed that he should execute the Banqueting House commission. Much had changed in the intervening years to make Jones's vision, as he subdivided the ceiling into nine compartments, no longer apposite.

King James I, whose continuing reign the ceiling was probably first intended to glorify, was dead. His son, in his first years as king had rejected his father's guiding principle, 'Beati Pacifici'. Now, having had peace forced upon him, Charles I determined that a memorial to celebrate his father's reign should be commissioned for the Banqueting House, thus acknowledging that his father was henceforth to be his exemplar in his conduct of foreign affairs.

By 1629 there already existed two written programmes for the ceiling. Both had proposed that the central oval should depict the dynastic achievement of James's reign: the Union of the Crowns of Scotland and England. In this sketch, Rubens rejected this idea and substituted the apotheosis of the King, borne up by Jupiter's eagle and assisted by Justice to be crowned by Minerva and Victory. Only to the left of James is Rubens's fluency halted, chiefly by the requirement to depict the Protestant King's spirituality. Rubens's ambivalence as a Catholic is betrayed by a mass of pentimenti.

Both programmes specified that this oval should be flanked by putti, animals and swags, to show, as one had it, 'the effects of publique union'. It had also proposed that triumphant Personifications of the King's public persona should occupy the corner ovals. Rubens depicts Liberality and Discipline triumphant over Avarice and Impudence, and below – upside down – Knowledge (Minerva) and Heroic Virtue (Hercules) vanquishing Ignorance and Envy.

Always economical with materials, Rubens here used a typical Antwerp panel – one on which he had sketched ideas, probably for the Medicis' commission that he was soon to abandon. These he partially wiped away, but traces are visible if the panel is turned on to its right side.

In order to use all the space available, he did not sketch the seven designs as they would be arranged in the ceiling. In fact he had insufficient room at top and bottom to elaborate the sequence of putti, etc., as friezes. If he had executed them in their predestined place, on either side of the central oval, he would not have had enough space for the Personifications which were to occupy the corners. Crucial to his vision of the whole ceiling is the depiction of the lower pair of Personifications upside down. Rubens had realised that, because of the proportions of the room, the canvases immediately above the spectator as he or she entered could only be viewed from the far end.

Much of Rubens's subsequent preparatory work has been lost, including, perhaps, grisaille sketches for the two other rectangular compositions that bestride the central oval – the Union and King James's 'Good Government' – and, certainly, the modello for the whole ceiling sent to Charles for his approval. Extant are thirteen coloured modelli, most produced for assistants to follow when working on the canvases; there must have been more.

James would have relished Rubens's introduction of Minerva – the goddess of wisdom – as the unifying presence in the programme. She appears here and as the King's inspiration in the Union and 'Good Government'. Thus Rubens by his sense of theatre and mastery of the lingua franca of allegory stamped his genius on the great project. In this elaborate working draft, we witness the first stage in what was to be Rubens's Baroque panegyric to James I and the expression of Charles I's revisionist foreign policy as King of Great Britain. Rubens was knighted by the art-loving King before his return to Antwerp.

EXH: *Art Treasures Centenary, European Old Masters*, City of Manchester Art Gallery 1957 (90); *Oil Sketches and Smaller Pictures by Sir Peter Paul Rubens*, Agnew's 1961 (27); Tate Gallery 1972 (39); *Rubens, Drawings and Sketches*, British Museum 1977 (179)
LIT: Oliver Millar, *Rubens: The Whitehall Ceiling*, Charlton Lecture, 1958; Julius S. Held, *The Oil Sketches of Peter Paul Rubens: A Critical Catalogue*, Princeton, 1980, I, pp.187–90, pp.199–201 no.133, pp. 217–18; Gregory Martin, 'The Banqueting House Ceiling – Two Newly Discovered Projects', *Apollo*, vol.139, 1994, pp.29–34; Gregory Martin, 'Rubens and King James I', *Shop Talk: Studies in Honor of Seymour Slive*, 1995 (forthcoming)

GM

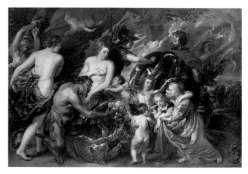

fig.60 Peter Paul Rubens, 'Peace and War' 1629–30, oil on canvas. *Trustees of the National Gallery, London* Rubens painted this political allegory in London and presented it to Charles I. Its theme sums up the purpose of his diplomatic mission there.

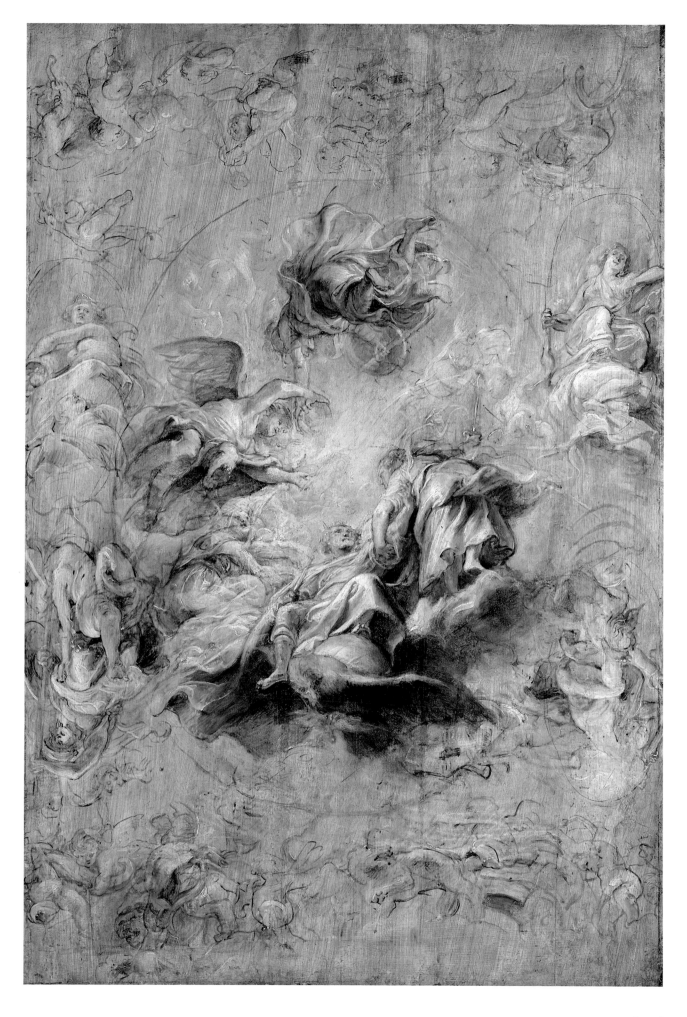

CORNELIUS JOHNSON
1593–1661

152 Thomas, 1st Baron Coventry
1631

Oil on canvas 124.5 × 100.3 (49 × 39½)
Inscribed 'LORD COVENTRY' left;
signed 'C.J. fecit | 1631.' right
PROV: ...; probably 1st Earl of Claren-
don (1609–1674); 4th Earl of Claren-
don, at Cornbury House, by 17 June
1722 (when noted in the Library,
Vertue, VI, p.6)
The Earl of Clarendon

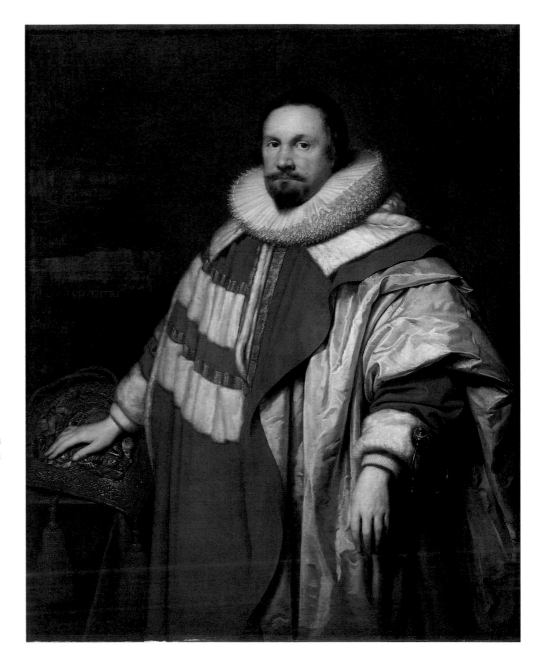

Coventry (1578–1640) had been appointed
Lord Keeper by Charles I in 1625, and is portrayed here in that role, in the parliamentary
robes of a baron. His right hand rests on the
bag containing the Great Seal. In April 1631,
the year of this painting, he presided as Lord
High Steward at the trial of Lord Audley.

Coventry evidently sat to Johnson a number of times and signed portraits of varying
dates survive. Johnson's earliest known three-
quarter-length is a signed portrait of Coventry, dated 1623; another is signed and dated
1627, with a signed replica dated 1629. A
half-length, signed and dated 1634, remains in
the possession of his descendant the Marquess
of Bath, and the National Portrait Gallery
owns another of Coventry with the Speaker's
mace; signed and dated 1639, the year before
his death. A three-quarter-length portrait of
Coventry's second wife, Elizabeth Aldersey,
facing to the left like the present portrait, is
known in two versions, of 1630 and 1631,
both signed by Johnson.

The present portrait is one of Johnson's
finest works and indicates his ability to convey private personality in a public image. It
predates Van Dyck's return to England the
following year, when the prolific Johnson was
at the height of his success. In 1631, Johnson
signed a full-length portrait of Charles I
(Duke of Devonshire, Chatsworth) which is
an exact version of Daniel Mytens's images of
Charles (e.g. that in the Metropolitan Museum, New York). In December 1632 Johnson
was appointed a picture maker to Charles I,
but the arrival of Van Dyck evidently had a
major impact on his patronage. In the early
1630s he retired to Bridge in Kent, where he
painted members of the principal local families. In 1643, after the outbreak of the Civil
War, he left England and continued his career
in the Netherlands.

Coventry, a staunch Protestant, was trained
as a lawyer. In March 1617 he was knighted
and appointed Solicitor General. In 1621 he
became Attorney General and in November
1625 Lord Keeper of the Great Seal. Created
Baron Coventry of Aylesborough, Worcs, in
1628 he seems to have had a contemporary
reputation for moderation and integrity. By
his two wives, he left ten children.

This picture was presumably purchased by
the first Lord Clarendon, who wrote that
Coventry 'knew the temper, disposition, and
genius of the kingdom most exactly ... He
had, in the plain way of speaking and delivery, without much ornament of elocution, a
strange power of making himself believed'
(*Dictionary of National Biography*, 1908, IV,
p.1286).

EXH: *National Portrait Exhibition*, 1866 (642)
LIT: Lady Theresa Lewis, *Lives of the Friends and Contemporaries of Lord Chancellor Clarendon ...* 1852, III,
no.44; A.J. Finberg, 'Chronological List of Portraits by
Cornelius Johnson', *Walpole Society*, vol.10, 1922, p.21,
no.52; Robin Gibson, *The Clarendon Collection*, 1977,
no.54

KH

ANGLO–DUTCH SCHOOL

153 London from Southwark

*c.*1630

Oil on panel 57.7 × 85.7 (22¾ × 33¾)
Inscribed: 'D^{F}B' is incised on the back
of the painting
PROV: Granville Leveson Gower (2nd
Earl Granville); Earl Granville's sale,
Christie's, 11 June 1892 (121); Colnaghi;
bt Samuel Montague, MP; presented to
Whitechapel Library Commissioners,
July 1892; Council of the Metropolitan
Borough of Stepney, 9 Nov. 1900
(powers transferred from Whitechapel
Library Commissioners in accordance
with London Government Act 1899);
London Borough of Tower Hamlets
(Globe Town Neighbourhood);
Christie's sale, 13 July 1991 (66), with-
drawn from sale; purchased from Tower
Hamlets by the Museum of London
with a grant from the MGC/V&A Pur-
chase Grant Fund, the Museum's acqui-
sitions and Trust funds and with private
donations
*Museum of London. Purchased with a Grant
from the MGC/V&A Purchase Grant
Fund*

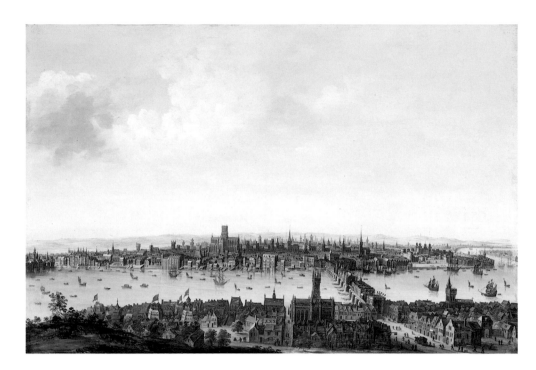

This is the earliest surviving oil painting with London as its sole subject. It shows the city in one breadth, from Whitehall to the Tower, without resorting to the sixteenth-century formula of 'running' the view in multi sections. For the first time, too, the city is set, jewel-like, in a huge sky: this departs from the traditional formula of the strip composition which concentrated on London's river banks and reduced sky and river to 'bands' of anec-dotal interest. This is also the last glimpse of London before the almost total destruction of the City in the Great Fire of 1666, and the last painted prototype showing the City and Westminster in a single image.

The meaning of the painting depends upon its place in the chronological framework of early views of London. Topographical detail should offer vital clues in this respect but this type of panoramic view is extremely complex and born from a tradition which involved more copying than direct observation. Irene Scouloudi's catalogue of panoramic views of London between 1600 and 1666 has made quite clear that out of 110 views of the capital produced between these dates only two rely on direct observation: the John Norden view prepared in 1600, and the 1647 prospect by Wenceslaus Hollar. Scouloudi's meticulous work on the topography of all these images

has uncovered a number of irreconcilable dis-crepancies based on the concurrent processes of copying and updating such views. The final assessment of this particular image led her to date the topography to around 1600.

The painting, on the other hand, was attributed to Claude de Jongh (see fig.54 on p.202) and tentatively dated 1627. However the existence of prints identical to the paint-ing and the unquestionable reliance of all these images on earlier published sources encouraged historians to consider printed images the more accurate representations. Moreover, the only secure date we have for this group of early views comes from the engraving by Matthew Merian found in J.L. Gottfried's 1638 German Atlas *Neue Cosmica Archontologia*. A few years later, the painting lost its attribution to Claude de Jongh and therefore its date, as a result of which its sta-tus plummeted: it was dated *c.*1650 and was assumed to be a copy of the Merian print (see *Image of London* 1987).

Also in the minds of historians and art his-torians, the painting was almost indistinguish-able from its sister version in the collection of the Duke of Devonshire; this was compound-ed by a cataloguing error which described both works as being on canvas whereas the painting under review is on Baltic oak. On this occasion, the support turned out to be of great significance for although the den-drochronological analysis (tree ring dating) of

the painting could not date the painting pre-cisely enough (1625–55), the following data was of great interest.

Board from Baltic countries was in pre-dominant use in northern Europe from 1300 to 1650. However, in the first half of the sev-enteenth-century, the Hanseatic League declined and with it the source of supply of Baltic oak entering England. This meant that there was a change in the type of oak used for panels; concurrently panel painting was also superseded by painting on canvas.

Another feature of this panel is the fact that it bears a panelmaker's inscription on the back. As a result of the work of Belgian researchers on Flemish panelmakers, the inscription 'D^{F}B' was identified as being the mark of Franchois De Bout from Antwerp. Franchois I was the son of Flips Debout, a panel maker who died in 1625. The data, however, is tentative and this attribution as well as his period of work have had to be deduced. The dates ascribed to his career (1637–1643 or 4) seem too late in the case of this painting, which on technical grounds is very close to another work on panel in the collection of the Museum of London, 'A View of Greenwich', securely dated to the 1620s on costume and topographical grounds. Both paintings share the same way of texturing the ground and preparing the panel with under-drawing.

It is not known whether the work was

painted in London using imported materials or painted in Antwerp using preparatory drawings: its early history is a mystery. However the presence of pentimenti is of interest: the repositioning of a tower on London Bridge (across from Nonsuch House) or of the church tower of St Lawrence Pountney on the north bank shows that correctness mattered more than a seemingly realistic appearance.

Much has been made of the 'mistake' the painting contains and which is common to all images in the Merian category: the depiction beyond the Tower of London of a non-existent river bend. The usual explanation is that a dock was misread as a river bend in a reprint of Visscher's 1616 panoramic view of London. The reprint is undated but was assumed to date from *c*.1620. However, this unexpected bend could have originated with the present work and be the result of the compression of the view for the small format of the painting. Panoramas of London taken from the south required artists to work from the only height available to them: the tower of the church of St Mary Overy, later to become Southwark Cathedral. As the artist has found a way of moving Whitehall from behind his back to the front of the painting on the left, similarly he could have brought closer in, next to the Tower, the river bend which lies further east between Wapping and the Isle of Dogs. These are important clues about the manufacture of a small-format image, the impact of which was such that it affected all subsequent views of London.

The links between the images in the Merian group have been discussed in some detail (Galinou 1994) and have shown that all derive from a single prototype. For reasons of technique, support and also format, the painting under review is very likely to have come first. The ground-breaking devices of giving the city a sky and of compressing the view into a single image belong to the realm of painters, not printmakers: cityscape painting was born in London.

EXH: *The Image of London: Views by Travellers and Emigrés 1550–1920*, Barbican Art Gallery 1987, pp.16–17, 109

LIT: Irene Scouloudi, *Panoramic Views of London 1600–1666*, 1953; three unpublished reports commissioned or supervised by the Museum of London: Nick Eastaugh, 'The Museum of London Project on 17th century Topographical and other Paintings on Panel', 1992; Ian Tyers's Dendrochronology Reports (DEN02/92 & REP03/91); Louisa Goldsmith, 'Topographical Painting in 17th Century London', Courtauld Institute 1993; Valerie Cumming, 'Some Observations on a Recent Acquisition', *International Journal of Cultural Property*, vol.2, 1993; Mireille Galinou, 'Acquisition in Focus' *Apollo*, vol.140, 1994; Mireille Galinou, 'Acquisition and Analysis', *Interdisciplinary Science Reviews*, April 1995; Mireille Galinou and John Hayes, *London in Paint*, Museum of London (forthcoming 1996)

MG

The Methods and Materials of Three Tudor Artists: Bettes, Hilliard and Ketel

Rica Jones

The broad European context in which sixteenth-century court oil painting flourished has yet to be reflected in the number of published technical studies. There are so few of them that anyone embarking on the subject must respect above all the need for fact before theories. But, if the caveats attending interpretation are many, it remains that there can hardly be a period more in need of detailed information on technique. This distant age is short on documentary sources. In his great, pioneering survey of Tudor and Jacobean painting, *The English Icon*,[1] Roy Strong lists 358 paintings, of which only about seventy are either signed or securely documented to an artist. In the analysis of style there is no substitute for a pair of keen eyes; but, with such a scarcity of documentary evidence to reinforce the results, the microscope can be put to good use, particularly in gaining access to the complex underlayers of paint, never meant to be seen as discrete elements with the naked eye but nonetheless essential to the final image. There are other problems to solve; all paintings alter naturally with age but over four hundred years these highly wrought images have suffered more than average change, not least from the harsh methods of cleaning sometimes used in the past. With or without this complication, we are often far removed from the subtleties of the artist's original effects and intent.

In this study, then, the work of three Tudor artists has been examined and analysed in detail for clues to its original production and appearance. Stylistically these painters are very different: Bettes was clearly associated with Holbein; Hilliard in the mind's eye embodies the very essence of iconic Elizabethan portraiture; and finally Ketel represents a northern Continental strain different again from either. The section on each painter has been written up under the sub-headings: support, ground, underdrawing and paint, followed in all three by a discussion of the results. Of more general conclusions as yet there can be none. One hopes this exhibition might promote more technical study of this particular phase of northern European art.

John Bettes, 'An Unknown Man in a Black Cap' (no.10)

The Support and Ground

The basic structure of the panel has been described in the catalogue entry (no.10). There has been no significant disjoining or splitting. Some of the background paint on the attached piece is reticulated in a way that suggests excessive heat. Fire then might be the reason for the reduction in size; attack by woodworm is another possibility.

The gesso ground is composed of natural chalk (calcium carbonate) with a small amount of gypsum (calcium sulphate) mixed up and bound together in animal glue size. It was applied evenly all over the front of the panel and has a smooth surface with just a trace of diagonal marking from the brush or spatula (fig.ii). There does not appear to be an isolating layer of oil or glue size on top of it, which might have been applied to make the ground less absorbent.

Underdrawing

There is a fine outline drawing of the face, done in what looks like graphite directly onto the white ground or onto the pink underlayer described below. It has the appearance of a sure hand working freely rather than using a cartoon for transfer.[2] These lines describe the contours of the features; there is no attempt at shading. Although more apparent now than they would have been at first (oil paint becoming more transparent with time),

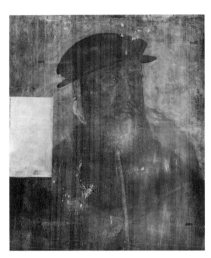

fig.i X-radiograph of 'An Unknown Man in a Black Cap'. Note the horizontal dowels in each joint. They were inserted during the manufacture of the panel. The white oblong is caused by the signature section on the back.

their presence beneath the visible pink flesh-paint would always have helped establish the structure of the face. A dark line or mark beneath a thin layer of lighter paint will lose its own character and read simply as a cool, pearly tone of the overlying colour. An example here is the bluish line marking the receding angle between the nose, brow and eye-socket; it is created almost entirely by dark strokes of underdrawing showing through the

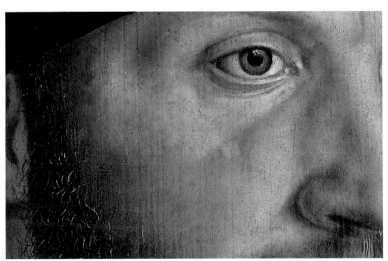

fig.ii Detail of face between nose and ear, in normal light

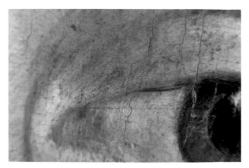

fig.iii His left eye photographed through the microscope at ×7 magnification, showing lines of underdrawing showing through the paint and particles of vermilion mixed in the 'white' of the eye

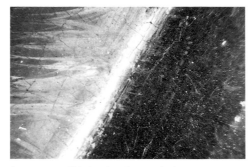

fig.iv Centre of black jacket photographed at ×10 magnification, showing the red underpainting

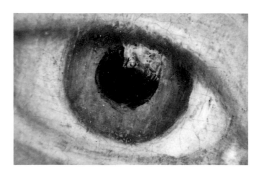

fig.vi His right eye photographed at ×7 magnification

paint (fig.iii). Probably the graphite drawing extended to the whole figure, but it is no longer visible beneath the thick paint.

Paint Layers

For the first stage of painting the artist took the pigments vermilion, red lead, white lead, ivory black and azurite,[3] and with linseed oil mixed up a pinkish red colour or colours. This was either a coloured priming to modify and seal the white ground layer or a broadly modelled monochrome underpainting with which to establish the bulky structure of the figure against the background. With the stereo-microscope it is visible beneath the background, hat, black coat and brown fur (fig.iv), but whether it extended to the face is not known. It was certainly leanly bound in linseed oil and, although basically opaque, used thinly to gain the benefit of the reflective white ground. It was allowed to dry before the artist resumed painting. From this point onward, however, the structure varies considerably from area to area, and, as it is impossible to know the relative sequence of all the subsequent layers, each part of the design will be described separately from start to finish. The binding-medium appears to have been linseed oil throughout. Analysis of the black jerkin and of all the separate layers in the background revealed pure linseed oil, that is not pre-treated in any way to make it thicker.[4]

The jerkin and hat are composed of two colours, near-black and dark grey, mixed up on the palette from ivory black and white lead and worked together wet-in-wet on the painting. There is no evidence of brushwork here, perhaps the better to point up the fur collar. Here red, yellow and brown ochres were mixed with white lead and applied wet-in-wet with broad, streaky strokes, becoming most expressive (and most unusual for the time) on his right shoulder (fig.v).

The face and beard were worked up from dark to light, starting with the shape of the beard and the shaded side of the face from his right eye to the ear. In these areas the structure of the face was blocked in with very thin, opaque, reddish-brown tones, inclining to gingery at the moustache and front of the beard. The main pink flesh colours are composed of white lead mixed on the palette with varying amounts of vermilion and black. These opaque tones were then applied thinly, wet-in-wet to the reserve left for the front of the face and drawn very lightly over the boundary of the previously shaded areas. On top of the pink tones, the

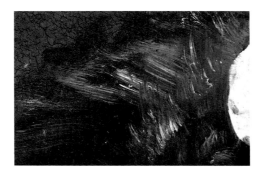

fig.v Detail of brushwork in fur collar and discoloured smalt in background

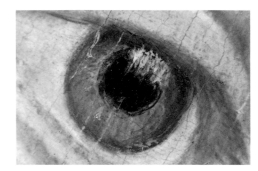

fig.vii His left eye photographed at ×7 magnification

highlights of the face were intensified with a very light flesh colour and some of the lines around the eyes were darkened with light brown. The shadows at the temple were mixed from white lead, lake, azurite, vermilion, black and yellow ochre. This bluish, opaque paint was applied on top of the flesh tone at the temple and over the shadowed area towards the ear, making a subtle tonal link with the bluish lines caused by the underdrawing around the nose (fig.ii). The eyes have some distinctive technical features, the principal being the use of a flesh tone, white lead mixed with vermilion, for the 'white' of the further eye (fig.iii). The irises were also painted in a darkish flesh tone before the greyish-greens of the visible layer were sketched in with a fine brush (fig.vi). Highlights of white lead were added to the black pupils with quick, overlapping strokes and scratches (figs.vi, vii). All this lively, minutely scaled brushwork, surrounded as it is by smoothly applied flesh tones, combines with the superb draughtsmanship to create the intense power of this gaze. The beard was darkened with shades of brown before the wiry hair was rendered with wavy strokes of paint made principally from the pigment, lead-tin yellow (fig.viii). This bulky pigment was used to make a flowing paint, which, when applied with a fine brush, would retain the brushstroke exactly (fig.ix).

The background, after the red underpainting had dried, was covered with a layer of bluish-grey paint, mixed up from white lead, azurite, chalk, black and yellow ochre. Although opaque in itself, it was applied streakily so that the red underlayer would warm it slightly. When this greyish layer was dry, the whole background was given two thick coats of the blue pigment, smalt, with oil (figs.x–xiv). Smalt is a translucent, glassy pigment, similar to the blue of stained-glass windows.

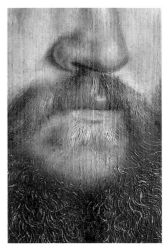

fig.viii Detail of face and beard in slightly raking light to show varied surface textures. Also shows underdrawing around nose

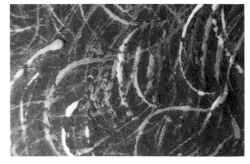

fig.ix The beard photographed in slightly raking light at ×7 magnification to show strokes of lead-tin yellow mixtures

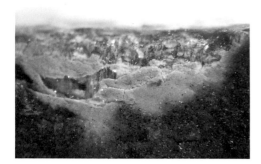

fig.x Tiny paint loss in the background at the top edge, photographed at ×20 magnification, to show grey under-painting beneath the smalt and, just visible beneath that, red underlayer and white ground

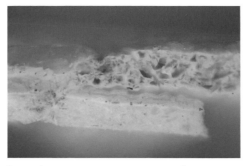

fig.xii The same cross-section at ×250 magnification in ultra-violet light, showing the smalt more clearly

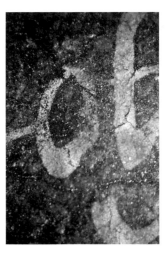

fig.xv Detail ('oh' of Johan) of original signature photographed at ×20 magnification. Note the splaying of the horizontal stroke crossing the upright gold line. Patchy quality is due to discoloured smalt on top of the gold

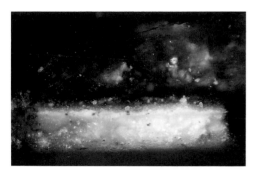

fig.xi Cross-section of paint from the background, photographed in polarised light at ×250 magnification. From the bottom: white ground; red underlayer; grey underlayer and, shearing away from the rest, a thick layer of discoloured smalt

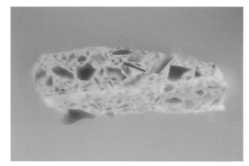

fig.xiii Cross-section from background at ×250 magnification in ultra-violet light, showing the two layers of smalt

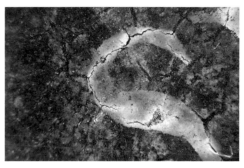

fig.xvi 'S' of Su[ae] to the right of the figure, photographed at ×10 magnification. Smalt on top of gold, mostly discoloured

Although it can be striking when first applied, it rarely lasts intact in an oil binder, becoming dis-coloured and unattractive as we see here. There are no green, brown or yellow pigments in this back-ground; these colours are the progressive effects of decaying smalt and the yellow is mainly aged oil, the smalt in these areas being largely transparent now. The discolouration of this pigment in oil is a very complex process involving changes in the chemistry and optical properties of the whole paint film.[5] Light is a triggering factor and this can be seen in no.10, where the original top edge, always shielded by the frame, has discoloured much less than the rest. From seventeenth-century manuals of painting we know that, because of these deficien-cies and also being a tricky pigment to handle as a paint, smalt was sometimes applied by a method known as strewing. Drying oil was painted over the relevant area; then, while this was tacky, loose smalt was sifted over its surface, sticking to the oil layer but not being engulfed by it. Though the opaque layer so produced was more reliable than the translucent film of smalt mixed as a paint, it is still inclined to discolour. We therefore cannot know for sure which method or methods were used here, though the treatment of the gilded inscriptions, which is described below, suggests that at least the second layer and probably both were applied as paint.

Both signatures are in gold against the smalt background but the methods of gilding are differ-ent. Microscopic examination of the signatures in comparison with the inscriptions on the front sug-gests that the lower signature is the earlier. This lower signature is either in gold leaf or gold paint.

fig.xiv A reconstruction of the blue background, using the same layered structure and similar materials, made in 1995 by Angela Geary

If the former it would have been applied using a mordant or gold size, a thin tacky substance laid onto the dried substrate and then covered with gold leaf. If the latter, gold would have been reduced to a powder by various means, mixed with a suitable binding-medium and used as an ink.[6] What might be the marks of a splayed nib are vis-ible on figure xv. A most striking feature is that once the gold had set it was painted over with a layer of smalt in oil, probably the second of the two layers present on the background. This layer is still visible here and there, though mostly dis-coloured to the point of transparency. The same is

true of the inscription on the front. Done in gold leaf applied to the background with a mordant, it was then painted over with the smalt mixture,[7] giv-ing glittery, bluish-green writing in keeping with the resplendent blue surrounding it. The smalt is just visible now as a transparent or slightly brown film (fig.xvi). Most of the light penetrating this layer on top of the gold would have been reflected straight back again, resulting in a very high rate of degradation, which, as noted above, goes through sludgy green, brown and yellow before becoming translucent. This progression, in conjunction with the presence of discoloured varnish layers, is almost certainly the reason why the other signature exists: the original was simply becoming illegible. And similarly a duplicate inscription was once made on the front, using the method of gilding employed for the upper signature. This time the mordant was a thick, creamy-orange coloured oil paint, painted onto the background and then gild-ed with leaf (fig.xvii). There are no traces of smalt on top of it. At some point in the past the dupli-cate inscription was cleaned off the front but not before it had had time to leave its own peculiar mark on the background. The letters 'DNI' fol-lowed by a repetition of the date, now very faint, can just be seen in patchy dark green below the gilded inscription on the left of the figure (fig.xviii). With the microscope traces of the creamy-orange mordant are visible within these green letters. This is the remains of the duplicate

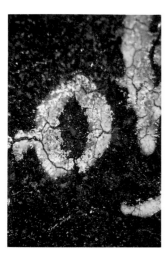

fig.xvii Detail ('oh' of Johan) of later signature, showing orange-coloured mordant with remains of gold leaf. Photographed at ×20 magnification

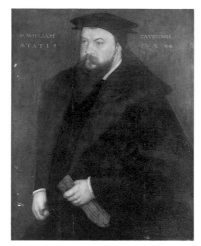

fig.xix John Bettes, 'Sir William Cavendish' c.1545, oil on panel. *The Trustees of the Chatsworth Settlement on loan to the National Trust, Hardwick Hall*

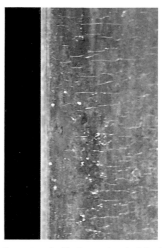

fig.xx Detail of background at the left edge showing, from left to right: red underlayer; greeny-blue azurite; discoloured smalt on top

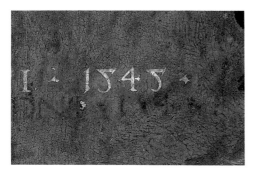

fig.xviii Detail of inscription to the left of the figure, showing the discoloured 'ghost' inscription below the original

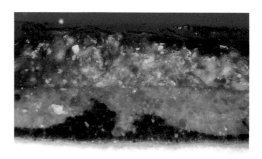

fig.xxi Cross-section through the background at the top right corner, photographed in polarised light at ×400 magnification. From bottom: part of the white ground; unpigmented oil layer; red underlayer; dark grey opaque layer; two applications of azurite with a few red particles; smalt mixed with white lead; (barely distinct) varnish and overpaint

he would learn the results of superimposing different colours and also how to optimise the physical characteristics of each pigment. Once apprised of the basic principles, the painter could then select and develop them as suited himself.

How then do the techniques used in this painting compare with those in works attributed to Bettes and also with pictures by Holbein, often cited as his master? The 'Portrait of Sir William Cavendish' (Hardwick Hall[9]) (fig.xix) and the 'Portrait of Sir William Butts' (Museum of Fine Arts, Boston)[10] have both been given to Bettes on stylistic grounds.[11] The Cavendish painting is partially obscured by discoloured varnish and patchy glazes of later repainting but, taking this into account, its background is a dull brownish green (fig.xx). Originally, as revealed in a cross-section taken at the top right corner, it was bright, probably opaque blue. This was achieved with two layers of azurite mixed with white lead and some red ochre followed by a layer of smalt mixed with white lead (fig.xxi). At the site of the sample these layers lie on top of streakily applied dark grey, but examination at the left edge suggests this was not continuous. Beneath this is an unbroken layer of pinkish-red, mixed from chalk, vermilion, black, yellow ochre and white lead. This red paint is present also beneath the hat, black coat and gloves, but it is not clear whether it occurs also beneath the face. It certainly goes under the cuff and edges of the hand holding the glove. It is separated from the white ground beneath it (chalk in animal glue) by an unpigmented priming of drying oil, as noted altogether absent in the Tate picture. Similar, though, is the 'white' of Sir William's right eye (the farther away from us), which has visible particles of vermilion mixed with the white lead. The techniques used in the irises and pupils look similar too, though here the highlight is on the iris, in keeping with the different angle of the head. Unfortunately the discoloured varnish obscures the detection of underdrawing beneath the flesh tones. The beard has none of the crisp, wavy strokes of lead-tin yellow found in the Tate picture; instead it is painted wet-in-wet with very smooth descriptive brushstrokes.

The bluish-green background of 'Sir William Butts' in Boston is composed of three successive

inscription, now only a shadow in the smalt it protected for a while from damage by light. The initial 'A' of 'AETATIS' is sometimes just visible in the equivalent position on the right.

The essential function of applying different colours in layers was to exploit the full optical properties of pigments which are never truly opaque when painted in thinnish films. It was a means of obtaining a wide range of colours with a fairly limited palette and without the overall deadening of tone that results when many different pigments are mixed up together and applied in a single thickness. Translucent pigments bound in an excess of oil (a glaze) and applied on top of an opaque colour will brighten or darken but always enrich its tone. Less obviously, perhaps, an apparently opaque colour, such as one mixed with white lead, can be modified by a different opaque colour lying beneath it. This depends on the same principle as that described for the underdrawing. Called the 'turbid medium effect', it is based on the fact that the same colour will appear warmer when painted over a lighter tone and cooler when laid over a darker one. So the red undermodelling, found here as beneath so many other black draperies of the period, warms up its sombre tone and gives a sense of depth without preventing our reading it as august black. With this method of painting, therefore, the painter had at his disposal the means of creating superb tonal effects: pearly whites and half-tones, glowing colours and enriched blacks.[8] To make the most of this facility he would have needed good training, during which

layers of colour on top of a white ground made of chalk in animal glue. The first is a pink underpainting or priming composed of white lead mixed with vermilion. Next comes an opaque dark grey (white lead and carbon black) and the final layer (or at least the final extant layer, the painting having suffered much damage in the past) is blue composed of smalt mixed with white lead. Fine linear underdrawing is visible through the flesh tones of the face and hands and the 'white' of the eyes is composed of white lead and vermilion.

Holbein's 'Lady with a Squirrel and a Starling' (no.4)[12] and the 'Edward, Prince of Wales' (no.6)[13] have been examined for technique at their respective galleries. The Lady's blue background is made up of two layers of azurite mixed with white lead (in oil) and applied on top of the white ground. This is chalk in animal glue and it is isolated from the paint layers by a priming of unpigmented oil. Prince Edward's blue background is different again. Here smalt was applied in oil on top of a salmon-pink priming painted directly onto the white ground. It would have been purplish-blue originally; now it has faded to grey. The underdrawing of the face was done on top of the salmon-pink layer, probably with a brush. The Lady's underdrawing, also probably in paint or ink, was done directly on top of the white ground.

So in just five paintings we have a wide variety

of techniques. Every blue background is different and we know that close followers of Holbein produced yet more, including the use of the blue pigment indigo.[14] Further studies will only add to the range. Holbein's technique generally appears to be full of variety, too much so for a comparison with three paintings by Bettes to have much significance, particularly when we know so little about contemporary practices at home and abroad. In assessing Bettes himself, however, we are on surer ground, as these three works from the 1540s display more similarities than differences. On a white chalk ground he laid on a pinkish red underlayer in which the principal colouring pigment is vermilion, from the particle sizes almost certainly derived from the naturally occurring mineral, cinnabar, rather than from its manufactured equivalent. This same pigment is the main colour in the pink fleshtones and it occurs also in the 'whites' of the eyes, this latter a most unusual feature. The backgrounds, though varied in construction, share an opaque, grey-toned interlayer between the red underpainting and the main layers of colour. In the Tate and Boston paintings this layer is continuous; in the Cavendish portrait it occurs patchily. Finally, we have smalt as the principal blue, though used differently in each. In the Tate painting he was almost certainly exploiting its translucent qualities to give a thick, dark, glassy surface which must have made a rich complement to the smooth, rubicund face. Its use over gold leaf is so far unprecedented, though an intriguing reference, 'How thow shalt laye thy Azure or byse upon thy goldc letters',[15] in the notebook of John Guillim, a sixteenth-century heraldic painter, suggests that in that branch of painting at least it was a known device. Whether it also provides us with a clue to Bettes's origins is debatable. In the Cavendish portrait the original effect is harder to envisage. It is traditional to underpaint azurite (found in the penultimate layer) with red or pink to reduce its greenish hue, and here it is also mixed with reds to enhance this effect. Presumably it made a substantial undertone to the opaque layer of smalt on top. In the Boston painting the smalt is also opaque.

Clearly the artist set store by this pigment which in the centuries since then has acquired an unfortunate mythology. Smalt was much used in seventeenth-century painting, despite its impermanence in oil which was by then well known. Inexpensive compared to ultramarine and azurite, it has become labelled as a poor substitute: cheap and inferior. With this in mind how might we then interpret its presence in Bettes's backgrounds? The answer is that according to the evidence from the time, we are not justified in attaching any mythology to it. Until the end of the sixteenth century we do not know what anybody thought about it. Haydocke in his translation of Lomazzo's treatise on painting (1584), published in England in 1598, lists smalt with ultramarine and azurite as the blues used in oil-painting.[16] The first reference with comments is by Nicholas Hilliard in *A Treatise Concerning the Arte of Limning* of about 1600. Discussing the pigments suitable for miniature-painting he says: 'For limning, the darkest and highest blue is Ultramarine of Venice. Of the best I have paid three shillings and eightpence a carat, which is but four grains – eleven pounds ten shillings the ounce; and the worst, which is but bad, will cost

two shillings and sixpence the carat – seven pounds ten shillings the ounce. Instead whereof we use smalt, of the best; blue bices [azurite] of divers sorts …'[17] So when even the limners found ultramarine too expensive for their background blue, we might not wonder at its absence from most blue backgrounds in oil. Some evaluation of its cost can be made by referring to Ketel's prices in the 1570s of £5 for a full-length painting and £1 each for portrait heads, such as those exhibited here (nos.58–60).[18] Comparing it to the scanty available data on contemporary wages, in the 1590s an agricultural bailiff could expect to earn about £2 a year and a labourer £1 6s 8d.[19] Although we know there was inflation in the second half of the sixteenth century, there is no reason to suppose that comparative prices from the earlier decades differed significantly. Throughout this century ultramarine was mined in Afghanistan and brought via the silk routes to Venice, whence it was distributed to Europe, and the complex methods needed to extract the pigment from the mineral did not alter.[20] This blue then, the most prized by painters for its intrinsic qualities as a pigment, was in the luxury goods class and in large quantities must have been way beyond the price range of most artists and sitters. The ultramarine background in Holbein's 'Henry VIII' (see no.8, fig.23)[21] represents truly princely wealth and when we find the same artist using smalt for the background of 'Edward, Prince of Wales' (no.6), painted as a New Year's gift to the boy's father, it is not the lack of ultramarine we should question but rather what is the significance of this particular alternative?

Azurite and indigo are both greenish blues, no good for making bright blues of a purplish cast which is one of the factors for which ultramarine was valued by painters. The best grades of smalt had the required purplish hue and this is the most likely reason for its use in this period (particularly for 'Edward, Prince of Wales', muted purple tones being consistent with the dynastic pose and costume). How far painters like Bettes and Holbein were aware of its long-term deficiencies is hard to say. The early history of smalt is obscure. To date the earliest known use of the pigment is in gluetempera on Dieric Bouts's 'Entombment' (National Gallery, London) of about 1455.[22] Bound in oil it has so far been found on only one painting significantly earlier than those described here, Michael Pacher's 'Early Fathers' altarpiece in Munich, painted about 1483, and a Parmigianino altarpiece, also in Munich, which cannot date after 1540. By the mid-sixteenth century it was in use both north and south of the Alps, having been analysed on paintings by Bruegel the Elder, and several Venetian artists. We do not know how long it takes to discolour significantly but, even if it had happened within a few decades, there is no certainty that the knowledge would have been widespread by the time Holbein and Bettes were using it. So, pending further studies, we might be wise to withhold the traditional twentieth-century view of smalt and concentrate instead on its positive qualities. Accessibly priced, richly toned, good for opaque and translucent work in large areas, it might have been a most exciting addition to the palette of any painter who, like Bettes, was sensitive to all the intrinsic qualities of paint and keen to push them to splendid and very personal effect.

Attributed to Nicholas Hilliard, 'Elizabeth I' (no.34)[23]

Support and Ground

The support is an oak panel composed of three vertical boards, the central wider than the laterals. The butt-joints, which have split apart in the past, are now reglued and reinforced with oak buttons, replacing earlier battens. There has been various subsidiary splitting, the most serious being down the middle of the central board from the top edge to the neckline (fig.xxii). Like the joints the old splitting has been rejoined and reinforced on the back. Exposed woodworm channels in the back of the central board indicate that the panel has been planed down.

The ground is composed of two layers, the first a thick application of chalk bound in animal glue size,[24] the second a very thin priming of white lead in drying oil. Apart from the losses associated with splitting in the support, it is in excellent condition.

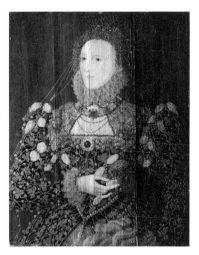

fig.xxii Queen Elizabeth I in raking light to show structure and damage in the panel

Underdrawing

The artist began work with an outline drawing of the contours of the face, the eyes, nose and mouth, done in black crayon or graphite directly onto the white priming. Then he changed his mind, adjusting the features upwards and narrowing the face (fig.xxiii). This pentimento is clear in infrared examination and may also be discerned with the naked eye. Very heavy outline drawing is present also in the hands, where the black lines showing through the flesh tones help create the structure of the fingers and knuckles. Done more delicately it exists also in both necklaces, where every element is outlined (fig.xxiii). Some of these lines were left deliberately unpainted to help describe the structure. The priming was also left unpainted here and there to create a different sort of white from that used for the large pearls (fig.xxiv). Now, with the darkening of this layer and in the presence of a discoloured varnish, these little elements look orangey-brown (fig.xxv). No other drawing is visible in the picture but the paint is very dense and, as will be seen, the methods of painting the intricate patterning on the dress were quite different from those used for the jewellery.

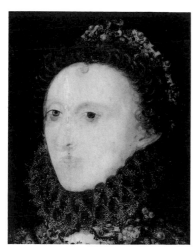

fig.xxiii Infrared detail of Elizabeth's face, showing pentimento drawing

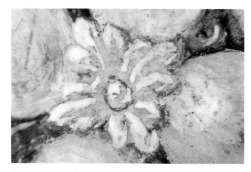

fig.xxv Detail, photographed at ×7 magnification, of the four pearls on the right of fig.xxiv. Underdrawing visible, also unpainted ground in centre, now looking orangey brown. Strokes of lead-tin yellow in central motif

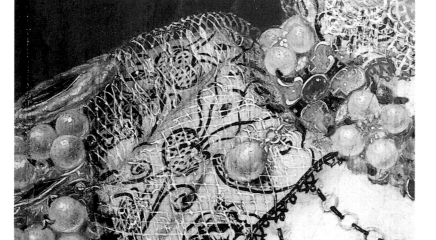

fig.xxiv Detail of her right shoulder

Paint Layers

As with Bettes, each part of the design will be described separately from start to finish, regardless of how the artist might have sequenced his work.

Damaged by the splitting of the central board and possibly also by overcleaning and fading, the face is the least well preserved area of the picture. Although the lineaments and basic field of colour are the artist's own, we are not in a position to assess what the original finish might have been, for apart from the yellowed varnish there are two types of overpainting on the face: opaque and translucent. The first, applied to disguise the pentimento and the damages caused mainly by the split, is fairly precisely located and therefore not too much of a problem. It is the translucent glazing in the eye sockets, at the end of the nose, in the lips and all along the chinline[25] which obscures the original construction in these areas. Clearly this painter favoured a linear definition rather than shadows. This is evident from the eyes (fig.xxvi) and the long line of the nose, which is formed only by underdrawing showing through the paint and probably never consisted of more, 'for the line without shadow showeth all to good judgement; but the shadow without line showeth nothing'.[26] What we cannot know is how much modelling there might have been in the areas where later glazing exists, and also whether colouring might have been lost from the flesh tone (or 'carnation'[27] as the painter would have described it). Scanning the surface with a microscope we can detect a few particles of vermilion and lake in the white lead matrix. Their distribution looks about even but it is possible that there has been fading of the lake, which one would expect to be the pigment used for pink cheeks, if they had ever existed.[28]

We cannot tell what sort of preparatory drawing was done for the black dress but it is clear that the whole thing was painted dead black first of all. The pigment is lamp black and the binder is a drying oil combined with a natural resin. Then the lines of the lattice and the overall shape of each leaf appear to have been painted in very lightly before the thick strokes representing each stitch in the embroidery were applied. Figures xxvii and xxviii show respectively a detail of the embroidery

from the bottom edge and a cross-section from the same site. Here, where the paint has been protected from light by the frame, we see the original colours, now faded elsewhere to neutral whites. The body and outline stitching of each leaf were in soft orange, mixed from white lead, red lead, lake and lead-tin yellow. The stitching within the leaves and the highlights were in two yellow tones, the lighter (unchanged) a mixture of lead-tin yellow and white lead, the darker a similar mixture warmed up with red lead and lake. These are the two pigments whose fading has caused the changes. This has robbed us not only of an effect

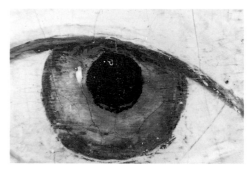

fig.xxvi Her right eye photographed at ×7 magnification, all original paint except for the small greyish patch at the lower left corner which is overpaint to disguise the pentimento drawing of the first eyes. This can still be seen beneath the brown paint of the iris. Hilliard wrote 'be sure … that the circle of the sight be perfect round'

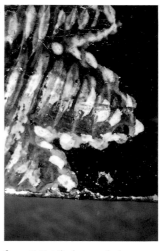

fig.xxvii Detail, photographed at ×7 magnification, of unfaded area of embroidery, bottom edge

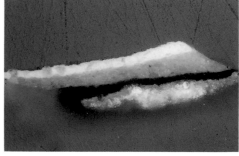

fig.xxviii Cross-section of the same unfaded area, photographed in polarised light at ×250 magnification. From bottom: sliver of white ground; thin priming of lead white in oil; black paint of dress; orange paint of edge stitching of leaf; yellow highlight

even richer than we have now but also of some very subtle overall patterning. Figure xxix shows the right edge of the skirt where the leaves, being in a shaded area, were painted in dark orange made from mixtures of ochres with only a small proportion of red lead. They have faded much less than the rest, consequently increasing the three-dimensional effect. Originally the embroidered design would have existed in sharper counterpoint with the flat, hooped patterns made by the pearls, an effect now more appreciable in black and white photography than in reality. Change has occurred also in the triangle of petticoat; now silver grey it was originally patterned in pink made by a glaze of lake on top of the grey tones (fig.xxx). Fading of lake has also occurred slightly in the rosette motif at the centre of the lower necklace and possibly in the fiery reds throughout the jewellery. These were created with vermilion glazed over with lake. The green of the rose leaves has also begun to go brown.[29] All in all though, we are exceptionally fortunate in having retained so much intact (fig.xxxi). The background too is in good condition apart from areas associated with splitting. It was painted principally in one layer composed of vermilion mixed with white lead, black and ochres, all ground extremely finely. This then appears to have been scumbled over with a very thin layer, slightly lighter in tone, applied last of all except for the veil which was painted on top of it. The plume was first painted mid-grey (white lead with ivory black) before the lighter and darker lines were put in discretely with similar mixtures.

Analysis of the binding media has proved very significant.[30] As noted the black dress is in oil mixed with resin. The yellow and orange patterning upon it, however, is bound in an emulsion made from egg, oil and wax. This would have produced a thick paint which lent itself to fine, detailed work while retaining volume and precise lines. It is more than probable that the sharply raised, linear and dotted patterning of white and yellow that we find throughout the period (John Bettes's wiry beard for example) was done with similar binders. The paint of the plume is the same egg-oil emulsion and the grey petticoat (though not its pink glaze) is also in a proteinaceous paint.[31] The background, however, appears to be in straight oil.[32] Analysis of the pearls yielded drying oil,[33] though not which type, so we cannot confirm Hilliard's note in his treatise that 'the satin ceruse grinded with oil of white poppy whiteneth up pearls in oil colours most excellently'.[34] Satin ceruse, according to the treatise, is one of three grades of ceruse, a white pigment whose basis (rarely clear from any writings of this period) is probably chalk. It has been noted that the faces in Hilliard's miniatures, for which he recommended the coarsest grade of ceruse, present hardly any resistance to X-ray, indicating the presence of chalk rather than white lead.[35] If this is so, then ceruse cannot be confirmed in this painting. The white used for the pearls is principally white lead; hardly any chalk is visible in analytical microscopy and the same is true of the face, hands and plume. But this is not to detract from the attribution to Hilliard, whose hand is so surely evident in the regular rhythms of the brushstrokes (figs.xxxii, xxvii), the linear conception and the extraordinary

detailing of such tiny elements as the phoenix's head (fig.xxxiii). Twenty-odd years elapsed between this painting and the writing of his treatise, years that might represent all sorts of changes in technique.

One other feature of this technique deserves mention as a prevailing trait in contemporary portraiture: the lack of gold or silver in the painting of the costume. There are no precious metals in this painting, not because the Queen's dress would not have contained them, but because the means of depicting them had become more painterly. Instead of finding gold or silver leaf glazed over with translucent paint, as in the costumes of Holbein's 'Edward, Prince of Wales' or Master John's 'Mary I as Princess' (no.11), we have opaque pigments, principally lead-tin yellow, used tonally to describe the effects of gold thread. The stiff poses and flat patterning of Elizabethan portraiture may hearken back deliberately to medieval times, but the techniques by then were modern and painterly, albeit a very linear, English version. While we cannot know how far financial restraints were involved in this development in England, it is nonetheless entirely in keeping with post-High Renaissance oil painting.

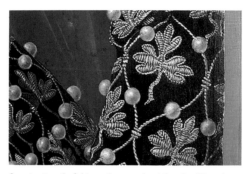
fig.xxix Detail of skirt and arm at the right edge. Note the unfaded edge, also the unfaded leaves at the edge of the skirt, painted in ochres

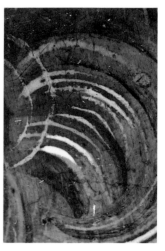
fig.xxxii A lock of hair photographed at ×7 magnification

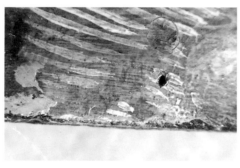
fig.xxx Bottom edge of petticoat, showing unfaded lake in a test clean revealing also the true tone of the whites and greys without discoloured varnish. Photographed at ×7 magnification

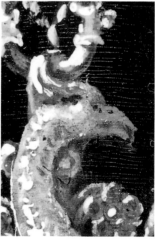
fig.xxxiii Detail of phoenix's head, photographed at ×7 magnification

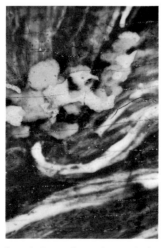
fig.xxxi Centre of rose, photographed at ×10 magnification, showing red lake glaze on top of thick white impasto and lead-tin yellow dotted on for the stamens

Three Portraits by Cornelis Ketel: Alice, Joan and Robert Smythe 1579–80 (nos.58–60)[36]

Supports and Grounds

All three are painted on single oak panels. Alice's and Robert's have the grain running vertically and appear to have been cut radially from a curved tree; the grain of Joan's is horizontal but again is curved. They are about 5 mm thick and the back edges are tapered to 2 mm via a wide bevel. All are strong, though Robert's has lost a narrow wedge of wood from the right edge and lower corner. This has been replaced.

The ground on each is a thick, smooth application of chalk bound in animal glue size. This was then sealed with an unpigmented film of drying oil.

Underlayer

Between the ground and the visible paint layers of each portrait is a fairly thick, opaque grey, mixed up in drying oil principally from white lead, charcoal black and red ochres. It is discernible here and there through the paint layers and was also studied in cross-sections, but even so it is not entirely clear whether it was applied as a priming or a broad monochrome undermodelling.[37] If an undermodelling then the variations in tone are only slight, though the overall colour does vary from painting to painting; Joan's is darker than Alice's and Robert's is very light and yellower. Neither could it have been at all detailed; the bold horizontal and diagonal brushstrokes going right across Joan's face and ruff occur in this layer, making no reference at all to her features. On the other hand it is barely present beneath Joan's black gown and veil, though substantial beneath Alice's. This would indicate that it was tonal and was used to describe the broad silhouettes of each part of the design. Pending further studies, however, we can call it no more than an underlayer, all the while noting its principal visible effect: to create the bluish half-tones in the face.

There appears to be no underdrawing as such. Examination with the microscope indicates that the contours of the features and shading of the head were sketched in roughly on top of the grey with very thin, light brown oil paint.

Paint Layers

The pink flesh tones are composed of white lead mixed on the palette with varying amounts of vermilion, lake and black.[38] The brown shadows used to delineate the features were mixed similarly but with large amounts of lake and a brown pigment, probably Cologne Earth. All these opaque tones were used thinly and were brushed into one another with busy strokes, sometimes following the contours of the head, sometimes hatching across them. As mentioned above, the grey underlayer, already dried, was left visible or just skimmed over in order to create bluish half-shadows (figs.xxxiv–xxxvi). This use of the turbid medium effect, combined with the visible evidence that the whole face was done wet-in-wet (fig.xxxvii), indicates a very swift worker who, once he had achieved an acceptable likeness, could well have completed the face in one sitting.

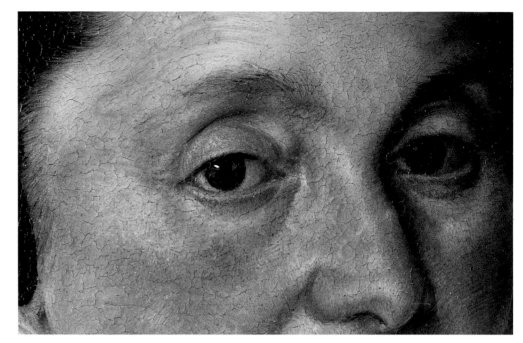

fig.xxxiv Detail of Alice's face

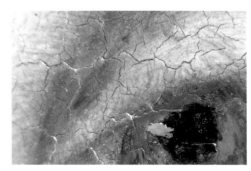

fig.xxxv Alice's left eye ×7 magnification, showing fine, wet-in-wet brushwork and brown shadow and grey underpaint forming the half-tone next to it. Grey of iris is later repainting

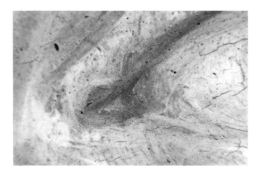

fig.xxxvi Joan's left eye ×7 magnification

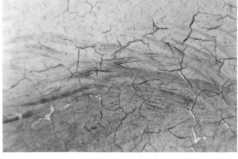

fig.xxxvii Alice's eyebrow showing wet-in-wet brushwork

For Alice's and Joan's black costumes, the artist took ivory black, white lead and probably umber (for its properties as a good drier in oil) and mixed up a few black tones to be used mainly wet-in-wet. Joan's bodice, though, has very dark grey patterning applied on top of the general black, but this is very hard to see now in ordinary lighting. For the fine muslin partlet and horizontal black lace beneath it the artist appears first to have applied a pale flesh tone. While this was wet he worked in thick white lead and when this was dry he painted on the black tracery of the lace. Then, taking more white lead, he made the long streaky strokes from the ruff to the top of the bodice, partially obscuring the lace. The gold chains were painted in three layers, first a mixture of ochres, umbers and ivory black with finely ground glass (to make these pigments dry faster in oil). This described the overall shape of the necklace and was applied on top of the white- or black-painted costume. The first brushstrokes describing the links were mixed from lead-tin yellow, red and yellow ochres and white lead. The highlights, applied last, are lead-tin yellow mixed with white lead (fig.xxxviii).

Robert's buff jacket has suffered considerable change. The basic opaque yellow mixture, which was applied on top of the grey underpainting, consisted of white lead, yellow ochre, black, brown, azurite and lake, the latter in large quantities. In the strip normally protected by the frame it has retained its warm buff appearance; elsewhere the lake has faded, making the jacket appear yellower than it was originally. A more serious change has occurred in the vertical and diagonal patterning. Figure xxxix shows one of these stripes as it crosses the line made by the sight-edge of the frame. In the protected area the stripe is green, indicating it is probably the pigment, copper resinate,[39] which usually turns brown with time. For the braid and buttons Ketel took thick mixtures of azurite, black and white lead and dotted in the texture. Then he glazed it with a copper resinate mixture, now

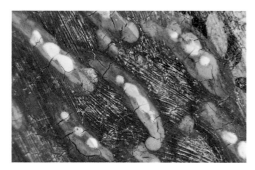

fig.xxxviii Joan's chain ×7 magnification

turned brown (fig.xl). The horizontal stripes were originally done in black hatching which has been overcleaned in the past. The backgrounds of all three are basically one opaque layer of a complex mixture containing white lead, azurite, chalk, ivory black, lake, gypsum, red, yellow and brown ochres and red lead bound in oil. The gilded inscriptions were applied to the background with a mordant which looks like a greyish-brown oil paint, applied thickly (fig.xli).

As noted in no.55, Ketel is recorded in later years back in Holland to have painted with his thumb, fingers or feet, a practice we have assumed was not adopted for the English portraits. He does, however, appear to have continued using grey underpainting for his later Dutch works.[40] His liking for speedy procedures, as revealed here by his use of the grey underlayer to create his half-tones and the quick wet-in-wet brushwork on the faces, is also evident in the later practice of producing drawings of portrait-poses minus individual faces,

presumably to be used as patterns in the studio.[41] Here there is no doubt that a grey underlayer would have helped even up any tonal differences resulting from a 'piece-work' approach. A grey ground was adopted by Godfrey Kneller a century later for very similar reasons.[42] Speed, however, is only an ancillary reason for his use of the turbid medium effect. All three painters examined here, like the rest of their contemporaries, used it to a greater or lesser extent even if only through the underdrawing. It is one of the fundamental techniques of painting throughout this period and is the main cause of the luminous, pearly faces that still arrest our attention in the shadows of a country-house corridor. When, a few decades later, Rubens came to use it so triumphantly for his iridescent flesh tones,[43] he was drawing on a long tradition, one which, with the death of the workshop or studio training, has been largely lost to more recent centuries.

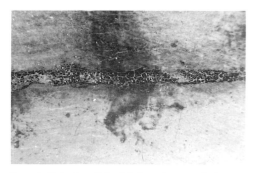

fig.xxxix Stripe from Robert's jacket as it crosses the line of the frame rebate. Green pigment discoloured to brown

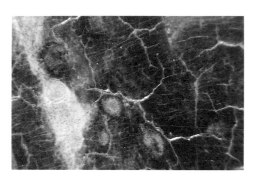

fig.xl Braid on Robert's jacket ×10 magnification

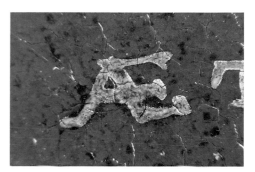

fig.xli Joan's inscription ×7 magnification

Notes

Specific acknowledgments of the many people who contributed to the research are given in the notes. In addition I would like to thank Sarah Cove and Alan Cummings, Iain McClure and his staff and students at the Hamilton Kerr Institute, especially Clare Chorley, Malcolm Rogers and Kai Kin Yung, Martin Wyld, Katharine Stainer-Hutchins, and Anne Ruggles.

1   Roy Strong, *The English Icon: Elizabethan and Jacobean Portraiture*, 1969.
2   For Holbein's use of transferred drawings see Susan Foister's essay, pp.21–6 above, and other articles cited in the notes.
3   Analysis of pigments throughout has been in dispersion by polarised light microscopy followed in many cases by EDX (Energy Dispersive X-ray) analysis, this latter carried out by Dr Joyce Townsend to whom I am very grateful. Raman spectroscopy of red lead was kindly done by Dr Marcus Daniels, Department of Chemistry, University of London.
4   This analysis by FTIR (Fourier Transform Infrared Spectrometry) microscopy and MS-GC (Mass Spectrometry Gas Chromotography) was carried out at the National Gallery, London. I am very grateful to Dr Jennifer Pilc and Raymond White for these results.

5   For the nature and discolouration of smalt see: J. Plesters, 'A Preliminary Note on the Incidence of Discolouration of Smalt in Oil Media', *Studies in Conservation*, vol.14, 1969, pp.62–74; R.D. Harley, *Artists' Pigments c.1600–1835: A Study in English Documentary Sources*, 1982, pp.53–6; A. Roy (ed.), *Artists' Pigments: A Handbook of their History and Characteristics*, National Gallery of Art, Washington 1993, pp.113–29.
6   For methods of gilding on oil paint see D.V. Thompson, *The Materials and Techniques of Medieval Painting*, New York 1936, pp.199–229.
7   A sample of this transparent layer, examined in transmitted light microscopy, revealed fragments of discoloured smalt.
8   For an excellent discussion of layered colours in works attributed to William Larkin, see S. Cove, 'The Materials and Techniques of Paintings Attributed to William Larkin (1610–1620)', unpublished thesis, Courtauld Institute 1985.
9   This painting is owned by the Trustees of the Chatsworth Settlement, to whom I am grateful for permission to examine it. The following people deserve thanks for assisting the process: Peter Day, Alison Devlin, Karen Hearn, Alastair Laing, Simon Murray, Tina Sitwell and Sarah Staniforth.
10 Information on the structure of the portrait is princi-

pally from a conservation report of 1935 by George Stout containing analytical work by Rutherford J. Gettens. I am grateful to Karen Hearn for finding it and greatly indebted to Rhona Macbeth who recently examined the painting in Boston to confirm similarities to the Tate painting.
11 Strong 1969, pp.65–8.
12 All technical information on this painting is from S. Foister, M.Wyld and A.Roy, 'Hans Holbein's "A Lady with a Squirrel and a Starling"', *National Gallery Technical Bulletin*, vol.15, 1994, pp.6–19.
13 All technical information on this painting is from S.O. Hand, *German Painting of the Fifteenth through Seventeenth Centuries*, National Gallery of Art, Washington 1994, pp.83–91.
14 Foister, Wyld and Roy 1994, p.9.
15 J. Murrell, 'John Guilliam's Book: A Heraldic Painter's Vade Mecum', *Walpole Society*, 1993–4, pp.1–51. This reference (p.12) in common with most in the book is for painting in aqueous media. 'Azure' may be ultramarine. 'Byse' is azurite.
16 G.P. Lomazzo, *A Tracte Containing the Artes of Curious Paintinge, Carvinge and Buildinge*, trans. R. Haydocke, Oxford 1598, p.99.
17 For early references to smalt, see M.K. Talley, *Portrait Painting in England: Studies in the Technical Literature*

before 1700, New Haven 1981. The Hilliard extract is from the version with modernised spelling and punctuation in the parallel text *A Treatise Concerning the Arte of Limning*, eds. R.K.R. Thornton and T.G.S. Cain, 1981, pp.93–5.

18 I am grateful to Karen Hearn for this information.

19 M. Campbell, *The English Yeoman under Elizabeth and the Early Stuarts*, New Haven 1942, p.398. The wages quoted are for Hertfordshire. The scales were set annually by justices for every shire. Those for East Riding of Yorkshire for the same work are £1 13s 4d and £1 3s 4d per annum respectively. I am grateful to Dr Graham Loud for this information.

20 Harley 1982, pp.43–6.

21 Foister, Wyld and Roy 1994, p.9.

22 This and the following information on occurrence is from Roy 1993, pp.122–3.

23 I am grateful to staff of the National Portrait Gallery, London, for permission to examine this painting, which arose from a proposal that the picture might be cleaned. After taking stock of the face we decided not to clean but to do a thorough technical study.

24 I am grateful to Sarah Vallance of the Department of Chemistry, University of Northumbria at Newcastle for analysis of this binder by HPLC (High Performance Liquid Chromotography).

25 Also obscured by the later glazing are points of lace, painted in white onto the flesh tone along the chin-line.

26 Hilliard, *Arte of Limning*, p.85 (see n.17 above).

27 From the Italian 'carnagione' (complexion); ultimately from the Latin 'caro, carnis' (flesh) (*Oxford English Dictionary*).

28 Hilliard also recommends red lead for very fair complexions (*Arte of Limning*, p.91). Like the same pigment in the patterning this may have been present but have faded.

29 This particular green has yet to be identified. As it appears to occur frequently in the period, it will be the subject of a future publication.

30 I am very grateful to Marianne Odlyha of the Department of Chemistry, Birkbeck College, London, for analysis of the binding medium in the black, yellows, orange and white plume by FTIR microscopy and Differential Scanning Calorimetry.

31 Staining of a cross-section with AB2 (Amido Black 2) was positive in the grey paint.

32 This film would not stain with AB2.

33 I am very grateful to Dr Jennifer Pilc of the National Gallery for this analysis by FTIR microscopy. Although the type of drying oil remains unidentified, there is certainly no egg in the pearls.

34 Hilliard, *Arte of Limning*, p.91. Poppy oil yellows less than linseed although, as Hilliard went on to note, it takes longer to dry.

35 J. Murrell, *The Way Howe to Lymne*, 1983, p.66.

36 I am very grateful to the owner of these paintings for permission to examine them in such detail.

37 It is mentioned as a 'ground' in W. Stechow, 'Sonder Borstel oft Pinseel', *Gelder*, 1973, pp.310–11. I am grateful to Karen Hearn for this reference.

38 The yellowish highlights on Johanna's and Robert's faces are patches of later overpainting.

39 EDX analysis showed copper.

40 Stechow 1973, p.310.

41 J.R. Judson, 'A New Insight into Cornelis Ketel's Method of Portraiture', *Master Drawings*, vol.1, no.4, Winter 1963, pp.38–41.

42 R. Jones, 'The Artist's Training and Techniques', *Manners and Morals*, exh. cat., Tate Gallery 1987, pp.24–5.

43 H. Ruhemann, *The Cleaning of Paintings*, 1968, pp.349–51.

Glossary

Animal glue size: Brown, water-based glue made by extracting collagen from entrails, hide, tendons or bones of animals.

Azurite: Also known as Bice. Bright, greenish blue prepared from naturally occurring mineral of the same name (basic copper carbonate). Artificial varieties have been known since the Middle Ages. Most of the azurite found in these paintings looks natural in origin.

Binding-medium/binder: In these paintings the glue or oil with which the pigments in the ground and paint, respectively, are bound together to form a film.

Black: Range of pigments from a variety of sources, for example burnt animal bones and ivory (both referred to here as ivory black), charcoal, candle-soot (lampblack)

Chalk: Natural or manufactured form of calcium carbonate, white in colour and used in powdered form as a filler for gesso and some paint.

Cross-section: Tiny sample of paint mounted in resin and then ground down sideways to reveal the layered structure.

Cut: The way a plank of wood is removed longitudinally from the trunk. Radially cut planks are cut at right angles to the concentric rings making up the trunk, tangentially cut planks at a tangent to them.

Drying oil: Organic oils which dry by oxidation to form a tough, waterproof film. They may be made more siccative by various methods such as heating with lead but in this catalogue drying oil simply designates linseed, walnut or poppy oil, all of which were available during the period.

Gesso: Lean, white paint made from chalk (calcium carbonate) or gypsum (calcium sulphate) bound in animal-glue size and applied to the support as a ground for painting upon.

Gold: Precious metal used in painting beaten into airily thin sheets (leaf) or reduced to a powder.

Grain/wood grain: Linear pattern made on the face of a wooden plank by its cutting in relation to the rings.

Graphite: Form of carbon used since the Middle Ages for drawing.

Ground: Mixture of pigments leanly bound in glue or oil and applied as a single, unmodulated colour to the canvas or panel in readiness for painting.

Gypsum: Naturally occurring calcium sulphate. Used in gesso more commonly than chalk south of the Alps. Also used as a base for lakes.

Lake: Translucent, bluish-red pigments made by precipitating natural dyestuffs onto transparent bases such as gypsum or alum to make a pigment. Dyestuffs at this period could be from insects or plants.

Lead-tin yellow: Pale, lemon-toned yellow (lead stannate) which in oil forms a bulky paint.

Limning: The art and practice of painting miniatures.

Ochres: Range of yellow, red and brown pigments made principally from naturally occurring earths (iron oxides).

Panel: Smooth square or rectangular piece of wood used as a support for painting. Sometimes composed of a single piece, more usually made up of several boards or planks glued together at butt joints.

Pentimento/pentimenti: Artist's alteration showing through overlying paint layers.

Priming: Layer of a single colour painted all over the ground to modify its tone. Although it may be applied unevenly it covers the whole prepared support without any reference to the design about to be placed upon it.

Red lead: Bright orangey-red pigment (tetroxide of lead), also known as minium. Not always stable.

Reserve: Area of picture left unpainted so that it may be put in later, eg. a face or mass of background trees against sky.

Smalt: Glassy blue pigment of which the basic colouring matter is cobalt. Its large particle size and chemical instability in oil causes sinking and discolouration.

Support: Panel or canvas used for painting.

Ultramarine: Very costly blue pigment made from semi-precious stone, lapis lazuli.

Underdrawing: Initial linear design applied to the ground or priming.

Undermodelling/underpainting: Initial painted design, usually applied thinly in muted or monochrome tones.

Vermilion: A bright red pigment either made from the natural mineral, cinnabar (mercuric sulphide), or its manufactured equivalent.

Wet-in-wet: Method of painting whereby colours are mixed up on the palette and worked into one another while wet on the painting.

White lead: A dense white pigment (lead carbonate) which until the twentieth century has been the principal white used in oil painting.

Bibliography

All books published in London unless otherwise stated

Ainsworth, M., '"Paternes for Phisioneamyes": Holbein's Portraiture Reconsidered', *Burlington Magazine*, vol.132, pp.173–86

Airs, M., *The Making of the English Country House, 1500–1640*, 1975

Anglo, S., *Images of Tudor Kingship*, 1992

Antwerp, exh. cat., Hessenhuis, Antwerp 1993

Art before the Iconoclasm, exh. cat., Rijksmuseum, Amsterdam 1986

Aston, M., *England's Iconoclasts*, I, Oxford 1988

Avery, C., 'Hubert Le Sueur, the Unworthy Praxiteles of King Charles I', *Walpole Society*, vol.48, 1980–2, pp.135–209

Béguin, S., *et al, La Galérie François Ier au Château de Fontainebleau* (special issue of *Revue de l'Art*), Paris, 1972

Betcherman, C.R., 'Balthasar Gerbier in Seventeenth-Century Italy', *History Today*, May 1961, pp.325–31

Betcherman, C.R., 'The York House Collection and its Keeper', *Apollo*, vol.92, 1970, p.250

Between Renaissance and Baroque: European Art 1520–1600, exh. cat., City Art Gallery, Manchester 1965

Boynton, L. (with commentary by P. Thornton), 'The Hardwick Inventory of 1610', *Furniture History*, vol.8, pp.1–40

Bracken, S., 'The Patronage of Robert Cecil, 1st Earl of Salisbury 1591–1612', unpublished MA report, Courtauld Institute 1993

British Portrait Miniatures, exh. cat., Arts Council, Edinburgh 1965

Brown, C., *Van Dyck*, Oxford 1982

Campbell, L., *The Early Flemish Pictures in the Collection of Her Majesty the Queen*, Cambridge 1985

Chaney, E. and Mack, P. (eds.), *England and the Continental Renaissance: Essays in Honour of J.B. Trapp*, Woodbridge 1991

Chirelstein, E., *Painting in Focus: The Allegory of the Tudor Succession*, [leaflet, n.d.], New Haven

Christian IV and Europe, exh. cat., 19th Council of Europe Exhibition, Denmark 1988

Collins Baker, C.H., *Lely and the Stuart Portrait Painters*, 2 vols., 1912

Corbett, M., and Lightbown, R., *The Comely Frontispiece: The Emblematic Titlepage in England, 1550–1660*, 1979

Croft Murray, E., *Decorative Painting in England 1537–1837*, I, 1962

CSP Ireland, *Calendar of State Papers Ireland 1509–1596*, ed. H.C. Hamilton 1860–90; *1596–1601*, ed. E.G. Atkinson 1893–1905; *1601–3*, ed. R.P. Mahaffy, 1912; *1603–6*, ed. C.L. Russell and J.P. Prendergast, 1872

CSP Domestic, *Calendar of State Papers, Domestic Series, 1547–80 and 1581–90*, ed. R. Lemon, 1856. *Calendar of State Papers, Domestic Series, of the Reign of Elizabeth, 1590–1601*, ed. M.A. Everett Green, 1869. *Calendar of State Papers, Domestic Series, of the Reign of James I, 1601–10*, ed. M.A. Everett Green, 1857–70

CSP Foreign, *Calendar of State Papers, Foreign Series, 1547–53*, ed. W.B. Turnbull, 1861, 1558–60, ed. R.J. Stevenson, 1865

Cust, L., 'Foreign Artists of the Reformed Religion Working in London from about 1560 to 1660', *Proceedings of the Huguenot Society of London*, vol.7, 1901–4, pp.45–52

Davies, R., 'An Inventory of the Duke of Buckingham's Pictures etc. at York House in 1635', *Burlington Magazine*, vol.10, 1907, p.376

Dawn of the Golden Age: Northern Netherlandish Art 1580–1620, exh. cat., Rijksmuseum, Amsterdam 1993–4

Dorsten, J.A. van, 'Steven van Herwyck's Elizabeth (1565)', *Burlington Magazine*, vol.111, 1969, pp.143–7

Dorsten, J.A. van, *The Radical Arts*, Leiden 1973

Downes, K., *Rubens*, 1980

Edmond, M., 'New Light on Jacobean Painters', *Burlington Magazine*, vol.118, 1976, pp.74–83

Edward Alleyn: Elizabethan Actor, Jacobean Gentleman, Dulwich Picture Gallery 1994

Eichberger, D., and Beaven, L., 'Family Members and Political Allies: The Potrait Collection of Margaret of Austria', *Art Bulletin*, June 1995, pp.225–48

Englefield, W.A.D., *History of the Painter-Stainers Company*, 1923

Europe and the Orient, Berliner Festspiele, Martin-Gropius Bau, Berlin 1989

Evett, D., *Literature and the Visual Arts in Tudor England*, Athens, Georgia, and London 1990

Ferguson, M.W., Quilligan, M., and Vickers, N.J., *Re-writing the Renaissance: The Discourses of Sexual Difference in Early Modern Europe*, Chicago 1986

Fiamminghi a Roma 1508–1608, exh. cat., Palais des Beaux-Arts, Brussels, and Palazzo delle Esposizioni, Rome 1995

Finberg, A.J., 'A Portrait of Prince Charles by Robert Peake', *Walpole Society*, vol.9, 1920–1, pp.89–95

Finberg, A.J., 'Cornelius Johnson', *Walpole Society*, vol.10, 1921–22, pp.1–37

Firenze e Inghilterra, Florence 1971

Foister, S., *Drawings by Holbein from the Royal Library, Windsor Castle*, 2 vols., New York 1983

Ford, B. (ed.), *The Cambridge Guide to the Arts in Britain*, Cambridge 1989, vols.3, 4

Fryer, P., *Staying Power: The History of Black People in Britain*, 1984

Gent, L., *Picture and Poetry, 1560–1620: Relations between Literature and the Visual Arts in the English Renaissance*, Leamington Spa 1981

Gent, L., and Llewellyn, N. (eds.), *Albion's Classicism*, 1995 (forthcoming)

Gittings, C., *Death, Burial and the Individual in Early Modern England*, 1984

Godfrey, R.T., *Wenceslaus Hollar*, exh. cat., Yale Center for British Art, New Haven 1994

Gordon, D.J., *The Renaissance Imagination: Essays and Lectures*, ed. S. Orgel, Berkeley and Los Angeles 1975

Greenblatt, S., *Renaissance Self-Fashioning from More to Shakespeare*, Chicago 1980

Groos, G.W., *The Diary of Baron Waldstein, a Traveller in Elizabethan England*, 1981

Hamilton, A., *The Family of Love*, Cambridge 1981

Harding, G.P., and Moule, T., *Portraits of Illustrious Persons in English History*, 1869

Hasted, E., *The History and Topographical Survey of the County of Kent*, 2 vols., Canterbury 1778–99

Haydocke, R., *A Tracte containing the Artes of curious Paintinge Caruinge & Buildinge*, Oxford 1598

Haynes, D.E.L., *The Arundel Marbles*, Oxford 1975

Hayward, J.F., 'English Firearms in the 16th Century', *Journal of the Arms and Armour Society*, vol.3, 1959–61, pp.117–41

Held, J., 'Rubens's Glynde Sketch and the Installation of the Whitehall Ceiling', *Burlington Magazine*, vol.112, 1972, pp.274–81

Helgerson, R., *Forms of Nationhood: The Elizabethan Writing of England*, Chicago 1992

Hepburn, F., *Portraits of the Later Plantagenets*, Woodbridge 1986

Hervey, M.F.S., 'Notes on a Tudor Painter – Gerlach Flicke', *Burlington Magazine*, vol.17, 1910 (2 parts)

Hind, A.M., *Engraving in England in the 16th and 17th Centuries*, Part I: *The Tudor Period*; Part II: *The Reign of James I*, Cambridge 1952, 1955

Historic Manuscripts Commission Calendar of the Manuscripts in the Possession of the Most Hon. the Marquis of Salisbury, K.G., 1883–1976, 24 vols.

Hodnett, E., *Marcus Gheeraerts the Elder*, Utrecht 1971

Holbein and the Court of Henry VIII, exh. cat., National Gallery of Scotland, Fitzwilliam Museum, Cambridge, and National Portrait Gallery, London 1993–4

Houghton, W.E., 'The English Virtuoso in the Seventeenth Century', *Journal of the History of Ideas*, vol.3, 1942

Howard, M., *The Tudor Image*, 1995

Howarth, D., 'Charles I and the Gonzaga Collection', in *Splendours of the Gonzaga*, exh. cat., Victoria and Albert Museum 1982

Hulse, C., *The Rule of Art: Literature and Painting in the Renaissance*, Chicago and London 1990

Inigo Jones: Complete Architectural Drawings, exh. cat., Royal Academy 1989

Jenkins, M., *The State Portrait*, New York 1947

Jonson, B., *Ben Jonson, The Works*, ed. C.H. Herford and P. Simpson, Oxford 1925–52, 11 vols.

King, J.N., *Tudor Royal Iconography*, Princeton 1989

Kuile, O. ter, 'Daniel Mijtens', *Nederlands Kunsthistorisch Jaarboek*, vol.20, 1969, pp.1–106

Leslie, M., 'The Dialogue between Bodies adn Souls: Pictures and Poesy in the English Renaissance', *Word and Image*, vol.1, 1985, pp.16–31

Lebel, G., 'British–French Artistic Relations in the 16th Century', *Gazette des Beaux-Arts*, vol.32, 1948, pp.278 et seq.

Levy, F.J., 'Henry Peacham and the Art of Drawing', *Journal of the Warburg and Courtauld Institutes*, vol.37 1974, pp.174–90

Lindley, D. (ed.), *The Court Masque*, Manchester 1984

Lingard, J.B., 'The Houses of Robert Cecil, 1st Earl of Salisbury 1595–1612', unpublished MA report, Courtauld Institute 1981

Lloyd, C., and Thurley, S., *Henry VIII: Images of a Tudor King*, Oxford 1991

Lockyer, R., *Buckingham: The Life and Political Career of George Villiers, 1st Duke of Buckingham, 1592–1628*, 1981

Louvre, Département des Peintures, *Les peintures de Hans Holbein le Jeune au Louvre*, Paris 1985

Lytle, G. and Orgel, S., *Patronage in the Renaissance*, Princeton 1981

McCracken, G., 'Dress Colour at the Court of Elizabeth I: An Essay in Historical Anthropology', *Canadian Review of Sociology and Anthropology*, vol.22, 1985, pp.515–33

Martin, G., 'The Banqueting House: Two Newly Discovered Projects', *Apollo*, vol.139, 1994, pp.24–35

Mellen, P., *Jean Clouet*, 1971

Melville, Sir James, of Halhill, *Memoirs of his own Life M.D.XLIX–M.D.XCIII*, Edinburgh 1827

Millar, O., *Rubens: The Whitehall Ceiling*, Charlton Lecture, Oxford 1952

Millar, O., 'Some Painters and Charles I', *Burlington Magazine*, vol.104, 1962, pp.325–30

Millar, O., 'Van Dyck in London', *Burlington Magazine*, vol.110, 1968, pp.307–11

Mr Cartwright's Pictures, exh. cat., Dulwich Picture Gallery 1987–8

Mowl, T., *Elizabethan and Jacobean Style*, 1993

Murrell, J., 'John Guillim's Book: A Heraldic Painter's Vade Mecum', *Walpole Society*, vol.57, 1995, pp.1–51

Newman, J., 'The Politics of Architecture', in *Culture and Politics in Early Stuart England*, Sharpe and Lake (eds.), 1994

Nichols, J., *The Progresses and Public Processions of King James I*, 1828

Nichols, J., *Illustrations of the Manners and Expences of Antient Times in England in the Fifteenth Sixteenth and Seventeenth Centuries*, 1797

Norgate, E., *Miniatura*, ed. M. Hardie 1919

Orgel, S., 'The Royal Theatre and the Role of the King', in Lytle and Orgel, *Patronage in the Renaissance*, Princeton 1981

Palme, Per, *Triumph of Peace*, Diss., Uppsala 1956

Parry, G., *The Golden Age Restor'd*, 1981

Peacock, J., 'New Sources for the Masque Designs of Inigo Jones', *Apollo*, vol.107, 1978, pp.89–111

Peacock, J., 'Inigo Jones's Stage Architecture and its Sources', *Art Bulletin*, vol.64, 1982, pp.195–216

Peacock, J., 'The Politics of Portraiture', in *Culture and Politics in Early Stuart England*, ed. K. Sharpe and P. Lake, Basingstoke 1994

Peck, L. Levy (ed.), *The Mental World of the Jacobean Court*, Cambridge 1991

The Peopling of London, exh. cat., Museum of London 1993

Pettegree, A., *Foreign Protestant Communities in Sixteenth-Century London*, Oxford 1986

Piper, D., 'The 1590 Lumley Inventory: Hilliard, Segar and the Earl of Essex I, and II', *Burlington Magazine*, vol.99, 1957, pp.224–231, 299–303

Piper, D., 'Some Portraits by Marcus Gheeraerts II and John de Critz Reconsidered', *Proceedings of the Huguenot Society of London*, vol.10, 1960, pp.210–29

Poole, Mrs R.L., 'An Outline of the History of the De Critz family of Painters', *Walpole Society*, vol.2, 1912–13, pp.45–68

Portraits from Welsh Houses, exh. cat., National Museum of Wales, Cardiff 1948

Prag um 1600, Kunsthistorisches Museum, Vienna 1988

Privy Council, *Acts of the Privy Council, 1547–70*, ed. J.R. Dasent, 1890–1904

The Queen's Pictures: Royal Collectors through the Centuries, National Gallery, London 1991

Ransome, D.R., 'Artisan Dynasties in London and Westminster in the Sixteenth Century', *The Guildhall Miscellany*, vol.2, 1960–8, pp.236–47

Rodney, J.M., 'The Earl of Salisbury and Henry Prince of Wales', in *Washington State University Research Studies*, vol.30, 1965, pp.56–63

Scarisbrick, D., *Tudor and Jacobean Jewellery*, 1995

Shakeshaft, P., 'The English Ambassadors in Venice 1604–39', unpublished MA report, Courtauld Institute 1979

Sharpe, K., *Criticism and Compliment: The Politics of Literature in the England of Charles I*, Cambridge 1987

Simpson, R., 'Sir Thomas Smith and the Wall Paintings at Hill Hall, Essex: Scholarly Theory and Design in the Sixteenth Century', *Journal of the British Archaeological Association*, vol.130, 1977, pp.1–20

Smuts, M., *Court Culture and the Origins of a Royalist Tradition in Early Stuart England*, Pennsylvania 1987

Splendours d'Espagne et les villes Belges 1500–1700, exh. cat., Palais des Beaux-Arts, Brussels 1985

Starkey, D. (ed.), *Henry VIII: A European Court in England*, 1991

Stopes, C.C., 'Daniel Mytens in England', *Burlington Magazine*, vol.17, 1910, p. 160

Strong, R., 'Queen Elizabeth, the Earl of Essex and Nicholas Hilliard', *Burlington Magazine*, vol.101, 1959, pp.145–9

Strong, R., and Dorsten, J.A. van, *Leicester's Triumph*, Leiden and London 1962

Strong, R., *Nicholas Hilliard*, 1975

Strong, R., *The Cult of Elizabeth: Elizabethan Portraiture and Pageantry*, 1977

Strong, R., 'Sidney's Appearance Reconsidered', in *Sir Philip Sidney's Achievements*, ed. M.B.J. Allen, D. Baker-Smith and A.F. Kinney, New York 1990, pp.3–19

Sutton, D., 'Thomas Howard, Earl of Arundel and Surrey as a Collector of Drawings', *Burlington Magazine*, vol.89, pp.3–9, 32–7, 75–7

Talley, M.K., *Portrait Painting in England: Studies in the Technical Literature before 1700*, Paul Mellon Centre 1981

Thomas Howard, Earl of Arundel, exh. cat., Ashmolean Museum, Oxford 1985

Thomson, W., *A History of Tapestries in England*, 1906, reprinted 1974

Thornton, P., *Seventeenth-century Interior Decoration in England, France and Holland*, New Haven and London 1978

Trapier, E. du Gué, 'Sir Arthur Hopton and the Interchange of Pictures between Spain and England in the Seventeenth Century', *Connoisseur*, vol.164, 1967, pp.239–43 and vol.165, pp.60–3

Trevor-Roper, H., *Princes and Artists: Patronage and Ideology at Four Habsburg Courts 1517–1633*, 1976

Van Dyck: Drawings, exh. cat., Pierpont Morgan Library 1991

Van Dyck in England, exh. cat., National Portrait Gallery 1982–3

Van Dyck: Paintings, exh. cat., National Gallery of Art, Washington 1990

Velde, C. van der, *Frans Floris (1519/20–1570), Leven en werk*, 2 vols., Brussels 1976

Von Bruegel bis Rubens, Wallraf-Richartz-Museum, Cologne, and Kunshistorisches Museum, Vienna 1992

Waterhouse, E., 'Venetian Paintings in Seventeenth-century England', *Italian Studies*, vol.7, 1952

Watson, F.J.B., 'On the Early History of Collecting in England', *Burlington Magazine*, vol.85, 1944, p.223.

Watson, K. and Avery, C., 'Medici and Stuart: A Grand Ducal Gift for Henry Prince of Wales', *Burlington Magazine*, vol.115, 1973, pp.493–507

Watt, T., *Cheap Print and Popular Piety 1550–1640*, Cambridge 1991

Wedgwood, C., *The Political Career of Peter Paul Rubens*, 1975

Wells-Cole, A., *Barbarous and Ungraceful Ornament: The Use of Continental Prints in Elizabethan and Jacobean England*, London and New Haven 1996 (forthcoming)

Wenceslaus Hollar, exh. cat., British Museum 1983

Whinney, M., *Sculpture in Britain, 1530 to 1830*, Harmondsworth 1964

White, C., *The Dutch Pictures in the Collection of Her Majesty the Queen*, Cambridge 1982

Wiffen, J., *Historical Memoirs of the House of Russell*, 1833

Wilks, T.V., 'The Picture Collection of Robert Carr, Earl of Somerset Reconsidered', *Journal of the History of Collections*, vol.1, 1989, pp.167–77

Wood, J., 'Inigo Jones, Italian Art, and the Practice of Drawing', *Art Bulletin*, vol.74, 1992, pp.247–70

Wood, J., 'Van Dyck and the Earl of Northumberland: Taste and Collecting in Stuart England', in Barnes, S. and Wheelock, A. (eds.), *Studies in the History of Art*, vol.46, Washington 1994

Wood, L., 'The Portraits of Anne of Denmark', unpublished MA report, Courtauld Institute 1981

Woodward, J., *Tudor and Stuart Drawings*, 1951

Yates, F., *Astraea: The Imperial Theme in the Sixteenth Century*, 1975; re-issued 1993

Yates, F.A., *The Valois Tapestries*, 2nd ed., 1975

Chronology

COMPILED BY SUSAN BRACKEN

	ENGLAND	ELSEWHERE
1520	Henry VIII meets Charles V at Dover and Canterbury and François I at the Field of the Cloth of Gold.	Süleyman I becomes Sultan of Ottoman Empire (–1566). Excommunication of Luther. Death of Raphael (b. 1483). Magellan rounds Cape Horn. Charles V crowned Holy Roman Emperor at Aix-la-Chapelle. Michelangelo begins New Sacristy, S. Lorenzo, Florence.
1521	Execution of Edward Stafford, Duke of Buckingham. Henry VIII publishes *The Assertion of the Seven Sacraments* (condemns Luther) and is named Defender of the Faith.	Süleyman takes Belgrade. Death of Pope Leo X (elected 1513). Death of Josquin des Pres (b. 1450).
1522	Wolsey makes unsuccessful attempt to become Pope.	Election of Pope Adrian VI (–1523).
1523		Election of Pope Clement VII (–1534). Deaths of Perugino (b. *c.*1450) and Luca Signorelli (b. *c.*1450). Titian paints 'Bacchus and Ariadne' and Parmigianino 'Self-Portrait in a Mirror'.
1524	Wolsey made Papal Legate.	James V becomes King of Scotland (–1542). Peasants' Revolt in Germany. Pietro Aretino expelled from Rome. Giulio Romano begins Palazzo del Te, Mantua.
1525	Wolsey gives Hampton Court to Henry VIII. Tyndale translates New Testament into English.	French defeated at Battle of Pavia; François I taken prisoner. Correggio begins 'Assumption', Parma Cathedral. Death of Vittore Carpaccio (b. *c.*1460).
1526	Hans Holbein the Younger visits England (–1528).	Turks defeat Hungarians at Mohacs. Dürer paints the 'Four Apostles'.
1527	Treaty of Westminster between England and France (against Charles V). Henry VIII decides to divorce Catherine of Aragon. Holbein paints 'The Family of Thomas More' [see no.76].	Ferdinand of Habsburg named King of Hungary (–1564). Imperial troops sack Rome and imprison Clement VII. Death of Machiavelli (b. 1469).
1528	England declares war on Charles V.	Death of Dürer (b. 1471), Matthias Grunewald (b. *c.*1475) and Palma Vecchio (b. *c.*1480). Publication of *The Courtier* by Baldassare Castiglione.

	ENGLAND	ELSEWHERE
1529	Legatine court considers Henry VIII's request for divorce, but powers revoked and investigation removed to Rome.	Turks besiege Vienna. Treaty of Cambrai.
1530	Wolsey arrested for treason and dies. St James's Palace begun.	Alessandro de'Medici, Duke of Florence (–1537). Charles V crowned in Bologna by Clement VII. Titian paints 'Death of St Peter Martyr'. Death of Quentin Metsys (b. *c.*1465).
1531	Henry VIII named Protector and Supreme Head of the church and clergy of England. Sir Thomas Elyot, *The Boke Named the Governour*.	Deaths of Andrea del Sarto (b. 1486) and Tilman Riemenschneider (b. *c.*1460). Great Comet (Halley's) sighted in Europe.
1532	Submission of the English clergy. Sir Thomas More resigns as Lord Chancellor. William Warham, Archbishop of Canterbury, dies. Holbein returns to England.	Rabelais, *Pantagruel*, book 1. Machiavelli's *The Prince* published (written 1513).
1533	Henry VIII marries Anne Boleyn and daughter Elizabeth is born. Cranmer becomes Archbishop of Canterbury.	Death of Ariosto (b. 1474) and Lucas van Leyden (b. *c.*1494). Titian paints Charles V.
1534	Act of Supremacy.	Election of Pope Paul III (–1549). Society of Jesus founded. Rabelais *Gargantua*. Death of Correggio (b. *c.*1489). Michelangelo commissioned to paint 'Last Judgement'.
1535	Execution of Thomas More and Cardinal Fisher for opposing Supremacy of Henry VIII.	Charles V conquers Tunis.
1536	Death of Catherine of Aragon; execution of Anne Boleyn. Henry VIII marries Jane Seymour. Suppression of monasteries begins. Pilgrimage of Grace begins (anti-Reformation rebellion led by Robert Aske). Holbein appointed court painter to Henry VIII.	Tyndale burnt at stake in Netherlands. Reginald Pole named Cardinal. Death of Erasmus (b. 1465).
1537	Death of Jane Seymour shortly after birth of Prince Edward. Suppression of Pilgrimage of Grace.	Cosimo de'Medici becomes ruler of Florence. Publication of Serlio's 'Five Books of Architecture' begins. Sansovino begins Venice Library.

	ENGLAND	ELSEWHERE
1538	Excommunication of Henry VIII finalised (begun 1533). Destruction of shrines including that of Thomas à Becket.	James V of Scotland marries Marie de Guise. Death of Albrecht Altdorfer (b. c.1480). Titian paints 'Venus of Urbino' and 'François I'.
1539	Publication of Coverdale's 'Great Bible'. Holbein paints 'Anne of Cleves' [no.66].	
1540	Henry VIII marries Anne of Cleves; the marriage is annulled and he marries Catherine Howard. Execution of Thomas Cromwell. English Bible to be in every parish church.	Society of Jesus recognised. Deaths of Parmigianino (b. 1503) and Rosso Fiorentino (b. 1494).
1541	Execution of Margaret Pole, Countess of Salisbury (niece of Edward IV, mother of Cardinal Archbishop). Henry VIII declared King of Ireland.	
1542	Execution of Catherine Howard. Battle of Solway Moss.	Holy Office established.
1543	Henry VIII marries Catherine Parr. Holbein dies (b. 1497/8).	Mary Stuart becomes Queen of Scotland (–1587). Death of Copernicus (b. 1473). Titian paints 'Pope Paul III'.
1544	Sinking of the *Mary Rose*. Henry VIII re-founds St Bartholomew's Hospital. 'Master John' paints 'Mary I as Princess' [no.11].	
1545	Death of John Taverner (b. 1495). Thomas Tallis, musician at the Chapel Royal. John Bettes the Elder paints 'Unknown Man in a Black Cap' [no.10].	Council of Trent commences (–1563).
1546		Michelangelo appointed architect of St Peter's. Deaths of Martin Luther (b. c.1483), Antonio da Sangallo the Younger (b. 1485) and Giulio Romano (b. 1492).
1547	Execution of Henry Howard, Earl of Surrey [see no.14]. Death of Henry VIII (b. 1491); accession of Edward VI (–1553), with uncle Edward Seymour, Duke of Somerset, as Lord Protector.	Death of François I; accession of Henri II (–1559). Charles V defeats Protestants at Muhlberg. Coronation of Ivan IV ('The Terrible') (–1584). Deaths of Pietro Bembo (b. 1470) and Sebastiano del Piombo (b. 1485).

	ENGLAND	ELSEWHERE
1548	Death of Catherine Parr.	Publication of Ignatius Loyola's *Spiritual Exercises*. Tintoretto paints 'The Miracle of the Slave'. Titian paints 'Charles V on Horseback'.
1549	Thomas Seymour executed for high treason; the Protectorate is dissolved and Somerset is sent to the Tower. Act of Uniformity (only the English Prayer Book is to be permitted).	Andrea Palladio begins building the Basilica, Vicenza. Hans Eworth paints 'A Turk on Horseback' [no.22].
1550	William Cecil made Secretary of State.	Election of Pope Julius III (–1555). Vasari's *Lives* (1st edition).
1552	Somerset executed.	
1553	Lady Jane Grey proclaimed Queen for 9 days at death of Edward VI; accession of Mary I.	Death of Lucas Cranach I (b. 1472).
1554	Wyatt's Rebellion against the Queen's marriage to Prince Philip of Spain which takes place in July. Execution of Wyatt. Execution of Jane Grey. Princess Elizabeth sent to the Tower. Antonis Mor visits England and paints Queen Mary's portrait [no.16].	
1555	Burning of heretics begins; Bishops Latimer and Ridley burnt. Thomas Cranmer removed as Archbishop of Canterbury.	Peace of Augsburg (religion of each state of the Empire to be determined by its ruler). Election of Pope Paul IV (–1559). Christopher Plantin begins to print in Antwerp.
1556	Cranmer burned at stake; Cardinal Pole Archbishop of Canterbury.	Abdication of Charles V (retires to monastery of Yuste). Philip becomes King of Spain (–1598). Death of Ignatius Loyola (b. 1491). Death of Aretino (b. 1492). Andrea Palladio illustrates Barbaro's *Vitruvius*.
1557	England declares war on France.	
1558	England loses Calais to France. Deaths of Mary I and Cardinal Pole. Accession of Elizabeth I (–1603).	Death of Charles V. Mary, Queen of Scots, marries the Dauphin (François). John Knox, *The First Blast of the Trumpet Against the Monstrous Regiment of Women*.
1559	Treaty of Câteau-Cambresis (England, France and Spain). Matthew Parker becomes Archbishop of Canterbury. England sends help to Scottish Lords to expel French. Elizabethan Acts of Supremacy and Uniformity.	François II becomes King of France (–1560). Establishment by Paul IV of Index of forbidden books (–1966). Election of Pope Pius IV (–1565).

	ENGLAND	ELSEWHERE		ENGLAND	ELSEWHERE
1560		Charles IX becomes King of France (–1574), with Catherine de'Medici as Regent [see no.72]. Eric XIV becomes King of Sweden (–1568, declared unfit to reign). Church of Scotland established. Uffizi founded. Death of Bandinelli (b. 1493).	1569	Duke of Norfolk arrested on suspicion of treason [see no.27]. Revolt of Northern earls (Northumberland and Westmoreland) in support of Mary, Queen of Scots.	Cosimo de'Medici created Grand Duke of Tuscany. Mercator's Map of the World. Death of Brueghel the Elder (fl. 1561).
1561	Sir Thomas Hoby translates *Il Cortigiano*. St Paul's Cathedral struck by lightning; spire damaged.	Mary, Queen of Scots returns to Scotland. Madrid declared capital of Spain. Tulips brought to Europe. Portrait of 'Eric XIV of Sweden' (attributed to Steven van der Meulen) [no.47].	1570	Excommunication of Elizabeth I. Duke of Norfolk released. Roger Ascham, *The Scholemaster*; translation of *Euclid's Elements of Geometry* (with Preface by John Dee).	Death of J. Sansovino (b. 1486). Palladio publishes *Quattro Libri*.
1562	Elizabeth I has smallpox; almost fatal.	John Hawkins begins slave trade to America. French Wars of Religion begin.	1571	William Cecil created Lord Burghley. Ridolfi Plot discovered (to overthrow Elizabeth and replace her with Mary, Queen of Scots). Royal Exchange opened.	Turks invade Cyprus and are defeated at Battle of Lepanto. Deaths of Benvenuto Cellini (b. 1500) and Vasari (b. 1512).
1563	Doctrine of 39 Articles (of faith). Poor Relief Laws. 1st English edition of Foxe's *Book of Martyrs*. John Shute, *First and Chief Groundes of Architecture*.	Council of Trent ends. Building of the Escorial begins. Veronese completes the 'Marriage Feast at Cana'. Tasso's *Rinaldo* published.	1572	Burghley appointed Lord Treasurer. Duke of Norfolk executed for part in Ridolfi Plot. Poor Law passed. Births of John Donne and Ben Jonson. Society of Antiquaries founded. Nicholas Hilliard paints miniature of 'Elizabeth I' [no.69].	St Bartholomew's Day Massacre (of Huguenots in Paris). Dutch war of Liberation begins, William of Orange elected Stadholder. Election of Pope Gregory XIII (1585). Deaths of John Knox (b. c.1505) and François Clouet (b. 1522).
1564	Robert Dudley created Earl of Leicester [see no.49]. Shakespeare and Marlowe born.	Accession of Emperor Maximilian II (–1576). Death of Calvin (b. 1509). Death of Michelangelo (b. 1475). Tintoretto begins decoration of Scuola Grande di S. Rocco. Building of Tuileries begins.	1573	Sir Francis Walsingham made a Secretary of State [see no.118]. Birth of Inigo Jones. George Gower paints 'Sir Thomas Kytson' [no.53] and 'Lady Kytson' [no.54].	Veronese paints 'Feast in the House of Levi' and appears before the Inquisition.
1565		Mary, Queen of Scots marries Henry Stuart, Lord Darnley (great-grandson of Henry VII). Siege of Malta.	1574	First Catholic missionary priests in England. Cornelis Ketel paints 'A Man of the Wachendorff Family' [no.55].	Henri III becomes King of France (–1589). Death of Maerten van Heemskerk (b. 1498).
1566		Election of Pope Pius V (–1572). Unrest and iconoclasm in Netherlands. Murder of Rizzio, secretary to Mary, Queen of Scots. She gives birth to son James (later VI of Scotland and I of England). Selim II becomes Sultan (–1574). Death of Nostradamus. Building of S. Giorgio Maggiore begins (designed by Palladio).	1575	Elizabeth I declines sovereignty of Netherlands. Christopher Saxton, *County Atlas of England and Wales*. Federico Zuccaro does chalk studies of 'The Earl of Leicester' and 'Elizabeth I' [nos.99 and 100].	
1567	Portrait of 'William Brooke, 10th Lord Cobham and his Family' (British School) [no.51].	O'Neill's rebellion in Ireland. Murder of Darnley. Mary, Queen of Scots, marries James Hepburn, Earl of Bothwell and is forced to abdicate in favour of her son. Alba arrives in Netherlands. Philibert de l'Orme's *Architecture*.	1576		Rudolph II becomes Emperor (–1612). Spaniards sack Antwerp. Frobisher searches for North-West Passage. J.A. du Cerceau, *Les Plus Excellents Bastiments de France*. Death of Titian (b. c.1488).
1568		Mary, Queen of Scots flees to England. English College founded at Douai to train Jesuit missionaries for work in England. Vignola begins the church of the Gesu, Rome. Vasari's *Lives* (2nd ed.).	1577	Francis Drake begins circumnavigation of the globe. Holinshed's *Chronicles* (2nd ed. 1587).	Birth of Rubens. Church of Il Redentore, Venice, begun to designs by Palladio.

	ENGLAND	ELSEWHERE		ENGLAND	ELSEWHERE
1578		James VI assumes throne of Scotland. Bothwell dies in prison in Denmark. Duke of Parma becomes Governor of Netherlands. Building of Pont Neuf, Paris, begins.	1589	Marlowe writes *Jew of Malta* (?). Custodis paints 'Elizabeth Brydges' [no.63].	Catherine de' Medici dies, Henri III murdered. Henri of Navarre becomes King of France (assassinated 1610). James VI of Scotland marries Princess Anne of Denmark. Galileo lectures on mathematics at Pisa.
1579	George Gower paints 'Self-Portrait' [no.57].		1590	Edmund Spenser's *Faerie Quene* published. Sidney's *Arcadia*. Death of Walsingham. 'The Lumley Inventory' is prepared [no.105].	Cupola and lantern of St Peter's completed by Domenico Fontana. Election of Pope Gregory XIV (–1591).
1580	Drake completes circumnavigation.	Montaigne's *Essais* published. Death of Palladio (b. 1508). Venetians import coffee from Turkey.	1591	Robert Cecil knighted.	Excommunication of Henri IV.
1581	Marriage negotiations between Elizabeth I and Duke of Anjou. Execution of Edmund Campion. Drake knighted.	Tasso's *Gerusalemme Liberata* published.	1592	Death of Hatton.	Election of Pope Clement VIII (–1605). Death of Montaigne (b. 1533).
1582		Philip II conquers Portugal. Gregory XIII reforms calendar. First English colony in Newfoundland.	1593	Marlowe murdered.	Henri IV becomes a Catholic.
1583	Throckmorton Plot discovered (to replace Elizabeth I with Mary, Queen of Scots). John Whitgift, Archbishop of Canterbury.		1594	Tyrone's uprising in Ireland. Marcus Gheeraerts the Younger paints 'Captain Thomas Lee' [no.120].	Birth of Prince Henry in Scotland. Deaths of Tintoretto (b. 1518), Mercator (b. 1512) and Palestrina (b. 1525). Birth of Nicolas Poussin (–1665).
1584		William of Orange assassinated. Fyodor I becomes Czar of Russia (–1598).	1595	Raleigh sails in search of El Dorado and returns.	Dutch colonise East Indies. Muhammed III becomes Sultan (–1603).
1585	Earl of Leicester leads expeditionary force to Netherlands. Death of Thomas Tallis (b. 1505).	Sixtus V elected Pope (–1590). Antwerp loses pre-eminence to Amsterdam. Grenville begins to colonise Virginia (abandoned 1586). John Davis, trying to find North-West Passage, discovers Davis Straits. Death of Ronsard (b. 1525).	1596	Death of Drake. Cecil made Principal Secretary. First water closets installed.	
			1597	Robert Devereux, 2nd Earl of Essex made Earl Marshal [see no.121]. Act for transportation of felons.	
1586	Babington Plot discovered – to replace Elizabeth I with Mary, Queen of Scots, whose trial then begins. Severe corn shortage. Camden's *Britannia* published.	Abbas the Great becomes Shah of Persia (–1628). Sir Philip Sidney killed at Zutphen and Leicester's troops forced to surrender. El Greco begins 'Burial of Count Orgaz'.	1598	Death of Burghley. John Stowe's *Survey of London*.	Death of Phillip II of Spain; Philip III becomes King (–1621). Boris Godunov seizes power in Russia (–1605). Freedom of worship granted to French Protestants (–1685) ('Edict of Nantes'). Birth of Bernini (–1680).
1587	Execution of Mary, Queen of Scots reluctantly authorised by Elizabeth I. Sir Christopher Hatton, Lord Chancellor. Marlowe writes *Tamburlaine* (?).	Drake 'singes the King of Spain's beard' (attacks Cadiz and destroys many ships).	1599	Essex made Lord Lieutenant of Ireland; returns without permission and is arrested. Death of Spenser. Birth of Oliver Cromwell (–1658).	James VI writes *Basilikon doron* (on divine right of kings). Births of Anthony Van Dyck (–1641) and Velásquez (–1660).
1588	Spanish Armada sets sail in May, is sighted in July and is defeated [see nos.43 and 44]. Elizabeth I rallies troops at Tilbury. Death of Leicester.	Christian IV becomes King of Denmark (–1648). Assassination of Guise brothers. Death of Veronese (b. c.1528).	1600	East India Company founded.	Birth of Prince Charles in Scotland (later Charles I of England). Giordano Bruno burned as a heretic.
			1601	Essex tried and executed. Cecil begins secret negotiations with James VI.	Birth of future Louis XIII (–1643). Death of Tycho Brahe (b. 1546).

	ENGLAND	ELSEWHERE
1602	Bodleian Library opens.	Dutch East India Company founded.
1603	Death of Elizabeth I; accession of James I. Arrest of Walter Raleigh. Robert Peake paints 'Elizabeth of Bohemia' [no.126].	Ahmed I, Sultan (–1617). Tokugawa family become Shoguns of Japan (–1867).
1604	Somerset House Conference produces peace treaty with Spain. James I adopts title 'King of Great Britain, France and Ireland'.	French East India Company founded. Van Mander begins *Het Schilderboek.*
1605	Gunpowder Plot discovered. Francis Bacon, *The Advancement of Learning.*	Election of Pope Paul V (–1621). Cervantes, *Don Quixote,* Part I.
1606		Birth of Rembrandt (–1669).
1607	Anti-enclosure riots in Midlands. Parliament rejects Union with Scotland. Ben Jonson writes *Volpone.*	Monteverdi writes *Orfeo.*
1608	Thomas Coryat travels to Italy. Birth of John Milton (–1674).	French colony established in Quebec. Death of Giambologna (b. 1524).
1609		12 years' truce between Spain and Netherlands. Expulsion of the Moriscos from Spain. Death of Annibale Carracci (b. 1560). Blue Mosque begun. Tea introduced to Europe.
1610	Michiel Jansz. van Miereveld paints 'Sir Edward Cecil, later Viscount Wimbledon' [no.137].	Assassination of Henri IV; Marie de'Medici becomes Regent for Louis XIII. Henry Hudson explores Hudson River. Deaths of Caravaggio (b. 1571) and Adam Elsheimer (b. 1578).
1611	Authorised Version of Bible published. Order of Baronets established.	Dutch establish trade with Japan. Gustavus Adolphus elected King of Sweden.
1612	Death of Robert Cecil. Death of Henry, Prince of Wales.	Death of Emperor Rudolph II; accession of Mathias (–1619).
1613	Marriage of Frederick V, Elector Palatine and Princess Elizabeth ('the Winter Queen'). Robert Carr (later Earl of Somerset) favourite of James I; his secretary, Overbury imprisoned in Tower, is poisoned. Globe Theatre burnt and rebuilt.	Michael Romanov elected Tsar (–1645). Amsterdam Exchange built.
1614	John Webster, *The Duchess of Malfi.* Raleigh, *The History of the World.* Death of Robert Smythson (b. 1536).	Death of El Greco (b. 1541).
1615	Camden's *Annale.*	Salamon de Brosse begins Palais de Luxembourg, Paris. Galileo appears before the Inquisition. Cervantes, *Don Quixote,* Part II.
1616	Raleigh released from Tower to lead expedition to Guiana in search of gold. Death of Shakespeare. Somerset and wife condemend to death for Overbury murder, but pardoned. Sale of peerages begins. Charles invested Prince of Wales. Inigo Jones designs the Queen's House, Greenwich, but work stopped 1618.	Richelieu becomes Secretary of State. Death of Cervantes (b. 1547).
1617	Pocahontas received at court; dies shortly before return to Virginia. Death of Isaac Oliver. Paul van Somer paints 'Anne of Denmark' [no.139].	Births of Murillo (–1682) and Peter Lely (–1680)
1618	Francis Bacon, Lord Chancellor. Earl of Suffolk dismissed as Lord Treasurer and imprisoned for embezzlement. Execution of Sir Walter Raleigh on return to England. Inigo Jones begins Banqueting House, Whitehall (–1622).	Defenestration of Prague; Thirty Years' War begins.
1619	Death of Anne of Denmark. William Harvey first lectures on circulation of blood. Deaths of Nicholas Hilliard (b. c.1547) and Richard Burbage (b. 1567)	Accession of Ferdinand as Emperor (–**1637**), but opponents favour Elector Palatine. Unrest in France (–**1631**). Birth of Cyrano de Bergerac (–**1655**).
1620	Secret Anglo-Spanish Treaty; Prince of Wales and Infanta to marry. *The Mayflower* sails for America.	Battle of the White Mountain; Elector Palatine's Army defeated.
1621	Commons revive impeachment; Lord Chancellor Bacon impeached. James I quarrels with Commons. Anthony Van Dyck probably paints 'Thomas Howard, Earl of Arundel' [no.146].	Philip IV becomes King of Spain (–1665). Election of Gregory XV (–1623).
1622	Arrest of John Pym, MP, for criticising King.	Birth of Molière (–1673)
1623	Buckingham and Prince of Wales travel incognito to Spain; marriage terms not agreed. 'First Folio' of Shakespeare's plays.	Election of Urban VIII (–1644). Velásquez made court painter to Philip IV.
1624	Commons impeach Lord Treasurer Cranfield.	Dutch found New Amsterdam (New York).

	ENGLAND	ELSEWHERE		ENGLAND	ELSEWHERE
1625	Death of James I; accession of Charles I (executed 1649). Marriage of Charles I and Henrietta Maria of France. Mytens appointed Court Painter. Rubens paints the 'Duke of Buckingham' [no.115].	Vincent de Paul founds Order of Sisters of Mercy.	1628	Oliver Cromwell elected MP for Huntingdon. Buckingham assassinated. William Laud becomes Bishop of London.	Shah Jehan, Great Mogul (–1658). Taj Mahal begun.
1626	Commons try to impeach Buckingham; Charles dissolves Parliament. Death of Francis Bacon (b. 1561). Birth of John Aubrey (–1697).		1629	Charles dissolves Parliament (–1640). Rubens visits London on diplomatic peace mission.	
1627		Buckingham leads disastrous expedition to relieve La Rochelle. Japan excludes all foreigners (–1852). Collegium de Propaganda Fide founded in Rome. Death of Duke of Mantua; succession disputed.	1630	Birth of future Charles II (–1658).	
			1631	Death of John Donne (b. 1572)	
			1632	Birth of Christopher Wren (–1723). First coffee shop opens in London. Anthony Van Dyck paints 'Charles I and Henrietta Maria' [fig.3].	

Lenders

Numbers refer to catalogue entries

Her Majesty The Queen 2, 5, 13, 19, 29, 32, 64, 93–7, 113, 124, 143, 150
Graphische Sammlung Albertina, Vienna 115
Rijksmuseum, Amsterdam 18, 55, 101
Musée des Beaux Arts, Angers 26, 104
The Worshipful Society of Apothecaries of London 44
Ashmolean Museum, Oxford 114
The Marquess of Bath 51
Trustees of the late Countess Beauchamp 68, 90–2
The British Museum 99, 100
Burghley House Collection 81
University of Cambridge 128
National Museum and Gallery, Cardiff 35
The Earl of Clarendon 50, 152
Statens Museum for Kunst, Copenhagen 78, 142
Courtauld Institute Galleries, London 23
Delman Collection, San Francisco 61
The Duke of Devonshire 106–12
Scottish National Portrait Gallery, Edinburgh 117, 131
English Heritage 135, 136
Fitzwilliam Museum, Cambridge 65, 70, 84, 87, 89, 103
The J. Paul Getty Museum, Malibu, California 146
National Maritime Museum, Greenwich 74, 126
Edward Harley Esq. 46
Mrs Drue Heinz 134
Collection of the Huddleston Family 15
Trustees of Lamport Hall 139
Museum of London 153
National Gallery, London 4
National Portrait Gallery, London 11, 12, 14, 20, 31, 34, 45, 69, 71, 77, 80, 98, 102, 118, 119, 140, 141
Mauritshuis, The Hague 7, 82
The National Trust (Charlecote Park) 133
The National Trust (Hardwick Hall) 52
The National Trust (Powis Castle) 138

Norfolk Museums Service (The Ancient House Museum, Thetford) 123
The Rt. Hon. Earl of Powis 86
Museo del Prado, Madrid 21
Private Collections 9, 16, 22, 24, 25, 27, 41, 42, 49, 57–60, 75, 83, 85, 88, 122, 125, 129, 144, 149, 151
Railways Pension Fund 67
Galleria Nazionale d'Arte Antica, Rome 8
The Earl of Scarbrough 36–9
Trustees of the Earl of Scarbrough's Children's Settlement 105
Sidney Sussex College, Cambridge 48
Pinacoteca Nazionale, Siena 40
Nationalmuseum, Stockholm 47
Tate Gallery, London 10, 28, 30, 53, 54, 120, 145, 147
Marquess of Tavistock and Trustees of the Bedford Estate 130
Trinity College, Cambridge 121
Palazzo Reale, Turin 127
Mr Tyrwhitt-Drake 43
Victoria and Albert Museum, London 66, 72, 76, 79, 116
Kunsthistorisches Museum, Vienna 17
National Museums and Galleries on Merseyside (Walker Art Gallery, Liverpool) 56, 137
National Gallery of Art, Washington 6
Woollahra Trading Co. Ltd 33
Yale Center for British Art 132

Photographic Credits

Index

Ways of Giving to the Tate Gallery

The Tate Gallery attracts funds from the private sector to support its programme of activities in London, Liverpool and St Ives. Support is raised from the business community, individuals, trusts and foundations, and includes sponsorships, donations, bequests and gifts of works of art. The Tate Gallery is an exempt charity; the Museums & Galleries Act 1992 added the Tate Gallery to the list of exempt charities defined in the 1960 Charities Act.

DONATIONS

There are a variety of ways through which you can make a donation to the Tate Gallery.

Donations All donations, however small, will be gratefully received and acknowledged by the Tate Gallery.

Covenants A Deed of Covenant, which must be taken out for a minimum of four years, will enable the Tate Gallery to claim back tax on your charitable donation. For example, a covenant for £100 per annum will allow the Gallery to claim a further £33 at present tax rates.

Gift-Aid For individuals and companies wishing to make donations of £250 and above, Gift-Aid allows the gallery to claim back tax on your charitable donation. In addition, if you are a higher rate taxpayer you will be able to claim tax relief on the donation. A Gift-Aid form and explanatory leaflet can be sent to you if you require further information.

Bequests You may wish to remember the Tate Gallery in your will or make a specific donation In Memoriam. A bequest may take the form of either a specific cash sum, a residual proportion of your estate or a specific item of property, such as a work of art. Certain tax advantages can be obtained by making a legacy in favour of the Tate Gallery. Please check with the Tate Gallery when you draw up your will that it is able to accept your bequest.

American Fund for the Tate Gallery The American Fund was formed in 1986 to facilitate gifts of works of art, donations and bequests to the Tate Gallery from the United States residents. It receives full tax exempt status from the IRS.

INDIVIDUAL MEMBERSHIP PROGRAMMES

Friends

Friends share in the life of the Gallery and contribute towards the purchase of important works of art for the Tate.

Privileges include free unlimited entry with a guest to exhibitions; *tate: the art magazine*; private views, events and art courses; 'Late at the Tate' evening openings; exclusive Friends Room. Annual rates range from £22 to £60.

Tate Friends Liverpool and Tate Friends St Ives offer local events programmes and full membership of the Friends.

Fellows

Fellows support the acquisition of works of art for the British and Modern Collections of the Tate Gallery. Privileges include invitations to Tate Gallery receptions, curatorial talks and behind-the-scene tours, complimentary catalogues and Joint or Family membership of the Friends. Annual membership ranges from £100 to £500.

The Friends of the Tate Gallery are supported by Tate & Lyle PLC.

Further details on the Friends and Fellows in London, Liverpool and St Ives may be obtained from:

Membership Office
Tate Gallery
Millbank
London SW1P 4RG

Tel: 0171-887 8752

Patrons of the Tate Gallery

Patrons of British Art support British painting and sculpture from the Elizabethan period through to the early twentieth century in the Tate Gallery's collection. They encourage knowledge and awareness of British art by providing an opportunity to study Britain's cultural heritage.

Patrons of New Art support contemporary art in the Tate Gallery's collection. They promote a lively and informed interest in contemporary art and are associated with the Turner Prize, one of the most prestigious awards for the visual arts.

Annual membership of the Patrons ranges from £350 to £750, and funds the purchase of works of art for the Tate Gallery's collection.

Privileges for both groups include invitations to Tate Gallery receptions, an opportunity to sit on the Patrons' acquisitions committees, special events including visits to private and corporate collections and complimentary catalogues of Tate Gallery exhibitions.

Further details on the Patrons may be obtained from:

Membership Office
Tate Gallery
Millbank
London SW1P 4RG

Tel: 0171-887 8743

CORPORATE MEMBERSHIP PROGRAMME

Membership of the Tate Gallery's Corporate Membership Programme offers companies outstanding value-for-money and provides opportunities for every employee to enjoy a closer knowledge of the Gallery, its collection and exhibitions.

Membership benefits are specifically geared to business needs and include private views for company employees, free and discount admission to exhibitions, discount in the Gallery shop, out-of-hours Gallery visits, behind-the-scenes tours, exclusive use of the Gallery for corporate entertainment, invitations to VIP events, copies of Gallery literature and acknowledgment in Gallery publications.

Tate Gallery Corporate Members

Partners
British Gas plc
The British Petroleum Company p.l.c.
Ernst & Young
Glaxo Wellcome p.l.c.
Manpower PLC
J.P. Morgan & Co. Incorporated
Reed Elsevier
Unilever

Associates
BUPA
Channel 4 Television
Drivers Jonas
Global Asset Management
Lazard Brothers & Co Limited
Linklaters & Paines
Merrill Lynch
Refco Overseas Ltd
Salomon Brothers
Schroders plc
Simmons & Simmons
THORN EMI

CORPORATE SPONSORSHIP

The Tate Gallery works closely with sponsors to ensure that their business interests are well served, and has a reputation for developing imaginative fund-raising initiatives. Sponsorships can range from a few thousand pounds to considerable investment in long-term programmes; small businesses as well as multi-national corporations have benefited from the high profile and prestige of Tate Gallery sponsorship.

Opportunities available at Tate Gallery London, Liverpool and St Ives include exhibitions (some also tour the UK), education, conservation and research programmes, audience development, visitor access to the Collection and special events. Sponsorship benefits include national and regional publicity, targeted marketing to niche audiences, exclusive corporate entertainment, employee benefits and acknowledgment in Tate Gallery publications.

Tate Gallery London: Principal Corporate Sponsors
(alphabetical order)

The British Land Company PLC
1993, *Ben Nicholson**
The British Petroleum Company plc
1990–6, *New Displays*
Channel 4 Television
1991–6, *The Turner Prize*
Ernst & Young
1994, *Picasso: Sculptor/Painter**
J.P. Morgan & Co. Incorporated
1995, *Willem de Kooning**
Nuclear Electric plc
1993, *Turner: The Final Years*
1994, *The Essential Turner*
1995–7, *The Nuclear Electric Turner Scholarships*
Pearson plc
1992–5, Elizabethan Curator Post
1995, *Dynasties: Painting in Tudor and Jacobean England 1530–1630*

Reed Elsevier
  1994, *Whistler*
Tate & Lyle PLC
  1991–5, Friends Marketing Programme
Volkswagen
  1991–6, The Volkswagen Turner
    Scholarships

*Tate Gallery London: Corporate
Sponsors* (alphabetical order)

ABN AMRO Bank
  1994, *Turner's Holland*
AFAA, Association Française d'Action
Artistique, Ministère de Affaires Etrangères,
The Cultural Service of the French
Embassy, London
  1993, *Paris Post War: Art and
    Existentialism 1945–55*
Agfa Graphic Systems Group
  1992, *Turner: The Fifth Decade**
Beck's
  1992, *Otto Dix*
  1994, *Rebecca Horn*
  1995, *Rites of Passage*
Blackwall Green Ltd
  1994, Frames Conservation
The British Printing Company Ltd
  1994–5, sponsorship in kind
Calor Gas
  1994, *Turner's Holland*
The Government of Canada and The
Canadian High Commission, London
  1995, *Rites of Passage*
  1995, *Art Now – Geneviève Cadieux*
CDT Design Ltd
  1995–6, *Art Now*
Classic FM
  1995–6, Regional tour of David
    Hockney's 'Mr and Mrs Clark and
    Percy' (in kind)
Clifton Nurseries
  1991–5, Christmas Tree (in kind)
Deutsche Bank A.G.
  1994, *Rebecca Horn*
Digital Equipment Co Limited
  1993, Library and Archive
    Computerisation
Alfred Dunhill Limited
  1993, *Sir Edward Burne-Jones:
    Watercolours and Drawings*
The German Government
  1992, *Otto Dix*
The Guardian
  1995, *Rites of Passage* (in kind)
Häagen-Dazs Fresh Cream Ice Cream
  1995–6, *Art Now*
The Hiscox Group
  1995, Friends Room
The Independent
  1992, *Otto Dix* (in kind)
  1993, *Paris Post War: Art and
    Existentialism 1945–55*
  1994, *Rebecca Horn* (in kind)
J.R.F. Panels
  1994, Christmas Tree (in kind)
Makro
  1994, *Turner's Holland*
Pro Helvetia
  1995, *Through Switzerland with Turner*
Russell & Chapple Ltd
  1994, Christmas Tree (in kind)
W.H. Smith Ltd
  1994, Sponsorship-in-kind
SRU Limited
  1992, *Richard Hamilton**
Sun Life Assurance Society plc
  1993, *Robert Vernon's Gift*

Swiss National Tourist Office
  1995, *Through Switzerland with Turner*
THORN EMI
  1993, *Turner's Painting Techniques*
  1995, *Centre Stage* education project
TSB Group plc
  1992, *Turner and Byron*
  1992–5, *William Blake* display series
  1995, Paintings Conservation

*Tate Gallery of Modern Art:
Corporate Sponsors*
(alphabetical order)

Ernst & Young
  1995, *Tate Gallery of Modern Art:
    Selecting an Architect*

*Tate Gallery Liverpool: Corporate
Sponsors* (alphabetical order)

American Airlines
  1993, *David Hockney*
Beck's
  1993, *Robert Gober*
Canadian High Commission, London and
Government of Canada
  1993, *Elective Affinities*
Girobank plc
  1995, *Primary Cooking* Education booklet
Ibstock Building Products Ltd
  1993, *Antony Gormley*
Ian Short Partnership
  1995, *Testing the Water*
Korean Air
  1992, *Working with Nature* (in kind)
The Littlewoods Organisation plc
  1992–5, *New Realities*
Merseyside Development Corporation
  1992, *Myth-Making*
  1992, *Stanley Spencer*
MOMART plc
  1991–5, The Momart Fellowship
North West Water Group PLC
  1994, Corporate Membership Brochure
David M Robinson Jewellery
  1994, *Venus Re-Defined*
Royal Liver Assurance
  1995, Making It
Samsung Electronics
  1992, *Working With Nature*
Tate & Lyle PLC
  1995, Tate Friends Liverpool
    membership leaflet

*Tate Gallery St Ives: Corporate
Sponsors* (alphabetical order)

Barclays Bank PLC*
  1995, *Porthmeor Beach: 'A Century of Images'*
First Class Pullman, InterCity*
  1993–4, *Annual Displays*
Northcliffe Newspapers in Education*
  1995–6, Education Programme
South Western Electricity plc (SWEB)*
  1993–4, Education Programme

*denotes a sponsorship in the arts,
recognised by an award under the
Government's 'Pairing Scheme'
administered by the Association for
Business Sponsorship of the Arts.

TATE GALLERY FOUNDING
BENEFACTORS (date order)

Sir Henry Tate
Sir Joseph Duveen
Lord Duveen
The Clore Foundation

TATE GALLERY PRINCIPAL
BENEFACTORS (alphabetical order)

American Fund for the Tate Gallery
Calouste Gulbenkian Foundation
Friends of the Tate Gallery
The Henry Moore Foundation
National Art Collections Fund
National Heritage Memorial Fund
The Nomura Securities Co., Ltd
Patrons of New Art
Dr Mortimer and Theresa Sackler
  Foundation
St Ives Tate Action Group
The Wolfson Foundation and Family
  Charitable Trust

TATE GALLERY
BENEFACTORS (alphabetical order)

The Baring Foundation
Bernard Sunley Charitable Foundation
Gilbert and Janet de Botton
Mr Edwin C. Cohen
The Eleanor Rathbone Charitable Trust
Esmée Fairbairn Charitable Trust
Foundation for Sport and the Arts
GEC Plessey Telecommunications
The Getty Grant Program
Granada Group plc
The Paul Hamlyn Foundation
John and Olivia Hughes
The John S. Cohen Foundation
The John Ellerman Foundation
The Kreitman Foundation
John Lewis Partnership
The Leverhulme Trust
Museums and Galleries Improvement Fund
Ocean Group plc (P.H. Holt Trust)
Patrons of British Art
Peter Moores Foundation
The Pilgrim Trust
Mr John Ritblat
The Sainsbury Family Charitable Trusts
Save & Prosper Educational Trust
SRU Limited
Weinberg Foundation

TATE GALLERY DONORS
(alphabetical order)

London

Professor Abbott
The Andy Warhol Foundation for the
  Visual Arts, Inc
Lord Attenborough CBE
BAA plc
Friends of Nancy Balfour OBE
Balmuir Holdings
The Hon. Robin Baring
B.A.T. Industries plc
Nancy Bateman Charitable Trust

Mr Tom Bendhem
Mr Alexander Bernstein
Janice and David Blackburn
Michael and Marcia Blakenham
Miss Mary Boone
The Britwell Trust
Card Aid
Carlsberg Brewery
Mr Vincent Carrozza
Mrs Beryl Carpenter
Cazenove & Co Charitable Trust
Charlotte Bonham Carter Charitable Trust
Christie, Manson & Woods Ltd
The Claire Hunter Charitable Trust
The Clothworkers Foundation
Mrs Elisabeth Collins
Mr R.N. Collins
Giles and Sonia Coode-Adams
Mrs Dagny Corcoran
C.T. Bowring (Charitable Trust) Ltd
Cognac Courvoisier
Mr Edwin Cox
Anthony d'Offay Gallery
Mr and Mrs Kenneth Dayton
Mr Damon and The Hon. Mrs de Laszlo
Madame Gustava de Rothschild
Baroness Liliane de Rothschild
Deutsche Bank AG
Miss W.A. Donner
Mr Paul Dupee
Mrs Maurice Dwek
Elephant Trust
Eli Broad Family Foundation
Elizabeth Arden Ltd
European Arts Festival
Evelyn, Lady Downshire's Trust Fund
Roberto Fainello Art Advisers Ltd
The Flow Foundation
First Boston Corporation
Foreign & Colonial Management Limited
Miss Kate Ganz
Mr Henry Geldzahler
Ms Laure Genillard
Mr and Mrs David Gilmour
The German Government
Goethe Institut
Sir Nicholas and Lady Goodison
  Charitable Settlement
Mr William Govett
Mr and Mrs Richard Grogan
Gytha Trust
Mr and Mrs Rupert Hambro
Miriam and Peter Haas Foundation
Mrs Sue Hammerson
The Hon. Lady Hastings
The Hedley Foundation
Mr and Mrs Michael Heseltine
Mr Rupert Heseltine
Horace W. Goldsmith Foundation
Harry Kwellek Charitable Trust
Mr Robert Horton
Hurry Armour Trust
Idlewild Trust
The Italian Government
Sir Anthony and Lady Jacobs
Mrs Gabrielle Keiller
James and Clare Kirkman Trust
Knapping Fund
Mr and Mrs Richard Knight
Mr and Mrs Jan Krugier
The Leche Trust
Robert Lehman Foundation, Inc
The Helena and Kenneth Levy Bequest
Mr and Mrs Gilbert Lloyd
Mr and Mrs George Loudon
Mr and Mrs Lawrence Lowenthal
Mail on Sunday
Mr Alexander Marchessini
The Mayor Gallery
Midland Bank Artscard
Mr and Mrs Robert Mnuchin